DATE DUE FOR RETURN

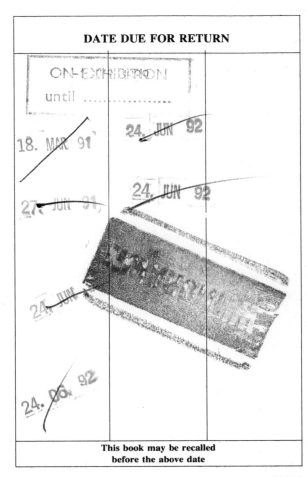

ON EXHIBITION

until ....

18. MAR 91

24. JUN 92

27. JUN 91

24. JUN 92

24. JUN

24. DEC 92

This book may be recalled
before the above date

90014

Companion to Charles Lamb

By the same author

Peppercorn Papers: *A Miscellany on Books and Book Collecting*

The Laughing Philosopher: *A Further Miscellany on Books,*
Booksellers and Book Collecting

Index to the London Magazine, with Frank P. Riga

Companion to Charles Lamb

A GUIDE TO PEOPLE AND PLACES
1760–1847

by
Claude A. Prance

Mansell Publishing Limited

ISBN 0 7201 1657 0

Mansell Publishing Limited, 6 All Saints Street, London N1 9RL

First published 1983
© Claude A. Prance 1983

Distributed in the United States and Canada by The H.W. Wilson
Company, 950 University Avenue, Bronx, New York 10452

Illustration facing title page by
Charles Edmund Brock, by courtesy of
J.M. Dent & Sons Limited, from Charles
Lamb, *Last Essays of Elia*, Dent, London, 1899

British Library Cataloguing in Publication Data

Prance, Claude A.
    Companion to Charles Lamb.
    1. Lamb, Charles, *1775–1834*—Friends and
    associates   2. Lamb, Charles, *1775–1834*—
    Homes and haunts
    I. Title
    824'.7   PR4863
    ISBN 0–7201–1657–0

Composition in Bodoni by Filmtype Services Limited,
Scarborough, North Yorkshire

Printed in Great Britain at the
University Press, Cambridge

*I own that I am disposed to say grace upon twenty other occasions
in the course of the day besides my dinner. I want a form for setting
out upon a pleasant walk, for a moonlight ramble, for a friendly
meeting, or a solved problem. Why have we none for books, those
spiritual repasts—a grace before Milton—a grace before Shakespeare—a devotional exercise proper to be said before reading the
Fairy Queen?*

Charles Lamb, 'Grace Before Meat'

*He chose his companions for some individuality of character which
they manifested. Hence, not many persons of science, and few
professed* literati, *were of his councils. They were, for the most part,
persons of an uncertain fortune . . . . His* intimados, *to confess a
truth, were in the world's eye a ragged regiment. He found them
floating on the surface of society; and the colour, or something else,
in the weed pleased him. The burrs stuck to him—but they were
good and loving burrs for all that. He never greatly cared for the
society of what are called good people.*

Charles Lamb, 'A Character of the late Elia'

*I will, however, admit that the said Elia is the worst company in the
world in bad company, if it be granted me that in good company he
is nearly the best that can be. He is one of those of whom it may be
said,* Tell me your company, and I'll tell you your manners.

William Hazlitt, 'On Coffee-House Politicians'

Lamb then named Sir Thomas Browne and Fulke Greville, the friend of Sir Philip Sidney, as the two worthies whom he should feel the greatest pleasure to encounter on the floor of his apartment in their nightgown and slippers, and to exchange friendly greeting with them.

William Hazlitt, 'Of persons one would wish to have seen'

I am naturally, beforehand, shy of novelties; new books, new faces, new years—from some mental twist which makes it difficult in me to face the prospective.

Charles Lamb, 'New Year's Eve'

And take my word for this, reader, and say a fool told it you, if you please, that he who hath not a dram of folly in his mixture, hath pounds of much worse matter in his composition.

Charles Lamb, 'All Fools' Day'

I am in love with this green earth; the face of town and country; the unspeakable rural solitudes, and the sweet security of streets.

Charles Lamb, 'New Year's Eve'

Antiquity! thou wondrous charm, what art thou? that, being nothing, art every thing! When thou wert, thou wert not antiquity—then thou wert nothing, but hadst a remoter antiquity, as thou called'st it, to look back to with blind veneration; thou thyself being to thyself flat, jejune, modern! What mystery lurks in this retroversion? or what half Januses are we, that cannot look forward with the same idolatry with which we ever revert! The mighty future is as nothing, being every thing! the past is every thing, being nothing!

Charles Lamb, 'Oxford in the Vacation'

Contents

Preface

As a reference to the friends and acquaintances, the places and matters associated with Charles and Mary Lamb, it is hoped this book will help readers to appreciate more fully the background to the Lambs' lives and work. In dictionary format are brief biographical details of the people the brother and sister knew and associated with, along with the ways in which they were associated. As one of Lamb's great interests was the theatre, most of the actors and actresses he mentions in his writings who were acting during his lifetime are included. Some of them were friends, but many were known to him only by their stage appearances. Those he mentions who died before or soon after he was born have been excluded, since his comments would not have been his own impressions.

Among the non-biographical entries are such places as the South Sea House, Pentonville's Chapel Street, Dove Cottage, Christ's Hospital and the houses lived in by the Lambs; such organizations as the Amicable Society of Blues, the Gregynog Press and the Charles Lamb Society; and such miscellanea as literary histories that refer to Lamb, memorials to Lamb, holidays taken by the Lambs and portraits of the Lambs. Included as well are Lambs's editors, illustrators of his works and details of books about him.

It is not intended to make this a volume of notes to his writings, since that has been done often before, particularly in editions of the *Essays of Elia*. No attempt has been made to trace quotations or explain allusions, for which the reader is referred to E.V. Lucas's superb and exhaustive edition of the *Works of Charles and Mary Lamb*, or to other good editions. Many of the editions are listed in this book and most have some annotation.

Because Lamb's circle of friends included many distinguished people, references to him in books about them are legion; it is almost impossible to read a book about Coleridge, Hazlitt, Leigh Hunt, Wordsworth, Southey, Godwin or even Keats and Shelley and members of their circles without finding numerous references to Charles Lamb. Although many of these books are mentioned in the *Companion*, usually under the names of the authors, this is not a bibliography of the Romantic Movement or even of Charles Lamb; many such books, of necessity, are omitted. Lamb's name also appears in most histories of English literature and encyclopaedias; some of the more important are mentioned here. Books about London frequently mention Charles Lamb; as they are useful in setting the scene to his life and times, some are included.

Articles about the Lambs that appear in periodicals are listed when
the authors are included. For further details the reader should consult
such books as *The English Romantic Poets and Essayists*, edited by
C.W. and L.H. Houtchens, 1957 (revised edition, 1966; third
edition, edited by Frank Jordan, 1972), or the *Annual Bibliography*
issued by the *Keats-Shelley Journal*. No doubt the bibliography of
Lamb studies being prepared by Professor Duane Schneider will also
be invaluable.

Although it is obvious that there are certain deliberate omissions
from the *Companion*, this book provides much information about
Charles Lamb, his friends and his background not readily available
elsewhere. It will supplement the reading of annotated editions of the
essays and letters, since far as is known no similar book on Charles
Lamb has been published before.

My work on the *Companion* began some thirty years ago. Research
was first done in the Library of the University College of North Wales,
Bangor, and continued in the Reading Room of the British Museum
(now the British Library). Other work intervened and the project was
laid aside for many years. When it was resumed the main source was
my own collection of Eliana of about 700 volumes and my general
collection of some 6,000 volumes of English literature, supplemented
by research in the Library of the University of Malta, the British
Council Library formerly on Malta, the Gozo Public Library, the
Charles Lamb Society's library and the National Library of Australia.
To the librarians of all those libraries my grateful thanks are given for
much valuable help. Acknowledgement is also given to the respective
editors of the *C.L.S. Bulletin*, now the *Charles Lamb Bulletin*, for
much information gathered from that useful periodical which has
been of great help in writing this book. Thanks are given to my wife
for considerable help in reading the proofs.

Any writer on the works of Charles Lamb as a whole is bound to
be indebted to E.V. Lucas's standard edition issued by Methuen and
the later volumes of letters published by Dent and Methuen. Both
William Macdonald (Dent) and Thomas Hutchinson (Oxford University Press) have published editions of great value, and for this book
those of Ainger, Kent, Fitzgerald, Moxon, Shepherd and some others
have been drawn upon; but the debt is greatest to Lucas. Generally
his edition of the *Letters*, 1935, has been used for reference, bearing
in mind the corrections in the text noted by later writers. A revised
edition of the letters is being prepared by Professor Edwin W. Marrs,
Jr., of the University of Pittsburgh, Volumes 1 and 2 of which were
published in 1975–6 and Volume 3 in 1978; but it will probably be
several years before all the volumes have appeared. Lucas's edition
is thus the latest and most complete available edition at present.

Abbreviations

ABC	*American Book Collector*
ALS	Autograph Letter Signed
ARA	Associate of the Royal Academy
BC	*Book Collector*
CBEL	*Cambridge Bibliography of English Literature*
CG	Covent Garden Theatre
CH	Christ's Hospital
CLB	*Charles Lamb Bulletin*
CLS	Charles Lamb Society
CLSB	*Charles Lamb Society Bulletin*
DL	Drury Lane Theatre
DNB	*Dictionary of National Biography*
ELH	*Journal of English Literary History*
ELN	*English Language Notes*
FR Hist S	Fellow of the Royal Historical Society
FRS	Fellow of the Royal Society
FSA	Fellow of the Society of Antiquaries
HLQ	*Huntington Library Quarterly*
KC	King's Counsel
K-SJ	*Keats-Shelley Journal*
LCC	London County Council
Lucas *Works*	*The Works of Charles and Mary Lamb.* Edited by E.V. Lucas. London. Methuen, 1903–1905. 7 volumes.
Lucas *Life*	*The Life of Charles Lamb* by E.V. Lucas. London. Methuen, 1905.
Lucas *Letters*	*The Letters of Charles and Mary Lamb.* Edited by E.V. Lucas, London. Dent and Methuen, 1935. 3 volumes.
Marrs	*The Letters of Charles and Mary Anne Lamb.* Edited by Edwin W. Marrs, Jr. Ithaca and London. Cornell University Press. Volumes 1–3, 1975–1978.
MLN	*Modern Language Notes*
MLQ	*Modern Language Quarterly*
MP	*Modern Philology*
NPG	National Portrait Gallery
OUDS	Oxford Union Dramatic Society
OUP	Oxford University Press
PMLA	*Publications of the Modern Language Association of America*

PQ	*Philological Quarterly*
PULC	*Princeton University Library Chronicle*
QC	Queen's Counsel
RA	Royal Academy, Royal Academician
RADA	Royal Academy of Dramatic Art
RAMC	Royal Army Medical Corps
RBA	Royal Society of British Artists
RES	*Review of English Studies*
STC	Samuel Taylor Coleridge
TLS	*Times Literary Supplement*

Companion to Charles Lamb

Abington, Frances, 1737–1815. English actress, née Frances Barton. After being a flower girl and a street singer she took to the stage and appeared at the Haymarket in 1755. Following a period at the Smock Alley Theatre, Dublin, she acted for many years at Drury Lane with Garrick, although he disliked her. She was the first Lady Teazle, which became one of her favourite parts. She also played with success such parts as Lady Betty Modish in *The Careless Husband* and Miss Prue in *Love for Love.* Among her other parts were Desdemona, Beatrice, Ophelia, Olivia, Portia, Millamant, Miss Hoyden, Lydia Languish, Polly Peachum and Lucy Lockit. She moved to Covent Garden in 1782 and remained there for eight years. She retired from the stage in 1790, but returned and did not finally retire until 1799. She was said to be one of the greatest comic actresses of all time. She was known to many famous people and is mentioned by Horace Walpole.

Lamb refers to her favourably in his piece 'The New Acting' in *The Examiner,* 1813. In his essay 'On the Artificial Comedy of the last Century' he says that she had been succeeded by Miss Farren as Lady Teazle wnen he first saw the play. In 'The Old Actors', as printed in *The London Magazine,* October 1822, he describes Charles Mathews's gallery of theatrical portraits and writes of one picture 'the screen scene in Brinsley's famous comedy, with Smith and Mrs Abingdon, whom I have not seen.' Presumably he may mean only in *The School for Scandal,* for he could well have seen her during the period of her return to the stage between 1790 and 1799. Lamb generally spells her name 'Abingdon'. Crabb Robinson records in his *Diary* that he had dinner with her on 16 June 1811 and, although not impressed by her face, he found her pleasant and alert and he listened to her memories of those she had known on the stage.

Adams, Dr Joseph, 1756–1818. Physician of Hatton Garden, formerly an apothecary. M.D. Aberdeen 1796. Editor of the *Medical and Physical Journal.* Wrote *Observations on Morbid Poisons,* 1795 and *Memoirs of the Life & Doctrines of the late John Hunter,* 1816. Crabb Robinson records in his *Diary* that Dr and Mrs Adams attended a party on 21 June 1811 with Charles and Mary Lamb, Barron Field and others, at which Lamb made his pun about punsters having no pockets 'they carry only a ridicule.' Adams recommended Coleridge to the care of James Gillman in 1816.

Adams, Sarah, *see* Sarah Flower

Adcock, Arthur St John, 1864–1930. Author and editor. Editor of *The Bookman,* 1923–30. Wrote *The Booklover's London,* 1913, which has references to Lamb. Other works include *Famous Houses*

& *Literary Shrines of London*, 1912, *From a London Garden*, 1903, and *London Etchings*, 1904.

Aders, Charles. A merchant who lived in Euston Square and possessed a valuable collection of pictures. He was a friend of Lamb, Coleridge and Crabb Robinson. In 1831 Lamb wrote a poem to 'C. Aders Esq. On his Collection of Paintings by the Old German Masters' which started 'Friendliest of men, Aders . . .'. In 1827 Lamb's poem 'Angel Help' had been inspired by a drawing owned by the Aders. There are many references to Charles Aders in Crabb Robinson's *Diary* and a few in Lamb's letters. At Lamb's request Aders found a place in his counting house for young Thomas Westwood. In a letter to C.W. Dilke, March 1832, Lamb refers to 'my friend Aders' who had opened to the public at the Suffolk Street Gallery his collection of old Dutch pictures.

Among Aders's many friends was William Blake from whom he purchased copies of the *Songs of Innocence and Experience*. Mrs Aders was a daughter of Raphael Smith, the engraver and painter. Coleridge addressed his poem 'The Two Founts' to her.

Ades, John I., b.1925. Professor of English Language and Literature, Southern Illinois University, Edwardsville, U.S.A. Author of 'Charles Lamb as a Literary Critic' (Doctoral Dissertation, Cincinnati 1963). Contributed 'Charles Lamb—Romantic Criticism & Aesthetics of Sympathy' to *Delta Epsilon Sigma Bulletin*, Southern Illinois University, December 1961; 'Charles Lamb's Judgment of Byron & Shelley' to *Papers on English Language & Literature*, Winter 1965; to the *Charles Lamb Bulletin*, 'Criticus Redivivus: The History of Charles Lamb's Reputation as a Critic', July 1972, 'Thomas Hood "Two Parts Methodist to one of humourist",' July 1974, and 'Perfect Sympathy: Lamb on Hogarth', April 1975; and to the *Wordsworth Circle*, Winter 1977, 'Friendly Persuasion: Lamb as a critic of Wordsworth'.

Aickins, The. In his essay 'The Old Actors' as it appeared in the *London Magazine*, Charles Lamb, in describing Charles Mathews's gallery of theatrical portraits, mentions 'the two Aickins, brethren in mediocrity.'

James Aickin, d.1803. Played at Smock Alley Theatre, Dublin, and Canongate Theatre, Edinburgh, before coming to Drury Lane and the Haymarket. At one time he was deputy manager at Drury Lane. He retired in 1800. In 1792 he fought a duel with John Philip Kemble because he thought he had been unfairly treated by Kemble as manager of Drury Lane. He is said to have been an excellent actor in such parts as an honest steward or affectionate father.

Francis Aickin, d.1805. A tragedian. Played with Sarah Siddons in Dublin in 1783; was also with Tate Wilkinson and was manager of a theatre at Liverpool. Mrs Siddons played at his benefit at Covent Garden. He was said to be a good supporting actor in manly, polite roles. At one time he also had a business as hosier in York Street, Covent Garden.

Both the Aickins had winning manners. One played Rowley in the original production of *The School for Scandal*. Crabb Robinson records dining with one of them at Holcroft's house in 1799. Francis was nicknamed 'Tyrant Aickin' and the other 'Belly Aickin'.

Aikin Family. The whole family were close friends of Crabb Robinson who introduced most of them to the Lambs. For Lucy Aikin, see the next entry.

Dr John Aikin, 1747–1822. Miscellaneous writer and physician, wrote a large number of pamphlets, translations and miscellaneous works, some in conjunction with his sister, Mrs Barbauld, Editor of Sir Richard Phillips's *Monthly Magazine*. Among his friends were Southey, James Montgomery, Erasmus Darwin and Priestley.

Anna Letitia Aikin, 1743–1825. Sister of John, see Mrs Barbauld.

Arthur Aikin, 1773–1854. Chemist and scientific writer. Son of Dr John Aikin. In 1811 Crabb Robinson asked him for help in relieving the financial difficulties of George Burnett. From 1803 to 1808 he edited the *Annual Review*, a literary periodical, to which Dr Aikin, Lucy Aikin, Mrs Barbauld, Robert Southey and William Taylor contributed.

Charles Rochemont Aikin, 1775–1847. A well known doctor and scientist. A son of Dr John Aikin. He married Anne, daughter of Gilbert Wakefield, a fact unknown to Lamb when he made his unfortunate remark to her that Wakefield had a peevish face. Charles Aikin was the 'little Charles' of his aunt, Mrs Barbauld's *Early Lessons*.

Aikin, Lucy, 1781–1864. Daughter of Dr John Aikin and niece of Mrs Barbauld. She wrote a volume of poems, *Epistles on Women*, 1810; a novel, *Lorimer*, 1814; and then turned to historical works. *Memoirs of the Court of Elizabeth* appeared in 1818, *Memoirs of the Court of James I* in 1822 and *Memoirs of the Court of Charles I* in 1833. She also wrote children's books, and in 1823 published *Memoir of John Aikin with Selections of his Miscellaneous Pieces*. She contributed a memoir of her aunt to Mrs Barbauld's *Works* in 1825 and the 'Memoir of Elizabeth Benger' to the latter's *Memoirs of the Life of Anne Boleyn* in 1827. In 1843 she wrote a *Life of Addison*.

She was a friend of the Lambs and Crabb Robinson and the latter records in his *Diary* on 9 May 1812 that he read 'Mr H——' at Mrs Barbauld's to Mrs and Miss Aikin and they were high in praise of it. On 28 May 1814 he went with Charles Lamb to Dr Aikin's and he notes that Miss Aikin admired 'both the wit and the fine face of Lamb.'

She was a noted conversationalist and wrote some admirable letters that were praised by Crabb Robinson. *Memoirs, Miscellanies and Letters of Lucy Aikin*, published in 1864, included her correspondence with William Ellery Channing, the Unitarian minister. She seems to have been critical of the Lake poets, particularly Southey.

Ainger, Alfred, 1837–1904. Author and editor. The son of an architect, he was educated at King's College, London, and Trinity College, Cambridge. He first studied law but turned to the church and was ordained in 1860; later he became a canon of Bristol Cathedral. In 1894 he was appointed Master of the Temple and chaplain to Queen Victoria, and then to Edward VII. Ainger was a noted wit with a large circle of friends, among whom were Charles Dickens, Leslie Stephen and Alfred Tennyson. He was possessed of considerable dramatic ability and was a most successful lecturer, particularly on Shakespeare. Many of his lectures were delivered at the Royal Institution. Several of his sermons were published, and he wrote a life of George Crabbe in 1903.

His best known work concerns Charles Lamb and in 1882 his biography of Lamb was published in the English Men of Letters series. His *Lectures and Essays*, 1905, edited by H.C. Beeching, included essays on Shakespeare as well as on 'The Letters of Charles Lamb', 'How I traced Charles Lamb in Hertfordshire', 'Nether Stowey', 'Coleridge's Ode to Wordsworth' and 'Charles James Mathews'. Some of these pieces had been contributed to *Macmillan's Magazine*. He also wrote the article on Lamb in the *Dictionary of National Biography*. To the *English Illustrated Magazine* in 1886 he contributed an article 'Charles Lamb in Hertfordshire', which is not the same as printed in his *Lectures and Essays*. The magazine article contained a number of illustrations by E.H. Fitchew.

His most extensive work was his edition of Charles Lamb's writings in six volumes over the period 1883–88. In 1900 this edition was issued as an *edition-de-luxe* in twelve volumes with additional letters. Ainger's edition was an excellent work, but he deliberately omitted whole pieces of which he disapproved. Among these were 'A Vision of Horns', 'Unitarian Protests', 'The Pawnbroker's Daughter', 'The Defeat of Time', 'Cupid's Revenge' and 'The Reminiscences of Jude Judkins'. It is, however, a very attractive edition to read. Edith Sichel has aptly described Ainger's work on Lamb when she said that he wrote as a lover and a friend, not as a scholar or student. His notes are literary, not learned.

In 1890 Ainger preached a sermon on Charles Lamb at Widford Church. He also wrote an article in *Glasgow Bazaar News* in December 1889 on *The Fortunate Blue Coat Boy*, a curious romance mentioned by Lamb. The two chapters in Edith Sichel's *The Life & Letters of Alfred Ainger*, 1906, devoted to Lamb make fascinating reading and show his method of acquiring material for his books.

Ainsworth, William Harrison, 1805–82. Novelist. In 1825 was studying law as a pupil of Jacob Phillips of Kings Bench Walk in the Inner Temple; qualified as a solicitor, but gave up the law for literature. Married a daughter of John Ebers, publisher, who at one time was manager of the Opera House. Ainsworth had also been a magazine editor and a publisher. He had a great admiration for Lamb's work and dedicated his volume of poems, *The Poems of Cheviot Tichburn*, 1822, to Lamb. As a publisher he issued Laman Blanchard's *Lyric Offerings*, 1828, which was also dedicated to Lamb. Of this book the latter wrote 'I shall put them [the poems] up among my poetical treasures'. Ainsworth also contributed to the *London Magazine* in 1822. Lamb and Ainsworth did not meet until 1824, but they had corresponded at least since 1822 when Ainsworth had sent the manuscript of the Tichburn poems to Lamb for criticism and permission to dedicate them. Ainsworth lent Lamb some books in 1823, and soon after he came to London in 1824 the two met. Ainsworth, while so enthusiastic over Lamb's work, was a little disappointed at the meeting: he had formed an idealistic picture of Elia, and to his friend James Crossley he confessed, 'What a *bona fide* Cockney he is!' He told the story that James Browne, the editor of *Constable's Edinburgh Magazine*, once introduced Ainsworth to some friends as the *nephew* of Charles Lamb! Lamb gave Ainsworth an introduction to Wordsworth.

Aitken, John, 1793–1833. An Edinburgh bookseller who had been a bank clerk with the East Lothian Bank until it failed in 1822. Lamb wrote to him on 5 July 1825 in reply to a letter from Aitken and offered him 'Rosamund Gray' which Aitken printed in his *Cabinet; or The Selected Beauties of Literature* in 1831. Other of Lamb's works which had been reprinted in previous issues of the publications were 'Dream Children' and 'On the Inconviences resulting from being Hanged.' Aitken was editor of *Constable's Miscellany* and occasionally contributed to periodicals himself. On 24 October 1831 Lamb wrote to Moxon asking for Aitken's town address which he had lost. Moxon would have known him when they both worked for the publishers Hurst, Chance & Co.

Albatross, The. A play by Howard Koch based on incidents from the lives of Charles and Mary Lamb. Presented on 4 November 1963 at the Theatre Royal, Stratford, London E.15. The part of Charles Lamb was played by Emrys James and that of Mary Lamb by Olive McFarland. The play was withdrawn after one week. *C.L.S. Bulletin*, No.

175. states that the play grossly distorts known facts. A review in the *Financial Times* stated 'people of the time, Coleridge, Hazlitt appear, in a welter of clichés and literary name-dropping, but are never real.' The title of the play implies that Mary Lamb is the albatross hung about her brother's neck.

Alfoxden. A large house three miles from Nether Stowey in Somersetshire which was rented by Wordsworth and his sister in 1797–8. It was a beautiful old mansion in a large park with seventy head of deer. They paid £23 a year rent. Here the Wordsworths moved from Coleridge's cottage at Nether Stowey in July 1797. They had been on a visit to Coleridge but were so attracted to him that they decided to live in the Quantock country where they enjoyed his society almost daily. While at Nether Stowey they had met Lamb, who spent a week's holiday with Coleridge in July 1797. It is almost certain that Lamb must have walked over to Alfoxden to look at the house with the Wordsworths, and on the day they moved in he returned to London.

During Wordsworth's period here he composed some of his best known poems and together with Coleridge planned *The Lyrical Ballads*. Hazlitt visited the poets here, as did John Thelwall. It was the visit of the latter reformer that aroused the suspicions of the authorities who sent a Government spy down to watch the poets.

There were difficulties over the lease of the house and the poets were not understood by the country people, a fact which was mainly responsible for the Wordsworths leaving Alfoxden in June 1798.

Allen, Robert, 1772–1805, 'Bob Allen'. Army surgeon and journalist. Educated at Christ's Hospital with Lamb and Coleridge. Proceeded to University College, Oxford, with a C.H. Exhibition in 1792. A friend of Southey, he introduced him to Coleridge, and was one of those interested in Pantisocracy. He was also a friend of John Stoddart and William Godwin. As a journalist he wrote for *The Oracle, The True Briton, The Star* and *The Traveller*, but succeeded with none of them. He married a widow with daughters of his own age; when she died in 1796 he was appointed Deputy Surgeon of the 2nd Royal Dragoons in Portugal. Later he practised in England, and when he died of apoplexy in 1805 he was on the medical staff at Sudbury.

Lamb writes of him in his essay 'Christ's Hospital Five and Thirty Years Ago', where he mentions his happy laugh and handsome face, and he tells of Allen's journalistic efforts in 'Newspapers Thirty Five Years Ago'. Leigh Hunt in his *Autobiography* also refers to Allen's handsome face.

Allsop, Thomas, 1795–1880. A silk merchant who later became a stock broker and made a considerable fortune. A friend of Lamb and

Coleridge and described as the 'favourite disciple' of Coleridge, whom he first met in 1818. He frequently sent presents of game to Lamb and Coleridge. He first met Lamb in 1820 and was named as one of Lamb's executors in the will of 1823, but the later will omits his name. In 1825 the Lambs joined the Allsops in lodgings at Enfield. In 1827 Allsop seems to have been in some financial difficulty.

Mrs Allsop was a most charming and intelligent woman who made her home so attractive to her husband's friends that it was a favourite resort of Lamb, Hazlitt, Barry Cornwall and others of their circle. Lucas prints a number of short notes from Lamb to Allsop. In 1836 Allsop published his *Letters, Conversations and Recollections of S.T. Coleridge* which contain some good stories of Lamb, but some distortions of Coleridge. He attended Mary Lamb's funeral in 1847.

Allsop held radical opinions and was the friend of Robert Owen, Cobbett and Mazzini. He achieved considerable fame in his middle years by his reforming activities; he came into conflict with the Government, which at one time offered £500 for his apprehension, but this was later withdrawn. He also lived in the U.S.A. for a few years.

Allsop is sometimes confused with Thomas Alsop, at one time a clerk in the Ordnance Office, a n'er-do-well, who married Fanny Daly, the eldest daughter of Mrs Jordan, the actress. Fanny Alsop went on the stage and her husband went to India in 1813 to avoid his debts; she died in 1821. Lamb's friends, who spelt their name differently, were mostly well-to-do and attractive people.

Allston, Washington, 1779–1843. American historical painter and poet. Educated at Harvard. Came to London in 1801 and entered the Royal Academy as a student of Benjamin West. In 1804 he went to Paris with C.R. Leslie and then to Rome where he became friendly with Coleridge. From 1809 to 1811 he was in America, then returned to England. In 1819 he was elected Associate of the Royal Academy.

He painted a portrait of Coleridge, now in the National Portrait Gallery, and Coleridge praised his paintings. His two best known pictures are *Jacob's Dream* and *Uriel in the Sun*. He wrote *The Sylphs of the Seasons and other poems* in 1813 and *Monaldi*, a romance, in 1841.

When in Rome Allston was known by the German artists there as 'The American Titian'. In England he was friendly with Wordsworth, Southey and Fuseli. Crabb Robinson records in his *Diary* that he met Allston on 30 April 1818 at Monkhouse's when Lamb and Haydon were there. There are stories of Lamb in J.B. Flagg's *Life and Letters of Washington Allston*, 1892. Lamb copied five of Allston's sonnets on painters into one of his Commonplace Books. Allston married the sister of R.H. Dana, the novelist, as his second wife.

Alsager, Thomas Massa, 1779–1846. Musical and financial writer for *The Times*. At one time he had a manufactory and bleaching ground near the King's Bench Prison, but he gave it up when, as a great lover of music, he became music reporter on *The Times*. He also wrote for the paper the 'State of the Money Market' section for many years and was responsible for collecting mercantile and foreign news. He was a shareholder in the paper.

Alsager was an intimate friend of Crabb Robinson and of Lamb, and frequented the latter's evening parties. Lamb presented him with a copy of his *Works*, 1818. In 1823 Alsager gave £10 to the fund raised by Lamb for William Godwin's benefit. At one time he lived opposite Horsemonger Prison and when Leigh Hunt was there, convicted of libel, Alsager sent over his first day's dinner. Talfourd describes him as 'stately and courteous' and Leigh Hunt as 'the kindest of neighbours', a man of business who contrived to be a scholar and a musician.

In a letter to Leigh Hunt in 1829 or 1830 (*C.L.B.*, July 1981), Lamb writes, 'Alsager is in a flourishing house, with a wife and children about him, in Mecklenburg Square—almost too fine to visit'. Alsager owned a beautiful copy of the folio edition of Chapman's *Homer* which he lent to Charles Cowden Clarke and John Keats in 1816. It was after reading this copy that Keats composed his famous sonnet 'On First Looking into Chapman's Homer.' In 1838 Alsager wrote to Crabb Robinson in an attempt to obtain employment for Lamb's old friend, Martin Burney. It was in Alsager's house that the first English performance of Beethoven's Mass in D was given in October 1832, conducted by Ignaz Moscheles.

Amicable Society of Blues, The. A society of those educated at Christ's Hospital founded in 1775 on the basis of an earlier society dating back to the seventeenth century. The first meeting of the Amicable Society was held at the Nag's Head Tavern in Leadenhall Street on 3 March 1775. One of the objects of the Society was to hold a dinner or supper to commemorate the royal founder of Christ's Hospital, Edward VI.

In January 1817, Lamb's essay on Christ's Hospital from the *Gentleman's Magazine* was read at a meeting and as a result he was asked to dine with the Society, which he did as a guest at the London Tavern, Bishopsgate Street, on 11 February. It is thought this was the occasion of his only public speech; it started and finished with the word 'Gentlemen', and as he says 'and there I stopped'. There appears to be no evidence that Lamb was a member of the Society, although he joined the Benevolent Society of Blues, a charitable society founded in 1824.

Among the members of the Amicable Society were many Old Blues who were schoolfellows of Lamb's, including Henry Woodthorpe and

A.W. Trollope, both of whom held office in the Society. The Society twice entertained Coleridge to dinner, in 1789 and 1790, while he was still a Grecian in the school.

A writer in the *Times Literary Supplement* for 3 July 1924, himself an Old Blue, said, 'But the claim of the Amicable Society of Blues to immortality does not rest on the company of immortals: it is intrinsic and derives from the nature of the Religious, Royal and Ancient Foundation of Christ's Hospital, of whose enduring vital spirit it is one of the most distinctive embodiments.'

Amyot, Thomas, 1775–1850. Antiquary, son of a watchmaker in Norwich and clerk to a well known firm of solicitors there. He became law agent to William Windham, M.P., and later his private secretary. On Windham's death he was appointed Registrar in London of the West Indian Slaves. He became Treasurer of the Society of Antiquaries and was himself F.S.A. Amyot assisted in founding the Camden Society and was associated with the Percy and Shakespeare Societies. He contributed to the *Transactions of the Society of Antiquaries* and he edited a play, *The Taming of the Shrew*, on which Shakespeare had founded his comedy.

A close friend of Crabb Robinson, he had also known Dr Parr. Robinson records in his *Diary* on 24 February 1811 that Amyot and the Lambs were among the party to supper.

Anderson, Gertrude Alison, 1875–1924. Lamb scholar. Friend of Major S. Butterworth, P.P. Howe, Edmund Blunden and F.A. Downing, all of whom were students of Charles Lamb's works. Mrs Anderson compiled a considerable quantity of notes on Lamb and intended to edit an edition of Lamb's letters, but died before she could bring her work to completion. Part of it comprised the letters of Thomas Manning to Charles Lamb which she had collected. These passed to Major Butterworth who in turn made them over to P.P. Howe, who was able to publish them in 1925 as *The Letters of Thomas Manning to Charles Lamb. Edited by G.A. Anderson.*

All students of Lamb owe a deep debt of gratitude to Mrs Anderson for her detailed and accurate work on his writings, the results of which she was happy to pass on to others. This debt is acknowledged by E.V. Lucas in the introduction to his edition of the *Letters* in 1935, where he prints a short biography of Mrs Anderson by her son; this is carried further in the same introduction by a quotation from Edmund Blunden, who writes on her scholarship and detailed researches and mentions that she was compiling as part of her work on Lamb biographies of his friends. In an obituary notice in *The Bookman*, October 1924, F.A. Downing wrote that Mrs Anderson was 'in touch personally and by correspondence with those interested in her subject all over the world'. A further notice appeared in *The London Mercury*,

October 1924, in which it is mentioned that she was an accomplished artist. She was also three times British Lady Chess Champion. Her extensive collection of Eliana was given to the Keats Museum, Hampstead, by Edmund Blunden.

Mrs Anderson contributed valuable articles to a number of periodicals:

The Bookman
1921   Some Charles Lamb Relics, July.
1924   Edward White of the India House, and a new portrait of Lamb, April.
The Times Literary Supplement
1924   Poems by a sister, 1812, wrongly attributed to Mary Lamb, August 21.
The London Mercury
1922   Some Unpublished Letters of Lamb, November.
1925   Lamb and the two G.D's., February.
1928   On the Dating of Lamb's Letters, August.
The Blue (Christ's Hospital)
An account of Leigh Hunt's collection of locks of hair.

Anderson, Dr James, 1739–1808. Economist, author and authority on farming. Editor of *Recreations in Agriculture, Natural History, Arts and Miscellaneous Literature*, 1799–1802, published in monthly parts. Introduced to Lamb by George Dyer in 1800 and a friend of Jeremy Bentham. Anderson applied to Lamb for poems for his magazine and Lamb gave him three extracts from *John Woodvil* which were subsequently included. Anderson complained to Lamb of being 'disappointed by Ministers', probably referring to his employment by Pitt in 1784 to survey the fisheries, for which he maintained he was never paid. He also wrote other agricultural works and edited *The Bee, or literary weekly intelligencer*, 1791–4.

Anthony, Katharine. American author. Wrote *The Lambs: A Study of Pre-Victorian England*, 1948 (New York, 1945). It reprints Mary Lamb's essay 'On Needle-Work'. In this book the author attempts to apply psychoanalysis to the relationship between Charles and Mary Lamb and to their association with Emma Isola; her views are rejected by most writers on Lamb, although Stephen Southwold (Neil Bell) made similar suggestions in 1940.

Arnold, Samuel James, 1774–1852. Dramatist and theatre manager. Son of Dr Samuel Arnold, the composer. Wrote a number of plays, some of which were produced at the Haymarket, Drury Lane, and the Lyceum. Arnold was manager of the Lyceum around 1809 and later became manager of Drury Lane. He produced some of his own operas at the Lyceum. Hazlitt adversely criticized his play

King's Proxy in 1816 and said 'Mr Arnold writes with the fewest ideas possible', but he described his *Two Words* as a 'delightful little piece'. In 1824 Arnold produced at the Lyceum, then known as the English Opera House, a version of Weber's *Der Freischütz* which had been refused at Covent Garden and Drury Lane.

Arnold married the daughter of H.J. Pye, the Poet Laureate. Lamb's friend, William Ayrton, married Arnold's sister Marianne. Arnold was a Fellow of the Royal Society and a magistrate. He had also written a novel *The Creole. or the Haunted Island* in 1796. He was a leading member of the Beef Steak Club where he was called 'the Bishop' and he was on the committee of the Garrick Club.

Arnold was a friend of Lamb's and in the letter of 9 February 1823 to John Howard Payne about the latter's play *Grandpapa*, Lamb says 'I am thick with Arnold'. In 1824 he wrote a letter thanking Arnold for some tickets and in 1827 he wrote to Mrs Arnold returning a recipe for omelette soufflée. Arnold was said to be living at Boulogne in 1837 owing to the deranged state of his affairs.

In October 1946 a portrait in oils said to be of Mary Lamb by S.J. Arnold was included in a sale catalogue at Sothebys, but withdrawn before sale.

Arnold's son, Thomas James Arnold, a barrister and man of letters, was an intimate friend of Thomas Love Peacock and son-in-law of T.J. Hogg.

Arnold, William Harris, 1854–1923. American book collector. Wrote *Ventures in Book Collecting*, 1923, which contains references to copies of Lamb's works owned by Arnold and some A.L.S. Among these were copies of *Elia* inscribed to John Clare and J.S. Munden. These volumes are also listed in the Sale Catalogue of Arnold's library issued in 1924 where a facsimile of the Munden inscription is given. He also wrote *First Report of a Book Collector*, 1898.

Artaxerxes. Opera by Thomas Augustine Arne, English composer, first performed at Covent Garden on 2 February 1762. It was founded on Metastasio's *Arteserse* and the libretto is an English translation of this work by the composer. It was said to be a very poor translation. The opera was, however, very popular and continued to be performed for about eighty years.

This was the first play seen by Charles Lamb as he tells in his essay 'My First Play'. Lucas thinks it was on 1 December 1780 which he states was the only occasion on which it was followed by 'Harlequin's Invasion', as mentioned by Lamb. Lucas prints a copy of the Drury Lane playbill in his edition of *Elia* in which it is stated that the part of Artaxerxes sung by Mrs Baddeley and that of Mandane by a 'young Lady'. The late Basil Francis stated in a lecture on the theatre that Lamb saw the play in 1781 and that Mandane was sung by Miss Anna

Philips. Lamb himself could not remember the names of those who took part. Boaden says Miss Philips first appeared as Mandane on 11 November 1780 when she was scarcely seventeen.

Asbury, Jacob Vale, 1792–1871. Doctor of medicine, living at Enfield who attended Emma Isola in 1830. Lamb was at a party at his house, probably about the same time, and next day wrote a letter apologising to the doctor and his wife for drinking too much. It is one of Lamb's most amusing letters which indicates that Dr Asbury was an understanding man with a sense of humour. A letter from E.V. Lucas in the *Times Literary Supplement* on 20 March 1937 reproduces a photograph of Asbury. Lamb wrote acrostics to both the doctor and his wife, Dorothy. He is mentioned also in Lamb's letter to Moxon on 25 April 1833 and in one of 7 May 1933 to Rev. James Gillman, the son of Coleridge's friend. Lamb's acrostic is for 'Joseph' Vale Asbury, but Lucas in his letter to the *T.L.S.* gives the name as Jacob.

Ashton, Helen, b.1891. Novelist, author with Katharine Davies of *I Had a Sister*, 1937, which contains a chapter on Mary Lamb. Others included are Dorothy Wordsworth, Caroline Herschel and Cassandra Austen.

Atherstone, Edwin, 1788–1872. Poet and novelist. Wrote poems: *The Last Days of Herculaneum*, 1821; *A Midsummer Day's Dream*, 1824; and *The Fall of Nineveh*, issued in 1828 and continued in additional books over many years. He also wrote two novels, *The Sea Kings in England*, 1830, and *The Handwriting on the Wall*, 1858.

P.G. Patmore in his book *My Friends and Acquaintances*, 1854, states that in 1826 he attended an evening party at Leigh Hunt's and Lamb was present with Atherstone and Mary Shelley. It was on this occasion that Lamb praised Dryden and Davenant. Atherstone was a friend of John Martin, the painter; they are said to have worked in friendly rivalry, for both in their separate arts conceived work on a grandiose scale. Lamb refers to Martin in his essays and letters.

Ayrton, William, 1777–1858. F.R.S., F.S.A. Musical critic and impressario. Son of Dr Edmund Ayrton, the musician. William Ayrton was musical director of the King's Theatre, Haymarket, and an original member of the Royal Institution and the Athenaeum Club. He edited *The Harmonicon* and Charles Knight's *Musical Library*.

A friend of Lamb and a frequent visitor to his evening parties. In April 1817 Lamb wrote to Ayrton to thank him for two musical evenings, one of which was to hear *Don Giovanni*, and shortly afterwards sent a letter in verse on the same subject. When in 1818 Lamb gave Ayrton the two volumes of his *Works*, the latter had a similar

volume of blank pages prepared in which he pasted cuttings of some
of Lamb's later work and called it *Works Volume III*.

Lamb's verses 'Free Thoughts on Several Eminent Composers',
which were inspired probably by either Ayrton or Novello, were sent
to more than one of Lamb's friends. Hazlitt called Ayrton 'the Will
Honeycomb of our set', and Lamb in his 'Letter to Robert Southey'
in 1823 called him 'the last and steadiest left me of the little knot of
whist-players that used to assemble weekly at the Queen's Gate . . .
and called Admiral Burney friend.' Lamb also mentions him in his
essay 'A Chapter on Ears'. He gave Ayrton an inscribed copy of *Elia*
in 1823 which is now in the Harvard Library.

Ayrton married Marianne Arnold, the daughter of Dr Samuel
Arnold, the composer, and sister of Lamb's friend, S.J. Arnold, the
theatrical manager. Ayrton's sister became Mrs Paris of Cambridge,
at whose house the Lambs first met Emma Isola.

Ayton, Richard, 1786–1823. Essayist and playwright. Educated at
Macclesfield Grammar School. Studied law but gave it up for
literature. In 1811 he came to London and wrote several plays: *What
can I be?* and *The Six Physicians* were produced at Covent Garden
without much success, but two translations from the French, *The
Rendezvous* and *The Ladies among themselves*, were popular at the
English Opera House. He also wrote the text of the first two volumes
of W. Daniell's *Voyage round Great Britain in 1813*, 1814–25,
having accompanied Daniell on the voyage.

In 1822 and 1823 Ayton contributed a number of excellent essays
to the *London Magazine* signed 'R.A.', which were reprinted as a
book by Taylor & Hessey in 1825 under the title *Essays and Sketches
of Character*, with a portrait by Richard Westall and a memoir,
probably by George Darley. The book was offered by C. Templeman
in his catalogue as a remainder in 1858. However, it had been praised
by the *Monthly Repository*, and the *Monthly Review* wrote 'Interesting and delightful essays, which by their force of truth, and vivid
illustrations, forcibly remind us of Hazlitt; and by their quaint, tick-
lish, and temeritious humour, of Lamb'.

Although there appears to be no record that Lamb knew Ayton, it
is quite possible that they met as contributors to the *London*. George
Darley seems to have been a friend and during his ill health in the
1820s Ayton was attended by Taylor & Hessey's friend, Dr Darling,
well known to many 'Londoners'.

Babb, Mr. An old friend and admirer of Lamb's mother. A meeting
with him by Mary Lamb at John Rickman's house in 1803 and the
memories it invoked, brought on an attack of her malady. The incident is mentioned by Coleridge in a letter to his wife on 4 April

1803. There is a reference to Mr Babb in Mary Lamb's letter to Sarah Stoddart of 23 October 1806.

Babson, Joseph E. American author and editor. In 1863 he reprinted a number of Lamb items in *The Atlantic Monthly*, and in 1864 issued them in book form as *Eliana: Being the Hitherto Uncollected Writings of Charles Lamb*. It is an important collection which was published first in Boston and then in London the same year by Moxon. Babson also collected Leigh Hunt's 'Wishing-Cap Papers' and published them as *A Day by the Fire and Other papers, Hitherto Uncollected* in 1870. See *Tom Folio: Joseph E. Babson*, 1947, a leaflet printed by Edwin B. Hill.

Bacon, Sir James, 1798–1895. Judge. Called to the Bar of Gray's Inn 1827; became a Bencher of Lincolns Inn 1846. At first travelled the home circuit, later developed a large practice in conveyancing, chancery and bankruptcy. Vice Chancellor in 1870. Retired from the Bench in 1886. In 1827 he had married Laura Frances Cook of Enfield. In his early days he is said to have been sub-editor of *The Times*.

In Edith Sichel's *Life of Ainger*, 1906, 226, is quoted a letter from Bacon to Ainger written about 1890 in which he states that he had known Lamb and was introduced to him by John Dibdin. He says he again met Lamb shortly after Dibdin's death at Godwin's house. He describes himself as a Lamb student living in lofty chambers in Gray's Inn Square when he prevailed on Godwin, his wife and Mary Shelley, to bring Charles and Mary Lamb to visit him. He adds that he thinks it was in 1824 or 1825. As Dibdin died in 1829 it may have been later. Bacon was ninety-two when he gave Ainger his reminiscences, but he describes what he calls several most agreeable evenings when J.H. Reynolds, Wainewright and Charles and Edwin Landseer were present and Lamb 'shed around a spirit of mirth'. Crabb Robinson refers to Bacon occasionally in his *Diary* as Mr Bacon, Q.C., and later as Commissioner of Bankrupts.

Badams, Louisa, b.1806. Daughter of Thomas Holcroft, the dramatist, she became a schoolmistress. Her mother married James Kenney after her first husband's death. Louisa married John Badams, a manufacturing chemist and the friend with whom Carlyle stayed at Birmingham in 1827. Some of Lamb's most amusing letters were addressed to her, including one of 31 December 1832 giving the possibly fictitious account of Lamb suspected of complicity in the murder of Mr Danby of Enfield, and another of 20 August 1833 about Emma Isola's wedding. In 1829 Lamb sent her his 'Instructions for Playing Whist' included as part of a letter to her. Mary Shelley gives a most attractive picture of her as Louisa Holcroft in a letter to Leigh

Hunt in Italy in 1823. John Badams helped Lamb in 1831 when there was difficulty over Coleridge's pension.

When the Badams were first married they lived at Enfield near the Lambs and it was at their house in 1831 that Carlyle met Charles Lamb. Louisa was described by the Carlyles as 'very pretty and lively and clever', but Carlyle thought the marriage unsatisfactory. Badams seems to have been dissipated and Carlyle reports him as drinking too much brandy. Lamb wrote a letter in 1829 addressed to 'Dr J. Badams'.

Baddeley, Robert, 1732–94. English actor. Originally a pastry cook and then a valet. First appeared at Drury Lane in 1761. Fought a duel with David Garrick's brother and was the last actor to wear the royal livery of scarlet and gold as one of the King's Servants. The original Moses in *The School for Scandal*, this was perhaps his most famous part. Also played Fluellen and Grumio, as well as Canton in Colman's *The Clandestine Marriage* and Brainworm in *Every Man in his Humour*. He excelled in representing footmen. By his will he left a fund for poor actors and money for a cake and wine to be consumed at Drury Lane annually on Twelfth Night, a rite still kept up.

Lamb mentions him in 'Barbara S——' and in 'On Some of the Old Actors'.

Baker, Herschel, b.1914. American professor of English at Harvard. Author of *William Hazlitt*, Cambridge, Mass., 1962, which contains many references to Charles Lamb. Also wrote *John Philip Kemble: The Actor in his Theatre*, 1942.

Baldwin, Robert. Publisher, senior partner in the firm of Baldwin, Cradock & Joy of 47 Paternoster Row, London. A Liveryman of the Stationers' Company and a member of the Court of Stationers. The firm was responsible for issuing *The Lady's Magazine* and *The Colonial Journal* and on 1 January 1820 started *The London Magazine*. They sold it to Taylor & Hessey in 1821 after the death of the editor, John Scott.

Lamb wrote several letters to Baldwin about his contributions to the *London Magazine*. In January 1823 Lamb told Barton that Baldwin 'has not paid me up yet', but some payment must have been made for in a letter of 2 January 1821 he acknowledges Baldwin's 'second dft for £20'. Lamb does not seem to have had dealings with Baldwin after the sale of the *London*. The firm of Baldwin & Cradock, as it later became, eventually got into financial difficulties and was absorbed by Simpkin, Marshall & Co.

Ball, Samuel. At Christ's Hospital with Lamb, later an Inspector of Teas at Canton and an employee of the East India Company. Lamb in two letters to Manning in 1806 asks him if he has met Ball in China.

Markham in his 'Memoir of Thomas Manning' states that Manning's
great friend and companion in Canton was Samuel Ball; he adds that
Ball was a member of the Athenaeum Club and lived to be nearly a
hundred.

In a letter to Bernard Barton on 1 December 1824 Lamb tells him
that he has asked his friend Ball in Canton to get some Chinese jars
for John Mitford. In 1827–9 Ball was in Italy with his friend Manning.
Samuel Ball wrote *Observations on the expediency of Opening a
Second Port in China* in 1817 which was reprinted in 1840. In 1848
he published *An Account of the Cultivation & Manufacture of Tea
in China* which contains a contribution by Thomas Manning.

Balmanno, Robert, 1780–1861. Journalist and later a Customs
House employee. Born in Aberdeen, but lived in London in the 1820s.
He and his wife, Mary, were friends of the Lambs, Thomas Hood,
Thomas Moore and Sir Thomas Lawrence. Balmanno was also a
friend and executor of Fuseli. He was secretary to the Artists'
Benevolent Fund and at one time lived in Craven Street near the
Hoods. About 1830 he and his wife emigrated to America where he
was employed in the Brooklyn Customs House. From America he
wrote letters to Mary Cowden Clarke in admiration of her literary
work. He formed a collection in four volumes of Stothard's engravings and he was one of the original subscribers for the plates of Blake's
The Book of Job.

Mrs Balmanno, who was an artist, poet and composer, published
in 1858 her book *Pen and Pencil* which contained interesting accounts of both the Lambs and the Hoods. She also contributed the
section on Pocahontas to Mary Cowden Clarke's *World-Noted
Women*.

Bannister, John 'Jack', 1760–1836. English actor and comedian.
Son of Charles Bannister, actor and singer who played with Garrick.
Was first a student of painting at the Royal Academy, then an actor.
Was encouraged by Garrick and first appeared at the Haymarket. He
was an excellent actor, appearing at Drury Lane where he played
many famous parts, and at one time was acting manager there. His
best known parts were Sir Fretful Plagiary, Sir Anthony Absolute,
Tony Lumpkin, Captain Absolute and Dr Pangloss. His friends included Rowlandson, Morland and Gainsborough. Bannister retired
from the stage in 1815.

He is one of Lamb's favourite actors and is mentioned in 'On Some
of the Old Actors', 'Old China', 'Stage Illusion', 'The New Acting' and
in 'The Old Actors' (the part in the *London* not reprinted in *Elia*).
Bannister appeared with Mrs Bland in one of Lamb's favourite plays,
Morton's *The Children of the Wood*. Leigh Hunt described him as
'the first low comedian on the stage'. In 1831 Bannister sat as the

model for Uncle Toby for C.R. Leslie's picture of *Uncle Toby and the Widow Wadman.*

Barbauld, Anna Letitia, 1743–1825. Poetess, born Anna Aikin and a sister of Dr John Aikin. A blue stocking who had a knowledge of French, Italian, Latin and Greek. In addition to her poems she wrote books for children and edited a fifty-volume collection of the British novelists. She collaborated with her brother in some of her books. In 1811 she wrote her poem 'Eighteen Hundred and Eleven' in which she prophesied some future traveller from the Antipodes contemplating the ruins of St Pauls from a broken arch of Blackfriars Bridge. Among her many friends were Crabb Robinson, Wordsworth, Walter Scott, Samuel Rogers and George Dyer. Crabb Robinson records in his *Diary* that he visited Mrs Barbauld in 1812 and read to her Lamb's' Mr H——, which she appeared to enjoy. It was at her house in 1821 that Lamb made his *faux pas* about Gilbert Wakefield. George Dyer was on the way to dine with Mrs Barbauld when he walked from Lamb's house into the New River.

Lamb called Mrs Barbauld, Mrs Inchbald and Mrs Godwin (who used the name of Baldwin as a publisher) 'the three bald women'. He was critical of Mrs Barbauld's books for children: 'Damn them! I mean the cursed Barbauld Crew, those Blights and Blasts of all that is Human in man and child.' He had not met Mrs Barbauld at the time of this outburst which occurs in a letter to Coleridge in October 1802. When they did meet he seems to have liked her.

Baring, Sir Francis, 1740–1810. London merchant and banker. Founder of Baring Bros & Co; Director of the East India Company from 1779 and Chairman in 1792–3. Miss Ann Manning in her *Family Portraits*, 1861, states that Sir Francis Baring was persuaded by Joseph Paice to procure Lamb his situation with the East India Company. He was described by Lord Erskine as 'the first merchant in Europe'.

Barnes, Thomas, 1785–1841. Editor of *The Times*. Educated at Christ's Hospital 1796–1804, a contemporary there of Leight Hunt. Proceeded to Pembroke College, Cambridge, and then was admitted student of the Inner Temple. He was a pupil of Joseph Chitty, the famous lawyer, but gave up the law after two years for journalism. He became dramatic critic to *The Times*, then its Parliamentary reporter and finally editor in 1817. He contributed to Leigh Hunt's *Reflector* and *Examiner* and also to *The Champion*. His position as editor of *The Times* was such that Lord Lyndhurst described him as 'the most powerful man in the country'.

Among Barnes's friends were Lamb, Leigh Hunt, Barron Field, Horace and James Smith, Theodore Hook and Charles Mathews.

During the early years of the century he was a frequenter of Lamb's rooms in the Temple. Talfourd gives an excellent account of a discussion in 1816 between Lamb and Barnes on Shakespeare, and how the latter praised Lamb's writings on the subject. Barnes was probably the author of the obituary notice of Lamb which appeared in *The Times* on 29 December 1834.

Leigh Hunt describes Barnes when a young man as remarkable for his good looks, his attainments in Latin and English and his love of bathing and boating. He was also a good cricketer.

Barnett, George Leonard, b.1915. American professor, Indiana University, U.S.A., now retired. Author of *Charles Lamb: The Evolution of Elia*, 1964, which also discusses Lamb MSS in various libraries, the relationship of Lamb's letters to his essays and how his writing was affected by his business career. Professor Barnett also contributed the sections on bibliographies, editions and biographies of Charles Lamb to *The English Romantic Poets and Essayists. A Review of Research and Criticism*, edited by C.W. and L.H. Houtchens, 1957, revised editions 1966 and 1972. In 1976 appeared his excellent book *Charles Lamb* in Twayne's English Authors Series. Among his contributions to periodicals are:

P.M.L.A.
1945   Dating Lamb's contributions to the *Table Book*, June.
1946   First American review of Charles Lamb, June.
M.L.Q.
1948   A Critical Analysis of the Lucas edition of Lamb's letters, September.
1952   Charles Lamb to John Britton: an unpublished letter, December.
1956   An unpublished review by Charles Lamb, December.
1959   Charles Lamb's part in an edition of Hogarth, December.
H.L.Q.
1943   An unpublished poem by Charles Lamb, May.
1955   Corrections in the text of Lamb's letters, February.
1956   Charles Lamb and the Button Family: An unpublished poem and letter, February.
1962   A disquisition on Punch & Judy attributed to Charles Lamb, May.
Notes & Queries
1962   The correct date of a Lamb letter, May.
Studies in Romanticism
1965   The pronunciation of Elia.
Coranto
1965   Lamb's Mortifying Applial: Payments from the London Magazine.

Charles Lamb Bulletin
1975   The history of Charles Lamb's Reputation, April/July.
1978   'That Cursed Barbauld Crew' or Charles Lamb and Children's
       Literature, January, Ernest Crowsley Memorial Lecture.

Barrington, Daines, 1727–1800. Barrister of the Inner Temple.
Fourth son of John Shute, first Viscount Barrington. Called to the
Bar, 1750; became a Bencher in 1777. Well known during his lifetime
as an antiquary, he was F.S.A. and F.R.S., but his antiquarian work
was ridiculed by Horace Walpole and Peter Pindar. He is best known
today for being the recipient of many letters from Gilbert White, the
naturalist, later printed as part of *The Natural History of Selborne*.
Barrington was partly the inspirer of that work. A friend of Dr Johnson and an original member of his Essex House Club, he was also a
friend of the poet Gray and of Bishop Percy. Barrington contributed
many papers to the Transactions of the Royal Society.
    He was one of Lamb's 'Old Benchers', described in the essay as 'an
oddity'. He lived at 5 Kings Bench Walk. In his essay Lamb mentions
Barrington's brother, a bishop: this was a younger brother who
became successively Bishop of Landaff, Salisbury and Durham.
Another brother was an Admiral. Barrington was one of the Counsel
for the Crown in the trial of Mary Blandy at Oxford. It was on her
execution that, as related by Lamb, Samuel Salt's unfortunate
remark was made to her relative.

Barry, James, 1741–1806. Painter. Elected Royal Academician in
1773, but expelled from the Royal Academy in 1799 on account of
his 'Letter to the Dilettanti Society.' Among his most famous pictures
was the 'Death of General Wolfe.' In 1775 he published *An Inquiry
into the Real and Imaginary Observations to the Acquisition of the
Arts in England.* Although he made many enemies by his attacks on
other artists, among whom were Sir Joshua Reynolds, he seems to
have retained the latter's friendship and that of Edmund Burke.
    Lamb refers to him in his essay on Hogarth, but does not agree with
Barry's views. He copied some passages from Barry's work into his
Commonplace Books. Barry was a member of Dr Johnson's Essex
House Club.

Barry Cornwall. *See* B.W. Procter.

Barrymore, William, 1758–1830. A favourite actor at Drury Lane
and the Haymarket. He first appeared in London in 1782 and in 1799
was the original Pizarro in Sheridan's play at Drury Lane to Mrs
Siddons's Elvira. On 13 December 1800 he acted at Drury Lane in
Godwin's unsuccessful play, *Antonio*. He played Aurelius in W.H.
Ireland's *Vortigern*. In May 1818 he opened the Royal Coburg

Theatre with his own melodrama *Trial by Battle or Heaven Defend the Right*. He also produced the play.

Lamb refers to him in his essay 'On Some of the Old Actors' where he says 'Orsino, by Mr Barrymore—What a full Shakespearean sound it carries! how fresh to the memory arise the image and the manner, of the gentle actor.' He also mentions him in his letter to Manning on 5 December 1806 as playing in Holcroft's *Vindictive Man* at Drury Lane. Leigh Hunt in *The Examiner* in 1836 refers to him as 'a regular strutting king.' Crabb Robinson in his *Diary* on 20 May 1815 has the non-committal statement 'Barrymore as Pierre requires no observation', in *Venice Preserved* at Covent Garden.

Bartley, George, 1782?–1858. Comedian. First appeared in London at Drury Lane in 1802 where he played Orlando. In 1803 he played Polydore in *The Orphan*. In 1806 he was Mr Bevil in Lamb's 'Mr H——'. He subsequently acted with success in the provinces but in 1815 had returned to Drury Lane where he acted Falstaff. With his wife he went to America where they were successful. On his return he played at Covent Garden and the Lyceum, and in 1829 was stage manager at Covent Garden. In 1850 he played Falstaff at Windsor Castle. He was treasurer of the Covent Garden Theatrical Fund. R.H. Barham said he married a Miss Smith, said to be a good tragic actress, somewhat resembling Mrs Siddons.

Barton, Bernard, 1784–1849. Quaker poet. After having worked in a shop, been a coal and corn merchant and a private tutor in Liverpool, in 1809 he became a clerk in the private bank of Dykes & Alexander at Woodbridge, Suffolk, and remained there the rest of his life. Barton had two sisters and one step brother; the elder sister, Maria Hack, was the author of many children's books.

Bernard Barton was an active member of the Woodbridge Book Club, notable for having blackballed *The Essays of Elia*. Among Barton's friends were Southey, Allan Cunningham, Capel Lofft, Charles Lloyd, John Mitford, Edward FitzGerald, John Linnell and, of course, Charles Lamb. Barton and Lamb first met in 1822 and there are a number of interesting letters from Lamb to Barton. The best known is that in 1823 in which Lamb advised him, in no uncertain terms, not to give up the bank and try to support himself by his writings: 'Keep to your bank and your bank will keep you.' Fotunately Barton followed this advice, which had also been given to him by Byron in 1812.

Barton was a contributor to the *London Magazine* and among the many items he sent was a sonnet 'To Elia'. He also wrote 'Fireside Quatrains to Charles Lamb', which was published in his *New Year's Eve* in 1828. Lamb gave Barton a presentation copy of *The Last Essays of Elia*. In 1824 Lamb had sent verses for the album of Lucy

Barton, the poet's only daughter. After her father's death she married Edward FitzGerald, the poet.

Barton's favourite books included some authors beloved by Elia, such as Goldsmith, Cowper, Bunyan, John Woolman and Izaak Walton. He was also fond of Gilbert White, Evelyn, Sir Walter Scott and was particularly delighted to quote Boswell's *Johnson*. One of Barton's hobbies was the collection of snuff boxes.

Many volumes of poems appeared from Barton's pen, among which were *Metrical Effusions*, 1812, about which he wrote to Byron, *Poems*, 1820; *Napoleon & Other poems*, 1822; *Poetic Vigils*, 1824; *A New Year's Eve*, 1828; and with his daughter, *The Reliquary*, 1836.

Barton lived in various lodgings in Woodbridge, one of which was at the house of Anne Knight, a Quaker widow, to whom he introduced Lamb. Later he moved into the bank house. In 1824 members of the Society of Friends subscribed £1,200 for his benefit and in 1846 Sir Robert Peel, with whom he had dined, procured him a pension of £100 a year. Edward FitzGerald wrote a memoir of Bernard Barton.

Barton, Lucy, 1808–98. Daughter of the Quaker poet, Bernard Barton. Visited Lamb with her father in 1823. In 1824 Lamb wrote a short note to Lucy Barton as a postscript to a letter to her father and the same year he sent verses for her album. *Selections from Bernard Barton's Poems & Letters* were edited by his daughter and published in 1849 with a memoir by Edward FitzGerald. In 1856 she married FitzGerald, but they separated the same year. In 1892 she wrote some reminiscences of Lamb for E.V. Lucas which he refers to in his *Life of Lamb*.

Barton, Thomas, d.1791. Barrister of the Inner Temple. Called to the Bar in 1737 and became a Bencher in 1775. He had chambers in King's Bench Walk and is one of Lamb's 'Old Benchers'.

Bartram, Ann. *See* Ann Simmons.

Bauer, Dr Josephine. American author of the University of Maryland. Author of *The London Magazine 1820–29* (Anglistica Series), Copenhagen, 1953, which contains many references to Charles Lamb.

Beard, John, c.1716–91. English singer and actor. Handel composed some of his finest tenor roles for him. He married the daughter of John Rich, manager of Covent Garden, and later became joint proprietor and acting manager of the theatre. He was President of the Beefsteak Club.

Lamb mentions him in his piece 'Playhouse Memoranda' in *The Examiner* in connexion with the first play he saw, *Artaxerxes*. But as Beard retired in 1767, eight years before Lamb was born, Lucas believes he probably set down the name as that of a well known actor, for he earlier says that he does not remember the names of the cast. Beard had, however, played in *Artaxerxes* and in *The Jovial Crew* and *Love in a Village* and was a frequent singer at Ranelagh. He also played Macheath in *The Beggar's Opera*.

Beaumont, Sir George Howland, 1753–1827. Connoisseur, patron of art and landscape painter. Educated at Eton and New College, Oxford M.P. 1790–96. Said to be a descendent of Francis Beaumont, the Elizabethan dramatist. Lived at Coleorton Hall, Leicestershire, but also had a house in Grosvenor Square, London.

He knew Dr Johnson and was an intimate friend of Sir Joshua Reynolds. He was also friendly with Coleridge, Haydon, Southey, Wordsworth and Samuel Rogers and Constable. As a considerable patron of artists and men of letters he encouraged Constable and helped Coleridge to establish *The Friend* and to procure a pension. He also assisted the painters Haydon, John Jackson and J.R. Cozens. Byron satirized him in 'The Blues' and he was devoted to a theory that a good picture must be brown, which amused some of his fellow artists.

He was largely responsible for the establishment of the National Gallery with pictures from J.J. Angerstein's collection, among which were the six pictures comprising Hogarth's *Marriage a la Mode* and his self portrait, all known to Lamb. He also gave some pictures from his own collection including some by the artist Claude, one of which he was so much attached to that he asked to have it returned for him to retain during his lifetime.

There appears to be no record of meetings between Beaumont and Lamb, but the help given to Coleridge and Haydon must have been the subject of discussion in the Lamb circle. Lamb also was a lover of Claude's landscapes and Hazlitt tells us that they were frequently discussed at Lamb's evening parties during which Beaumont's name was no doubt mentioned.

Becky. The Lamb's servant. Talfourd describes her as 'an old petted servant' and it seems that she was of an intensely practical mind which could not distinguish between the genius and the ordinary man. She had the good of her employers at heart, but was used to 'give them a bit of her mind' for their own good. P.G. Patmore in his *My Friends and Acquaintances*, 1854, has a long and amusing account of her benevolent tyranny and he calls her an excellent person in all respects. The Lambs in turn were kind to her and tried to find a situation for her father. She was a great friend of Dash, Hood's dog, who sometimes lived with them. Eventually she left to be married, about 1829. In his essay 'Thoughts on Presents of Game &c' in *The Athenaeum* in 1833, Lamb refers to her under the name of 'Mrs

Minikin'. Becky had been servant to the Hazlitts before she went to the Lambs and W.C. Hazlitt suggests that her name may have been Tomlinson. Crabb Robinson in his *Diary* on 9 May 1829 notes that she was ill-tempered and had been 'a plague and a tyrant' but had been with the Lambs for many years.

Bedingfield, Mrs. Lamb's letter to Ollier in October 1826 encloses the manuscript of a novel by Mrs Bedingfield which he is asked to show to Colburn. He says Hazlitt thought well of her writing. In another letter he says she is coming to tea. In a letter of 21 May 1827 he says she has invited Ollier to tea, and writing to Charles Cowden Clarke on 2 February 1829 he says Mary Lamb 'likes Mrs Bedingfield much'; presumably he here means her writings. Lucas says a Mrs Bryan Bedingfield wrote a novel called *Longhollow: a Tale of the West* published by Whittaker in 1829; this may have been the same person. She may have been a friend of Matilda Betham.

Bell, Neil. *See* Stephen Southwold.

Benevolent Society of Blues, The. A society of those educated at Christ's Hospital founded in 1824 with the object of granting pensions or temporary assistance to those old Blues who were in need, and to the widows and orphans of old Blues who were in distress. Charles Lamb was a member. A later society than the Amicable Society of Blues, which was founded in 1775.

Benger, Elizabeth Ogilvie, 1778–1827. Novelist, poet and biographer. Born at Wells, Somerset, the daughter of a purser in the Navy on Admiral Keith's ship. In 1791 she wrote a poem 'The Female Geniad'. She is said to have acquired a knowledge of Greek, Latin, Italian, Spanish and German. In 1800 she came to London and made vigorous attempts to get to know the Lambs. Charles Lamb wrote an amusing letter about her to Coleridge in April 1800, in which he calls her 'Miss Benje or Benjey' and says 'It seems she is one of your authoresses, that you first foster, and then upbraid us with', and he adds that he was luckily in time to prevent her and Mary Lamb 'exchanging vows of eternal friendship'. She was a friend of Miss Sarah Wesley, Coleridge's disciple and Charles Wesley's daughter. She was greatly admired by George Dyer and the Lambs talked him into thinking he was in love with her, but they did not succeed in a similar course with Miss Benger. She was a member of the Aikin-Barbauld circle and friendly with Robert Smirke, the painter. Engravings from his paintings were used to illustrate her long poem 'On the Slave Trade', 1809.

Among her other works were two novels, *Marian* and *The Heart and the Fancy*, 1813; a translation of Klopstock's letters, 1814; and a series of memoirs including those of Elizabeth Hamilton, John

Tobin, the dramatist, Anne Boleyn, Mary Queen of Scots and Elizabeth of Bohemia. Madame de Staël described her as 'the most interesting woman she had seen during her visit to England'. She is said to have been full of enthusiasm and vivacity and a good talker. She died in reduced circumstances.

In *A Book for a Rainy Day*, J.T. Smith prints from his album, verses entitled 'Impromptu Lines by Miss Benger, on the paucity of information respecting the life and character of Shakespeare'. Her friend Lucy Aikin wrote a Memoir of her which appeared in Miss Benger's *Memoirs of Anne Boleyn*.

Bensley, Robert, ?1738–1817. Actor. Played at Drury Lane, Covent Garden, and the Haymarket. His best known parts included Malvolio, Pierre in *Venice Preserved* and Evander in Murphy's *The Grecian Daughter*, in which he played with Mrs Siddons. He retired in 1796. One of Lamb's favourite actors, he is praised highly in the essay 'On Some of the Old Actors', where Lamb says 'Of all the actors who flourished in my time . . . Bensley had most swell of the soul, was greatest in the delivery of heroic conceptions, the emotions consequent upon the presentment of a great idea to the fancy.'

Bensusan, Samuel Levy, b.1872. Author and editor. Wrote *Charles Lamb: His Homes & Haunts*, 1910, and similar volumes on Shakespeare and Wordsworth for Jack's *Homes & Haunts* series. He also wrote a volume on Coleridge for the *Peoples' Books* in 1913. He wrote numerous other books on travel, the countryside and art and edited *The Jewish World* 1897–8. It is said that Lamb writing from India House to a firm named Bensusan & Co invariably addressed them as "Sir—Madam."

Benyon, Thomas, or Bennion. Taylor & Hessey's porter. As such he met many of the London Magazine circle. There are letters from him to John Clare and he acted as Clare's guide in London. He also occasionally guided Lamb home after a party, and a letter from Hessey to Taylor describes the amusing difficulty of Lamb insisting he could find his own way home and Thomas watching for a favourable opportunity to bundle him into a coach and see him home. Thomas Hood states Benyon contributed to the *London Magazine*, but there is no evidence of this and it is probably one of Hood's jokes. Benyon's letters indicate that he was unskilled in writing.

Betham Family. Rev. William Betham, 1749–1839, was an antiquary who married Mary Damant of Boston, Lincs, and had a family of fifteen children noted for their stature and good looks. He lived for most of his life at Stonham Aspel, Suffolk, as headmaster of a school, but resigned in 1833 when presented to the rectory of Stoke Lacy near

Hereford. He had a fine library. In Lamb's letter to Landor in 1833
he says 'the measureless Bethams. I know a quarter of a mile of them.'
He also refers to them in his 'Lepus Papers' in the *New Times*, in
1825. Among the fifteen children were:

William Betham, 1779–1853. Eldest son, antiquary and Ulster
King of Arms. Knighted in 1812. Author of antiquarian books.

Charles Betham. With East India Company. On his return from
India and marriage became Landor's tenant at Llanthony in 1812.
Referred to by Lamb in a letter to Landor as one of your 'Welsh
annoyancers.'

George Betham. With East India Company.

John Betham. Captain with East India Company.

Robert Graham Betham. With East India Company.

Edward Betham, d.1809. With East India Company.

Frederick Betham. At one time with East India Company, but
later lived with Charles at Llanthony and a source of annoyance to
Landor.

Mary Matilda Betham. Minature painter. *See* separate entry.

Anne Betham, d.1833. She left a legacy of £30 to Mary Lamb in
1833.

Barbara Betham. *See* separate entry.

Other children were Alfred, Emma and Mary Betham.

Betham, Barbara, b.1800. Sister of Matilda Betham and fifth
daughter of Rev William Betham. Mary Lamb wrote a most interesting letter to her in 1814, in which she describes the finding of the four
unused rooms in their Inner Temple abode, one of which became
Charles's study, the walls of which he covered with prints. Lamb
commented that Barbara Betham's face had 'more cloud and sun-
shine in it than any he knew.' She appears to have been a pupil at Mrs
Holcroft's school but ran away from it.

Betham, Ernest. Author. Editor of *A House of Letters*, 1905, which
contains many references to the Lambs and he prints some of their
letters to the Betham family.

Betham, Mary Matilda, 1776–1852. Minature painter and author.
Eldest daughter of Rev William Betham. She had received Italian
lessons from Agostino Isola at Cambridge and was a self-taught
minature painter. She did minatures of George Dyer, Randal Norris,
Mrs Coleridge and her daughter Sara. In a note to Sara Hutchinson
in 1816 Lamb passes a message through Wordsworth to De Quincey
that Matilda Betham charged three guineas for a *Virgin and Child*.
She was a correspondent of Coleridge, Southey and the Lambs, and
Coleridge addressed a poem to her. Lamb gave her some of his books
inscribed 'Matilda Betham with Charles Lamb's old love.' She wrote

some 'Bridal verses' for the Moxons in 1833. When George Dyer became blind she used to read to him. She gave Talfourd some recollections of Lamb's conversation, particularly of his puns.

Matilda Betham published *Elegies*, 1797; *Poems*, 1808; and *Lay of Marie*, 1816. The latter book was read in manuscript by Lamb who praised it; there are several letters about it printed by Lucas. It was also praised by Southey and Allan Cunningham. She also published *Biographical Dictionary of the Celebrated Women of every Age and Country*, 1804.

Betty, William Henry West, 1791–1874. Actor. Master Betty was a child prodigy known as the Young Roscius who was very popular in 1804–5, playing at Covent Garden and Drury Lane. He appeared in all the great tragic roles of Shakespeare. His popularity waned and he was hissed when he played Richard III. Lamb mentions him in his essay 'Detached Thoughts on Books and Reading' in the *London Magazine* in a paragraph not reprinted in the *Elia* volume.

Bibliographies. The principal bibliographies of Charles Lamb are:

E.D. North in B.E. Martin, *In the Footprints of Charles Lamb*, 1891.
Luther S. Livingston, *A Bibliography of the First Editions in Book Form of the Writings of Charles and Mary Lamb, published prior to Charles Lamb's death in 1834*. New York, 1903. 54 illustrations (facsimiles of autograph letters and title pages).
J.C. Thomson, *Bibliography of the Writings of Charles and Mary Lamb. A Literary History*. Hull, 1908.
Thomas Hutchinson, 'Bibliographical List 1794–1834' in Volume I of *The Works of Charles Lamb*. Oxford University Press, 1908.
Charles Lamb Society Bulletin. 1935 to date.
Edmund Blunden in *Cambridge Bibliography of English Literature*. Volume III, 1940. Includes items in periodicals. Also Volume V Supplement, 1957, by Richard E. Morton.
W.L. Renwick in *English Literature 1789–1815*. Volume IX of The Oxford History of English Literature. Oxford University Press, 1963.
Ian Jack in *English Literature 1815–1832*. Volume X of The Oxford History of English Literature. Oxford University Press, 1963.
George L. Barnett and Stuart M. Tave in *The English Romantic Poets and Essayists. A Review of Research & Criticism*. Edited by C.W. and L.H. Houtchens. New York, 1957. Later editions, 1966 and 1972. Of the section on Charles Lamb, Barnett wrote on bibliographies, editions and biographies and Tave on criticism. This valuable book includes the lesser known items often difficult to trace. It also draws attention to the annual bibliographies appearing in such publications as *P.M.L.A.*,

E.L.H., P.Q., E.L.N. and to some exhibition catalogues. Roy Park in *The New Cambridge Bibliography of English Literature,* Volume 3, 1969. Includes items in periodicals. Much bibliographical information can also be found in the sale catalogues of Lamb collectors such as W.H. Arnold, A. Edward Newton, Dean Sage, Charles Scribner, Harry B. Smith, John A. Spoor, W.T. Wallace and T.J. Wise (*see* The Ashley Library Catalogue, Volume 3, 1923), as well as in the publications concerning large libraries, e.g. Harvard, Princeton and the University of Texas. There is also the catalogue of the Charles Lamb Society Library, 1949, a new edition of which is being prepared. Useful information is sometimes found in *Book Prices Current, Book Auction Records, American Book Prices Current* and in Sothebys' and other auctioneers' catalogues. Selected bibliographies are given in some of the many volumes on Lamb, the most important of which are mentioned in Barnett & Tave. The *Keats-Shelley Journal* bibliographies are also useful. A bibliography of Lamb studies from 1900 is being prepared by Professor Duane Schneider of the Department of English, Ohio University, U.S.A.

Biddle, Moncure. American lover of Lamb's work. Author of *A Christmas Letter. Charles Lamb,* Moncure Biddle & Co, Philadelphia, 1938, which contains a facsimile of the letter from Lamb to Wordsworth that introduced W. Harrison Ainsworth (No. 522 in Lucas). This is a pamphlet of thirty-eight pages by Biddle intended as a Christmas gift for his friends; other illustrations are Charles Lamb by Hazlitt, and by Hancock, Lamb's portrait of Milton and of the East India House.

Bigod, Ralph. *See* John Fenwick.

Bird, William. Schoolmaster. Lamb attended Bird's Academy in Bond Stables, off Fetter Lane, about 1781. Mary had been there before him. As mentioned in Lamb's letter to Hone's *Every-Day Book* in 1825, Captain Starkey was an assistant there. The school is described in Lamb's letter.

Birrell, Augustine, 1850–1933. English author and politician. Educated at Amersham Hall School and Trinity College, Cambridge. Called to the Bar at Lincolns Inn, and was Quain professor of law at University College, London. Liberal M.P., became President of the Board of Trade and Secretary of State for Ireland. He married as his second wife Mrs Lionel Tennyson, daughter of Frederick Locker (Locker-Lampson).

Augustine Birrell was described by S.M. Rich writing in 1931 as 'the doyen of Elians'. He was the guest of honour at the first Cambridge Charles Lamb Dinner in 1909, and as President of the Elian Club was Chairman of its first dinner at the Cheshire Cheese, Fleet Street, on 6 November 1925.

He wrote an introduction to the Temple Library edition of *The Essays of Elia* in 1888 and it was reprinted in the Dent edition illustrated by C.E. Brock in 1899 and several times since. Hugh Walpole described the introduction as 'Birrell's delightful preface'. In 1902 he wrote the volume on *William Hazlitt* for the English Men of Letters series and it has many references to Lamb. Of his books of essays those which refer to Lamb are *Obiter Dicta*, 1884, 'Truth Seeking'; *Obiter Dicta 2nd Series*, 1887, 'Charles Lamb'—a review of Ainger's edition, which was reprinted by Arthur L. Humphreys in a most beautifully produced booklet entitled *A Rogue's Memoirs &c* in 1912; and *Res Judicatae*, 1892, 'The Letters of Charles Lamb' (also a review of Ainger's edition). Other volumes are *Essays about Men, Women & Books*, 1894; *In the Name of the Bodleian*, 1905; *More Obiter Dicta*, 1924, which contains an essay on Coleridge; and *Et Cetera*, 1930, with 'No Crabb, No Christmas', an essay on Crabb Robinson. In 1920 he wrote *Frederick Locker-Lampson. A Character Sketch*, an interesting volume on the well known book collector. Birrell also wrote for the English Men of Letters series a volume on *Andrew Marvell*. An autobiography, *Things Past Redress*, was published in 1937, but there is little about his Elian interests in it. He also wrote a short introduction for Blackie's Wallet Library edition of *The Essays of Elia*.

Birrell became well known as a man of letters and essayist, his writing being marked by grace and humour. Some critics have written contemptuously of Birrell's essays and stated that they were nick-named 'birrelling' by a few reviewers. It may be worth noting that the *Encyclopaedia Britannica*, fourteenth edition, published when Birrell was still alive, gives a different view: 'In the House of Commons, his light but pointed humour led to the coining of a new word 'birrelling'. R.C.K. Ensor in the *D.N.B.* states that the criticism of Birrell's writing as superficial is unfair and that he was able 'to write entertainingly on a dull subject, the reverse practice to that of some of his critics.'

Blacket, Widow. *See* Mrs Smith.

Blackwood, William, 1776–1834. Edinburgh publisher. After being a bookseller and working with publishers in Edinburgh and Glasgow, he went to London and worked for three years in Cuthill's bookshop, which was noted for its catalogues. In 1804 he returned to Edinburgh and started his own business, after a time turning to publishing and becoming John Murray's agent in Edinburgh.

In 1817 he founded *Blackwood's Edinburgh Magazine*, and after

a bad start took over the editorship himself. With the help of John
Wilson, J.G. Lockhart and James Hogg he made it highly successful.
In addition to publishing the works of his three chief assistants on the
magazine he issued books by D. Moir, John Galt and Susan Ferrier.
He also published the *Edinburgh Encyclopaedia* and Alison's *History
of Europe*. It was through a quarrel with *Blackwood's Magazine* that
John Scott, the editor of the *London Magazine*, lost his life in 1821.
Charles Lamb wrote several short notes to William Blackwood and
contributed to 'Maga' as *Blackwood's Magazine* was called.

Blake, William, 1757–1827. Poet and painter. Crabb Robinson
records a party at Lamb's in July 1811 where Southey talked about
Blake whom he had recently visited. Southey admired his work but
thought him mad. In May 1824 Lamb wrote one of his best letters to
Barton in which he praised Blake's work greatly. Bernard Barton
wrote several letters about Blake's pictures to John Linnell, Blake's
friend, and the latter presented Barton with one of Blake's illustrations to Dante. Crabb Robinson also noted that he had given Lamb
a 'Catalogue of a Blake exhibition', with which the latter was delighted. He also gave him a print of Blake's Canterbury Pilgrims' which
Lamb preferred to Stothard's. Robinson states that Lamb declared
Blake's description was the finest criticism he had ever read of
Chaucer's poem.

The plates for the illustrations to Lamb's *Tales from Shakespeare*
are said to have been engraved by Blake who at that time was a
journeyman engraver who did work for William Godwin. In 1824
Lamb sent Blake's poem 'Chimney Sweeper' to James Montgomery
for his volume *The Chimney Sweeper's Friend*.

Blakesware. A mansion near Widford in Hertfordshire, the 'Blakesmoor' of Lamb's famous essay. The house was originally built in
1640 and in 1683 became the property of the Plumer family, who
owned it until Lamb's time. After the death of his mother in 1778
William Plumer maintained the house, but himself lived at Gilston.
Lamb's maternal grandmother, Mary Field, was in charge at Blakesware as housekeeper until her death in 1792.

After William Plumer's death in 1822 Blakesware was pulled down
as Lamb relates in his essay. There are also descriptions of the house
and garden in Mary Lamb's tale of 'The Young Mahometan' in *Mrs
Leicester's School*, in Charles Lamb's *Rosamund Gray* and in 'Dream
Children'. In his letters to Southey on 31 October 1799 and to Barton
on 10 August 1827, he also mentions the house. Reginald Hine in his
Charles Lamb and his Hertfordshire, 1949, has a very full description of the old house based largely on his discovery of the sale
catalogue of the contents in 1822. From this he is able to reconstruct

the fifty-nine rooms of the mansion and to bring before our eyes the house as Lamb saw it as a child, a truly fascinating experience.

Blanchard, Samuel Laman, 1804–45. Author, who had also been a clerk, dramatic critic, actor, proof reader, editor and Secretary to the Zoological Society. His volume of poems *Lyric Offerings,* 1828, published by W. Harrison Ainsworth, was dedicated to Charles Lamb, who praised the book and told Blanchard in a letter of 9 November 1828 he would 'put them up among my poetical treasures'. It was also praised by Browning. Blanchard later took Lamb's essays as a model for his own and contributed some 'Popular Fallacies', after Lamb's death, to the *New Monthly Magazine.*

In 1831 Blanchard became acting editor of the *Monthly Magazine* and in 1832 editor of *The True Sun.* Later he edited the *Court Journal* and *The Courier* and from 1841 wrote for *The Examiner.* Among his friends were T.N. Talfourd, B.W. Procter, Douglas Jerrold, Leigh Hunt, Macready, Charles Dickens, J.B. Buckstone, Harrison Ainsworth and L.E. Landon. Blanchard's *Sketches from Life,* 1846, refers to Lamb.

Bland, Mrs Maria Theresa, 1769–1838. Jewish actress and singer. Born Ida Romani (Romanzini). Was a well known ballad singer at Ranelagh and Vauxhall, and was attached to the Drury Lane Company for many years. She appeared in many operas of the time, including *Inkle and Yarico, The Pirates, The Iron Chest* and particularly in Thomas Morton's *The Children of the Wood* with Jack Bannister.

She is described as pock-marked, squat and thick set, but she charmed by the pure silvery tones of her voice. When she appeared on the stage with Charles Dignum, who was squat and clumsy, they drew from Charles Lamb the exclamation 'And lo, two puddings smoked upon the board!' She was among the well known singers who appeared at the celebrated performance of Giardini's oratorio 'Ruth' at Ranelagh in 1792 when some of the tickets cost £100. She married George Bland, brother of Mrs Jordan, with whom she had acted in Dublin.

Mrs Bland was a mezzo soprano; Lamb tells Manning in a letter of 2 January 1810 he heard her sing the ballad 'She's sweet fifteen' in boy's clothes, and added 'I sometimes think the lower notes in my voice are like Mrs Bland.' Lamb also refers to her in his essay 'Old China' where he makes Mary Lamb say that when they used to sit in the pit they saw Mrs Bland and Bannister in *The Children in the Wood.* In later years he saw Fanny Kelly in this play.

Blandy, Mary, d.1752. Daughter of Francis Blandy, attorney. Convicted of poisoning her father and hanged at Oxford in 1752. Referred to by Lamb in his essay 'The Old Benchers of the Inner Temple' where he recounts Samuel Salt's *faux pas* in mentioning her name to a relative of hers at the time she was executed.

Bloomfield, Robert, 1766–1823. Peasant poet. First a shoemaker, later a bookseller. Had an appointment in the Seal Office which he had to resign on account of ill health. His best known work *The Farmer's Boy*, 1800, was published with the help of Capel Lofft. It was an immediate success and 26,000 copies were sold in three years. Other works included *Rural Tales*, 1802; *Wild Flowers*, 1806; and *May Day with the Muses*, 1822.

Lamb first met him through George Dyer and was not impressed; but in 1823 George Daniel took Bloomfield to dine with Lamb, who then liked him. He did not think much of Bloomfield poetry, and in a letter to Manning on 3 November 1800 he had said that he thought the author of *The Farmer's Boy* had a poor mind and added 'he makes me sick'. Bernard Barton wrote 'Verses to the Memory of Bloomfield, the Suffolk Poet', which were printed in his *Poetic Vigils* in 1824.

Bloxam, Samuel Anthony. A friend of Lamb who was also educated at Christ's Hospital. On 19 July 1826 Lamb wrote to the Rev Edward Coleridge, nephew of S.T. Coleridge, to thank him for kindness to Bloxam's son, Frederick, Lamb may have been assisting him to get into Eton, where Edward Coleridge was a master. On 9 September 1826 Bloxam dined with Lamb, Coleridge and Frederic Reynolds, according to Lamb's letter of that date to J.B. Dibdin.

Lucas in a note to the July letter in his 1905 edition of the *Letters* states that Lamb and Bloxham were at Christ's Hospital together, but in the 1935 edition he omits this and states 'I do not trace Bloxam'. It looks as if he had overlooked his earlier note, which repeats the information given by W.C. Hazlitt in the Bohn edition of the *Letters* and is no doubt correct since Hazlitt says he was given the facts by J.B. Bloxam, Samuel Bloxam's nephew. The latter only states the the two were educated at Christ's and 'very probably contemporaries'. In his *Life of Charles Lamb* Lucas states that 'Bloxam was an old acquaintance whose son Lamb had recommended for Christ's Hospital.'

It may be worth mentioning that in a note in Jack Simmons's *Southey*, 1945, 232, is a reference to the scheme of Pantisocracy as being first proposed in the rooms of Matthew Bloxam, an undergraduate of Worcester College. A Rev Richard Bloxam married Sir Thomas Lawrence's sister, Anne, in 1796.

Blunden, Edmund Charles, 1896–1974. Poet and critic. Educated at Christ's Hospital and Queen's College, Oxford. Served in the First World War as a lieutenant and awarded the Military Cross. Wrote many fine volumes of poetry. Awarded the Hawthornden Prize for *The Shepherd*. Professor of English at Tokyo, 1924–27. Fellow and Tutor of Merton College, Oxford. In 1943 joined the staff of *The Times Literary Supplement*. Head of Department of English at University of Hong Kong, 1955. Professor of Poetry at Oxford 1966–68. Has also written much first class criticism, fascinatingly on cricket and is an authority on the works of Charles Lamb. Was a Vice President of the Charles Lamb Society and a member of the Committee which edited *The Christ's Hospital Book* in 1953.

In 1934 Blunden gave his library of 900 volumes to the Hampstead Central Library and the collection is kept at the Branch Library adjacent to Keats House. His many books about Lamb and his contemporaries include:

John Clare: Poems chiefly from manuscript, edited E. Blunden and A. Porter, 1920.
Christ's Hospital: a retrospect, 1923.
Madrigals and chronicles: being newly found poems by John Clare, 1924.
Shelley and Keats as they struck their contemporaries, 1925.
Leigh Hunt's 'Examiner' examined, 1928.
The Last Essays of Elia, edited by E. Blunden, notes by F. Page, 1929.
Leigh Hunt: a biography, 1930.
Sketches in the life of John Clare written by himself, 1931.
Votive Tablets, 1931.*
Charles Lamb and his contemporaries, 1933.
Charles Lamb: his life recorded by his contemporaries, 1934.
Coleridge: studies by several hands, edited by E. Blunden and E.L. Griggs, 1934.
Keats's Publisher: a memoir of John Taylor, 1936.
'Bibliography of Charles Lamb' and 'Leigh Hunt' in *Cambridge Bibliography of English Literature*, Volume III, 1940.
Shelley: a life story, 1946.
John Keats, 1950, British Council pamphlet.
The Christ's Hospital Book, introduction by E. Blunden, 1953.
Charles Lamb, 1954, British Council pamphlet.
'Charles Lamb' article in *Chambers Encyclopaedia*. Revised edition, 1973.

Among Blunden's articles in periodicals are:

The London Mercury
1921   New Sidelights on Keats, Lamb and others, from the letters of J. Clare.
1923   Clare on the Londoners, February.
The Nation
1928   Elia's G.D., May 5.

The Spectator
1935   Review of E.V. Lucas's edition of Lamb's Letters, September
       13. Reprinted *C.L.S. Bulletin*, July 1956.
The Argosy
1935   Charles Lamb, an Appreciation, January.
The Times Literary Supplement
1928   Lamb's Mr Sea-Gull, September 20.
1937   A Lamb Mystification, June 12.
1941   Thomas Barnes 1785–1841: Literary Diversions of an
       Editor, May 10. As a member of the staff 1943–7 and Assis-
       tant Editor 1949–55 Blunden must have written much for the
       T.L.S., but at that time reviews were anonymous.
Essays and Studies (English Association)
1937   Elia and Christ's Hospital.
Essays by Divers Hands (Royal Society of Literature)
1942   Leigh Hunt's Eldest Son.
C.L.S. Bulletin
1936   The November Hour—poem, April.
1937   Lines to Charles Lamb—poem, October.
1941   Obituary notice of Fred Edgcumbe, October.
1944   An Elian's Petition, January.
1945   On C. Lamb's Birthday 1945—poem, April.
1947   Mary Lamb Memorial Address, May.
1948   Charles Lamb and the Japanese, July.
1957   Prologue—poem, July.
1965   Mary Lamb 1764–1847, A Bicentenary Tribute, January.
1965   A.C.W. Edwards 1881–1964, March.
Keats-Shelley Memorial Bulletin
1951   Letters from Charles and Mary Cowden Clarke to Alexander
       Main 1864–86.
1964   John Taylor 1781–1864.
Review of English Literature (Leeds)
1960   The Poet Hood, January.

Boas, Frederick Samuel, 1862–1957. English philologist.
Educated at Clifton College and Balliol College, Oxford. Vice
President of the English Association and Fellow and Professor of the
Royal Society of Literature. Professor of English History and
Literature, Queen's College, Belfast, Inspector of L.C.C. Education
Department. Author of *Queen Elizabeth in Drama and Related
Studies*, 1950, which contains a chapter on 'Charles Lamb and the
Elizabethan Drama.' Also wrote *Shakespeare and his Predecessors*,
1896; *University Drama in the Tudor Age*, 1914; *Marlowe and his
Circle*, 1929; *An Introduction to Stuart Drama*, 1946; *An Introduc-
tion to Tudor Drama*, 1933; and *Sir Philip Sidney*, 1955.

Contributed to the *Cambridge History of English Literature*, Volumes V and VI, and to the *Encyclopaedia Britannica*, fourteenth edition.

Bookstalls. We know from many references in Charles Lamb's writings that he was a constant frequenter of bookstalls. It is doubtful if he ever paid many visits to booksellers who dealt in volumes of high cash value, but probably he gazed in their windows and may have occasionally ventured inside to browse over their stock and handle their treasures. That he sometimes visited the larger shops is shown by his letter to Coleridge in September 1802, when he writes that he hunted at Lackington's for Milton's *Prose Works*. James Lackington's famous and enormous shop known as the 'Temple of the Muses' was in Finsbury Square and the stock was large; in 1794 he is said to have issued a catalogue listing 100,000 volumes. Although he dealt largely in remainders, he would have had many other books to tempt such as Lamb.

Charles Lamb bought his books to read and re-read, annotate, lend to his friends and discuss with them. He was not concerned about first editions, but liked good ones. Condition was a small consideration.

His journeys to and from his office in Leadenhall Street were often delayed by poring over bookstalls, many of which lay in his way. There were stalls in Barbican, in Wardour Street; Exeter Change had bookstalls on the ground floor, and other good bookstalling areas were Little Britain, Clare Market, Holborn, Moorfields, Fleet Street, St Paul's Churchyard, Paternoster Row, Princes Street, Poultry and Seven Dials. Since Lamb's interests were mainly in old books he probably paused only out of curiosity at Thomas Tegg's nightly book auctions at 111 Cheapside, for the books were mostly remainders.

Lamb also found much pleasure in browsing in the print sellers' shops and he writes of his 'old friend Carrington Bowles', whose shop was in St Paul's Churchyard; no doubt most of the booksellers also displayed prints.

Sometimes he acted as book agent for his friends (unpaid), who were not lucky enough to have London's many bookstalls available to them. In a letter to Wordsworth in October 1804 he tells of searching for a number of books the poet wanted. He writes that 'Ben Jonson is a guinea book. Beaumont & Fletcher in folio, the right folio not now to be met with.' He is looking for the old poets and dramatists, particularly Massinger, without much success; he says Marlowe's plays and poems have completely vanished but 'Congreve and the rest of King Charles's moralists are cheap and accessible.'

One of his earliest eulogies of London, that in his letter to Manning on 28 November 1800, lists among the many pleasures of the City 'old bookstalls, Jeremy Taylors, Burtons on Melancholy, and Religio Medicis on every stall.'

Perhaps his most famous reference to the old bookstalls is in the essay 'Old China', where he tells of his purchase of the folio Beaumont & Fletcher from Barker's shop in Covent Garden. Later Lamb was to live at No 20 Great Russell Street which was Barker's address, but by that time the old bookseller was no longer there. How Lamb would have loved to live over a bookshop with the bookseller for your friend, as did the hero of E.V. Lucas's *Over Bemertons*.

What is perhaps a rather unusual type of purchase for Charles Lamb is recorded in his copy of the *Noctes Atticae* of Aulus Gellius, where he noted that it was bought at Horne Tooke's sale. John Horne Tooke's library was sold by King & Lochee of Tavistock Street in 1813, the sale occupying four days.

After his retirement in 1825 Lamb was not in Central London very often. At first all was freedom and as he says in his essay 'The Superannuated Man' he found himself at eleven o'clock in the day in Bond Street when he would formerly have been on his office stool, and he adds 'I digress into Soho, to explore a bookstall'. He came to Leadenhall Street at least each quarter to draw his pension, an ideal time to browse on a bookstall. He tells Barton of one of these visits in a letter of 25 March 1829 when he found on stalls in Barbican 'the old Pilgrim's Progress with the prints—Vanity Fair &c—now scarce' and 'the whole theologic works of Thomas Aquinas' and he adds how his arm ached with lugging it a mile to the stage, but the burden was a pleasure.

Again in still later years he came to London once a month to dine with Cary at the British Museum and breakfast with Crabb Robinson next morning. We can be sure that he did not neglect the bookstalls on these occasions, for the pleasure of browsing is something few booklovers ever outgrow. *See also* Lamb's Library.

Boston Bibliophile Society. This American society of book collectors published, for members only, an edition of *The Letters of Charles Lamb* in five volumes. It comprised one folio volume with twenty-two facsimile letters and four volumes octavo of text. It had an introduction by Henry H. Harper and explanatory notes on the facsimiles by Richard Garnett. The title page is dated 1905, the reverse of the title has 'Copyright 1906', but the *British Museum Catalogue* gives 1907 as the date of publication. This edition contains 746 letters, but has been described as 'seriously inaccurate'.

Bowles, Henry Carington. At least five members of the Bowles family bore the same Christian names and three of them could have known Lamb. The first lived 1724–93 and is referred to by Lamb in a letter to Thomas Manning in September or October 1801 (Marrs II 25). The second lived 1763–1830 and is the most likely to have known Charles Lamb personally. Both were print sellers and

publishers at 69 St Pauls Churchyard. The third was born in 1801
and lived until 1852.

Lamb refers to 'my old friend Carrington [sic] Bowles' in his essay
'On the Artificial Comedy of the last Century' and again in his
'Recollections of a late Royal Academician', where he says the shop
'exists still for the poorer sort of caricatures'. Perhaps he had in mind
the sketch of Elia by Brook Pulham to which Procter objected. He
adds that George Dawe's father worked for Bowles, and in a footnote
to his poem 'To Bernard Barton. With a Coloured Print' he again
mentions Bowles. The print was the work of George Morland's father
who also worked for Bowles.

There is a tradition that Carington Bowles used to entertain Lamb
at Myddleton House, Enfield where he lived, but although it may well
be true, no evidence has been found to support it.

There is a water colour of the shop by Robert Dighton in the Victoria & Albert Museum.

Bowles, William Lisle, 1762–1850. Divine, poet and antiquary.
His sonnets were much praised by the young Coleridge and were
discussed in Lamb's early letters to Coleridge. Bowles was Rector of
Chicklade, Wiltshire, at the time, but removed to the rectory of
Dumbleton, Gloucestershire, in 1797 and later was Vicar of Bremhill,
Wiltshire.

In his essay 'Mrs Battle's Opinions on Whist' Lamb claims to have
sent Bowles notes on Mrs Battle's observations on the game of Ombre
for inclusion in his edition of Pope, but they were not included and
the story may be an invention.

Bowring, Sir John, 1792–1872. Author, translator, linguist and
traveller. Editor of the *Westminster Review* with Henry Southern.
Later became Consul at Canton and Governor of Hong Kong.
Contributed to the *London Magazine*. Crabb Robinson records that
he met him at Lamb's house in July 1824 in company with Taylor,
Hessey, Clare and C.A. Elton. Bowring was a Fellow of the Royal
Society. Among Bowring's publications were *Batavian Anthology*,
1824; *Ancient Poetry and Romances of Spain*, 1824; *Specimens of
the Polish Poets*, 1827; and *Poetry of the Magyars*, 1830.

Boyer, Rev. James (also spelt Bowyer), 1736–1814. Upper Master
at Christ's Hospital during Lamb's schooldays. Was himself educated
at the school and proceeded to Balliol College, Oxford, returning to
Christ's in 1767 as Under Grammar Master. He retired in 1799, and
was made a Governor of Christ's Hospital. He held various livings
including that of Colne Engaine. Lamb gives a detailed description
of him in his essay 'Christ's Hospital Five and Thirty Years Ago'. Both
Coleridge and Leigh Hunt also wrote sketches of their old schoolmas-

ter. Boyer kept a *Liber Aureus* in which boys had to copy English essays or verses which he liked. Lamb appeared in it once and Coleridge several times. In 1799 Thomas Stothard painted a picture of the St Matthews Day ceremony at Christ's Hospital in which Boyer figures prominently. In addition to Lamb's essay, there are references to Boyer in his letters and most writers on Christ's Hospital refer to him. Some publications that mention him are Coleridge's *Biographia Literaria* and *Table Talk*; Leigh Hunt's *Autobiography*; E.H. Pearce's *Annals of Christ's Hospital*, 1901; Edmund Blunden's *Christ's Hospital*, 1923; P.J. Boyer's *James Boyer: A Memoir*, 1936; *C.L.S. Bulletin*, Nos. 191 and 194; *The Christ's Hospital Book*, 1953.

Boynton, Percy Holmes, 1875–1946. American author. Professor of English Literature at University of Chicago. Wrote *London in English Literature*, Chicago 1913, which contains a chapter 'The London of Lamb and Byron'.

Bradford, Gamaliel, 1863–1932. American author. Wrote *Bare Souls*, 1925, which contains a chapter on Charles Lamb.

Braham, John, 1774–1856. English tenor of Jewish parentage, born John Abraham in London. Was a pupil of Leoni Lee. First appeared at Covent Garden in 1787, later at the Bath concerts. Appeared in Storace's opera *Mahmoud* in 1796 and the following year sang at all the principal opera houses in Italy. He returned to England in 1801 and again appeared at Covent Garden where he became the principal tenor. He appeared in Weber's *Der Freischütz* and *Oberon*, and also in *William Tell* and *Don Giovanni*. He is said to have held undisputed supremacy alike in opera, oratorio and concert room for about forty years. He also composed music, including the famous song 'The Death of Nelson' in 1811. The opera *Kais*, composed by Braham and Reeve, was produced at Drury Lane in 1808. Braham recanted from the Jewish faith and turned Christian, a fact mentioned by Lamb in his 'The Religion of Actors', while another reference occurs in the essay 'Imperfect Sympathies'. His singing was praised highly by Lamb in his letters to Manning on 26 February 1808 and 2 January 1810. In the first Lamb says 'I was insensible to music till he gave me a new sense.' He is also mentioned in Lamb's essay 'on the Custom of Hissing at the Theatre'.

Braille Editions. Among the many Braille editions available for the blind are the following works of Charles Lamb: *The Essays of Elia*, *Tales from Shakespeare*, *Charles Lamb: Prose & Poetry* (Selected by George Gordon). Also available are Lamb's *Letters*, E.V. Lucas's *Life of Charles Lamb* and Edmund Blunden's *Charles Lamb and his Contemporaries*.

Brains Trusts. The Charles Lamb Society has held three Charles Lamb Brains Trusts in which questions set by the members were answered by a panel. They were:
November 1943, reported *C.L.S. Bulletin*, January 1944.
December 1944, reported *C.L.S. Bulletin*, January 1945.
December 1945, reported *C.L.S. Bulletin*, January 1946.

Brent, Charlotte. Mary Lamb tells Sara Hutchinson in a letter in November 1816 that she and Miss Brent had set out to find lodgings in the country, as Mary thought a change of scenery would improve Charles's health. Miss Brent was the sister of Mrs John Morgan. The Morgans were old friends of the Lambs and of Coleridge.

Brewer, Luther A. American book collector, with a famous Leigh Hunt collection. Published in 1924 *Some Lamb and Browning Letters to Leigh Hunt*. Edited by L.A. Brewer. Cedar Rapids, Iowa. Author of a number of small annual volumes mostly about Leigh Hunt, among which were *Around the Library Table*, 1920; *Stevenson's Perfect Virtues as Exemplified by Leigh Hunt*, 1922; *Leigh Hunt's Letter on Hogg's Life of Shelley with other Papers*, 1927; *Joys and Sorrows of a Book Collector*, 1928; *Some Letters from my Leigh Hunt Portfolio, with Brief Comments*, 1929. He also published *My Leigh Hunt Library: The First Editions*, 1932, and *My Leigh Hunt Library: The Holograph Letters*, 1938. Brewer's Leigh Hunt collection is now at the University of Iowa.

Bridget Elia. The name under which Charles Lamb refers to his sister, Mary Lamb, in his published writings. It occurs in the essays 'Mackery End', 'Old China', 'Mrs Battle's Opinions on Whist' and 'My Relations'.

Briscoe, John Potter, b.1848. Librarian and antiquary. Published Lamb's *Prince Dorus* at Nottingham in 1896 in the series 'Nottingham Sette of Odde Volumes.' He also contributed to *The Bibliographer* and *The Bookworm*.

British Museum. Since Charles Lamb lived for so much of his life within easy reach of the British Museum it is probable that he visited it quite early in his career. From 1804 to 1807 he was using the Reading Room for his researches into old plays and had been recommended for his ticket by William Godwin. In December 1806 Mary Lamb in a letter to Mrs Clarkson mentions that Charles is proposing to work at the Museum for Wordsworth. In June 1807 Charles tells the Clarksons that he is spending part of his holidays at the Museum preparing his *Dramatic Specimens* which were published in 1808. For these he worked much from the collections of old plays by Robert Dodsley and Thomas Hawkins, which no doubt he had at home; but for the plays he could not find there he searched the Garrick collection at the Museum. For such authors as Jonson, Beaumont & Fletcher and Massinger he would have used the copies in his own library. Since the British Museum Reading Room was open only from 10:00 AM to 4:00PM and closed on Saturdays, Lamb could only make use of it during his holidays.

We appear to have no record of Lamb's use of the Museum again until after he retired from the East India House in 1825, although he may well have done so occasionally. About 1826 when the novelty of abundant leisure had worn off, he again visited the Reading Room, remembering the riches of the Garrick Plays, of which he had not been able to take full advantage on his previous visits. This time he was recommended for his ticket by his friend, H.F. Cary. He tells Bernard Barton in a letter of 26 September 1826 'I am going thro' a course of reading at the Museum . . . It is a sort of office to me; hours, 10 to 4, the same. It does me good.'

Lamb filled two note books with extracts and worked his material up for weekly contributions to William Hone's *Table Book* in 1827. The first item as printed is prefaced by a letter from Lamb to the Editor in which he says that sitting, as he has been doing in Montagu House (the original building of the Museum), 'is like having the range of a Nobleman's Library, with the Librarian to your friend. Nothing can exceed the courteousness and attention of the Gentleman who has the chief direction of the Reading Room here; and you scarce ask for a volume before it is laid before you.' The officer in charge at this time was John Cater, who was designated 'Clerk of the Reading Room'. Although Lamb does not mention him, Thomas Maurice, Assistant Keeper of the Manuscripts until 1824, was an old Christ's Hospital boy.

The Reading Room that Lamb knew was not, of course, the great domed structure of later years. Part of the old Montagu House, in 1803 the main Reading Room was much smaller, and demand for its use outgrew the available space. When it had moved to larger and to additional rooms about 1809, the number of readers was nearly 2,000 a year. When Lamb used the Museum in 1826 a further move had been made and the number of readers had risen to about 22,000 a year. Hours, too, had been extended and shortly afterwards the Room was kept open from 9:00 AM until 7:00 PM during the summer. During Lamb's time two books were permitted at a time and readers pulled a bell rope for attention.

Lamb ceased to be a regular reader at the British Museum in October 1827, but he now had other attractions there than the Reading Room. The Rev H.F. Cary had been appointed an Assistant Keeper of the Printed Books at the Museum in 1826, and moved from his house in Chiswick, where Lamb used to visit him, to appartments in the Court-yard of the British Museum. No doubt during 1826–7

Lamb sometimes passed from his researches in the Reading Room to Cary's house. A few years later he had established a regular monthly visit to the Assistant Keeper. Several letters from Lamb to Cary exist, in one of which in 1834 Lamb apologises for his indiscretions 'To be seen deliberately to go out of the house of a clergyman drunk!' and he elaborates amusingly 'from a kingly repository of science, human and divine, with the primate of England for its guardian . . . Could all those volumes have taught me nothing better!'

Lamb does not mention that he met any of his friends in the Reading Room, but some of them certainly used it at the same time as he did. Godwin had worked there on his *Life of Chaucer* just before Lamb in the early part of the century, John Payne Collier about 1808, George Dyer periodically, H.F. Cary about 1812. Sir Walter Scott was also there about 1806–7 and around the time Lamb was preparing his material for Hone's *Table Book*, a colleague from East India House, Thomas Love Peacock, also used the Reading Room. Two of the most famous readers there, Carlyle and Macaulay may have been seen by Lamb, although their principal work at the Museum was done after he had ceased to attend. A *London Magazine* contributor who was there in 1827 was George Darley. He told Cary that he often sat next to Lamb, but was too shy to make himself known. Cary soon remedied this by inviting Darley to his house to meet Lamb.

The British Museum gave Lamb pleasure and the information he sought during his lifetime. After his death it continued its services by obtaining and preserving important books and manuscripts of his for the benefit of posterity. Notable among its treasures are Lamb's copy of the folio Beaumont & Fletcher with manuscript notes by Lamb and Coleridge, his Milton and the two note books used for the *Dramatic Specimens*.

Britton, John, 1771–1857. Writer on archaeology, topography and architecture. At one time he worked in a tavern as a cellarman, then as a clerk in an attorney's office, meanwhile writing many books. Among these were *Beauties of Wiltshire*, 1801–25; *Beauties of England & Wales*, 18 volumes; *Cathedral Antiquities*, 15 volumes; and *Memoir of Aubrey*, 1845. Some of his early books were published by Vernor & Hood, one partner of the firm being the father of Thomas Hood, the poet and Lamb's friend. Britton was an active member of the Royal Literary Fund.

In his *Autobiography*, 1850, Britton wrote that he was often at parties at Thelwall's house and met Lamb there together with Godwin, Holcroft, Dr Wolcot, Kenney and others. In 1937 a note by John H. Birss appeared in *Notes & Queries* about a letter from Lamb to Britton which had appeared in the sale catalogue of E.A. Denham in New York. This letter, which is now in the New York Public Library, was printed in full by G.L. Barnett in *M.L.Q.* in 1952.

Brock, Charles Edmund, 1870–1938. Artist, book illustrator and portrait painter. Educated at the Higher Grade School, Cambridge, and in the studio of Henry Wiles, sculptor of Cambridge. He drew much for magazines, including *Punch* and the *Graphic*, but is best known as a book illustrator. Among the many books he illustrated are Hood's *Comic Poems*, 1893; *Gulliver's Travels*, 1894; *Westward Ho!*; Thackeray's *Complete Works*; Jane Austen's *Works*; A.G. Gardener's *Pebbles on the Shore*; William Canton's *W.V. Her Book*; *The Household of Sir Thomas More*; *The Broad Highway*; *The Vicar of Wakefield* with H.M. Brock; and 'John Gilpin'.

When in 1899 J.M. Dent decided to issue an illustrated edition of Lamb's *Essays* he commissioned C.E. Brock to do the work. He tells in his *Memoirs* with what fear and trembling he approached the hazardous enterprise of interpreting Lamb's whimsical, delicate humour, and of the 'exquisite sympathy' which Brock showed in the finished work. Both *The Essays of Elia* and *The Last Essays of Elia* appeared in 1899 in perhaps the most attractive format of any edition. The same illustrations were used with some new ones in Macdonald's edition of Lamb's *Works* which Dent issued in 1903, and again in the *Collected Essays of Charles Lamb* edited by Robert Lynd in 1929. Dent also used some of the illustrations in other publications, such as R.L. Hine's *Charles Lamb & his Hertfordshire* 1949.

Charles Brock had also illustrated an edition of *Mrs Leicester's School* for Wells, Gardner, Darton & Co.

Henry Matthew Brock, 1875–1960. Charles's youngest brother was also an artist and the work of the two brothers was very much alike. H.M. Brock's drawings have a clearer and firmer line, but generally Charles's work is perhaps the more attractive. H.M. Brock drew the cover illustration for *Elia and his friends* by Anna M. Pagan (based on the Maclise portrait of Lamb), and a few illustrations to *The Fancy and Humour of Charles Lamb*, a tiny volume published by Seeley & Co. Ltd. in 1908. He also did much work for J.M. Dent, illustrating the 'Breakfast-Table' series of Oliver Wendall Holmes in 1902; *Essays of Leigh Hunt*, 1903; *Essays of Douglas Jerrold*, 1903; and *Sir Roger de Coverley & other Essays from The Spectator*, 1905.

Both brothers were members of the Royal Institute of Painters in Water-Colours.

Brooks, Elmer Leroy, b.1917. Professor of English, Indiana State University. American author of 'Studies in the London Magazine', an unpublished doctoral dissertation, Harvard 1954.

Broughton, James. Clerk in the East India Company, Under Clerk to the Clerk to Committee of Shipping. Of Clements Inn. Friend of William Godwin and J. Brook Pulham and almost certainly known to Lamb. Broughton and Pulham were co-editors of *British Stage and*

Literary Cabinet and from 1817 to 1822 Broughton was sole editor. In 1830 he wrote for the *Gentleman's Magazine* articles entitled 'Of the Dramatic Writers who Preceded Shakespeare' which contains much about his favourite Marlowe.

Broughton, William Grant, 1788–1853. Clerk in the Treasurer's Department at East India House, 1807–14, ranking just above Lamb's friend, Pulham. Resigned in 1814 and went to Cambridge University where he was Sixth Wrangler in 1818. Ordained the same year and became Archdeacon of New South Wales. Was the first Bishop of Australia and Metropolitan of Australasia. Buried in Canterbury Cathedral. There seems no record that he was friendly with Lamb, but it is probable that they were known to one another when at East India House. It is likely that he was also known to Lamb's friend Barron Field.

Brown, Charles Armitage, 1786–1842. In early life a Russian merchant, later an author. Friend of Keats, C.W. Dilke, Leigh Hunt, Hazlitt, Joseph Severn and Landor. Introduced Keats to Fanny Brawne. Contributed to Leigh Hunt's *The Liberal*: a paper 'Les Charmettes and Rousseau' at one time wrongly attributed to Charles Lamb, and another 'On Shakespeare's Fools' which has been incorrectly attributed to Charles Cowden Clarke. He also contributed to the *New Monthly Magazine*. His serio-comic opera *Narensky* was acted at Drury Lane under Arnold's management in 1814 with Braham in the chief part. His best known work is a book on Shakespeare's Sonnets published in 1838, and dedicated to Landor. He also wrote for *The Examiner* in 1823 a story entitled 'La Bella Tabaccaia'.

Brown's name is known today mainly because of his close friendship with Keats. Although it is not known if he ever met Lamb, he could well have done so through their mutual friends, particularly Hazlitt and Leigh Hunt. Crabb Robinson notes in his *Diary* on 6 October 1830 that Hazlitt 'left his books with Brown' (Hazlitt had died on 18 September 1830).

Brown, Frances. Lamb wrote verses for her album and sent them to her in a letter in November 1833. From a letter to the Moxons on 29 November it seems that her step-father was a pawnbroker named Barrow in Gray's Inn Lane. She was engaged to a Mr White and Lamb's verse has the line 'May your fame, and fortunes, Frances *Whiten*, with your *name*.'

Brown, John Mason, 1900–69. American dramatic critic in New York. Editor of *The Portable Charles Lamb* (Viking Press, New York), 1949, which contains a thirty-seven page introduction on Charles Lamb. Author of many books, including *Seeing More Things*, 1949, which has references to Lamb and *Still Seeing Things*,

1951, which in the chapter 'The Shorn Lambs', reprints his introduction to *The Portable Charles Lamb*. Other books include *Morning Faces*, *The Art of Playgoing* and *The American Theatre 1752–1934 as seen by its critics* and *Letters from the Green Room Ghosts*, 1934.

Browne, W.G.R. Artist. In 1890 the famous colour printer Edmund Evans issued *Toasted Leaves or 'Tudoces Fragrans'. An Essay on the Origin of Tea. By the shade of Charles Lamb*. It is humorously illustrated by W.G.R. Browne. The author appears to be Owen A. Gill.

Brunton, Anne, 1768–1808. Actress. Daughter of John Brunton, actor and manager of theatres in Brighton and in Birmingham. She appeared at Bath in 1785 as Euphrasia and later at Covent Garden. She retired from the stage in 1792 and married Robert Merry of 'Della Cruscan' memory. After his death in 1798 she went to America where she was a successful actress and re-married.

Lamb refers to 'Miss Brunton' in his Popular Fallacy 'That You Must Love Me, and Love my Dog.'

Other members of the family were on the stage and have sometimes been confused with Anne Brunton by Lamb's editors, particularly with Elizabeth, who was her niece. They are Anne, 1768–1808, Mrs Merry; Louisa, 1782–1860, Countess of Craven; and Elizabeth, 1799–1860, Mrs Yates. All three appeared on the stage under their maiden names. Miss Brunton, presumably Elizabeth, spoke the epilogue by Barry Cornwall to J. Sheridan Knowles's play *Virginius* at Covent Garden in 1820.

Bruton Family. Lamb's maternal grandmother was Mary Bruton, who married Edward Field in 1736. Her sister Ann married James Gladman in 1747 and they lived at Mackery End farmhouse. Mary Field's daughter, Elizabeth, was Lamb's mother. *See* separate entries for Mary Field, Elizabeth Lamb, Gladman family and Mackery End.

Buchan, Earl of, 1742–1829. David Steuart Erskine was the eleventh earl and brother of Lord Erskine, the Lord Chancellor and of Henry Erskine, both of whom were noted at the Scottish Bar. David Erskine was eccentric, but by careful living had restored the family fortunes which had sunk. He published in 1792 *Essays on the Lives and Writings of Fletcher of Saltoun and the poet Thomson* and earlier he had published *Plan for the better Regulation of the Peerage in Scotland*, 1780, and *An Account of the Life, Writings & Inventions of John Napier of Merchiston* (with Walter Minto) in 1787.

Lamb wrote an amusing letter to John Rickman on 9 January 1802 telling him that George Dyer had 'at last met with a madman more mad than himself—the Earl of Buchan.' George brought the Earl to call on Lamb, but Charles was out and Mary was washing. Lamb says he is to have breakfast with 'the mad Lord on Sunday', and is studying manners.

Crabb Robinson called on the Earl in 1821 at Dryburgh Abbey, the family estate, and was favourably impressed by his host and his mansion and grounds.

Buffam, The Misses. These ladies lived at 34 Southampton Buildings, Chancery Lane where they let rooms. The Lambs lived there for a few weeks in 1809 while waiting to move into No. 4 Inner Temple Lane. Again in 1830 they were living there and, in fact, after they had moved out of London used the Buffam's house as their headquarters whenever they stayed in town. William Hazlitt had also lodged there at one time. In a letter to Moxon in February 1831 Lamb asks him to collect some books from the Buffams and return them to Novello and Talfourd. J.M. Turnbull in the *Times Literary Supplement* of 20 March 1930 mentions a copy of Lamb's *Album Verses* inscribed 'Miss Emily Buffam from the Author'.

Bunbury, Sir Charles, d.1821. Thomas Charles Bunbury was described by Crabb Robinson as a 'beau-ideal of an English sportsman who was also well known as a Whig politician and a man of honour.' He succeeded his father as sixth Baronet in 1764. He had been Secretary of the Legation in Paris under Lord Hertford and in 1765 was appointed Secretary to Lord Weymouth in Ireland. He was devoted to the turf and for some years had the finest stud in England, being noted for owning the winner of the first Derby. He married Lady Sarah Lennox in 1762 at the private chapel in Holland House. His estate was at Milden Hall, Suffolk, and he was reputed to be one of the handsomest men of his day.

Crabb Robinson records an amusing incident of meeting Bunbury when he was with Lamb, and the latter insisting that it was Sheridan and that he had always known him as such. As Robinson says, he had robbed Lamb of an agreeable image by destroying the misapprehension.

Burnett, George, 1776–1811. Miscellaneous writer who followed many occupations unsuccessfully. He was a Unitarian minister, studied medicine, was a tutor, an Army surgeon and a hack writer to Sir Richard Phillips, the publisher. He died in poverty at a workhouse. Burnett was at Balliol with Southey, who introduced him to Coleridge and he was one of the party who were to follow Pantiscocracy. In 1795 he lodged with Coleridge at Clevedon. Burnett was later employed by John Rickman on the census. He is referred to from time to time in Lamb's letters, and Lamb tried to help him. Burnett succeeded George Dyer as tutor to Lord Stanhope's sons, but not for long. His chief works were *A View of the Present State of*

Poland, 1807, and *Specimens of English Prose Writers to the End of the Seventeenth Century*, 1807. For the latter book he repeatedly called on Lamb for assistance and advice. (See also *Charles Lamb Bulletin*, October 1977.)

Burney, Charles, the Younger, 1757–1817. Classical scholar and schoolmaster. Son of Dr Charles Burney, the historian of music, and brother of Admiral James Burney and Fanny Burney. He was educated at Charterhouse, Caius College, Cambridge and King's College, Aberdeen. The young Charles Burney opened a school at Hammersmith and then in 1793 moved to Greenwich. Among his pupils at Greenwich Academy were Thomas Griffiths Wainewright and Edward Foss, both of whom were distantly related to Burney. He was also Chaplain to the King and at one time was editor of the earlier *London Magazine* (not that to which Charles Lamb contributed). He also wrote for the *Monthly Review*.

After his death in 1817 Crabb Robinson records in his *Diary* that he was at a dinner party with his nephew, Martin Burney, and Charles Lamb, when the latter maintained that Martin had eaten enormously 'on account of his grief' for his uncle.

Charles Burney had a vast library of classical books which were subsequently purchased by the British Museum for £13,500. It also included theatrical prints from the time of Elizabeth. Burney is said by Dr Doran to have kept a school at Gosport where Liston, the actor, had been an usher.

Burney, Edward Francisco, 1760–1848. Artist, son of Richard Burney and cousin of Fanny Burney and Admiral James Burney. His early work was praised by Sir Joshua Reynolds and he exhibited some illustrations to *Evelina* at the Royal Academy. He also did illustrations to a number of books, including Admiral Burney's *Discoveries*, *Gay's Fables*, Glover's *Leonidas*, Richardson's and Smollett's novels and the *Abrabian Nights*. He also did illustrations for the *World*, *Tatler*, *Guardian* and *Adventurer*, and he did twelve copper engravings of the months for Ackermann's *Forget Me Not*, the first of the Annuals. Subsequently he did illustrations for many of these publications.

Lamb mentions him as 'my kind friend ... E.B.' in his essay on Valentine's Day, who sent a valentine to a girl living opposite whom he did not know and watched her open it from his window. He was always distinguished for his gentle and unassuming manners. In Lamb's Key he is mistakenly given as Fanny Burney's half-brother, instead of cousin. Nine of his drawings are reproduced in R. Brimley Johnson's *Fanny Burney and the Burneys*, 1926.

Burney, Admiral James, 1750–1821. British sailor. Son of Dr

Charles Burney, the historian of music. Brother of Fanny Burney and Charles Burney, the younger, the classical scholar. He had been a pupil of Eugene Aram and Hood's poem is said to be founded on Burney's recollections of Aram. First went to sea in 1760 and served in North America and the Mediterranean. Sailed with Captain Cook, 1772–4. Promoted Lieutenant 1773. Sailed with Cook on the Captain's third voyage and on the latter's death came home in command of the Discovery. Appointed Commander in 1780 and Captain in 1782. He came home from the East Indies on account of ill health, did not receive another appointment and was placed on the retired list. Appointed Rear Admiral in 1821.

Burney was noted for his honesty and humour and when he received command of the Latona in 1781 Dr Johnson wrote to Mrs Thrale 'I question if any ship upon the ocean goes out attended with more good wishes than that which carries the fate of Burney.'

During his retirement he started to write his history of the South Seas. The first volume of *A Chronological History of the Voyages and Discoveries in the South Seas or Pacific Ocean* appeared in 1803 and the last of the five volumes in 1817. In 1819 he published *A Chronological History of the North Eastern Voyages of Discovery . . . .* Burney also wrote *An Essay by way of Lecture, on the Game of Whist* published in 1821 (reprinted in R. Brimley Johnson's *Fanny Burney and the Burneys*, 1926).

Lamb and Burney first met in February 1803 at Rickman's house and he and his wife, Sarah, said to be the original of Lamb's Mrs Battle, became intimate friends of the essayist and his sister. All four were devoted to whist and much frequented each others houses for whist parties. The Burneys lived at 26 James Street, Buckingham Gate. Martin Burney, their son, became one of the Lambs' closest friends. Lamb has numerous references to the Burneys in his writings. In his essay 'The Wedding' he amusingly describes his behaviour at the wedding of the Admiral's daughter, Sarah.

In 1803 Captain, as he then was, and Mrs Burney went with the Lambs for a holiday to Cowes in the Isle of Wight, and in 1811 Mary Lamb visited Mrs Burney when she was staying at Richmond.

Burney was a Fellow of the Royal Society and read papers to the members. Among his friends were Sir Joseph Banks and, of course, most of the members of the Lamb circle, particularly Rickman, Ayrton and Crabb Robinson. He was friendly with Hazlitt until the latter adversely criticized the novels of Fanny Burney, the Admiral's sister. Southey gives a picture in a letter in 1804 of Burney at Rickman's 'smoking after supper, letting puffs at one corner of his mouth and puns at the other.'

Burney, Martin Charles, 1788–1852. Barrister, son of Admiral Burney and nephew of Fanny Burney. Southey's letter of 11 June

1804 sketches Martin Burney: 'The Captain (he was not then Admiral) hath a son—begotten according to Lamb, upon a mermaid; and thus far is certain, he is the queerest fish out of water.' When articled to Sharon Turner, the latter said of him 'a man of great honour and integrity. He never told me a lie in his life.' Martin Burney suffered from facial paralysis as a child, but his brain was not affected. Thomas Westwood described him as 'the ugliest of men, hugest of eaters, honestest of friends.'

The Lambs had great affection for Martin and Procter said that he was found at their house more often than any other person. There are affectionate accounts of him in Lamb's writings and in those of several of his circle. Lamb dedicated the second volume of his *Works* 1818 to Martin Burney. Hazlitt frequently played racquets with him.

He was employed by Rickman at the House of Commons in 1821, but was dismissed as unsatisfactory; he was re-instated with the help of the Lambs and Mrs Rickman. Crabb Robinson records in 1829 that Martin Burney 'by his injudicious call to the bar and habits of indulgence had brought himself to a state of great want'. He adds that Lamb was able sometimes to procure employment for Martin through Rickman and Alsager.

In 1816 he married Rebecca Norton, a maidservant, but the marriage was kept secret for five years. Crabb Robinson describes it as an unfortunate marriage, and they separated about 1831. As a barrister he travelled the Western Circuit and used to read briefs for Sir Thomas Wilde, later Lord Truro. He helped Wilde with his election campaigns at Newark, for which Lamb is supposed to have written election verses.

Writing to Sarah Hazlitt on 24 May 1830 Lamb said of Martin Burney 'So he goes on harassing about the way to prosperity and losing it—With a long head but somewhat a wrong one—harum scarum—why does not his guardian angel look to him? he deserves one—maybe he has tired him out.'

Martin Burney seems to have got into some trouble of which Matilda Betham told Lamb in July 1833, and the latter tells Moxon he is unable to do anything, but arranges to pass some letter on to Martin's brother-in-law. Little is known of Martin's later years, but it is doubtful if they were happy. Miss Mann states that in 1849 he was living at 26 St James's Street, Westminster, with a housekeeper named Anne Macguinnis, to whom he left his property in his will. (*See also* W.C. Hazlitt's *The Lambs*, 1897, 35).

Burney, Sarah, 1758–1832. Wife of Admiral James Burney and the younger daughter of Thomas Payne, the famous bookseller of the Mews Gate. She was the mother of Martin Burney and of Sarah Burney, who married her cousin, John Payne, a bookseller with his father.

Mrs Burney and her husband were close friends of the Lambs and she is thought to be the original of Lamb's Mrs Battle who so loved a game of whist. They frequented each others houses and in 1803 spent a holiday together. In a letter to Sarah Hazlitt on 2 October 1811 Mary Lamb writes that she is going to pass a week with Mrs Burney who was at Richmond recovering from an illness.

Burney, Sarah, the Younger, b.c.1793. Daughter of Admiral James Burney and Sarah Burney. Married her cousin John Thomas Payne in April 1821 at St Margaret's, Westminster, the service being conducted by Rev. Charles Parr Burney, cousin of the bride. Sarah Burney is the heroine of Lamb's essay 'The Wedding', and both Lamb and his sister attended at the church which he disguises as St Mildred's, Poultry. Sarah when a child was the little girl that Lamb said ate so many apples that 'no ordinary orchard would be a jointure for her.'

Burney, Sarah Harriet, c.1770–1844. Novelist. Youngest daughter of Dr Charles Burney, the historian of music, and his first wife. Stepsister of Fanny Burney and Admiral James Burney. Among her books are *Clarentine*, 1796; *Geraldine Fauconbridge*, 1808; and *Tales of Fancy*, 1816. She also translated from the Italian and was a good French scholar. Her friends included Crabb Robinson and W.S. Landor. After her father's death she lived in Florence for a time. She bequeathed some of her property to Martin Burney, the son of her step-brother, the Admiral.

Her book *Tales of Fancy* contained her story 'Country Neighbours' which inspired Lamb's sonnet 'To Miss Burney, on her Character of Blanch.' G.E. Mainwaring in *My Friend the Admiral*, 1931, prints a letter from Admiral Burney's wife to her daughter in which it is stated that she and Sarah Harriet Burney dined with the Lambs in April, 1821.

Burrell, Fanny. English singer who married and became a Mrs Gold or Gould. Lamb wrote a notice of *Don Giovanni in London* for *The Examiner* in November 1818 which praised Miss Burrell for her acting. In a letter to Mrs Wordsworth of 18 February 1818 he included her in the famous passage about Fanny Kelly: 'and yet reserve in some "corner of my mind" some darling thoughts all my own— faint memory of some passage in a Book—or the tone of an absent friend's Voice—a snatch of Miss Burrell's singing—a gleam of Fanny Kelly's divine plain face.' Lamb also mentions her in his letter to Manning of 28 May 1819. He had pasted a portrait of her into his Commonplace Book in which he also inserted a copy of his review of Miss Burrell in *Don Giovanni in London*.

Macdonald says in a note to this piece that Fanny Burrell was an occasional visitor to the Lambs at Great Russell Street and he suggests that the review may have brought about their acquaintance. Talfourd states that Fanny Burrell was one of Lamb's favourites at this time, the others being Fanny Kelly and Munden. (A 'Jack Burrell' is mentioned in Lamb's piece 'A Character of the late Elia', but it is not known if he was a relation).

Butterworth, Samuel. Major. R.A.M.C. and a noted Lamb scholar. In his Introduction to the three volume edition of the *Letters of Charles Lamb*, 1935, E.V. Lucas states that Butterworth wrote several letters to him about his shortcomings 'and he was usually right'. Major Butterworth was an Army surgeon and carried the accuracy necessary for such a profession into his hobbies which were of a literary nature. His researches into Lamb's works have been of enormous help to several generations of Lamb students, as is well acknowledged by P.P. Howe in the Foreword to his and Mrs Anderson's edition of *Thomas Manning's Letters to Charles Lamb*.

Unfortunately no book appears to have been published by Butterworth, but he contributed largely to periodicals, such as *The Athenaeum, The Academy, Notes & Queries* and particularly *The Bookman*. In the latter publication there are fifty-nine contributions by him between May 1914 and February 1923. Most were reviews, but some were articles containing the results of his researches into Lamb's works and the *London Magazine* circle. In nearly all his reviews he manages to slip in a reference to or a quotation from Elia.

Much of his research was contained in note books, many of which have disappeared, but two were acquired by S.M. Rich and are now in the Charles Lamb Society Library, as is Butterworth's fully annotated copy of Lucas's *Letters of Charles Lamb*, 1905, which belonged to Ernest G. Crowsley. Rich also obtained a number of newspaper cuttings which had belonged to Butterworth and they also passed to the C.L.S. library.

Major Butterworth was living in Carlisle in 1903, but at the time of his death about 1934, he was living in Southsea and a large part of his Elia collection was bought by George Seaford, the bookseller of Arundel Street, Portsmouth. The best of the books were sorted out and sold to a London dealer for £75, eventually Francis Edwards Catalogue No. 594 (June 1936) contained as item 665 'The Major Butterworth Collection of Books, Manuscript Notes, Excerpts, Cuttings &c relating to Charles Lamb' amounting to 137 volumes for which £125 was asked. The collection included a copy of Coleridge's *Remorse* 3rd edition, 1813, inscribed by Charles Lamb to Barron Field, thirteen albums of letters, deeds, cuttings, reviews &c. and many other desirable items. It is believed that the collection went to America. Some thirty volumes of Eliana of lesser importance were acquired by the present writer from Seaford's shop, all enriched with Butterworth's careful notes. Alas the shop was destroyed by bombing in 1941 and the stock lost, among which must have lurked many items of interest overlooked when the original sorting was done.

Major Butterworth was a friend of Mrs G.A. Anderson, that inspired commentator and researcher on Lamb, and she passed to him her Manning material, most of which was subsequently used by P.P. Howe when he published Manning's letters in 1925.

Edmund Blunden has said that Major Butterworth was his Commanding Officer at one period of his Army service and in his review in the *Spectator* of Lucas's edition of the *Letters*, 1935, refers to Butterworth 'who used, I understand, to serve out pills to the Border Regiment with one hand while he explicated Lamb's pages with the other.' In his book on *Christ's Hospital*, 1923, Blunden acknowledges the loan from Butterworth of W.P. Scargill's scarce book *Recollections of a Blue-Coat Boy*, 1829, which was dedicated to Lamb. In his *Thomas Hood: His Life and Times* published as long ago as 1907 Walter Jerrold acknowledges help from Butterworth.

Major Butterworth wrote the chapter on Lamb in F.W. Hackwood's *William Hone: his Life and Times*, 1912. R.W. King acknowledges help from Butterworth in his *The Translator of Dante* which is full of Lamb references. Some of Butterworth's contributions to periodicals are:

Academy & Literature
1903   Letter about the review of Lucas's edition of the *Works* in *The Academy* on 13 June 1903, June 20.
——   'The Date of Charles Lamb's Birth', December 19.
1904   Further letter about Lamb's birth, January 16.
——   'A Lamb Letter.'

The Athenaeum
1903   Review of the early volumes of Lucas's and Macdonald's editions of the *Works*, unsigned but attributed to Butterworth on style and context, July 18.
1913   'Lamb's Manuscript copy of Coleridge's Sonnet "Fancy in Nubibus".'

The Bookman
1914   *Letters to Lady Alwyne Compton 1869–81. From Thomas Westwood*, December. Supplement. Mentions Lamb and Mrs Reynolds.
1916   *William Wordsworth* by George McLean Harper, May.
1918   *The Early Life of Robert Southey 1774–1803* by William Haller, September.
——   Wordsworth's Academic Honours, November.
1920   Coleridge: *Biographia Literaria ... Wordsworth: Prefaces and Essays*, edited by George Sampson, May.
——   Coleridge's 'Marine Sonnet', July.

—— *Mary Russell Mitford and her Surroundings* by Constance Hill, August.

—— *The Christ's Hospital Anthology* by S.E. Winbolt, December.

1921 Charles Lamb: Some New Biographical and Other Details, July.

—— *Wordsworth's French Daughter* by George McLean Harper, October.

—— *The Early Life of Wordsworth* by Emile Legouis, October.

1922 Charles Lamb: A Few More Details, March.

—— The Old 'London Magazine' and Some of its Contributors, October.

1923 *Blake, Coleridge, Wordsworth, Lamb &c. being Selections from the Remains of Henry Crabb Robinson*. Edited by E.J. Morley, February.

Cambridge Review

1912 Article on a portrait of George Dyer and his dog, May 30. The portrait was reproduced in Wherry's *Cambridge and Charles Lamb*, 1925.

Notes & Queries

1906 Item explaining reference to Battin in Lamb's letter of 8 March 1830 to Gillman, 24 March 1906.

Edmund Blunden in his *Christ's Hospital* 1923 (161) mentions a Lady Butterworth who presented a portrait of Leigh Hunt to the school. It is not known if she was a relation.

Button, Eliza. Lucas mentions in the *Life* a man who claimed to be related to a cousin of Charles Lamb named Eliza Button, and says perhaps this has some connexion with the cottage Button Snap in Hertfordshire which Lamb owned. Reginald Hine found that the Button family had long been established in Hertfordshire and in Lamb's day a Joseph Button was a flourishing malster in Hitchin. (Curiously the *D.N.B* lists a Sir William Button who died in 1655 and who was the eldest son of William Button of Alton and Jane, daughter of John Lamb of Wiltshire).

Button Snap. A thatched cottage with about three-quarters of an acre of ground and an old thatched barn at West Mill, Buntingford, near Puckeridge, Hertfordshire. The cottage was left by Francis Fielde, Lamb's godfather, to his wife, and in August 1812 she conveyed it to Charles Lamb. The tenant was then a Mr Sargus. Miss Mann states in the *C.L.S. Bulletin*, No. 122, that Francis Fielde purchased the cottage in 1779 for £40, but R.L. Hine in his *Charles Lamb and his Hertfordshire* gives the amount as £20. In 1815 Lamb sold it for £50 to Thomas Greg and a relative of his some years later presented it to the Royal Society of Arts. In 1949 this Society sold it for £400 to the Charles Lamb Society, the present owners.

The reason for Lamb's sale of the cottage within three years of inheriting it is not known, but it has been suggested by R.L. Hine that Lamb needed the money to lend to a friend, probably Godwin or Hazlitt, and points out that Hazlitt witnessed Lamb's signature to the conveyance of sale.

The cottage bears two plaques commemorating Lamb's ownership. The first was placed there by Mrs Greg in 1901 and reads:

From the 21st August 1812 to the
25th February 1815
This Cottage and Garden of
'Button Snap'
Was the property of
Charles Lamb, the Essayist.
Essays of Elia 'My First Play.'

Another plaque was placed on the cottage in 1954 by the Charles Lamb Society:

This Cottage was acquired
From the
Royal Society of Arts
by the
Charles Lamb Society
And dedicated to Elia's
Memory
3rd September, 1949.

In 1965 the Medallion portrait of Charles Lamb formerly on the Westminster Bank building at Southampton Buildings, Chancery Lane, was re-erected at Button Snap. It bears the following inscription:

This Medallion of Charles Lamb
was presented to the Charles Lamb Society
by the
Westminster Bank Ltd
on its removal from their premises
at Southampton Buildings, Chancery Lane
London
4th February 1965

Reginal Hine records in his book on Lamb that the family of Ives lived for two generations in Button Snap. *See C.L.S. Bulletin*, Nos. 85, 154 and 185.

Bye, Tommy. Clerk at East India House in the Accountant's Office with Lamb. Lamb's letter to John Chambers, probably in 1818, states Bye was publishing a volume of poems which are most like 'what we might have supposed Petrarch to have written if Petrarch had been a fool!' In 1819 Lamb recounts in a letter to Manning of 28 May that Bye had been dismissed for drunkenness after 36 years' service, his salary of £600 per annum being reduced to a pension of £100. Mrs Anderson stated in the *London Mercury* in 1928 that Bye's case was reconsidered in 1820 by the General Court and his pension increased to £300.

When Lamb's colleague P.S. Dupuy, published a translation from the French in 1795 Bye subscribed for five copies.

Byron, Lord, 1788–1824. Poet. Friend of Shelley, Leigh Hunt and Thomas Moore. Helped Leigh Hunt to start *The Liberal* in 1822 when both were in Italy. In his *English Bards and Scotch Reviewers* Byron has references to Lamb and a footnote describes Lamb and Lloyd as 'the most ignoble followers of Southey & Co.' In 1816 Lamb told Wordsworth that Coleridge was printing Christabel 'by Lord Byron's recommendation to Murray.' When Lamb was attempting to raise a fund for Godwin's benefit in 1823 Byron gave £26. 5s., and he had given £30 to the fund for John Scott's widow, after the editor of the *London Magazine* had been killed in a duel in 1821. When Byron died Lamb referred to him in a letter to Barton and expressed his poor opinion of his lordship's work. Lamb did, however, praise Byron's 'Vision of Judgment.' In 1825 Lamb wrote an epigram 'On the Arrival in England of Lord Byron's Remains' printed in *The New Times.*

Campbell, James Dykes, 1838–95. Author. Born in Glasgow. Worked with a manufacturer of pottery and in 1860 went to Canada for his firm. His leisure was devoted to literature, particularly Tennyson's works. When he returned to England in 1862 he started his own business, subsequently went to India and then to Mauritius. In 1878 he married a daughter of General Chesney, who commanded the island. He retired in 1881 and returned to London.

Among his friends were Mrs Procter and Robert Browning. He was Honorary Secretary of the Browning Society. In his later years his main literary work concerned Coleridge and his friends which, of course, included Lamb. He contributed many valuable articles to periodicals and wrote a fine life of Coleridge which formed the introduction to his edition of Coleridge's *Poetical Works*, 1893. It was republished as a separate book in 1894 as *Samuel Taylor Coleridge; a Narrative of the Events of his Life.*

An edition of Lamb's *Dramatic Specimens* was issued in the London Library series in 1907 edited by Campbell. The sale catalogue of his library issued in 1904 included an interleaved copy of his life of Coleridge with numerous manuscript notes and printed extracts. Among his contributions to periodicals are:

The Athenaeum
1888   Lamb on Cooke's Richard III (August 4).

1889   Reviewing Oneself (August 3). Concerns Lamb's review of the Latin Poems of Vincent Bourne.

——   Moxon's 'Englishman's Magazine' and 'Reflector' (December 7).

1891   A Letter of Charles Lamb (June 13). To Coleridge—No. 17 in Lucas.

——   Lamb's John Woodvil (October 31 and November 14).

1893   Leigh Hunt on Himself (March 25).

1894   Lamb's Specimens (August 25).

——   Lamb's Lines to Sara & S.T. Coleridge (September 8).

Illustrated London News

1891   An Account of Boyer's *Liber Aureus* which contained a poem by Lamb (December 26).

1892   Article on the Prologue to Coleridge's Remorse (October 22).

——   'Lamb's Prologue to "The Wife"', (September 24).

Canning, George, 1770–1827. Tory statesman. Prime Minister in 1827. In 1798 wrote a satirical poem 'The New Morality' for *The Anti-Jacobin* which referred to Coleridge, Southey, Lamb and Lloyd. In 1802 Lamb wrote an epigram on Canning and John Hookham Frere for the *Morning Post* and he referred to Canning again in 1820 in his 'Sonnet to Matthew Wood' in *The Champion.* Canning at one time had chambers at 2 Paper Buildings, Inner Temple. He met Southey and Wordsworth in the Lake District in 1825.

Carlisle, Sir Anthony, 1768–1840. Surgeon at Westminster Hospital. Friend of Lamb. He was Professor of Anatomy at the Royal Academy and Surgeon-extraordinary to the Prince Regent. He wrote a number of books on medical subjects and also lectured; in 1820 and 1826 he delivered the Hunterian lectures at the College of Surgeons, of which he was long a member of the council.

Carlisle repeated to Lamb the Quaker incident at Andover which appears in the essay 'Imperfect Sympathies', and in his letter to Barton on 11 March 1823 Lamb describes Carlisle as 'the best story teller I ever heard'. In August 1830 Lamb wrote a letter to Carlisle thanking him for sending a pamphlet he had written. He is also referred to in Lamb's essay 'Ellistoniana'.

Carlyle, Thomas, 1795–1881. Historian and essayist. Contributed the 'Life of Schiller' to the *London Magazine.* Friend of Edward Irving and Mrs Montagu, and knew Lamb, Coleridge and Hazlitt. Wrote for the *Edinburgh Review* and *Fraser's Magazine.* Carlyle's friend J. Badams married Louisa Holcroft who was well known to Lamb. Carlyle visited Lamb in July 1824 with Irving and in 1831 there occurred another visit after which Carlyle recorded in his *Diary* his ill-tempered comments on Lamb, November 2.

Cartwright, Charles. Deputy Accountant-General at the East India House in Lamb's time. Mentioned by Lamb in his letter to Coleridge of 1 July 1796 where he states Cartwright objected to his obtaining leave at that time.

Cary, Francis Stephen, 1808–80. Artist, youngest son of Rev. H.F. Cary, the translator of Dante and the friend of Charles Lamb. He was a student at Sass's Art Academy and eventually became director of it. He had been a pupil of Sir Thomas Lawrence.

Lamb wrote to him on 21 December 1833 about a picture by Hogarth. In 1834 he painted the portrait of Charles and Mary Lamb which is now in the National Portrait Gallery.

Cary, Henry Francis, 1772–1844. Scholar and translator. educated at Christ's Church, Oxford. Vicar of Abbot's Bromley, later became afternoon lecturer at Chiswick and curate of the Savoy. In 1826 was appointed an Assistant Keeper of the Printed Books at the British Museum and remained there until 1837 when he resigned after failing to obtain the appointment of Keeper, a position which went to Antonio Panizzi. At Chiswick he lived in Hogarth's house and later had apartments in the Court-yard of the British Museum, adjoining the Reading Room. Landor, who had been a schoolfellow, wrote verses to Cary on his appointment in Bloomsbury.

Cary published *Sonnets & Odes* in 1788, *Ode to General Kosciusko* in 1797 and his most famous work, his translation of Dante's *Inferno* in 1805. He then completed the translation of the remainder of *The Divine Comedy* and published it in 1814. This work was highly praised by Coleridge, who persuaded Taylor & Hessey to publish a second edition in 1819. These publishers more than once thought of Cary as a possible editor for new magazines they proposed to issue, and when in 1821 they bought the famous *London Magazine* his name was again before them for this purpose. Eventually Taylor decided to edit the magazine himself, but Cary became a frequent contributor and sent poems, a 'Continuation of Dr Johnson's Lives of the Poets', criticism and translations of the 'Early French Poets' and papers on early Italian poets as well as on Latin and Greek literature. Lamb praised the 'Early French Poets'. Some of these essays and translations were afterwards collected and published in 1846 as *Lives of the English Poets from Johnson to Kirke White* and *Early French Poets*. Cary also published his translation of the *Birds of Aristophanes* in 1824 and *Pindar in English Verse* in 1833.

Cary's friends included Miss Seward in his early days, and later Coleridge, Lamb, Procter, Hood, Clare and Wainewright. He first met Lamb about 1819 or 1820, probably through Coleridge, and they became close friends. In 1823 Lamb visited Cary at his house at Chiswick and Cary visited Lamb's house from time to time. In later years the friendship became even closer and in 1833 and 1834 there was an arrangement for Lamb to visit Cary at the British Museum regularly every third Wednesday, breakfasting with Crabb Robinson next morning. Cary's rooms at the Museum became a resort of poets and, in addition to the friends mentioned, Darley, Talfourd and, on their occasional visits to London, Wordsworth and Southey were often found there.

Cary seems to have been popular, although of a retiring nature. Lamb described him as a 'model of a country Parson, lean (as a curate ought to be), modest, sensible'; Procter as 'mildest and most amiable of men' and Hood as 'mild and modest Cary', while in a letter to Manning in 1832 Lamb calls him 'the flower of clergymen'.

A number of letters from Lamb to Cary exist, one in October 1823 in which Lamb asks if Cary can give him a bed for a night; then in August 1824 he thanks Cary for a gift of his translation of the *Birds*. In 1828 Lamb invites Cary to Enfield and tells him that Allan Cunningham and Darley will be there. When in May 1831 Cary gave Lamb a copy of Euripides the result was a Latin letter of thanks, while in September 1833 Lamb tells Cary that he and Mary Lamb are reading the 'Inferno' in Italian with the help of Cary's translation. Lamb's longest letter to Cary came in 1834 when he wrote a most amusing letter of apology for his misdeeds: 'But to be seen deliberately to go out out of the house of a clergyman drunk! a clergyman of the Church of England too! ... I am de-vited to come on Wednesdays.' Lamb's last letter that we have was written on 22 December 1834 to Mrs Dyer about a book he had borrowed from Cary and which he had left at her house. On the book being returned to Cary after Lamb's death, he wrote his 'Lines to the Memory of Charles Lamb'. Subsequently he composed the lines engraved on Lamb's tombstone. When Cary died in 1844 he was buried in Poet's Corner, Westminster Abbey, next to Dr Johnson.

R.W. King in his fine biography of Cary, *The Translator of Dante*, 1925, gives much information about the friendship with Lamb.

Catalani, Angelica, 1780–1849. Italian soprano and opera singer. Made her first appearance in Venice in 1797. First appeared in London in 1806 at the King's Theatre. She remained in England for seven years where her marvellous voice brought her high praise and enormous fees. Vincent Novello acted as her pianist and conductor in London. She later became manager of the Italian opera in Paris. For nearly thirty years she sang at all the great opera houses in Europe. In 1824 and 1828 she again sang in England, but retired in the latter year to a villa at Florence.

Lamb mentions her in his essay 'On the Custom of Hissing at the Theatre' where he writes that 'Syren Catalani charms and captivates us. 'It is not likely that he often heard her at the opera, but she also sang at concerts, and was noted for her rendering of 'God Save the King' and 'Rule Britannia'. Not all her audience appreciated to the full the charm of her voice: Dr Busby said 'One of the most striking characteristics of Madame Catalani's voice is—force. Indeed, distance is absolutely indispensable to the true enjoyment, to the forming a true notion, of her wonderful powers.' In a letter of March 18 1811 from Mary Lamb to Matilda Betham it is stated that Coleridge dined with her on one occasion.

Caulfield, Thomas, d.1815. Actor, comedian and mimic at Drury Lane. Also played at the Haymarket and eventually went to America where he died. He is mentioned by Lamb in his letter to Manning on 23 April 1802. He was the brother of James Caulfield, the author, antiquary and print seller.

Cecil, Algernon, b.1879. Barrister, Inner Temple. Educated at Eton and New College, Oxford. Author of *Essays in Imitation*, 1910, which contains 'Mrs Battle's Opinions on Bridge' and 'An Essay in Apology', both imitations of Elia.

Cecil, Lord David, b.1902. Critic. Goldsmith's Professor of English Literature at Oxford. President of the Charles Lamb Society 1944–55. Lectured to the Society from time to time on Charles Lamb. Trustee of the National Portrait Gallery. Author of *The Stricken Deer*, 1929; *Jane Austen*, 1935; *The Young Melbourne*, 1939; *Lord M*, 1954; *Poets and Story Tellers*, 1949; *Two Quiet Lives*, 1948; and *The Fine Art of Reading*, 1957.

Chambers, Charles, died c.1857. Educated at Christ's Hospital, probably a little later than Lamb. Son of the Rev. Thomas Chambers, Vicar of Radway-Edgehill, Warwickshire. Became a Naval surgeon and after his retirement from the Navy practised at Leamington. Lamb wrote an amusing letter to him in September 1817 partly in praise of fish. His brother, John Chambers, was a colleague of Lamb's at the East India House.

Chambers, John, d.1872. Son of Rev. Thomas Chambers. Educated at Christ's Hospital after Lamb's time. Was a clerk at the East India House. About 1818 Lamb wrote an amusing letter of office news to Chambers who appears to have been absent through illness; this letter contains the humorous reference to Tommy Bye's poems. Some of Chambers's recollections of Lamb were printed in *MacMillan's Magazine* in 1879 by his executor, Algernon Black. W.C. Hazlitt in his *The Lambs* says John Chambers rode to the India House on a white horse and was so punctual that people regulated their watches by his movements. He is the 'Ch——' referred to in Lamb's essay

'The Superannuated Man'. Canon Ainger stated that John Chambers was one of Lamb's most intimate friends in the office. The writer of a letter in the *Times Literary Supplement* of 5 September 1958 states that John Chambers's London address was Radway Cottage, Lee Green S.E.

Chambers, Rev. Thomas. Vicar of Radway-Edgehill, Warwickshire. Father of Charles and John Chambers, friends of Lamb. He is the 'sensible clergyman in Warwickshire' mentioned in Lamb's 'Thoughts on Presents of Game &c', who used to allow 'a pound of Epping to every hare'. W.C. Hazlitt says he left a diary recording little beyond the dinners he used to eat, and is said to have cured the gout with lobster and port.

Charles and Mary. *See* Plays about Charles Lamb.

Charles Lamb Centenary Memorial Appeal 1934–5. *See* Memorials to Charles Lamb (St Sepulchre).

Charles Lamb Memorial Plaque. *See* Memorials to Charles Lamb.

Charles Lamb Society. Founded 1 February 1935 at a meeting at Essex Hall, Strand, largely through the enthusiasm of Ernest George Crowsley. The first officials of the Society were: President, Sir Arthur Quiller-Couch; Chairman of Council, Walter Farrow; Vice Chairman, S.M. Rich; Hon. Treasurer, Miss Mizpah Gilbert; Hon. Secretary, Ernest G. Crowsley; Editor of *C.L.S. Bulletin*, S.M. Rich.

The objects of the Society are defined as 'To study the life, works and times of Charles Lamb and his circle. To stimulate the Elian spirit of friendliness and humour. To form a collection of Eliana.' The activities of the Society comprise periodical meetings, lectures, visits to places associated with Lamb and his contemporaries, the issue of some publications concerning Lamb, the holding of an annual dinner or lunch on or near Lamb's birthday, February 10, at which well known personalities are guests and propose the toast of 'The Immortal Memory'. There is also a Dramatic Group which presents plays. The Society owns Button Snap, the cottage in Hertfordshire which belonged to Lamb, and periodically supervises the upkeep of Mary Field's grave at Widford.

Among the Society's publications are:

C.L.S. Bulletin. Nos. 1–216, 1935–72. Renamed *Charles Lamb Bulletin, New Series.* January 1973 to date. Editors: S.M. Rich, 1935–47; H.G. Smith, 1948–72; Basil Savage, 1972–77; Basil Savage & M.R. Wedd, 1977–79; M.R. Wedd, 1979–.

Annual Reports. 1935–71 (printed) 1972 to date (duplicated).

Charles Lamb and Emma Isola by Ernest Carson Ross. Elian Booklet No. 1 1950. 40.pp.

Catalogue of the C.L.S. Collection of Eliana. 1949. 19.pp. Prepared by F.E. Sandry. Revised and enlarged edition being prepared.

The Society maintains its Library at the Guildhall Library, London. Opened in 1955 it was kept at the Central Library, Edmonton, and comprised 1,600 items, accumulated by the Society since 1935. Among notable additions have been the collections of J.M. Turnbull (350 items), S.M. Rich (over 750 items) and George Wherry; E.J. Finch's bequest of hundreds of prints; and the bequest of Ernest G. Crowsley. The total number of volumes now exceeds 2,000, plus many miscellaneous items.

Presidents of the Society
Sir Arthur Quiller-Couch, 1935–44.
Lord David Cecil, 1944–55.
Professor Geoffrey Tillotson, 1956–69.
Dr Ian Jack, 1970–80.
Dr John Stevens, 1980–   .

Guests of Honour at the Birthday Celebrations
1936   Sir Arthur Quiller-Couch.
1937   Lord Plender.
1938   Frank Swinnerton.
1939   Viscount Finlay.
1940   S.M. Rich.
1941   J.P. Collins.
1942   No guest, but the toast of 'The Immortal Memory' proposed by Herbert Grant Smith.
1943   Professor Willard Connely.
1944   James Agate.
1945   Lord David Cecil.
1946   A.C.W. Edwards.
1947   R.H. Mottram.
1948   Professor Basil Willey.
1949   Lord David Cecil.
1950   H.L.O. Flecker.
1951   Professor Ifor Evans.
1952   Lord David Cecil.
1953   Professor Geoffrey Tillotson.
1954   Helen Darbishire.
1955   Walter Farrow.
1956   Professor Geoffrey Tillotson.
1957   C.M.E. Seaman.
1958   Sir George Rostrevor Hamilton.
1959   Sir Sydney C. Roberts.
1960   Professor Geoffrey Tillotson.

1961 Lord Birkett of Ulverston.
1962 Professor Basil Willey.
1963 Professor Douglas Grant.
1964 Frank Swinnerton.
1965 Professor Ian Jack.
1966 Professor Edmund Blunden.
1967 Dr Elsie Smith.
1968 Mollie Sands.
1969 Henry Cecil Leon.
1970 William Kean Seymour.
1971 Professor William A. Armstrong.
1972 David Newsome.
1973 Dr Josephine Bauer.
1974 Professor John Wain.
1976 Professor J.E. Morpurgo.
1977 Professor Lionel Elvin.
1978 Professor Ian Jack.
1979 C. Reginald Watters.
1980 Dr John Beer.
1981 Professor Brian Morris.
1982 Elizabeth Tucker.

Plays Presented

The dramatic group was founded in 1946 with Ernest G. Crowsley as chairman to 1970.

1946 *The Wife's Trial*, Charles Lamb.
—— *The Man Without a Foe*, P. Mann and A. Macdonald.
1947 *The Pawnbroker's Daughter*, Charles Lamb.
1948 *A Convivial Evening at Charles Lamb's*, Frank Hallam.
—— *Charles and Mary*, Joan Temple.
1949 *What a Lass*, Basil Francis.
1950 *Mr H——*, Charles Lamb
1951 *Chinese Crackling*, Basil Francis.
1952 *She Stoops to Conquer*, Oliver Goldsmith.
1953 *Charles and Mary*, Joan Temple.
1954 *Harriot*, Basil Francis.
1955 *The Magpie or the Maid*, Isaac Pocock.
1957 *Lover's Vows*, Elizabeth Inchbald.
1958 *Tom Thumb*, Henry Fielding.
1959 *Mr H——*, Charles Lamb.
1960 *Only a Clerk*, E.G. Crowsley.
1964 *Modern Antiques*, John O'Keeffe.

The Society produced Christmas Cards between 1957 and 1966 which carried illustrations of the Charles Lamb Medal, Portrait of John Lamb Senior, Caricature of Charles Lamb by Daniel Maclise,

East India House, Christ's Hospital and the Charles Lamb bust at Christ's Church.

Chasles, Philarète, 1798–1873. French critic. Librarian of the Bibliothèque Mazarin and later Professor of Comparative Literature at the Collège de France. Wrote 'Le Dernier Humoriste Anglaise' in the *Revue des Deux Mondes* in 1842 in which he describes meeting Charles Lamb at the office of Valpy, the publisher, in 1818. He also published *Études de littérature comparée*, 1846–75 (20 volumes).

Chatterley, Louisa, 1797–1866. Actress, born Louisa Simeon, married the actor William Simmonds Chatterley in 1813. Said to be excellent in comedy and to be the best representative of French women on the stage in her time. She has been described as a minor actress less remembered than her husband, but she was praised by T.L. Peacock. Crabb Robinson in his *Diary* in 1821 describes her as 'very pleasing' and again praised her in 1829. She played Dorinda in *The Beaux' Stratagem* at Covent Garden in 1828.

Lamb mentions her in his 'New Pieces at the Lyceum' in *The Examiner* in 1819 and says 'We did not know Mrs Chatterley's merits before; she plays with downright sterling good acting.'

Chilcott, Tim. A member of the Department of English, United States International University, Ashdown Park, Sussex. Author of *A Publisher and his Circle*, 1972, which deals with John Taylor, the publisher of *The London Magazine*, and has many references to Charles Lamb. Contributed 'De Quincey and *The London Magazine*' to *Charles Lamb Bulletin*, January 1973.

Childs, John, c.1783–1853. Well known printer of Bungay, Suffolk. He wrote to Lamb in 1834 asking where he could obtain a copy of *The Essays of Elia*. Lamb offered to lend him the book in return for a pig. According to Talfourd, Childs sent a turkey instead of a pig, but Lucas prints a note from Lamb in 1834 thanking Childs for a pig. For many years Childs issued a cheap series of reprints known as the 'Imperial Octavo editions of Standard Authors' which subsequently passed to H.G. Bohn. In May 1823 William Hone wrote verses to John Childs which he inserted in a copy of his *Ancient Mysteries* given to the printer. Childs replied in verse and inserted a copy in the book, printed in *The Bibliographer* 1882. A copy of *John Woodvil*, 1802, sold at Sothebys on 20 December 1938 was inscribed to Childs. It is marked 'Revd. Sept 26—1834' according to the sale catalogue. Lucas *Letters*, 1935, reproduces the inscription as Letter No. 1016.

Chimney Sweeper's Friend and Climbing Boy's Album, The. Published in 1824, edited by James Montgomery, with illustrative designs by R. Cruikshank, it is a miscellany of verse and prose, original and borrowed. Montgomery asked Lamb for a contribution. This was declined, but Elia sent a copy of Blake's poem 'The Chimney Sweeper' to Montgomery for insertion. In transcribing it Lamb altered line five by a 'sly blunder', changing 'Little Tom Dacre' into 'Little Tom Toddy'. Statements have been made by later writers that Lamb is supposed to have had a hand in editing the book, but no evidence to support this seems forthcoming.

Chorley, Henry Fothergill, 1808–72. Music critic and novelist. Born of Quaker parents. Wrote musical criticism for *The Athenaeum* from about 1830 and eventually became one of its chief reviewers. Wrote a number of novels and some plays.

Chorley wrote the text of *The Authors of England: a Series of Medallion Portraits of Modern Literary Characters, engraved from the Works of British Artists by Achille Collas,* 1838. Chorley's part is described as 'Illustrative Notices' and among those included were Byron, Coleridge, Lamb, Shelley, Scott, Moore, Southey and Wordsworth. The book was published by Tilt and a second edition appeared in 1861. The portrait head of Lamb was by H. Weekes, and there is a letter in the National Library of Scotland (Ms. 1706/38) from Allan Cunningham dated 28 January 1827 asking Moxon for facilities for Weekes to do the portrait. Chorley was a friend of Mrs Hemans, Dickens, Macaulay, Procter and Lady Blessington. He wrote for *The Athenaeum* obituary notices of Mary Lamb, Thomas Hood, George Darley, Miss Mitford, Samuel Rogers and N.P. Willis.

Christ's Hospital, the Blue Coat School. Originally in Newgate Street, London, but now at Horsham, Sussex. The school was founded by Edward VI in 1553 as a home for orphans and other poor children, but its character has changed and it had developed in time into one of the most famous schools in England. The City of London as a corporate body, the City Companies and the Lord Mayor and Aldermen have all taken an affectionate and generous interest in the school to its great benefit.

The buildings were largely destroyed in the Great Fire, but were partly rebuilt by Wren. In 1902 the school moved to Horsham and the old building was demolished. From 1683 until 1902 there was a preparatory school at Hertford, when it moved to Horsham. There is a Christ's Hospital school for girls at Hertford.

The school in Lamb's time was divided into the Writing School, which prepared boys for the great trading houses; the Navigation or Royal Mathematical School, founded by Charles II and with which Samuel Pepys was much conerned (he was a Governor of the School), which trained boys for the Navy and Merchant Service; and the Grammar School, where Greek and Latin were studied and from which boys passed to the Universities. Both Coleridge and Lamb were in the Grammar School. Lamb passed through the forms of Little and Great Erasmus in the Under School, into that of the Deputy Grecians. Edmund Blunden thought he may have proceeded further to become 'a boy with the Grecians'. Lamb was at the school from 1782 until 1789, Coleridge from 1782 to 1791 and Leight Hunt from 1791 to 1799.

Much fame has come to Christ's Hospital through the many notable men who have been educated there: from William Camden in Elizabethan times to the famous trio of Coleridge, Lamb and Leigh Hunt, and on to Edmund Blunden and J.E. Morpurgo in our own times.

Lamb wrote about the school in the *Gentleman's Magazine* for June 1813 (reprinted in his *Works*, 1818) and in his essay 'Christ's Hospital Five and Thirty Years Ago' in the *London Magazine* in November 1820 (reprinted in *The Essays of Elia*). Coleridge wrote of it in *The Courier* for 15 July 1811, in *Biographia Literaria*, 1817, and in his *Table Talk*, published in 1835. Leight Hunt referred to it many times in various periodicals, including *The Examiner*, *The Indicator*, *The New Monthly Magazine* and in his *Lord Byron and some of his Contemporaries*, 1828, and in his *Autobiography* in 1850. Most of these pieces are reprinted by R. Brimley Johnson, himself an old Blue, in his *Christ's Hospital*, 1896.

The affection in which Christ's Hospital is held by those educated there is shown in the many books written about the school, a long list of which is included in *The Christ's Hospital Book*, 1953. Among the most interesting are R. Brimley Johnson, *Christ's Hospital*, 1896; E.H. Pearce, *Annals of Christ's Hospital*, 1901; Edmund Blunden, *Christ's Hospital: A Retrospect*, 1923; and *The Christ's Hospital Book*, 1953. See also 'Christ's Hospital in Lamb's time and my own' by Frank Ledwith, contributed to the *Charles Lamb Bulletin*, October 1978.

Lamb's schoolfellows at Christ's Hospital included Robert Allen, army surgeon; Samuel Ball, East India Company at Canton; Samuel Bloxam; John Colborne, Field Marshal, Baron Seaton; S.T. Coleridge, poet; William Evans, East India House; Robert Favell, army officer; F.W. Franklin, Christ's Hospital Master at Hertford; C.V. Le Grice, clergyman; Samuel Le Grice, army officer; J.M. Gutch, author and editor; John Maunde, clergyman and translator; T.F. Middleton, Bishop of Calcutta; Thomas Mitchell, translator of Aristophanes; George Richards, poet; William Robinson, East India House; Henry Scott, died in Bedlam; Lancelot P. Stephens, Christ's Hospital Master; T.S. Surr, novelist; Marmaduke Thompson, clergyman; A.W. Trollope, Christ's Hospital Master; E. Thornton, diplomatist; James White, clerk at Christ's Hospital and advertising agent; Thomas White; William Winch, army officer; and H. Woodthorpe, Jnr, town clerk of London. In addition there were others at the school either just before Lamb's time or just after, who became friends, such as Thomas Barnes, George Dyer and Leigh Hunt. There were some at the school just after Lamb who may have been known to him because of the fame they achieved during his lifetime; such were James Scholefield, the Greek professor; John Rogers Pitman, the preacher and author; and the novelist W.P. Scargill, who may have sent a copy of his book on Christ's Hospital to Lamb, although the latter denied receiving it. Later Blues who showed a particular interest in Charles Lamb and wrote about him are R. Brimley Johnson, S.E. Winbolt, Edmund Blunden and J.E. Morpurgo. *See* separate entries for Amicable Society of Blues, Benevolent Society of Blues, Lamb Medal, Memorials to Charles Lamb. Some of Lamb's schoolfellows also have separate entries.

Clairmont, Clara Mary Jane (Claire), 1798–1879. Daughter of Mrs Clairmont, second wife of William Godwin. She accompanied Mary Godwin to the Continent when the latter eloped with Shelley, and she remained with them there, returning to England in 1816. She then pursued Byron and lived with him for three years when their child, Allegra was born. She later lived in Russia, Italy and Paris. It is highly probable that Lamb met her at the Godwin's house from time to time, and she records in her *Journal* on 1 March 1818 that Mary Lamb 'pays us a visit' (i.e. at the Shelley's house). Shelley left her a legacy.

Clapton, G.T. Author and editor. Edited *Selected Letters of Charles Lamb*, 1925, which has a long introduction including short biographies of Lamb's friends.

Clare, John, 1793–1864. Northamptonshire peasant poet. Was employed in a variety of labouring work and later attempted to be a small farmer, but was unsuccessful. Lived in poverty for much of his life. As a youth he managed to procure a copy of Thomson's *Seasons* which he studied ardently and began to write his own verses. Enlisted in the Militia but it was soon disbanded. In 1819 Henry Drury, a bookseller of Stamford, saw his poems and, thinking highly of them, helped Clare to get them published. They appeared in 1820 as *Poems, descriptive of Rural Life* with Taylor & Hessey and Drury as publishers. Octavius Gilchrist, who knew Clare, wrote at Taylor's request, an account of the poet which appeared in *The London Magazine* in January 1820. Subsequently Gilchrist reviewed the book in the *Quarterly Review* which greatly helped the sale of the volume.

In March 1820 Clare first visited London, accompanied by Gilchrist and on the day of his arrival Madame Vestris sang at Covent Garden one of his poems that had been set to music by Haydn Corri; Rossini wrote the music for another. While in London Clare dined at Taylor's house and met Cary and Reynolds. He also met in London

Lord Radstock and Mrs Emmerson, both of whom were to help him considerably in the future.

Clare's second volume of poems *The Village Ministrel and Other Poems* appeared in September 1821, but was not so successful as the first. Taylor visited Clare in October and his 'A Visit to John Clare' appeared in the *London Magazine* in November. In May 1822 Clare again visited London and was a guest at one of the famous 'Magazine dinners' attended by the contributors. It may have been at this time that he first met Lamb, although the well known short note to T.G. Wainewright printed as No. 386 in Lucas *Letters*, 1935, and there erroneously addressed to Procter, is tentatively dated May 1821. If this date is correct it is probable that they met earlier or Lamb would hardly say 'The *Wits* (as Clare calls us) ... '. Subsequent visits to London occurred in May-July 1824 and February-March 1828, during the first of which he became friendly with Allan Cunningham and visited Lamb at Colebrooke Cottage where Crabb Robinson met him on July 6.

Clare's third volume of poems *The Shepherd's Calendar; with Village Stories, and Other Poems* was issued in 1827 and in 1835 appeared *The Rural Muse*. In 1837 he showed signs of insanity and was placed in a private asylum in Epping Forest, subsequently being moved to the County Lunatic Asylum at Northampton, where he remained until his death in 1864. He continued to write poetry during his confinement.

Lamb and Clare met only during the latter's visits to London. In 1822 Clare had sent Lamb gifts of his *Poems* and *The Village Ministrel* and in return Elia sent the two volumes of his *Works* and a copy of *Tracts* by Sir Thomas Browne, which had just appeared edited by James Crossley. In his letter of 31 August 1822 Lamb offered Clare advice on his poetry, suggesting he should reduce the amount of 'rustick Cockneyism' in his work. He also tells Clare that he has visited France and eaten frogs. In August 1822 Clare had contributed to the *London* a sonnet 'To Elia' and in 1831 he sent another to Hone's *Year Book*. Clare does not seem to have met Lamb during his last visit to London for he says in a letter to Cary in 1830 that he has not seen him since 1824 and does not know where he is living. During 1828, however, he did visit Cary at the British Museum, again met Allan Cunningham, and contributed to *The Anniversary* which Cunningham was editing.

Thomas Hood has left in his *Literary Reminiscences* a vivid account of a London Magazine dinner, with Clare in his 'bright, grass-coloured coat, and yellow waistcoat' and Lamb in his black, and of them walking home arm in arm to the amusement of the populace. Clare himself left manuscript notes of the 'Londoners' in which he includes both Charles and Mary Lamb (they are printed in Blunden's

Sketches in the Life of John Clare, 1931). In his *Journal* in October 1824 Clare noted 'Lamb's best poetry is in Elia.'

Clarke, Charles Cowden, 1787–1877. Author, theatre critic, lecturer and musician. Friend of Lamb, Hazlitt, Coleridge, Leigh Hunt, George Dyer and Keats. The latter was a pupil at the school kept by Clarke's father, John Clarke. Charles Clarke married Mary Victoria Novello, a daughter of Vincent Novello, and he was a frequent visitor to the Novellos' musical evenings. He had been a publisher with Henry Hunt, Leigh Hunt's nephew, and later joined with J. Alfred Novello in the family music business. A number of letters from Lamb to Clarke survive. Lamb wrote a sonnet for the album of Mrs Towers, Clarke's sister and Keats wrote an 'Epistle to Charles Cowden Clarke' in 1816. About 1828 Charles Cowden Clarke and his wife stayed with the Lambs at Enfield.

Clarke became well known for his lectures on Shakespeare which were published. He also edited John Nyren's *Young Cricketer's Tutor* and Clarke and Nyren frequently met at the Novello's parties. *The Atlas* for 11 January 1835 prints a notice on Charles Lamb which Edmund Blunden thought was possibly by Clarke.

Clarke, John, 1757–1820. Originally a lawyer's clerk, later a schoolmaster. Father of Charles Cowden Clarke. Had as pupils at his school at Enfield John Keats and Edward Holmes, the biographer of Mozart. Friend of George Dyer, who had been an usher with Clarke at a school at Northampton. It is said that they both courted the same girl, and Clarke was accepted. This caused no breach in their friendship, nor in that of Dyer for Clarke's son. *See also Keats-Shelley Journal* XXVIII, 1979.

Clarke, Mary Victoria Cowden, 1809–98. Authoress, daughter of Vincent Novello who married Charles Cowden Clarke in 1828. In 1845 she published her *Complete Concordance to Shakespeare* after sixteen years' work on it. She collaborated with her husband on a number of books, one of which was *Recollections of Writers*, 1878, that refers to the Lambs; there are further references in her *My Long Life*, 1896. As a girl she had been taught Latin by Mary Lamb and both she and her husband were close friends of the Lambs.

Clarkson, Thomas, 1760–1846. English reformer and anti-slavery agitator. Educated at St Paul's School and St John's College, Cambridge. He became Vice-President of the Anti-Slavery Society. Among his works were *A Portraiture of Quakerism*, 1806; *History of the ... Abolition of the African Slave Trade*, 1808; and the *Life of William Penn*, 1813. But he was not himself a Quaker. He was the author of a large number of books largely concerned with the reform of abuses.

Clarkson's wife was Catherine Buck, a childhood friend of Crabb Robinson, who described her as 'the most eloquent woman I have ever known, with the exception of Madame de Staël.' She introduced Crabb Robinson to Charles Lamb, and also to Coleridge and Wordsworth. The Clarksons lived in the Lake District near Wordsworth and in 1802 the Lambs stayed with them there. In 1807 after they had moved to Bury St Edmunds the Lambs again stayed with them. There are numerous references to the Clarksons in Lamb's letters and both Charles and Mary Lamb wrote interesting letters to them. It was with their son, Tom, as accomplice that Mary Lamb robbed a cherry tree.

Coaching. Charles Lamb was a great pedestrian, often walking twenty miles a day. Yet he was not a great traveller and his journeys were limited mainly to his annual month's leave with an occasional trip to such places as Cambridge to see friends. Only once did he leave England, but his annual holidays usually necessitated a coach journey. In his early days coach travel was most uncomfortable, for the roads were bad, coaches slow and inn keepers often difficult to those who did not travel in their own coaches or by postchaise.

Lamb's earliest journeys would have been those he took with Mary to visit relatives in Hertfordshire, when they would have travelled by stage coach. The famous York Road took them most of the way and coaches left London frequently, passing through Shoreditch, Stoke Newington, Tottenham, Edmonton, Enfield, Waltham and on to Ware before they would leave the main coach to make their way to Widford and possibly Blakesware to visit their grandmother.

Again Charles Lamb would have taken the same road on his visits to Cambridge which may have been as early as 1791, possibly in 1794 when Coleridge left Cambridge, and certainly in 1801, 1815, 1819 and 1820. Mary describes the journey in 1815 in a letter to Sara Hutchinson and tells how the coach driver was the famous 'Hell Fire Dick' (Richard Vaughan). He drove half way to London on one coach and then brought the London coach back to Cambridge to the 'Sun' in Trumpington Street. She says they travelled on the outside, which passengers did who could not afford the higher inside fare. A fine view was obtained of the countryside in fair weather, and as they went in August possibly they were lucky in this, but the jolting and discomfort would shock modern travellers.

The Lambs, whose journeys were mostly by stage coach, would have also have travelled on the equally famous Holyhead Road when going to Birmingham to see the Lloyds, and on later journeys may have alighted at Redbourn to visit Thomas Manning. Lambs's visit to Nether Stowey in 1797 to see Coleridge would have been by means of the Bath Road and the journeys to Winterslow to see Hazlitt probably were made by the Exeter Road, and in the Salisbury Long Coach which took forty eight hours for the double journey. In 1782 Parson

Woodforde paid £2. 2s. for two inside places on the Salisbury coach and 10s. 6d. for one outside place.

During Lamb's life the time for coach journeys was reduced. In 1764 London to Newcastle took six days, but by 1785 it had been reduced to three days; London to Birmingham was two days in 1752, but only nineteen hours in 1785; while London to Manchester had dropped from four and one-half days in 1754 to twenty-eight hours in 1788. The first mail coach was introduced in 1784 running from London to Bristol in sixteen hours, passengers paying 28s. About this time the journey from London to Brighton took eleven hours, but 'flying' coaches did it in eight hours and the single journey cost from 14s. to 16s.

Most routes were covered by rival coaches and the competition between the drivers was keen and often dangerous. The aim was to do the journey in the shortest possible time to attract passengers. When the Lambs went with the Burneys to the Isle of Wight in 1803 they probably travelled by the Portsmouth Road for part of the way, although they actually took the packet from Southampton. This road was served by the Portsmouth Regulator which left the Angel, St Clements, in the Strand at 8:00AM and arrived at the George in Portsmouth at 5:00 PM. the same day, and also by the Rocket from Belle Sauvage, Ludgate Hill, the Light Post Coach, the Portsmouth Telegraph and other coaches.

Lamb must have seen many changes in coach travel during his lifetime, not only greatly increased speed and lighter coaches, but also an increase in the number of vehicles: in 1821 on the Brighton Road alone twenty coaches a day left London for the coast, and on other roads they were equally numerous. Frequently the coach carried items of news, as of famous victories in the wars, catastrophies and unusual happenings: at Christmas time they were full of parcels; on May Day they were decorated. Travelling in the early nineteenth century was still hazardous to modern minds, but there was some enjoyment if one could overcome the cold and the jolting.

In several letters Lamb complains of the discomforts: 'I am so tired with my journey, being up all night . . . ' after the Winterslow return journey in 1809. 'No more night travelling' in 1810 and 'Travelling is not good for us.' As he grew older and after he retired in 1825 he walked more and travelled less, but there must always have been glamour and excitement about a coach journey and the start from the inn yard, which may have distracted one's mind from the unpleasant aspects.

Cobb, James, 1756–1818. Dramatist. Secretary of the East India Company 1814–18. Author of many plays including farces and comic operas. Among these were *The First Floor*, 1787; *Poor Old Drury*, 1791; *Poor Covent Garden*, 1792; and *Paul and Virginia*: *A*

Musical Entertainment, 1800. His play *The Haunted Tower*, 1789, contained the famous song 'The Roast Beef of Old England'. Miss Tyrer, later Mrs Liston, played the part of Fidelia in his comic opera *Pirates* at Drury Lane in 1801. He was a member of the Beefsteak Club and a friend of Sheridan, for whom he wrote a prelude on the removal of the Drury Lane Company of actors to the King's Theatre, preparatory to the rebuilding. Cobb was a man of ability and humour.

He does not seem to have been mentioned by Lamb, but he was a colleague who achieved considerable fame during his lifetime. Like T.L. Peacock a little later, his position in the East India Company was that of an important official. He seems, like Lamb, to have been an admirer of the actress Miss Pope, for he wrote a prologue for one of her benefits and his first play was produced for another.

Coe, Mrs Elizabeth, c.1818–1903. Elizabeth Hunt, later Mrs Coe, was a pupil at the Misses Norris's school Goddard House, Widford. She remembered Charles Lamb when he visited the school between 1827–32 and she gave her reminiscences of the visits to E.V. Lucas, who printed them in *The Athenaeum* on 7 June 1902 and again in his *Life of Charles Lamb*.

Colborne, John, 1778–1863. Field Marshal. Educated at Christ's Hospital, 1785–89 and at Winchester. Entered the Army as an ensign in 1794. Became military secretary to Sir John Moore. Served in Egypt and in the Peninsula War. Colborne, then a Colonel, commanded the 52nd Light Infantry at Waterloo and led the charge which routed the Old Guard. He has been credited with having won the Battle of Waterloo, but it is said that Wellington never gave him fair credit for his charge.

He held the appointment of Lieutenant Governor of Guernsey in 1821 and of Upper Canada in 1828. He was created Baron Seaton in 1839 and became a Field Marshal in 1860. Although this distinguished soldier is unlikely to have come in contact with Lamb after he left school, no doubt Elia was aware of his exploits. Among its collection of Eliana, Harvard now has an autograph of Colborne's.

Colburn, Henry, d.1855. Publisher. Issued the *New Monthly Magazine* in 1814, also started the *Literary Gazette* in 1817 and the *Court Journal* in 1828. Lamb contributed 'Popular Fallacies' to the *New Monthly* in 1826, the editor of which was Thomas Campbell from 1820 when a new series began. Colburn published the first edition of *Evelyn's Diary* in 1818 and *Pepys's Diary* in 1825. He also published Theodore Hook's *Sayings and Doings* in 1824 and is remembered for his series of 'Colburn's Modern Standard Novelists' 1835–41. Among the authors he published were Bulwer Lytton,

Horace Smith, Captain Marryat, G.P.R. James, Harrison Ainsworth and Benjamin D'Israeli.

Lamb wrote some letters to Colburn, one on 25 September 1827 recommending Moxon, but the latter was not employed by Colburn. In a letter to P.G. Patmore on 10 April 1831 Lamb expressed dislike of Colburn 'Coal-burn him in Beelzebub's deepest pit.'

Coldwell, Joan, b.1936. Associate Professor of English, McMaster University. Contributed 'The Playgoer as critic: Charles Lamb on Shakespeare's Characters' to the *Shakespeare Quarterly*, Spring 1975. Editor of *Charles Lamb on Shakespeare*, 1978.

Cole, Mr. Lamb wrote a letter in 1831 to a Mr Cole thanking him for a copy of Aristotle and enclosing verses for his daughter's album. They were printed in *The Athenaeum* on 7 January 1832 under the title of 'The Self Enchanted'.

In a letter to Hone in July 1827 Lamb had mentioned a friend of Moxon's named Cole, who was the author of the *History of Weston Favell*; Hone printed an extract from this book in *The Table Book* II, 366−9, and he had also mentioned Cole in Volume I, 526. This was John Cole, 1792−1848, a bookseller and antiquary of Northampton and Scarborough.

In his notes to the 1831 letter Lucas states that the Cole referred to there may have been R. Cole, a master of the Free Grammar School at Andover and author of Greek text books, or it could have been John Cole of the 1827 letter. A 'John Cole' published *Memoirs of Mrs Chapone* in 1839 and a 'Jack Cole' is mentioned in 'A Character of the late Elia.' Sophia Holcroft married a Mr Cole of Exeter.

Colebrooke Cottage, Islington. The Lambs moved in 1823 from Russell Street to Colebrooke Cottage, Colebrooke Row, Islington. Lamb in a letter to Barton on 2 September 1823 describes the house as 'a cottage, for it is detach'd; a white house, with 6 good rooms.' He added 'I feel like a great Lord, never having had a house before.' It had three stories and the New River then ran at the front door. There was a garden of which Lamb boasted to his friends, and George Daniel stated that this first stimulated Lamb's interest in gardening, and he 'planted, pruned and grafted', and was especially fond of anemones and roses. He paid £45 a year rent for the house.

It was here that Lamb challenged Theodore Hook to a race round the garden, but Hook 'pursy and puffy ... whose gait was like the hobbling of a fat goose in attempting to fly, declined the contest, remarking that he could outrun nobody but the constable.' Other friends visited him here and the Hoods lived nearby at 5 Lower Street. Vincent Rice, a colleague at East India House, who witnessed Lamb's will, lived at 3 Ruffords Row and Lamb's cousin, Charles Lovekin, the bookbinder, at Windsor Place.

From this house George Dyer, in broad daylight, walked straight into the New River; an incident forming the subject of some of Lamb's most amusing letters and his essay 'Amicus Redivivus'. For a few weeks in August 1825 William Hone lived in Colebrooke Cottage when the Lambs were on a visit to Enfield. They finally left the house in September 1827 when they moved to Chase Side, Enfield.

Many changes have taken place since Lamb's day. The New River is now covered in and the garden has disappeared. Wilmot Harrison, writing in 1889, stated that a soda-water manufactory occupied the garden. This was started by John Webb, the founder of John G. Webb & Co Ltd., of South Lambeth. To him the Lambs sold some of their furniture when they left Islington, and a chair which belonged to Lamb was presented by the Company to the Charles Lamb Society.

A house still exists there which is known as 'Charles Lamb's House', but William Kent, writing in the *C.L.S. Bulletin* in May 1962 stated he had the assurance of Mr F.V. Hallam, Secretary of the Islington Antiquarian Society, that Lamb's cottage disappeared long ago; what is there now is a house not a cottage. He added that although the plaque was still on the house, it should read 'In a cottage on this site Charles Lamb lived.' Kent had also written to the *Times Literary Supplement* about this on 26 September 1958. The existing house seems to have been variously described as No. 19 Camden Terrace and 64 Duncan Terrace. An illustration of the cottage as it was in Lamb's time, taken from a contemporary water-colour drawing, appears in E.V. Lucas's *Life of Charles Lamb*, 1905.

Coleridge, David Hartley, 1796–1849. Author, eldest son of S.T. Coleridge. Won a Fellowship at Oxford but was deprived of it through misbehaviour. Became an unsuccessful journalist and then a schoolmaster at Ambleside. Contributed poems and essays to the *London Magazine*. Published *Biographia Borealis* in 1833 comprising lives of Lancashire and Yorkshire worthies. His sonnets, published in 1833, are said to be among the finest in English literature. In 1840 he edited the works of Massinger and Ford. He was nicknamed 'The Philosopher' by Lamb. Like his father, Hartley Coleridge was of outstanding ability, but suffered from a similar lack of will power and direction.

Some of his essays have a strong resemblance to those of Charles Lamb and are nearly as attractive. They were republished by his brother, Derwent, in 1851. Major Butterworth in *The Bookman,* July 1921, attributed to him the review of *The Last Essays of Elia* in the *Quarterly Review* of July 1835, but the *Wellesley Index to Victorian Periodicals* gives this to Henry Nelson Coleridge.

Coleridge, Derwent 1800–83. Second son of S.T. Coleridge, nick-named 'Pi-pos' by his family. He was ordained in 1825, became a schoolmaster and author. He was friendly with W.M. Praed, Macaulay and Bulwer. In 1822 he contributed to the *Quarterly Magazine*. Edited the *Poems and Essays* of his brother Hartley and included a memoir. He also edited Praed's *Works*. For a time he was a schoolmaster at Helston, Cornwall, where he had Charles Kingsley as a pupil; in 1841 he was appointed the first principal of St Mark's College, Chelsea. Dean Stanley declared him to be the most accomplished linguist in England: it was said that he could read at least a dozen languages.

Coleridge, Rev. Edward, 1800–83. Youngest son of Colonel James Coleridge and nephew of S.T. Coleridge. Went up to Corpus Christi College, Oxford in 1818, became a Fellow of Exeter College in 1823 and was a master at Eton from 1824–57. In 1862 he was Vicar of Mapledurham. He was a contemporary at Oxford of his cousin Harley. In a letter of 9 December 1825 S.T. Coleridge invites him to the Gillman's at Highgate and says that he had secured Charles Lamb and Edward Irving to meet him, and hoped to induce Blanco White to come as well. On 19 July 1826 Lamb wrote to Edward Coleridge to thank him for kindness to a friend's child. This was Samuel Bloxam, and W.C. Hazlitt states in his edition of Lamb's *Letters* that Bloxam's son, Frederick, was on the foundation at Eton, probably through the help of Edward Coleridge and Charles Lamb.

Coleridge, The Hon. Gilbert, 1859–1953. Barrister and sculptor. Great-great-nephew of S.T. Coleridge. Third son of Lord Chief Justice Coleridge. Educated at Eton and Trinity College, Oxford, and one of the founders of the O.U.D.S. Called to the Bar in 1886. Appointed Assistant Master of the Crown Office. Retired in 1921. Exhibited his sculpture at R.A. and R.B.A. He executed a bas relief of S.T. Coleridge for Jesus College, Cambridge and a plaque of Charles Lamb for Christ's Hospital.

Coleridge, Henry Nelson, 1798–1843. Author and barrister. Son of Colonel James Coleridge and nephew and son-in-law of S.T. Coleridge, having married the poet's daughter, Sara, in 1829. Educated at Eton and King's College, Cambridge. Was literary executor of S.T. Coleridge. Contributed to *The Etonian*, March 1821, an essay 'On Charles Lamb's Poetry', signed 'G.M.' He edited Coleridge's *Literary Remains, Aids to Reflection, Confessions of an Enquiring Spirit* and *Biographia Literaria*. He also recorded Coleridge's *Table Talk* which he published in 1835. He contributed to the *Quarterly Review* and is said to have written there the review of *The Last Essays of Elia* in July 1835, although Major Butterworth gave this to Hartley Coleridge. He also wrote *Six Months in the West Indies*, 1825.

Coleridge, Samuel Taylor, 1772–1834. Poet, philosopher and critic. Educated at Christ's Hospital at the same time as Charles Lamb: the two became lifelong friends. After Mary Lamb, perhaps Coleridge was the most important person in Charles Lamb's life, at least during his early years. Because of his addiction to opium Coleridge placed himself under the care of Dr James Gillman of Highgate in 1816 and lived with him for the rest of his life. The main events in Coleridge's life are:

1772   S.T. Coleridge born at Ottery St Mary, October 21.

1782   Entered Christ's Hospital, July.

1791   Left Christ's Hospital, September. Entered as sizar at Jesus College, Cambridge, February 5. Came into residence at Cambridge, October.

1793   Fled from Cambridge, went to London and enlisted in 15th Dragoons in December.

1794   Discharged from the Army and returned to Cambridge, April. Visited Oxford and met Southey, June. Trip to Wales with John Hucks, July. Became engaged to Sara Fricker. Pantisocracy proposed. In December left Cambridge without a degree.

1794–5   At 'Salutation & Cat' in Newgate Street and met Charles Lamb again, December 1794–January 1795.

1795   Went to Bristol and met Joseph Cottle. Lectured at Bristol. Married Sara Fricker on October 4 and went to live at Clevedon.

1796   Tour of the north of England to obtain subscribers for *The Watchman*, published this year. Met Charles Lloyd at Birmingham during tour. *Poems on Various Subjects* published in April with four sonnets by Charles Lamb. Hartley Coleridge born September 19. The Coleridge's moved to Nether Stowey on December 31. Coleridge met the Wedgwoods during this year.

1797   Second edition of *Poems* published in June with poems by Charles Lamb and Charles Lloyd. Coleridge visited the Wordsworths at Racedown and they moved to Alfoxden to be near S.T.C. Charles Lamb visited Coleridge at Nether Stowey when the Wordsworths were there in July. Coleridge composed part of 'Christabel', 'The Ancient Mariner' and 'Kubla Khan'.

1798   Coleridge and Hazlitt met. Berkeley Coleridge born May 14. *Lyrical Ballads* published in September and Coleridge and Wordsworth left for Germany.

1799   Coleridge returned to England. Berkeley Coleridge died February 10.

1799–1800   Coleridge again in London, writing for the *Morning Post* and met Lamb.

1800   In July removed with his family to Greta Hall, Keswick. Wrote second part of 'Christabel'. Derwent Coleridge born September 14. *Wallenstein* published.

1801   Second, revised edition in two volumes of *Lyrical Ballads* published in January.

1802   The Lambs visited Coleridge at Keswick, August. Tour of Wales with Thomas Wedgwood in November–December. Sara Coleridge born December 22.

1803   Coleridge with the Wordworths in Scotland in August.

1804   Coleridge sailed for Malta in April.

1805   Left Malta in September.

1805–6   Visited Sicily, Naples and Rome.

1806   Returned to England and went to stay with Lamb, later moving to *The Courier* office in the Strand.

1807   Met his wife and family at Bristol and spent the summer with them. Met Thomas De Quincey.

1808   Lectured at the Royal Institution on Shakespeare and other English poets, January to June. At Allan Bank, Grasmere.

1809–10   Published *The Friend*. Living in Wordsworth's house at Allan Bank, Grasmere.

1810   Living in London with Basil Montagu, then with the Morgans.

1810–12   Lectured on Shakespeare, Milton and other subjects.

1811   Wrote for *The Courier*.

1813   *Remorse* produced at Drury Lane in January and published.

1813–14   Lectures at Bristol on Shakespeare and Milton.

1814–16   Coleridge at Calne with the Morgans.

1816   On April 16 Coleridge entered Gillman's house as a patient and friend. *Christabel, Kubla Khan and The Pains of Sleep* published by Murray.

1817   *Sibylline Leaves, Lay Sermons* and *Biographia Literaria* published.

1818   Lectured in Fetter Lane on Shakespeare and other subjects. Met Thomas Allsop.

1825   *Aids to Reflection* published.

1828   Collected edition of *Poetical and Dramatic Works* published. Tour of the Rhine with the Wordsworths in June-July.

1829   Sara Coleridge married Henry Nelson Coleridge.

1833   Coleridge visited Cambridge with the British Association, June.

1834   S.T. Coleridge died July 25. Second edition of *Collected Poems* published, edited by H.N. Coleridge. Mrs S.T. Coleridge died in 1845.

Volume I of Lamb's *Works*, 1818, was dedicated to Coleridge. *The British Museum Catalogue* (Extract published 1947) contains a list of the books there annotated by Coleridge, as does the Bibliography by J.P. Anderson included in Hall Caine's *Life of Samuel Taylor Coleridge*, 1887.

Coleridge, Sara, c.1773–1845. Wife of S.T. Coleridge; they were married in 1795. Born Sara Fricker, sister of Robert Southey's wife; another sister married Robert Lovell. In 1796 Lamb wrote verses 'To Sara and her Samuel'. Some verses 'The Silver Thimble' are printed in S.T. Coleridge's *Poems* where they are signed 'Sara', but Mrs Coleridge told her daughter many years later that she wrote but little of these verses.

Coleridge, Sara, 1802–52. Only daughter of S.T. Coleridge, was brought up by her uncle, Robert Southey, and married her cousin Henry Nelson Coleridge in 1829. All accounts of her appearance and manner indicate that she was a most charming person, as well as an accomplished scholar. She translated Dobrizhoffer's *Account of the Abipones* from Latin in 1822 to pay for her brother Derwent's college education. She also translated *Memoirs of the Chevalier Bayard*, 1825, and wrote *Pretty Lessons in Verse for Good Children*, 1834, and a fairy tale *Phantasmion* in 1837, which contains many attractive lyrics.

Coleridge, The Hon. Stephen, b.1854. Great-great nephew of S.T. Coleridge. Hon. Secretary of the Anti-Vivisection Society. Author of *Quiet Hours in the Temple*, 1924, which contains chapters on 'The Temple in the Reign of Charles Lamb' and 'Henry Crabb Robinson keeps a Diary in the Temple.' Other works include *Letters to my Grandson on the Glory of English Prose, Letters to my Grandson on the Glory of English Poetry, A Morning in my Library* and *Memoirs*. He contributed to the *Contemporary Review, Fortnightly Review* and other periodicals.

Collett, William, d.1832. A clerk at East India House in the Accountant's Office with Lamb, next in rank to Du Puy. Samuel McKechnie in the *C.L.S. Bulletin* No. 83, stated that he was awarded a pension of £550 at the age of fifty-eight and died on the last day of his service. In his letter in August 1832 to Walter Wilson, Lamb states that Collett is dead.

Collier, John Dyer, 1762–1825. Originally a Spanish wool merchant, but turned to literature. He edited *The Monthly Register* and *Critical Review* and also did reviews for *The Times* and *The Morning Chronicle*. He was the father of John Payne Collier, the Shakespearean scholar. He was a close friend of Crabb Robinson who lived with the Colliers for some years, and there are numerous references to him and his family in Robinson's *Diary*. Among Collier's friends were Coleridge and Wordsworth. He was introduced to Charles Lamb by Robinson, who records going with the Lambs and the Colliers to Covent Garden to see *Cato* in 1811.

At Mrs Clarkson's instigation Collier obtained for Hazlitt a situation as parliamentary reporter on *The Morning Chronicle* in 1812, and Lamb wrote a letter to Collier at the time recommending Hazlitt. In January 1823 he wrote to Mr and Mrs Collier thanking them for a present of a pig, and in November 1824 he wrote to Mrs Collier acknowledging a similar gift. Mary Lamb had written to her earlier, possibly in 1814, about a situation as a mantua maker for a sister of Mrs Coleridge.

Collier, John Payne, 1789–1883. Shakespearean critic and editor of old plays. Son of John Dyer Collier. He succeeded his father as a reporter on *The Times* from 1809–21. In 1811 he became a student of the Middle Temple and in 1816 married Mary Louisa Pycroft, formerly of Edmonton. He became a member of the staff of *The Morning Chronicle*.

Collier had a remarkable knowledge of the Elizabethan poets, probably stimulated by Charles Lamb and by his friendship with Rodd, the antiquarian bookseller. He published much valuable work, but unfortunately some of it was subject to the suspicion of his having tampered with the text.

Collier was a friend of Lamb and in 1820 sent him his *Poetical Decameron*; in his letter of thanks Lamb wrote 'I like books about books.' In 1823 he sent Lamb a copy of his *A Poet's Pilgrimage* which contains a 'Dedicatory Poem to C.L.' Collier frequently mentions Lamb in his *Old Man's Diary* 1871. Collier wrote *The History of English Dramatic Poetry*, 1831, mentioned by Lamb in his letter on 14 June 1831 to Moxon. Collier took shorthand notes of Coleridge's lectures in 1811–12.

Collins, John Philip, 1870–1954. Journalist. For many years with *Birmingham Post*, subsequently with the *Pall Mall Gazette* and *Pall Mall Magazine*, and was London correspondent to various overseas papers. Wrote reviews for *The Bookman*. Edited Charles Morley's *Travels in London*. Collins was a friend of the artist Hugh Thomson and wrote on 'The Art of Hugh Thomson' in *The Bookman* in 1913. Succeeded Augustine Birrell as President of the Elian Society and was later its Secretary. A founder member of the Charles Lamb Society and at one time its Honorary Auditor. Member of the Charles Lamb Centenary Memorial Appeal Executive Committee 1934–5.

Collins was a contributor to the *C.L.S. Bulletin* and was the author of 'Of Masks and Faces. A Letter as from the Late Elia' in that publication in January 1942. He also delivered a lecture on 'The Press of Charles Lamb's Day' which was reprinted in the *City Press* on 10 September 1942. In 1945 he gave a lecture on 'The Godwins'.

Colman, George, the Younger, 1762–1836. Dramatist, educated at Westminster and Oxford. Son of George Colman, dramatist, theatre manager and friend of Garrick. The younger Colman wrote many plays, including *Inkle and Yarico*, 1787; *The Iron Chest*, 1796; *The Heir at Law*, 1797; *Bluebeard*, 1798; and *John Bull*, 1803. Like his father he became manager of the Haymarket. His character of Dr Peter Pangloss in *The Heir at law* was a favourite part with comedians and has become famous. In 1824 he was appointed Examiner of Plays and as such was rigorous and prudish, in contrast to the license in his own works. Lamb mentioned him in 'The Religion of Actors.'

Contemporary Events. Charles Lamb's writings for publication seldom refer to contemporary events. His letters occasionally have passing references, but the general impression gathered from his work is that he was little concerned with the great events which occurred during his lifetime of fifty-nine years. This is not, of course, a true picture, for it would have been impossible to live in London and to frequent such company as that of Coleridge, Hazlitt, Rickman, Godwin, Crabb Robinson and Leigh Hunt without hearing much of life around him and discussions of the questions of the day.

Possibly the Gordon Riots of 1780 made little impact on him at the age of five, or even the French Revolution at fourteen, although the latter event must have left some mark on almost all Englishmen of the time. A few of the events likely to have been discussed at his home, at school, at the East India House, and particularly among the friends of his leisure hours were:

1793   Execution of Louis XVI.
1795   Acquittal of Warren Hastings.
1798   Battle of the Nile.
1802   Peace of Amiens.
1804   Napoleon–Emperor
1805   Battles of Trafalgar and Austerlitz
1807   Abolition of the Slave Trade
1812   Murder of Spencer Perceval
———   Napoleon invades Russia
1815   Waterloo
1819   Peterloo Massacre
1820   Death of George III
———   Trial of Queen Caroline
1821   Death of Napoleon
1827   University of London founded

1830   Death of George IV
1831   Reform Bill

In his early days Lamb wrote a few political epigrams and paragraphs and there are references to Napoleon and Nelson in his letters. He so far supported Queen Caroline as to write verses to her champion Matthew Wood. In a letter to George Dyer on 20 December 1830 he has much to say about rick burning. We know, too; that he read Cobbett's *Political Register*, Leigh Hunt's *Examiner*, the monthly magazines and the great quarterlies, all of which dealt with current affairs. Generally, however, his heart was not in such subjects. He tells us in his essay 'Detached Thoughts on Books and Reading' that he read the newspapers, but in a paragraph in the essay in the *London Magazine*, not reprinted in the *Elia* volume, he adds 'I generally skip the Foreign News, the Debates—and the Politics.'

Cook, Elsie Thornton. Author, wrote *Justly Dear: Charles and Mary Lamb. A Biographical Novel*, 1939, *Speaking Dust: Thomas and Jane Carlyle* (a novel), *They Lived: A Brontë Novel, Sir Walter's Dogs* and a number of books dealing with the Royal Family and the Kings and Queens of England.

Cooke, George Frederick, 1756–1811. English actor. Played much in the provinces but also appeared at the Haymarket and at Covent Garden. Although of considerable ability and good in villainous parts, he was unreliable. Among his best parts were Richard III, Shylock, Iago and Sir Giles Overreach. He also played Othello, Lear, Macbeth, Falstaff, Hamlet, Sir Peter Teazle, Joseph Surface and Pierre.

Lamb wrote a criticism of Cooke's Richard the Third at Covent Garden which was printed in *The Morning Post* for 8 January 1802. Lucas also prints from the same paper a piece on Cooke as Lear at Covent Garden which he thinks is by Lamb. In a letter to Robert Lloyd on 26 June 1801 Lamb also wrote much about Cooke.

Cottle, Amos Simon, c.1768–1800. Antiquarian, brother of Joseph Cottle, publisher of Bristol. A neighbour of George Dyer in Clifford's Inn. He wrote *Icelandic Poetry*, 1797, which contains a long prefatory poem by Southey. He is immortalized by Byron in *English Bards and Scotch Reviewers* by the lines:
      Oh! Amos Cottle—Phoebus! What a name
      To fill the speaking trump of future fame!
In a note to the poem Byron described the Cottles as 'sellers of books they did not write, and now writers of books that do not sell.' Lamb's letter of 9 October 1800 to Coleridge refers to him.

Cottle, Joseph, 1770–1835. Author and publisher of Bristol. He issued the early work of Coleridge, Southey and Charles Lloyd. He also published *The Annual Anthology* which in 1799 contained Lamb's poem 'Living without God in the World.' In 1798 he issued *The Lyrical Ballads*.

Joseph Cottle wrote a number of volumes of poems, of which *Alfred, an Epic Poem*, 1801, went into several editions and is particularly mentioned by Lamb in a letter to Coleridge in October 1800. In 1837 Cottle issued *Early Recollections, chiefly relating to the late Samuel Taylor Coleridge*, reprinted in 1847 as *Reminiscences of Coleridge and Southey*. It is a valuable work but is not notable for accuracy.

He was a friend of Lamb, who in the letter of 9 October 1800 to Coleridge, wrote a most amusing account of his visit of condolence to Cottle on the death of his brother, Amos, and the rapidity with which Cottle overcame his grief. In 1819 Lamb wrote to him about the portrait of Cottle which he had borrowed for his friend William Evans, and he comments on Cottle's poem 'Messiah'. A further letter on 26 May 1820 refers to Cottle's 'Fall of Cambria'. There are other references to Cottle in Lamb's letters to his friends.

Coulson, Walter, 1794–1860. Barrister, journalist and editor. Reporter for the *Morning Chronicle*, later a Parliamentary reporter,. Editor of *The Globe* 1823–5. Called to the Bar 1828, became a Q.C. and then a bencher of Gray's Inn. Subsequently he was a Parliamentary Counsel and draughtsman for the Home Office. He was noted for his erudition and was known as the 'walking encyclopaedia'. He was a disciple of Jeremy Bentham and at one time his amanuensis.

Among his friends were Lamb, Hazlitt, T.J. Hogg, Leigh Hunt and Crabb Robinson, as well as James Mill, Francis Place, R.H. Barham and T.L. Peacock. Coulson was godfather to Hazlitt's son and later was responsible for finding employment for the boy with the *Morning Chronicle*, standing sponsor for him with Martin Burney.

Crabb Robinson records on 17 June 1815 finding Coulson in a party with Lamb, and on 9 December the same year he notes that at Alsager's he met Lamb, Hazlitt, Coulson and Ayrton. Again on 9 April 1822 Robinson records calling at Lamb's and finding Coulson there.

He was one of Sarah Hazlitt's chief advisers in her negotiations for divorce in 1822. Walter Coulson's brother, William, was an eminent surgeon. He married Maria, daughter of Ann Bartram, Lamb's 'Alice W——' (Ann Simmons). He was on the staff of *The Lancet*.

Counting-House Clerk, The. A play by Michael Voysey broadcast by the B.B.C. on 7 September 1956 which conerns the life of Charles Lamb. (A copy of the T.V. Script is in the Library of the Charles Lamb Society).

Courtney, Winifred F. Contributed to the *Charles Lamb Bulletin* 'Charles Lamb in New York 1974', April 1974; 'Charles Lamb and Ann Simmons', January 1975; 'Lamb, Gillray and the ghost of Edmund Burke', October 1975; and 'New Lamb Texts from *The Albion*', January, April & October 1977. Mrs Courtney's attention was drawn to some copies of *The Albion* in Bath Municipal Library by Professor Carl Woodring and she attributes a number of items to Charles Lamb. She is working on a biography of the young Lamb.

Coventry, Thomas, 1713–97. Barrister, one of Lamb's 'Old Benchers of the Inner Temple.' He was a director of the South Sea Company and M.P. for Bridport. Miss Ann Manning stated in her *Family Portraits* that Coventry had placed Lamb in the Blue Coat School and when he left found him a situation in Joseph Paice's office until he could get into the South Sea House. It seems, however, that Samuel Salt and Timothy Yeats were also concerned. Paice was also a director of the South Sea Company. Coventry had a house at North Cray Place, Kent, and employed Capability Brown to landscape the grounds.

Craddock, Thomas. Author of *Charles Lamb*, 1867, a book of 216 pages printed at the private printing office of William Dawbarn & Company of Liverpool, where the author lived.

Craig, William James, 1843–1906. Shakespeare scholar and philologist. Educated at Trinity College, Dublin. In 1876 appointed Professor of English language and literature at University College, Aberystwyth. Subsequently a private tutor. Editor of The *Oxford Shakespeare*, 1892 (Oxford Edition of Standard Authors), with R.H. Case edited the 'Arden Shakespeare'. Edited *The Essays of Elia* and *The Last Essays of Elia* in 1897 for Dent's 'Temple Classics' series. The general editor of this series was Israel Gollancz, and it was his suggestion that these volumes contain no introductions 'to come between readers and their favourite authors.' Notes were to be confined to the smallest limits, but in fact Craig's notes to the Elia volumes are fairly satisfactory. They are based to some extent on those of Ainger.

Lucas several times acknowledges help from Craig in tracing quotations in Lamb's works, and for notes on the names and words in the Burton fragments. In 1902 Lucas and Craig visited Elizabeth Coe at Berkhampsted. As a child she had been a pupil of the Misses Norris at Goddard House, Widford, and she gave them some reminiscences of Lamb which Lucas published in *The Athenaeum* on 7 June 1902 and again in the *Life of Charles Lamb*. Craig was a friend of Edward Dowden and a member of the Savage Club.

Crane, Walter, 1845–1915. Artist: portrait painter and miniaturist. Apprenticed to W.J. Linton, the wood engraver, influenced by Ruskin and the Pre-Raphaelites as well as Japanese prints. Exhibited at the R.A. in 1862 his picture *The Lady of Shalott*. Concentrated much on book illustration and did much work for Edmund Evans, the famous colour printer. Crane was a friend of William Morris and collaborated with him in the page decoration of *The Story of the Glittering Plain* published by the Kelmscott Press.

In 1901 he decorated for Cassell & Company an edition of Lamb's essay 'Rejoicings upon the New Year's Coming of Age' published with the title *A Masque of Days*.

Crawford, Ann, 1734–1801. Actress. Born Ann Street at Bath, she married an actor named Dancer, then the more famous Spranger Barry and, after his death in 1777, she married a Mr Crawford. She was particularly good in the part of Millamant and was notable as Lady Randolph in *Douglas*. She appeared under Garrick's management at Drury Lane; at the Stratford-upon-Avon Jubilee she was the Tragic Muse. She retired from the stage in 1798.

Lamb's footnote to his essay 'Barbara S——' states that the incident he relates was told to him of herself by Mrs Crawford in 1800, but in a letter to Barton in April 1825 he says 'I never saw Mrs Crawford in my life' and, in fact, the story was told to him by Fanny Kelly, to whom the incident occurred when she was a child; she wrote a letter to Charles Kent in 1875 confirming this. Lamb also confessed in his letter to Wordsworth in May 1825 that he had gleaned the story from Miss Kelly.

Cresswell, Daniel, 1776–1844. Divine and mathematician. Educated at Trinity College, Cambridge, where he became a Fellow, took pupils and lived there for many years. In 1822 he was presented to the Vicarage of Enfield and in 1823 was appointed a justice of the peace for Middlesex. He was a Fellow of the Royal Society, and published works on mathematics and some sermons.

Lucas in the notes to his edition of the *Poems and Plays* quotes J. Fuller Russell's statement that Lamb suppressed *Satan in Search of a Wife* because the Vicar had married a tailor's daughter, and doubts if Russell is correct. However, according to his letter to Moxon in 1830 (No. 866 in Lucas) he had sent Cresswell a copy for consideration since he says it 'was imputed a lampoon on HIM!!!' There does not appear to have been any trouble, for in 1831 he is writing to Cresswell enclosing acrostics for his wife's album and for her friend Sarah Thomas.

In Lamb's account of his meeting with the murderers of Danby he tells Louisa Badams that next morning he was summoned before Dr Cresswell, presumably in his magisterial capacity.

Crossley, James, 1800–83. Scholar, lawyer and book collector.

Born in Halifax, but was articled in Manchester to the legal firm of which Thomas Ainsworth, the father of the novelist, William Harrison Ainsworth, was the head. Later Crossley became a partner in the firm and a most successful lawyer, but his leisure was devoted to literary and antiquarian pursuits. He also amassed a large collection of books said to number about 100,000, many being rare and valuable volumes.

When Crossley was in London in 1822 and 1823 to complete his legal training he had a letter of introduction to Charles Lamb from Harrison Ainsworth. Crossley called on Lamb at his office and also met him elsewhere and heard talk on Milton. He recorded his recollections of Lamb for Canon Ainger to include in his volume on Elia published in 1882. Lamb and Crossley would have had much to talk about, for the young lawyer was keenly interested in Sir Thomas Browne, Thomas Fuller and the early dramatists; in 1822 he edited a tiny volume of Browne's *Tracts*, which included also *Hydriotaphia*. It was a copy of this book which Lamb presented to John Clare in August 1822 and since he states in his letter that it is a duplicate, he may have had one given him by Crossley. Another link would have been Lamb's beloved Temple, for Crossley was then a pupil of Jacob Phillips, a noted conveyancer, whose office was in King's Bench Walk.

James Crossley contributed to a number of periodicals, including *Blackwoods Magazine*, *The Retrospective Review*, *The Gentleman's Magazine* and later to *Notes & Queries*. To these publications he sent articles on Sir Thomas Browne, Thomas Fuller, Sir Philip Sidney and Quarles, all of whom were among Lamb's favourites. Although Crossley became a very learned man, he published few books, mainly those he edited for the Chetham Society, of which he was the founder and for a time honorary librarian.

Crossley knew many famous people, among whom were Thomas De Quincey (another Manchester celebrity), Charles Dickens, John Forster and D'Israeli. He maintained with Harrison Ainsworth a lifelong friendship and supplied him with information for some of his novels. He seems to have been a most amiable scholar who was always ready to place his learning and his library at the service of others.

Crossword Puzzles. *The Bookman*, November 1930, contains a crossword puzzle based on Charles Lamb. The solution was given in the issue for January 1931. This was No. 1 of a series of literary crossword puzzles by 'Procrustes' that included among the subjects Goldsmith, Donne, Defoe, Dryden, the Lake Poets, Pepys, Byron, Dr Johnson, Chaucer and Montaigne, as well as on London, Ancient Greece and Rome. The *C.L.S. Bulletin* for July 1972 contains an Elian Crossword Puzzle, the solution being published in the next issue. (No. 216)

Crown Office Row, Inner Temple. Charles Lamb was born at No. 2 Crown Office Row, Inner Temple on 10 February 1775 and lived there until 1792. The chambers, which overlooked Inner Temple Gardens, belonged to Samuel Salt, for whom Lamb's father, John Lamb Senior, worked as a clerk and servant. Salt owned two sets of chambers there, in one of which the Lambs had lived for a number of years before Charles Lamb's birth. John Lamb Junior was born there in 1763 and Mary Lamb in 1764. After Salt's death in 1792 the family left the Temple and are next found at No. 7 Little Queen Street.

Nos. 4, 5 and 6 Crown Office Row were rebuilt in the early 1860s but No. 2 was still standing until the night of 11–12 May 1941 when the whole of Crown Office Row was badly damaged by bombs and what remained had to be demolished. The memorial tablet to Lamb was broken but not destroyed. After the war Crown Office Row was rebuilt and a memorial tablet was again affixed there in 1958. The wording on it reads

Charles Lamb
was born in the Chambers
which formerly stood here
10th February, 1775
'Cheerful Crown Office Row (place of my kindly
engendure) . . . a man would give something
to have been born in such places.'

The quotation is from Lamb's essay 'The Old Benchers of the Inner Temple.'

On the lawn of Inner Temple Gardens outside Crown Office Row is a statue of a boy at the edge of a fish-pond which was erected in 1930 and on the book which the boy is holding are the words from Lamb's essay 'Lawyers were children once . . .'. The sculptor was Miss Margaret Wrightson. The iron gates erected in 1730 leading to the gardens opposite Lamb's birthplace still survive there.

During the period from October 1782 to November 1789 when at Christ's Hospital, Lamb was able to visit Crown Office Row only on holidays, but it was always his home to which he looked with the greatest affection.

As a footnote to Elia, it may be recorded that in the 1930s the name of M.D. Lyon, the Cambridge and Somerset wicket keeper and batsman, appeared on the lintel of No. 2 Crown Office Row. Lamb himself never mentions cricket, although one of his Bruton cousins was an excellent cricketer, and Lamb may have met that famous man, John Nyren, at his friend Novello's house. At least two of Lamb's devotees, E.V. Lucas and Edmund Blunden, would have noted with interest the association of the Lyon and the Lamb.

Crowsley, Ernest George, 1902–70. Founder of the Charles Lamb Society and its first General Secretary, 1935–70, he was for many years the main spring of the Society's activities. In his will he left substantial legacies in money and books to the Society. Part of the legacy was for a new edition of the Catalogue of the Charles Lamb Society's Library.

The Society has established a series of annual Ernest Crowsley Memorial Lectures. Those given are as follows:

1. October 1972. Charles Lamb and S.T. Coleridge, by Professor Basil Willey. *C.L.B.*, January 1973.
2. October 1973. Charles Lamb and the Romantic Style, by Hugh Sykes Davies. *C.L.B.*, January 1974.
3. October 1974. The Authentic Voice: Lamb and the Familiar Letter, by Professor R.A. Foakes. *C.L.B.*, January 1975.
4. October 1975. Charles Lamb and the Critical Tradition, by Dr Roy Park. *C.L.B.*, July 1976.
5. October 1977. The Romantic Humourist, by Dr J.E. Stevens. *C.L.B.*, April 1978.
6. September 1978. 'That Cursed Barbauld Crew' or Charles Lamb and Children's Literature, by Professor George L. Barnett. *C.L.B.*, January 1979.
7. October 1979. The Musician and the Nightingale: Charles Lamb and the Elizabethan Drama, by Professor Angus Easson. *C.L.B.*, January 1980.
8. October 1980. 'We are in a manner *marked*', Images of Damnation in Charles Lamb's Writings, by Jane Aaron. *C.L.B.*, January 1981.
9. October 1981. Lamb and Wordsworth. The Story of a Remarkable Friendship, by Professor Alan G. Hill. *C.L.B.*, January 1982.

Cruikshank, George, 1792–1878. Artist, caricaturist and etcher. Son of Isaac Cruikshank, also a famous caricaturist. He illustrated a great number of periodicals and among other books, Pierce Egan's *Life in London*, 1821; *Grimm's Popular Tales*, 1824–6; Dicken's *Sketches by Boz* and *Oliver Twist*; as well as works by Harrison Ainsworth and Thackeray. Cruikshank was largely discovered by William Hone and illustrated work by him. In 1831 he did the woodcuts for Lamb's *Satan in Search of a Wife*. There appears to be no evidence that Lamb and Cruikshank ever met, although the artist lived for many years in Islington.

Cruikshank, John. Land agent to Lord Egmont at Nether Stowey. He was the first treasurer of the fund raised to help Coleridge when the *Watchman* failed in 1796. Lamb visited his house during his stay at Nether Stowey and in his letter to Coleridge in July 1797 states that he behaved in Cruikshank's house like a sulky child from lack of practice among people. Lucas notes that Cruikshank had married a Miss Budé on the same day that Coleridge had married Sara Fricker.

Cruikshank, William Cumberland, 1745–1800. Anatomist, educated at Edinburgh and Glasgow universities. In 1796 he attended Lamb's brother, John, when he injured his leg. Cruikshank had been Dr Hunter's pupil, assistant and partner and he applied for the appointment of Professor of Anatomy in the Royal Academy, but in spite of Dr Johnson's recommendation to Sir Joshua Reynolds, he was not successful. He had attended Johnson in his last illness without accepting any fee, and in the Doctor's will he left him a book which he could choose from Johnson's library.

Cunningham, Allan, 1784–1842. Scottish poet and man of letters. At one time a stone mason, he came to London in 1810 and became a parliamentary reporter. In 1814 he was secretary and assistant to Francis Chantry, the sculptor, a position he held until Chantry's death in 1841.

Cunningham contributed much to periodicals, including *Blackwood's Magazine*, *The London Magazine*, *Edinburgh Magazine* and *The Athenaeum*. To the *London* he sent many poems and tales: between 1820 and 1824 more than sixty items can be traced to him in that journal, many signed with the signature 'Nalla'. With Dilke, Hood and Reynolds he became part owner of *The Athenaeum*. In 1829 he edited *The Anniversary* for John Sharpe and may possibly have edited Sharpe's *London Magazine* the same year. Among Cunningham's books are *Traditional Tales of the English & Scotch Peasantry*, 1822; *Sir Marmaduke Maxwell*, 1822; *The Songs of Scotland, Ancient & Modern*, 1825; *Paul Jones. A Romance*, 1826; *Lives of the most Eminent British Painters, Sculptors & Architects*, 1829–33; *The Maid of Elvar*, 1833; and Burn's *Works* in 1834. His *Songs of Scotland* contained his famous song 'A Wet Sheet and a Flowing Sea'. In 1833 he contributed to *The Athenaeum* his 'Biographical and Critical History of the Literature of the last fifty years' which contained references to Charles Lamb; it was republished in 1834.

Cunningham had many friends, including Sir Walter Scott, James Hogg, William Jerdan and Thomas Carlyle. He was particularly friendly with his fellow contributors to the *London*, chief among whom were Lamb, Darley and Clare. Lamb described him in his 'Letter to Southey' as 'the large-hearted Scot', and among his friends he was known as 'honest Allan'. William Jerdan said he was 'straight forward, right-minded, and conscientious, true to himself and to others.'

Cunningham sometimes attended Lamb's evening parties: there is a letter in 1821 inviting him to 20 Russell Street, and another inviting

Cary in 1828, told him that 'our old chums of the London, Darley and Cunningham' were coming to Enfield.

Curling, Jonathan. Author and publisher. Wrote *Janus Weathercock: The Life of Thomas Griffiths Wainewright 1794–1847*, 1938, which contains many references to Charles Lamb.

Dalston. In *The Ambulator*, 1820, Dalston is described as 'a pleasant hamlet in Hackney parish, two miles N.E. from London, celebrated for its nurseries.' Here the Lambs took rooms at 14 Kingsland Row, Dalston, first for a holiday and later to avoid the continual interruptions of visitors which occurred at their more permanent residences in Inner Temple Lane and Great Russell Street. They stayed there for about ten weeks in 1816 and retained these lodgings for several years. Crabb Robinson mentions visiting them there in December 1820 and there are records of them at Dalston in 1822 and 1823. Lamb invited William Hone there in May 1823.

In a letter to Barton on 17 August 1824 Lamb has a curious reference to the whole family of his landlord at his 'place of rustication', beating one another. Presumably this was at Dalston. When they moved to Islington the Lambs gave up the Dalston lodgings. In the essay 'The Old South Sea House' which appeared in the *London Magazine* in 1820 there is a reference to Dalston, and to Kingsland in 'The Old and the New Schoolmaster', but neither refers to Lamb's lodgings.

In his letter to Hazlitt on 19 February 1806 Lamb reports an earlier attempt to avoid interruptions. He says 'Have taken a room at 3s. a week, to be in between 5 & 8 at night, to avoid my *nocturnal* alias *knock-eternal* visitors.' Lucas says we do not know where the room was and suggests possibly in the Temple. In her letter to Sarah Stoddart in March 1806 Mary Lamb reports that Charles could not endure the solitariness of the room and had said he could write just as well at home.

Danby, Benjamin. d.1832. Lamb relates in a letter to Louisa Badams on 31 December 1832 that he entered the Crown & Horseshoe at Enfield on December 19 to get a drink, and was spoken to by some men who were playing dominoes there. One of them claimed to be a Mr Danby and to have known Lamb in the Temple, where his father had been a hairdresser. Lamb remembered the father. After a time Lamb left the inn, but that night Danby was murdered, and next morning Lamb was called before the magistrate and questioned, but was not detained. The three men who had been with Danby were Johnson, Fare and Cooper, who were all charged with the murder and tried at the Old Bailey. Fare was acquitted,

Cooper turned king's evidence, but Johnson was convicted and hanged.

W.C. Hazlitt relates this incident in his *Charles & Mary Lamb*. 1874, adding that he had the facts from the lips of one of the ladies with the Lambs on the evening of the murder. Ainger in his edition of the *Letters* says 'another of Lamb's elaborate fictions'. although he admits that the murder did take place. E.V. Lucas thought the story was probably true. There was a wig maker named Danby who worked in the Temple as Lamb relates. The magistrate before whom Lamb appeared was Dr Cresswell, according to the letter to Louisa Badams.

Dance, George, 1741–1825. Architect and surveyor. Lucas in the *Life of Charles Lamb*, 1905, II, 293, states that a drawing by Dance said to be of Charles Lamb was in America. but from a photograph of it he does not believe it to be Lamb. *A Collection of Portraits sketched from Life since the year 1793 by G. Dance & engraved in imitation of the original drawings by William Daniell* appeared in 1811–14. It was reissued in 1854. George Dance was the architect who rebuilt Newgate Prison in 1770 and he was responsible for the front of Guildhall, London. He was a foundation member of the Royal Academy.

Daniel, George, 1789–1864. Antiquary. dramatist. poet and book collector. Originally a stock broker's clerk. he continued in a commerical career for most of his life. but devoted his leisure to literature. Daniel edited the forty-eight volumes of John Cumberland's *British Theatre*, 1826–61, and wrote satirical verse and plays. as well as *Merrie England in the Olden Time*. 1842. In 1818 Miss Kelly played in his *Doctor Bolus* at the English Opera House. He possessed a valuable library, rich in Shakespeare (all four folios) and Elizabethan books and black letter ballads. When sold in 1864 it realized £15,865. Daniel also owned many literary and theatrical relics.

He first met Lamb in 1817 and as he lived in Islington they were neighbours for some years. On one occasion Daniel took Robert Bloomfield, the peasant poet, to dine with Lamb. He included some interesting reminiscences of Lamb in his *Love's Labours Not Lost*. 1863, reprinted by Elkin Mathews in 1927 as *Recollections of Charles Lamb*.

Darley, George, 1795–1846. Poet. dramatic critic and mathematician. Educated at Trinity College. Dublin. A friend of Lamb, Cary, Clare and Procter. Thomas Westwood describes him as 'scholar and poet, slow of speech and gentle of strain: Miss Kelly's constant shadow in her walks among the Enfield woodlands.' Together with Mary Lamb he taught Latin to Fanny Kelly. A frequent contributor to the *London Magazine* from 1821–25 under various pseudonyms, the chief of which was 'John Lacy' for his articles on contemporary drama, which he criticized strongly. He also contributed to the magazine poems and his best known story 'Lilian of the Vale'.

His works include *Errors of Ecstasie*, 1822, and *Labours of Idleness*, 1826; the latter book included his most popular lyric 'I've been roaming', which was set to music by C.E. Horn and frequently sung by Miss Paton. Darley also edited Beaumont & Fletcher's plays. He contributed articles and art criticism to *The Athenaeum*.

Darley was friendly with most of the London Magazine circle and attended the periodical dinners given by the publishers. Like Lamb he had a slight impediment in his speech and was an admirer of the Elizabethan dramatists. Between 1826 and 1828 he wrote for John Taylor, the publisher, a series of popular scientific treatises on mathematics.

Lamb praised his contributions to the *London* in a letter to Barton on 10 February 1825, and in April 1828, in a letter to Cary he says that Darley is coming to visit him at Enfield. In a letter in June 1828 from Darley to Cunningham he mentions having stayed with Lamb for two days and speaks of Lamb as 'so devilish idle'. In March 1829 Lamb sent Barton a copy of Darley's *Sylvia* which he describes as a 'Very poetical poem'.

Abbott prints in his *Life and Letters of George Darley*, 1928, some amusing lines written by Darley in May 1830 from the British Museum Reading Room addressed to Cary and asking for a meal. They are of the kind which would have appealed to Lamb strongly and show that Darley's sense of fun was much akin to Lamb's. In September 1833 Lamb writes to Cary that he is reading something he calls 'Darley's act' and complains of the author's handwriting. When in 1827 Darley applied for the Professorship of English Literature at the newly founded University of London, both Lamb and Cary wrote testimonials for him, but he was unsuccessful.

From 1830 to 1835 Darley travelled in France, Italy, Holland and Germany, visiting picture galleries for much of the time.

Darling, George, ?1782–1862. A Scottish doctor of medicine who came to London and had among his patients a number of literary men and artists. He had a house at 29 Brunswick Square. He was a personal friend of both John Taylor and J.A. Hessey for much of their lives and also attended many of the contributors to the *London Magazine*. He was present at some of the magazine dinners given by the publishers. It is said that he was also a contributor to the magazine, but nothing of his has been traced there.

Among his patients were John Keats, John Clare, John Taylor, Richard Ayton, William Hazlitt, George Darley, B.R. Haydon and Thomas De Quincey. He attended John Scott, the first editor of the

London, following the fatal duel. He seems to have been of a generous nature and attended some of his literary patients without charge. He gave £5. 5s. to the fund for John Scott's widow and he was a member of the Committee which received donations for Mrs Scott. He also contributed to a fund for Clare in 1841. Although described by Reynolds as 'Bleak Dr Darling' this does not seem to have referred to his pocket. He was also a benefactor to the National Gallery.

In December 1824 Taylor & Hessey announced as forthcoming *A Practical Treatise on Diseases of the Liver* . . . by George Darling, but it does not seem to have appeared. However he did publish *An Essay on Medical Economy*, 1814, and a pamphlet *Instructions for Making Unfermented Bread*, 1846.

It is not recorded that he and Lamb met, but as a close friend of both Taylor and Hessey and of Lamb's friends, it seems almost certain that they did meet. Thomas Benyon in a letter to Clare records that Darling was present at a London Magazine dinner in March 1824, but that Elia was absent on that occasion owing to illness.

Darling had made several voyages as surgeon in the East India Company's service before settling in general practice.

Dash. Thomas Hood's dog, a large and very handsome animal. In 1827 Dash was 'staying on a visit' to the Lambs, who were themselves staying at Enfield. Probably Hood thought the country better for a large dog than the metropolis. Dash was an especial favourite of the Lambs and accompanied Charles on his long walks, but behaved extremely badly, disappearing for long periods to Lamb's consternation. It is recorded that he was a perfect slave to the dog and walked often in Regent's Park because it was Dash's favourite walk, although he did not like it himself.

On one occasion at Enfield Dash chased sheep and when the owner protested Charles answered 'Hunt *Lambs* sir? Why he has never hunted *me*.' At last Dash's whims were too much for Charles and he was piloted across the streets of London to P.G. Patmore's house, with a plea for Patmore to look after him. Under his new master he reformed and became a model dog, although sometime in 1828 he seems to have been in Edward Moxon's possession. Dash was a particular friend of the Lamb's servant, Becky.

When the Lambs decided to rent a house at Enfield the fact was announced to the house agent by Dash proceeding them carrying in his mouth the board with the legend 'This House to Let'. There are numerous glimpses of the dog in Lamb's letters in 1827–28 and one particularly amusing letter to Patmore in June 1827 has much about him and Patmore's reply is largely concerned with Dash. The fullest details of Dash are given by Patmore in his *My Friends and Acquaintances*, 1855. Hone's *Every-Day Book* for 14 July 1825 contains a letter entitled 'Dog Days' signed 'Pompey' which is thought to be by Lamb.

Davies, Katharine. *See* Helen Ashton.

Dawe, George, 1781–1829. Portrait painter and mezzotint engraver. Son of Philip Dawe, a mezzotint engraver. Studied at the Royal Academy schools and became well known as a portrait painter. He was made A.R.A. in 1809 and R.A. in 1814. He painted portraits of Princess Charlotte of Wales and the Duke of Wellington and many other well known people, including William Godwin and Coleridge. In 1819 he went to Russia and remained there nine years, painting nearly four hundred portraits. He is said to have become very wealthy.

Lamb mentions him in his letter to Hazlitt on 10 November 1805 in connexion with the picture of *Samson*, and again in a letter to Manning on 5 December 1806. In January 1809 he wrote to Dawe declining the offer of a ticket for an anatomical lecture. In Moxon's *Englishman's Magazine* in 1831 Lamb wrote 'Recollections of a late Royal Academician' which contain some amusing stories of Dawe's eccentricities. Lamb considered Dawe a poor painter, a view probably not shared by his sitters or he would not have been so successful financially. In the *Library of Fine Arts* for October 1831 is a letter signed 'Vindex' protesting at Lamb's article and saying that Lamb was often indebted to Dawe for a dinner. Mrs Anderson who mentions this in her article 'Lamb and the two G.D's' in *The London Mercury* in February 1925 was unable to say who 'Vindex' was.

In August 1831 Lamb wrote to Moxon about the essay in *The Englishman's Magazine* confirming that it was a portrait of George Dawe and that he had heard many of the anecdotes from the painters 'Daniels and Westall'. Dawe was nicknamed 'The Grub' by his acquaintances, for reasons obvious from Lamb's essay.

Among Dawe's friends were George Morland whose life he wrote, Charles Lamb and Coleridge. The latter, in a letter to his wife on 21 April 1812, says Dawe is visiting the Lake District and asks Mrs Coleridge to receive him 'as a friend'. He adds that he is a very modest man and praises him for his innocence, but has no higher opinion of his work as an artist than Charles Lamb had. Dawe was buried in St Paul's Cathedral.

Dawson, George, 1821–76. English divine, a well known Birmingham preacher. Educated at Glasgow University. Author of *Biographical Lectures*, 1886, which includes essays on Charles Lamb, Thomas Hood, Coleridge and Wordsworth. Edited the *Birmingham Morning News* 1871–76.

Dawson, William James, 1854–1928. Clergyman, poet, prose writer and lecturer. Author of *The Makers of Modern Prose*, 1899, which contains a chapter on Charles Lamb. With C.W. Dawson edited *The Great English Essayists*, 1909.

Deacon, William Frederick, 1799–1845. Journalist and author. Educated at Dr Valpy's school at Reading where he had T.N. Talfourd for a schoolfellow. Principal contributor to Gold and Northhouse's *London Magazine*, 1820–21. Author of the fictitious account of a dinner supposed to have been given by Baldwin, Cradock & Joy to their contributors, which was printed in Gold's *London* in March 1821, at which Charles Lamb is described as reciting 'Songe to Fancy, By Good Master Webster'. Deacon wrote in the magazine under the name of 'Paul Clutterbuck'. In 1824 Deacon wrote *Warreniana*, a collection of poems in praise of Warren's Patent Blacking. These included parodies of Byron, Coleridge and others. Charles Lamb figures in it in a pastoral masque—a parody of Charles Wells.

Deacon later became editor of *The Sun* and wrote for *Blackwoods*. He was the author of *The Innkeeper's Album*, 1823 (sketches of Wales), *November Tales* and *The Exile of Erin*, 1835, which was very popular. William Hone published his first book. Deacon was a schoolfellow of T.G. Wainewright.

De Camb, Vincent. Actor. Brother of Marie Thérèse de Camp, the actress who married Charles Kemble, and of Adelaide de Camp also an actress. He played Goldfinch in Holcroft's *The Vindictive Man* at Drury Lane in November 1806 when the play failed. Lamb's letter to Manning of 5 December 1806 describes him as 'a vulgar brother of Miss de Camp' and as 'a fellow with the make of a jockey and the air of a lamplighter.' The writer of the Drama article in the *London Magazine* in August 1821, probably J.H. Reynolds, wrote 'Mr De Camp has a rambling style of acting, but he is lively and unaffected and is a fit inhabitant of comic ground.' It seems that his ability was doubtful and Crabb Robinson records seeing him at the Lyceum on 30 March 1811 in *Weathercock* and says he is by no means an excellent performer. Lamb was with him at the time. In 1820 de Camp was manager of the Newcastle theatre.

Delpini, Carlo Antonio, d.1828. Clown and theatre manager. An Italian who became famous in his day in pantomime at Drury Lane, Covent Garden, and the Haymarket. He was also stage manager at the Opera. In 1774 engaged by Garrick for Drury Lane. He was responsible for the mechanical arrangements for pantomimes at Covent Garden and the Haymarket in which he acted. He played the hero in *Robinson Crusoe* with Grimaldi as Friday, and he was in the original production of Sheridan's *The Critic* in 1779. Lamb mentions him in his Popular Fallacy 'That You Must Love Me, and Love my Dog', where he states that Robert Merry, the Della Cruscan, at one time intended to marry Delpini's daughter. Among his other assignments was that of arranging the entertainments for George IV at Brighton.

De Morgan, Sophia Elizabeth. *See* Sophia Elizabeth Frend.

De Quincy, Richard, 'Pink'. Sailor brother of Thomas De Quincey who had led a highly adventurous life. He ran away from school to sea and after serving on a merchantman was captured by pirates and forced to serve under the Black Flag for two years. He escaped from them somewhere in the River Plate and subsequently falling under the eye of Sir Horace Popham became a midshipman in the Royal Navy. Later he experienced a Danish prison where he languished about eighteen months before there being an exchange of prisoners.

Thomas De Quincey relates in his *Autobiography* an amusing incident of a meeting between Charles and Mary Lamb and him and his brother at an exhibition in Bond Street where two large and splendid pictures by Salvator Rosa were shown, and of the violent reaction of his brother, 'Pink' to the pictures: 'D—— the fellow! I could do better myself.' accompanied by the ejaculation of a quid of tobacco at the picture. 'Pink' was not a connoisseur of art, although he admired Benjamin West's *Death and his Pale Horse* and always attended an exhibition of pictures when he could.

De Quincey, Thomas, 1785–1859. Essayist and miscellaneous writer. Friend of Lamb, Coleridge, Southey, Wordsworth and John Wilson. Lived much in the Lake District. Frequent contributor to the *London Magazine* in which his famous 'Confessions of an English Opium-Eater' first appeared. He also contributed to *Blackwoods, Tait's, Edinburgh Literary Gazette* and *Hogg's Instructor*. Lamb figures in several of De Quincey's voluminous writings, particularly in his review in 1848 of Talfourd's *Final Memorials* (Masson V, 215–58) and earlier in his 'London Reminiscences' (Masson III, 34–92). De Quincey is such an important figure in English literature that numerous books and articles have been written about him, many of which refer to Lamb. A list of sources is given in *C.B.E.L.* and *The English Romantic Poets and Essayists*, 1966.

Derocquigny, Jules. Author of *Charles Lamb: sa vie et ses oeuvres.* Lille 1904. This book is praised highly by Barnett and Tave in *The English Romantic Poets & Essayists*.

Dibdin, Charles, the Younger, 1768–1833. Charles Isaac Mungo Dibdin (or Pitt) was the son of Charles Dibdin the dramatist, actor and song writer who wrote 'Tom Bowling' and 'The Lass that loves a Sailor'. His mother was Harriet Pitt, the actress. The younger Charles was a prolific dramatist and wrote over 200 pieces. He also wrote *Life in London* ... *Tom & Jerry*, 1821; *Comic Tales*, 1825; and *History and Illustrations of the London Theatres*, 1826. He was proprietor and manager of Sadler's Wells theatre, for which he wrote many plays and songs. His comic opera *The Farmer's Wife* is one of his best known works. Lamb wrote to his son, John Bates Dibdin, on 11 January 1825 about a copy of *Comic Tales* the author had sent him, and he reviewed it in *The New Times* of 27 January 1825. In 1827 Dibdin wrote verses for Emma Isola's Album.

Dibdin, John Bates, c.1799–1829. Son of Charles Dibdin, the Younger. As a clerk with a London shipping office, Dibdin used to call at East India House and so met Lamb. In 1823 he discovered that he was the author of the Elia essays and they became friends. In 1827 Dibdin wrote verses for Emma Isola's Album. Lamb wrote an amusing letter to him in 1823 about his Elia pseudonym and a number of light hearted letters followed. Dibdin was the nephew of Thomas Frognall Dibdin, the bibliographer and author of books on book collecting. He was a brother of Henry Edward Dibdin, musician and artist.

Diction. Although many others have adopted an archaic diction, none has done so more successfully or quite in the same style as Lamb. A most interesting study of his work from this aspect is Tsutomu Fukuda's *A Study of Charles Lamb's Essays of Elia*, Tokyo, 1964; while George Sampson's *Seven Essays*, Cambridge 1947, in an essay 'On Playing the Sedulous Ape' analyses Lamb's 'Old China' and points out that in none of the seven categories defined by examiners in English does this essay qualify for a pass, although it is one of the most delightful in English literature.

E. V. Lucas in the Index to the *Letters*, 1935, gives a list of the 'Odd Words' used by Lamb and an article on 'The Diction of Charles Lamb' by Louise Griswold appeared in the *Quarterly Journal of the University of North Dakota* in April 1927. A most valuable and enlightening study of Lamb, the craftsman and the stylist is contained in Professor George L. Barnett's *Charles Lamb: the Evolution of Elia*, 1964. An earlier study is the article 'A Chip from Elia's Workshop' by J. Milton French contributed to *Studies in Philology* in 1940.

Lamb's famous remark 'Damn the age, I will write for antiquity' was made when the editor of *The Gem* rejected his poem 'The Gypsy's Malison' on the grounds that it would 'shock all mothers'.

Dignum, Charles, ?1765–1827. Tenor singer. Was a chorister at the Sardinian Chapel. Trained by Thomas Linley. First appeared at

Drury Lane in 1784 in *Love in a Village* and remained attached to that theatre for most of his life. Also appeared in Storace's operas *The Haunted Tower*, 1789; *No Song, No Supper*, 1790; and *The Pirates*, 1792. Dignum took part at Covent Garden in the first performance of Haydn's *Creation*. He also sang at Ranelagh and Vauxhall. He was a composer and publisher of his own music.

When Dignum, who was short and fat, appeared on the stage with Mrs Bland, who was equally squat, they drew from Lamb an amusing comment on their appearance (*See* Mrs Bland). Lamb mentions him in his essay 'The Old Actors' as it appeared in the *London Magazine* in October 1822.

Dilke, Charles Wentworth, 1789–1864. Antiquary, critic and editor, worked in the Navy Pay office, but devoted his leisure to literature. Friend of Keats, Leigh Hunt, Charles Armitage Brown, Hood and Reynolds. He also knew Shelley. He contributed to *The London Review, London Magazine, New Monthly, Retrospective Review* and *The Athenaeum*. Of the latter journal he was proprietor and from 1830 supreme editor. He published a continuation of Dodsley's *Collection of Old English Plays*, 1814–16.

During Dilke's editorship of *The Athenaeum* Lamb sent contributions to the journal and Lucas prints several letters from Lamb to Dilke, mostly about the articles or paragraphs he had sent. In July 1834 Dilke asked Lamb to write about Coleridge's death for *The Athenaeum*, but Lamb felt too upset to do so.

Dircks, Rudolf. Librarian, Royal Institute of British Architects. Edited with an introduction *Plays and Dramatic Essays by Charles Lamb*, 1893, and *Sheridan's Plays*, both for the Scott Library series. Contributed to the *Art Journal, Saturday Review* and *Outlook*.

Dobell, Bertram, 1842–1914. Antiquarian bookseller and man of letters. Opened his first shop with a capital of £10 and in 1876 printed his first catalogue of second-hand books. Moved to Charing Cross Road, London, in 1887. He was particularly successful in his literary discoveries, the greatest of which was the poetical work of Thomas Traherne. He befriended the poet James Thomson for many years.

Dobell's publications include some of Thomson's works which he edited, *Shelley's Letters to Elizabeth Hitchener*, 1908; the *Poetical Works of William Strode*, 1907; *Goldsmith's A Prospect of Society*, 1902; *Traherne's Poetical Works*, 1903; and *Centuries of Meditation*, 1908. He also published a number of volumes of his own poems. His valuable *Catalogue of Books Printed for Private Circulation* was published in 1906, and a specimen of it had been issued as early as 1891.

A particularly interesting work was Dobell's *Sidelights on Charles*

Lamb, 1903. In this he published the results of his research into a set of *The London Magazine* of the 1820s, and he reprinted a number of pieces which he attributed to Lamb. Although not all of them have been acknowledged by later editors of Lamb, Dobell did valuable work and his gleanings from the *London* and other sources on Lamb and his friends are of great interest. His book reproduces in facsimile Lamb's poem 'The Three Graves'.

Among his contributions to periodicals were:

The Athenaeum
1903   Lamb's Trouvailles, October 24, about 'Munden's Farewell.'
1906   Some Unpublished Letters of Charles Lamb, May 5.
Notes & Queries
1889   Article on a playbill of *Mr H*——, 1822. August 3.

He also contributed to the *Quarterly Review*.

Dobrée, Bonamy, b.1891. Professor of English Literature, University of Leeds, 1936–55. Author of *English Essayists*, 1946 (Britain in Pictures series), which includes references to Lamb, Hazlitt, De Quincey and Coleridge. He also wrote a number of other books on English literature, including *Restoration Comedy*, 1924; *Restoration Tragedy*, 1929; and *English Literature in the Early Eighteenth Century 1700–1740* (Volume VII of the Oxford History of English Literature).

Dodd, James William, 1734–96. English comedian described as 'the most perfect fopling ever placed upon the English stage.' Appeared at Drury Lane in 1777 as the original Sir Benjamin Backbite in *The School for Scandal*. Famous as Sir Andrew Aguecheek, and in such parts as Tattle, Bob Acres, Slender, Fribble and Lord Foppington. When not on the stage Dodd was a serious man who possessed a fine library of Elizabethan literature which was sold at his death; parts were bought by the King, the Duke of Roxburghe and John Kemble.

He was one of Lamb's favourite actors and is referred to in the essay 'On Some of the old Actors' where Lamb tells the story of James White's meeting with Dodd in the street. He also mentions him in his piece 'The New Acting' in *The Examiner* of 18 July 1813, in the essay 'On the Artificial Comedy of the Last Century', in 'The Death of Munden' and in 'Barbara S——.'

Dodwell, Henry, d.1837. Clerk in the Accountant's Department with Lamb at East India House. Lamb wrote several letters to him, one in July 1816 when he was on holiday at Calne, Wiltshire, another on 7 October 1827 from Enfield which mentions a number of Lamb's former colleagues at East India House. In a letter to another colleague

Chambers, in 1818 Lamb mentions Dodwell's monopoly of *The Times* in the office and writing to Walter Wilson in December 1822 he describes Dodwell as willing but slow. He also refers to 'Do——' in the essay 'The Superannuated Man' who is probably Dodwell. Lamb wrote a charade on the name Dodwell starting 'My first is that which infants call their Maker.'

Donne, William Bodham, 1807–82. Educated at Bury St Edmunds Grammar School where he had as schoolfellows James Spedding, Edward FitzGerald and John Mitchell Kemble, the Anglo-Saxon scholar. Donne proceeded to Caius College, Cambridge. He contributed to the *Edinburgh Review, Quarterly Review, Fraser's Magazine, British and Foreign Review* of which Kemble was editor and the *Saturday Review*. He published *Essays upon the Drama,* 1858. In 1852 he became librarian of the London Library and in 1857 Examiner of Plays.

Among his friends were Bernard Barton, Crabb Robinson, Edward FitzGerald, William Taylor of Norwich and George Borrow. Lamb's letter of 21 April 1830 to Mrs Williams is addressed to Donne's house, where perhaps she was staying. Her husband, the Rev. Williams, had been Donne's tutor at one time. It does not seem that Lamb and Donne ever met, but they must have known of one another.

Dorrell, William. A friend of Lamb's father who is said by Charles Lamb to have cheated the family of about £2,000. He was one of the witnesses to the will of John Lamb Senior and earlier in 1761 he had been one of the three witnesses to the wedding of John Lamb and Elizabeth Field. Miss Mann in *C.L.S. Bulletin* Nos. 146 and 198 has printed some further facts about Dorrell among which she mentions that he was a well-to-do grocer related to the Fields. The name Dorrell occurs in Lamb's essay 'New Year's Eve' and in the poem 'Going or Gone'.

Dove Cottage, Grasmere. Originally a wayside inn, Wordsworth and his sister moved into this cottage, which is in a lakeland village in Westmorland, in December 1799, and remained there until 1808. Coleridge with his wife and son, Hartley, stayed at Dove Cottage from June 29 to July 24, 1800, and he was again in Grasmere in 1808. When the Wordsworths left the cottage was taken over by De Quincey and his family and he lived there until 1830. The graves of both Wordsworth and Hartley Coleridge are in the churchyard at Grasmere.

When on their visit to the Coleridges in August 1802 the Lambs stayed for a few days in Dove Cottage at the invitation of the Wordsworths, although the poet and his sister were abroad at the time.

Dowden, Mrs Isaac. *See* John Lamb, Junior.

Dowton, William, 1764–1851. English actor. Trained as an architect but turned to the stage. First appeared in London in 1796. An excellent actor in such parts as Sir Anthony Absolute, Sir Peter Teazle and Hardcastle; he was famous as Falstaff and also played Malvolio and Shylock. He was praised by Hazlitt and Leigh Hunt and by the Cowden Clarkes, who thought very highly of his acting in the part of Cantwell. For his benefit in 1817 he appeared as Mrs Malaprop in *The Rivals*. Although a fine experienced actor Dowton would not allow his name to be printed on the playbills larger than those of the other players, even though he was playing the lead. Lamb wrote of him in *The Examiner* in 1813 in his pieces 'The New Acting', 'Brome's Jovial Crew' and 'Bickerstaff's Hypocrite'; he also mentioned him in 'The Death of Munden' in *The Athenaeum*.

Druitt, Mary, d.1801. At John Rickman's request Lamb wrote on Mary Druitt his 'Epitaph on a young lady who lived neglected and died obscure.' She died of consumption at the age of nineteen and was buried at Wimborne. Rickman had also asked Southey for an epitaph on her, but he refused. Lamb's verses are not on her tombstone. Lamb sent this epitaph to both Manning and Wordsworth and printed it in *The Morning Post* on 7 February 1804. He also wrote an alternative version and sent it to Rickman in February 1802. Lamb did not know Mary Druitt.

Duncan, Maria Rebecca, ?1780–1858. Actress. First with Tate Wilkinson at York and played Sophia in *The Road to Ruin*. Acted at Edinburgh, Glasgow and Liverpool. Appeared at Drury Lane in 1804 as Lady Teazle to Charles Mathews's Sir Peter and Elliston's Charles Surface. Among her other parts were Rosalind, Miss Hardcastle, Lydia Languish and Letitia Hardy. She created the role of Juliana in Tobin's *The Honeymoon*, her most famous part. She was also well known as Lady Teazle and Beatrice, and appeared as Mrs Sullen in *The Beaux's Stratagem*. She remained at Drury Lane from 1804 to 1818 and then appeared at Covent Garden. She returned to Drury Lane in 1820 and retired about 1829. She had played many of Mrs Jordan's parts. In 1812 she married James Davison and after that date appeared in her married name. She is said to have had an excellent voice, almost good enough for opera.

Leigh Hunt wrote much in her praise and others who praised her were Hazlitt and Talfourd. Charles Lamb mentions her in his letter to Manning of 5 December 1806 as playing in Holcroft's *Vindictive Man* and taking the part intended for Mrs Jordan. She also played in Henry Siddons's *Time's a Tell-Tale* at Drury Lane in 1807. Mary Lamb's letter to Matilda Betham of March 1811 mentions her as playing 'famously' in Marianne Chambers's new play *Ourselves*.

Dunstan, Sir Jeffry, ?1759–97. A dealer in old wigs, elected as the unofficial 'Mayor of Garret.' Garret Common was a district between Wandsworth and Tooting and the 'Mayor' was supposed to protect the rights of the inhabitants. Mock elections were held and became a popular entertainment. In 1796 Dunston was ousted from his office by 'Sir' Harry Dimsdale, a muffin-seller and dealer in tinware. Lamb's sketch in Hone's *Every Day Book*, 1826, is entitled 'Reminiscences of Sir Jeffery Dunstan'.

Du Puy, Peter Solomon, c.1769–c.1829. Clerk in the Accountant's office at East India House with Lamb; he also acted as Dutch translator. Became second clerk at a salary of £1,130 per annum. Translated from the French M. Gorjy's *Sentimental Tablets of the Good Pamphile*, 1795. Lamb's letter to Coleridge of 14 June 1796 mentions some of Du Puy's curious translations and how Lamb 'had much trouble in licking the book into any meaning at all.' Tommy Bye, a colleague of later fame, took five copies of the book and Lamb took one. In his letter to Walter Wilson in August 1832 Lamb states that Du Puy is dead.

Dyer, George, 1755–1841. Scholar, poet and man of letters. Son of John Dyer, a 'citizen and shipwright of London'. Educated at Christ's Hospital, became a Grecian and head of the School, which he left in 1774, passing to Emmanuel College, Cambridge. After taking his degree he became an usher in a school at Dedham, Essex; then a tutor in the family of Robert Robinson, the Baptist minister, whose life he wrote and who persuaded him to become an Unitarian. Subsequently he was an usher in Dr Ryland's school at Northampton, where he had John Clarke, father of Charles Cowden Clarke as a colleague.

In 1792 he came to London and took rooms in Clifford's Inn where he remained for the rest of his life. One of his neighbours was Amos Cottle, brother of Coleridge's publisher. Here Dyer began his career of scholarship and hack work. He wrote innumerable articles for periodicals, among which were the *Critical Review, Reflector* and *Monthly Magazine*; he edited Valpy's many volumes of the classics, and published his own books. These included *An Inquiry into the Nature of Subscripton to the Thirty Nine Articles*, 1789; *A Dissertation on the Theory of Benevolence*, 1795; and *History of the University & Colleges of Cambridge*, 1814. His *Life of Robert Robinson*, 1796, was described by both Wordsworth and Samuel Parr as one of the best biographies in the language. His first volume of poems appeared in 1792, followed by others in 1801 and 1802.

At one time tutor in Lord Stanhope's family, 'Citizen Stanhope' appointed Dyer one of his ten executors, a position which he hastily disclaimed. On 3 May 1824 Dyer married Honour Mather, a widow, who looked after him well. Towards the end of his life he became

blind and among the friends who used to read to him were Matilda
Betham and Crabb Robinson. When he died H.F. Cary wrote an
epitaph at the widow's request. She lived to the age of one hundred,
dying in 1861. Dyer had a brother, John Dyer, a lighterman, who
inherited £1,000 in 1805 at the same time as George received £250.
A niece, probably a daughter of this brother, looked after him before
his marriage.

Dyer had many friends, including Joseph Jekyll, one of Lamb's
'Old Benchers'. He was well known in the Lamb circle, and although
his eccentricities made him a figure of fun, his simplicity and good-
ness of heart caused him to be a great favourite among them. Lamb
first met him about 1796 and some of Lamb's choicest writing
describes George Dyer's amusing activities. The famous letter to
Manning on 27 December 1800 describes the burning of the preface
to the *Poems*, 1801; that to Rickman, probably in November 1801,
gives the account of Dyer's illness from lack of food and subsequent
recovery under Lamb's ministrations. In 1823 Sarah Hazlitt received
in a letter the first account of George's immersion in the New River.
This formed the subject of the famous essay 'Amicus Redivivus' in
The London Magazine in December 1823, but Dyer had figured in an
earlier essay 'Oxford in the Vacation' in the same magazine. It was
this latter essay which caused Dyer to write a letter of mild protest
about some of Elia's facts.

In a letter of 17 February 1802 Southey told Rickman that the
Lambs had talked Dyer into believing he was in love with Elizabeth
Benger, but that they failed in their attempt to interest her in Dyer.
Many of his friends have left descriptions of the immortal George
besides Lamb's famous sketches. Hazlitt in his essay 'On the Look of
a Gentleman' described him as 'One of God Almighty's Gentlemen',
while Leigh Hunt made him the subject of his 'Jack Abbot's Breakfast'. One of E.V. Lucas's best essays is the chapter on George Dyer
in his *Life of Charles Lamb*. As Lamb wrote 'with a head uniformly
wrong and a heart uniformly right' he is a perennial attraction, and
among the many publications which have devoted space to him are:

Life of Charles Lamb by E.V. Lucas, 1905.
Letters of Charles & Mary Lamb, E.V. Lucas, 1935.
Men, Women and Books by Leigh Hunt, 1847.
Recollections of Writers by C. & M. Cowden Clarke, 1878.
Essays of Elia, 1823.
Last Essays of Elia, 1833.
Diary of Henry Crabb Robinson, E.J. Morley, 1938.
Cambridge and Charles Lamb, G.E. Wherry, 1925.
George Dyer by A.E. Newton, 1938, a pamphlet.
Dictionary of National Biography
Gentleman's Magazine, 1841.

The Bookman, July 1921.
The London Mercury, 1925.
Charles Lamb Bulletin, April 1982.

In 1835 George Dyer wrote obituary notices of Charles Lamb in *The Christian Reformer* and the *Gentleman's Magazine.* He also wrote a piece in Hone's *Every Day Book,* 'The New River at Hornsey', in which he referred to Lamb's cottage at Islington as 'endeared to me ... by its being the abode of "as much virtue as can live"'.

East India House. The headquarters of the Honourable East India Company where Charles Lamb worked from 5 April 1792 to 29 March 1825. The Company was founded at the end of the sixteenth century by English merchants in order to compete with the Dutch in the Spice Islands. Queen Elizabeth incorporated it by Royal Charter in 1600. The Company grew and through its vast trading activities with India and elsewhere in the Far East, it became enormously powerful and wealthy. However during the nineteenth century its powers were reduced by various acts of Parliament, and after Earl Grey's act of 1833 ended its monopoly of the valuable trade with China, it ceased to be a trading concern and exercised only administrative functions. In 1858 all Indian administration was passed to the Crown.

The building in which Lamb worked was at Nos. 12–21 Leadenhall Street. It was erected in 1726, but certain additions were made from time to time; for example in 1799 an Ionic portico and an east wing were added. Although Lamb was working there at the time he does not seem to have mentioned them in his letters. East India House was demolished in 1862. The fine library of oriental books belonging to the company passed to the India Office in Whitehall.

For thirty-three years Charles Lamb was a clerk in the Accountant's Office, retiring with a pension in 1825. During his service there the Company was still a huge trading concern and an enormous amount of merchandise passed through its warehouses, and there were periodical auctions in its sale rooms. Lamb was concerned with the accounts for this business which covered such items as tea, indigo, drugs and piece-goods, and he had to attend the sales to record the transactions.

In the accountant's office he worked at a desk seated on a high stool and with him were six clerks in a compartment known as a compound, which Lamb defined as 'a collection of simples'.

Although he sometimes had much work to do and worked late in the evening, many were the occasions when he was not fully occupied and, in fact, wrote much of his correspondence at the office, often on East India Company stationery. It is said that those clerks who arrived before 10:00AM were given breakfast, and that some rode to their

office on their horses. Lamb, of course, lived near enough to Leadenhall Street for most of his life to walk there. In spite of the drudgery
of much of the work and of his complaints in his letters to his friends,
he seems to have been reasonably happy there and to have liked his
colleagues, with whom he was popular. Although he looked forward
greatly to his retirement, it was not the success he had hoped for.

The staff at East India House was considerable and Lamb is unlikely to have known personally many outside his own department.
He does mention his colleagues in his letters occasionally, sometimes
wrote to them and mentioned them in his published writings. Among
those employed in the Accountant's Office he refers to are Thomas
Bye, Thomas S. Cabell, Charles Cartwright (Deputy Accountant
General), John Chambers, William Collett, Henry Dodwell, Thomas
Dowley, Peter S. Du Puy, Francis J. Field, James Chicheley Hyde
(1761–1838), William Marter, John Matthie (d.1836), W.D. Plum-
ley (1787–1848), William Richardson (Accountant General), Harry
Rouse, Charles Ryle, C.W. Smith, Henry Wadd (?1784–1834), Ed-
ward White, C.H. Winfield, and T. Woodruff. Others to whom Lamb
referred are Samuel Ball (later at Canton), Bland, Peter Corbet, Jack
Cole, William Evans (Baggage Warehouse), George Friend, John
Gardner (Porter), Charles Greenwollers (1764–1831), Huddy, Ker-
shaw, John Kiddell (Clerk to the Private Trade Warehouse), George
Medley (1784–1827), Martin Minns (Porter and Doorkeeper), J.
Ogilvie, Thomas Love Peacock (Examiner's Department), R.B. Pitman (Extra Clerk), J. Brook Pulham (Military Correspondence), Vin-
cent Rice (Transfer Accounts Office), William Robinson (Transfer
Office), Savory, Joseph Thompson (d.1854), Truss (?Clerk to the
Committee of Lawsuits), Walter Wilson, R. Wissett (Clerk to the
Committee of Warehousing), and Samuel Wolfe (Chief Clerk). A few
occupied two positions, such as Du Puy who was Dutch translator as
well as a clerk in the Accountant's Office.

The British Museum has been called 'a nest of singing birds'
because of the members of staff who were poets. East India House has
also been a nursery of writers, foremost among whom was Charles
Lamb, but there are other writers around his time who achieved fame
in a variety of fields. Among these were John Hoole, the translator of
Tasso; James Cobb, playwright; Peter Auber, historian; Thomas
Love Peacock, poet and novelist; the two Mills; and Lamb's friend,
Walter Wilson, who wrote on Defoe.

Editors of Lamb's Works. The principal editors are:

Alfred Ainger. 1883–88, 6 vols. 1900, 12 vols. (*edition-de-luxe*).
J.E. Babson. 1864, *Eliana*.
Bertram Dobell. 1903, *Some Sidelights on Charles Lamb*.
Percy Fitzgerald. 1875, 6 vols, often reprinted.

William C. Hazlitt. 1868–70, edition appeared under name of Thomas Purnell.

Thomas Hutchinson. 1908, 2 vols. Reprinted 1924 and 1934.

Charles Kent. 1876, Reprinted 1889.

E.V. Lucas. 1903–5, 7 vols. Reprinted 1912, 6 vols.

William Macdonald. 1903, 12 vols.

Edward Moxon. 1835, *Prose Works*, 1836, *Poetical Works*. Often reprinted.

Thomas Purnell. *See* W.C. Hazlitt above.

R.H. Shepherd. 1874.

T.N. Talfourd. 1840, often reprinted.

See also under Works

Excellent accounts of the various editions are given in the General Preface to Volume I of Macdonald's edition, in Volume I of Hutchinson's edition and in *The English Romantic Poets & Essayists*. Revised editions, 1966 and 1972.

Edmonton, Walden Cottage. In May 1833 the Lambs moved from the Westwood's house at Chase Side, Enfield to a cottage in Church Street, Edmonton. This was occupied by Mr and Mrs Walden, who looked after mild cases of mental illness and was a sort of private asylum. Walden was formerly a keeper at a neighbouring 'Bethelhem'. Mary Lamb had been nursed at the Waldens before during one of her attacks and as these were becoming more frequent and prolonged Charles felt it would be better for her to live there permanently. So that they should be together he decided to live under the same roof.

The house still exists, at one time known as Bay Cottage, it is now called Lamb Cottage, and has a long narrow garden in front. It was at this house that Charles Lamb died on 27 December 1834, after an injury caused by a fall in the street, which was followed by erysipelas. After her brother's death Mary Lamb remained at the Walden's until 1841 when she moved to a house in St Johns Wood occupied by Mrs Parsons, a sister of her former nurse, Miss James.

Edwin, Elizabeth Rebecca, c.1771–1854. Actress. Born Elizabeth Richards, she married the actor, John Edwin, the younger. She had played in Dublin and appeared at Covent Garden in 1789, subsequently joining Tate Wilkinson's company in the provinces. In 1792 she played at the Haymarket with her husband. She appeared frequently in the provinces and in addition to the Haymarket was seen in London at the Adelphi and the Surrey. After her husband's death in 1805 she appeared with the Drury Lane Company. She retired early, but owing to financial losses returned to the stage and in 1821 was again at Drury Lane (in Sheridan's *Duenna*). She was excellent in both comedy and farce and is described as a pleasing comedian in the line of Mrs Jordan. Lamb mentions her in his piece

'Mrs Gould (Miss Burrell) in "Don Giovanni in London" ' in which he saw her during 1818.

Edwin, John. **John Edwin the elder**, 1749–90. English actor famous for his comic songs. Was very successful at Bath and later at the Haymarket and Covent Garden. Said to be a good reliable actor, among his best parts were Dogberry, Launcelot Gobbo, and Sir Anthony Absolute. When he died Munden succeeded to his parts.

John Edwin the younger, 1768–1805. Comedian, son of the above. As a child playéd with his father at Bath and at the Haymarket. First appeared at Covent Garden in 1788. He was well known in Munden's part of 'Nipperkin' and was praised by Tate Wilkinson. He was a friend of Lord Barrymore and directed his amateur theatricals at Wargrave, Berkshire.

Lamb refers to Edwin in 'On the Acting of Munden' but it is not certain which Edwin he has in mind. He also mentions him in Barbara S——, and in 'The Old Actors' as it originally appeared in the *London Magazine*.

Elia, Bridget. *See* Mary Lamb.

Elia, F. Augustus, d.1820. Italian clerk at the South Sea House. Wrote *Considération sur l'état actuel de la France au mois de juin 1815*. Lucas *Letters*, II, 303, states this tract was reprinted in *Letters from Originals at Welbeck Abbey*, 1909. In his letter of 30 June 1821 to John Taylor Lamb tells him that he took the name of Elia as his pseudonym from that of a fellow clerk at the South Sea House. When Lamb wrote the old Elia was dead. It is in this letter that Lamb says call him 'Ellia'. See *Charles Lamb Bulletin*, January 1978, 104 for explanation of pronounciation from the name of Elia del Medigo.

Elia, James. *See* John Lamb, Junior.

Elian Club, The, or Elian Society. As an outcome of suggestions made at the Inner Temple Charles Lamb Centenary Dinner on 30 March 1925 The Elian was founded by those who served on the Committee for that function. Prominent among these was F.A. Downing, the first secretary of the club. It was founded in 1925 and the intention was to limit the number of members to fifty-nine (Charles Lamb's age at the time of his death), but subsequently additional members were elected, although possibly to replace those who had either died or resigned.

The main object was to have periodical meetings, including a dinner, at which addresses were given by members or guest speakers; sometimes discussion only took place between members. On certain occasions members could bring guests and there were ladies nights from time to time. The first dinner was held at the Cheshire Cheese, Fleet Street on Friday, 6 November 1925. Some of the officials were:

Presidents and Chairman: Rt. Hon. Augustine Birrell, J.P. Collins, E. Charles Fâche, J.G. Wilson.
Vice Chairman: E.J. Finch.
Secretaries: F.A. Downing, J.P. Collins, S.M. Rich.
Treasurer: J.N. Hart.

Membership of The Elian at 15 January 1926 was:
Rt. Hon. Augustine Birrell (President), statesman and essayist.
J.C. Squire, poet, critic and editor of *The London Mercury*.
A. St. John Adcock, journalist, editor of *The Bookman*.
G.K. Chesterton, essayist, novelist and poet.
C.E. Lawrence, joint-editor of *The Quarterly Review*.
Robert Lynd, essayist, literary editor of *The News Chronicle*.
Walter de la Mare, poet and novelist.
Rt. Hon. J.M. Robertson, politician and critic.
W. Kean Seymour, poet and banker.
Dr Hubert Norman, doctor of medicine and bibliophile.
Alfred Noyes, poet.
Eugene Mason, poet and essayist.
Gerald Gould, journalist and poet.
John Freeman, poet and critic.
Thomas Sharp, poet.
Cecil Palmer.
R. Cobden-Sanderson, publisher.
Geoffrey Dearmer, poet.
John Henderson.
F.G. Bettany, dramatic critic of *The Illustrated London News*.
E.V. Knox, humorist and later editor of *Punch*.
Clennell Wilkinson, journalist and author.
H.M. Tomlinson, novelist, travel writer and critic.
Philip Tomlinson, writer for *TLS*.
J.G. Wilson, bookseller, chairman of Bumpus.
Walter Jerrold, miscellaneous writer, author of *Thomas Hood and his Times*.
E. Gilpin.
S.M. Ellis, biographer and journalist.
Dr George Wherry, surgeon, author of *Charles Lamb and Cambridge*.
George Sampson, educationist and man of letters.
James Bone, journalist, London editor of *The Manchester Guardian*.
W.H. Pratt.
Edmund Blunden, poet and critic.
John Hassall, artist.

E. Charles Fâche.
T. Michael Pope.
A.J. MacDowell.
Milton Waldman, author and publisher, assistant editor of *The London Mercury*.
A.G. Gardiner, journalist and essayist, editor of *Daily News*.
B. Anderson.
G.L. Stampa, artist.
George Morrow, artist.
Robin Flower, scholar and poet; Deputy Keeper of Manuscripts, British Museum.
Rolf Bennett, novelist.
John Hart.
E.J. Finch, print collector and Lamb scholar.
W.W. Jacobs, short story writer.
Keighley Snowden, novelist and journalist.
W.L. Courtney, editor of *The Fortnightly Review*.
James Milne, literary editor of *The Daily Chronicle*.
R. Ellis Roberts, on the staff of *Pall Mall Gazette*.
James Greig.
J.M. Bulloch, editor of *The Graphic*.
Gerald Barry, editor of *The Saturday Review*.
R.P. Cowl, man of letters.
J.P. Collins, journalist.
Crawford Snowden.
J.B. Priestley, novelist, dramatist and essayist.
F.A. Downing, business man and Lamb collector.

Fifty-nine members in all. Some later members included Lewis Melville, Herman Finck, R.L. Hine, W. Henderson, Basil Francis, Kenneth Willis Cotton and S.M. Rich. The Club commissioned the portrait bust of Charles Lamb erected on the wall of Christ's Church, Greyfriars, London, which was unveiled by Lord Plender on 5 November 1935. Meetings of The Elian ceased in 1940.

Ellis, Stewart Marsh. Author of *Mainly Victorian*, 1925, which includes a chapter 'Some New Charles Lamb Letters'. These are to Fanny Kelly and the portrait of her by Drummond is reproduced. The article originally appeared in *The Saturday Review* in June 1915. Other works include *William Harrison Ainsworth and his Friends*, 1911, which has many references to Lamb. Ellis contributed to numerous periodicals including *The Fortnightly Review*, *The Bookman*, *Saturday Review*, *Contemporary Review*, *The Times Literary Supplement*, *Chambers' Journal* and *Sunday Times*.

Elliston, Robert William, 1774–1831. Actor. Educated at St Paul's School, Covent Garden. Originally intended for the church, he found that his interests lay in the theatre. Appeared at Bath in 1791 and later at York. First played in London in 1796 at the Haymarket and subsequently often at Drury Lane, where he became one of the most popular actors of the day. In 1809 he was lessee of the Surrey Theatre and from 1819 to 1926 he was manager of Drury Lane. His first production there was King Lear with Kean. Madame Vestris was one of his stars during this period. He became bankrupt in 1826, but afterwards recovered his position by his successful production in 1829 of Douglas Jerrold's *Black-Eyed Susan* at the Surrey with T.P. Cooke as William.

Some of his best parts were Doricourt, Charles Surface, Ranger, Hamlet, Romeo, Hotspur and Falstaff. He played the title role in Lamb's play Mr H—— when it was produced at Drury Lane in 1806.

Elliston was known to Lamb personally and Raymond in his *Memoirs of Elliston* recounts a trip which Lamb made with Munden and Elliston to Warwick Castle. At that time Elliston had opened a circulating library at Leamington Spa for his sons, but sometimes dealt with borrowers there himself, as humorously described by Raymond. (*See* Fitzgerald's edition of Lamb's *Works*, IV, 425—Enfield edition). Elliston also played in Henry Siddons's *Time's a Tell Tale* at Drury Lane for which Lamb had written an epilogue.

He was one of Lamb's favourite actors and Elia wrote for Moxon's *Englishman's Magazine* in 1831 his 'Reminiscences of Elliston' which he re-arranged and reprinted in the *Last Essays of Elia* in 1833 as 'To the Shade of Elliston' and 'Ellistoniana'. Lamb says in the latter essay that his acquaintance with Elliston was slight, and that he first met him in the Leamington Spa library; he recounts several other meetings with and anecdotes of the great actor. It is in this essay that he tells of the occasion on which Elliston dined with him in the Temple, and on Lamb's apology for the humbleness of the fare, which comprised haddock followed by mutton, gave the notable reply 'I too never eat but one thing at dinner', then after a pause 'reckoning fish as nothing'. As Lamb said 'The manner was all' and the anecdote should be read in full as written in Lamb's incomparable style.

Lamb has high praise for Elliston both as a man and as an actor. Leigh Hunt placed him second only to Garrick in tragedy. Elliston liked to be known as 'the great leasee'. Lamb also mentions him in his piece on 'Mrs Gould (Miss Burrell) in "Don Giovanni in London".'

Elmes, James, 1782–1862. Architect and antiquary. Educated at Merchant Taylors School and at the Royal Academy, where he gained the silver medal for architectural design in 1805. Vice President of the Royal Architectural Society in 1809. Published a number of books on architecture as well as *London in the Nineteenth Century* and *A Topographical Dictionary of London & its Environs*. He edited

Annals of the Fine Arts, which in July 1819, printed Keats's 'Ode to a Nightingale'. The publication also printed his 'On a Grecian Urn' and his sonnets 'To Haydon' and 'On Seeing the Elgin Marbles'. Elmes with Haydon championed the Elgin Marbles. He was a friend of both Haydon and Keats.

In his contribution to *Notes & Queries* in 1859 he mentioned Lamb as a friend and that he met him at evening parties at Haydon's house. He says 'Lamb and Haydon were often like boys, so boisterous in their mirth and hilarity.'

Elton, Sir Charles Abraham, 1778–1853. Author and translator. Educated at Eton and entered the Army. He published *Poems*, 1804; *Tales of Romance and other Poems*, 1810; *Specimens of Classical Poets*, 1814; *Remains of Hesiod*, 1815; *The Brothers, a Monody*, 1820; and *Boyhood and other Poems*, 1835. In 1812 he edited Habington's *Castara*. He was a frequent contributor to the *London Magazine* over the signatures of 'Olen' and 'An Idler'. In August 1821 his 'Epistle to Elia' was printed in the *London* and in August 1824 he contributed 'The Idler's Epistle to John Clare' which contains a reference to Charles Lamb.

Crabb Robinson records meeting him at Lamb's house in 1824 in company with Taylor, Hessey, Clare and Bowring. Lamb wrote to Elton in 1824 thanking him for some books he had sent. Lamb copied Elton's 'Epistle to Elia' into one of his Commonplace Books.

Elwin, Malcolm, 1903–73. Author. In 1952 edited with an introduction *The Essays and Last Essays of Elia* for Macdonald's Illustrated Classics series. He has also edited the *Autobiography and Journals of B.R. Haydon*, 1950, and De Quincey's *Confessions of an English Opium Eater*, 1956. Other works include *The Playgoer's Handbook to Restoration Drama*, 1928; *Savage Landor*, 1941; *De Quincey*, 1935; *Old Gods Falling*, 1939; *The First Romantics*, 1947; *Landor: A Replevin*, 1958; *The Noels and the Milbankes*, 1967; and *Lord Byron's Wife*, 1974.

Emery, John, 1777–1822. English actor. Originally in a theatre orchestra. Played with Tate Wilkinson's Company. First appeared at Covent Garden in 1798, subsequently at the Haymarket, but returned to Covent Garden and remained there until his death. Hazlitt said 'in his line of rustic characters he is a perfect actor,' and of his acting he also wrote 'It is impossible to praise it sufficiently because there is never any opportunity of finding fault with it.' His greatest success was as Tyke in Morton's *School of Reform*; other parts for which he was well known were: Zekiel Homespun in Colman's *Heir at Law*, Giles in *The Miller and his Men*, Caliban, Dogberry and Sir Toby Belch. He was also an excellent musician and an artist who exhibited his pictures frequently at the Royal Academy between 1801–17. Lamb praises him in his 'Stage Illusion'.

Emma Isola's Album. This was a book containing manuscript contributions from a number of well known people, it was separate from her Extract Book. Lamb was largely responsible for obtaining contributions from his friends. At one time the Album was cut up for the value of the autographs and W.C. Hazlitt, writing in 1886, said that when he saw it, it contained only nine items. He quotes from a Quaritch Catalogue of 1884 that listed thirty-two items and says there were probably many more in the book. Lucas lists them more fully in his *Letters of Lamb*, 1912, but again from Quaritch's Catalogue, which he dates 1886.

The Album was later acquired by John A. Spoor of Chicago and the catalogue of the sale of his library at the Parke-Bernet Galleries, New York, in 1939 gives a fuller description of the contents that had been re-assembled until thirty-six items were included. A facsimile reproduction is given of Keats's poem 'To my Brothers'. The text is also given of some other important items, including a facsimile of Lamb's poem 'What is an Album?' The price realized at the sale was $22,700.

Today the Album is one of the greatest of the Lamb treasures in the Harvard Library. Professor Carl Woodring gave interesting details of it in the *Harvard Library Bulletin* in 1956. Among the authors who either contributed or from whom items were acquired and inserted were Joanna Baillie, Bernard Barton, Matilda Betham, Campbell, H.F. Cary, Allan Cunningham, George Darley, Charles Dibdin, J.B. Dibdin, George Dyer, James Hogg, Hood, Leigh Hunt, Keats, Landor, Locker Lampson, Moore, Moxon, Procter, Rogers, Southey, Talfourd, Tennyson, Wordsworth and, of course, Lamb himself. There are several contributions from some authors. The Album also contained letters, portraits and cuttings.

Emma Isola's Extract Book. Charles Lamb compiled for Emma Isola an Extract Book, which contained original poems by him, and a number of items copied from some of his favourite authors. There were thirty-four items mainly in his handwriting. Lucas was able to examine the book, when in 1903 it was in the possession of the Misses Moxon, Emma Isola's daughters.

Lucas lists the poems, other than Lamb's, in his *Life of Charles Lamb*, 1905, and the authors include Coleridge, Drummond, Knowles, Marlowe, Marvell, Moxon, Prior (four quotations), Raleigh, Strode, Thurlow, Tickell, Waller, Walton and Wither, besides a number of traditional verses.

In 1934 Henry Sotheran Ltd of Piccadilly offered pages from this Extract Book (there called an Album) for sale for £1,150 as a collection. Unfortunately they were not sold as a whole, but as separate pages. Sotheran's Piccadilly Notes No. 13 reproduced in facsimile the pages offered for sale. Emma Isola's Album was a separate production by Lamb containing contributions from his friends.

Encyclopaedias and Reference Books. Most encyclopaedias and biographical reference books have articles on Charles Lamb. Among the most interesting are:

Encyclopaedia Britannica. 14th edition, Vol. 13, article by Ainger and Lucas. Article in 1973 edition by Ian Jack.
Chambers Encyclopaedia. 1973, Vol. VIII, article by Edmund Blunden.
Chambers Biographical Dictionary. 1953.
The Caxton Encyclopaedia. 1960, Vol. IV.
Compton's Encyclopaedia. Chicago, 1969, Vol. 13.
Dictionary of National Biography. Vol. XI, article by Ainger.
Oxford Junior Encyclopaedia. Vols. V & XII, 1971, 1972.
Everyman's Encyclopaedia. 1913, Vol. VIII & later editions.
Who's Who of Children's Literature, Brian Doyle, 1968.

Many foreign language reference books include Lamb; for example *Enciclopedia Italiana*, 1933, Vol. XX, article by Mario Praz.

Enfield. Crabb Robinson records that he took Charles Lamb to Enfield in July 1814 when they spent the day with his friend Anthony Robinson who lived there. This is probably Lamb's first recorded visit to Enfield. The Lambs lived in three houses in Enfield:

Mrs Leishman's, The Chase, Enfield, now known as Clarendon Cottage, No. 17 Gentleman's Row. Mrs Leishman let lodgings and in July 1825 the Lambs stayed there with the Allsops for some weeks. Again in the summer of 1827 they stayed there by themselves from May until the autumn.

The Poplars, No. 87 Chase Side, Enfield. The Lambs moved here permanently from Colebrooke Cottage, Islington, in September 1827. Thomas Hood who visited them there described it as a 'bald-looking yellowish house, with a bit of garden.' Lamb said he was told the house had cost £1,100 to build and he paid a rent of £35 a year exclusive of rates. P.G. Patmore records that while in this house Lamb completely neglected the garden, which he described as in the condition of a school playground 'never having been touched by spade or hoe for the two years they occupied the place.'

No, 89 Chase Side, Enfield. now called Westwood Cottage. The Lambs finding Mary Lamb's attacks more frequent and housekeeping a worrying matter, moved from No. 87 Chase Side, next door to the Westwoods at No. 89 in October 1829. Here they were satisfied for a time, but eventually tired of their landlord and his wife and left the house in May 1833 for Edmonton.

Evans, William. Cashier at the South Sea House (Deputy Cashier 1791). Lamb refers to him in his essay 'The South Sea House' as 'one Evans, a Cambro-Briton' and the description is one of Lamb's best character sketches. A magazine entitled *The Cambro-Briton* was started in 1820 about the time Lamb wrote his essay for the *London Magazine*.

Evans, William. Clerk in East India House, was at Christ's Hospital with Lamb and Coleridge. Brother of Mary Evans with whom Coleridge was in love in 1794. Evans was the proprietor of *The Pamphleteer* and introduced Talfourd to Lamb. He extra-illustrated a copy of Byron's *English Bards and Scotch Reviewers*, and it was for this book that in 1819 G.F. Joseph painted Lamb's portrait. William Evan's mother befriended Coleridge when he was at Christ's Hospital. Lamb has an amusing story of him in his letter to Wordsworth of 1 February 1806 in that he confused Edmund Spenser with the Hon. William Spencer. Lamb later used the story in *The Reflector* in 1811 in his 'On the Ambiguities Arising from Proper Names.'

Evening Parties. Lamb's famous evening parties started in 1806, for he tells Manning in a letter of 5 December 1806 'Rickman and Captain Burney are well; they assemble at my house pretty regularly of a Wednesday—a new institution.' He was then living at Mitre Court Buildings, Inner Temple, and the neighbourhood was convenient for his friends who dropped in from time to time, sometimes after the theatre. The day was changed to Thursday later and by 1814 it was altered from a weekly to a monthly event. No doubt the strain on Mary Lamb's health as well as the stimulation to convivality on the part of Charles were the main causes of the alteration. Perhaps Lamb's happiest time was when he lived in the Inner Temple, for after he moved to Colebrooke Cottage in 1823 he was not so accessible to his friends.

Vivid account of these parties have been left by several of his friends, notably by William Hazlitt in his essays 'On the Conversation of Authors' and 'Of Persons one would wish to have seen'; by Leigh Hunt in *The Examiner* in 1824 'A Walk in Covent Garden'; by Talfourd in *Final Memorials* in 1848; and by B.W. Procter in *Charles Lamb: A Memoir* in 1866.

Exeter Change. A building on the north side of the Strand erected in 1676 on the site of the Earl of Exeter's house. It contained shops and part was used as a menagerie from about 1773. It stood somewhere near the present Strand Palace Hotel.

Lamb refers to it in his eulogy of London in the letter to Manning in February 1801, and Mary Lamb tells Barbara Betham in 1814 that 'The Lions still live in Exeter Change.' In the joint letter of 9 January 1821 from Charles Lamb and Emma Isola to Miss Humphreys, Emma says she has been taken to see 'the wild beasts at Exeter Change.' The building was demolished in 1829 in a Strand improvement.

Moxon in his obituary notice of Lamb in *Leigh Hunt's London Journal* stated that Lamb could never pass the place where Exeter Change had stood without emotion. For Lamb the disappearance of Exeter Change had spoilt a reality in John Gay, whose body was said to have lain there in state in 1732.

Faint, Joseph, d.1833. Chief butler to the Hall Society of the Inner Temple. Brother of Randal Norris's wife. When he died he left money to Norris's widow and children so that they were able to give up Goddard School at Widford. In his position at the Inner Temple he must have been well known to Lamb in his early days. Joseph Jekyll the Bencher told Lamb that he had much regard for Faint.

Farley, Charles, 1771–1859. Actor and dramatist. For many years was concerned with the pantomimes at Covent Garden. Noted for inventing ingenious mechanical devices for them and as a theatrical machinist he was without rival in his time. He instructed Joseph Grimaldi and assisted Thomas Dibdin in the composition of *Harlequin and Mother Goose* which played for ninety-two nights at Covent Garden in 1806–7 and made Grimaldi famous. Among Farley's best known parts were Grindoff in *The Miller and his Men*, Robinson Crusoe and Timour the Tartar, which were masterpieces of melodramatic acting. Farley's acting was of the old fashioned, noisy style with much gesture. He also played Jeremy in *Love for Love* and Lord Trinket in *The Jealous Wife*. He retired from the stage in 1834. He also wrote airs, glees and choruses for pantomimes and in 1821 was responsible for *Henry IV Part II. Arranged by Mr Farley, with four additional scenes representing the Coronation in the Abbey*.

Lamb refers to him in 'Barrenness of the Imaginative Faculty in the Productions of Modern Art' and 'On the Acting of Munden'.

Farren, Elizabeth, ?1759–1829. English actress. First appeared in London at the Haymarket in 1777 as Miss Hardcastle, then moved to Drury Lane. She eventually succeeded to Mrs Abington's parts of fine ladies, to which she was particularly suited. She played Berinthia, Angelica, Elvira, Hermoine, Olivia, Portia, Lydia Languish, Millamant, Juliet and Lady Betty Modish. She was especially famous as Lady Teazle.

Hazlitt refers to her as 'Miss Farren with her fine-lady airs and graces, with that elegant turn of her head and motion of her fan and tripping of her tongue.' She received high praise as an actress from Horace Walpole and many others. In 1797 she married the Earl of Derby and left the stage.

She was one of Lamb's favourite actresses and he refers to her in his essay 'On the Artificial Comedy of the Last Century.'

Farren, William, 1725–95. Actor. Appeared at Drury Lane from 1776 to 1784 and at Covent Garden from then until his death. He was the original Careless in *The School for Scandal* and also played the Earl of Leicester in *The Critic* in 1779. He was a successful Shakespearean actor. His son William Farren, 1786–1861, was also an actor, but since Lamb's reference to Farren in 'The Old Actors' is to the portrait in Charles Mathews's gallery, it is probable that the elder Farren is intended.

Farrow, Walter, 1867–1964. Chairman of the Council of the Charles Lamb Society, 1935–64.

Fauntleroy, Henry, 1785–1824. Banker sentenced to death for forgery and hanged on 30 November 1824. He was a partner in the bank of Marsh, Sibbald & Co of Berners Street, London, and was responsible for a series of forgeries over about ten years, until the bank failed in 1824. Lamb refers to Fauntleroy in his letter to Barton on December 1 of that year; he makes great play of the subject for Barton's amusement. His paper 'The Last Peach' which was printed in the *London Magazine* in April 1825 also refers to Fauntleroy.

A curious entry appears in Caroline Fox's *Journals* under the date of 25 October 1839 about the advertisement which appeared shortly after Fauntleroy was hanged: 'To all good Christians! Pray for the soul of Fauntleroy.' When asked if he knew anything about it Lamb claimed to have paid seven and sixpence for it.

Favell, Robert, 1775–1812. Army officer. Was at Christ's Hospital with Lamb and Coleridge, where he was a Grecian. Went to Pembroke College, Cambridge, but is said to have left because he was ashamed that his father was a house painter. Favell wrote to the Duke of York for a commission in the Army which was given to him in the 61st Foot 1st Battalion. He fought in the Peninsula War and was killed at Salamanca.

Favell was an advocate of Pantisocracy with Coleridge and Southey, and wrote a poem on the subject. Lamb mentions him in his essay on Christ's Hospital and in 'Poor Relations' where he is described as 'W——.' Lamb also states that he was at Oxford instead of Cambridge.

Note. There seems some confusion about Favell's christian name among modern writers. Lucas in the *Life* and elsewhere calls him

Joseph, whereas Maurice Carpenter in *The Indifferent Horseman* gives Samuel, as does F. Page in the notes to his edition of the *Last Essays of Elia*, and Jack Simmons in his *Southey*. Both his contemporaries, who should know, Coleridge and Leigh Hunt, call him Robert, and they are followed by the reliable James Dykes Campbell.

Fawcett, John, 1768–1837. Comedian and dramatist. Educated at St Paul's School. Apprenticed to a linen draper, but ran away to the stage. Appeared at Covent Garden in 1791; played Caleb in *He Would Be a Soldier* and Jerry Sneak in Foote's *Mayor of Garratt*. In 1794 he appeared at the Haymarket and in 1796 played Falstaff at Covent Garden for Pope's benefit. In 1799 he was stage manager at the Haymarket. He became well known in such parts as Job Thornberry in Colman's *John Bull* and as Dr Pangloss. Among his other parts were Bartolo to the Figaro of Liston in *The Barber of Seville* in 1818, and Rolamo in John Howard Payne's *Clairi, the Maid of Milan* in 1823. He was excellent as Lord Ogleby, Sir Peter Teazle and Touchstone. He retired from the stage in 1830. For many years he was treasurer of the Covent Garden Theatrical Fund.

Talfourd praised him and said 'in representations of bluff honesty and rude manly feelings, he had no rival.' Leigh Hunt commented on his grating laugh. He is mentioned by Lamb in 'The Religion of Actors' and in his letter to Hazlitt on 15 January 1806. Fawcett also wrote plays and collaborated with Dibdin.

Fawcett, Millicent Garrett, 1847–1929. A leader of the Women's Suffrage movement. Became Dame Millicent Fawcett, but sometimes wrote under the name of Mrs Henry Fawcett. Her husband, who was blind, was Professor of Economics at Cambridge. She was author of *Some Eminent Women of Our Times*, 1889, which included Mary Lamb and Dorothy Wordsworth. She also wrote *Life of Sir William Molesworth*, 1901.

Feilde, Rev. Mathew, 1748–96. Master of the Lower School at Christ's Hospital in Lamb's time. Educated at Christ's Hospital and Pembroke College, Cambridge; became a Fellow of Pembroke. He held a number of livings among which were those of Rector of the united churches of St Anne and St John Zachary, Aldersgate; Vicar of Ugley, Essex; and Curate of Berden. He was buried in the cloisters of Christ's Church in 1796. He left a wife and seven children. Lamb states in a footnote to his essay on Christ's Hospital that Feilde wrote a play *Vertumnus and Pomona* which was accepted by Garrick, but was not a success. Blunden stated that it was acted for one night at Covent Garden in 1782.

Lamb mentions him in his essay 'Christ's Hospital Five and Thirty Years Ago' where he describes him as an easy going man who did not trouble himself much about his pupils: 'There was now and then the formality of saying a lesson.' Leigh Hunt in his *Autobiography* states 'a man of more handsome incompetence for his situation perhaps did not exist.'

Fell, Ralph. d.1814 Author. Convivial friend of Lamb and John Fenwick. Wrote *A Tour through the Batavian Republic during the Year 1800*, 1801, and *Memories of the Public Life of Charles James Fox*, 1808. Fell was introduced to Lamb by Godwin. In a letter to Rickman in 1801 Lamb states Fell is writing a comedy, but in another letter he adds that he has stopped because someone told him it had no merit. In September 1802 writing to Manning he states that 'Fell, my other drunken companion . . . is turned editor of a Naval Chronicle.' In a letter in January 1804 (not 1803 as Lucas dates it) Lamb asks Rickman for a place for Fell 'a decayed Literatus' and adds 'here is a young man of solid but not brilliant genius . . . not the worse (I hope) for knowing Latin and Greek.' In 1802 Fell was living in Pentonville.

Fenwick, Elizabeth, d. c.1840. Wife of John Fenwick, one of Lamb's 'drunken companions'. In an endeavour to provide for her family, for her husband was continually in debt, she followed many occupations, and was a schoolmistress, translator, governess, author of children's books and manager of William Godwin's publishing venture, The Juvenile Library. She also wrote a novel entitled *Secrecy*. In 1820 Godwin issued *Leçons pour les Enfans. Traduit de l'Anglais par L'Abbé le Februre*, by Mrs Fenwick. She was a friend of Mary Wollstonecraft and with Mary Hays nursed her during her last illness. Like Charles Lamb she detested the second Mrs Godwin. In addition to William Godwin, she numbered among her friends Thomas Holcroft, Sarah Hazlitt, Mary Hays and the Lambs. Both Charles and Mary Lamb helped her from time to time and occasionally she stayed with them with her children.

In a letter in July 1803 Mary Lamb tells Dorothy Wordsworth of Fenwick's misfortunes and adds 'I have a great affection for Mrs Fenwick.' Crabb Robinson records in his *Diary* on 10 December 1811 'Mary Lamb dined with us . . . In the evening Charles Lamb, Manning [i.e. James Manning] and Mrs Fenwick. A pleasant evening.' In a letter of 24 May 1814 to Mary Hays, Mrs Fenwick mentioned that she had thought of Mary Lamb as guardian for her son, Orlando, but did not approach her about it because Charles was fearful of the state of his sister's health.

Mrs Fenwick seems to have been a warm hearted and courageous woman constantly struggling against odds. In 1814 she left England permanently to join her daughter in Barbados, and carried on the struggle to earn a livelihood there, which included assisting at a school run by her daughter. Later she lived in New York where she died.

She had two children, Eliza and Orlando. The daughter was coached by Thomas Holcroft and became an actress, first playing in private theatres, but in 1810 appearing for a season at Covent Garden with John Philip Kemble. In October 1811 she accepted an offer to go with Mr Dyke's company to Barbados, and stayed with the Lambs just before her departure. While in the West Indies she married a man named Rutherford, who turned out to be no better than her father. He abandoned her fairly soon and returned to England. In 1818 he called on William Godwin who was not favourably impressed. Lamb, writing to Sir John Stoddart in August 1827, tells him that Eliza Fenwick is now dead and that Mrs Fenwick is the sole support of her four grandchildren. He describes Rutherford as 'lurking about the pothouses of Little Russell Street.' Just before Eliza Fenwick went to Barbados Lamb wrote an address for her to deliver from the stage.

E.V. Lucas stated that he had seen in America a copy of the *Essays of Elia* inscribed by Lamb to Mrs Fenwick and her daughter, Eliza, so there must have been some correspondence between them and the Lambs during their residence in Barbados.

Fenwick, John. d.1820. Author and editor. He was owner and editor of *The Albion* on which he worked with his brother; he later edited *The Plough* and *The Statesman*. In 1794 he translated the *Memoirs of Charles François Duperier-Dumouriez* and in 1800 his farce *The Indian* was produced at Drury Lane. Fenwick also wrote a pamphlet about the Rev. James O'Coigley who was executed in 1798. He was one of Charles Lamb's early and undoubtedly disreputable companions; was continually in need of money and was imprisoned for debt. Although dissolute and lacking in principle, it seems that he was a man of some education, and Miss Wedd in *The Fate of the Fenwicks*, 1927, describes him frequently reading in a Greek Testament he carried about with him.

Thomas Holcroft's *Diary* has several references to Fenwick among which is a note on 24 October 1798 'Mr and Mrs Fenwick to dinner: promised my endeavours towards procuring money to set up a day school for her.' On November 2 he has the not unexpected note 'Advanced Fenwick £3 to supply his wife with necessaries.'

Fenwick was introduced to Lamb by William Godwin. For a short time in 1801 Lamb worked with Fenwick on *The Albion* and he gives an amusing account of his experiences in his essay 'Newspapers Thirty-Five Years Ago'. Lamb's letter of 9 January 1802 to John Rickman states that Fenwick was extravagantly spending on entertainments the money he had collected for his publication *The Plough*, partly from the Duke of Northumberland. Mary Lamb, therefore christened the magnificent new hats of his wife and daughter 'Northumberland hats'. In January 1806 Lambs tells Hazlitt that Fenwick, who is hiding from his creditors in the country, is coming to London to surrender himself to prison and that he hopes to get the Rules of the Fleet; in February 1808 he was again in the Fleet Prison. Fenwick abandoned his wife and family and fled to Canada.

The most famous reference to him is in the essay 'The Two Races of Men' where he is described as 'my old friend, Ralph Bigod, Esq' who was a leading member of 'the great race'—the borrowers. Lamb's character sketch has conferred immortality on his friend, whose favourite aphorism was that 'money kept longer than three days stinks.' He also figures in 'The Praise of Chimney-Sweepers' where it is mentioned that Fenwick and Lamb acted as waiters at James White's annual feast for the sweeps. There is also a reference in the essay 'Confessions of a Drunkard' which looks as if it applies to Fenwick and his boon companion, Ralph Fell. Fenwick is described by Lamb as of a cheerful open exterior and a quick jovial eye, and he had many friends, even if as Lamb maintains, they were mostly feeders of his exchequer. Among the more permanent friends were Godwin, Holcroft and Lamb.

Field, Barron, 1786–1846. Barrister. Entered at Inner Temple 1809 and in 1812 was living at No. 4 Hare Court, Temple. He was called to the Bar in 1814 and for some years practised as a barrister on the Oxford Circuit. His father was apothecary to Christ's Hospital and his brother, Francis John Field, was a clerk in East India House, while another brother, Frederick, had been educated at Christ's Hospital after Lamb's time. At one time Barron Field was dramatic critic to *The Times* and he contributed to *The Reflector* and *Quarterly Review*. In 1811 he compiled an analysis of Blackstone's *Commentaries*.

He was a friend of Lamb, Leigh Hunt and Crabb Robinson and there are numerous references to him in Robinson's *Diary*. For a time he was advocate-fiscal in Ceylon, but in 1816 sailed for New South Wales, arriving in Sydney in February 1817. Here he became Judge of the Supreme Court of New South Wales. He remained in Australia until 1824 when he returned to England and resumed practice at the Bar, but soon left it to become Chief Justice at Gibraltar.

While in Australia Field contributed to the *London Magazine* and in September 1824 his 'Narrative of a Voyage from New South Wales' appeared there. In 1819 he had published in Sydney his *First Fruits of Australian Poetry* and he sent a copy to Lamb who reviewed it in *The Examiner* on 16 January 1820. Later Field reprinted the 'First Fruits' in his *Geographical Memoirs of New South Wales*, published in 1825. Earlier he had published *Hints to Witnesses in Courts of Justice* and had written an introduction to the *Memoirs of James Hardy Vaux*. He also wrote a farce *The Antiquary* and with John

Payne Collier edited the *Dramatic Works of Thomas Heywood* in 1842.

There does not seem to be any record of when Lamb and Field first met, but it may have been early in Lamb's life; they were certainly intimate friends and Crabb Robinson records in his *Diary* that he often met Field in company with Lamb, either at the latter's rooms or at parties elsewhere. Field accompanied Lamb on a visit to Mackery End in 1815.

No early letters from Lamb to Field appear to exist, probably because they lived near one another. After Field went to Australia Lamb wrote to him a letter on 31 August 1817 which is a sketch for the Elian essay 'Distant Correspondents' which appeared in the *London Magazine* in March 1822. Other letters followed, that of 22 September 1822 tells of Lamb's visit to France and the incident of Talma and the bellows. In 1827 Lamb tells Field of his refusal to write a detailed description of Charles Mathews's collection of theatrical portraits.

Field was also a friend of John Murray and in 1826 at Lamb's request, gave Hood a letter of introduction to the publisher. Lamb wrote verses to Field's wife and to his sisters, Esther and Mary Louisa. After Lamb's death Barron Field wrote a notice of him for the *Annual Biography and Obituary* for 1835. Field claimed to be a descendant of Oliver Cromwell.

Field, Esther. Daughter of Henry Field and sister of Barron Field. Lamb wrote verses to her in the form of an acrostic.

Field, Francis John. Clerk at East India House with Lamb, brother of Barron Field.

Field, Henry, Senior, 1755–1837. Treasurer to the Apothecaries' Company. From 1807 he was apothecary at Christ's Hospital. He was a member of the Society of Apothecaries, lectured to them and helped to introduce examinations for them. He contributed to medical journals and wrote *Memoirs, historical and illustrative of the Botanick Garden at Chelsea, belonging to the Society of Apothecaries of London*, 1820. He had six sons and two daughters. Among the former were Barron Field, Francis John, Henry and Frederick Field. Lamb wrote verses for the two daughters, Mary Louisa and Esther Field.

It was at Henry Field's house that an amateur performance of Richard II was given in 1824 for which Lamb wrote an epilogue. It was at this time that Lamb made his joke concerning Mr Negus, 'Hand him round!'

Field, Henry, Junior. Surgeon. Brother of Barron Field, who in 1824 lived 'a few doors west of Christ's Church Passage, Newgate Street.' He attended Lamb professionally in 1825.

Field, Mary c.1713–92. Lamb's maternal grandmother, née Bruton. Reginald Hine discovered that she married Edward Field, a gardener, on 14 September 1736. She entered the service of the Plumer family and from 1766 to 1792 was housekeeper at Blakesware House, near Widford, Hertfordshire. She is buried in Widford Churchyard and her grave is maintained by the Charles Lamb Society.

Lamb has a number of references to his grandmother. His poem 'The Grandame' was written in 1796; there are also references in the Elian essay 'Dream Children' and in his short piece 'Saturday Night'. Descriptions of Blakesware are given in the essay 'Blakesmoor in H——' and by Mary Lamb in the story 'The Young Mahometan' in *Mrs Leicester's School*. Another sister of Mary Field, who had married a Gladman, lived at Mackery End farmhouse. (*See* R.L. Hine's *Charles Lamb and his Hertfordshire*, 1949, and Miss Mann's articles in *C.L.S. Bulletin* Nos. 198 and 199).

Field, Mary Louisa. Second daughter of Henry Field to whom Lamb wrote verses. Sister of Barron Field. When an old lady living at Hastings she gave Canon Ainger some reminiscences of Lamb.

Fielde, Francis, d.1809. One of Lamb's godfathers. An oilman with a shop at the corner of Featherstone Buildings, Holborn. Fielde owned the cottage Button Snap at Buntingford, which he left to his wife, who conveyed it to Lamb in 1812 to fulfil her husband's wishes. Fielde provided the tickets for Lamb's first play, *Artaxerxes* at Drury Lane about 1780. Fielde was a friend of R.B. Sheridan; Lamb says Sheridan brought his first wife, the beautiful Maria Linley, to Fielde's house when he eloped with her from Bath, and that Lamb's parents were present when he arrived.

Fielde supplied oil for the illumination of the 'orchestra and various avenues' of Drury Lane and thus received free admission to the theatre. He was a friend of John Palmer, the comedian, and he is described by Lamb as 'the most gentlemanly of oilmen.'

Fields, Annie Adams, 1834–1915. American authoress. Second wife of the publisher and author James T. Fields. She was a prominent literary figure and established a literary *salon* in her home. In 1894 she published *A Shelf of Old Books* which contained a long chapter on Leigh Hunt and in a later chapter 'From Milton to Thackeray' she tells of the interesting volumes in her husband's library. Among these were Charles Lamb's copy of *The Rape of the Lock* given to Fields by Moxon, copies of Lamb's own books and autograph letters of Lamb. She was the author of a number of books among which were *James T. Fields: Biographical Notes and Personal Sketches*, 1881; *Authors & Friends*, 1896; and her *Memories of a Hostess*, a diary edited by M.A. De.W. Howe and published in 1922.

Fields, James Thomas, 1817–81. American publisher, author and book collector. First a clerk in a bookseller's shop, but later became partner in the publishing firm of Ticknor & Fields, later known as Fields, Osgood & Co. His firm published some of the chief American writers, as well as many well known English authors. He published the first collected edition of De Quincey's works and from 1861 to 1871 he edited *The Atlantic Monthly*. When he retired he devoted himself to lecturing and writing, and he gave lectures on both Charles Lamb and Longfellow. He was a friend of many authors and was well known to the Cowden Clarkes.

Field wrote some interesting essays and literary reminiscences. Of these *Yesterdays with Authors*, 1872, includes a chapter on Wordsworth in which he tells of his visit to the poet in the Lake District and that they talked about Charles Lamb and Hazlitt; in the earlier 1871 Boston edition there was a chapter on 'Barry Cornwall and some of his friends' which referred to Lamb. In *Underbrush*, 1877, he has the long and attractive chapter 'My Friend's Library' in which he writes of the occasion when Moxon showed him the volumes of Charles Lamb's library then in his possession, and he tells how the whole Moxon family stood round and 'told stories of Lamb's enthusiasm' over the *Life of the Duke of Newcastle*. He has too an account of the copy of Pope's *Rape of the Lock* which Lamb found on a bookstall for sixpence and carried home to supply the missing pages in his beautiful handwriting. Fields' book also contains a final chapter 'To Leigh Hunt in Elysium'.

Finch, Edward James, 1865–1955. Elian scholar and collector of books and prints. One of the founder members of the Elian Society and a former Vice Chairman. A member of the Charles Lamb Society 1936–55. Honorary Founder Curator of the Southgate Museum. Member of the Lamb Centenary Memorial Appeal Executive Committee 1934–5.

Finch was known as a collector of prints about London and he had a special collection devoted to the life and work of Charles Lamb. Some of these were used from time to time in exhibitions concerning Lamb's period, and prints from Finch's collection were used to illustrate the famous Gregynog Press edition of the *Essays* in 1931 and also to illustrate the edition in Macdonald's Illustrated Classics series in 1952. In 1951 Finch presented his collection of several hundred prints on Lamb and London to the Charles Lamb Society and it is accommodated in their library. Basil Francis in his *Fanny Kelly of Drury Lane*, 1950, acknowledges the help given him by Finch in the research for his book.

Finch, Jeremiah Stanton, b.1910. American Professor of English at Princeton University. A Lamb scholar. Author of *Sir Thomas*

Browne, 1950. Contributed to the *Princeton University Library Chronicle*:

1945   Charles Lamb's Companionship ... in Absolute Solitude. Concerns Emma Isola and gives details of manuscripts at Princeton.
1946   The Scribner Lamb Collection.
1947   Lamb's copy of the *History of Philip de Commines*.

FitzGerald, Edward, 1809–83. Poet and translator. Educated at King Edward's School, Bury St Edmunds, and Trinity College, Cambridge. Friend of Bernard Barton and in 1856 married Barton's daughter, Lucy. In 1849 he wrote a memoir of Barton. His other works include *Euphranor*, 1851; *Six Dramas of Calderon*, 1853; and *The Rubaiyat of Omar Khayyam*, 1859.

Lamb admired his poem 'The Meadows of Spring' contributed to Hone's *Year Book* in 1831. When the poem was reprinted in *The Athenaeum* in 1831 the editor implied that it might be by Lamb. The latter refers to the poem in his letter to Moxon in August 1831. FitzGerald related the story of Thackeray putting one of Lamb's letters to Barton to his forehead with the words 'Saint Charles'.

Among FitzGerald's friends were James Spedding, W.B. Donne, Thackeray, Frederick Tennyson and Carlyle. It is not recorded that he ever met Lamb, but they must have known of one another through their mutual friend, Barton, and no doubt FitzGerald saw some of the matchless letters to Barton. FitzGerald compiled a short chronology of Lamb's life which he sent to J.R. Lowell in 1878 and stated that 'Pollock calls my paper "Cotelette d'Agneau a la minute".' It was printed in *Euphranor and Other Miscellanies*, 1900, and reprinted in *C.L.S. Bulletin*, No. 43 Supplement.

Fitzgerald, Percy Hetherington, 1834–1925. Irish writer. Educated at Trinity College, Dublin. Was called to the Irish Bar, but subsequently came to London and pursued a literary career. Contributed to Dickens's *All the Year Round* and *Household Words*. He was a voluminous writer and among his books are: *Charles Lamb: his Friends, his Haunts and his Books*, 1866; *The Life, Letters and Writings of Charles Lamb*, edited by Percy Fitzgerald, 6 volumes 1875; *The Art of the Stage as set out in Lamb's Dramatic Essays*, 1885; *Memoirs of Charles Lamb*, edited and annotated by Percy Fitzgerald (Talfourd's *Memoir* re-arranged), 1892; *Little Essays, Sketches, and Characters by C.L. Selected from his Letters*, 1884; *Afternoon Lectures on Literature and Art*, 1864 (contains 'Two Essayists; Charles Lamb and Charles Dickens'); and *Recreations of a Literary Man*, 1882. He also wrote *The Life of Laurence Sterne*, 1864; *The Life of David Garrick*, 1868; *The Kembles*, 1871; *A New*

History of the English Stage, 1882; *Lives of the Sheridans*, 1886; *Memoirs of an Author*, 1894; and *The Book Fancier*, 1886.

Flaxman, Mary Ann, Maria, 1768–1833. Artist, sister of John Flaxman, the sculptor. Exhibited at the Royal Academy, 1786–1819. Among her pictures were *Ferdinand and Miranda*, 1789, and *Sappho*, 1810. She is thought to have done the designs for *Prince Dorus* and *Beauty and the Beast*, both published by Godwin in 1811 and attributed to Lamb.

Flower, Sarah, 1805–48. Poet, daughter of Benjamin Flower, who was editor of *The Cambridge Intelligencer* and who published Coleridge's 'Ode on the Departing Year', and latterly lived at Dalston. After the death of her father in 1829 she lived with the family of W.J. Fox and contributed to *The Monthly Repository*, then conducted by Fox. Her contributions were signed 'S.Y'. The Cowden Clarkes in *Recollections of Writers* relate seeing her give an excellent dramatic performance in a private house of scenes presenting Shakespeare's heroines. In 1837 she appeared at the little Richmond Theatre as Lady Macbeth, Portia and Lady Teazle. Later she appeared at the Bath Theatre. She was said to have had a rich contralto voice as well as acting ability. She married William Bridges Adams, an inventor and eminent engineer.

Among her contributions to *The Monthly Repository* in 1835 was a long account of an evening with the Lambs and Coleridge at Colebrooke Cottage (Reprinted in Bertram Dobell's *Sidelights on Charles Lamb*, 1903). She also wrote hymns, including 'Nearer my God, to Thee'. One of her best known poems was her drama *Vivia Perpetua*, 1841. Among her friends were Browning, Macready and W.J. Fox. Her sister, Eliza Flower, composed *Musical Illustrations of the Waverley Novels*, and most of Sarah Flower's hymns were set to music by her sister.

Foote, Maria, c.1797–1867. English actress, daughter of the manager of a theatre at Plymouth. She played Juliet at the age of thirteen and appeared at Covent Garden in 1814 in Mrs Inchbald's *The Child of Nature*, playing at that theatre every season up to 1824–5. Among her parts were Beatrice, Ophelia, Desdemona and Rosalind. Her first appearance at Drury Lane was in 1826. She was the original Isidora in Barry Cornwall's *Mirandola*. She was an actress of limited abilities, but was attractive and renowned for her beauty and grace which secured her constant engagements.

She also achieved notoriety through her love affairs, one of which was with Colonel Berkeley, another was with 'Pea Green' Hayes, against whom she brought a breach of promise action and obtained

£3,000 damages. She retired from the stage in 1831 and became the Countess of Harrington.

Lamb mentions her in his letter of 22 October 1822 to John Howard Payne when describing Payne's play *Ali Pacha* at Covent Garden. He wrote 'Miss Foote looked helpless and beautiful and greatly helped the piece.' She played Helena in it. She is also mentioned by Reynolds and Hood in their 'Ode to Joseph Grimaldi, Senior' in *Odes and Addresses to Great People*, 1825, and Lamb quotes the verses in his review of the book in *The New Times* in 1825.

Forster, John, 1812–76. Biographer and historian. Educated at University College, London. Barrister of the Inner Temple, but relinquished the law for literature. In 1829 he met Leigh Hunt and became dramatic critic of the *True Sun*, and later for *The Examiner*. Wrote for *The Courier, Athenaeum* and *Edinburgh Review*. He edited Moxon's *Reflector* and subsequently became editor of *The Examiner*. He also wrote for *Lardner's Encyclopaedia* and later was editor of the *Daily News*.

In 1834 he had chambers at 58 Lincoln's Inn Fields, to which many literary men came. At one time he was engaged to Letitia E. Landon, and Lamb in a letter in 1833 tells Forster to bring her to visit him.

Forster was an able writer; he wrote lives of Goldsmith, Landor, Dickens and others. Both Lamb and Leigh Hunt were among his friends. He was at Lamb's house in January 1834 when Macready was also there to supper.

Lucas notes that among Crabb Robinson's papers was a letter from Barron Field in 1835 on the subject of a biographer for Lamb and Field wrote 'But heavens preserve us from a monster of the name of Forster.' John Forster wrote two articles on Lamb in the *New Monthly Magazine* in 1835 which were reprinted in Baudry's European Library edition of *The Essays of Elia* in Paris in 1835, and also in Galignani's volume of the prose in the same year. Forster bequeathed his large collection of about 18,000 books and pamphlets to the Victoria and Albert Museum.

Fortunate Blue-coat Boy, The. In his essay 'Christ's Hospital Five and Thirty Years Ago', included in the *Elia* volume, Lamb has a reference to the books read by the Christ's Hospital boys in his time. He says 'We had classics of our own ... Peter Wilkins—the Adventures of the Hon. Capt. Robert Boyle—the Fortunate Blue Coat Boy—and the like.'

Of these Peter Wilkins was the well known *The Life and Adventures of Peter Wilkins, A Cornish Man* by Robert Paltock, first published in 1751 (available this century in Everyman's Library). Another Blue Coat Boy who thought highly of this book was Leigh Hunt, who wrote on it in his *A Book for a Corner*. Captain Boyle's book has not withstood the years as well, but probably the least well known is *The Fortunate Blue-Coat Boy*.

The full title is *The Fortunate Blue-Coat Boy: or Memoirs of the Life and Happy Adventures of Mr Benjamin Templeman; Formerly a Scholar in Christ's Hospital. By an Orphanotrophian*, and it appeared in two volumes in 1760. It tells of an orphan's adventures as a school boy about 1730. There is much about his school days and while still at Christ's Hospital he attracts the attention of the young widow of a rich citizen, who heard him sing in Christ's Church, and he marries her within a short time. The author was the Rev. James Penn.

Canon Ainger had a copy of the book, but does not seem impressed with it, although he wrote about it in the Glasgow University *Bazaar News* in 1889. In more recent years Edmund Blunden has given a long quotation from the book in his *Christ's Hospital*, 1923. Macaulay is said to have known the book by heart.

Foster, Sir William, b.1863. Registrar and Superintendent of Records, India Office 1907–23, Historiographer 1923–7. Author of *The East India House: its story and associations*, 1924, which includes many references to Charles Lamb. He wrote many books about India.

Foxon, David. Assistant Keeper in the Department of Printed Books at the British Museum. Contributed to *The Book Collector*, Spring 1957, 'The Chapbook Editions of the Lamb's Tales from Shakespeare.'

Francis, Basil, d.1968. Author, novelist and contributor to theatrical magazines. Formerly Hon. Treasurer of the Society for Theatre Research. Contributor to the *C.L.S. Bulletin*. A member of the Elian Society and the Charles Lamb Society.

Wrote *Fanny Kelly of Drury Lane*, 1950, and three plays of Elian interest: [*What a lass . . .*, 1949; *Chinese Crackling*, 1951; and *Harriot*, 1954]. In the production of *What a lass . . .* in 1949 by the Dramatic Group of the Charles Lamb Society, Basil Francis played the part of Charles Lamb. He also compiled the indexes to *The Benefit System in the British Theatre* by St Vincent Troubridge, 1967.

Frank, Robert, b.1939. Associate Professor of English, Oregon State University. Author of *Don't Call Me Gentle Charles! An Essay on Lamb's Essays of Elia*, Oregon State University Press, 1976.

Franklin, Rev. Frederick William, d.1836. Schoolmaster. At Christ's Hospital with Lamb (C.H., 1783–93), the 'Fine frankhearted Fr——' of the Elian essay on Christ's Hospital. He proceeded to Pembroke College, Cambridge; in 1801 he became Grammar Master at the Blue Coat School at Hertford. He resigned in 1827 on being presented to the living of Albrighton in Shropshire.

Lamb visited him on his first visit to Cambridge and in 1815 on a subsequent visit, showed Mary Lamb Franklin's rooms which she describes in a letter to Sarah Hutchinson. In 1824 Lamb dined with Franklin at Hertford and defended Coleridge to him from a supposed scandal concerning Mrs Gillman. He relates the happening amusingly in a letter to Sara Hutchinson. Franklin in addition to being a school-master was also chaplain to the county gaol and administered to the last moments of Thurtell, the murderer, and received as a gift from him a gold watch.

Fraser's Magazine, 1830–69, new series 1870–82. Edited by William Maginn in 1830. Published by James Fraser, but named after Hugh Fraser, joint proprietor with Maginn. Contributors included Thomas Carlyle, T.L. Peacock, Charles Kingsley, Thackeray and W.H. Ainsworth. In 1835 the magazine included Daniel Maclise's portrait of Charles Lamb with a notice of Lamb's death by William Maginn. The sketch of Lamb is reprinted with additional text by William Bates in *The Maclise Portrait Gallery of Illustrious Literary Characters*, 1898.

French, Joseph Milton. Author. Editor of *Charles Lamb: Essays and Letters*, New York, 1937. Among his contributions to periodicals are:

Studies in Philology
1933   Lamb and Spenser (with F. Hard).
1934   Lamb and Milton.
1940   A Chip from Elia's workshop.
Journal of the Rutgers University Library
1948   Article on Charles Lamb.

He also wrote various books and articles on Milton and edited *Four Scarce Poems of George Wither*, 1931.

Frend, Sophia Elizabeth. Eldest daughter of William Frend, mar-ried Augustus De Morgan, the mathematican, in 1837. Was mother of William De Morgan, the novelist. Lamb wrote verses for her Album and an acrostic 'To S.F.' She wrote *Memoirs of Augustus De Morgan*, 1882. In 1895 her daughter edited Mrs De Morgan's *Three Score Years and ten* which contains stories of George Dyer's eccentricities.

Frend, Rev. William, 1757–1841. Mathematican, Unitarian and reformer, at one time Rector of Longstanton. Fellow and Tutor of Jesus College, Cambridge, who was banished from the University in 1793 for writing an Unitarian tract. He was a friend of Lamb, Crabb

Robinson and George Dyer, and the latter's executor. Lamb wrote verses to Frend's daughter and lines to William Frend. For fifteen years Frend issued his *Evening Amusements, or Beauty of the Heavens displayed*, 1804–18; he had also published *Principles of Algebra*, 1796–9, with an Appendix by Baron Maseres, who is mentioned in Lamb's essay 'The Old Benchers of the Inner Temple'. Frend was tutor to Malthus the economist. At one time he was pursued by Mary Hays who wrote him many letters, said to have been used by her in her novel *Memoirs of Emma Courtney*.

Frere, John Hookham, 1769–1846. Diplomat, translator and author. Educated at Eton where he was a friend of Canning. Passed to Cambridge and became a Fellow of Caius. He was a clerk in the Foreign Office and subsequently became Under Secretary for Foreign Affairs. He was also Envoy to Portugal and Ambassador to Spain. He contributed to *The Anti-Jacobin*, but is best known for his translations from Aristophanes. Lamb wrote an epigram on Canning and Frere in *The Morning Post* in retaliation for their verses mentioning him in *The Anti-Jacobin*. For that magazine Frere wrote the greater part of the 'Loves of the Triangles' and shared with Canning the authorship of 'The Friend of Humanity and the Knife grinder'. He also contributed to Ellis's *Specimens of the Early English Poets* and to Southey's *Chronicle of the Cid*. When there was difficulty over Coleridge's pension after the death of George IV, Frere helped him financially and made attempts to obtain sinecure posts for him towards the end of his life.

Frickers, The. Daughters of Mrs Fricker of Bristol, the widow of a small manufacturer who had failed in business. Edith Fricker, d.1837, married Robert Southey; Sara Fricker, d.1845 married S.T. Coleridge; and Mary Fricker married Robert Lovell. Two other unmarried daughters, Eliza and Martha, were friends of Mary Lamb who visited them occasionally when they worked in London.

Fryer, Maria, d. c.1848. Friend and schoolfellow of Emma Isola. Lucas prints three letters from Lamb to Miss Fryer, two written in 1831 and one in 1834. The latter has an account of Mary Lamb while ill. Lamb also recommends to her Walton's *Angler*. J.S. Finch in his article 'Charles Lamb's Companionship ... in Almost Solitude' (*P.U.L.C.*, 1945) prints eight unpublished letters from Charles Lamb and one from Mary Lamb to Maria Fryer. Lamb's sonnet 'Harmony in Unlikeness' printed in *Album Verses* refers to her as 'The fair Maria'. The family lived at Chatteris between Bury and Cambridge and Emma Isola stayed with them occasionally.

Fukuda, Tsutomu. Professor of English in Kobe University. Author of *A Study of Charles Lamb's Essays of Elia*, Tokyo, 1964, which contains a foreword by Professor George L. Barnett. The book is divided into two parts, the first of which is concerned with Lamb's style 'Lamb the Verbal Magician', and the second is entitled 'Lamb the frolic and the gentle'. The book has one index of subjects and another of words and phrases. Professor Fukuda is also the author of papers on 'Charles Lamb as an Accountant', 'Lamb's Humanity' and 'Charles Lamb's Character Sketches.' (Possibly unpublished).

Fulleylove, John, 1845–1908. Artist, member of the Royal Institute of Painters in Water Colours. Exhibited much in London from 1871–93 and has pictures in the Victoria and Albert Museum and a number of provincial galleries. Bronze Medal in Paris in 1899. Illustrated with Herbert Railton *In the Footprints of Charles Lamb* by Benjamin Ellis Martin, 1891. The drawings also appeared in *Scribner's Magazine* in March and April, 1890, to illustrate Martin's article there.

Garnett, Richard, 1835–1906. Librarian, poet and critic. Keeper of the Printed Books at the British Museum. Dr Garnett wrote the explanatory notes on the facsimiles in the elaborate Boston Bibliophile Society edition of *The Letters of Charles Lamb* issued about 1905. He was the author and editor of many books, a number of which dealt with some of those known to Charles Lamb. Among them were *Relics of Shelley*, 1862; *Select Letters of P.B. Shelley*, 1882; *Confessions of an English Opium Eater*, with notes of De Quincey's conversations by Richard Woodhouse, 1885; *Prologue to Hellas*, P.B. Shelley, 1886; *Shelley and Lord Beaconsfield*, 1887; *Life of Carlyle*, 1887; *Tales and Stories of Mary Wollstonecraft Shelley*, 1891; *The Collected Works of Thomas Love Peacock*, 10 volumes, 1891–2; *William Blake. Painter and Poet*, 1895; *Poems of S.T. Coleridge*, 1898; ' *Original Poetry by Victor and Cazaire*, P.B. and Elizabeth Shelley, 1898; *'Thomas Moore' Anecdotes*, 1898; *Essays of an Ex-Librarian*, includes chapters on Coleridge, Shelley, Beckford, Thomas Moore and T.L. Peacock, 1901; *Journal of Edward Ellerker Williams*, 1902; *Browning's Essay on Shelley*, 1903; *Life of Coleridge*, 1904; *Letters of T.L. Peacock to Edward Hookham and P.B. Shelley*, 1910; *Letters about Shelley*, 1917.

Garnett also wrote with Sir Edmund Gosse *English Literature. An Illustrated Record* in four volumes, 1903–4. Volume IV which dealt with the Lamb period was written by Gosse. There are many contributions by Garnett in the *Dictionary of National Biography*. Garnett also wrote the article on Charles Lamb in *Celebrities of the Century*, 1890 (revised edition). His most famous book is *The Twilight of the Gods*, 1888, a volume of short stories; but the service which would perhaps have been most appreciated by Lamb, could he have availed himself of it, was the editing by Richard Garnett of the British Museum *General Catalogue of Printed Books*, 1881–89.

Garrick Plays. David Garrick, the celebrated actor, bequeathed his famous collection of English plays to the British Museum in 1779. He had acquired much of the collection from Cartwright's books at Dulwich. Charles Lamb made great use of these plays at the Museum, first for his *Dramatic Specimens* published in 1808, and later for his contributions to Hone's *Table Book* in 1827.

Gattie, Henry, 1774–1844. Actor and singer. Appeared in Bath in 1807, then in London at the Lyceum in 1813 under S.J. Arnold. He was a member of the Drury Lane company from 1813 until his retirement in 1833. He was famous for old man parts, particularly Monsieur Morbleu in Moncrieff's *Monsieur Tonson*, first played at Drury Lane in 1821. He was said to be the best Dr Caius of his time. Hazlitt praised him as Old Barnacle in *The Romp* at Drury Lane in 1817. He is mentioned by Lamb in his essay 'Stage Illusion', and is called 'Gatty' by Lamb.

Charles Cowden Clarke in *Recollections of Writers*, 1878, states that the brothers Gattie—Frederick, William, Henry and John Byng Gattie—were friends of Leigh Hunt and Vincent Novello. It is probable that Lamb met them at Novello's house. Hunt wrote a 'Sonnet to Henry Robinson, John Gattie and Vincent Novello', admonishing them for being late for an appointment. When Henry Gattie retired from the stage he opened a cigar shop at Oxford frequented by many members of the university who appreciated his dry humour.

Gifford, William, 1756–1826. Critic, poet and editor. After a short time at sea he was apprenticed to a cobbler, but because of his ability was befriended and eventually sent to Oxford. He published *The Baviad*, 1794, a satire against the Della Cruscans and *The Maeviad*, 1795, a satire against minor dramatists. He edited the works of Massinger, Ford and Ben Jonson. Editor of *The Anti-Jacobin* and later of the *Quarterly Review*, 1809–24, he bitterly attacked the 'Cockney School of poetry'. In addition to attacks on Keats and Hazlitt, he referred to Lamb's comments on Ford in the *Dramatic Specimens* as 'the blasphemies of a maniac'. Southey wrote to Gifford in protest and the latter replied that he had used the words in ignorance of Lamb's history. In 1814 Lamb's review of Wordsworth's *Excursion* appeared in *The Quarterly Review*. Lamb says Gifford had made so many alterations 'that charm if it had any is all gone: more than a third of the substance is cut away .... Every warm expression is changed for a nasty cold one.'

In 1816 Gifford persuaded Murray not to publish the two volumes of Lamb's works which the Olliers issued in 1818. In 1819 Lamb had a sonnet in *The Examiner*, 'St Crispin to Mr Gifford'. In 1820 Gifford reviewed John Clare's poems favourably in the *Quarterly*. Among Gifford's friends were Grosvenor Bedford, Southey's friend and Octavius Gilchrist.

Gilchrist, Anne, 1828–85. Authoress. Wife of Alexander Gilchrist, who wrote the *Life of William Blake*, which was completed by his widow. Mrs Gilchrist wrote the volume in the Eminent Women series on *Mary Lamb* in 1883. It reprints Mary Lamb's essay 'On Needle-Work' from the *British Lady's Magazine*.

Gilfillan, George, 1813–78. Poet and critic, educated at Glasgow University. Author of *A Gallery of Literary Portraits*, 1845, which includes Charles Lamb, Godwin, Hazlitt, De Quincey, Wordsworth, Allan Cunningham, Keats, Southey and others. These sketches had originally appeared in his friend, Thomas Aird's *Dumfries Herald*. A *Second Gallery of Literary Portraits*, 1850, included Byron, Hood, Mary Shelley, Leigh Hunt, Thomas Moore and others. A third series was issued in 1854. Gilfillan wrote many books including lives of Sir Walter Scott and Burns. He also edited the Library Edition of *Poets of Britain* in forty-eight volumes, 1853–60. Among his friends were 'Christopher North', De Quincey and Carlyle.

Gill, Owen A. *See* W.G.R. Browne.

Gillman, Dr James, 1792–1839. Surgeon at Highgate in whose house Coleridge lived from 1816 until his death in 1834. Coleridge came to Gillman as a patient in an attempt to break the habit of taking laudanum; he remained with the doctor as a friend. Lamb and many of Coleridge's other friends visited him at Gillman's house. Mrs Coleridge and her daughter, Sara, were there in 1822–3. Crabb Robinson maintained in 1816 that Gillman had treated him with rudeness and Lamb had a similar comment, but the Gillmans did all they could to make Coleridge comfortable, even building a fine new study for him, and helping with a new edition of his poems. In return he gave Gillman the benefit of the 1828 edition and praised the doctor and his wife in his will.

When Lamb was ill in 1825 Gillman attended him, and the alleged rudeness could not have amounted to much, for writing of Coleridge's death in 1834 Lamb said 'I love the faithful Gillmans more than while they exercised their virtues towards him living.' Lamb's letter to Gillman in 1830 has the memorable reference to the 'golden works of the dear, fine, silly old angel', that is, Thomas Fuller. In 1838 James Gillman published through William Pickering *The Life of Samuel Taylor Coleridge*. It was to be in two volumes, but only one was ever issued.

Gillman, Rev. James, 1808–77. Son of Dr James Gillman, Coleridge's friend. At one time a schoolmaster, he later became Rector of Barfreston, Kent, and subsequently Vicar of Holy Trinity Church, Lambeth. Lamb wrote to him on 7 May 1833 about an appointment Gillman wished to obtain at Enfield.

Gillman, Russell Davis. Editor of *The Letters of Charles Lamb*, 1905, published in George Newnes Thin Paper Classics edition. Frontispiece by A.S. Hartrick, title page illustrated by Garth Jones.

Gillray, James, 1757–1815. Caricaturist. Produced many political caricatures. He drew the cartoon to illustrate the poem 'The New Morality' in The *Anti-Jacobin Review* in 1798 which depicted Charles Lloyd and Charles Lamb as 'Toad and Frog'. The verse by Canning which accompanied the drawing had

> C------ge and S--th-y, L---d, and L--b and Co.
> Tune all your mystic harps to praise LEPAUX!

La Révellière-Lepaux was a French politician who was hostile to the Christian religion.

Gisburne, Mary. In *Blackwood's Magazine* in 1829 Lamb printed two sets of verses, one in May entitled 'The Christening' and a second 'For the Album of Miss——, French Teacher at Mrs Gisborn's School, Enfield.' Mary Gisburne kept a ladies school at Enfield and married Charles May. W.C. Hazlitt in his *Mary and Charles Lamb*, 1874, states that both the families of the Mays and the Gisburnes lived in Enfield, where Charles May's brother, Dr May, was headmaster of The Palace School. Charles and Mary Lamb were sponsors to the child of Charles and Mary May who was christened on 25 March 1829.

Gladman Family. Mrs Gladman was born a Bruton. She was the sister of Mary Field, Lamb's grandmother and thus his great aunt. She lived at the farmhouse at Mackery End, Hertfordshire. In his essay with this title Lamb also refers to Gladman and Bruton cousins. Much information about the Gladman family is contained in Miss Mann's article in the *C.L.S. Bulletin*, No. 199, and in Hine's *Charles Lamb and his Hertfordshire*.

Glover, Julia, 1779–1850. Actress. Born Julia Betterton, she claimed descent from the great Betterton. Appeared on the stage as a child in Fielding's *Tom Thumb*. Played at York and first appeared in London at Covent Garden in 1797. She was most successful at Covent Garden, Drury Lane, and particularly at the Haymarket. Among her parts were Mrs Candour, Mrs Malaprop and Mrs Heidelberg. She was the original Alhadra in Coleridge's *Remorse* in 1813.

In 1814 at Drury Lane she played the Queen in *Richard III* to Kean's Richard and Emilia to his Othello. In 1816 she played as leading lady with Kean in *A New Way to Pay Old Debts*. She also appeared as Hamlet, fairly successfully, but failed in the part of Falstaff. She played with Liston in *Paul Pry* in 1825.

She has been described as a very famous actress and was praised by many of the critics of the day. Macready called her 'a rare thinking actress'. Lamb refers to her rather disparagingly in his 'The New Acting' in *The Examiner* in 1813.

Goddard House. The school at Widford, Hertfordshire, run by the daughters of Randal Norris. Lucas obtained interesting reminiscences of the school and Lamb's visits to it from Mrs Coe (Elizabeth Hunt) who had been a pupil there, which he prints in his *Life of Charles Lamb*.

Godwin, Mary Jane. Second wife of William Godwin, whom she married in 1801. She was a widow, a Mrs Clairmont, who already had two children, Charles and Jane Clairmont. She was largely responsible for the establishment of the Juvenile Library which published the Lambs' children's books. She seems to have had some ability and was able to make translations, but she was generally disliked by members of the Lamb circle. Lamb said she had alienated all Godwin's old friends; he called her 'the bad baby' and 'a very disgusting woman'. She is the original of his sketch 'Tom Pry's Wife'. Other friends who equally disliked her were Mrs Fenwick, at one time manager of the Juvenile Library, Robert Lloyd and Mary Godwin. The latter was glad to flee with Shelley to avoid her.

When Mrs Godwin's daughter, Jane Clairmont, accompanied Mary and Shelley, her mother pursued her to France, but was unable to persuade her to return.

Kenneth Cameron in his *Shelley and his Circle* maintains that Mrs Godwin has been maligned and he states that Aaron Burr who knew her well in 1808 described her as 'A sensible, amiable woman' and was impressed by her kindness and generosity. Wordsworth evidently thought well of her also for he inscribed a copy of his *Yarrow Revisited* to her 'in token of a sincere regard'.

Godwin, Mary Wollstonecraft. *See* Mary Wollstonecraft Shelley.

Godwin, William, 1756–1836. Philosopher and novelist. At one time a Presbyterian minister, but on a change in his theological views he resigned his pastorate and devoted himself to literature. An advocate of political and social reform, his most famous work *Inquiry Concerning Political Justice*, 1793, advocated the overthrow of authority and abolition of marriage. In 1797 he married Mary Wollstonecraft by whom he had a daughter, Mary, who became the second wife of the poet Shelley. Godwin's wife died in 1797, and in 1801 he married Mrs Mary Jane Clairmont.

Godwin's works included several novels: *Caleb Williams*, 1794; *St Leon*, 1799; *Fleetwood*, 1804; and *Cloudesley*, 1830. He also wrote a *Life of Chaucer*, 1803; *An Essay on Sepulchres*, 1808; and the *Lives of the Necromancers*, 1834.

Although Lamb and Godwin were not intimate friends the association between them was fairly constant and its importance was increased by the publication of a number of the Lambs' books for children from the Juvenile Library. (*See* separate entry). Charles Lamb wrote the Epilogue to Godwin's tragedy *Antonio*, which was produced by Kemble at Drury Lane on 13 December 1800 and hopelessly damned. Lamb tells the story in a passage in his essay 'The Old Actors' in the *London Magazine* in April 1822 which was omitted from the *Elia* volume. Lamb also wrote a prologue for Godwin's tragedy, *Faulkener*, produced at Drury Lane in 1807.

Lamb was several times responsible for helping Godwin in his financial difficulties: in 1822 he helped to raise a subscription for him and gave £50 to it. William Macdonald in the notes to his edition of *The Essays of Elia*, 1903, describes Godwin in a memorable phrase 'a notably naïve and generous-minded borrower.'

Lucas records that Lamb once said Godwin had read more books that were not worth reading than any man in England. Many books have been written about Godwin and more about his son-in-law, Shelley, and a number of them refer to his association with Charles Lamb.

Godwin, William, Junior, 1803–32. Journalist and illustrator, son of William Godwin and Mary Jane Clairmont. He was a reporter on *The Morning Chronicle*. He was heartily disliked by Crabb Robinson, who tells us that Godwin's son inspired Lamb's Lepus paper 'Many Friends' which appeared in the *New Times* in 1825. He wrote a novel, *Transfusion*, which his father published after the son's death from cholera in 1832. Kegan Paul states he was 'much loved by his friends.'

Gordon, George Stuart, 1881–1942. Merton Professor of English at Oxford. President of Magdalen College, Oxford. Educated at Glasgow University and Oriel College, Oxford. In 1920 he wrote the centenary article on *The Essays of Elia* for the *Times Literary Supplement*. It was reprinted with alterations as the introduction to his *Charles Lamb: Prose & Poetry*, 1921, which had notes by A.M.D. Hughes. Gordon contributed other articles to the *T.L.S.* from time to time, some of which were collected in *The Lives of Authors*, 1950. There are references to Lamb in *The Letters of George S. Gordon 1902–1942*, 1943, and in his *The Discipline of Letters*, 1946. His

More Companionable Books, 1947, reprints talks for the B.B.C. and includes 'The Humour of Charles Lamb', 'Lamb's Letters' as well as chapters on Walton, Sterne and Cowper.

In a letter to Florence Nixon on 17 September 1920 Gordon writing of Lamb's letters said 'I have read and read them for fifteen years, and the only fault I find in them is that they make all other Letters seem poor and thin.' Gordon also wrote *English Literature and the Classics*, 1912; *Shakespeare's Comedy & other Studies*, 1944; and the introduction to *Third Leaders Reprinted from The Times*, 1928.

Gould, Mrs. *See* Fanny Burrell.

Grabianski, Janusz. Polish artist. In 1969 J.M. Dent published *Ten Tales from Shakespeare* for which Grabianski chose and illustrated ten of 'Lamb's Tales'. Among the pictures were scenes of Venice, Elsinore, Prospero's realm and Fairyland.

Grant, Arthur. Author of *In the Old Paths. Memories of Literary Pilgrimages*, 1913, which contains a chapter on 'Wheathampstead and Charles Lamb.' Also wrote *Rambles in Arcadia* which deals with Lamb's Hertfordshire.

Grant, Mary, b.1740. A nurse mentioned several times in Charles and Mary Lamb's letters, first in June 1804, again in July 1805. In Mary Lamb's letter to Sarah Hazlitt on 7 November 1809 she states that 'Nurse' is now established in the 'Incurable Ward'. Major Butterworth found out that she was admitted to Westminster Hospital in September 1809. She is again mentioned in Lamb's letter to Manning on 2 January 1810. Possibly she may have helped the Lambs during Mary's illnesses.

Grasmere. *See* Dove Cottage.

Grattan, Thomas Colley, 1792–1864. Travel writer, novelist and poet, who for some years lived in France and Belgium. He did translations from contemporary French poets, and contributed to the *Westminster* and *Edinburgh Reviews* and the *New Monthly Magazine*. He was at one time British Consul at Boston, U.S.A. He wrote several novels including *Traits of Travel, or Tales of Men and Cities*, 1829, and *The Heiress of Bruges*, 1830. He also wrote *Highways and Byways, or Tales of the Roadside, picked up in the French Provinces by a Walking Gentleman* in 1823, with a second series in 1825 and a third in 1827. He sent a copy of the first series to Lamb who mentions it in a letter of 9 February 1823 to John Howard Payne. Grattan was then living in Paris and Lamb writes 'Tell Mr Grattan I thank him for his book, which as far as I have read it is a very *companionable one.* 'Perhaps Lamb met Grattan on his visit to Paris in 1822. In a postscript to his letter to James Kenney in September 1823 Lamb has 'Pray tell Mr Grattan I sh'd have been better pleased if he had taken a meal with me. I hope he will do so another time.'

Gray, Miss. Actress. A pupil of Fanny Kelly. Lamb's letter to Miss Kelly on 6 July 1825 thanks her for tickets for Miss Gray's performance at the English Opera House. S.J. Arnold had also sent tickets and, from Lamb's remarks, it seems that Miss Gray was known to him. (The letter is printed in part in Lucas 1935 and in full in Holman's *Lamb's 'Barbara S——*, 1935.) A further reference to her is given in a letter to Coleridge on 22 March 1826 when Lamb describes Miss Gray's manners with 'her kitten eyes.'

Gregynog Press. A private press established in 1923 at Gregynog, Newtown, Monmouthshire, by Gwendoline and Margaret Davies for the production of beautiful books. It ceased to exist in 1940, but during its life printed forty-two books. In February 1931 it issued *Elia and the Last Essays of Elia* in two volumes. The book was printed in Baskerville type on Japanese vellum, with wood engravings by Horace W. Bray from Elia prints lent from the collection of Edward J. Finch. 260 copies were bound in grey buckram and sold at five guineas and 25 copies in rich brown levant morocco, price ten guineas.

Greta Hall. A house near Keswick in the vale of Derwentwater, on the bank of the river Greta and about a mile from the lake. Coleridge lived here from August 1800 to the autumn of 1803. In August 1802 the Lambs visited the Coleridges at Greta Hall for three weeks, staying also with the Clarksons for a few days in Dove Cottage, although the Wordsworths were absent. Lamb has left a fairly full account of the visit in his famous letter to Manning on 24 September 1802 and he also referred to it in a letter to Coleridge on September 8.

Great Hall comprised two houses under one roof, part occupied by the landlord, Mr Jackson. In 1803 Robert Southey and his family moved there sharing the Coleridges' part of the house. After the landlord left and when Coleridge left later in the year, Southey and his family occupied the whole building. With him lived Mrs Lovell, who was his wife's sister and Mrs Coleridge and her children. Southey lived there until his death in 1843.

Sara Coleridge, S.T.C.'s daughter, who was born in the house in December 1802, has left a detailed description of it in a letter to her daughter written specially for the 'Recollections of the Early Life of Sara Coleridge', printed in the *Memoirs and Letters of Sara Coleridge*, 1873 (Third Edition).

Greville, Mary Ellen, Gerbini. *See* Francis Maria Kelly.

Griggs, Earl Leslie, 1899–1975. Professor of English, University of California. Vice President of the Charles Lamb Society since 1950; lectured to the Society in 1956 on 'Coleridge and his friends' in which he said that Lamb was in no way inferior to Coleridge. In 1972 he gave the first Ernest G. Crowsley Memorial Lecture on 'Charles Lamb and Coleridge'. Author of *Hartley Coleridge, his Life & Work*, 1929; *Letters of Hartley Coleridge*, 1936 (with Grace Evelyn Griggs); and *Coleridge Fille: A Biography of Sara Coleridge*, 1940. Professor Griggs edited the *Collected Letters of S.T. Coleridge*, 6 vols., 1956–71. He also edited with Edmund Blunden *Coleridge: Studies by Several Hands*, 1934. He has frequently contributed to periodicals, mainly articles on the Coleridges: among these are *M.P.*, *M.L.N.*, *H.L.Q.*, *R.E.S.*, and *English*.

Grimaldi, Joseph, c.1778–1837. The famous clown. Played at Drury Lane, Covent Garden, and Sadler's Wells. Perhaps the most celebrated clown on the English stage. In 1818 he had purchased an eighth share in Sadler's Wells and later was assistant manager there. He retired in 1823 and was succeeded at Covent Garden by his son. Hood addressed verses to him in his *Odes and Addresses* and in 1828 wrote a speech for the clown's farewell performance.

Lamb refers to him as 'our Joe—the immortal Grimaldi' in his review of the *Odes and Addresses* in *The New Times*. He also mentions him in his essay 'The Religion of Actors' in *The New Monthly Magazine*. His son, Joseph S. Grimaldi, who played Friday in *Robinson Crusoe* in 1814 died in 1832, aged 30.

Gutch, John Mathew, 1776–1861. Journalist, law stationer, bookseller and later a banker. Educated at Christ's Hospital with Lamb and Coleridge. In 1800 Gutch, then a law stationer in Southampton Buildings, Chancery Lane, offered the Lambs rooms in his house, which they accepted gratefully. Shortly afterwards Lamb visited Gutch's family at Oxford and was much impressed with the colleges and buildings. Gutch's father was the Rev. J. Gutch, antiquary and Registrar of Oxford University. Cardinal Newman was once one of his curates at St Clements.

In 1803 Gutch went to Bristol and became proprietor and printer of *Felix Farley's Bristol Journal*. It was in this journal that Lamb's letter in praise of Fanny Kelly's acting appeared in 1819. Gutch issued two catalogues as a second hand bookseller in 1810 and 1812. From 1828 to 1830 he was joint editor of *The New Times*. His published works included *Caraboo: Narrative of a Singular Imposition ...*, 1817; an edition of Wither's *Juvenilia*, 1820; *Observations ... upon the Writings of the Ancients ...*, 1827; and *A Lyttel Geste of Robyn Hode*, 1847. The latter volume mentions Lamb in connexion with George Wither.

Gutch possessed a valuable library, rich in George Wither. He printed privately an interleaved copy of Wither's poems which he lent to Lamb who annotated it and returned it. The amusing story of further annotation by a Dr John Nott is fully told in Lucas's edition of the *Miscellaneous Prose*, 1903. Gutch's book, which subsequently belonged to Swinburne who told the story of it in his *Miscellanies* in 1886, is also notable for containing the account which Brook Pulham wrote on the flyleaf of the volume of Lamb's adventures in the stocks at Barnett. Lamb told the story in the 'Confessions of H.F.V.H. Delamore Esq' in the *London Magazine* in April 1821. A later owner of the Wither volume was the American collector J.A. Spoor. Numerous letters from Lamb to Gutch are printed in Lucas's edition and there are references to him in Lamb's letters to his other friends.

Guthkelch, A. Senior English Master, Bancroft's School and Lecturer in English at King's College, London. In 1906 George Bell & Sons published *Charles Lamb: Essays and Letters. Selected and edited by A. Guthkelch*. The book contains a useful sketch map of Lamb's London in 1800.

Hall, Samuel Carter, 1800–89. Author and editor. Born at Waterford and came to London in 1821. Was literary secretary to Ugo Foscolo in 1822, a Parliamentary reporter at the House of Lords in 1823 and a member of the Inner Temple. Although entered a student in 1824 he was not called to the Bar until 1841. Edited *The Amulet*, 1826–36; *Literary Observer*, 1823; *New Monthly Magazine*, 1830–36; *The Book of Gems of Poets and Artists*, 1838. Founded *The Art Journal* in 1839 and edited it until 1876. Published *A Book of Memories of Great Men and Women of the Age, from Personal Acquaintance*, 1871. Both the *Book of Gems* and the *Book of Memories* include Lamb, and the latter book has memories of most of Lamb's friends. Hall says he first met Lamb in Fleet Street and during 1827 or 1828 met him several times at the Gillmans'.

Hallward, N.L. Professor of English Literature and Principal of the Ravenshaw College, Cuttack, India. Editor with S.C. Hill of Macmillan's edition of *The Essays of Elia*, 1895, and *The Last Essays of Elia*, 1900.

Hancock, Robert, 1730–1817. Engraver at Battersea Enamel Works, then draughtsman and engraver at the Worcester Porcelain Works. He was one of the proprietors of the works from 1772 to 1774. Later became an engraver in mezzotint. He engraved portraits after Sir Joshua Reynolds. In later life he lived at Bristol and about 1798 drew crayon portraits of Charles Lamb, Wordsworth, Southey and Coleridge which were engraved by R. Woodman for Cottle's

Reminiscences. The originals were purchased for the National Portrait Gallery.

Hardy, Thomas, 1752–1832. Scottish bootmaker and radical politician. Came to London in 1774 and opened a shop at No. 9 Piccadilly. In January 1792 he founded The London Corresponding Society to promote parliamentary reform. The subscription was a penny a week. From its original nine members it spread until it was said to have 30,000 members. In 1794 Hardy, Horne Tooke, Holcroft, Thelwall and others were arrested on a charge of high treason. Hardy's trial began in October and lasted eight days when he was acquitted as were the others. Erskine was the principal defence counsel and Sheridan was a witness for the defence. At the dinner to celebrate the acquittal the Earl of Stanhope ('Citizen' Stanhope) presided. From 1797 Hardy had moved to a shop in Fleet Street.

Charles Lamb wrote a letter to him on 24 April 1824 about a novel by Miss Hazlitt that Hardy seems to have been helping her to publish. He was a friend of William Godwin and was known to William Hone.

Hare, Julius Charles, 1795–1855. Clergyman and essayist. Educated at Charterhouse and Cambridge. Fellow of Trinity, 1818. About 1819–20 he studied law and had chambers in Hare Court, Temple, but soon abandoned it. Appointed to a living at Hurstmonceaux in Sussex, he became Archdeacon of Lewes and a Chaplain to the Queen. With his brother, Augustus, he published *Guesses at Truth*, 1827.

Thomas Hughes in his *Memoir of Daniel Macmillan*, 1882, relates that Julius Hare once attended a dinner and sat next to Lamb, who praised De Quincey also at the dinner. Lucas thinks it was a *London Magazine* dinner, for in 1824 Hare had contributed to the *London* a review of Landor's *Imaginary Conversations*. He had acted for Landor, who was in Italy, in the negotiations with Taylor & Hessey who published the book. Hare had a remarkable library of some 12,000 volumes, especially rich in German literature.

Harley, John Pritt, 1786–1858. Actor and singer. Frequently played at Drury Lane and at one time was stage manager of the Lyceum. First appeared at the English Opera House in 1815 and at Drury Lane later the same year. In 1816 he played Bobadil in *Every Man in his Humour* to Kean's Kitely. He succeeded to many of the parts of his friend, Bannister, when the latter retired from the stage. In 1833 he became Master and Treasurer of Drury Lane Theatrical Fund. When Braham opened St James's Theatre in December 1835 Harley joined the company as chief comedian and stage manager. In 1838 he was with Macready at Covent Garden and afterwards with Madame Vestris and Charles Mathews.

Harley, who had a counter tenor voice, was very popular as a comic singer. He is said to have played Shakespeare's clowns with 'rich natural humour'. Being very thin he was known sarcastically as 'Fat Jack'. Lamb mentions him in a letter to Hone in July 1825, 'I have sent up my petit farce altered; and Harley is at the theatre now. It cannot come out for some weeks.' This was *The Pawnbroker's Daughter* which was rejected. In May 1829 Lamb wrote to Harley at Kenney's suggestion offering the song 'A Sentimental Butcher' from the farce for him to sing at his benefit. Harley had a passion for collecting walking sticks and more than 300 were included in his effects when sold.

In his essay 'The Old Actors' in the *London Magazine* Lamb has a reference to the elder Harley, presumably a relation of John Pritt Harley.

Harlowe, Sarah, 1765–1852. Actress. Although she had married Godolphin Waldron, prompter of the Haymarket and an actor himself, she played under the name of Mrs Harlowe. She appeared at Sadler's Wells as a singer and actress. First appeared at Drury Lane in 1790, and played at the Haymarket as well. She frequently acted chambermaids, romps, shrews and old women. In 1806 she played the Maid to Melisinda in Lamb's Mr H—— at Drury Lane. Among her best parts were Lucy in *The Rivals* and Widow Warren in *The Road to Ruin*. She also played many of Mrs Jordan's parts. In 1826 she retired from the stage.

Harness, Rev William, 1790–1869. Author. Educated at Harrow where Byron was a schoolfellow. Passed to Christ's College, Cambridge. Was Curate at Kelmeston, Hants, had a chapel at Hampstead and was minister and evening lecturer at St Anne's, Soho. Wrote reviews for the *Quarterly Review*, edited Shakespeare's *Works*, 1825, a 'family' edition of Massinger's plays in 1830 and Ford's *Dramatic Works* in 1831. His tragedy *Welcome and Farewell* was privately printed in 1837. His *Life of M.R. Mitford* was published in 1870.

Among his friends were Mrs Siddons, Fanny Kemble, Mr and Mrs Charles Kean, Southey, Wordsworth, M.R. Mitford, Joanna Baillie, Harriet Martineau, Catherine Fanshawe and Byron.

In 1823 Lamb wrote to Harness returning as unacceptable a manuscript the latter wanted to publish in the *London Magazine* that he had sent to Lamb as an important contributor to the periodical. John Payne Collier stated that he met both Lamb and Miss Mitford at a dinner at Harness's house in 1832, when Lamb made his 'Witch of End-door' joke.

Harrison, Frederic, 1831–1923. Lawyer and philosopher. Educated at King's College, London, and Wadham College, Oxford.

Called to the Bar in 1858. Lectured in Oxford, Cambridge and Chicago. Author of *Tennyson, Ruskin, Mill and other literary estimates*, 1899, that contains 'Lamb and Keats', an address on the unveiling of the portraits of Lamb and Keats at the Passmore Edwards Free Library at Edmonton. Among his other works were *Studies in Early Victorian Literature*, 1895, and *The Choice of Books*, 1903. In the latter book, in an essay on 'Historic London', he quotes Carlyle's remark that 'it is next to an impossibility that a London-born man should not be a stunted one', and Harrison adds the comment that the long catalogue of the 'stunted ones' includes Chaucer, Milton, Ben Jonson, Spenser, Pope, Byron, Keats, Bacon, Sir T. More, Bentham, Gibbon, Lamb, Turner and Disraeli.

Harrison, Wilmot. Author of *Memorable London Houses*, 1889, 3rd edition enlarged 1890. This refers to Charles Lamb's residences in Russell Street and Islington.

Hart, Hannah. *See* Robert Lloyd.

Harvey, William, 1796–1866. Artist and wood engraver. Born at Newcastle and apprenticed to Thomas Bewick, whom he assisted with his woodcuts for Aesop's *Fables*. He came to London in 1817 and became a pupil of B.R. Haydon, and executed on wood the large cut of the 'Death of Dentatus' by Haydon. In 1824 he relinquished engraving and devoted himself to designs for wood cuts and copper plates.

Among his best designs are those for the *Arabian Nights*, the vignettes for Northcote's *Fables*. He also illustrated *Knight's Shakespeare*, *The Babes in the Wood*, *The Blind Beggar of Bethnal Green* and Hood's *Eugene Aram*. He did the illustrations for W.F. Mylius's *A First Book of Poetry*, 1811, which contained poems by Charles and Mary Lamb, as well as for editions of *Mrs Leicester's School*, 1825, and *Tales from Shakespeare*, 1831.

Hathaway, Matthias. Steward at Christ's Hospital from 1790 to 1813 when he retired. He succeeded John Perry who was steward at the school in Lamb's time. Hathaway is mentioned in Lamb's essay on Christ's Hospital. Leigh Hunt, who was at Christ's Hospital after Lamb, states that he was nicknamed 'the Yeoman' because Shakespeare's father-in-law of the same name was described as 'a substantial yeoman.' Hathaway was a member of the Committee of the Benevolent Society of Blues. The Steward was a most important member of the school staff who carried out most of the administrative work.

Haven, Richard, b.1924. Professor of English, University of

Massachusetts, Amherst. Contributed 'The Romantic Art of Charles Lamb' to *Journal of English Literary History*, 1963.

Hawkes, Charles Pascoe, b.1877. Barrister of the Inner Temple. Registrar in the Supreme Court. Educated at Dulwich College and Trinity College, Cambridge. Was also an artist and cartoonist. Author of *Chambers in the Temple*, 1930, which contains a plan of the Temple. There are only a few references to Lamb in the book, but its subject and atmosphere make it of interest to Elians. Hawkes also wrote other books and contributed to *Punch*, *The Times*, *Sunday Times*, *XIX Century* and *Cornhill*.

Hayden, John Olin, b.1932. Professor of English, University of California. Author of *The Romantic Reviewers 1802–1824*, 1972, and editor of *Romantic Bards and British Reviewers*, 1972.

Haydon, Benjamin Robert, 1786–1846. Historical painter and writer on art. Studied at the Royal Academy schools. Won prizes with his pictures the *Death of Dentatus* and *The Judgement of Solomon*. He had a stormy career in which he quarrelled with the Royal Academy and although he painted many pictures, he did not receive all the praise he felt due to him. Among his best known pictures were *Christ's Entry into Jerusalem*, 1820; *Lazarus*, 1821–3; *Punch*, 1829; *Wellington at Waterloo*, 1839; and the *Banishment of Aristides*, 1846. He also did portraits of Leigh Hunt, and Wordsworth, both of which are in the National Portrait Gallery. He was among those who championed the Elgin Marbles when they came to England.

Haydon wrote a number of works on art and his *Lectures on Painting and Design* were published in two volumes in 1844–6. He contributed the article on Painting to the seventh edition of the *Encyclopaedia Britannica*. He is best remembered for his *Autobiography and Memoirs*, one of the most delightful of literary journals and full of references to his friends.

Haydon was twice imprisoned for debt and when in 1823 his effects were sold, his friends Thomas Barnes, Dr Darling, Sir George Beaumont and Wilkie bought items at the sale so that he would have something to start work with when he came out of the King's Bench Prison.

Among Haydon's friends were Keats, Lamb, Hazlitt, Wordsworth, Horace Smith, Samuel Rogers, M.R. Mitford and T.N. Talfourd. In 1812 he attended the curous christening party of William Hazlitt's son. James Elmes writing in *Notes & Queries* in 1859 stated that 'Lamb and Haydon were often like boys, so boisterous in their mirth and hilarity.' In 1817 occurred the famous party in Haydon's studio where Lamb misbehaved himself in teasing John Kingston, the

Comptroller of Stamps. The guests there included Wordsworth, Monkhouse, Keats, Ritchie and John Landseer.

In 1820 Lamb wrote both Latin and English verses in *The Champion* on Haydon's picture of *Christ's Entry into Jerusalem*. Haydon sometimes introduced portraits of his friends and others into his historical pictures. In this one are the heads of Wordsworth, Hazlitt, Keats, Newton and Voltaire. In his *'Examiner' Examined* Edmund Blunden wrote that in this picture are 'some of the women of the Keats circle waiting to be recognized', and in Appendix III in *The Life and Death of Benjamin Robert Haydon* by Eric George it is mentioned that 'Lamb too is said to be there.' (Second edition 1967). In a letter in the *Times Literary Supplement* of 25 January 1947 Willard Pope states that he cannot identify Lamb, but that William Bewick and probably J. Hamilton Reynolds are there. Verses in praise of Haydon's paintings were written by many of his contemporaries including Keats, Wordsworth, J.H. Reynolds, Leigh Hunt and M.R. Mitford.

In 1846 because of the poor response to his numerous works Haydon committed suicide.

Hays, Mary, c.1763–1843. Author, political and moral reformer. Friend of Mary Wollstonecraft, William Godwin and Crabb Robinson. The latter described her in his *Diary* as 'my old friend' and in August 1819 gives there a summary of her character. She was acquainted with Coleridge, Southey and George Dyer and she wrote a number of love letters to Charles Lloyd. Lamb refers to Lloyd's curious letter to her in his letter to Manning in February 1800. He also mentions her in his letter to Rickman in December 1816. She wrote a novel *Memoirs of Emma Courtney* said to contain her love letters to Godwin and William Frend. Charles Lloyd attacked her in his novel *Edmund Oliver*. In a letter to Matilda Betham in September 1811 Lamb wrote

> G——forbid I should
> pass my days
> with Miss H——ys

George Dyer mentions her in his *Memoirs of the Life and Writings of Robert Robinson*, 1796, as a woman of considerable literary merit, and as Robinson's 'sensible friend', although not all would agree with Dyer, who believed ill of no one. She seems also to have been known to Gilbert Imlay and Henry Fuseli. She is said to be the original of Bridgettina in Elizabeth Hamilton's novel *The Memoirs of Modern Philosophers*, 1800. Mary Hays herself wrote *Female Biography; or Memoirs of illustrious and celebrated Women of all ages and countries* in 1803 in six volumes.

Hayward, Abraham, 1801–84. Essayist and translator. Educated at Blundells School, Tiverton, studied law at the Inner Temple and called to the Bar in 1832. Became a Q.C. Well known as a raconteur. Contributed frequently to periodicals, especially the *Quarterly Review*. Published several volumes of essays, a book on whist and *The Art of Dining*, 1852. In 1833 he published a translation of Goethe's *Faust* to which Wordsworth had contributed a preface. Hayward sent a copy of this translation to Lamb; Crabb Robinson records in his *Diary* on 9 April 1833 that Lamb thought it well done. Hayward was editor of the *Law Magazine*.

Hazlitt, John, 1768–1837. Miniature painter. Elder brother of William Hazlitt. Studied under Sir Joshua Reynolds. He exhibited at the Royal Academy from 1788–1819. Among his portraits were those of his brother and sister, William and Margaret Hazlitt, S.T. Coleridge, Charles Kemble, 'Clio' Rickman and Joseph Lancaster. His friends included Thelwall, Stoddart, Godwin and Holcroft. His wife was a Miss Mary Pearce of Portsea and in a letter to Mrs S.T. Coleridge on 13 October 1804, Mary Lamb describes her as 'a pretty good humoured woman'. They had a daughter, Mary, who was a great favourite with the Lambs. Mary Lamb's letter of 7 November 1809 to Sarah Hazlitt has the comment that John Hazlitt 'has been very disorderly lately' with further elaboration. He was said to be a hard drinker.

Hazlitt, Margaret, 'Peggy', 1771–1844. Sister of John and William Hazlitt. Like her two brothers she also painted pictures. She was a great favourite of her brother, William, and of Mary Lamb, who mentions her in a letter to Mrs S.T. Coleridge on 13 October 1804. Peggy Hazlitt wrote a manuscript biographical sketch and diary of the early history of the Hazlitt family. Some of her pictures are in the Maidstone Museum. Her portrait by John Hazlitt is reproduced in W.C. Hazlitt's *Four Generations of a Literary Family*, 1897.

Hazlitt, Mary. Daughter of John Hazlitt, the miniature painter, and niece of William Hazlitt. She was well known to the Lambs; she was so fond of Charles that when a child she used to stop strangers in the street to tell them that 'Mr Lamb is coming to tea.' There is a letter from Lamb to her on 24 July 1823 in which he undertakes to read the manuscript of a novel she had written. In a letter to Thomas Hardy in April 1824 Lamb refers to her novel and states she is going as a governess to Dawlish. Later she opened her own school at Enfield and Lamb wrote to Walter Wilson in August 1832 asking if he could help her by finding pupils.

Hazlitt, William, 1778–1830. Critic and essayist. Began his career as a theological student and was then an artist before turning to literature. Met Coleridge in 1798 as recorded in his brilliant essay 'My

First Acquaintance with Poets', printed in *The Liberal* in 1823. In 1808 he married Sarah Stoddart, a great friend of the Lambs and sister of John Stoddart, later Chief Justice of Malta. They were divorced in 1822 and he married Mrs Bridgewater in 1824; she left him in 1827. Lamb attended Hazlitt's first wedding when Mary Lamb was bridesmaid.

Lamb and Hazlitt first met in 1804 through Coleridge and, although Hazlitt was of a 'prickly' nature, they remained friendly for most of their lives. In 1804 he painted Lamb's portrait which is now in the National Portrait Gallery. He was a frequent visitor to the Lambs' house and his essay 'On the Conversation of Authors' gives one of the best pictures we have of Lamb's Thursday evening parties. In 1812 Hazlitt lectured on the History of English Philosophy at the Russell Institution and at the Surrey Institution in 1818 on poetry. He contributed his 'Table Talk' and other essays to the *London Magazine* and wrote dramatic criticism for it.

In 1809 the Lambs visited the Hazlitts at Winterslow near Salisbury and repeated the visit in 1810. Lamb in his 'Letter of Elia to Robert Southey' published in the *London Magazine* in October 1823 wrote 'I think W.H. to be, in his natural and healthy state, one of the wisest and finest spirits breathing.' Hazlitt dedicated his *Characters of Shakespeare's Plays* to Lamb. As Lamb said in his letter to Southey, Hazlitt quarrelled with a great many people, but not always in bad temper. He was once knocked down by John Lamb, Charles's brother, after an argument on the colours of Holbein and Vandyke, but bore him no ill feelings.

Among Hazlitt's chief works are *The Round Table*, 1817; *Characters of Shakespeare's Plays*, 1817; *A View of the English Stage*, 1818; *Lectures on the English Poets*, 1818; *Lectures on the English Comic Writers*, 1819; *Table Talk*, 1821–2; *The Spirit of the Age*, 1825; and *The Plain Speaker*, 1826. In 1823 he published his *Liber Amoris* which tells of his infatuation with Sarah Walker.

Hazlitt has numerous references to Lamb in his writings which include those in his essays 'On the Conversation of Authors' (*Plain Speaker*), 'On the Pleasure of Hating' (*Plain Speaker*), 'My First Acquaintance with Poets' (*The Liberal* and *Literary Remains*), 'On Persons One Would Wish to Have Seen' (*Literary Remains*), 'On Great and Little Things' (*Table Talk—Bohn*), 'On Familiar Style' (*Table Talk*). Lamb helped Hazlitt with his *Select British Poets*, 1824, and in the first edition were some of Lamb's poems, but they were omitted in later editions with the work of all contemporary poets owing to copyright difficulties. In *The Spirit of the Age* Hazlitt has a chapter on Elia.

Hazlitt's importance as an essayist is such that much has been written about him and most of the books mention Lamb. Lists of the principal authorities are contained in the *Cambridge Bibliography of*

English Literature, P.P. Howe's *Life of William Hazlitt*, 1947, Herschel Baker's *William Hazlitt*, 1962, and in the section on Hazlitt by Elisabeth W. Schneider in *The English Romantic Poets & Essayists*, 1966.

Hazlitt, William Carew, 1834–1913. Bibliographer and author. Eldest son of William Hazlitt ('Registrar') and grandson of William Hazlitt, the essayist. Educated at Merchant Taylors' School and after following various occupations was called to the Bar at the Inner Temple in 1861. He wrote many books on bibliographical subjects, such as *A Handbook to the Popular, Poetical and Dramatic Literature of Great Britain*, 1867, and *Bibliographical Collections and Notes*. Among his main works were: a new edition of Dodsley's *Select Collection of Old Plays*, 1874–76; *Shakespeare's Library*, 1875; and *Poems and Plays of Thomas Randolph*, 1875. He also wrote books on coins; *The Confessions of a Collector*, 1897; *The Book Collector*, 1904; and edited the works of old English authors. He wrote several volumes for Eliot Stock's fascinating series 'The Book Lover's Library' among which were *Old Cookery Books*, *Gleanings in Old Garden Literature*, 1887, and *Studies in Jocular Literature*, 1890, the latter volume mentions Charles Lamb.

As a descendant of William Hazlitt, he was particularly interested in the essayist and his friends: among his books and essays on this subject were:

Memoirs of William Hazlitt: with Portions of his correspondence, 1867.
Works of William Hazlitt, 7 vols, 1869–86.
Mary and Charles Lamb: Poems, Letters and Remains, 1874.
Essays and Criticism by Thomas Griffiths Wainewright. Now first collected with some account of the author, 1880.
Offspring of Thought in Solitude: Modern Essays, 1884 (Includes 'Coleridge Abroad' and 'Charles Lamb').
Letters of Charles Lamb, 1886.
Four Generations of a Literary Family, 1897.
The Lambs: their Lives, their Friends and their Correspondence, 1897.
Lamb and Hazlitt. Further Letters and Records, 1900.
The Hazlitts, 1911.
The Later Hazlitts, 1912.
'Charles Lamb: Gleanings After his Biographers' in *Macmillan's Magazine*, 1867.
'Unpublished Letters of Charles Lamb' in *Cornhill Magazine*, December 1892.
'Hazlitt from Another Point of View' in Richard Le Gallienne's edition of *Liber Amoris*, 1894.

W.C. Hazlitt claimed to have done most of the editorial work on the four volume edition of Lamb's works and correspondence which appeared in 1870. Owing to a dispute with the publishers it was taken out of his hands before he could read the proofs and one volume only appeared in 1868 with an introduction by George Augustus Sala. In 1870 it was reissued with three more volumes with a prefatory essay by Thomas Purnell under the title of *The Complete Correspondence and Works of Charles Lamb*. William Macdonald has pointed out in the General Preface to his edition of Lamb's *Works* that W.C. Hazlitt has done a great deal to give new information about Lamb to the world, but because he was not noted for accuracy, the debt to him is not generally recognized.

Heard, Miss. Actress. Daughter of William Heard, playwright and author of *The Snuff Box*. Miss Heard spoke the epilogue to Godwin's *Antonio* on 13 December 1800. Lamb's comment in his letter to Manning on the same date was that his epilogue 'was intended for Jack Bannister to speak; but the sage managers have chosen Miss Heard, —except Miss Tidswell, the worst actress ever seen or *heard*.'

Hedges, Henry. Clerk at East India House. Lamb's letter of 9 August 1815 to Southey says 'there is a man in my office, a Mr Hedges, who proses it away from morning to night and never gets beyond corporal and material verities' and adds that he uses an imaginary dialogue with Hedges as a cure for insomnia. A copy of the Second Edition of Coleridge's *Poems* inscribed by Hedges, who states Lamb gave it to him, is at Harvard with Hedges's copies of *Rosamund Gray* and *Blank Verse*.

Henderson, John, 1747–85. Actor. Originally apprenticed to a jeweller and silversmith. Garrick gave him a letter of introduction to the manager of a theatre in Bath and he appeared there in 1772 as Hamlet. He became a successful actor and in 1777 played Shylock at the Haymarket. He subsequently played at Drury Lane and Covent Garden and appeared in Edinburgh with Mrs Siddons. He was a great success as Falstaff, Sir Giles Overreach and Shylock. He was also well known as a reader, famous for his reading of John Gilpin.

Lamb mentions him in 'The Old Actors' in the *London Magazine* where he says 'There is Henderson, unrivalled in Comus, whom I saw at second hand in the elder Harley'. Lamb was only ten years old when Henderson died.

Henderson was a well known amateur artist and a collector of Hogarth's works. He had great admiration for Sterne and was nicknamed 'Shandy' by his friends. Gainsborough, who painted his portrait, was one of his friends. With Tom Sheridan he wrote a 'Practical Method of Reading and Writing Poetry.' During the last ten years of his life he was said to be one of the finest actors in England.

Henshaw, 1723–1822. A gunsmith, one of Charles Lamb's godfathers. In a letter to Cowden Clarke in 1821 there is a reference to 'your friendly Henshaw face' and in another letter to Mrs John Lamb on 22 May 1822 Henshaw is mentioned. According to Lucas's note he died on 28 July 1822 in his hundredth year. In a letter of 13 November 1810 to Dorothy Wordsworth, Lamb says William Henshaw is dead aged fifty-six. This was the son of Lamb's godfather, who had failed in business three times.

Hessey, Rev. Francis. Classical scholar, son of J.A. Hessey, publisher of the *London Magazine*. Educated at Merchant Taylors School and St John's College, Oxford. Was first a schoolmaster with his father at Hampstead, became Principal of the Collegiate School, Huddersfield, and later Head Master of Kensington School. Lamb wrote verses for Francis Hessey when he was a schoolboy at Merchant Taylors. They were entitled *Suum Cuique* (or *Cuique Suum*) and were to be read at the School Election Day. Lucas prints a translation of the verses by Francis Hessey in *Poems and Plays*, 1903, and another by E.V. Knox in his edition of the *Letters* in 1935.

Hessey, James Augustus, 1785–1875. Publisher, partner in the firm of Taylor and Hessey, who issued the *London Magazine* from 1821 to 1825. Later he became a book, print and picture auctioneer and then a schoolmaster. Nicknamed 'Mistessey' by Keats. Hessey had been originally employed by Lackington and Allen, booksellers of Finsbury Square, where he met his future partner, John Taylor. Lamb wrote epigrams for Hessey's sons when they were schoolboys. He also wrote a number of letters to Hessey, mostly about his contributions to the *London Magazine*.

Hessey, Rev. James Augustus, 1814–92. Clergyman and schoolmaster, son of J.A. Hessey, publisher of the *London Magazine*. Educated at Merchant Taylors School and St John's College, Oxford. Public Examiner at Oxford 1842. He became Head Master of Merchant Taylors School 1845–70, Archdeacon of Middlesex in 1875 and was Chairman of the S.P.C.K. He wrote theological works. Lamb wrote verses for James Hessey when he was a schoolboy entitled *Breves esse laboro* which were to be read at the School's Election Day.

Hewlett, Maurice Henry, 1861–1923. Novelist and poet. Called to the Bar in 1891 but did not practise. Author of *Last Essays of Maurice Hewlett*, 1924, containing an essay 'One of Lamb's Creditors', which concerns James Howell. His first and best known novel was *The Forest Lovers*, 1898; he also wrote *In a Green Shade*,

1920, and *Wiltshire Essays*, 1921; the latter volume contains an essay on John Clare.

Hill, Constance. Author of *Good Company in old Westminster and the Temple*, 1925, which is founded on the early recollections of Anne Lefroy, daughter of John Rickman. There are many references to Lamb. Her other works include *The House in St Martin's Street* (chronicles of the Burney family), *Fanny Burney at the Court of Queen Charlotte, Mary Russell Mitford and her Surroundings, Juniper Hall, Jane Austen: Her Homes and Her Friends* and *Maria Edgeworth and her Circle in the Days of Bonaparte and Bourbon*.

Hill, Edwin Bliss, 1866–1949. American newspaper editor, printer and Lamb scholar. At one time news editor of *Detroit Journal*, he later worked with the United States Reclamation Service in Texas. Was owner of the oldest continuously operated private press in the United States. Friend of E.V. Lucas, Herbert F. West and Vincent Starrett. During his long life Hill printed a number of items on his private press, many of them written by himself. His interests were many, but in particular included H.D. Thoreau and Charles Lamb. In the check list of his publications printed in *The American Book Collector* there are more than 200 items, of which about fourteen concern Charles Lamb. See *The American Book Collector*, October 1967, for 'The Search for Edwin B. Hill' by Adrian Goldstone, 'Edwin Bliss Hill' by Gertrude Hill Muir and 'A Check-List of items published by the Private Press of Edwin B. Hill' by John Myers Myers, with additions by Gertrude H. Muir.

Hill, S.C. Professor of English Literature, Hoogly College. Editor with N.L. Hallward of Macmillan's editions of *The Essays of Elia*, 1895, and *The Last Essays of Elia*, 1900.

Hill, Thomas, 1760–1840. Drysalter, book collector and *bon vivant*. Part proprietor of the *Monthly Mirror*. A general busybody, noted for his faculty of finding out what everyone did. Said to be the original of Theodore Hook's 'Hull' in *Gilbert Gurney* and the 'Paul Pry' of John Poole. He had a large library, but had little knowledge of its contents other than the titles. He gave dinners to many literary people and was popular, but was made the object of ridicule by his friends. He was partly responsible for helping Robert Bloomfield to fame and Henry Kirke White contributed to his *Monthly Mirror*. This was edited for Hill by Edward Dubois, a witty and classically minded barrister.

Lucas prints two short notes from Lamb to T. Hill, whom he thinks was Thomas Hill. It has been suggested that Lamb had Hill in mind when he wrote his Lepus paper 'Tom Pry' in *The New Times* in February 1825. Among Hill's friends were the Kembles, Hook,

Campbell, Dubois, the Hunts, Barron Field and many other literary men who attended his 'Sydenham Sundays'. He was described by Leigh Hunt as a 'jovial bachelor, plump and rosy as an abbot.'

Hine, Reginald, L., 1883–1949. Solicitor and author. Educated at Kent College, Canterbury and the Leys School, Cambridge. F.S.A., F.R. Hist S. Author of *Charles Lamb and his Hertfordshire*, 1949, containing much valuable information not hitherto accessible. Probably his best known book is *Confessions of an Un-common Attorney*, 1945, but he also wrote other books full of fascinating antiquarian material. He was the author of *Anima Celtica*, 1912; *The Cream of Curiosity*, 1920; *The History of Hitchin*, 1927–9; *Hitchen Worthies*, 1932; and *Relics of an Un-common Attorney*, 1951, which contains a memoir by Richenda Scott. Both the *Confessions* and the *Relics* refer to Lamb. Hine was a member of the Elian Society and of the Charles Lamb Society.

He owned one of Lamb's Common-place Books which had formerly belonged to Frederick Locker and he gives an account of it in his *Charles Lamb and his Hertfordshire*. He also owned some volumes which were in the Richard Jackson collection and were said to have belonged to Lamb. Reginald Hine's widow presented them to the Charles Lamb Society.

Hodge, Arthur William, d. 1811. Lamb in his essay 'Christ's Hospital Five and Thirty Years Ago' refers to 'one H——' who tortured his schoolfellows and kept an ass in secret at the school. Lamb suggests it might be the planter who was brought to the gallows for whipping a slave to death. In Lamb's Key he gives 'H—' as Hodges. Edmund Blunden has examined the facts and in his essay 'Elia and Christ's Hospital' in *Essays & Studies*, 1937, states that a William Hodges was at Christ's and in 1783 left to be bound to Jacob Wilkinson. The Hon. Arthur William Hodge was hanged in 1811 in the West Indies as stated above. Blunden observes that the case is not quite clear, but it seems as if Lamb's memory was mainly correct. An 'Edward Huggins', a West Indian planter, was acquitted about 1812 of a charge of inhuman whipping of slaves.

Hodgkins, Thomas. Manager of William Godwin's Juvenile Library in Hanway Street, off Oxford Street from 1805 to 1808. Lamb's *King and Queen of Hearts* was published with Hodgkins's name on the title page in 1805, since Godwin thought it would affect the sale of children's books adversely if his name appeared on them as publisher. Hodgkins was dismissed as unsatisfactory.

Hogg, Thomas Jefferson, 1792–1862. Barrister and author. Educated at Durham Grammar School and University College, Oxford. A friend of Shelley, and because of his association with Shelley's pamphlet *The Necessity of Atheism*, he was sent down from Oxford

at the same time as Shelley. He then studied law and was called to the
Bar in 1817. In 1832 he contributed to the *New Monthly Magazine*
some reminiscences of Shelley at Oxford. In 1858 he published two
volumes of a life of Shelley, but it was unfinished because the Shelley
family objected to it and withdrew the material they had provided for
the work. Hogg was also the author of *The Memoirs of Alexy
Haimatoff*, 1813. He contributed to the *London Magazine* in 1825
and 1826 a series of articles entitled 'Journal of a Traveller on the
Continent' later reprinted as *Two Hundred and Nine Days*. He also
contributed to the *Westminster Review, Edinburgh Review, Monthly
Chronicle, The Liberal*, and *New Monthly Magazine*.

Among Hogg's friends were Leigh Hunt, T.L. Peacock, Keats,
Walter Coulson, Shelley and Mary Shelley. Hunt introduced Hogg to
the Lambs about 1818. Charles Cowden Clarke in his *Recollections
of Writers* records meeting Hogg at Lamb's house when the latter
produced one of his worst puns on Hogg's name. Hogg's daughter,
Prudentia, married as her first husband Thomas James Arnold, son
of Samuel James Arnold, the theatrical manager and friend of Charles
Lamb. Miss Winifred Scott in her *Jefferson Hogg*, 1951, sees
similarities of style between Hogg's autobiographical essays and the
Elia essays.

Holcroft, Fanny, d.1844. Daughter of Thomas Holcroft, the dramatist, by his third wife. She published her translation of the *Memoirs
of the Life of the Great Condé* in 1807. She also made translations
from Alfieri, Calderon and Lessing which were published around
1805–7 and she wrote a novel *Fortitude and Frailty* published in
1817 in four volumes. Her father dedicated his play *The Vindictive
Man* to her. She was also a musician.

Lamb mentions her in his letter in January 1823 to John Howard
Payne when he says she is bringing a 'literary lady' to see him. In July
1825 in a letter to Coleridge he says she has just come in 'with her
paternal severity of aspect.' Crabb Robinson records finding her at
the Lambs in 1824. Her step-sister, Louisa, married John Badams,
Carlyle's friend.

Holcroft, Harwood. 'Harwood' is mentioned in the letters of Charles
and Mary Lamb in 1822–3. Lucas states that this was Harwood
Holcroft, presumably a relation of Thomas Holcroft, possibly a
grandson.

Holcroft, Louisa. *See* Louisa Badams.

Holcroft, Sophia, b.1775. Daughter of Thomas Holcroft, the
dramatist, by his second wife. She married a Mr Cole of Exeter about
1793. Lamb wrote a letter to her in September 1822 after his visit to
France, when he had stayed with the Kenneys at Versailles.

Holcroft, Thomas, 1745–1809. Dramatist, novelist and translator. Had been a pedlar, cobbler, Newmarket stable-boy, schoolmaster and actor. Although entirely self educated he was an excellent French scholar and had a phenomenal memory. In 1783 he was Paris correspondent of the *Morning Herald*. He wrote many plays and novels and edited *The Theatrical Recorder*. His best known play was *The Road to Ruin*, 1792. He also wrote the popular song 'Gaffer Gray'. In 1794 Holcroft was imprisoned for high treason with Hardy, Horne Tooke, Thelwall and others.

He was a friend of Lamb, who described him in his 'Letter to Robert Southey' as 'one of the most candid, most upright and single-meaning men.' His play *The Vindictive Man* failed at Drury Lane a few nights before Lamb's Mr H— in 1806. Crabb Robinson records in his *Diary* that a meeting of Holcroft's friends was held after his death to try to raise a subscription for his family. He lists Godwin, Stothard, Nicholson, Dawe, Thelwall and Lamb as attending and adds that most of them were more likely to need help themselves. He says he contributed £20 and believes £500 was raised.

Holcroft's widow, Louisa, his fourth wife, married James Kenney, the dramatist, also a friend of Lamb. *The Memoirs of Thomas Holcroft* were continued by William Hazlitt and published in 1816. Mrs Holcroft at one time kept a school; among her pupils were Barbara Betham, who ran away, and Annette Lane to whom Lamb wrote a letter at the end of 1822.

Holcroft, Thomas, Junior. Son of Thomas Holcroft, the dramatist. Was a clerk at the House of Commons with John Rickman, but was dismissed by his employer in 1819. Lamb wrote to Basil Montagu to try to find work for the boy; eventually Crabb Robinson, Anthony Robinson and Lamb raised enough money to send him to his brother, Villiers Holcroft, in India. He must have returned by 1824 for Lamb then writes to him to thank him for orders and an offer to accompany the Lambs, presumably to a theatre.

Holidays. Charles Lamb's earliest holidays were no doubt those taken with his parents when he was a child, most probably into Hertfordshire. Sometimes he was accompanied by his brother and sister; we know that Mary Lamb took him to visit their aunt and cousins at Mackery End and their grandmother at Blakesware. From Christ's Hospital there were bathing excursions to the New River and he mentions once setting out alone in an unsuccessful attempt to discover the source of the river.

Of later holidays there are frequent references in his letters. As a clerk at East India House he seems to have been entitled to a month's holiday a year, at least in his later years. In her book *The Lambs*, Katharine Anthony states that £10 of Lamb's salary was earmarked by the Company as holiday money. A list of the known holidays is as follows:

1782–3　Hertfordshire
1790　Margate. Lamb's reference in his essay 'The Old Margate Hoy' seems to indicate this was about 1790.
1791–4　Cambridge. Lucas thought Lamb visited Cambridge while Coleridge was there, staying with F.W. Franklin, but the exact date is uncertain.
1797　Nether Stowey. A week with Coleridge in July visiting Bristol and meeting Southey at Burton.
1798　Birminghan in June, a fortnight with the Lloyds.
1799　Hertfordshire in October, visiting Blakesware and Widford, and Cambridge in December.
1800　Hertfordshire at Whitsun.
　　　　Oxford staying with J.M. Gutch's family.
1801　Cambridge in January, Margate in September.
1802　Keswick to visit Coleridge in August, also visiting Grasmere and seeing the Clarksons.
1803　Isle of Wight with the Burneys staying at Cowes.
1804　Richmond visiting Windsor and Hampton.
1805　Harrow and Egham for three or four days.
1806　Holiday at home to finish the *Tales from Shakespeare*.
1807　Bury St Edmunds in June visiting the Clarksons. Part of this year's holiday was spent at the British Museum working on the *Specimens*.
1808　No evidence of holidays away from home, but few letters exist for this year. Probably some time was spent at the Museum as in the previous year.
1809　Winterslow in October to visit Hazlitt when they went to Wilton, Salisbury and Stonehenge.
1810　Winterslow in July to visit Hazlitt, accompanied by Phillips and Martin Burney, visiting Oxford on the return journey.
1811　A month's holiday at home. Mary Lamb went to Richmond for a week with Mrs Burney in October.
1812　In August Lamb acquired Button Snap. He mentions journeying down to take possession, perhaps this was his holiday this year.
1813　Crabb Robinson mentions that Mary Lamb was taken ill at Windsor. Possibly they had been spending their holiday there (June 11).
1814　Harrow and excursions on the banks of the Thames, possibly to Henley.
1815　Mackery End with Barron Field. Cambridge in August by coach driven by 'Hell Fire Dick.'
1816　Calne, Wiltshire in June–July staying with the Morgans and

visiting Bath and Bristol.

1817 Brighton with the Morgans.

1818 Birmingham in June, visiting the Chambers family, but Charles also saw the Lloyds.

1819 Cambridge in August.

1820 Cambridge in July–August.

1821 Margate in May–June.

1822 France in August. They sailed from Brighton to Dieppe. Mary Lamb was taken ill on the road to Amiens and remained there. Charles Lamb went on to Paris. Miss James was with Mary Lamb.

1823 Hastings, stopping at Tunbridge Wells on the journey and visiting Knole and Penshurst.

1824 Holiday spent at home with visits to Ware, Kingston and Watford.

1825 Lamb retired from East India House in March 1825 and no doubt regarded the rest of the year as all holiday. In July they went to Enfield to stay with the Allsops. Charles was ill for most of the summer.

1826 In September Lamb was visiting the British Museum to read the Garrick plays.

1827–9 After his retirement Lamb seldom went far as all was now holiday. Living in the country he walked many miles daily, visiting Widford, Waltham Cross and numerous places within twenty miles of Enfield.

1830 Although not a holiday Lamb went to Bury St Edmunds in April to bring back Emma Isola who had been ill.

1831–4 During these years the health of both Charles and Mary Lamb was not good, and they did not feel it advisable to venture far from home. There were, however, various trips to London from the country.

Although there appears to be no record of all the holidays, Lamb wrote in his essay 'The Old Margate Hoy' in 1823, 'We have been dull at Worthing one summer, duller at Brighton another, dullest at Eastbourne a third.' Moxon in his 'Recollections' in 1835 states that the Lambs had spent holidays at Twickenham, Hampton Court, Cheshunt, Southgate, Ware, Tottenham, Winchmore and the banks of the Lea. No doubt these would have been day excursions only during holidays spent at home, or after Charles's retirement. R.W. King in his book on H.F. Cary suggested that from 1827 onwards the Lambs may have used Cary's Chiswick house as a summer resort. Cary had by then gone to live at the British Museum. From about 1816 the Lambs had taken lodgings for the summer at 14 Kingland Row, Dalston, but these were given up when they moved to Islington.

Hollingshead, John, 1827–1904. Journalist and theatre manager. Great nephew of Sarah James, Mary Lamb's nurse. Originally a journalist, he contributed to the *Cornhill* and was on the staff of Dickens's *Household Words*. He was dramatic critic of the *Daily News* and wrote for *Punch*. Stage manager of the Alhambra in 1865, then manager of the Gaiety. Produced the first Ibsen play to appear in London. In his *My Lifetime*, 1895, he has memories of the Lambs collected from his great aunt, Miss James and her sister, Mrs Parsons, both of whom had nursed and looked after Mary Lamb. He claimed that when a child he had seen Charles Lamb. At one time he owned Lamb's letter of 20 July 1819 in which he proposed marriage to Fanny Kelly and he sold it to *Harper's Magazine* in 1903. It is now in the Henry E. Huntington Library in Pasadena. There are minor references to Lamb in Hollingshead's *According to My Lights*, 1900.

Holman, Joseph George, 1764–1817. Actor and dramatist. Originally intended to enter the church but turned to the stage. He first appeared at Covent Garden in 1784 remaining there until 1800. Later he went to America and became manager of Charlestown Theatre. Holman was said to be at his best as Lord Townely in *The Provoked Husband*. Among his plays which were produced at Covent Garden were *Abroad and at Home,* 1796; *The Votary of Wealth,* 1799; and *The Gazette Extraordinary,* 1811. He also wrote *The Red-Cross Knights,* a play founded on Schiller's *Robbers* which was produced at the Haymarket in 1799.

Lamb mentions him in his essay 'The Old Actors' in the *London Magazine* where he says 'Holman with the bright glittering teeth in Lothario, and the deep paviour's sighs in Romeo—the jolliest person ("our son is fat") of any Hamlet I have yet seen, with the most laudable attempts (for a personable man) at looking melancholy.'

Holman, L.E. Author of *Lamb's 'Barbara S——'* 1935, a biography of Fanny Kelly.

Holmes, Edward, 1797–1859. Organist, pianist, writer on music and teacher of music. Originally apprenticed to a bookseller. Had been at John Clarke's school when Keats and Charles Cowden Clarke were there. Holmes was a music pupil of Vincent Novello and lived with the family for a time. His best known work is the *Life of Mozart,* 1845; he also wrote *A Ramble among the musicians of Germany,* 1828, and a *Life of Purcell*. He was music critic to *The Atlas* in 1826 and contributed to the *Musical Times, Fraser's Magazine* and *The Spectator*. Was known to Lamb who often met him at the Novello's house and called him 'bonny Holmes'. He was a friend of Leigh Hunt and Charles Cowden Clarke. With Novello he raised a subscription for Mozart's widow and went to Germany to present it to her in 1828.

Hone, William, 1780–1842. Author, bookseller and publisher. He wrote many political satires and in 1817 was tried for blasphemy but acquitted. In 1820 he championed Queen Caroline and published a form of prayer for her and her 'Letter to the King.' Among his many works were a *Life of William Cobbett*, 1816; *Ancient Mysteries*, 1823; *The Every-Day Book*, 1825–6; *The Table Book*, 1827–8; and *The Year Book*, 1832. Hone was largely responsible for the discovery of George Cruikshank.

Lamb and Hone were acquainted from at least 1819 and a number of letters between them exist. In a letter in May 1823 Lamb thanks Hone for the present of a book, possible *Ancient Mysteries*, published that year and invites him to dinner. Lamb adds 'I shall beg your acceptance (when I see you) of my little book.' This was probably the *Elia* volume. In 1825 Lamb lent his house at Islington to Hone while he and his sister were at Enfield.

Hone's *Every-Day Book*, which was dedicated to Lamb, contained contributions by Elia, and Lamb wrote verses to Hone which were printed in the *London Magazine*. Lamb also contributed to Hone's *Table-Book*, the most important item being the series of 'Extracts from the Garrick Plays.' Hood's caricature of Mary Lamb was printed in the Table-Book in 1827. Lamb also contributed to the *Year-Book*.

In 1826 Hone was in the King's Bench Prison for debt, where he lived for three years carrying on his editorial work from there. In 1830 he was again in difficulties and friends, of whom Lamb was prominent, placed him in the Grasshopper Coffee House at 13 Gracechurch Street, but he did not prosper. In his later years he was converted by Edward Irving and devoted much of his time to Evangelical religion.

Mrs Anderson stated that Matilda, Hone's wife, had a print shop in Russell Court, from which she issued some of her husband's publications, possibly this was carried on by Hone's daughter, not his wife.

Hood, Thomas, 1799–1845. Poet, novelist and comic writer. Born in London, the son of Thomas Hood, bookseller of the firm of Vernor and Hood in the Poultry. Was apprenticed to his uncle an engraver, but gave up the work for literature. Became sub-editor of the *London Magazine* when it was taken over by Taylor & Hessey in 1821 and remained with them until about 1825. As a result he became the friend of many well known literary figures including Lamb, Hazlitt, De Quincey, J. Hamilton Reynolds and John Clare. He contributed to the magazine a number of poems and some prose pieces. In 1825 Hood married Jane Reynolds, the sister of John Hamilton Reynolds.

The same year he published his *Odes and Addresses to Great People* in collaboration with J.H. Reynolds. It was so successful that he followed it with *Whims and Oddities* in 1826, and in 1829 started *The Comic Annual*. He published in 1827 *The Plea of the Mid-*

summer Fairies . . . and other Poems, some of which had appeared in the *London*. This volume was dedicated to Charles Lamb. He had also published a novel *Tylney Hall* in 1824. *Hood's Own* was started in 1839 which contained reminiscences of the London Magazine circle. Among his best remembered poems are 'The Song of the Shirt', 'The Dream of Eugene Aram' and 'The Bridge of Sighs'.

Lamb and Hood were great friends and the latter was a frequent visitor to the Lambs' parties. In a letter to T.C. Grattan in 1837 Hood stated that he spent three evenings a week with Lamb when they were neighbours. The Hoods lived twice at Islington, first at Lower Street until 1827 and later at Upper Street from 1830–32. In 1828 the Hoods stayed with the Lambs at Enfield.

In 1825 Lamb reviewed Hood's *Odes and Addresses to Great People* in *The New Times*. When Hood's child died in 1827 Lamb wrote his poem 'On an Infant Dying as Soon as Born' which was printed in Hood's publication *The Gem* in 1829. In 1827 Hood made the caricature of Mary Lamb getting over a stile which was sent by Lamb to Hone's *Table-Book*. Lamb also paraphrased part of Hood's poem *The Plea of the Midsummer Fairies* for the *Table-Book* under the title of 'The Defeat of Time'. In *The Gem* in 1829 Hood wrote a parody in Lamb's style entitled 'The Widow' and signed it 'C Lamb.'

Hood became dramatic critic of *The Atlas* in 1826 and soon after *The Athenaeum* was founded he became part proprietor with others who included C.W. Dilke, J.H. Reynolds and Allan Cunningham. In 1841 he became editor of *The New Monthly Magazine*.

Hood was responsible for Lamb acquiring a dog. 'Dash' belonged to Hood but was said to be 'staying on a visit' with Lamb. P.G. Patmore described it as large and handsome, but of an extravagantly errant nature to the no little vexation of Lamb who was afraid of losing it. (*See* separate entry).

After Lamb's death the Hoods sometimes visited Mary Lamb.

Hook, Theodore Edward, 1788–1841. Novelist and dramatist. Noted for his witty conversation and practical jokes. Was editor of *John Bull* and the *New Monthly Magazine*. Appointed accountant general and treasurer at Mauritius in 1813, but owing to his lack of supervision deficiencies occurred and he was finally imprisoned from 1823–5, although he does not seem to have been criminally guilty himself.

Although they were acquainted he does not appear to have been a particular friend of Lamb's. George Daniel records that Hook and Lamb met once at the Old Queens' Head in Islington and the two repaired to Colebrooke Cottage, where Lamb proposed a race round the garden, an event which Hook's figure precluded. Lamb's jest of 'Hook and I' occurs in his letter to Manning of 26 February 1808.

Hopkins, Richard. Cook of Trinity Hall and Caius College, Cambridge. Lamb in his letter in February 1805 to Manning describes him as 'Dick Hopkins, the swearing scullion of Caius' who became cook to the two colleges. He seems to have sold brawn direct to the public, and Lamb pretended that brawn sent to him by Manning had been a gift from Hopkins.

Houses lived in by the Lambs. During their life together Charles and Mary Lamb lived in more than a dozen houses. Owing to Mary's attacks they were sometimes obliged to move house more often than other people, for they were to some extent marked. Most of their moves, however, were merely normal changes due to routine circumstances. The more or less permanent rooms or house they inhabited were:

1775–92	No. 2 Crown Office Row, Inner Temple.
1792–96	7 Little Queen Street, Lincolns Inn Fields.
1797–99	45 Chapel Street, Pentonville.
1799–1800	36 Chapel Street, Pentonville.
1800–1801	27 Southampton Buildings, Chancery Lane.
1801–1809	16 Mitre Court Buildings, Inner Temple.
1809	34 Southampton Buildings, Chancery Lane.
1809–17	4 Inner Temple Lane.
1817–23	20 Russell Street, Covent Garden.
1823–27	Colebrooke Cottage, Islington.
1827–29	87 Chase Side, Enfield.
1829–33	89 Chase Side, Enfield, The Westwoods.
1833–34	Bay Cottage, Church Street, Edmonton, The Waldens.

In the first two of these addresses Charles and Mary Lamb lived with their parents; later they rented lodgings, and it was not until 1823 when the move to Colebrooke Cottage was made that they actually had a house to themselves. The Waldens' house at Edmonton was a sort of private mental home in which Charles felt it would be best for his sister to live in view of her increasingly frequent attacks. He decided to live there as well so that they could then be more often together.

In 1816 in order to avoid the 'knock eternal' of visitors at their London rooms, they took lodgings at 14 Kingsland Row, Dalston and retained them for several years. They also stayed at Mrs Leishman's in Enfield several times.

Writing to Thomas Hood on 18 September 1827 Lamb said 'To change habitations is to die to them, and in my time I have died seven deaths. But I dont know whether every such change does not bring with it a rejuvenescence.' The only houses which still stand more or less as Lamb knew them are the two Enfield houses and that at Edmonton.

After Lamb's death Mary Lamb continued to live at the Walden's house, but moved in 1841 to Alpha Road, Regents Park (either No. 20 or No. 41) with Mrs Parsons, a sister of her former nurse, Miss James.

Housman, Laurence, 1865–1959. Dramatist, novelist and book illustrator. Younger brother of A.E. Housman, the poet and scholar. Author of *Cornered Poets: a book of Dramatic Dialogues*, 1929, which includes 'Charles! Charles!', a version of the Haydon dinner at which Charles Lamb misbehaved.

Howe, Percival Presland, 1886–1944. Author and publisher. Educated at University College School. Partner with Martin Secker, the publisher. Wrote *The Life of William Hazlitt*, 1922, reprinted 1928 and 1947. Edited *The Complete Works of William Hazlitt*, 1930–4, 20 volumes, centenary edition, a reissue of the Waller-Glover edition with additional material and notes; *New Writings by William Hazlitt. Collected by P.P. Howe*, 1925; *New Writings. Second Series*, 1927. Howe issued *The Letters of Thomas Manning to Charles Lamb*, edited by G.A. Anderson, 1925, but left incomplete at her death. He edited *The Best of Hazlitt*, 1923, and contributed the bibliography of Hazlitt to *C.B.E.L.* Howe reviewed for *The Globe* and wrote dramatic criticism for *The Outlook* and *Truth*. Among his contributions to periodicals are:

Fortnightly Review
1916 Hazlitt & Liber Amoris.
       Hazlitt's Second Marriage.
1919 Hazlitt & Blackwood's Magazine.
The London Mercury
1935 Lamb's Letters Complete.
Times Literary Supplement
1935 Lamb and Hazlitt (September 26).

Howe, Will David. American author. Wrote *Charles Lamb and His Friends*, New York, 1944. Has also edited *Selections from William Hazlitt*, Boston, 1913.

Hudson, Robert, 1732–1815. English tenor, musician and composer. Taught music at Christ's Hospital in Lamb's day. He composed the music for James Boyer's Easter hymns sung at the school. Lamb mentions him in a letter to Coleridge as 'little Hudson, the immortal precentor of St Paul's.' The letter is dated by Lucas'? June 1803', but in the *Records of the Amicable Society of Blues* it is printed as 22 June 1800. As a young man Hudson sang at Ranelagh and Marylebone Gardens. In 1755 he was assistant organist at St Mildred's, Bread Street; in 1756 Vicar Choral of St Paul's Cathedral;

and from 1773 until 1793 he was almoner and master of the children of St Paul's.

Hughes, Arthur Montague D'Urban, b.1873. Editor and author. Professor of English Language and Literature at Birmingham University. Member of the staff of Oxford University Press. Educated at St Edmund's School, Canterbury, and St John's College, Oxford. Editor with D. Nichol Smith of the Clarendon Series of English Literature. For the volume on *Charles Lamb: Prose & Poetry*, 1921, Hughes wrote the notes, with the introduction by George Gordon. Among other works edited by Hughes are Carlyle's *Frederick the Great* and *Past and Present*, 1918; Shelley's *Prometheus Unbound*, 1910; Tennyson's *Poems of 1842*, 1914; *Selections from Burke*, 1921; *Selections from Cobbett*, 1923; *Milton: Poetry & Prose*, 1920; and *Shelley: Poetry and Prose*, 1931. He also wrote *Theology of Shelley*, 1938, and *The Nascent Mind of Shelley*, 1947.

Hughes, T. Rowland. Author of 'The London Magazine' an unpublished doctoral dissertation, Jesus College, Oxford 1931. Contributed to the *London Mercury*, April 1930, 'John Scott: Editor, Author and Critic.'

Hull, Thomas, 1728–1808. Actor and playwright. Acting manager at Covent Garden. He was the founder of the Theatrical Fund and a great friend of Tate Wilkinson. He played Gloucester to G.F. Cooke's Lear at Covent Garden in 1802 and Lamb refers to him in his review of the production in the *Morning Post* on 9 January 1802 where he says he was 'natural and impressive'. He wrote a tragedy *Henry II* or *Fair Rosamund*.

Hume, Joseph, 1767–1843. Clerk in the Victualling Office at Somerset House. A friend of Lamb, Hazlitt, Crabb Robinson and Godwin. In 1807–8 an elaborate joke was concocted between Lamb and Hume involving a fictitious report of the death of William Hazlitt. Several of Lamb's letters to Hume refer to it. The story is told in full in W.C. Hazlitt's *Lamb and Hazlitt*, 1900, and although the victim played his part, the joke seems in questionable taste.

Lamb was acquainted with the whole Hume Family. He mentions him in a postscript to his essay in the *London Magazine*, 'A Complaint of the Decay of Beggars in the Metropolis', which was omitted when the essay was republished in the *Elia* volume. It seems that Hume had an original draft of the celebrated 'Beggar's Petition' by Rev. Thomas Moss. In 1832 Lamb wrote a letter to Hume's daughters, Amelia, Caroline, Julia, Augusta and Louisa. At that time the family lived in Percy Street, Bloomsbury. Hume published a translation of Dante's *Inferno* in 1812 and *A Search into the Old Testament . . .* in 1841.

Humphreys, Miss. An aunt of Emma Isola who lived at Cambridge. On 9 January 1821 Charles Lamb and Emma Isola wrote a joint letter to Miss Humphreys. Lamb's letter of 27 January 1821 is addressed to 'Miss Humphreys, with Mrs Paris, Trumpington Street, Cambridge.' Mrs Paris was William Ayrton's sister. Lamb's letter to Moxon on 13 September 1833 seems to indicate some misunderstandings between Emma and her aunt, who appears to have written an unpleasant letter to Moxon's sister.

Hunt, James Henry Leigh, 1784–1859. Essayist and poet. Educated at Christ's Hospital, entered 23 November 1792 and left 20 November 1799. Became a clerk in the War Office from 1803 to 1808, when he resigned to edit his brother's publication *The Examiner*, which had just started. The Hunt's were prosecuted in 1808 and 1811 for material published in it, but acquitted. In 1812 the two brothers were tried for libel on the Prince Regent whom they had described as a fat Adonis of fifty. They were convicted, fined and imprisoned. Leigh Hunt went to Horsemonger Lane Gaol, where he was allowed to have his family with him; he transformed his two rooms into a bower of flowers with a piano and a garden. Here he was frequently visited by his friends, prominent among whom were the Lambs. He continued to edit *The Examiner* while in prison, which he left in 1815.

Leigh Hunt's first volume of poems, *Juvenilia*, was issued by subscription by his father in 1801—Charles Lamb's brother, John, was one of the subscribers. In 1805 Hunt wrote theatrical criticism for *The News* (edited by John Hunt) and later for *The Times*. In 1810 came one of his most famous publications, *The Reflector*, but it only lasted for four numbers. *The Feast of the Poets* was issued in 1814 and during the next few years appeared *The Story of Rimini*, 1816; *Foliage*, 1818; *Hero & Leander and Bacchus & Ariadne*, 1819, as part of a three volume edition of his *Poetical Works*; and *Amyntas* in 1820. Another fine publication, *The Indicator*, was started in 1819.

During these years Hunt had become friendly with a number of interesting people. He met Shelley in 1811, Wordsworth in 1815, Keats in 1816; other friends included Barron Field, Haydon, Procter, Hogg and Peacock. In 1820 Keats was nursed at the Hunt's home and the following year Leigh Hunt and his family decided to move to Italy at the invitation of Shelley and Byron who were both already there. They did not arrive until 1822 and shortly afterwards Shelley was drowned. In 1822 Hunt issued *The Liberal* which, in addition to his own work, contained contributions by Shelley, Byron and Hazlitt, but it lasted for only four numbers.

Although by then not on good terms with Byron, on whom they were partly dependent, the Hunts remained in Italy until the end of 1825 when they returned to England. In 1828 Hunt founded *The*

Companion and published *Lord Byron and his Contemporaries*. The following year he founded *The Tatler*. In 1832 he published by subscription his *Poetical Works* and in 1834 started *Leigh Hunt's London Journal* which ran until the end of the next year.

During his later years he issued a number of volumes of great attraction, some designed to popularize English Literature, such as *Imagination and Fancy*, 1844; *Wit and Humour*, 1846 and *A Book for a Corner*, 1849. A volume of essays came in 1847, *Men, Women and Books*; *The Town* in 1848; and his *Autobiography* in 1850; to be followed by *Table Talk*, 1851, and *The Old Court Suburb* in 1855. He had by now become friendly with John Forster and Charles Dickens and was in contact with many famous people, some of whom helped him with his frequent financial difficulties.

Hunt records that he used to see Lamb when he was still a schoolboy at Christ's Hospital, and the latter visited his old school, but they did not meet until some years afterwards. Edmund Blunden thought they were friends by 1810 and perhaps earlier; they were certainly intimate by 1812 when Hunt was imprisoned, for the Lambs were their most frequent visitors at the gaol. It does not seem that Hunt was ever as close to Lamb as were Coleridge and Manning.

In 1814 Lamb wrote verses to Leigh Hunt's son, Thornton, 'To T.L.H. A Child' which appeared in *The Examiner* the following year. Lamb praised Hunt's poem *The Story of Rimini* and selected poems from his *Foliage* and *Amyntas* for Hazlitt's *Elegant Extracts*. In his 'Letter of Elia to Robert Southey' Lamb has a long piece on Hunt in which he describes him as 'one of the most cordial-minded men I ever knew, and matchless as a fire-side companion.'

Lamb contributed to Leigh Hunt's publications *The Reflector*, *The Examiner* and *The Indicator*. His papers in the first included such well known pieces as 'On the Genius and Character of Hogarth,' 'On the Custom of Hissing at the Theatre,' 'On Shakespeare's Tragedies' (there entitled 'On Garrick & Acting'), 'Specimens from the Writings of Thomas Fuller' and 'A Bachelor's Complaint of the Behaviour of Married People.'

Hunt wrote an 'Epistle to Charles Lamb' in verse which he printed in *The Examiner*; it tells how the Lambs were constant visitors in all weathers during the imprisonment. He has numerous other references to Lamb in his writings among which are:

Foliage, 1818 (reprints the 'Epistle' and Preface mentions Lamb's position as a writer in relation to Wordsworth and Coleridge).
The Examiner, March 1819 (review of Lamb's *Works*).
The Indicator, 1821 (reprints the review of Lamb's *Works* and has other references to Lamb).
The Literary Examiner, July 5 and 12, 1823 (describes Lamb's library in essay 'My Books').

Lord Byron and his Contemporaries, 1828 (high praise given to Lamb).

The Tatler, June 1831 (a review of Moxon's publications that mentions Lamb's *Satan in Search of a Wife*).

Leigh Hunt's London Journal, 1835 (obituary notice of Lamb which contains the memorable sentence 'He was only at his ease in the old arms of humanity', and numerous other references, some reprinted in *The Town* 1848).

Autobiography, 1850 (many references).

Table Talk, 1851 (reprints part of obituary from the *London Journal*).

Many of the references to Lamb mentioned above are reprinted in Edmund Blunden's *Charles Lamb: His Life Recorded by his Contemporaries*, 1934. Leigh Hunt's *Correspondence* was edited by Thornton Leigh Hunt in 1862.

In later years Lamb and Leigh Hunt do not seem to have met frequently and Crabb Robinson notes in his *Diary* on 29 October 1820, 'Leigh Hunt hardly belongs to this set and I very seldom saw him at Lamb's.'

Hunt, John, 1775–1848. Publisher and printer. Elder brother of Leigh Hunt. Was first apprenticed to Carew Reynell, printer of Pimlico. Published *The Reflector* jointly with his brother in 1811 and he was prosecuted with him for the libel on the Prince Regent. In 1824 he was fined £100 for a libel on George III for printing Byron's 'Vision of Judgment' in *The Liberal*. He started a number of journals, including *The News*, 1805; *The Statesman*, 1806; and *The Examiner*, 1808. He was friendly with Thomas Barnes, Thomas Mitchell and Barron Field and others of his brother's circle. Among the authors he published were Byron, Shelley, Hazlitt, Jeremy Bentham and Leigh Hunt.

Hunt, Thornton Leigh, 1810–73. Journalist. Eldest son of Leigh Hunt. Began his career as an artist. In 1814 Lamb wrote verses 'To T.L.H.' which were printed in Leigh Hunt's *Examiner*; the last line was 'Thornton Hunt, my favourite child.' His father included verses to him in his book *Foliage*, 1818. He is mentioned by Lamb in his 'Letter to Robert Southey' and in his essay 'Witches and other Night Fears'.

His journalistic work was extensive and he wrote for *The Atlas* and *Globe*, became acting editor of *The Spectator* and of *The Daily Telegraph*. He also started *The Leader* with G.H. Lewes. In 1845 he published a novel, *The Foster-Brother*, and he edited and published his father's *Autobiography*, his *Correspondence* and his *Poetical Works*. He also illustrated Leigh Hunt's *Captain Sword and Captain Pen*.

He was friendly with many of his father's famous friends, including the Lambs, Shelley, Keats, Jefferson Hogg, Charles Brown, John Forster and Vincent Novello, as well as Laman Blanchard and Edward Gibbon Wakefield. In Lucas's *Life of Lamb*, 1905, is reproduced a sketch from memory by Thornton Leigh Hunt in which he appears with his father, Hazlitt and Lamb.

Hunt, Wray, d.1897. Rector of Trowell, near Nottingham. Educated at Merton College, Oxford. Author of *Essays*, 1899, which contains his delightful 'A Letter to Charles Lamb'.

Hunter, John, 1745–1837. Classical scholar. Was private secretary to Lord Monboddo. He was Professor of Humanity in St Andrews' University, 1775–1835. He published editions of Livy, 1822; Horace, 1797; Caesar, Virgil and Sallust. He contributed a 'Sonnet to Elia' to *Friendship's Offering* in 1832. It was reprinted in Lucas's *Life of Lamb* and S.M. Rich's *The Elian Miscellany*.

Hutchinson, Joanna, 1780–1841. Sister of Mrs Wordsworth and Sara Hutchinson. Wordsworth wrote a poem 'To Joanna' in 1800. There are several references to her in Lamb's letters including one to 'Joanna's laugh', an incident in Wordsworth's poem.

Hutchinson, Mary, 1770–1859. Married William Wordsworth in 1802. She visited London with her husband in 1817 and again in 1823. She was a sister of Sara Hutchinson and a cousin of Thomas Monkhouse.

Hutchinson, Sara, 1775–1835. Sister of Mary Hutchinson, Wordsworth's wife. Lived near the Wordsworths when at Grasmere and became an invaluable helper to the family. Cousin of Thomas Monkhouse, Lamb's friend. Professor de Selincourt described her as a 'woman of considerable intellectual gifts, fully worthy to be the intimate friend of two great poets', i.e. Coleridge and Wordsworth. She was in love with Coleridge. Some of the most interesting letters written by both Charles and Mary Lamb were to Sara Hutchinson.

Hutchinson, Thomas. Editor. Among the works he edited are *The Works of Charles Lamb*, 2 vols, 1908; *Poetical Works of William Wordsworth*, 1895; *The Oxford Wordsworth*, 1910; *The Oxford Shelley*, 1921. He also contributed to *The Athenaeum* an article on *John Woodvil*, 28 December 1901, and 'Lamb and the Utilitarians', 16 August 1902. The latter piece concerns Lamb's Confessions of a Drunkard. A.E. Newton in his *Amenities of Book Collecting*, 1920, quotes a poem 'Ballade of a Poor Book-Lover' by Thomas Hutchinson, the last verse of which would have pleased Elia.

Tho' frequently to stall I speed,
The books I buy I like to read;
Yet wealth to me will never hie—
The books I read I like to buy.

Hutton, Laurence, 1843–1904. American author and critic. Author of *Literary Landmarks of London*, fourth edition, 1888. It contains an account of many of the places associated with Charles Lamb and there are numerous other references to him. Other of Lamb's friends dealt with are Coleridge, Godwin, Hazlitt, Hood, Leigh Hunt and Samuel Rogers.

Illustrators of Charles Lamb's Works. Few of Lamb's books were illustrated during his lifetime except the books for children. *The Essays of Elia* do not seem to have attracted the attention of artists until 1883 when the Islington edition was published in New York with eight engravings by R. Swain Gifford, James D. Smillie, Charles A. Platt and F.S. Church; but these artists were not notably successful as illustrators to Lamb's essays. After that date other editions followed with drawings by a number of others. *The Tales from Shakespeare* are rather different from Lamb's other works, for the illustrations are really to Shakespeare rather than to Lamb; a fact underlined by the inclusion in some editions of the *Tales* of work done for the plays themselves and not specially for editions of the Lambs' book.

Many early issues of Lamb's works had engraved frontispieces, some of which were by William Harvey, which illustrated merely one piece in the book; fully illustrated editions came only towards the end of the nineteenth century. The principal illustrators of Lamb's books included:

Blake, William. *Tales from Shakespeare*, 1807. Although the designs are said to be by Mulready, the engraving is thought to be Blake's work, and the strength of some of the illustrations may indicate that Blake's share was larger than is generally supposed. They are not perhaps among his best work.

Brock, Charles E. *Essays of Elia*, 1899; *Last Essays of Elia*, 1899; *Works* (Macdonald), 1903; *Collected Essays* (Lynd), 1929; *Mrs Leicester's School.*

Crane, Walter. *The Masque of Days*, 1901.

Cruikshank, George. *Satan in Search of a Wife*, 1831.

Cruikshank, Robert. *Tales from Shakespeare*, 1837.

Flaxman, Maria. *Prince Dorus*, 1811; *Beauty and the Beast*, 1811.

Fitchew, E.H. 'Charles Lamb in Hertfordshire' by Alfred Ainger in the *English Illustrated Magazine*, 1886.

Fulleylove, John with Herbert Railton. *In the Footprints of*

Charles Lamb by B.E. Martin, 1891 (originally published in *Scribner's Magazine*).

Gordon, E. *Essays of Elia,* 1894, Artists' edition—New York.

Green, Winifred. *Poetry for Children,* 1898, *Works* (Macdonald), 1903, Vol. VIII; *Mrs Leicester's School,* 1927.

Harvey, William. *Tales from Shakespeare,* 1831; *Mrs Leicester's School,* 1825.

Jones, A. Garth. *Essays of Elia,* 1901.

Martin, Frank. *Essays,* 1963, Folio Society.

Mulready, William. *The King and Queen of Hearts,* 1805, *Tales from Shakespeare,* 1807.

Murray, C.O. *Some Essays of Elia,* 1886; *A Dissertation upon Roast Pig,* 1895.

Rackham, Arthur. *Tales from Shakespeare,* 1899.

Railton, Herbert. *Essays of Elia* and *Last Essays of Elia,* 1888 (Temple Edition); *Six Etchings on Vellum,* 1890 (from the Temple edition); *In the Footprints of Charles Lamb* (Martin), 1891, with John Fulleylove; *Portfolio,* 1892, illustrations of the Temple. *Works* (Macdonald), 1903.

Robinson, W. Heath. *Tales from Shakespeare,* 1901.

Shepard, Ernest H. *Everybody's Lamb,* 1933.

Tawse, Sybil. *Essays of Elia,* 1910.

Waudby, Roberta F.C. *Mrs Battle's Opinions on Whist,* 1930, *Dream Children and the Child Angel; Witches and other Night Fears; The Praise of Chimney Sweepers.* (Each a separate pamphlet published by J.M. Dent).

Among the artist whose work has been used to illustrate the *Tales from Shakespeare,* although not done specially for that work, are: R. Anning Bell, 1899; H. Copping, 1901; Norman Carse, 1914; Edmund Dulac, 1914; Sir John Gilbert, 1877; A.E. Jackson, 1918; Sir James D. Linton, 1914; Frank Papé, 1923; H. Pillé 1902; Norman Price, 1905; G. Soper, 1923; and Hugh Thomson, 1914. In 1893 Aubrey Beardsley did a series of grotesques for *Bon-Mots of Charles Lamb and Douglas Jerrold,* but they can hardly be described as illustrations to Lamb's work. Paul Braddon did a number of water colour sketches of Elian topography which are now in the library of the Charles Lamb Society.

See separate entries for most of the artists, also 'Charles Lamb's Illustrators 1796–1967' by Claude A. Prance in *C.L.S. Bulletin,* July and October 1968 (reprinted in *The Laughing Philosopher 1976*).

Imlay, Fanny, 1794–1816. Daughter of Gilbert Imlay and Mary Wollstonecraft. She is described in Lamb's letter to Hazlitt of 10 November 1805 as 'sulky Fanny Imlay, alias Godwin'; Lamb adds, however, that Miss Dawe, who was painting her portrait, maintained that she was not sulky. Her life was difficult, for she lived with God-win and his second wife. She committed suicide in 1816.

Inchbald, Elizabeth, 1753–1821. Actress, dramatist and novelist. Her maiden name was Simpson and in 1772 she married Joseph Inchbald, an actor. Both she and her husband were friends of J.P. Kemble and when her husband died in 1779, Kemble wrote a Latin epitaph for him. In 1780 she refused an offer of marriage from Dicky Suett, the actor, and at one time J.P. Kemble also wanted to marry her.

She first appeared on the stage in the provinces and became a friend of both Mrs Siddons and Tate Wilkinson. She appeared at Covent Garden, but retired from the stage in 1789 and devoted her-self to literature. She wrote a number of sentimental comedies and some novels, the best known being *A Simple Story*, 1791, and *Nature and Art*, 1796. She edited *The British Theatre* in twenty-five volumes and *The Modern Theatre* in ten volumes.

She seems to have been very attractive, possessed of beauty, a sense of humour and wit. Mary Shelley said that when she came into a room the men forsook all other women and flocked round her. Godwin was one of her admirers.

Lamb included her in what he called 'the three bald women': Mrs Barbauld, Mrs Inchbald and Mrs Godwin, who used the name of Baldwin as a publisher. He did, however, tell Thomas Allsop that she was 'the only endurable clever woman he had ever known.'

Inner Temple Lane. In May 1809 the Lambs moved from 34 Southampton Buildings, Chancery Lane to No. 4 Inner Temple Lane. Lamb described the rooms to Coleridge in a letter of 7 June 1809, 'I have two rooms on third floor and five rooms above, with an inner staircase to myself and all new painted &c., and all for £30 a year.' Some rooms looked out on the trees and pump of Hare Court. It was here in 1814 that, as a result of the cries of a cat, they discovered four untenated rooms which they could use, and Mary furnished one of them as Charles's study so that he could work there away from inter-ruptions, and she and her brother decorated it with prints cut from their books. Mary Lamb relates the discovery in her letter to Barbara Betham on 2 November 1814.

They left the rooms in the autumn of 1817 for 20 Great Russell Street, Covent Garden. Lucas thinks that Lamb's Thursday evening parties were at their best during the eight years in Inner Temple Lane. Crabb Robinson notes under 1806 that Lamb then lived in a garret in Inner Temple Lane and that he saw there 'a greater number of excellent persons than I had ever seen collected in one apartment.' Robinson seems to have mistaken the house, for the Lambs were living at 16 Mitre Court Buildings, Inner Temple from 1801 to 1809 and then moved to 4 Inner Temple Lane via Southampton Buildings. Mary Lamb in her letter to Barbara Betham refers to the rooms as garrets.

The house as Lamb knew it was replaced in 1857 by a new building known as Johnson's Buildings because the Doctor lived in chambers on the site from 1760–65. Barron Field lived in Hare Court at one time.

Ireland, Alexander, 1810–94. Author and journalist. Born in Edinburgh. Originally in business, but later turned to literature. In 1846 became publisher and manager of the *Manchester Examiner*. Among his friends were Carlyle, Emerson, the Cowden Clarkes, Leigh Hunt and Robert Chambers. He was the author of *A Bibliographical and Critical Account of the Writings of William Hazlitt and Leigh Hunt. Preceded by a Chronological List of the Works of Charles Lamb,* 1868 (Dedicated to the Cowden Clarkes). He also wrote *Recollections of George Dawson and his lectures in Manchester in 1846–47,* 1882. His best known work today is *The Book-Lover's Enchiridion,* 1882; sixth edition, 1890. The latter work has as its sub-title 'Thoughts on the Solace and Companionship of Books' and is one of the most fascinating of anthologies. It contains nearly nine pages taken from Charles Lamb's writings. It was first published under the title of 'Philobiblos'.

Ireland also contributed to the *Manchester Examiner* in July 1847 an article on 'The Genius and Writings of Leigh Hunt.' In 1899 he edited a selection of Hazlitt's works prefaced by a memoir. He possessed a fine library, rich in early English authors, including all the seventeenth century editions of Burton's *Anatomy of Melancholy.* Ireland also had a fine collection of the works of Lamb, Hazlitt and Leigh Hunt, which with his Lamb papers is now in the Manchester Free Library.

Irving, Edward, 1792–1834. Scottish minister and schoolmaster. Preached at the Scotch Church, Hatton Garden where he drew large attendances. Later he had a church in Regent Square, but his views caused him to be ejected from the church and ultimately his deposition from the ministry. He then founded the Catholic Apostolic Church whose adherents were known as 'Irvingites'. Irving was admired by De Quincey, Coleridge, Canning and Scott. He had been tutor to Jane Welsh and wished to marry her, but she eventually married his friend, Thomas Carlyle. Mrs Basil Montagu was a friend. Irving was known to Lamb and Crabb Robinson records finding him with Carlyle at the Lambs in 1824, but adds that there was little sympathy between Irving and Lamb. Lucas prints a letter in 1828 from Lamb to Irving, and one from Irving in which he returns a book lent to him and Irving invites Lamb to come to look at his books.

Iseman, Joseph Seeman. Author of *A Perfect Sympathy: Charles Lamb and Sir Thomas Browne,* 1937 (Harvard Honors Thesis in English No. 10).

Islington. *See* Colebrooke Cottage.

Isola Family.
   Agostino Isola, c.1713–97. Grandfather of Emma Isola. Teacher of Italian and Spanish at Cambridge, a refugee from Italy. He published in 1778 *Pieces Selected from the Italian Poets, By Agostino Isola . . . and Translated into English Verse by some Gentlemen of the University* (2nd edition 1784); he also published other Italian authors, including Tasso's *Gerusalemme Liberata,* 1786, and Ariosto's *Orlando Furioso,* 1789. Lowndes calls this latter translation 'a very correct edition of the original.' Among Isola's pupils were Matilda Betham, William Hayley, T.J. Mathias, Wordsworth, Gray and Pitt.

Charles Isola, 1774–?1814. Esquire Bedell of Cambridge University. Son of Agostino Isola and father of Emma Isola. In 1803 he married Mary Humphreys. The Miss Humphreys mentioned in Lamb's letters was Emma's aunt and lived with William Ayrton's sister, Mrs Paris, at Cambridge. (The *C.L.S.B.,* No. 206 states Charles Isola died in 1814, Lucas in the *Life,* 1905 and 1921, gives 1823, and in *Letters,* 1935, has 1821.)
   Edward Isola. Son of Charles Isola and brother of Emma. Entered Christ's Hospital in 1814 where he was placed through the patronage of the Duke of Gloucester on the death of his father.
   Emma Isola. *See* separate entry.
   Frederick Isola. Son of Charles Isola and brother of Emma. Entered Christ's Hospital in 1821 under the patronage of the Duke of Gloucester.
   Harriet Isola. Daughter of Charles Isola and sister of Emma. Occasionally mentioned in Lamb's letters and one letter to her is printed by Lucas. Mrs Anderson suggested she was a governess in London. Lamb wrote an acrostic to her in 1833.

Isola, Emma, 1809–91, pronounced Ease-ola. Daughter of Charles Isola and granddaughter of Agostino Isola. She first met the Lambs at the house of Mrs Paris in Cambridge, probably when they spent their holiday there in 1820. By January 1821 she was visiting them and Mary took her to Covent Garden. As she was an orphan, the Lambs adopted her and she used to spend her school holidays with them, and they paid for her schooling at Mrs Richardson's at Dulwich. Both Charles and Mary Lamb helped to teach her French and Latin and Mary wrote verses 'To Emma, Learning Latin, and Desponding.' Crabb Robinson read Italian with her in 1832 and noted that Lamb was teaching her the language without knowing it himself. Lamb said that the first school present he gave her was Samuel Roger's *The Pleasures of Memory*.

In 1828 she became a governess in the family of Mrs Williams, the wife of the Rector of Fornham, Suffolk. There are further glimpses of her in the Lambs' letters about this time: her illness in 1830 when Lamb went to Fornham to bring her back: Landor's verses to her: reading Cary's *Danté* with the brother and sister and then her engagement to Edward Moxon, the publisher. The latter event brought forth Lamb's amusing letter to Moxon on his present of a watch; 'For god's sake, give Emma no more watches. *One* has turn'd her head.' The wedding took place in July 1833 by Special Licence and the honeymoon was spent in France. Lamb gave Emma his portrait of Milton as part of her dowry and in a letter to Moxon says he has transferred' stock to her. He had also made a new will some years earlier leaving all he had in trust for his sister and the residue to Emma.

Emma Isola had an Album and Lamb solicited his friends for contributions; many famous authors responded, and Lamb himself wrote verses for it. She also had an Extract Book made for her by Lamb. Lucas examined this and gave a list of the contents in his *Life of Charles Lamb*.

Edward Moxon died in 1858 and the publishing business was carried on as a trust, but by 1871 Emma Moxon was in financial difficulties and Lord Houghton appealed to Gladstone for a Civil List pension; since it was not forthcoming, a subscription was started to which Thomas Baring gave £50 'in memory of the pleasure he had had from Charles Lamb.' Eventually Emma moved to Brighton where she died on 2 February 1891. She left one son and five daughters.

That both Charles and Mary Lamb were very fond of Emma is certain and their letters contain many affectionate references. It has been suggested, however, that Charles was actually in love with his ward, notably by Neil Bell in his novel *So Perish the Roses*, 1940, and in Katharine Anthony's *The Lambs*, 1948. Professor E.C. Ross wrote a pamphlet *Charles Lamb and Emma Isola* in 1950 to combat the views expressed by Neil Bell and Miss Anthony. Professor Edith Johnson noted that Lamb's richest mental harvest—the Elia period—coincided with that when Emma Isola was adopted by the Lambs. Crabb Robinson noted in his *Diary* on 23 July 1832 that Lamb had described Emma Isola as 'the most sensible girl and best female talker' he knew.

Ives, Abigail. She kept a general shop in Widford and her speciality was Gibraltar Rock. Mrs Coe mentioned her in the reminiscences of Lamb she gave to Lucas (*See Life* II 174 and 'The Last to call him Charley' in *At the Shrine of Saint Charles*). Miss Mann in *C.L.S. Bulletin*, No. 146, describes her as a young woman still in her twenties when Lamb used to call at her shop on his visits to Goddard House, the Norris's school. Reginald Hine recorded that a family named Ives lived for two generations in the cottage of Button Snap.

Jack, Ian, b.1923. Professor of English literature in University of Cambridge. Fellow of Pembroke College, Cambridge. President of the Charles Lamb Society, 1970–80. Gave the address at the annual dinner to the Society in February 1965 and in March 1970 an address on T.L. Peacock. Author of *English Literature 1815–1832*, 1963, being Volume X in the Oxford History of English Literature. It contains many references to Charles Lamb and includes a bibliography. Other works include *Augustan Satire* and for the British Council 'Writers and their Work' series booklets on *Sir Walter Scott* and *Alexander Pope*. Wrote article on Lamb in *Encyclopaedia Britannica*, 1973 edition.

Jackson, Holbrook, 1874–1948. Journalist and literary historian. The complete bookman. In 1930 he published his great *The Anatomy of Bibliomania*: in the two indices there are more than forty references to Charles Lamb. Among his many other works are interesting volumes of essays and *The Fear of Books*, 1932; *The Printing of Books*, 1938; *Bookman's Holiday*, 1945; *The Reading of Books*, 1946; *Dreamers of Dreams*, 1948; and *Maxims of Books and Reading*, 1934. He also edited Burton's *The Anatomy of Melancholy* for Everyman's Library in 1932. Jackson had been editor of *T.P.'s Magazine*, *T.P.'s Weekly*, *The New Age* and *To-Day*. In 1951 Elkin Mathews Ltd, the booksellers, issued *A Memorial Catalogue of the Holbrook Jackson Library* with an appreciation by Sir Francis Meynell.

Jackson, Richard, d.1787. Barrister of the Inner Temple. Called to the Bar at Lincolns Inn in 1744. Became a Bencher in 1770. Was M.P. for New Romney and in 1782 a Lord of the Treasury. Known as the 'Omniscent Jackson' becuase of his extensive knowledge and remarkable memory. He is mentioned in Boswell's *Life of Johnson*. He is one of Lamb's 'Old Benchers' and in the essay an anecdote of his multifarious knowledge is related. He was Standing Counsel to the South Sea Company in 1764.

Jackson, Richard Charles, 1851–1923. Jackson claimed to be the grandson of 'Lamb's Captain Francis Jackson' according to an article in *The Times* on 30 July 1923. He was said to be an eccentric bachelor who lived alone at 185 Camberwell Grove, London, among 8,000 books and relics all in a state of filth and neglect. He claimed to possess relics of Lamb, Dr Johnson, Garrick and Blake. His possessions were sold by Goddard and Smith in 1923.

He stated he had been a pupil of Carlyle and that he was the original of Pater's *Marius the Epicurean*. Other references to him appeared in *The Times* on July 23 and 25, 1923, and in *Notes & Queries* on July 9 and August 13, 1927. The catalogue of the Jackson sale lists five pieces of furniture alleged to have belonged to Lamb as well as 116 volumes described as 'The Lamb Collection of Books.' It is not known if Jackson's claim was genuine, but a Francis Jackson was at Christ's Hospital in 1790, the year after Lamb had left. In R.L. Hine's *Charles Lamb and his Hertfordshire* it is stated that a Francis Jackson of the Red House, Mare Street, Hackney, bought Lamb relics at the Moxon sale in 1858 and some of them came into Hine's possession.

James, Sarah. Daughter of the Rector of Beguildy, Shropshire. A nurse at the Hoxton Mental Institution who acted as nurse to Mary Lamb from time to time and accompanied the Lambs on several holidays. She went with them to France in 1822 and to Hastings in 1823. From 1841 until her death Mary Lamb lived at the house of Mrs Parsons in St Johns Wood, a sister of Miss James, and it was here that a comfortable library-sitting room was fitted up for her and where Lamb's books were lodged until Mary's death. Miss James's great nephew was John Hollingshead, the theatre manager, who gives interesting reminiscences of Charles and Mary Lamb's last years in his book *My Lifetime*, 1895. He tells us that if Lamb had not returned home by a reasonable hour Sarah James put on her bonnet and went out to find him. Lucas prints one letter to Miss James and Lamb wrote an acrostic to her. Another sister of Miss James's, Mrs Trueman, is mentioned in a letter from Lamb to Basil Montagu, in which Lamb states there were four sisters, all nurses at Mr Warburton's, Hoxton.

Jameson, Robert S. Barrister, later a Colonial judge. Connected with Fraser's Magazine. His wife, whom he married in 1825, was Anna Brownell Jameson, well known as a writer on art and for her *Shakespeare's Heroines*, 1832, *Beauties of the Court of Charles II*, 1833, and many other books. They separated in 1829. Jameson had been a school friend of Hartley Coleridge at Ambleside and later met him in London. Hartley wrote four sonnets to him printed in the *London Magazine* in February 1823 and reprinted in his *Poems*, 1833. Crabb Robinson notes in his *Reminiscences* on 22 June 1815 that Basil Montagu helped Jameson when he came to London. He also notes in 1834 that when Jameson became rich he neglected to help Hartley Coleridge who was destitute.

Jameson conveyed Lamb's play *The Wife's Trail* to Mrs Charles Kemble in 1827. There are several references to him in Lamb's letters and in one on 29 August 1827 Lamb writes seeking a situation for Emma Isola and he sends Mary Lamb's best regards to Mrs Jameson.

In a letter to Barton on 28 August 1827 Lamb describes Jameson as 'a particular friend of mine and Coleridge' and it was in response to Jameson's request that Lamb sent him several sets of verses for inclusion in William Fraser's annual *The Bijou*, 1828. Only the 'Verses for an Album' were included. In 1828 Jameson and James Gillman superintended the production of an edition of Coleridge's poems issued by William Pickering. Thomas Allsop in his *Letters, Conversations and Recollections of S.T. Coleridge* relates that it was when returning from a visit to the Tower with Jameson that Lamb saw two Billingsgate fish women fighting and made his joke about Fair-lop-Fair.

Japp, Alexander Hay, 1837–1905. Scottish author and publisher. Also wrote under the pseudonym of 'H.A. Page'. Was known to Leigh Hunt. Wrote an article in the *Gentleman's Magazine* in 1881 on 'Charles Lamb's Humour'. Japp also wrote much on De Quincey and published *Thomas De Quincey: His Life & Writings*, 1877 (under the name of H.A. Page, and *The Posthumous Works*, 1891–3. He helped to edit the *Contemporary Review and Chambers's Cyclopaedia of English Literature*. His publishing venture lasted only from 1880 to 1882 and was taken over by T. Fisher Unwin.

Jekyll, Joseph, 1753–1837. Barrister and one of Lamb's 'Old Benchers'. He became a Bencher in 1805 and a Master in Chancery in 1815. In 1787 Jekyll had been elected M.P. for Calne, Wiltshire. In 1824 he was one of the founders of the Athenaeum Club with John Wilson Croker and Sir Humphry Davy. He had been one of the Counsellors for Jane Austen's aunt, Mrs Leigh Perrot, when she was tried in 1800 on the unjustified charge of shop-lifting.

Jekyll was a noted wit and diner out and wrote interesting and amusing letters. He published the *Letters of Sancho*, 1802, and *Facts and Observations relating to the Temple Church* as a quarto pamphlet in 1811. Jekyll had chambers at 6 King's Bench Walk. He was a friend of George Colman the Younger, of George Dyer and of the Norrises. When Randal Norris died in 1827 Jekyll was of assistance with the petition to the Temple Benchers which Crabb Robinson and Lamb organized and an annuity of £70 per annum was paid to the widow by the Inn. In 1833 Lamb sent Jekyll a copy of *The Last Essays of Elia* and then forwarded the letter of thanks to Mrs Norris as it mentioned her brother. In the letter Jekyll thanks Lamb for 'another volume of your delightful pen', so probably there was an earlier gift. Jekyll was named with George Dyer as one of the ten executors of the third Earl of Stanhope (Citizen Stanhope).

Jepson, Rowland Walter, b.1888. Headmaster of Mercer's School, Holborn. Educated at Shrewsbury School and Magdalene College,

Oxford. Edited *Selected Essays of Charles Lamb*, 1931, which has an excellent map of London in the time of Charles Lamb. He also edited *Selections from Lamb and Hazlitt*, 1940. Author of *The Writer's Craft*, 1927.

Jerdan, William, 1782–1869. Scottish journalist. Editor of the *Literary Gazette*. Had written for many publications including *The Morning Post, Pilot, British Press, Satirist* and the *Sun*. He attacked Lamb's *Album Verses* in the *Literary Gazette* in 1830. Leigh Hunt in *The Examiner* rallied to his defence and Southey was so annoyed at Jerdan's abuse that he sent to *The Times* verses 'To Charles Lamb on the Review of his Album Verses in the Literary Gazette.' Lamb wrote an epigram against Jerdan. Jerdan wrote his *Autobiography*, 1853, and *Men I Have Known*, 1866. He is also remembered as having seized Perceval's assassin in the lobby of the House of Commons in 1812.

Jerrold, Walter, 1865–1929. Journalist and author. Grandson of Douglas Jerrold of *Punch*. He was sub-editor of *The Observer* and later a member of the literary staff of the *Daily Telegraph*. He wrote several books about his famous grandfather: *Douglas Jerrold and Punch*, 1910; *Douglas Jerrold, Dramatist and Wit*, 1914; *Jerrold's Jest Book*; and in 1903 he edited *The Essays of Douglas Jerrold*. With M.H. Spielmann he wrote *Hugh Thomson: His Art, His Letters, His Humour and His Charm*, published in 1931.

Among his other works are *Bon-Mots of Charles Lamb and Douglas Jerrold*, edited by Walter Jerrold, 1904; *Charles Lamb*, 1905; *Life and Times of Thomas Hood*, 1907; *Thomas Hood and Charles Lamb*, 1930. He also wrote *The Autolycus of the Bookstalls*, 1902; *A Descriptive Index to Shakespeare's Characters*, 1905; and *A Book of Famous Wits*, 1912. He edited Thomas Hood's *Poems* and various volumes in the Temple Classics, Everyman's Library and World's Classics series; among these was Lamb's *Essays and Sketches* in the Temple Classics. His articles in periodicals included one in *The Athenaeum* on 30 June 1906 which printed some poems by Lamb, and to the *Cornhill Magazine* he contributed in November 1924, 'Charles Lamb and "The Laughing Philosopher"'.

Johnson, Edith Christina, d.1954. Professor of English, Wellesley College, U.S.A. Author of *Lamb Always Elia*, 1935, an excellent study of Lamb which also contains an extensive chapter on Thomas Manning. Contributed an article 'Lamb and Coleridge' to the *American Scholar* in 1937 and a letter on 'Lamb and Manning' to the *Times Literary Supplement* on 31 August 1946. In September 1948 Professor Johnson lectured to the Charles Lamb Society on 'Charles Lamb's adopted daughter'.

Johnson, Reginald Brimley, 1867–1932. Author, editor and publisher. Educated at Christ's Hospital. Published *Rosamund Gray and Barbara S——* by Charles Lamb in The York Library, c.1912?. Wrote introduction to *A Tale of Rosamund Gray and old Blind Margaret,* Golden Cockerel Press, 1928. Published *Christ's Hospital: Recollections of Lamb, Coleridge and Leigh Hunt. Edited by R. Brimley Johnson, with some account of its foundation,* 1896; *Leigh Hunt,* 1896; *Essays of Leigh Hunt* and *Poems of Leigh Hunt,* both volumes selected and edited by R. Brimley Johnson for Dent's The Temple Library, 1891; *Cambridge Colleges,* 1909; *Fanny Burney and the Burneys,* 1926; *Jane Austen,* 1927; *Story lives of XIXth century authors,* 1925; and *The Letters of Mary Russell Mitford,* 1925. He has also edited the novels of Jane Austen, Fanny Burney and Captain Marryat and numerous volumes for several popular series.

Johnston, Mrs, b.1782. Actress, wife of Henry Erskine Johnston, the 'Scottish Roscius'. Acted with her husband in Ireland and first appeared in London in 1797. She played in *The Children of the Wood* and as Ophelia at the Haymarket in 1798, and at Covent Garden she played Lady Macbeth. She was well known as Elvira in *Pizarro* and had played with Charles Kemble at the Haymarket; was Dorinda in *The Beaux Stratagem* at Covent Garden in 1801 and in 1809 played opposite Liston in *The Mountaineers.* Leigh Hunt describes her as 'a slight, handsome creature, with a formidable power of looking vixenish.' Lamb mentions her rather disparagingly in 'The New Acting'.

Jones, A. Garth. Artist and book illustrator. Studied in Manchester and in 1893 went to Paris. Has illustrated many books including works by Coleridge, Goldsmith, Swift, Marco Polo's *Voyages* and Keats's poems. In 1901 he illustrated an edition of *The Essays of Elia* which has become well known because of the excellence of his work. He also illustrated the title page of Russell Davis Gillman's edition of *The Letters of Charles Lamb* published by George Newnes in 1905.

Jordan, Dorothy, 1761–1816. Actress, the greatest comedienne of her time; she played at Drury Lane from 1785 to 1809. She reached the height of her beauty and fame about 1790 and at that time became the mistress of the Duke of Clarence, later William IV, with whom she lived for twenty years and bore him ten children. She continued to act until 1814. She was painted by Reynolds, Gainsborough, Hoppner and Romney. Among her best parts were Lady Teazle, Miss Hardcastle, Lydia Languish and Peggy in *The Country Girl.*

   She was a favourite actress of Lamb's and he praised her highly in his essay 'On Some of the Old Actors', in 'The New Acting' and again in his letter to J.M. Gutch on Miss Kelly which was published in *Felix Farley's Bristol Journal*. Lamb said Mrs Jordan was 'sent to teach mankind what it most wants, joyousness.' In his essay 'The Old Actors' in the *London Magazine* in October 1822, Lamb in describing Charles Mathews's gallery of theatrical portraits wrote 'and (Shakespeare's woman) Dora Jordan.' He also praised her in his review of Kenney's 'Debtor & Creditor' in *The Examiner* on 8 May 1814 where he calls her 'One of Shakespeare's ladies'. In his review are quoted verses 'Thalia to Mrs Jordan' which Edmund Blunden identified as by Lamb in his *Leigh Hunt's 'Examiner' Examined*. She was also praised by Coleridge, Hazlitt, Leigh Hunt and Mrs Inchbald.

Her eldest daughter, Fanny Daly, married Thomas Alsop, who is often confused with the Allsop who was the friend of Coleridge and Lamb.

Joseph, George Francis, 1764–1846. Portrait and historical painter. Entered the Royal Academy schools in 1784, elected A.R.A. in 1813. Exhibited at the Royal Academy from 1788. His pictures include *Return of Priam with the dead body of Hector* and *Procession at Calvary*, but he is chiefly a portrait painter; the National Gallery has his paintings of the Hon. Spencer Perceval and Sir Stamford Raffles. He painted Mrs Siddons as the Tragic Muse in 1797.

Joseph painted a water colour portrait of Lamb in 1819 for William Evans of the East India House and *The Pamphleteer*. It is now in the British Museum. There is also a water colour portrait of Lamb by Joseph done about 1830 which is now in the Huntington Library.

Juvenile Library, The. A publishing venture founded by William Godwin in 1805 at the suggestion of his wife. It started at Godwin's house in Hanway Street, opposite Soho Square with £100 borrowed from Thomas Wedgwood. Because of Godwin's known radical writings it was first carried on under the name of Thomas Hodgkins, Godwin's manager. For a time the business prospered and larger premises were acquired at 41 Skinner Street, Snow Hill, in 1807 to which Godwin and his family moved, while next door he rented other rooms to be used as a printing shop and warehouse. It included a bookshop which also sold maps, pens and stationery and he seems to have had agents for his publications in some large provincial towns, and to have issued catalogues.

Hodgkins appears to have been unsatisfactory as a manager and was dismissed, and the business was carried on under the name of Godwin's wife, M.J. Godwin. Elizabeth Fenwick, the wife of Lamb's 'Ralph Bigod', took Hodgkins place for a time. Godwin was an unsatisfactory business man, much given to borrowing, and there was always a lack of capital in the publishing business. By 1807 he was in financial difficulties and an appeal for subscriptions was launched which brought in £1,200, contributions being received from a number of well-known people. Unfortunately these financial crises occurred from time to time until finally he became bankrupt and the Juvenile Library ceased to exist around 1822. He moved to a house in the Strand where some bookselling or publishing seems still to have been done as from the Juvenile Library, although the stock of the original bookshop was acquired by Baldwin & Cradock and advertised by them. They seem to have acquired rights in the publications also for they brought out new editions of some of them. In 1828 they advertised a tenth edition of *Fables Ancient and Modern*, a seventh edition of *The Pantheon* and the tenth edition of *Mrs Leicester's School*.

Carl Woodring in the *Harvard Library Bulletin*, Spring 1956, describes Sir Richard Phillips as 'one of the underwriters for Godwin's Juvenile Library' and adds that some of the books issued from the Library bore the name of Tabart. One of these was *The Book of Ranks and Dignities*, 1805, which has as publisher the name 'Tabart & Co at the Juvenile & School Library 157 New Bond Street.' Phillips published Godwin's *Fleetwood* in 1805 and he contributed £100 to the appeal for Godwin in 1808.

The most famous books issued by the Juvenile Library were those by Charles and Mary Lamb: *The King and Queen of Hearts*, 1805; *Tales from Shakespeare*, 1807; *The Adventures of Ulysses*, 1808; *Mrs Leicester's School*, 1809; *Poetry for Children*, 1809; *Prince Dorus*, 1811; and *Beauty and the Beast*, 1811. Godwin also published school books by W.F. Mylius: *A School Dictionary of the English Language* and three books edited by Mylius, which reprinted poems from Charles and Mary Lamb's *Poetry for Children*. They were *The Junior Class Book*, 1809; *The Poetical Class Book*, 1810; and *The First Book of Poetry*, 1811.

Among other books issued by the Juvenile Library was William Hazlitt's *A New and Improved Grammar of the English Tongue* to which Godwin added his own 'Guide to the English Tongue', 1810. Godwin also wrote books for the Library under the pseudonyms of Edward Baldwin (his foreman) and Theophilus Marcliffe, among which were *Fables Ancient and Modern*, 1805 (the first book from the Juvenile Library); *The Pantheon; or History of the Gods of Greece and Rome*, 1806; histories of England, 1806, Rome, 1809, and Greece, 1811; *The Looking Glass*, 1805; and *The Life of Lady Jane Grey*, 1806. Books by other writers included *The Little Woman and the Peddlar*, 1805; *Gaffer Gray*, 1806; *Tom and his Cat*, 1806; *Stories from Old Daniel*, 1808; *Monsieur Tonson* and *Monsieur Nongtongpaw*. Mrs Godwin also translated tales from the French and Mrs Fenwick wrote a pamphlet entitled *A Visit to the Juvenile Library*.

The principal illustrator was William Mulready, but some of the drawings were by Maria Flaxman, the sister of the sculptor, and

William Blake is said to have done some of the engravings. At one time he worked as a journeyman engraver and may well have worked for Godwin.

As a footnote to Godwin's activities it may be mentioned that P.H. Muir in *The Book Collector*, Autumn 1973, stated that jigsaw puzzles, then called dissected puzzles, were stocked and advertised by the Juvenile Library.

Kean, Edmund, 1787–1833. English tragedian, perhaps the best known actor of his time, whose life and acting became legendary. He first appeared in London in 1814. Among his famous parts were Shylock, Barabas in Marlowe's *Jew of Malta* and Sir Giles Overreach in Massinger's *A New Way to Pay Old Debts*. Hazlitt's reviews in the *Morning Chronicle* did much for Kean's reputation. He was described as the greatest actor that ever trod the English stage. Crabb Robinson has many references to Kean in his *Diary* and records that he took Mary Lamb to see him in *Richard II*, in *A New Way to Pay Old Debts* and *Timon of Athens* during 1815–16.

Lamb mentions him in his rhymed letter to William Ayrton on 12 May 1817, but merely states that he and Kean were of the same height. He refers to him in 'The Hypocrite', 'New Pieces at the Lyceum' and in the *New Times* on 28 August 1820 there is the review of 'Mr Kean as Hamlet' which has been attributed to Charles Lamb by William Macdonald. 'To see Kean act' said Coleridge was 'like reading Shakespeare by flashes of lightning.'

Keats, John, 1795–1821. Poet. Friend of Leigh Hunt, Hazlitt, Shelley, Dilke and Cowden Clarke. He was a pupil at John Clarke's school at Enfield; other pupils included Charles Cowden Clarke and Edward Holmes.

Although Lamb and Keats met they were not close friends, but Lamb admired the latter's poetry and wrote a review of *Lamia, Isabella, The Eve of St Agnes and Other Poems* in the *New Times* in 1820 in eulogistic terms. Leigh Hunt recorded in his *Lord Byron and his Contemporaries*, 1828, Lamb's pleasure on reading *Lamia*, and Lamb also praised Keats's poetry to Wordsworth and others. Crabb Robinson noted in his *Diary* on 8 December 1820 that Lamb placed Keats 'next to Wordsworth, not meaning any comparison. They are dissimilar.'

Keats was at the famous party at Haydon's in December 1817 when Lamb teased the Comptroller of Stamps. Keats also attended Novello's musical evenings. Writing to Benjamin Bailey in November 1817 Keats mentions calling on Lamb. In a letter to George and Georgiana Keats about 1818 or 1819 Keats wrote that he was taken by Hunt to Novello's where he met Lamb and was 'devastated and excruciated with bad and repeated puns.'

Kelly, Frances Maria, Fanny, 1790–1882. Actress and singer. Niece of Michael Kelly the composer and singer. She first appeared on the stage at Drury Lane at the age of seven. Later she played in many parts associated with Mrs Jordan, mainly at Drury Lane. She acted with all the great players of her time, including John and Charles Kemble, Mrs Siddons, Mrs Jordan, Munden, Suett, Liston, Mathews, Bannister and Catalani. She was especially associated with Edmund Kean, her playmate in childhood, and was often the Ophelia to his Hamlet.

Her farewell performance at Drury Lane was in 1835 when she played Lisette in John Banim's *The Serjeant's Wife*, also acting Peggy in *The Country Girl* (Garrick's alteration from Wycherley's *Country Wife*), as a curtain raiser. After her retirement from Drury Lane she undertook provincial tours and subsequently started a school of dramatic art at the Strand Theatre, later transferred to a theatre built at the back of the house she then occupied in Dean Street, Soho. In this she had as patron the Duke of Devonshire, but the project was not successful due mainly, according to John Forster, to her lack of business sense. As an old woman Fanny Kelly is said to have become eccentric.

Lamb had seen her on the stage for some years before they met. The exact date is uncertain; it may have been by 1813 as suggested by her biographer, Basil Francis. Neil Bell in his novel *So Perish the Roses* included her in the 1806 supper party to celebrate 'Mr H——,' although he does not say on what evidence. They were certainly acquainted by about 1816 and probably met at Kenney's house earlier. The first letter from Lamb which mentions her is that to the Kenneys wrongly dated 1817 by Lucas instead of 1816 (No. 301). The first extant letter to her from Lamb appears to be that dated 31 December 1818 (No. 313 in Lucas which he dates October 31, 1818).

Lamb admired her acting greatly and often praised her in print; the following are the known items he wrote which refer to Fanny Kelly:

1813   *Examiner*, The New Acting (July 18).
——   *Morning Chronicle*, Sonnet to Miss Kelly ('You are not, Kelly, of the common strain'). Reprinted *Examiner*, 12 July 1818, and *Works*, 1818.
1818   *Examiner*, Paragraph following Leigh Hunt's review of 'A Word to the Ladies' (20 December). Reprinted Lucas *Letters* 1935 II 253.
1819   *Felix Farley's Bristol Journal*, Miss Kelly at Bath (January 30). Reprinted *Examiner*, 7 February 1819.
——   *Examiner*, Richard Brome's 'Jovial Crew' (July 4).
——   Isaac Bickerstaff's 'Hypocrite'. (August 1).
——   New Pieces at the Lyceum. (August 8).
——   *Morning Chronicle*, Sonnet to Miss Kelly on her performance

of Edmond in the 'Blind Boy' Reprinted *Examiner*, 14 November 1819; *Table Book*, 1827, and *Album Verses*, 1830.

1825 *London Magazine* (April) Barbara S——. Reprinted *Last Essays of Elia*, 1833.

In July 1819 Lamb proposed marriage to Fanny Kelly, but she did not feel she could accept him, mainly because of the taint of insanity in his family, although she did not give him this reason. They remained good friends, however, for the rest of his life and in 1827 she was staying at his house and continued to visit Mary Lamb after her brother's death. Lucas in the *Life* II 18 raises the query whether Lamb's proposal of marriage to Fanny Kelly had a bearing on his essay 'Dream Children', published in the *London Magazine* in 1822. Fanny Kelly died unmarried.

A number of letters exist from Charles and Mary Lamb to Fanny Kelly: in February 1818 Lamb's letter to Mrs Wordsworth has the phrase about 'a gleam of Fanny Kelly's divine plain face.' The review of Brome's 'Jovial Crew' contained the equally well known sentence 'What a lass that were ... to go a gipsying through the world with.' At one period she was taught Latin by Mary Lamb and George Darley. When the Lambs moved to Great Russell Street they were only a few yards from Fanny Kelly's residence in Henrietta Street.

John Hollingshead in his *My Lifetime*, 1895 I 11, states that Miss Kelly was of the Lamb's party which visited Paris in 1822. Hollinghead's aunt was Sarah James, the nurse who accompanied the party to France, and he must be relying on her reminiscences since he was not born at the time. There appears to be no other evidence of this and neither Miss Kelly's biographers nor E.V. Lucas mentions it. The Lambs had left London for France on 18 June 1822. Crabb Robinson, who was in Paris on August 18 when Mary Lamb was still there, does not mention it. In August Fanny Kelly was playing in 'Gil Blas' at the English Opera House.

Fanny Kelly was shot at on the stage of Drury Lane in February 1816 by the deranged George Barnett, a desperate admirer; some of the shot fell into Mary Lamb's lap. Barnett is said to have given her the alternative of a duel or marriage with him, and he ended his life in an asylum. A similar attempt is said to have been made on her life in Dublin, but her biographer, Basil Francis, could find no record of this.

Miss Kelly had a sister Lydia, also an actress, and Nancy Jackson, her half-sister, became Charles Mathews's second wife. In April 1829 a Mary Ellen Gerbini was born at Edinburgh who was referred to as Fanny Kelly's adopted daughter. There is some possibility that she was her illegitimate daughter and writers on Lamb and Fanny Kelly have argued about it for years. Lucas definitely states in a note to the *Letters* 1935 II 256 that she entered into a liaison: Basil Francis examined the evidence at some length and is not sure, but he obviously wishes to discredit the rumour. When Miss Kelly died she left all her property to Mary Gerbini, who had then changed her name to Greville. Lydia Kelly also made provision for Miss Greville in her will, who she named as 'daughter of Frances Maria Kelly, spinster.' A photograph of Miss Greville was reproduced in *The Bookman* in November 1926.

Most of Lamb's friends also admired Miss Kelly and John Hamilton Reynolds wrote the text of her well known solo performance 'Dramatic Recollections & Imitations'. She was praised by Hazlitt and Thomas Hood wrote 'Ode to Miss Kelly on her opening of the Strand Theatre.' This was printed in *The Atlas*. He also wrote several songs for her.

Kemble, Charles, 1775–1854. Actor. Brother of Mrs Siddons and John Philip Kemble. Was joint proprietor and manager of Covent Garden and later an examiner of plays. Father of Fanny Kemble, the actress. Among his best parts were Benedick, Mercutio, Mirabell and Charles Surface. He was not suited to tragedy which he wisely avoided, except for a successful playing of Romeo. When he played Mercutio at Covent Garden in 1829 his daughter, Fanny, played Juliet.

He sometimes attended Lamb's Thursday evening parties. In August 1827 Lamb sent his play *The Wife's Trial* to Kemble, but it was not accepted. Kemble married Marie Thérèsa de Camp, 1773–1838, an actress who had been a leading dancer at the Royal Surrey Theatre. She became well known as Edmond in *The Blind Boy* and Lady Elizabeth Freelove in her own *The Day after the Wedding*. Lamb refers to her in his essay 'Barbara S——' as 'ever good-humoured Mrs Charles Kemble', where he also says 'I have conversed as friend to friend with her accomplished Husband.'

Kemble, John Philip, 1757–1823. Actor. Described as the greatest tragedian of his time and as a great actor in the grand manner. He was manager of Drury Lane from 1788 and later at Covent Garden, 1803–17. Here he caused the O.P. Riots by raising the prices. Some of his best parts were Wolsey, Brutus, Cato and Coriolanus. He is said to have played more than 120 characters with Mrs Siddons and others. He was a favourite actor of Lamb's. In 1799 Lamb sent his play *John Woodvil* to Kemble who offered to pass it to the proprietors of Drury Lane. The copy sent was lost and Lamb supplied another, but after about a year it was returned as unsuitable. Lamb mentions Kemble as an actor in his essays 'On the Tragedies of Shakespeare ...', 'On Some of the Old Actors', 'On the Artificial Comedy of the Last Century', 'The Old Actors' and in 'Imperfect Sympathies'. Kemble played Antonio in Godwins' play of that name to which Lamb wrote an epilogue. Lamb tells the story of the failure of the play in a part of the essay 'On the Artificial Comedy . . .' originally printed in the *London Magazine* but omitted in the *Elia* volume. Kemble retired from the stage in 1817.

Kendall, Kenneth Everett, b.1913. Professor of English, University of Florida. Author of *Leigh Hunt's Reflector*, The Hague, 1971, which contains many references to Lamb and lists his contributions to *The Reflector*.

Kennedy, Mrs, d.1793. English contralto and actress. Was a pupil of Dr Arne. Formerly known as Mrs Farrell, she married Dr Kennedy in 1779. Appeared at Covent Garden in 1776 in *Caractacus* with Arne's music. She often sang at concerts and at Covent Garden, Drury Lane and Vauxhall. In 1791 she sang at a Fête at Frogmore. Her chief successes were in male parts, playing Artaxerxes in 1777, Belford in *Love Finds a Way* and Allen-a-Dale in *Robin Hood* in 1784. She was especially good as Captain Macheath in *The Beggar's Opera*. In 1788 she played Huncamunca in *Tom Thumb*.

Lamb mentions her in his piece 'Playhouse Memoranda' in *The Examiner* in connexion with the first play he saw *Artaxerxes*, although she does not seem to have been in the cast at the time.

Kenney, James, 1780–1849. Irish dramatist, son of James Kenney, one of the founders of Boodles' Club. Originally in a banking house, he later became a successful playwright who produced more than forty dramas and operas. His farce *Raising the Wind*, 1803, contained the famous character of Jeremy Diddler, while his play *Love, Law and Physic* gave Liston the part of Lubin Log. The most popular of his plays was *Sweethearts and Wives* at the Haymarket in 1823.

In 1812 he married the widow of Thomas Holcroft, who was a Frenchwoman, and they later went to live in France. There is a pleasing picture of the Kenney household at Versailles in a letter of 1823 from Mary Shelley to Leigh Hunt. In 1822 the Lambs stayed with the Kenneys at Versailles during part of their visit to France. James Kenney had been a close friend of Lamb's when he lived in England and a frequent visitor to his house. Kenney named his youngest son Charles Lamb Kenney.

Lamb wrote an epilogue to Kenney's farce *Debtor and Creditor* which was produced in April 1814 and he reviewed it in *The Examiner*. Lamb mentions Kenney in his essay 'The Two Races of Men' as having carried off the folio of the Duchess of Newcastle's *Letters*, but it was eventually returned. Kenney was also friendly with Godwin, Hazlitt, Leigh Hunt, Mary Shelley and Samuel Rogers. He was present on the occasion when John Lamb knocked Hazlitt down.

Kent, William Charles Mark, 1823–1902. Poet, biographer and miscellaneous writer. Barrister of the Middle Temple. Edited *The Sun* after W.F. Deacon and the *Weekly Register*. He wrote under the name of 'Charles Kent' and 'Mark Rochester'. In 1864 he wrote *Footprints on the Road* which refers to Leigh Hunt. He also wrote books on Burns, Lytton and Father Prout. In 1876 he edited a one-volume edition of *The Works of Charles Lamb* and it was several times reprinted. In his Prefatory Memoir he includes a letter he had received from Fanny Kelly in which she states that she related to Charles Lamb the incident which was used later in the essay 'Barbara S——'. Kent also printed in his volume, as by Lamb, a 'Comic Opera' from a manuscript in the British Museum, although most later editors reject this as Lamb's work. Kent also prints in his edition six facsimiles of Lamb's manuscripts, including part of the doubtful 'Comic Opera'. In his note to 'The Old Benchers of the Inner Temple' he makes the extraordinary statement that the Benchers mentioned by Lamb 'were with one or two exceptions purely imaginary characters.' He also did the notes to an edition of *The Essays of Elia* published by Routledge (n.d.).

Kent edited a selection of Leigh Hunt's work, *Leigh Hunt as Poet and Essayist*, 1889, and included his own reminiscences of Hunt who was a friend. Among his other friends were Charles Dickens, Lord Lytton, Charles Reade, Robert Browning, George Meredith and Matthew Arnold.

Kent, William Richard Gladstone, 1884–1963. Civil Servant who had also worked for the L.C.C. and London Passenger Transport Board. Well known as an authority on London, as a lecturer and guide. The author of about twenty-five books most of which concern London and several refer to Charles Lamb. He wrote under the name of 'William Kent'. A founder member of the Charles Lamb Society who occasionally lectured to it and guided parties around London.

Among his books which refer to Lamb are *An Encyclopaedia of London*, 1937, reprinted 1951, edited by W. Kent, who also wrote about three fourths of it; it contains many references to Lamb; *London Worthies*, 1939 (seven columns are devoted to Lamb); *London for Dickens Lovers*, 1935; *The Lost Treasures of London*, 1947 (numerous Lamb references); *London for the Literary Pilgrim*, 1949 (in addition to several pages on Lamb, there are five pages on S.M. Rich and his Lamb Room with its notable collection of Eliana— much of which is now in the Charles Lamb Society's Library).

Kent has written many other books on London among which are *London for Everyman*, 1931; *London for Shakespeare Lovers*, 1934; *London for the Curious*, 1946; *Mine Host, London*, 1948; and *London in the News*, 1954.

Kenyon, John, 1784–1856. Poet and philanthropist. Friend of

Coleridge, Southey, Wordsworth, Crabb Robinson, B.W. Procter, Landor, and Miss Mitford, but perhaps best known as the friend of Browning. Educated at Charterhouse and Cambridge. He frequently stayed at Nether Stowey with Coleridge's friend Poole. Kenyon met Lamb through Southey and sent Elia a pig with verses accompanying it. Lucas prints a letter to Kenyon in February 1834, but they had been known to each other for many years and Crabb Robinson's *Diary* states that in November 1820 he dined at Monkhouse's with the Wordsworths, the Lambs and Kenyon. John Kenyon published *A Rhymed Plea for Tolerance*, 1833; *Poems*, 1838; and *A Day at Tivoli with other Verses*, 1849. Robinson described him as having 'the face of a Benedictine monk and the joyous talk of a good fellow.'

Keymer, James. London bookseller and stationer of 142 Cheapside. John Forster asked Lamb to write something for Keymer's Album. Lamb wrote 'The Death of Coleridge' which Forster later quoted in his memorial article on Lamb in the *New Monthly Magazine* in February 1835. Bernard Barton wrote to Keymer on 4 January 1835 also giving a sketch of Lamb and asking Keymer for a copy of 'The Death of Coleridge'. Barton's letter to Keymer was published in *Notes & Queries*, 18 October 1879, and reprinted in Blunden's *Charles Lamb: His Life Recorded by his Contemporaries*, 1934. Keymer married the sister of Laman Blanchard and was a friend of W.C. Hazlitt.

Kiddell, John. Clerk to the Private Trade Warehouse-keeper at East India House. Lamb says in his letter of 8 October 1824 to J.A. Hessey that Kiddell owns the original letter of James Thomson which Lamb had sent for the *London Magazine*, where it was printed in November 1824.

King, R.W. Lecturer, University College of North Wales, Bangor. Author of *The Translator of Dante: The Life, Work and Friendships of Henry Francis Cary*, 1925, which contains much about Charles Lamb and the London Magazine circle. His numerous contributions to periodicals include:

Nineteenth Century
1923 Charles Lamb, Cary and the London Magazine (September and October).
Modern Language Review
1925–6 Italian Influence on English Scholarship during the Romantic Revival.
1956 Article on Shelley and Southey.
Review of English Studies
1928 Crabb Robinson's Opinion on Shelley.
1946 Review of Jack Simmons's Southey.

Times Literary Supplement
1953   The Text of Hazlitt (March 13 and 27, April 10).

He also contributed bibliographies to the *Cambridge Bibliography of English Literature*, including those for Thomas Campbell, Thomas Moore, Samuel Rogers, George Darley, Thomas Hood, W.M. Praed and F. Wrangham.

King, Thomas, 1730–1805. English actor and dramatist. First appeared at Drury Lane in 1748 under Garrick. He was the original Sir Peter Teazle and Puff. He was also very successful as Malvolio and Touchstone, but his best known part was as Lord Ogleby in 'The Clandestine Marriage'. He was later manager at Drury Lane under Sheridan. King was said to be one of the first actors to give naturalistic and life-like performances. He retired from the stage in 1802 and played Sir Peter Teazle at his benefit. Late in life he went into theatrical management in Bristol and at Sadler's Wells, but lost most of the considerable wealth he had accumulated. He also wrote a number of farces.

Lamb mentions him in his essay 'On the Artificial Comedy of the Last Century'. He was praised highly by Hazlitt who described his acting in later life as leaving 'a taste on the palate sharp and sweet like a quince; with an old hard, rough, withered face, like a johnapple, puckered up in a thousand wrinkles, with shrewd hints and tart replies.'

Kingston, John. Comptroller of Stamps. The victim of Charles Lamb's misbehaviour at Haydon's famous party in December 1817 where Kingston had been invited to tea. There are several references to him in Keats's letters, but he does not seem to have liked him. Wordsworth dined with Kingston subsequent to the famous party. *The London Kalendar* for 1815 lists John Kingston as Deputy Comptroller and Accomptant General. In November 1818 he was promoted to be one of seven commissioners of the Stamp Office, another was Henry Hallam. It is thought that Kingston retired from the Stamp Office about 1827.

Kirlew, Marianne. Author of *Famous Sisters of Great Men* published by Thomas Nelson. [n.d.] It includes Mary Lamb and Dorothy Wordsworth.

Knight, Anne. Quakeress who kept a school at Woodbridge with her sisters. A friend of Bernard Barton who lodged in her house at one time. He introduced her to the Lambs in 1825. There are numerous references to her in Lamb's letters and he seems to have given her a copy of *The Adventures of Ulysses* in 1827. She had a daughter named Emma.

Knight, Edward, 1774–1826. English comic actor and dramatist. Began his career as an artist. but gave it up for the stage. Played in the provinces including a period at York with Tate Wilkinson. First appeared in London in 1809 and played at both Drury Lane and the Lyceum. One of his best parts was Sim in O'Keeffe's *Wild Oats*. He was said to be the best actor of his day in sharp footmen and cunning rustics. He was the author of a musical farce *The Sailor and Soldier, or Fashionable Amusements*. 1805. He also re-set *The Committee* as *The Honest Thieves*.

Lamb mentions him in his essay 'On the Acting of Munden.' On 17 February 1816 Knight was playing at Drury Lane in *Modern Antiques; or the Merry Mourners* as leading man to Fanny Kelly when George Barnett fired at Miss Kelly from the pit. The Lambs were present on this occasion.

Knowles, James Sheridan, 1784–1862. Irish dramatist and actor. Had also been a soldier, doctor and schoolmaster. Was a cousin of R.B. Sheridan. He wrote many plays including *Caius Gracchus*, 1815; *William Tell*, 1825; and *The Love Chase*, 1837. The most successful was *The Hunchback*, 1832. For his play *The Wife* Lamb wrote both a prologue and an epilogue. He also wrote verses to Knowles on his tragedy of *Virginius*, 1820, which were published in the *London Magazine* for September 1820. In these he says 'Twelve years ago I knew thee, Knowles.' Macready played the lead in this play and J.H. Reynolds wrote a prologue and B.W. Procter an epilogue for it. His comedy *The Beggar's Daughter of Bethnal Green* was produced at Drury Lane in 1828.

Lamb copied into Emma Isola's Extract Book the 'Sonnet written on seeing Bewick's Chalk Drawing of the Head of Hazlitt' by Sheridan Knowles. Both Lamb and Hazlitt were friends of Knowles and in his *The Spirit of the Age* the latter called him the first tragic writer of his time. Knowles eventually left the stage and in 1843 became a Baptist preacher.

Lachlan, Sarah. Lamb mentions 'The Lachlans' in a letter to Moxon on 27 April 1833. and in August he wrote to Miss Lachlan about some papers to be handed to the Westwoods. Lucas says the Lachlans were neighbours at Enfield. but a fuller account of them is given by 'E.G.B.' in *Notes & Queries* of 10 May 1941, where an acrostic by Lamb to Sarah Lachlan is printed, and it is mentioned that it concerns a painting by Emma Isola. Lucas prints the poem in *Poems and Plays*, 1903, under the title of 'Un Solitaire.'

Lake, Bernard. Author of *A General Introduction to Charles Lamb*, Leipzig, 1903. This also deals with the relationship of Lamb and Robert Burton. Lake makes the comment that 'lovers of Lamb must become lovers of Burton.'

Lamb, Charles, 1775–1834. Born 10 February 1775 at No. 2 Crown Office Row, Inner Temple, the youngest child of John and Elizabeth Lamb. Christened by Rev. Mr Jeffs 10 March 1775. Godfathers: Henshaw, a gunsmith, and Francis Fielde, an oilman of Holborn. Educated first at Mr Bird's Academy, Bond Stables, Fetter Lane, London, about 1781. Entered Christ's Hospital 9 October 1782; left 23 November 1789. Worked in Joseph Paice's office, 27 Bread Street, probably between 1789 and 1791. Entered the South Sea House 1 September 1791 where he worked in the Examiner's Office. Left 8 February 1792. Entered East India House 5 April 1792. Retired 29 March 1825. Died Saturday, 27 December 1834, at Bay Cottage, Edmonton, and was buried on 3 January 1835 in Edmonton Churchyard. At the funeral were T.N. Talfourd, Charles Ryle, Edward Moxon and Thomas Allsop.

In a letter in the *Times Literary Supplement* of 7 March 1968 E.E. Duncan-Jones quotes from an unpublished journal of Rev. William Harness, Miss Mitford's friend, a remark by Charles Lamb that his grandfather had been a cobbler.

List of the principal books published:

1796   *Coleridge's Poems on Various Subjects* containing four poems by Lamb.
1797   *Coleridge's Poems.* Second Edition, containing poems by Lamb.
1798   *Blank Verse by Charles Lloyd and Charles Lamb, A Tale of Rosamund Gray and Old Blind Margaret.*
1802   *John Woodvil, a Tragedy.*
1806   *The King and Queen of Hearts.*
1807   *Tales from Shakespeare.*
1808   *Specimens of English Dramatic Poets who lived About the Time of Shakespeare, The Adventures of Ulysses.*
1809   *Mrs Leicester's School. Poetry for Children.*
1811   *Prince Dorus. Beauty and the Beast.*
1813   *Mr H——, or Beware of a Bad Name* (Philadelphia).
1818   *The Works of Charles Lamb.*
1823   *Elia. Essays which have appeared under that Signature in the London Magazine.*
1828   *Elia. Second Series* (Philadelphia). (Erroneously includes some essays not by Lamb).
1830   *Album Verses.*
1831   *Satan in Search of a Wife.*
1833   *The Last Essays of Elia*

See Chronology of Lamb's life.

Lamb, Elizabeth, c.1732–96. Wife of John Lamb, senior, and mother of Charles, Mary and John Lamb, junior. She was the daughter of Mary Field, housekeeper of Blakesware House, Ware, Hertfordshire. She is described as tall and stately, resembling Mrs Siddons. Mary Lamb in her letter of 21 September 1803 to Sarah Stoddart refers to her mother as 'a perfect gentlewoman'. On 22 September 1796 she died as a result of a knife wound inflicted by her daughter, Mary, in a fit of madness. She was buried at St Andrews, Holborn.

Elizabeth Field married John Lamb in 1761 and had seven children: Elizabeth, 1762; John, 1763; Mary Anne, 1764; Samuel, 1765; Elizabeth, 1768; Edward, 1770; and Charles, 1775. Only John, Mary and Charles reached maturity. Miss Mann has revealed many facts about the Field family (*C.L.S. Bulletin*, No. 146) among which is that there were Quakers in the family.

Lamb, John (Senior), ?1722–99. Father of Charles, Mary and John Lamb. Waiter to the Inner Temple and until 1792 servant and assistant to Samuel Salt, Bencher of the Inner Temple. He was appointed Second Waiter in 1756 and First Waiter in 1772. On 29 March 1761 he married Elizabeth Field, at St Dunstan's Church; the witnesses were William Dorrell who gave away the bride, Bennett Thomason and Mary Field. At the time of Charles Lamb's birth the family lived at No. 2 Crown Office Row, Inner Temple. When Samuel Salt died in 1792 John Lamb continued as First Waiter until his death. Salt left John Lamb £500 South-Sea Stock in his Will and £200 to Mrs Lamb. In his latter days John Lamb became enfeebled and was rather exacting to Charles. When he died he was buried in the churchyard of St Andrews, Holborn, April 1799.

John Lamb wrote *Poetical Pieces on Several Occasions* which is reprinted in Lucas's *Life of Charles Lamb* with a portrait of the author. Lamb's references to his father occur in his poem 'Written on the Day of my Aunt's funeral' included in *Blank Verse*. A detailed sketch is included in the essay 'On the Old Benchers of the Inner Temple' where he is referred to under the name of 'Lovel', and he is mentioned in Lamb's letters.

In Charles Lamb's library was a volume of *Hudibras* with John Lamb's signature on the title and two volumes of *The Guardian* that had belonged to his father. John Lamb was a keen angler. Lucas *Letters*, 1935 II 318 states that John Lamb's will proves that Charles Lamb had two aunts—presumably John Lamb's sisters.

Lamb, John (Junior), 1763–1821. Elder brother of Charles Lamb. Samuel Salt procured his entry into Christ's Hospital in 1770 where he remained eight years. Salt also obtained for him his employment with the South Sea Company. By 1792 he had become Deputy Accountant, on the promotion of John Tipp to Accountant, and later followed him to become Accountant, with a suite of rooms allotted to him.

John Lamb was Bondsman for his brother at East India House. In 1796 he injured his leg seriously. Late in life he married a widow, Mrs Isaac Dowden, with one or more children. She died in May 1825. In his Will made in July 1821 John Lamb appointed his brother as executor and trustee of his estate. When Mary Lamb stabbed her mother in 1796 John Lamb attempted to confine her permanently to an asylum, a move resisted by Charles.

His father's book *Poetical Pieces on Several Occasions* has a poem 'A Letter from a child to his grandmother' signed 'John L—b the less.' In *Poetry for Children*, published in 1809 as by the author of *Mrs Leicester's School*, there was one poem 'The Beggar Man' by John Lamb; in Charles Lamb's *Works* published in 1818 was a poem 'To John Lamb Esq. Of the South Sea House', while he figures in Lamb's essays 'My Relations' and 'Dream Children' as James Elia. Both essays give detailed pictures of him. In *The First Book of Poetry*, the editor, W.F. Mylius, included John Lamb's poem 'The Beggar Man'.

John Lamb wrote a pamphlet in 1810 'A Letter to the Right Hon. William Windham, on his opposition to Lord Erskine's Bill for the prevention of Cruelty to Animals.' He also contributed to *The Examiner*, and probably wrote the letter 'On the Custom of Stifling Children to Prevent their Catching Cold' in January 1814, and in November 1818 he wrote a letter on the Corn Laws of 1815.

He had a taste for pictures and after his death his collection was sold at Christie's in March 1822, realizing £336. Some pictures did not fetch the reserve place on them and were returned to the widow. A list of those sold is given in Mrs Anderson's article in *The Bookman* in July 1921. One picture, a portrait of Milton, which John Lamb bought in 1815 passed to Charles and was given by him to Emma Isola.

Although known to Charles Lamb's friends, he was not particularly popular with them. Crabb Robinson disliked him, and following an argument with Hazlitt about the colours of Holbein and Vandyke, John Lamb knocked the essayist down. There were, however, no bad feelings as a result of this, for as Hazlitt commented, he did not mind a blow, 'nothing but an *idea* hurts me.' Talfourd described John Lamb as 'jovial and burly'.

Lucas prints one letter written on 22 May 1822 from Charles Lamb to his brother's widow and Mary Lamb added a footnote.

Miss Mann has discovered that John Lamb was buried on 7 November 1821 at St Martin Outwich. The church stood on the corner site at the junction of Threadneedle Street with Bishopsgate, but was demolished in 1874.

John Lamb's name appears among the list of subscribers in some editions of Leigh Hunt's *Juvenilia*.

In a letter written to Thomas Allsop, probably in 1819, Charles Lamb seeks employment for a youth he describes as his 'God Son, a nephew.' Mrs Anderson commented that if Lamb really meant 'Nephew', he can only have referred to a natural son of his brother, John. Mrs Anderson in an article in *The Bookman* in July 1921 states that 'We have a hint from Crabb Robinson that John Lamb had irregular connections, who would have to be provided for, as well as his widow.' In a letter of 11 July 1830 (No. 854 in Lucas), Lamb refers to 'Mrs Dowden my Niece' who lived at Brighton.

Lamb, Mary Anne, 1764–1847. Elder sister of Charles Lamb. Born 3 December 1764. Baptized 30 December 1764 by Rev. Mr Humphreys. Educated at William Bird's Academy, Bond Stables off Fetter Lane. Worked as a mantua maker until 1796 and in that year on 22 September she stabbed her mother in a fit of insanity. Her mother died as a result and Mary was confined in an asylum at Islington from 1796 to 1797. She recovered in the Spring of 1797 and lived in lodgings at Hackney. She had a relapse at the end of 1797, but again recovered and in 1799, after the death of her father, she returned to live with Charles. She was subject to periodical attacks of insanity for the rest of her life, attacks which became more frequent and of longer duration as she became older. Although her brother John wished to confine her permanently to an asylum, Charles resisted this and undertook her care for the rest of his days.

Much of her life was normal and the brother and sister lived in amity. In 1808 Mary was bridesmaid at the wedding of William Hazlitt and Sarah Stoddart. She frequently accompanied Charles on his holidays and in 1822 went with him to France, but suffered an attack of her malady and had to remain there until she recovered. She was often accompanied on such journeys by Sarah James, a professional nurse and friend. In June 1833 she received a legacy of £30 from Anne Betham, a friend. She died 20 May 1847, at a house in Alpha Road, St Johns Wood, and was buried in Edmonton Churchyard with her brother. Mourners at her funeral were T.N. Talfourd, Charles Ryle, Edward Moxon, Crabb Robinson, John Forster, Thomas Allsop, Martin Burney and an uninvited guest named Mockshay (? Moxey).

She is the 'Bridget Elia' mentioned in some of Charles Lamb's essays and is referred to in 'Mrs Battle's Opinions on Whist', 'Mackery End in Hertfordshire' and 'Old China', and of course in the letters. She also wrote a number of interesting letters herself. In *Recollections of Writers* by Charles and Mary Cowden Clarke 1878 it is stated that when Mary Lamb was asked if she remembered Garrick, she replied 'I saw him once, but I was too young to understand much about acting. I only knew I thought it was mighty fine.' Her books and writings include:

1807   *Tales from Shakespeare.* Jointly with Charles, Mary wrote the comedies.

1809   *Mrs Leicester's School.* Mary wrote all the tales except Maria Howe, Susan Yates and Arabella Hardy, which were by Charles.

1809   *Poetry for Children.* Written jointly with Charles. Helen Repentant too late—a poem 1800. Printed *John Woodvil,* 1802. Reprinted, *Works,* 1818 and *London Magazine,* September 1824.

Verses on the birth of Hazlitt's son, 1811. 'There lives at Winterslow a man.' Printed in W.C. Hazlitt's *Lamb and Hazlitt,* 1900. Reprinted Lucas *Life,* I 312. Hazlitt does not name the author, but Lucas attributes the verses to Mary Lamb.

On Needle-Work, *The British Lady's Magazine,* 1815.

Dialogue Between a Mother and Child, *Works,* 1818.

Lines, suggested by a Picture of Two Females by Leonardo Da Vinci, *Works,* 1818.

Lines, on the same Picture being removed to make place for a Portrait of a Lady by Titian, *Works,* 1818.

Lines, on the celebrated Picture by Leonardo Da Vinci, called the Virgin of the Rocks. 'Maternal lady with the virgin grace,' *Works,* 1818.

Salome, *Works* 1818.

A Lady's Sapphic, *The Champion,* 4 November 1820.

What is Love? *The Keepsake,* 1829.

To Emma learning Latin, *Blackwood's Magazine,* June 1829.

Verses at the end of Charles Lamb's 'Free Thoughts on Several Eminent Composers', Written in Vincent Novello's Album about 1830. Printed by Lucas. *Poems & Plays* 1903.322.

In Miss Westwood's Album, *Notes & Queries,* 4 June 1870.

Lines on the loss of Captain John Wordsworth, 1805. Reprinted, Lucas, 1903. William Macdonald in his edition of Lamb's *Works,* 1903, attributed *Beauty and the Beast* to Mary Lamb.

Mary Lamb was a favourite among her brother's friends. Talfourd said she was remarkable for the sweetness of her disposition, the clearness of her understanding and the gentle wisdom of all her acts and words. Talfourd quotes Hazlitt as saying she was the only reasonable woman he knew. Leigh Hunt in his 'Blue Stocking Revels' refers to her fine brain. Hood and Proctor both praised her intellect, and to Crabb Robinson who had criticized Hazlitt to her, she replied 'You are rich in friends. We cannot afford to cast off our friends because they are not all we wish.' In his *Diary* on 11 December 1814 Crabb Robinson praised her style in *Mrs Leicester's School.*

Lamb, Sarah, c.1712–97. Charles Lamb's 'Aunt Hetty', his father's eldest sister, who remained unmarried. She lived with the Lambs until the tragedy of 1796, then went to live with a rich relation, but soon returned to her nephew's rooms. She had a sister who lived in The Borough. Lamb gives glimpses of his kind hearted old aunt, with whom he was a favourite, in his essays 'My Relations', 'Poor Relations', 'Witches and other Night Fears' and in the story 'The Witch Aunt' in *Mrs Leicester's School*. She is also mentioned in the 'Dissertation upon Roast Pig', in the Elia essay on Christ's Hospital and in his letters. He wrote verses 'Written on the day of my aunt's funeral' which were printed in his *Blank Verse* in 1798. She was buried at St Andrews, Holborn.

Sarah Lamb's favourite reading was Thomas à Kempis and a Roman Catholic Prayer Book. Basing her theory on this Katharine Anthony suggests that she may have been a Catholic.

Lamb Dinners. J.C. Squire wrote in the *Westminster Gazette* in 1925 that when the English want to organize or celebrate something they exclaim 'We had better have a dinner.' There have been many occasions when lovers of Charles Lamb's works have wished to commemorate his birthday, the date of his retirement, his death or some of his writings by some function. This has usually been a dinner or lunch, although there have been many meetings to celebrate Lamb unaccompanied by manducation. Many of these occasions have become famous and some information on them may be interesting.

London Tavern, 1817. On 11 February 1817 The Amicable Society of Blues held a dinner at the London Tavern at which Charles Lamb was the guest of honour of his old schoolfellows. This is thought to be the occasion when his speech was limited to the one word 'Gentlemen.' Unfortunately little information is available on this function, but it is recorded in the Society's minutes.

Taylor and Hessey's functions, 1822–3. Although the publishers of the *London Magazine* gave dinners to their contributors, they were not specially for the benefit of any one contributor, but it is likely that the dinner held soon after the publication of the *Elia* volume at the end of 1822 would be something of a celebration for Charles Lamb. At least those attending are likely to have drunk his health.

Swinburne Dinner, 1875. In January 1875 Edmund Gosse drew Swinburne's attention to the joint anniversaries of Lamb and Landor occurring that year. It was suggested in *The Athenaeum* that some celebration should take place. Accordingly on 10 February a dinner was held at a hotel in Soho and was organized by Algernon Charles Swinburne, as he put it 'to partake of our Passover feast in honour of a Lamb quite other than Paschal (as Carlyle might word it).' Those present were William Minto, Thomas Purnell, Theodore Watts and Edmund Gosse, with Swinburne in the Chair. The dinner may have been a success for Swinburne had ordered it 'with careless rapture', although Gosse called it a 'rough entertainment', but unfortunately the organizer had made no arrangements as to price. It is said that when the bill was presented five impecunious men of letters left with long faces. An amusing account of this function is printed in George Wherry's *Cambridge and Charles Lamb*, 1925.

Dykes Campbell dinner, 1888. Edith Sichel writing on Canon Ainger in the *Quarterly Review* for January 1905 mentions a dinner given by the Dykes Campbells in honour of the completion of Ainger's biography of Lamb in 1888. She writes that Ainger was permitted to compose the menu out of dishes mentioned by Lamb, with appropriate quotations for each. She adds 'the bill of fare as it originally stood swelled to such dimensions that his hostess had to beg him to curtail it in consideration of the cook. A fuller account with details of the menu is contained in Edith Sichel's *The Life & Letters of Alfred Ainger*, 1906.

Cambridge dinners 1909–14. From 1908 Charles Sayle, A.T. Bartholomew and George Wherry were responsible for the organization of Annual Dinners to be held at Cambridge in honour of Charles Lamb. The first dinner was held in 1909 and they continued until 1914. During these years many distinguished men attended as Chairmen, Guests or just Diners and a list of them is given in George Wherry's *Cambridge and Charles Lamb*, with much information on the functions and reports of the speeches. The Guests of Honour during these years were the Rt. Hon. Augustine Birrell, 1909; E.V. Lucas, 1910; Sir Walter Raleigh, 1911; Sir Edmund Gosse, 1912; Sir Henry Newbolt, 1913; and G.S. Street, 1914.

Inner Temple Hall Dinner, 1925. On 30 March 1925 the centenary of Lamb's retirement from East India House was celebrated by a dinner in the Hall of the Inner Temple, adjacent to Lamb's birthplace, No. 2 Crown Office Row. The Chairman was Augustine Birrell and the Hon. Secretary who organized the function was F.A. Downing. Many distinguished people attended, among whom were the Earl and Countess of Winterton, Sir Frederick and Lady Pollock and Lady Spencer Churchill. Literature was represented by A. St. John Adcock, Robert Lynd, G.K. Chesterton, J.C. Squire, E.V. Lucas, C.E. Lawrence, Clement Shorter and George Sampson. Augustine Birrell proposed the toast of 'The Immortal Memory of Charles Lamb', that of 'The D——d India House' by J.C. Squire and the East India House was defended by Earl Winterton, Under Secretary of State for India. Other speakers included Cecil Harmsworth, G.K. Chesterton, Hubert J. Norman, Mr Justice Shearman and George Sampson. As a result of suggestions made at this dinner the society known as The Elian was founded in 1925. The menu, complete with the Elian quotations, is printed in S.M. Rich's *The Elian Miscellany*, 1931, as is Augustine Birrell's speech.

Dinners organized by The Elian. A large part of the activities of The Elian included the holding of dinners. The first was at the Cheshire Cheese, Fleet Street, on 6 November 1925, and others followed at various hotels or restaurants during the next ten years or more. Members spoke on various Elian subjects and sometimes guest speakers were invited. The record of speakers includes the names of many Lamb scholars. For details of The Elian see separate entry.

The year 1934. This year, the centenary of Lamb's death, saw a number of commemorative functions. Among these was a luncheon on November 7 at Salters Hall in commemoration of Coleridge and Lamb, and a dinner at The Angel, Edmonton organized by The Elian. No doubt there were other events in London and the provinces, both public and private.

Charles Lamb Society dinners, 1935 onwards. This society, which was founded on 1 February 1935 by Ernest George Crowsley continues to flourish, and in addition to many meetings of members, holds a special dinner or luncheon on or about Lamb's birthday, February 10. Many famous people have attended as guests of honour and proposed the toast of 'The Immortal Memory.' *See* separate entry.

Lamb Medal. A silver medal instituted at Christ's Hospital in 1875 on the suggestion of the Rev. G.C. Bell, then Headmaster, was awarded for the best English essay by a Grecian. It was designed by A.B. Wyon and bears a relievo of Lamb on the face with the words 'Charles Lamb. b.1775. d.1834.' The reverse of the medal shows the School's arms with the words 'Christ's Hospital, English Essay Prize.' The name of the winner was engraved around the edge with the year of award. It was awarded annually until 1948; since that date it was replaced by an award of books. The original charcoal sketch for the medal is owned by Christ's Hospital. Illustrations of it are given in R.B. Johnson's *Christ's Hospital*, 1898; E.V. Lucas's *Elia and the Last Essays of Elia*, 1903; S.E. Winbolt's *Coleridge, Lamb and Leigh Hunt*, 1920; and the *C.L.S. Bulletin*, No. 135.

Lamb's Commonplace Books. Charles Lamb spent many hours recording in his Commonplace Books those passages from his reading which appealed to him most. He started probably when he was in his teens, for after the tragedy of 1796 he tells Coleridge in a letter of 10 December 1796, when he was only twenty-one, that he had destroyed his book of extracts from Beaumont and Fletcher 'and a thousand sources.' However he soon started others and some survived. E.V. Lucas says Lamb's best Commonplace Book was printed as the *Dramatic Specimens* in 1808. Of the others none has as yet been printed but some have been described.

As might be expected Lucas's *Life of Charles Lamb* contains much on his Commonplace Books (Appendix II 294–303). The first one he describes was from the six owned by Frederick Locker-Lampson (he states that three were owned by Godfrey Locker-Lampson in 1905). The content of this one was almost entirely made up of Elizabethan and Stuart lyrical poetry and old ballads, and he gives details of the Scottish and other ballads in it.

Next he gives very full details of that made out of a large paper copy (or the proof sheets) of *Holcroft's Travels* in which, as Crabb Robinson noted in his *Diary* in April 1833, Lamb had pasted extracts in manuscript and clippings out of newspapers. When Lucas wrote, this book was called 'Charles Lamb's Album', and was owned by Mrs Alfred Morrison. Lucas tells us that it also contained letters from *The Examiner* written by John Lamb, Charles's brother.

Some details of Locker-Lampson's six books were contained in the Catalogue of his books prepared by Quaritch in 1886. Again the Berg Collection at the New York Public Library contains another of Lamb's Commonplace Books, while one devoted solely to Lamb's contributions to Hone's *Table-Book* was sold in 1929 at the Jerome Kern sale for $48,000. Lamb's Note Books containing his Extracts from the Garrick Plays were presented by Edward Moxon to the British Museum in 1851.

More recently the late Reginald Hine bought at Sothebys in 1948 for £220 one of the Commonplace Books which had formerly belonged to Frederick Locker-Lampson. He described it in great detail in his *Charles Lamb and his Hertfordshire*, 1949, 280–97. This book comprised 106 pages and contained an index made by Dr Robin Flower of the British Museum. Lucas mentions in his edition of the *Letters*, 1935, that another Commonplace Book is in the Huntington Library and he gives details of the contents (I, 31).

Lamb's Grave. Lamb was buried in Edmonton Churchyard on 3 January 1835. The tombstone bears the following inscription composed by the Rev. H.F. Cary:

> Farewell, dear friend; that smile, that harmless mirth,
> No more shall gladden our domestic hearth;
> That rising tear, with pain forbid to flow,
> Better than words, no more assuage our woe;
> That hand outstretch'd, from small but well-earned store,
> Yield succour to the destitute no more:
> Yet art thou not all lost; thro' many an age,
> With sterling sense and humour shall thy page
> Win many an English bosom, pleased to see
> That old and happier vein revived in thee.
> This for our earth; and if with friends we share
> Our joys in heaven, we hope to meet thee there.

The grave was restored in 1897 by a member of the Christ's Hospital Club, Septimus Vaughan Morgan, as an inscription at the foot of the stone states. E.V. Lucas paid for the upkeep of Lamb's grave for some years and in his will he stated that he wished, after his death, the opportunity should be given to two of his friends, first to Herman Finck and then to Charles Walter Berry. In the event of their predeceasing him or being unwilling to undertake the upkeep, Lucas left a sum of thirty shillings a year in perpetuity for this purpose. Lucas died in 1938.

C.W. Berry undertook this service but died in 1941. In his will he left £200 to the Almoners of Christ's Hospital on trust, the income to be used for the upkeep of the grave. It was stated in 1971 that Edmonton Borough Council proposed to take over the Churchyard and transform it into a Garden of Rest.

Lamb's Key. Lamb's colleague and friend at East India House, R.B. Pitman, prepared a list of the initials and asterisks which occur in *The Essays of Elia*, 1823. Against each item Lamb wrote his interpretation and the sheet of paper, which was of the type used by Lamb when he wrote letters from India House, was pasted into Pitman's copy of the book. The list is as follows:

	Page	
M.	13	Maynard, hang'd himself.
G.D.	21	George Dyer, Poet.
H.	32	Hodges.
W.	45	
Dr. T——e	46	Dr Trollope.
Th.	47	Thornton.
S.	47	Scott, died in Bedlam.
M.	47	Maunde, dismiss'd school.
C.V.le G.	48	Chs. Valentine le Grice.
F.	49	Favell; left Cambrg because he was asham'd of his father, who was a house-painter there.
Fr.	50	Franklin, Gramr Mast., Hertford.
T.	50	Marmaduke Thompson.
K.	59	Kenney, Dramatist. Author of Raising Wind &c.
S.T.C.	60	Samuel Taylor Coleridge.
Alice W——n	63	Feigned (Winterton).
***	64	No meaning.
****	64	No meaning.
***	64	No meaning.
Mrs S.	87	Mrs Spinkes.
R.	98	Ramsay, London Library, Ludg. St; now extinct.

Granville S.	98	Granville Sharp.
E.B.	130	Edward Burney, half-brother of Miss Burney.
B.	141	Braham, now a Xtian.
*** *** ****	170	Distrest Sailors.
J——M.	195	Jekyll
Susan P.	198	Susan Peirson.
R.N.	206	Randal Norris, Subtreasr, Inner Temple.
C.	216	Coleridge.
F.	222	Field.
B.F.	238	Baron Field, brother of Frank.
Lord C.	243	Lord Camelford.
Sally W——r	248	Sally Winter.
J.W.	248	Jas. White, author of Falstaff's Letters.
St L.	268	No meaning.
B., Rector of ——	268	No meaning.

Pitman had also pasted a portrait of Lamb in the book and noted that it was the best extant in 1823.

The copy of *Elia* containing the key belonged to John Rogers at one time, and in his book *With Elia and his Friends*, 1903, he has a chapter entitled 'A First Edition of Elia—Lamb at Home' in which he has written a short sketch of Lamb at Colebrooke Cottage.

Most editors of the *Essays* have drawn on this Key in their notes, particularly W.C. Hazlitt, who prints it in his *Charles and Mary Lamb: Poems, Letters and Remains*, 1874; Alfred Ainger; and E.V. Lucas who also prints it. Rogers says that not too much reliance should be placed on the accuracy of the Key and that the manuscript bears evidence of hesitation and re-consideration 'there are in fact actual alterations in it by Lamb after it was apparently finished.' Lamb mistakenly states that Edward Burney was the half-brother of Miss Burney instead of her cousin.

Landon, Letitia Elizabeth, 1802–38. Poet. Wrote under the initials 'L.E.L.' Married George Maclean, Governor of Cape Coast Castle, West Africa. Wrote much for the *Literary Gazette* and other periodicals, particularly the Annuals, and published numerous volumes of verse. At one time she was engaged to John Forster, who in a note of late 1833, Lamb invites to his house and tells him to bring 'L.E.L.'.

Patmore relates that Lamb said she ought to be locked up and fed on bread and water until she stopped writing poetry. He did, however, refer to her as 'sweet L.E.L.' in his verses 'What is an Album?'

Landor, Walter Savage, 1775–1864. Poet and prose writer.

Educated at Rugby and Oxford. Owing to his ungovernable temper his life was one long series of quarrels. Among his books were *Gebir*, 1798; *Count Julian*, 1812; *Imaginary Conversations*, 1824–9; and *Pericles and Aspasia*, 1836. In 1808 he bought the estate of Llanthony Abbey, Monmouthshire. Lamb's friend, Charles Betham, was for a time his tenant there, but Landor quarrelled with him and Betham eventually sued him for libel. Owing to quarrels with the local authorities Landor was obliged to leave the estate. He had also fought in Spain against Napoleon. From 1814 until 1832 he lived in France and Italy, then returned to spend the summer in England. After again living in Italy he came to live for many years in Bath.

Lamb mentions Landor's poem *Gebir* in his letter to Southey of 31 October 1799 and there are other references in his letters. Landor was known to Lamb and expressed admiration for *Mrs Leicester's School* and *The Essays of Elia*. On 28 September 1832 Crabb Robinson records that he and Landor visited the Lambs at Edmonton and that Lamb gave Landor a copy of White's *Falstaff's Letters*. Landor commemorated this visit in verses to Elia 'Written after an Hour's visit', and also contributed to Emma Isola's Album. He expressed great admiration for her. Lamb sent Landor a copy of *The Last Essays of Elia* in 1833. When Landor heard of Lamb's death in 1834 he wrote his verses 'To the Sister of Elia' and sent them to Crabb Robinson.

Landseer Family. John Landseer, A.R.A., 1769–1852; Thomas Landseer, A.R.A., 1795–1880; Charles Landseer, R.A., 1799–1879. Edwin Henry Landseer. R.A. (1802–73). Keats stated in a letter of 5 January 1818 to his brothers, George and Thomas, that among those present at the famous party in Haydon's studio on 28 December 1817 was 'Landseer'. The name is not given in the account in Haydon's *Autobiography*. There seems some doubt as to which Landseer was present. Lucas in the *Life of Lamb* (Index) gives Thomas, in the notes to the *Letters*, 1935 II 466, he states he believes it to be Thomas. Sidney Colvin in his *Life of Keats* (Index) gives Edwin Landseer. In 1817 when the party took place Thomas was twenty-two, Charles eighteen, and Edwin fifteen. Their father, John, was a man of forty-eight and a friend of Haydon's. It seems likely, therefore, that John attended the party, although since all three boys were at that time pupils of Haydon, either Thomas or Charles could have been there. Kenneth Neil Cameron in *Shelley and his Circle* states it was John Landseer who came to the party.

Lane, Annette. Lamb wrote a letter to her on 31 December 1822 which invited her to visit him and his sister at 20 Russell Street. He mentions her as 'Mrs Kenney's pupil and Mrs Aders' friend.' Lucas notes that Mrs Anderson suggested she had been a schoolfellow of

Barbara Betham when they were both at Mrs Holcroft's school (Mrs Holcroft became Mrs Kenney).

Lang, Andrew, 1844–1912. Scholar, critic and poet. Educated Edinburgh Academy, Glasgow University and Balliol College, Oxford. A voluminous writer who produced many books of great charm and interest. He wrote introductions to a great many books, including Lamb's *Beauty and the Beast,* 1887, *The Adventures of Ulysses,* 1890, and *Tales from Shakespeare,* 1899. Among Lang's books are *Letters on Literature,* 1889, which contains a chapter and appendix on John Hamilton Reynolds and *Letters to Dead Authors,* 1886, which included 'To Master Isaak Walton'. He also wrote an introduction to an edition of the *Complete Angler,* 1896. Other works include translations of *The Iliad* with Walter Leaf and Ernest Myers, 1883, and of *The Odyssey* with S.H. Butcher, 1879. He was the author of *Oxford,* 1879; *The Library,* 1881; *Books and Bookmen,* 1886; and *Lost Leaders,* 1889.

Law, M.H. Author of *The English Familiar Essay in the Early Nineteenth Century,* Philadelphia, 1934.

Ledwith, Frank. Vice Chairman of the Charles Lamb Society. Lectured to the Society in November 1977 on 'Christ's Hospital in Lamb's time and my own' (Reprinted *Charles Lamb Bulletin* October 1978). Contributed 'The East India Company' to *Charles Lamb Bulletin,* July 1980. Author of *Ships that go bump in the night,* 1974, and *Ships afloat in the City,* 1977.

Lee, Leoni. d.1797. Well known Jewish musician and singer who trained John Braham, the singer, and is said to have adopted him. He eventually went to Jamaica where he died. Lamb mentions him in his 'Playhouse Memoranda' in *The Examiner,* in connection with the first play he saw *Artaxerxes.* Lee first appeared in the play in 1775, but was not in it when Lamb first saw it. He also appeared as Don Carlos in the original production of Sheridan's *The Duenna,* and because he was a Jew and would not appear on Fridays, the opera was not produced on that day.

Le Grice, Charles Valentine, 1773–1858. Clergyman. Friend and schoolfellow of Lamb and Coleridge. At Christ's Hospital 1781–92, left as Senior Grecian and proceeded to Trinity College, Cambridge. Ordained 1798. Married Mrs William Nichols, a wealthy widow of Trereife, Cornwall, in 1799, where he had been tutor to her son. Incumbent of St Mary's Church, Penzance, in 1806 and perpetual curate of Madron, Penzance 1806–31. Young Nicholls died in 1815, Mrs Nicholls in 1821 and Le Grice inherited all her property. His brother Samuel was also at Christ's and a friend of Lamb's.

Charles Le Grice wrote a pamphlet *A General Theorem for a ******* College Declamation* in 1796 which Lamb mentions in a letter to Coleridge in May 1796. He also wrote *An Imitation of Horace*, 1793; *Analysis of Paley's Principles of Moral and Political Philosophy*, 1795; a translation of Longus's *Daphnis and Chloe*, 1803, and many articles for magazines. He seems to have fallen foul of Coleridge in the *Critical Review* and also to have raised Wordsworth's ire.

Although Le Grice was very friendly with Lamb as a boy and spent some of his holidays at the Lamb's, they did not meet much after he went to Cornwall, but in 1833 Le Grice entertained Lamb at 'Johnny Gilpin's', that is the Bell at Edmonton. At this time he also visited Coleridge at Highgate. Lamb mentions Le Grice in his Elian essay on Christ's Hospital and in 'Grace Before Meat.'

Le Grice wrote a number of pieces on Charles Lamb and Coleridge. One of which was the memories of Lamb given to T.N. Talfourd for inclusion in *Letters*, 1837. A draft of the letter to Talfourd about this was printed in the *Charles Lamb Bulletin* in April 1974. Others include reminiscences of Lamb and Coleridge in the *Gentleman's Magazine* in May 1838; 'College Reminiscences of Coleridge' in the *Gentleman's Magazine*, December 1834, reprinted in 1842 and also included in Cottle's *Reminiscences of Coleridge and Southey*, 2nd Edition, 1848; *Sonnet on Charles Lamb leading his Sister to the Asylum*, 1849, printed as a broadside; *Recollections of Lamb*, 1850, and *Sonnet in Reminiscence of the Poet Coleridge*, 1852.

Crabb Robinson records in his 'Reminiscences' that in 1837 he dined with Le Grice who told him that he used to go to debating societies with Lamb.

Le Grice, Samuel, 1775–1802. Friend and schoolfellow of Lamb. At Christ's Hospital 1783–94. Younger brother of Charles Valentine Le Grice. Went to Trinity College, Cambridge. Wrote to the Duke of York for a commission in the Army and received it in the 60th Foot. He died in Jamaica. When the Lamb tragedy occurred in 1796 Sam Le Grice gave up much of his time to help Lamb in his trouble, particularly by his attention to Lamb's father. He is mentioned in several of Lamb's letters and in the Elian essay on Christ's Hospital. Leigh Hunt in his *Autobiography* has amusing stories of Le Grice's pranks as a schoolboy. He also said that Le Grice 'died a rake' but his brother protested to Hunt about this statement.

Leishman, Mrs. Keeper of lodgings at The Chase, Enfield, at which the Allsops stayed and in 1825 the Lambs were there also. During the summer of 1827 they stayed there again. Mrs Leishman's husband was Lamb's tailor and about 1832 seems to have lived at No. 2 Blandford Court, Pall Mall; Lamb's letter to Moxon in 1832 says

Leishman has moved and asks Moxon to pay his bill if he can find him.

Leonard, R.M. Editor of *The Book-Lover's Anthology*, 1911, which contains twenty-six references to Lamb as well as many to Hazlitt, Leigh Hunt, Coleridge, Southey and Wordsworth. Leonard also selected and edited *The Pageant of English Poetry* for the Oxford Standard Authors series.

Leslie, Charles Robert, 1794–1859. English painter. Born of American parents, and lived in Philadelphia where he was apprenticed to a bookseller. Came to London in 1811 and was admitted as a student of the Royal Academy. Famous for his pictures dealing with scenes from the great masters of fiction. Elected A.R.A. in 1821 and R.A. in 1826. He wrote a Life of his friend Constable and a *Handbook for Young Painters*. His *Autobiography* was published in 1860.

Leslie was acquainted with Coleridge and Lamb and other members of their circle. In his *Autobiography* he states that he first met Lamb at Morgan's house in Berners Street, and that he dined one day with Lamb at Gillman's when, returning with him in the stage-coach Lamb made his facetious remark about Mr Gillman's pudding.

Lewin, Walter. In 1890 Cope's Smoke Room Booklet No. 4, *Charles Lamb in Pipefuls*, was issued, selected and arranged by Lewin from Lamb's writings.

Lewis, J.G. Author of *The Evolution of Lamb's 'Ballad from the German'*, 1897, a pamphlet of twenty-one pages issued as Opusculum VI of *Ye Nottingham Sette of Odde Volumes*. Other works include *Christopher Marlowe: his Life and Works*.

Lewis, William Thomas, 'Gentleman Lewis', 1749–1811. English comic actor who earned his nickname for his elegance and affability. Appeared at Covent Garden in 1773 and remained there for the rest of his life, for twenty years as acting manager. He had been the first Falkland in *The Rivals*. He retired in 1809. He had been famous for rattling, hare-brained parts and particularly as Jeremy Diddler in Kenney's *Raising the Wind*. Leigh Hunt described him as the 'Mercutio of the stage' and 'the feather of the stage', and as one of the most delightful performers of his class. He was also highly praised by Hazlitt.

Lewis was present at the performance of *Mr H——* in December 1806, and Hazlitt records in his essay 'On Great and Little Things' in the *New Monthly Magazine* in February 1822 that he had said he could, with a few judicious curtailments, make it 'the most popular little thing that had been brought out for some time.' Lamb mentions him in 'The Death of Munden' (Munden the Comedian) contributed to the *Athenaeum* in 1832. There is also a reference to 'the restless fidgetiness of Lewis' in 'The Old Actors' which may refer to the same actor.

Liber aureus. The manuscript book kept by James Boyer, Upper Master of Christ's Hospital in Lamb's time, in which he allowed his scholars to transcribe exercises of 'more than ordinary merit.' James Dykes Campbell contributed an account of the book to the *Illustrated London News* for 26 December 1891. He states that the book was begun in 1783 and ended in 1799, the year of Boyer's retirement. Lamb's contribution was entitled 'Mille viae mortis' and being dated 1789 is thus his earliest known poem. Coleridge made a number of contributions to the book, one of which was his 'Monody on Chatterton.'

In an article 'A School Poem by Lamb' in *The Athenaeum* on 4 June 1904, H. Dugdale Sykes also gives details of the book and lists the following as among the contributors: C.V. Le Grice, S. Le Grice, Lancelot Pepys Stephens, Edward Thornton, A.W. Trollope, George Richards, Henry Scott, T.F. Middleton, John Maunde, R. Allen, Favell, M. Thompson and F.W. Franklin. He states that only four contributors were not mentioned in Lamb's essay on Christ's Hospital, presumably he means contributors during Lamb's period at the school for the book was used until 1799. It comprised three volumes.

Library, Lamb's. Charles Lamb in his essay 'Mackery End' writes that his sister, Mary, had been 'tumbled early, by accident or design, into a spacious closet of good old English reading, without much selection or prohibition, and browsed at will upon that fair and wholesome pasturage.' This was, no doubt, Samuel Salt's library and certainly Charles browsed there too—a salutary process which coloured many of his thoughts and is reflected in the books in his library. It is probable that Lamb and his sister also browsed on the books in the library at Blakesware during their visits to their grandmother. Some of these books are named in R.L. Hine's *Charles Lamb and his Hertfordshire*, 1949. As Lamb wrote in another essay 'When I am not walking, I am reading; I cannot sit and think. Books think for me.' In 'Mackery End' he gives something of his literary tastes 'Out-of-the-way humours and opinions—heads with some diverting twist in them—the oddities of authorship please me most.'

Leigh Hunt wrote in *The Literary Examiner* in 1823 that Lamb's library, though not abounding in Greek and Latin was anything but superficial. The depths of philosophy and poetry were there 'the innermost passages of the human heart.' Hunt continued 'It looks like what it is, a selection made at precious intervals from the bookstalls; now a Chaucer at nine and twopence, now a Montaigne or a Sir Thomas Browne at two shillings; now a Jeremy Taylor; a Spinoza; an old English Dramatist, Prior, and Sir Philip Sidney; and the books are "neat as imported"—in fact, they often still had the bookseller's ticket attached.'

Charles Lamb was not a book collector who hunted specially after first editions, although he liked good ones; he was a lover of literature who accumulated a number of old books because he loved to read and re-read them; to annotate them, and to lend and discuss them with his friends. Their condition was not of great importance to him. If a volume was badly in need of repair, it was patched up by a local cobbler. Although he had a cousin who was a bookbinder, there is no record that he made use of his services. Sometimes if a volume was incomplete, the missing pages were supplied by Lamb in manuscript. One such volume was the copy of Pope's *The Rape of the Lock* which Lamb bought for sixpence and, as Mrs J.T. Fields tells in her *A Shelf of Old Books*, restored the lacunae in 'his own beautiful handwriting.'

The booklover who treasures his volumes as things of beauty and handles them with loving care, will recoil with horror at Mary Lamb's account, in her letter to Barbara Betham in 1814, of the wholesale cutting out of plates from their books to decorate the walls of the newly discovered garret at Inner Temple Lane. Nevertheless, in spite of his disregard of the condition of his books, he was of almost all English writers, except perhaps Leigh Hunt, the most bookish.

Lamb's views on format are given in his essay 'Detached Thoughts on Books and Reading.' He could read Beaumont and Fletcher only in folio, 'the octavo editions are painful to look at.' Modern reprints of Burton were anathema to him. He confessed that he had 'no repugnances' and 'can read any thing which I call a book.' But he had certain 'books which are no books' not allowed in his library, generally 'all those volumes which "no gentleman's library should be without".'

To establish the contents of his library is now somewhat difficult, for we have no complete catalogue as a guide, as we have for many other writers. It seems that after his death the books remained in Mary Lamb's possession, but subject to the depredations of friends who wanted mementos of Elia. After her death the books passed, as Lamb intended, to Edward Moxon, the husband of Emma Isola. Apparently he was not concerned to preserve the collection, for he parted with sixty volumes to Charles Welford and they were sold in New York by Bartlett and Welford in 1848. W.C. Hazlitt stated that the amount realized was $479. Accounts of the sale differ and the position was investigated and set out in *The Harvard Library Bulletin* in Carl Woodring's 'Charles Lamb in the Harvard Library', 1956. The remainder of the books are said to have been destroyed by Moxon. Some, however, either those which escaped the holocaust, or which friends had abstracted earlier, crop up from time to time and generally find their way into institutional libraries.

The first partial list of Lamb's books must have been that prepared by the American booksellers in 1848. A list also appeared in *The Literary World* in the same year. Details were printed by W.C. Hazlitt in *Mary and Charles Lamb*, 1874 (some fifty-five items). In his *The Lambs*, 1897, Hazlitt states there were some errors in the earlier book and he gives a corrected list of the sixty items, with the names of some other books from Lamb's library. Here he gives the name of the booksellers as Welford and Scribner. In 1897 the Dibdin Club in New York reprinted the booksellers' list with additional books since discovered to have belonged to Lamb, including some annotated by S.T. Coleridge. W.C. Hazlitt in his *Lamb and Hazlitt*, 1900, included some additional books belonging to Lamb.

In 1905 E.V. Lucas published *The Life of Charles Lamb* and in Appendix III has a most fascinating chapter devoted to Lamb's library, mainly from Leigh Hunt, Hazlitt and Thomas Westwood. He then lists all those authors whose books he feels sure from Lamb's writings, remarks of friends and sale catalogues, must have been on his shelves, and he marks the actual works and sometimes the editions where he knows that the books were in Lamb's possession. It is an impressive list of more than 200 authors, and this does not include Lamb's favourite Elizabethan dramatists except those in composite volumes of old plays counted as one volume.

After Lucas's exhaustive account there seems little that later writers can add, except to describe in more detail the actual volumes belonging to Lamb, and as Lucas's list appeared in 1905, to add the books which have since been found to have been in his library. References to these are mostly found in the sale catalogues of collectors such as A.E. Newton and J.A. Spoor, and in the accounts of the Lamb treasures held by famous libraries. One of the most fascinating of the latter is Carl Woodring's 'Charles Lamb in the Harvard Library'. In this are described the eighteen works from Lamb's library that Harvard possessed in 1956, and fuller information is given than has been available before.

Many of Lamb's books have manuscript notes in his handwriting or in those of his friends. In his essay 'The Two Races of Men' he says of Coleridge 'Many are these precious MSS of his—(in *matter* oftentimes, and almost in *quantity* not infrequently, vying with the originals)—in no very clerkly hand—legible in my Daniel; in old Burton; in Sir Thomas Browne; and in those abstruser cogitations of the Greville.' A number of the notes are reproduced in Lucas's Appendix, with passages from Lamb's essays and letters on some of the volumes.

Lucas also gives a list of the books by Lamb's friends and contemporaries which he possessed. Some came as presentation copies from the authors and Lamb regarded many with mixed feelings. Thomas Westwood, who lived next door, has described how 'A Leigh Hunt . . .

would come skimming to my feet through the branches of the apple-trees ... the Plea of the Midsummer Fairies I picked out of the strawberry-bed.' As Lucas says, it was not that Lamb was indifferent to the literary doings of his friends, but on his shelves their works clashed with the Marlowes and Miltons that were his household gods. Procter writing in *The Athenaeum* in 1835 said that Lamb 'had more real knowledge of old English literature than any man' he ever knew.

There is an indication in a letter to Dilke in 1834 that Lamb's taste in reading may have widened as he got older. He asks Dilke for books to read and says 'Any light stuff: no natural history or useful learning' and he adds a postscript 'Novels for the last two years, or further back —nonsense of any period.' Possibly the novels were for his sister.

Crabb Robinson makes a fitting comment in his *Diary* on 10 January 1824, 'I looked over Lamb's library in part; such a number of first rate works of genius, but filthy copies, which a delicate man would really hesitate touching, is I think nowhere to be found. I borrowed several books.'

Lindsey, John. Biographer and novelist. Author of *Suburban Gentleman: The Life of Thomas Griffiths Wainewright, Poet, Painter & Poisoner*, 1942, which contains references to Charles Lamb.

Linnell, John,· 1792–1882. Artist. Student at Royal Academy Schools and obtained a Silver Medal there in 1807. A most successful landscape and portrait painter whose pictures are still exhibited in galleries in England, America and Australia. During the latter part of William Blake's life, Linnell befriended him and subsequently helped Blake's widow. Linnell taught painting to Mary Shelley, T.G. Wainewright and William Godwin's step-son, Charles Clairmont. His eldest daughter married the painter Samuel Palmer.

A.T. Story in his *Life of John Linnell*, 1892, states that Lamb and Linnell met at the house of Charles Aders. It is likely that they also met elsewhere for they had mutual friends, among whom were Bernard Barton and B.R. Haydon. William Mulready, who did the designs for the 1807 edition of Lamb's *Tales from Shakespeare* was a lifelong friend of Linnell's. Crabb Robinson had also met him and mentions him in his *Diary*. (*See* also 'Charles Lamb and John Linnell' by Claude A. Prance in the *Charles Lamb Bulletin*, October 1980).

Liston, John, 1776–1846. English comedian. Favourite actor and friend of Charles Lamb. Was at one time a schoolmaster and was said to have been an usher at Dr Burney's school at Gosport, and later a master at St Martin's Grammar School, Castle Street, Leicester Square. His early appearances in tragedy were unsuccessful, but later he becomes extremely popular as a comedian. He was the first leading comic actor to command a salary higher than a tragedian. Charles

Mathews maintained he was never known to smile. In private life he was melancholic and was interested in the study of theology, but he had only to appear on the stage to set the audience laughing. He was a quiet comedian and his face was no small part of his fortune.

Liston played much at the Haymarket, afterwards at Covent Garden and then at Drury Lane with Elliston. Under the management of Madame Vestris at the Olympic he was paid £100 a week and was said to have received £20 a night at one time. Liston was the favourite comedian of George IV. Hazlitt praised him on several occasions and in *The Champion* of 6 November 1814 wrote 'It has been objected with some truth that he is rather a humourist than an actor: if he is not a copy of anyone but himself, he is at least an exquisite original and wonderfully great in the character of Liston.' In *The Times* on 25 September 1817 he reviewed a performance of *Tom Thumb the Great* and wrote 'We consider Mr Liston as the greatest comic genius who has appeared in our time, and Lord Grizzle as his greatest effort.' John Liston was famous as Lubin Log in Kenneys' farce *Love, Law and Physic*, as Paul Pry and as Launcelot Gobbo. He is said to have made the fortune of several managers and authors.

Liston's wife, formerly Miss Tyrer, was also an actress and singer and a favourite in burlesque. She was very tiny, but according to Cruikshank's etching of her as Queen Dollalolla in Fielding's *Tom Thumb* she was also very fat. This became one of her best known parts. She died in 1854.

Liston and his wife were frequently to be found at the Lambs and sometimes at the Thursday evening parties. Mary Cowden Clarke relates often finding them at the apartments in Great Russell Street, Covent Garden. There is also a record of Liston dining with Lamb in 1826. Lamb praised Liston in his review of Kenney's *Debtor and Creditor* in *The Examiner* in May 1814. He also referred to him in his essay 'On the Acting of Munden' and in 'The New Acting'. In January 1825 his 'Biographical Memoir of Mr Liston' was printed in the *London Magazine*. This was, as Lamb said in a letter to Sara Hutchinson, 'from top to toe, every paragraph Pure Invention; and has passed for Gospel, has been republished in newspapers and in the penny play-bills of the Night, as an Authentic Account.' Liston was himself a great practical joker, with a quick wit and he was also a punster. An amusing review of Lamb's 'Memoir' appeared in the *London Magazine* for February 1825 in the form of a letter from 'Abraham Twaddler' who commented with humour on recent articles in the New Series of the magazine, and wished to see a similar Life of Lord Byron.

Liston retired from the stage in 1837 and died a rich man.

Little Queen Street, Lincoln's Inn Fields. The Lambs lived at No. 7 Little Queen Street, Lincoln's Inn Fields, Holborn, from about

1792 or 1793 until December 1796 when they moved to Pentonville. Lucas says they shared the house with a Mr and Mrs Weight. It was here that the tragedy occurred on 22 September 1796 when Mary Lamb in a fit of insanity, killed her mother. The street used to run south from High Holborn into Great Queen Street and is now merged in Kingsway. Hutton in his *Literary Landmarks of London*, 1888, says that behind the church in the playground of the church school 'was, in 1885, a tree standing in what had undoubtedly been Lamb's back garden.' Lucas, who was shown the stump of the tree later, is doubtful of the story.

Literary Histories that Refer to Lamb. The importance of Charles Lamb in English literature is such that his name appears prominently in almost all literary histories. The single exception, perhaps, being Taine's *History of English Literature*, which although extending to four volumes, fails to mention *The Essays of Elia* and has only passing reference to Lamb as the author of *John Woodvil* and as 'the restorer of the old drama.' A list of some of those which do him greater justice follows:

The Cambridge History of English Literature. Vol. XII, Chapter VIII by A.H. Thompson, 1914. (Also references in other volumes).
Oxford History of English Literature. Vol. IX, *English Literature 1789–1815* by W.L. Renwick, 1963. Vol. X, *English Literature 1815–1832* by Ian Jack, 1963.
A Survey of English Literature, 1780–1830, by Oliver Elton, 1912.
Illustrated History of English Literature by A.C. Ward, 1955, Vol. III.
A History of Nineteenth Century Literature 1780–1895 by G. Saintsbury, 1896.
Augustans and Romantics 1689–1830 by H.V.D. Dyson and John Butt, 1940.
A History of English Criticism by G. Saintsbury, 1911.
A Short History of English Literature by G. Saintsbury, 1898.
The Literary History of England XVIII–XIX Centuries by Mrs Oliphant, 1883.
English Literature: An Illustrated Record. Vol. IV by Edmund Gosse, 1903.
The Cambridge Bibliography of English Literature. Vols III and V., 1940 and 1957.
The New Cambridge Bibliography of English Literature. Vol. III, 1969.
The Age of Wordsworth by C.H. Herford, 1897.
The Pelican Guide to English Literature. Vol. 5, 1957.
A History of English Literature by E. Legouis and Louis Cazamian, 1930. Revised edition, 1947.

The Oxford Companion to English Literature. 3rd edition, 1946. Reprinted, 1960.
The Oxford Companion to the Theatre, 1951. 2nd edition, 1957.
The Outline of Literature. Edited by John Drinkwater. n.d., c.1923.
Chambers's Cyclopaedia of English Literature, 1901–3.
The Romantic Revival 1780–1830 by Percy Westland, 1950.
Cassell's Encyclopaedia of Literature, edited by S.H. Steinberg, 1953.
A Critical History of English Literature by David Daiches, 1960. Reprinted, 1968. Vol. IV, The Romantics to the Present Day.
A Literary History of England, edited by Albert C. Baugh, 1967. Reprinted, 1970. Book IV, The Nineteenth Century and After, 1789–1939, by Samuel C. Chew and Richard D. Altick.

Livingston, Luther S, d.1914. Bibliographer. In charge of the rare book department of Dodd, Mead & Co and the first custodian of the H.E. Widener Collection at Harvard. Author of *A Bibliography of the First Editions in Book Form of the Writings of Charles and Mary Lamb, published prior to Charles Lamb's death in 1834*, New York, 1903. There are fifty-four illustrations that include facsimiles of autograph letters, title-pages of Lamb rarities and portraits. The work was based on the famous Lamb collection of John A. Spoor of Chicago. Livingston also contributed to the *Bibliographer* in 1902 an article 'Some Notes on Three of Lamb's Juveniles.'

Lloyd, Charles (Senior), 1748–1828. Quaker banker and philanthropist of Birmingham. Partner in the firm of Taylors and Lloyds founded in 1765 and known as Birminghan Old Bank. Father of Charles, Robert, Olivia, Priscilla and a number of other children. Lived at Bingley Hall, Birmingham. Known to the Lamb circle through his children: Charles and Robert being friends of Lamb, while Priscilla married Wordsworth's brother, Christopher. He translated Homer and Horace and sent the manuscript of his Homer to Lamb, who made suggestions for its improvement and passed on some more made by a classical friend. Several letters from Lamb to Lloyd written about 1809–10 exist referring to the translation and one of 1812 on the Horace. On a visit to London in 1799 Lloyd had entertained Lamb to dinner. Robert Lloyd writing to Lamb in May 1803 says 'My father smokes, repeats Homer in Greek, and Virgil, and is learning, when from business, with all the vigour of a young man Italian.' He contributed his translations from Horace to the *Gentleman's Magazine*. Southey wrote to Lloyd in 1820 about the history of the Society of Friends and Wordsworth wrote in 1825 asking advice on investing £500.

Lloyd, Charles (Junior), 1775–1839. Poet. Eldest son of Charles

Lloyd, banker and philanthropist of Birmingham. Although originally intended for his father's bank he was not suited to this employment. After studying medicine he turned to literature and published his first volume of poems in 1795, followed by *Poems on the Death of Priscilla Farmer by her Grandson*, 1796; the second edition of Coleridge's *Poems* in 1797 with verses by Charles Lamb and Charles Lloyd added; *Blank Verse by Charles Lloyd and Charles Lamb* in 1798; *Edmund Oliver* (a novel), 1798; a translation of Alfieri in 1815; *Nugae Canorae*, 1819; *Desultory Thoughts in London*, 1821; a tragedy *The Duke of Ormond* in 1822; and *Poems* in 1823.

During the early part of his life Charles Lloyd was intimate with Coleridge and Lamb, in 1796 he lived with Coleridge at Bristol and visited Lamb in 1797 when the latter wrote verses 'To Charles Lloyd: An Unexpected Visitor.' *Poems on the Death of Priscilla Farmer* contained Lamb's poem 'The Grandame' and in *Blank Verse* was another poem by Lamb 'To Charles Lloyd.' He is also referred to in Lamb's poem 'The Old Familiar Faces.' In his novel *Edmund Oliver* Lloyd introduced Coleridge's experiences as Private Silas Tomkyn Comberbach, much to Coleridge's annoyance. Another whom he offended by his novel was Mary Hays who had been attracted to him. This book was dedicated to Lamb and published by Cottle. In his *Desultory Thoughts in London* Lloyd had verses on Lamb (Reprinted in Blunden's *Charles Lamb: His Life Recorded by his Contemporaries*, 1934).

Canning's satirical poem 'The New Morality' in *The Anti-Jacobin* associated Lamb and Lloyd together and they figure in Gillray's cartoon as Toad and Frog. In 1798 Lloyd seems to have been the cause of the quarrel between Lamb and Coleridge that produced Lamb's sarcastic 'Theses Quaedam Theologicae'.

Lloyd performed one great service to Lamb and to literature by introducing him to Thomas Manning—both Charles and Robert Lloyd were then at Cambridge studying with Manning. Lloyd lived for some years in the Lake District at Old Brathay and De Quincey gives a detailed picture of him from about 1808 in his *Reminiscences of the English Lake Poets*. To the cottage there came many visitors, including the Wordsworths, Coleridges, Southey and John Wilson (Christopher North), as well as De Quincey.

Charles Lloyd was subject to fits of mental instability and in 1815 was placed in an asylum at York for a time. By 1818 he had recovered, went to London and resumed his literary work. The following year he introduced Lamb to Macready the actor. In 1819 Lamb reviewed Lloyd's poems *Nugae Canorae* in *The Examiner* on 24–5 October. The volume of poems published in 1823 was Lloyd's last literary work to appear. His subsequent years were spent in France in a state of mental derangement.

Lloyd had married Sophia Pemberton in 1799 and they had several

children; the eldest was Charles Grosvenor Lloyd born in 1800. E.V.
Lucas printed in the *Life of Charles Lamb*, 1905.I.135, verses by
Lloyd beginning 'Oft when steals on the meditative hour' as about
Lamb, but Major Butterworth stated that these do not refer to Lamb
but to another friend, although he does not give the name.

Lloyd, Priscilla, 1782–1815. Daughter of Charles Lloyd, Senior,
the Quaker banker of Birmingham. Sister of Charles and Robert
Lloyd. She married Christopher Wordsworth, the poet's brother, in
1804. Her husband was a Norfolk rector, but shortly afterwards he
became Vicar of St Mary's, Lambeth, where most of Priscilla's married life was spent. In 1820 he became Master of Trinity College,
Cambridge.

Priscilla Lloyd was known to the Lambs. In 1798 Lamb sent her
and her brother, Robert, verses from *John Woodvil*, later the same
year he breakfasted with her and Coleridge. In 1800 there is a letter
to Manning in which Lamb says Priscilla is thinking of going to see
Sheridan's *Pizarro* 'under cover of coming to dine with me.' When
Robert Lloyd proposed to live with Lamb in 1799 Priscilla advised
him against it, 'He is too much like yourself.'

Priscilla Wordsworth had three children, two of whom were
Charles Wordsworth who became Bishop of St Andrews and Christopher Wordsworth, later Bishop of Lincoln. She was also the grandmother of John Wordsworth, Bishop of Salisbury. As Lucas said 'no
bad achievement for a Quaker's daughter.'

Lloyd, Robert, 1778–1811. Third son of Charles Lloyd, Senior, and
brother of Charles and Priscilla Lloyd. He was a friend of Lamb,
Coleridge and Manning. He was first apprenticed to a Quaker grocer
and draper in Saffron Walden in 1798, but did not like it. He left
home in 1799 because of differences with his father, went to London
and lived for a time with Lamb. The latter gave him some good advice
and eventually he returned home. In 1804 he married Hannah Hart,
daughter of a Quaker banker. In 1809 his father bought him a partnership in a bookselling and printing business in Birmingham, later
known as Knott and Lloyd.

Robert Lloyd first met Lamb in 1797. In 1798 Lamb sent him
verses from *John Woodvil*, not yet published. In 1809 Lloyd came to
London on business and seems to have had a great deal of social
activity: he went with Lamb to Captain Burney's, met Wordsworth,
went to the Opera House to see Mrs Siddons, dined with Lamb's
friend James White and saw Mrs Clarke, the Duke of York's mistress,
walking in Cheapside and observed that 'she has very fine large eyes.'

A number of letters exist from Lamb to Robert Lloyd, some are of
his best, one praises Walton's *Angler* greatly and another contains one
of his eulogies of London, while a third is about Jeremy Taylor. When

he died in 1811 Lamb wrote a 'Memoir of Robert Lloyd' which was printed in the *Gentleman's Magazine* in November 1811.

Lockhart, John Gibson, 1794–1854. Novelist and biographer. Barrister. Was one of the leading contributors to *Blackwood's Magazine*, possibly one of the editors with John Wilson (Christopher North). In 1820 he married Sophia, daughter of Sir Walter Scott. He became editor of the *Quarterly Review*, 1824–53. He wrote *Peter's Letters to his Kinsfolk*, 1819; the *Life of Burns*, 1828; and the *Life of Sir Walter Scott*, 1838.

In 1821 he challenged the editor of the *London Magazine*, John Scott, to a duel as a result of a quarrel between the *London* and *Blackwood's*. The duel did not take place, but Lockhart's second, Jonathan Christie, later issued a challenge to Scott. In the ensuing duel that took place on 16 February 1821, Scott was fatally injured and died a few days later. Scott sent Lamb a copy of his published statement on the quarrel, that Lamb acknowledged by letter stating that he heartily acquiesced in the conduct of the whole affair 'on OUR PART.'

Lofft, Capel. 1751–1824. Lawyer and philanthropist. Educated at Eton and Cambridge. Was a member of Lincoln's Inn and was called to the Bar in 1775. He edited Book I of Milton's *Paradise Lost* in 1792 and *Laura: An Anthology of Sonnets* in five volumes in 1814. Among his friends were Clarkson, Wilberforce, Godwin and Hazlitt and he is mentioned in Crabb Robinson's *Diary*. He was a patron of Robert Bloomfield. Byron ridiculed him in *English Bards and Scotch Reviewers* as 'the Maecenas of shoemakers and preface-writer general to distressed versemen . . .'.

Lamb does not appear to have met him, but he is mentioned several times in Lamb's letters. Sometimes his initials have been confused with those of Charles Lamb for he occasionally signed his writings 'C.L.' He had a son also named Capel Lofft, 1806–73, a classical scholar, poet, miscellaneous writer and barrister.

London. *See* Praise of London.

Lord, Alice, E. Author of *The Days of Lamb and Coleridge: A Historical Romance*. New York, 1893.

Lovegrove, William, 1778–1816. Actor. Started his career as a plumber but turned to the stage and became well known in comedy parts. He played at Bath and first appeared in London at the Lyceum in 1810 as Lord Ogleby in *The Clandestine Marriage*. He also appeared at Drury Lane and remained there until he retired. He was said to be an excellent actor and was good as Rattan in *Beehive* and particularly as Peter Fidget in *The Boarding House*. He was praised by Charles Mathews and Lamb praised him as Sir Andrew Aguecheek in his essay 'On Some of the Old Actors' in the *London Magazine* for February 1822. He also mentions him in his notice of Brome's *Jovial Crew* in *The Examiner* in 1819.

Lovekin, Charles, 1780–1827. Bookbinder. Cousin of Charles Lamb on his mother's side. Had a business at 10 Pemberton Row, Gough Square, Fleet Street, but died on 14 July 1827 at Windsor Place, Islington, where he had retired. In a letter of 3 June 1810 Mary Lamb tells Sarah Hazlitt that 'my poor relation the bookbinder' had lent them a Life of Lord Nelson. In a letter to P.G. Patmore on 19 July 1827 Lamb states that he has been at his cousin's funeral, and has an anecdote of the widow 'part howling, part giving directions' and of Mary falling through a chair. There are other references to the widow in letters in 1827. There is in America a copy of Lamb's *Works*, 1818, inscribed 'Mr C. Lovekin, from his friend and cousin the Author.'

The identification of Charles Lovekin as Lamb's cousin was made by Major Butterworth who published his discovery in *The Bookman* in July 1921, where he seems to imply that Lovekin may have been the son of a sister of Lamb's mother. E.V. Lucas wrote a pleasing conversation piece 'My Cousin the Bookbinder' which he published in his *Character and Comedy*, 1907, and reprinted with slight alterations in his *At the Shrine of St Charles* in 1934. Miss Mann stated in the *C.L.S. Bulletin*, No. 148, that Lovekin was buried at St Bride's Church, Fleet Street.

Lovel. The name under which Lamb refers to his father in his essay 'The Old Benchers of the Inner Temple'.

Lovell, Robert, ?1770–96. Friend of Coleridge and Southey. A Quaker, educated at Balliol College, Oxford. One of the advocates of Pantisocracy. Married Mary Fricker in 1794 and was thus the brother-in-law of both Coleridge and Southey. After the proposal to establish Pantisocracy on the banks of the Susquehanna had cooled, Lovell with Burnett wanted to establish it on a farm in Wales, but nothing came of it. In 1794 a volume appeared at Bath, *Poems: containing The Retrospect, Odes, Elegies, Sonnets &c by Robert Lovell and Robert Southey*, dated 1795. Coleridge had a poor opinion of Lovell's poems. Also in 1794 Coleridge, Southey and Lovell started to write a drama, the *Fall of Robespierre*. Each was to write one act, but Lovell's was not considered suitable and eventually Southey wrote two acts and Coleridge one. Lovell contributed sonnets to Coleridge's *Watchman* under the name of Moschus. He was also known to Thomas Holcroft, the dramatist, and wrote a letter to him on 11 December 1794 for advice on Pantisocracy. Lovell died of a fever in May 1796 and left a widow and one child, who subsequently lived with the Southeys. After Lovell's death Southey started to edit a collection of his poems, but the volume does not seem to have appeared.

Lowe, Willis Henry. A clerk at East India House, and a friend of both Charles Lamb and Charles Ryle. He is mentioned by Lamb in a letter to Edward Moxon on 17 October 1833 and he seems to have dined with Lamb just before that date; Lamb notes that his gentlemanly manners were the special admiration of their landlady, Mrs Walden.

In January 1835 Lowe certified at Somerset House that he knew Lamb well and that the Will of 1830 was in Lamb's handwriting.

Lucas, Edward Verrall, 1868–1938. Essayist and editor. Worked as a journalist. Has compiled numerous excellent anthologies and has written travel books, on art, many volumes of attractive essays and stories; considerably on cricket and on Charles Lamb. He edited the standard edition of Lamb's works and his letters. He became Chairman of Methuen & Co., Ltd., the publishers. His books on Charles Lamb and his contemporaries include:

Bernard Barton and his Friends. A Record of Quiet Lives, 1893.
Charles Lamb and the Lloyds, edited by E.V. Lucas, 1898.
The Essays of Elia, introduction by E.V. Lucas, 28 illustrations by
    A. Garth Jones, 1901; reprinted, 1914.
The Essays of Elia and the Last Essays of Elia, with an introduction
    by E.V. Lucas (The Little Library Series), 1902.
The Works of Charles and Mary Lamb, edited by E.V. Lucas, 7 vols.,
    1903–5; 6 vols., 1912.
The Life of Charles Lamb, 2 vols., 1905; 7th edition, 1921.
The Best of Lamb: Compiled by E.V. Lucas, 1914; 6th edition, 1934.
The Charles Lamb Day Book, compiled by E.V. Lucas, 1925.
*At the Shrine of Saint Charles. Stray papers on Lamb brought
    together for the centenary of his death in 1834,* 1934; reprinted from his many volumes of essays.
Coleridge, Lamb and the year 1834, 1934; Pamphlet issued in connexion with the N.P.G. Centenary Exhibition.
The Letters of Charles and Mary Lamb, edited by E.V. Lucas, 1935,
    3 vols.

Among Lucas's many contributions to periodicals, the following refer to Charles Lamb. Some others were collected in *At the Shrine of Saint Charles*

The Athenaeum
1901   A New Book by Charles Lamb, November 2.
1902   A Friend of Charles Lamb, June 7—Mrs Coe's recollections
    given to Lucas.

1904 Lamb's Letters on the Death of John Wordsworth, February 6.

1905 Lamb's Letters, June 3.

The Bookman

1903 Review of Bertram Dobell's *Sidelights on Charles Lamb*, May.

Cambridge Review

1910 Cambridge and Charles Lamb (The speech delivered by Lucas at the Lamb dinner in Cambridge in 1910), February 17. Reprinted in *Cambridge and Charles Lamb*, edited by George Wherry, 1925.

1911 Article on a letter from Lamb to Talfourd, probably written in 1819, June 7.

Cornhill Magazine

1898 Charles Lamb and Robert Lloyd: Some Unpublished Letters.

1905 G.D., Friend of Lamb

1910 Examination paper on the Works of Charles Lamb; reprinted in *Reading, Writing and Remembering*, 1932.

Fortnightly Review

1901 Two Notes on Charles Lamb, April.

Life & Letters

1932 The Last to Call him Charley, March.

London Mercury

1934 Recollections of Charles Lamb, by Walter Wilson, edited by E.V. Lucas, December.

Sunday Times

1936 A Review of Elia, March 1.

The Times

1934 Charles Lamb 1775–1834, November 7.

1937 Lamb's Doctor, March 20.

The Times Literary Supplement

1937 An Unpublished Letter of Charles Lamb, February 13.

—— Charles Lamb again, May.

Zigzag, the house magazine of Methuen Ltd.

1935 Editing Lamb, No. 1 Summer.

In his autobiography *Reading, Writing and Remembering. A Literary Record*, published in 1932, Lucas has one chapter entitled 'Concerning Lamb' that deals with his work on Elia. There are also numerous references to Lamb in other parts of the book.

Ludlow, Edmund. Mentioned by Lamb in his letter to Thomas Allsop on 5 October 1825. A writer, 'E.G.B.' in *Notes & Queries* of 10 May 1941 quotes from *Cope's Tobacco Plant* for September 1875 which refers to Edmund Ludlow and adds 'said by Coleridge to have been one of the most thoroughly honest men within my knowledge.'

Lynd, Robert Wilson, 1879–1949. Essayist and journalist. Educated at Queens' College, Belfast. Became literary editor of the *News Chronicle* and also wrote for the *New Statesman* over the signature 'Y.Y.' He is the author of a number of essays said to be in the Lamb tradition. Among these are *The Pleasures of Ignorance*, 1921; *Books and Authors*, 1923; *Solomon in all his glory*, 1923; *The Orange Tree*, 1926; *Both Sides of the Road*, 1934; and *Life's Little Oddities*, 1941.

For a number of years he was 'John O'London' of *John O'London's Weekly*. On 30 March 1929 he contributed an essay on Charles Lamb to that journal. From time to time he wrote on Lamb in his essays, for example in *Books and Authors*, in *John O'London's Weekly* and elsewhere. In 1929 he edited *The Collected Essays of Charles Lamb* in two volumes for J.M. Dent & Sons, a handsome edition with an introduction by Lynd, notes by William Macdonald and illustrations by C.E. Brock as well as twenty-four photogravure plates. Lynd also wrote the chapter on Charles Lamb in Leonard Russell's *English Wits*, 1940. He was one of the original members of The Elian.

Lytton, Edward George Earle Lytton Bulwer, 1803–73. Novelist and statesman. Entered Parliament in 1831 and rose to be Colonial Secretary in 1858. Made a baronet in 1837 and raised to the peerage in 1866. Among his best known works are *Pelham*, 1828; *Eugene Aram*, 1832; *The Last Days of Pompeii*, 1834; and *Rienzi*, 1835. He also wrote poems and plays. He was known to Crabb Robinson who noted in his *Diary* on 19 November 1834, that at Lytton's request he had promised to arrange a meeting with Lamb. There appears to be no record of such meeting and Lucas is doubtful if it ever took place. Lamb died just over a month later. Lytton's novel *Lucretia*, 1846, is partly based on T.G. Wainewright's life. In 1831 he was editor of the *New Monthly Magazine*.

Macaulay, Thomas Babington, 1800–59. Historian, essayist and statesman. Educated at Trinity College, Cambridge. Called to the Bar, 1826. Among Macaulay's famous essays was that reviewing Leigh Hunt's *The Dramatic Works of Wycherley, Congreve, Vanbrugh and Farquhar*. In the essay, which appeared in the *Edinburgh Review* in January 1841, he refers to Charles Lamb's essay 'On the Artificial Comedy of the Last Century', and praised Lamb's writings.

Macdonald, William. Scottish author and editor. In 1903 he edited for J.M. Dent the fine twelve volume edition of *The Works of Charles Lamb* and wrote introductions to most volumes. Frank Swinnerton has told in his *Autobiography*, 1937, how Macdonald, although a cripple and terribly handicapped, worked with great acumen on the huge task. Swinnerton, a friend of Macdonald, gave him help with the work. Dent described Macdonald as 'almost painfully analytic in his criticisms, but splendidly appreciative of all literary values, though at the same time tremendously prejudiced in his dislikes and judgements.'

Macdonald's notes were used in the *Collected Essays of Charles Lamb* edited by Robert Lynd in 1929. He also contributed to periodicals and in 1903 his two articles on 'Lamb's Trouvailles' appeared in *The Athenaeum*, August 8 and December 19. In a lecture to the Charles Lamb Society on William Macdonald in 1944 Frank Swinnerton described him as 'that rare phenomenon, an editor of imagination' and he added, 'No memoir of Lamb had made the man so comprehensible and so lovable as Macdonald's'. *See* separate entry Works.

McKenna, F. Wayne. Lecturer in English, University of Newcastle, New South Wales, Australia. Contributed to the *Charles Lamb Bulletin*, 'Charles Lamb on Acting and Artificial Comedy', April 1977, and 'Charles Lamb on Bensley', July 1977. Author of *Charles Lamb and the theatre*, 1978.

Mackery End. A farmhouse in Hertfordshire near Harpenden, the subject of one of Lamb's best known essays. The house still exists, but has been altered since Lamb's day. Nearby is a large house in which Lamb's great-aunt was housekeeper, as his grandmother was at Blakesware, but the essay concerns a visit to the farmhouse, then occupied by his cousins, the Gladmans. Mary Lamb has written of her earlier visits, possibly also with Charles as a child, in the story 'The Farmhouse' in *Mrs Leicester's School*. *See* R.L. Hine's *Charles Lamb in his Hertfordshire*, 1949; *C.L.S. Bulletin*, Nos. 119 and 152; and Douglas Cory-Wright's *Mackerye End in Hertfordshire*, privately printed 1955.

MacKinnon, Sir Frank Douglas, 1871–1946. Judge and author. Master of the Bench of the Inner Temple. Educated at Trinity College, Oxford. President of the Johnson Society of Lichfield in 1933. In 1927 the Clarendon Press published an edition of Lamb's essay 'The Old Benchers of the Inner Temple' with annotations by Sir F.D. MacKinnon. In this beautiful book the essay occupies nine pages and the annotations seventy-two pages. Both the essay and the annotations were reprinted in MacKinnon's *Inner Temple Papers*, 1948, which also included chapters on 'The Flying Horse Returns' and 'The Ravages of War 1939–45', the latter describing the damage done to the Inner Temple. Some of the chapters in this book had been contributed to the *Times Literary Supplement*:

1936 The Flying Horse Returns: Atonement to Elia, January 16.
—— In the Inner Temple: Four Inscriptions, October 14.

MacKinnon wrote *Grand Larceny*, 1937 (concerns the trial of Jane Austen's aunt); *The Murder in the Temple*, 1935; *On Circuit*, 1940; and he published an annotated edition of Fanny Burney's *Evelina* in 1930. He also wrote the chapter 'The Law and the Lawyers' in *Johnson' England*, 1933.

Mackintosh, Sir James, 1765–1832. Scottish publicist and philosopher. Took a degree in medicine at Edinburgh in 1787, but in 1795 was called to the Bar. Mackintosh's first wife whom he married in 1789 was Catherine Stuart, sister of Daniel Stuart, later editor of the *Morning Post*. In 1797 he married as his second wife, Catherine Allen, sister-in-law of Josiah and John Wedgwood; through them he introduced Coleridge to Daniel Stuart, and to the *Morning Post*. In 1799 he lectured at Lincoln's Inn on the law of nature and nations. In 1791 he had published his *Vindiciae Gallicae*, a reply to Burke's *Reflections on the French Revolution*, but later he became a friend of Burke and repudiated his own work. In 1801 Lamb wrote his epigram on Mackintosh's conduct which was published in his friend John Fenwick's paper *The Albion* and is rumoured to have caused its decease.

In 1803 Mackintosh was appointed Recorder of Bombay and did not return to England until 1812. He later became an M.P. and was Professor of Law and General Politics in the East India Company's College at Haileybury, where he was friendly with Malthus. Mackintosh also published *Dissertation on the Progress of Ethical Philosophy*, 1831; his *History of the Revolution in England* was published after his death, and produced one of Macaulay's famous essays. When Lamb was raising a subscription for Godwin in 1823 Mackintosh gave £10.

Maclean, Catherine Macdonald, d.1960. Lecturer in English Literature at the Universities of Edinburgh, Bristol and Wales. Author of *Born Under Saturn*, 1943, a biography of William Hazlitt. She also wrote *Dorothy Wordsworth: The Early Years*, 1932; *Dorothy and William Wordsworth*, 1927; and *Hazlitt Painted by Himself*, 1948. She edited a selection of Hazlitt's essays in 1949 and wrote introductions to the Everyman editions of Hazlitt's *The Round Table*, 1957, and *Table Talk*, 1959. She lectured to the Charles Lamb Society in September 1946 on 'William Hazlitt and the challenge of our time' and in April 1950 gave the Wordsworth Centenary Address to the Society. She also reviewed in the *C.L.S. Bulletin* in September 1959 W.H. Bonner's *The Journals of Sarah and William Hazlitt*, 1822–1831.

Maclise, Daniel, 1806–70. Irish artist. A historical painter who originally worked in a bank. He used the pseudonym of 'Alfred

Croquis'. When working in Ireland he attracted the attention of Sir Walter Scott when there on a visit. In 1827 he came to London and studied at the Royal Academy where he exhibited in 1829. Soon after the establishment of *Fraser's Magazine* in 1830 Maclise started to contribute sketches for the 'Gallery of Illustrious Literary Characters', and produced the famous Elia sketch. William Bates suggested that the artist had taken the head from the Brook Pulham etching.

Macready, William Charles, 1793–1873. English actor. First appeared in Birmingham in 1810. Was engaged at Covent Garden in 1816. One of the greatest of tragic actors, he is said to have been surpassed only by Garrick and equalled only by Kean. He became the leading actor at Drury Lane from 1823–26. He was manager of Covent Garden 1837–39 and of Drury Lane 1841–43. Among his best parts were those in *Rob Roy* and *Virginius*, but he was universally acclaimed as Lear, Hamlet and Macbeth. His last appearance was at Drury Lane in February 1851 when he played Macbeth. Following this a few days later a celebration dinner was held attended by 600 people, the stewards consisting of many of the famous, including Dickens, Thackeray and Tennyson, while of Lamb's friends there were Talfourd, Procter and John Forster. Tennyson had composed a special sonnet for the occasion.

Lamb first met Macready about 1820 or a little earlier through Charles Lloyd. Crabb Robinson records in his *Diary* that on 27 June 1820 he was at the Lambs and sat an hour there with Macready. When Macready played Virginius, Lamb liked the performance so much that he wrote some congratulatory verses to the author, J. Sheridan Knowles. In 'Barbara S——' Lamb states 'I have been indulged with a classical conference with Macready.' In his *Diary* Macready recorded Lamb's remark that he wished to draw his last breath through a pipe and expel it in a pun. On that occasion Macready had supper at Talfourd's (in January 1834) to meet Lamb, and others present were Forster, the Barron Fields and Moxon. In a letter in January 1823 Lamb tells J. Howard Payne that Macready had taught Frances Harriet Kelly (the *other* Miss Kelly). Macready was also acquainted with T.G. Wainewright and dined with him in Great Marlborough Street. In 1837 when Wainewright was in prison in Newgate, Macready recognized him with horror when he was visiting the prison with Forster and Dickens.

When Charles Lloyd was suffering from melancholia in 1818 his recovery was said to have been brought about by witnessing a performance by Macready in the part of Rob Roy in Isaac Pocock's dramatisation of Scott's novel. Lamb's friend Talfourd also had occasion to be grateful to Macready for his performance secured the success of Talfourd's play *Ion* at Covent Garden in 1836. He also played in Talfourd's other two tragedies *The Athenian Captive* and *Glencoe*.

Magazine Dinners. It was the custom in the eighteenth and nineteenth centuries for publishers occasionally to give dinners to their authors. James Boswell records that he and Dr Johnson were often entertained at the 'hospitable and well-covered table' of Charles and Edward Dilly in the Poultry, where he met a great number of literary men. In Charles Lamb's time John Murray, William Blackwood and other publishers gave similar dinners and Taylor & Hessey, the publishers of the *London Magazine*, were wont to entertain the contributors to their periodical. The monthly dinners were usually held at the publisher's office in Waterloo Place, Pall Mall, but in return some of the contributors occasionally held the festivities at their own houses. Although there is no record that Lamb ever held the dinners at his rooms he certainly attended at those held elsewhere.

There are vivid accounts of the functions which were marked by high spirits and wit. Among the most interesting are those given in the following books: Hood's 'Reminiscences' in *Hood's Own*, 1839; *Memoir of H.F. Cary* by Henry Cary, 1847; *Charles Lamb: A Memoir* by B.W. Procter, 1866; *Autobiographical Fragment* by B.W. Procter, 1877; *The Translator of Dante* by R.W. King, 1925; and *John Clare: A Life* by J.W. and A. Tibble, 1932. A rival publication, the *London Magazine* published by Gold and Northhouse in 1820–21, printed in March 1821 an account of an imaginary dinner supposed to have been given by Baldwin, Cradock & Joy to the contributors to their *London Magazine*.

Maginn, William, 1793–1842. Journalist. Contributed to *Blackwood's Magazine* and in 1830 became editor of *Fraser's Magazine* for which he wrote a notice on Charles Lamb to accompany Maclise's sketch. In this he suggested that Lamb's family was Jewish and his real name 'Lomb'!

Man, Henry, 1747–99. Author. Originally in business, but retired in 1775; and after his marriage in the following year entered the South Sea House, rising to be Deputy Secretary by 1793. He contributed to the *Morning Chronicle* and *London Gazette*. In 1770 he published a volume of essays, *The Trifler*, then *Cloacina: A Comi-Tragedy* and *Letters on Education* in 1775. *The Miscellaneous Works in Verse and Prose of the late Henry Man* was published in two volumes in 1802. Lamb mentions him with affection in his essay 'The South Sea House'. In a letter of 20 January 1825 to Sara Hutchinson he quotes Man's epigram from his *Miscellaneous Works* on Lord Spencer and Lord Sandwich, one of whom invented half a coat and the other half a dinner.

Mann, Phyllis G. Miss Mann has been particularly successful in her exploration of the by-ways of Eliana, particularly those concerning Lamb's relations and more obscure friends and acquaintances. Much of her work has been printed in the *C.L.S. Bulletin* as follows:

1949 Francis Fielde, November.
1952 Lamb, Elia and the Burneys, July.
1953 Mr Norris of the Bluecoat School, September.
1954 Mr Norris . . ., continued, March.
—— Mackery End, July.
1955 Button Snap: What Did Godfather Fielde pay for it?, January.
—— Mr Norris of the Bluecoat School, July.
1956 Lamb and Coleridge's Admission to Christ's Hospital, September.
—— The Rice Families, November.
1957 Charles Lamb's Governor, January.
1959 Notes by the Way, January.
1963 A New Gloss for 'The Wedding', March.
1968 Adventures in Research, April.
—— A Commentary on H.W. Gray's 'New Light on Charles Lamb', July.
1969 The Cox Family of Bankers by K.R. Jones (contains some details supplied to the editor by Miss Mann), October.

Other contributions to periodicals include:

The Times Literary Supplement
1950 A Friend of Hazlitt, December 1.
Keats-Shelley Memorial Bulletin (Rome)
1961 Further Notes on John Keats.

Miss Mann was joint author with Mr A. Macdonald of the play *The Man Without a Foe* (i.e. Charles Lamb), first produced by the B.B.C. in February 1945, and in January 1946 presented by the Dramatic Group of the Charles Lamb Society. She also contributed to the *Keats-Shelley Journal*.

Manning, Anne, 1807–79. Novelist. Author of *Family Pictures*, 1861, which contains a chapter on Charles Lamb and Joseph Paice. It also contains much interesting information on Paice and his family. Lucas states in the *Life of Charles Lamb* that Miss Manning had the story of Lamb's employment in Paice's office 'more or less directly from Mr Paice', but the *C.B.E.L.* lists her book as fiction. However, she states at the beginning that an earlier Joseph Paice was her great-grandfather and she seems to write of Lamb's friend from real knowledge. She was a voluminous writer who used the pseudonym of 'The Author of Mary Powell' from her book *The Maiden and Married Life* *of Mary Powell, afterwards Mistress Milton* (i.e. the poet's wife). Perhaps her best known book is *The Household of Sir Thomas More.*

Manning, Thomas, 1772–1840. Mathematician, linguist and traveller. Second son of the Rev. William Manning, Rector of Broome and Diss, Norfolk, at the former of which Manning was born. Owing to ill health he was educated at home, but went to Caius College, Cambridge, at the age of eighteen. He became a close student of the classics and of mathematics and showed unusual powers of mind, but because of an objection to oaths and tests did not take his degree. He remained at Cambridge as a mathematical tutor and among his pupils were Charles and Robert Lloyd. Among his friends were Porson, Baron Maseres, Sir George Tuthill and Dr Martin Davy, the Master of Caius.

While at Cambridge he became interested in the Chinese language; and early in 1802 he went to France to study Chinese under Dr Hagar, at the same time studying chemistry there. He was friendly with Carnot and Talleyrand and communicated ideas to the former which Carnot used in his treatises.

When the war with France was renewed he was detained by Napoleon, but through the help of his French friends, particularly Talleyrand, Napoleon was persuaded to issue a passport to Manning for China, with permission to visit England first. He continued to study Chinese in London and also studied medicine at Westminster Hospital. With the help of Sir Joseph Banks, the President of the Royal Society, he obtained a passage in an East India Company's ship and sailed from Portsmouth about the middle of 1806, arriving in Canton in 1807 where he lived in the English factory. Here he practised as a doctor and made plans for his attempts to enter China. In 1810 he left Canton for Calcutta, but officialdom was not helpful there and he decided to make the attempt alone, setting out for Tibet in 1811 disguised as a Tartar doctor and accompanied only by a single Chinese servant. He eventually reached Lhasa and met the Dalai Lama, remaining there for some months. He was obliged to leave, however, on orders from Peking and returned to Calcutta and thence to Canton.

In 1816 he went with Lord Amherst's Embassy to Peking as Chinese interpreter. Although they reached their destination, the object of the visit, a trade agreement, was not achieved. On the return journey Manning and the party were wrecked in the Straits of Gaspar, but no lives were lost. He then embarked for England and called at St Helena on the way, where he met Napoleon and talked with him.

Manning reached England a disappointed man and nothing was heard of his earlier project of a Chinese and English Dictionary. He retired first to a cottage at Puckeridge, Hertfordshire, and then to Redbourn near St Albans, where he lived in seclusion, although from time to time he visited London and stayed with his friend Sir George Tuthill, the physician. His cottage was sparsely furnished, but contained a large library of Chinese books. He is said to have brought a Chinese servant back with him. During 1827–29 he lived in Italy and was there with Lamb's East India Company friend, Samuel Ball, whom he had known in Canton. Later he returned to England and lived in another cottage at Dartford, Kent. In 1838 he had a paralytic stroke and moved to Bath for medical treatment. He died May 1840 and is buried in the Abbey Church, Bath.

Manning published nothing about his travels in Tibet and China and refused to speak of what he had seen there. Reginald Hine commenting on this in *Charles Lamb and his Hertfordshire*, remarked that 'With his immense learning he could be silent in fifteen languages.' However, some rough notes of his adventures were published as the *Narratives of the Mission of George Bogle to Tibet and of the Journey of Thomas Manning to Lhasa* in 1876, edited by Clements R. Markham. While at Cambridge Manning had published in two volumes *Introduction to Arithmetic and Algebra*, 1796 and 1798. This work was so much desired by George Dyer that he talked of buying a copy, but as Lamb said, George 'had not been master of seven shillings a good time' and Charles wrote to the author for a copy for him (letter of 21 August 1800). Manning also contributed mathematical articles to Volume VI of Baron Maseres's *Scriptores Logarithmici*, 1791–1807, and to the *Philosophical Transactions* in 1806. He revised the proof sheets of the House of Commons *Report on the Poor Laws* and wrote a treatise on the consumption of tea in Bhutan, Tibet and Tartary, and his description of the mode of preparing tea in Tibet was included in Samuel Ball's *Account of the Cultivation and Manufacture of Tea in China*, 1848. In his *Charles Lamb and his Hertfordshire*, Reginald Hine prints a Drinking Song composed by Manning.

In 1826 he contributed a series of Chinese Jests to the *New Monthly Magazine* that were submitted to the editor by Charles Lamb and the Olliers on Manning's behalf. They appeared in the same issues of the magazine as Lamb's 'Popular Fallacies' and some of Hazlitt's essays.

Lamb first met Manning at Cambridge in December 1799 through Charles Lloyd. From that time Manning became one of Lamb's most intimate friends and some of the very best of Lamb's letters were sent to Manning, particularly in the years before Manning went to China. Lucas prints fifty-two letters from Lamb to Manning and they include some of the gems of English epistolary art. Lamb sometimes sent Manning manuscript copies of his writings or included poems in his letters; some of the imitations of Burton, the 'Londoner', the prologue to 'Antonio', the poem 'Hester' and one of the eulogies of London are all in these letters. In 1800 he sent a manuscript copy of *John Woodvil* written out by himself and his sister.

Letters between the friends are most numerous from 1800 to 1806; after that the distance between England and China curtailed the correspondence. When Manning returned to England and was living relatively near at Redbourn, the paucity of letters may be because they saw one another frequently. The London coaches for Shrewsbury and Manchester passed through both Islington and Redbourn. (A coach leaving the 'Peacock' at Islington at 6.45 a.m. was at Redbourn at 9.13 a.m.)

From time to time Manning is known to have visited the Lambs and as late as 1825 stayed at Colebrooke Cottage. Crabb Robinson described Manning as 'a darling of Miss Lamb's', and Charles was lyrical in his praise of his friend, and said he was 'more extra-ordinary than Wordsworth or Coleridge.' Lamb's letters to Manning are full of fun and it was to him that he wrote in February 1808 of Wordsworth, 'He says he does not see much difficulty in writing like Shakespeare, if he had a mind to try it. It is clear, then, nothing is wanting but the mind.'

Manning gave Lamb the idea for his 'A Dissertation upon Roast Pig.' Alfred Ainger in his edition of *The Essays of Elia* suggests Manning may have got the story from Thomas Taylor, the Platonist, when the latter was translating Porphyry's *De Abstinentia*. This raises the interesting speculation as to whether the eccentric Greek scholar Taylor was a friend of the equally eccentric Manning. One of Taylor's friends was Thomas Love Peacock, another Greek scholar and later of East India House.

Thomas Allsop has recorded in his *Letters, Conversations and Recollections of S.T. Coleridge* (3rd edition, 1864) that he once witnessed Manning give 'an outburst of his *unembodied* spirit, when such was the effect of his more than magnetic, his magic power (learnt was it in Chaldea, or in that sealed continent . . .) that we were all rapt and carried aloft into the seventh heaven.' Allsop maintains that few persons had so great a share of Lamb's admiration, for to few did Manning vouchsafe manifestations of his *very* extraordinary powers.

Perhaps Lamb's friendship with Manning was on a rather lower level than that with Coleridge and Wordsworth. The letters, which are not particularly subjective, would seem to indicate this more mundane level: Lamb's bubble with humour and vitality, while Manning's show a love of banter and paradox. Although Manning left no written work that exhibited his genius, he stimulated Lamb to produce letters that are among the treasures of English literature. Manning described the Lambs as his best and dearest friends.

After Manning had become an invalid and moved to Bath, he was visited by Crabb Robinson, who had met him occasionally at the Lambs. Robinson notes in his *Diary* on 27 March 1840 that he, Landor and Miss Burney were in Bath and called on Manning. They found him cheerful and glad to see them and Landor was particularly struck with Manning's personal beauty.

A bust of Manning was done in 1805 or 1806 and there is a photograph of a bust reproduced in *The Bookman* for July 1921 and again in the volume of Manning's letters edited by Mrs G.A. Anderson. Manning's library is now a valued possession of the Royal Asiatic Society.

Manning's elder brother, William, married a daughter of William Sayer Donne, brother of Edward Charles Donne, Fellow of Caius College, Cambridge, and father of William Bodham Donne, the friend of Edward Fitzgerald.

We have been long able to read Lamb's matchless letters to Manning, but it was not until 1925 that *The Letters of Thomas Manning to Charles Lamb* were published. Although they are edited by Mrs Anderson, she had died the year before; P.P. Howe, the Hazlitt scholar, saw them through the press, wrote a foreword and, in fact, decided on the form the volume should take. With them before us we can appreciate more fully Lamb's letters, but those of his friend are not their equal in interest or in style.

Marrs, Edwin W. Jr. Professor of English, University of Pittsburgh. Professor Marrs is preparing a new edition of Lamb's *Letters*, the first volumes of which were published by Cornell University Press in 1975, 1976 and 1978. It is expected to consist of six volumes. He wrote 'Some Account of the Publishing History of the Lamb's letters, with notes of a new edition in progress' in the *Charles Lamb Bulletin*, April 1973.

Marshall, James. Hack writer, friend of William Godwin, who sometimes dealt with Godwin's business and practical affairs. He was a witness at the marriage of William Godwin and Mary Wollstonecraft at Old St Pancras Church in 1797. When in 1807 Godwin appealed for subscriptions to help pay his debts, Marshall organized the appeal, a service Godwin was able to return some years later when he raised a fund to save Marshall from a debtor's prison.

Lamb liked Marshall and said that 'a more god-like honest soul exists not in the world.' He was with him after the failure of Godwin's play *Antonio* in December 1800, and amusingly describes it to Manning in his letter of 16 December 1800. In his essay 'The Old Actors' in the *London Magazine* in April 1822 he says he sat in a box with Godwin and Marshall and gives a longer account of the failure. Lamb had contributed an epilogue to the play.

In a letter to Manning of 24 September 1802 Lamb complains that the second Mrs Godwin had alienated her husband's former friends. 'That Bitch has detached Marshall from the house, Marshall the man who went to sleep when the "Ancient Mariner" was reading, the old, steady, unalterable friend of the Professor.'

Marter, William. Clerk at East India House with Lamb. He was slightly senior to Lamb in service, but was transferred from the Accountant General's Office to the Baggage Warehouse in 1810 and retired in 1812. In 1823 he was living at Knockholt, near Sevenoaks. Mrs Anderson suggested that Marter was the clerk referred to in Mary Lamb's letter to Sarah Hazlitt of 7 November 1809 whereby Charles got £20 a year extra salary. In July 1824 Lamb wrote to Marter in reply to a letter asking for advice on suitable magazines for a club. With his letter Lamb sent a copy of his sonnet 'Work' first published in *The Examiner* in 1819 and reprinted in *Album Verses* in 1830.

Martin, Benjamin Ellis. American author. In March and April 1890 Martin contributed articles to *Scribner's Magazine* entitled 'In the Footprints of Charles Lamb', later republished as a book with the same title in 1891. It was a topographical biography illustrated by John Fulleylove and Herbert Railton, and it contains a Bibliography of Charles and Mary Lamb by E.D. North. Both Alfred Ainger and Dykes Campbell appear to have been critical of this book.

Martin, Frank Vernon, b.1921. Artist, engraver, etcher and book illustrator. Educated at Uppingham, Hertford College, Oxford and St Martins School of Art. Member of the Society of Wood Engravers. Has work in many galleries including the Victoria & Albert Museum and the Fitzwilliam Museum. Has done illustrations for the *Reader's Digest* and the Folio Society. Martin did most attractive wood engravings for the Folio Society edition of *Charles Lamb: Essays*, 1963.

Martin, John, 1789–1854. English painter. Noted for his large scale subjects and wild and rather fantastic compositions. First exhibited at the Royal Academy in 1812. His most famous work was *Belshazzar's Feast* exhibited in 1821. Other works include *The Fall of Babylon*, 1819; *Joshua*, 1816; *The Destruction of Herculaneum*, 1822; and *The Eve of the Deluge*, 1840.

Martin was a friend and favourite painter of Bernard Barton, and the latter in his *New Year's Eve*, 1828, has four poems on Martin's pictures, as well as a frontispiece showing his picture of *Christ Walking on the Water*. In his letters Barton discussed the artist with Lamb who was very critical of his work. Lamb also wrote on Martin in his essay 'On the Total Defects of the Quality of Imagination, observable in the Works of Modern British Artists' in *The Athenaeum* in January and February 1833, and later reprinted in the *Last Essays of Elia*. Lamb claimed that Martin lacked imagination, but others maintained that he had too much imagination. Martin received much praise and became famous in his own day.

Martin, Louisa, 1793–1858. Friend of Lamb, whom he called 'Monkey', from 'her diverting sportiveness in childhood'. In his letter to Hazlitt on 10 November 1805 Lamb relates how she claimed to be called 'Miss' at the age of twelve. In March 1809 Charles and Mary Lamb wrote a joint letter to her; Charles wrote a short note to her in July 1830 in which he gives her address as Chelsea College; on 22 February 1834 he wrote to Wordsworth asking for help for Louisa who was establishing a school at Carlisle. He calls the Martins 'the oldest and best friends I have left.' Before going to Carlisle Louisa Martin had been a governess for many years in the Devonshire household of Sir Thomas Acland, from whom she received a legacy. Later she had a school in Kensington High Street. A silhouette portrait of her appears in *The Bookman* for September 1921. Lamb wrote verses on Louisa Martin in 1806 entitled 'The Ape' which were printed in the *London Magazine* in October 1820, and further verses, 'The Change', were printed in Hone's *Year Book* in December 1831. They were later included in Lamb's *Poetical Works*, 1836, under the title of 'To Louisa M——, whom I used to call "Monkey".' According to Lamb's letters to her she must have known many of the members of the Lamb circle. Her two sisters, Sarah and Hannah, are mentioned in Mary Lamb's letters to her. Sarah married a Mr Fulton.

Maseres, Baron Francis, 1731–1824. Mathematician, historian and reformer. Cursitor Baron of the Exchequer. Was at school at Kingston-on-Thames where he had as schoolfellows Edward Gibbon, William Hayley and Gilbert Wakefield. Proceeded to Cambridge. Was called to the Bar in 1758. He was Attorney General of Quebec, 1766–69, where his fluent French was of help to him. He became a Bencher in 1774 and much of his life was spent in the Temple where he had chambers at No. 5 Kings Bench Walk.

Baron Maseres had met and did not like Dr Johnson. Among his friends was William Cobbett whom he visited when the latter was in prison in Newgate, always wearing his wig and gown in order, as he said, to show his abhorrence of the sentence. The Baron was the author of works on mathematics, on Canada, on historical subjects and he also wrote poetry.

He was one of Lamb's 'Old Benchers'. Lamb told Manning in a letter in April 1801, 'I live at No. 16 Mitre-Court Buildings, a pistol-shot off Baron Maseres.' Lamb added that the Baron's forte was the higher mathematics, whereas his own was poetry and *belles lettres*. Manning and Maseres must have been acquainted as fellow mathematicians at some period for the former contributed to Maseres's *Scriptores Logarithmici*. In his essay 'On the Old Benchers of the Inner Temple' Lamb states that the Baron wore the costume of the reign of George II all his life.

Masson, Flora. Author of the small volume on *Charles Lamb* in Jack's People's Books series, 1913.

Mather, Honor, 1761–1861. A widow who married George Dyer about 1825. She had inherited from her third husband chambers opposite Dyer in Clifford's Inn. A Devonshire woman, she seems to have made him an excellent wife and looked after him well. He told Crabb Robinson that 'Mrs Dyer is a woman of excellent natural sense, but she is not literate.' She would only agree to marry him after his friends had approved the match. Mrs De Morgan (Sophia Frend) relates how her father hurried to London in some alarm on hearing of the proposal, but was well satisfied on seeing the kindly nature of Mrs Mather. They were married at St Dunstan's-in-the-West, Fleet Street.

She lived until her one hundredth year; when Crabb Robinson visited her at that time she still had both eyesight and hearing, and spoke warmly of Charles and Mary Lamb. The last letter we have of Lamb's was one written to Mrs Dyer about Cary's copy of Phillips's *Theatrum Poetarum Anglicanorum* which he thought he had left at her house.

Mathews, Charles, 1776–1835. English actor, specializing in comic parts and later in one-man entertainments. He first appeared in Dublin in 1794, then at York under Tate Wilkinson and subsequently in London at the Haymarket, Covent Garden and Drury Lane. One of his best parts was Sir Fretful Plagiary and Leigh Hunt described his acting in this part as perfect. He also played Falstaff and Sir Peter Teazle. It has been estimated that he appeared in over 400 parts. He also wrote for the *Ladies Magazine* and was sub-editor of the *Thesbian Magazine*.

In 1808 he created his one-man entertainments that have been described as 'a whole play in the person of one man.' These brought him great fame and gave him an opportunity to display his outstanding talents for imitation. The performances were known as 'At Homes' and were gradually extended until they became short plays.

Charles Mathews's first wife was Eliza Strong, a school teacher, who died in 1802. His second wife, Anne Jackson, was a half sister of Fanny Kelly and herself an actress, but she retired from the stage in 1810. She published *Memoirs* of her husband in 1839 which mention Lamb. She also wrote *Anecdotes of Actors*, 1844. She died in 1869.

Lamb first met Mathews in May 1821 at a dinner at Gillman's at Highgate. Coleridge had wished the two to meet, but at first neither seemed quite to come up to the expectations of the other. Later Lamb was to say to Barron Field in 1827 'Mathews whom I greatly like— and Mrs Mathews, whom I almost greatlier like.' Mrs Mathews said at first impression Lamb's appearance was not prepossessing, but his head indicated great intellect. Later both she and her husband became very fond of Lamb. Mrs Mathews recorded in the *Memoirs* the amusing story of Lamb's dipping at the seaside.

In a letter to Barron Field in October 1827 Lamb declined a request to describe the theatrical portraits in Mathews's celebrated collection, on the grounds that he was unfitted for the task. In his essay 'The Old Actors' in the *London Magazine* in October 1822 Lamb had briefly described Mathews's gallery at Highgate, and stated it was 'the most delightful collection I ever gained admission to', and he gave some details which expressed his enthusiasm. In his essay 'Barbara S——' Lamb says he was conducted round the Mathews gallery by the owner himself. The pictures were also described by P.G. Patmore in his *British Galleries of Art*, 1824, and by most writers on the Garrick Club.

The collection was originally formed by Thomas Harris, manager of Covent Garden, and bought by Mathews after Harris's death, to form the nucleus of his own collection. When in 1833 Mathews was in financial difficulties his pictures were exhibited at the Queen's Bazaar in Oxford Street to attract purchasers, but the result was unsatisfactory. The catalogue for the exhibition was drawn up by Mathews's son, who included in it Lamb's comments on the pictures from his essay. After Mathews's death the collection was bought by Robert Durrant, who presented it to the Garrick Club. Both Mathews and his son were members of the Club.

Mathews, Charles James, 1803–78. Actor and dramatist, son of Charles Mathews the actor. Was first trained as an architect with Pugin, but abandoned this career for the stage. He had appeared in private theatricals but did not take to the stage professionally until 1835. He appeared at the Olympic in his own play *The Humpbacked Lover*, and also played with Liston. In 1838 he married Madame Vestris, who was herself well known as a dancer and singer and as manager of the Olympic. Together they took over the management of Covent Garden, and then moved to the Lyceum, but at neither theatre were they financially successful. Much later he toured Australia, America and India with success. One of his best parts was Dazzle in *London Assurance*. He also appeared at the Haymarket.

Mathews mentions in his *Autobiography* the many famous people he met at his father's house, including Charles Lamb, Coleridge who was their neighbour at Highgate and a daily visitor, Leigh Hunt, Moore, Byron and Scott.

On 26 April 1822 a private theatrical performance was organized by Mathews at the English Opera House and was attended by many people of fashion and intellectual celebrity. The programme started with Lamb's farce *Mr H*—— in which the name part was played by Captain Hill, 'an amateur of long practice at the Woolwich theatricals', who became a professional actor under the name of Benson Hill. The cast were Mr H——, Captain Hill; Landlord, Mr Gyles; Bevil, Mr C. Bryne; Melesinda, Mrs Weippart; Betty, Mrs Bryan. A prologue was written by James Smith and spoken by Captain Hill. The rest of the programme consisted of 'Le Comédien D'Etampes' in which Mathews both played and sang, and 'The Sorrows of Werther' by John Poole, a parody of Goethe, in which Mathews played Werther and his mother played Charlotte. Although there appears to be no record of Lamb's attendance at the production of his play, it seems likely that since both Charles and Anne Mathews and their son who organized it were friends, he would have been invited to see it.

Matthews, James Brander, 1852–1929. American essayist and dramatic critic. Educated at Columbia University where he became Professor of Literature, 1892–1900, and of Dramatic Literature, 1900–24. In 1891 he edited with an introduction and notes *The Dramatic Essays of Charles Lamb*. The introduction on 'Charles Lamb and the Theatre' occupies pages 7–31; there are few notes. Matthews wrote more than forty books, a number of which are about the theatre. Among them are *Actors & Actresses of Great Britain and the United States*, 5 vols., 1886 (with Laurence Hutton); *A Book about the Theatre*, 1916; *Shakespeare as a Playwright*, 1913; *Principles of Playmaking*, 1919; and *These Many Years*, 1917 (autobiography). He was dramatic critic for the *New York Times*. He has been called 'perhaps the last of the gentlemanly school of critics and essayists' in America.

Mattocks, Isabella, 1746–1826. English actress, daughter of the actor, Lewis Hallam. Married an actor named Mattocks who became manager of a Liverpool theatre. She is said to have first appeared at Covent Garden at the age of five. In 1761 she played Juliet, but became best known for country bumpkin parts, playing mainly at Covent Garden. She was particularly good as servants and citizen's wives and in low comedy. Her best parts included Betty Hint in *The Man of the World*, Mrs Racket, Mrs Brittle, Betty Blackberry, Mrs Cockletop in *Modern Antiques*. O'Keeffe praised her particularly as Betty Blackberry.

Lamb praised her in his 'The New Acting' in *The Examiner* and mentioned her in his essay 'The Old Actors' in the *London Magazine* in October 1822 as 'the sensiblest of viragos.' Crabb Robinson records in his *Diary* on 17 May 1815 going with Lamb to see Kenney's *The Fortunes of War* at Covent Garden when Mrs Mattocks was in the cast.

Maunde, John, c.1770–1813. At Christ's Hospital with Lamb. Ran away from the school and was expelled in 1789. He subsequently went to Paris and was imprisoned for four years by Robespierre. Later he studied at Oxford and took orders. He translated works from the French. Lamb mentions him in his essay 'Christ's Hospital Five and Thirty Years Ago' as 'ill-fated M——.' Harvard has John Maunde's copy of his translation *Rural Philosopher*, 1801, of James Delille's *Les Georgiques*.

May, James Lewis, 1873–1961. Author, editor and translator. Educated at University College School and in France. Was reader and literary adviser to John Lane, the publisher. Author of *Charles Lamb: A Study*, 1934. Vice President of the Charles Lamb Society and has lectured to members from time to time. He is best known as editor and translator of the works of Anatole France. In 1953 he edited with an introduction *Selected Essays, Letters and Poems by Charles Lamb* in Collins's New Classics series.

May, John, 1775–1856. Friend of Robert Southey who wrote many letters to him. They first met in Portugal in 1795 and their friendship was lifelong. May lived at Richmond. In 1821 when May lost his fortune through the mismanagement of a brother in Brazil, Southey offered him his entire savings. In a letter to Southey of 27 December 1798 Lamb mentions that May had made an offer, through Lloyd, of serving Lamb in some way at East India House by the interest of his friend Sir Francis Baring, the banker and a director of the Company. Lamb replied to Southey with thanks but declined the offer.

May, William. Landlord of the 'Salutation and the Cat' in Newgate Street, London, where Coleridge and Lamb used to meet in 1794–5. He is mentioned in several of Lamb's letters in 1796 and Lamb seems to have paid Coleridge's bill there. It was here in a small smoky room that they drank egg-hot, ate welsh rarebit and smoked a mixture of oronooko and herb tobacco—and of course, talked and talked.

Cottle has a story that a London innkeeper offered Coleridge free lodging if he would stay and just talk, as he would attract customers. Lucas says it could not have been May since his bill was unpaid by Coleridge, but could have been the landlord of the 'Angel' in Butcher Hall Street. Possibly this was after all the 'Salutation' and May only rendered his bill when Coleridge did not comply with his request to remain at the inn (and Lamb settled it).

Maynard, Thomas. In his essay on the South Sea House Lamb refers to 'mild, child-like pastoral M——.' He also mentions M——'s father as 'old surly M——, the unapproachable churchwarden of Bishopsgate.' According to Lamb's Key 'M——' stood for Maynard who hanged himself and who Lucas says was chief clerk in the Old Annuities and Three Per Cents until 1793. John M. Turnbull in *Notes*

& *Queries*, 14 December 1946, also suggests that 'M——' was Thomas Maynard which W.H. Phillips supplements in *Notes & Queries* of 15 February 1947.

Mellon, Harriot, 1777–1837. English actress. Was brought to Drury Lane from the provinces by Sheridan in 1795 and later acted Lydia Languish in *The Rivals*. She was very successful and popular in light, rather impertinent comedy parts and frequently under-studied Mrs Jordan. She also played at the Lyceum when Drury Lane was burnt down, but acted in Sheridan's Company for almost the whole of her stage life. In 1815 she retired on her marriage to Thomas Coutts, the banker; after his death she married the Duke of St Albans. When she died she left most of her enormous fortune to Lady Bur-dett's daughter, the grand-daughter of Thomas Coutts, and later the Baroness Burdett Coutts.

When Lamb's play *Mr H——* was produced at Drury Lane on 10 December 1806, Harriot Mellon played Melesinda, while Elliston played the title role. The following year when Henry Siddons's play *Time's a Tell-Tale* was produced on October 27, she played the leading part of Lady Delmar, some of the male parts were taken by Elliston, Charles Mathews and Palmer, all known to Lamb. After the first night Lamb's epilogue was withdrawn and another substituted for it. The play ran for nine nights.

Although there is no direct evidence that she and Lamb met, they must have seen one another at the rehearsals of *Mr H——*. In his letter to B.R. Haydon in October 1822 Lamb asks if it is likely Mrs Coutts would help Godwin who was in financial difficulties.

Memorials to Charles Lamb. Memorials usually comprise some-thing tangible and permanent, such as plaques, medals, pieces of sculpture or even a building; but those of an ephemeral nature, such as celebratory dinners and luncheons and meetings of societies to pay tribute to an author must also be mentioned. Those listed below are mostly of a permanent nature, but some other types are given al-phabetically elsewhere in this book.

Button Snap. The cottage at Buntingford, Herts, that once be-longed to Charles Lamb has three memorials on it to him.

1. A plaque placed there in 1901 commemorating his ownership.
2. A plaque placed there in 1954 stating that the cottage was acquired by the Charles Lamb Society from the Royal Society of Arts in 1949.
3. A terra cotta medallion portrait of Lamb removed from Southamp-ton Buildings, Chancery Lane.

See separate entry Button Snap for text of inscriptions.

Cambridge. In George Wherry's *Cambridge and Charles Lamb*, 1925, it is stated that a tablet was placed in 1913 on the house of Mr

Bays in Trumpington Street at which Lamb stayed in 1819. It is now No. 11 King's Parade.

Christ's Hospital.

1. A Lamb Medal was instituted in 1875 at Christ's Hospital and, until 1948 was awarded for the best English essay by a Grecian.

   See separate entry.

2. The Coleridge Memorial at Christ's Hospital comprises a small bronze group showing the figures of Lamb, Coleridge and Middleton. It illustrates the incident of Coleridge being found reading Virgil for pleasure during play hours. The statuette was subscribed for in 1872 and is held in rotation by the ward in which most prizes have been gained during the year. It is illustrated in R.B. Johnson's *Christ's Hospital*, 1896, and S.E. Winbolt's *Coleridge, Lamb and Leigh Hunt*, 1920.

3. A house at Christ's Hospital is named Lamb House in commemoration of Charles Lamb.

4. A bronze portrait plaque of Lamb, executed and presented by the Hon. Gilbert Coleridge, was placed on the wall of 'A' Block of Lamb House at Christ's Hospital. It was unveiled by Sir Arthur Quiller-Couch on 13 May 1939. An account of the ceremony appears in *C.L.S. Bulletin*, June 1939. The inscription reads:

   > Charles Lamb: b.1775. d.1834
   > A Gift to the School from the
   > Charles Lamb Society and the
   > Artist. God Save us all.

5. On 16 November 1959 *The Times* carried a notice of the death of Mr Oscar H.T. Dudley of Addlestone, Surrey, who left £2,500 to the Council of Almoners of Christ's Hospital for the purpose of founding an Exhibition for an Open Scholarship in Classics at Oxford; the choice to rest with the Headmaster of Christ's Hospital. The Exhibition was to be called 'The Charles Lamb Exhibition.'

Dr Williams's Library. University Hall, Gordon Square, London. The ground floor Hall was decorated with a fresco by Edward Armitage, R.A., showing Crabb Robinson and his friends. The painting showed him as the centre figure and there were portraits of Charles and Mary Lamb, Wordsworth, Coleridge, Southey, Hazlitt, Talfourd, Rogers, Godwin, Clarkson and Landor, among others. The Lamb portraits were based on the painting by F.S. Cary and are reproduced in E.V. Lucas's *At the Shrine of Saint Charles*, 1934, where the whole fresco is described. An illustration of most of the forty-seven figures is included in E.J. Morley's *The Life and Times* *of Henry Crabb Robinson*, 1935. The fresco was obliterated during re-decorations in 1958.

Edmonton.

1. Edmonton Church has a medallion tablet to Charles Lamb and William Cowper erected by Joshua W. Butterworth after a visit in 1888 of the London and Middlesex Archaeological Society.
2. Edmonton Churchyard, in which Charles and Mary Lamb are buried, has a gravestone over their tomb with H.F. Cary's inscription on it (reproduced in Lucas's *Life of Charles Lamb*, 1905).
3. The Charles Lamb Institute opposite the churchyard commemorates Lamb's name.
4. Edmonton Public Library has a sculptured medallion of Lamb, the work of Sir George Frampton and presented by J. Passmore Edwards in 1898. It was unveiled by Frederic Harrison at the same time as a memorial to Keats.
5. The library of the Charles Lamb Society at Edmonton Public Library in a special Lamb Room. Since this contains all Lamb's works, as well as a large collection of Eliana, it forms a permanent and extremely valuable memorial to Charles Lamb. Now moved to Guildhall, London.

Enfield. Plaques commemorating Charles Lamb have been placed on the three houses associated with him.

1. Mrs Leishman's, Clarendon Cottage, 17 Gentleman's Row.
2. The Poplars, 87 Chase Side.
3. Westwood Cottage, 89 Chase Side.

Essay Competition. In 1972 *The Wordsworth Circle*, a publication of Temple University, Philadelphia, instituted a Lamb Essay Competition. About 5,000 words were to be written dealing with the life and times of Charles Lamb.

Exhibitions.

1. In 1923 an exhibition of first editions of Lamb's works, autograph manuscripts and Eliana was held at the Grolier Club, 47 East 60th Street, New York, to commemorate the one hundredth anniversary of the publication of *The Essays of Elia*. It was opened by E.D. North.
2. In December 1934 an exhibition of Eliana was held on the first floor of J & E Bumpus's famous bookshop in Oxford Street, London, on the anniversary of Lamb's death. Material was drawn partly from the extensive collection made by the Company's director, J.G. Wilson, at one time President and Chairman of The Elian.
3. In 1935 an exhibition of books and manuscripts concerning Lamb was held in the University of Texas Library. A catalogue was issued, edited by R.H. Griffith.

4. In 1975 a Lamb Exhibition was held at the British Museum and at Christ's Hospital. No doubt there were many other exhibitions and celebrations in museums and libraries during the anniversary years and 1975 saw a further crop of these displays, including those by the B.B.C. and the British Council.

Hoxton.

William Kent in *London for the Literary Pilgrim* 1949, states that a bronze relief by Sir George Frampton, formerly at Hoxton Library, was removed to Shoreditch Town Hall, owing to bombing. *See* also Edmonton (4) above.

Inner Temple.

1. The Inner Temple Gardens have the Charles Lamb Memorial Fountain, comprising the figure of a boy at the edge of a fish pond on the lawn. He is holding a book on an open page of which is inscribed 'Lawyers were children once ...' from Lamb's famous essay. The statue was the work of Miss Margaret Wrightson and was erected in 1930. It is illustrated in E.V. Lucas's *At the Shrine of Saint Charles*, 1934, and in William Kent's *London for the Literary Pilgrim*, 1949.

2. A tablet commemorating Lamb's birth was placed on No. 2 Crown Office Row, but was broken during the bombing in 1941. A tablet was again affixed in 1958 on the new building. *See* separate entry Crown Office Row for text of the inscription.

Islington. A plaque has been placed on 64 Duncan Terrace, formerly Colebrooke Cottage, Colebrooke Row, stating that Lamb lived there from 1823–27. This should read that he lived in a cottage on this site.

Memorial Window. In a letter of 11 February 1891 Canon Ainger writing to J. Dykes Campbell asks 'What do you think, *candidly*, of the Lamb memorial window scheme?' Apparently it had been suggested that such a window should be placed in St Margaret's, Westminster, and Ainger stated that St Andrew's, Holborn would have the better claim. It does not seem to have materialized. (*Life of Ainger*, 1906, 251).

Panel. A carved panel of English oak depicting Charles and Mary Lamb, the work of Francis D. Bedford, was offered for sale for fifty guineas in 1945. The artist also designed the cover of E.V. Lucas's pocket edition of Lamb's *Works*, 1912.

St Sepulchre. A memorial portrait bust of Charles Lamb by Sir William Reynolds-Stephens was placed on the north wall of Christ's Church, Greyfriars, in 1935. It had been commissioned by The Elian Society, and in 1934 a public appeal had been made for funds for it. This was signed by Sir James Barrie, E.V. Lucas and Edmund Blunden; J.P. Collins and E.J. Finch were members of the Appeal Executive Committee. The bust was unveiled by Lord Plender on 5 November 1935. The Church was bombed during the war, but the bust survived. An account of a visit to the site shortly after the bombing is given by J.P. Collins in a Supplement to No. 50 of the *C.L.S. Bulletin* (April 1941). The bust was removed to Christ's Hospital, Horsham, for safety, but in 1962 it was placed on the re-built Watch House of the Church of St Sepulchre, Giltspur Street, London. The inscription was amended in 1965. An illustration of the bust with the original inscription appears in the *C.L.S. Bulletin* in January 1936.

Woolner Memorial. In Edward Moxon's edition of *The Essays of Elia*, 1867, there is a note stating that a subscription was being raised to erect a Monument to the memory of Charles Lamb in Edmonton Churchyard, 'to replace the tasteless headstone that now exists there. The Tomb and Bust will be executed by Thomas Woolner Esq., and subscriptions in furtherance of this object will be received by Messrs Moxon.' The note was reprinted in the single volume of Lamb's works issued by Moxon in 1868, but the memorial did not materialize.

Merriam, Harold. Author of *Edward Moxon: Publisher of Poets*, New York, 1939.

Meyer, Henry, 1782–1847. Artist and engraver. He was educated at Christ's Hospital, and was a nephew of Hoppner and a pupil of Bartolozzi. He was one of the founders of the Society of British Artists and was President in 1828. He was a friend of George Dyer. In 1826 he lived in Red Lion Square where on May 26 Crabb Robinson records finding Lamb sitting for his portrait. The picture was exhibited at the Royal Academy in 1826 and later came into the possession of the India Office. Lamb's letter to Barton of early 1827 (No. 652 in Lucas) mentions the portrait and tells an amusing story of Lamb's verses 'The Young Catechist' being written for a picture for which Meyer could not think of a title. It was later engraved with Lamb's verses attached. Leigh Hunt used this portrait of Lamb in his *Lord Byron and Some of his Contemporaries* and Lamb's letter to Hunt of 11 December 1827 refers to it.

Comments on the portrait of Charles Lamb and 'The Young Catechist' appeared in the *New Monthly Magazine* for 1 May 1827 and are reprinted in Edmund Blunden's *Charles Lamb: His Life Recorded by his Contemporaries*, 1934, where Blunden points out that reproductions of both pictures are contained in Lucas's large edition of Lamb's *Works*.

Middleton, Thomas Fanshaw, 1769–1822. Clergyman and editor. Educated at Christ's Hospital with Lamb and Coleridge (C.H. 1779–88). Three years older than Coleridge he acted as his friend and protector at school. He was responsible for kindling Coleridge's early interest in the *Sonnets* of W.L. Bowles. A story exists that Middleton found Coleridge reading Virgil in the playground at

Christ's Hospital and on inquiring if a lesson was being prepared, Coleridge replied that he was reading for pleasure. The answer when passed to James Boyer, the Upper Master, led to his taking a special interest in Coleridge.

Middleton proceeded to Pembroke College, Cambridge, which he left in 1792. He became Curate at Gainsborough and in 1792–3, editor of *The Country Spectator*, a weekly publication concerned mainly with rural England, the style of which resembled *The Rambler*. Most of it was written by Middleton. Subsequently he was editor of *The British Critic* and he also wrote poetry. Middleton became Rector of Tansor in 1795, Vicar of St Pancras in 1811 and Archdeacon of Huntingdon in 1812. In 1814 he was appointed the first Protestant Bishop of Calcutta, and in the *London Kalendar* for 1815 Middleton is listed as Bishop of Calcutta on the Bengal establishment of the East India Company. His salary was £5,000 a year. He founded Bishop's College, Calcutta, in 1820. Later he became a Governor of Christ's Hospital and there is a memorial to him in St Pauls.

Lamb described Middleton in his essay 'Christ's Hospital Five and Thirty Years Ago' as 'a scholar and a gentleman in his teens' and he refers to Middleton's published work *The Doctrine of the Greek Article applied to the Criticisms and Illustrations of the New Testament*, 1808. In 1872 a Coleridge Memorial was subscribed for which consisted of a statuette group of Lamb, Coleridge and Middleton. It is competed for annually at Christ's Hospital.

Milman, Constance. Author of *Through London Spectacles*, 1897, which contains chapters on 'Charles Lamb's Plays', 'The Thrice Noble Margaret Newcastle', 'Sir Thomas Browne' and 'The Temple Gardens.'

Mingay, James, 1752–1812. Barrister of the Inner Temple. Called to the Bar, 1775, a Bencher in 1785. Mingay lost his right hand in an accident when he was a boy and in his essay on the 'Old Benchers' Lamb describes him as 'Mingay with the iron hand.' He seems to have been a most successful barrister and a rival to the famous Erskine. *The Gentleman's Magazine* describes him as 'of a persuasive oratory, infinite wit, and most excellent fancy', but Lamb describes him as 'a blustering, loud-talking person.'

Mitchell, Thomas, 1783–1845. Classical scholar and tutor. Educated at Christ's Hospital with Leigh Hunt, Lamb having left just before Mitchell arrived. He left in 1802 for Pembroke College, Cambridge, and was later elected to a Fellowship at Sidney Sussex College. He contributed to both Leigh Hunt's publications, *The Reflector* and *The Examiner*. In the former his 'Inquiries Respecting Jack Ketch' was inspired by Lamb's 'On the Inconveniences of Being

Hanged' that had appeared in an earlier issue of the journal. In 1814 Leigh Hunt dedicated his *The Feast of the Poets* to Mitchell. His chief work was an excellent translation of the *Comedies of Aristophanes*, 1820–22. Mitchell also became a 'Quarterly Reviewer' and in 1813 contributed a series of articles on Aristophanes and Athenian manners. In 1813 he had dined with Leigh Hunt in Horsemonger Lane Gaol with Barnes, Byron, Brougham and Thomas Moore. Lamb mentions him in his letter of 31 August 1817 to Barron Field.

Mitford, Rev. John R., 1781–1859. Miscellaneous writer, scholar and book collector. Rector of Benhall, Suffolk, and a friend of Bernard Barton and Samuel Rogers. He is said to be a cousin of Mary Russell Mitford. He edited the works of many old poets, including Gray and Milton and he wrote the lives of the poets for the Aldine edition. He also published volumes of his own poetry and wrote on cricket, reviewing John Nyren's famous book for the *Gentleman's Magazine* in 1833. In 1840 he edited Vincent Bourne's *Poematia*, a favourite book of Lamb's, and included in it the latter's translation of 'Epitaphium in Canem.' He became editor of the *Gentleman's Magazine* in 1834.

He visited Lamb at Islington and there are references to him in Lamb's letters to Barton. In one he describes Mitford as 'a pleasant layman spoiled.' Lamb obtained for him some Chinese jars from Canton, through his friend Samuel Ball. In 1827 Mitford gave Lamb a copy of his *Sacred Specimens Selected from the Early English Poets*, and in 1832 wrote a 'Sonnet to Charles Lamb on his Poem called "Leisure"' which appeared in *Raw's Ladies Fashionable Repository*. In the *London Magazine* in June 1823 Mitford had a 'Sonnet addressed to Bernard Barton' which had been transmitted to the publishers through Lamb.

In the *Gentleman's Magazine* in 1835 Mitford reviewed Moxon's edition of *Rosamund Gray* &c, and the two volumes of the *Specimens of English Dramatic Poets* published that year. For the same periodical he wrote in 1838 some recollections of Lamb which he included in his review of Talfourd's edition of the *Letters*, and he reviewed there the *Final Memorials* in 1848.

Mitford was a keen book collector and when his library was sold in 1859–60 at Sothebys, the sale occupied twenty days and realized £4,846.

Mitford, Mary Russell, 1787–1855. Poet and novelist. Friend of T.N. Talfourd. Became famous as the author of *Our Village*, originally sketches contributed to the *Lady's Magazine*. She also contributed dramatic sketches to the *London Magazine* and wrote a tragedy *Julian* produced at Covent Garden in March 1823. She was said to be a cousin of Rev. John Mitford, scholar and editor of the *Gentleman's Magazine.*

She visited the Lambs occasionally, having met them at least as early as 1817. Crabb Robinson records meeting her there with Talfourd several times in 1824. On one occasion she came to Colebrooke Cottage to consult Lamb on a new play, probably *Rienzi* which the Lambs had read and praised. Lamb also praised *Our Village* and said that 'nothing so fresh and characteristic has appeared for a long-while,' a view passed on to her by Talfourd. She described Lamb in a letter to Sir William Elford in 1824 as 'the matchless Elia of the London Magazine' and said the Elia essays were 'incomparably the finest specimens of English prose in the language.' John Payne Collier records in his *Old Man's Diary* meeting the Lambs at the Rev. William Harness's house when Miss Mitford was there.

Mitre Court Buildings, Inner Temple. The Lambs moved to No. 16 Mitre Court Buildings from Southampton Buildings, Chancery Lane, on Ladyday, 1801. Lamb reported the move to Manning in his letter in April 1801. 'I live . . . a pistol-shot off Baron Maseres . . . . I can see the white sails glide by the bottom of King's Bench Walk as I lie in bed.' Mitre Court is at the north end of King's Bench Walk, but the present building dates from 1830. During the war some bombs fell in Mitre Court. In 1809 the Lambs left this house because the landlord wanted the rooms for himself, and they went to 34 Southampton Buildings until they could move into Inner Temple Lane.

Monkhouse, Thomas, 1783–1825. London merchant. Married Jane Horrocks, daughter of the M.P. for Preston. He was a cousin of Mary and Sara Hutchinson and thus a relation of Wordsworth by marriage. His literary dinners were very popular with Lamb's circle of friends, and Crabb Robinson records many of the functions. Monkhouse was present at the famous dinner at Haydon's in 1817 when Lamb teased the Comptroller of Stamps. In April 1823 he gave a dinner to a number of his friends of which Lamb wrote to Barton 'I dined in Parnassus with Wordsworth, Coleridge, Rogers and Tom Moore—half the Poetry of England constellated and clustered in Gloster Place.'

The Wordsworths accompanied Monkhouse on a tour of the Continent in 1820 and Crabb Robinson was with the party for some of the time. When Monkhouse died in 1825 Lamb wrote to Sara Hutchinson saying 'I had grown to like poor Monkhouse more and more.'

Montagu, Basil, 1770–1851. Barrister, author and humanitarian. He was the natural son of the fourth Earl of Sandwich and the beautiful Miss Martha Ray, whose lover, Hackman, murdered her in 1779 by shooting her as she was leaving Covent Garden Theatre. Hackman was later hanged and Boswell witnessed the execution. Fanny Kemble said that Montagu had inherited ability, eccentricity and personal beauty from his parents.

He was educated at Charterhouse and Christ's College, Cambridge, and was called to the Bar in 1798. He developed an extensive practice in chancery and bankruptcy. He became a K.C. in 1835 and was a member of the Athenaeum Club. He was appointed Accountant General in Bankruptcy and held the position until 1846.

Montagu married as his third wife the widow of Thomas Skepper. Mrs Montagu was attractive and popular with her husband's friends. She was praised by Edward Irving, Carlyle wrote letters to her and Hazlitt praised her conversation. Anne Skepper, her daughter by her first husband, married B.W. Procter and became famous in her own right as a wit.

Basil Montagu was an early friend of Coleridge and Wordsworth. In 1797 he toured Holland with William Godwin. Among his friends were Charles Lamb, Hazlitt, Leigh Hunt, Edward Irving, Crabb Robinson, Sir James Mackintosh and Dr Parr. He frequently figures in Crabb Robinson's *Diary*. He was also a friend of Mary Wollstonecraft and in 1817 Shelley employed him to defend the application from Westbrook to take his children away from the poet. It is said that as a boy he knew Dr Johnson and attended his funeral.

Montagu was the author of a number of legal works. He edited Bacon's *Works* in sixteen volumes over the period 1825–36, but it is said that his knowledge was insufficient for the task and Macaulay criticized it in a famous essay in the *Edinburgh Review*. He also published *Essays and Selections by Basil Montagu, Thoughts on Laughter* and a volume of selections from Jeremy Taylor, Hooker, Hall, Sir Thomas Browne, Fuller and others. Many of his literary works were published by William Pickering. He also contributed to the *Retrospective Review*.

In 1814 he wrote *Some Enquiries into the Effects of Fermented Liquors* which included Lamb's 'Confessions of a Drunkard'. Lamb was very friendly with the Montagus and with Anne Skepper. He relates in his essay 'Oxford in the Vacation' the story of George Dyer's absent-mindedness in calling at their house twice in one morning, although told they were absent from home. There is also a reference in 'Newspapers Thirty-Five Years Ago' to Basil Montagu, a teetotaller, in the passage 'we were none of your Basilian water-sponges . . . we were right toping Capulets.' Several letters from Lamb to the Montagus exist, one of which in 1827 to Mrs Montagu, contains Lamb's very amusing remarks on his reluctance to contribute to a memorial for Thomas Clarkson while he was still alive.

In 1802 the Wordsworths stayed with the Montagus; and in 1810 Basil Montagu, by indiscreet remarks, was the cause of a quarrel between Coleridge and Wordsworth. At one time Wordsworth was tutor to Montagu's son.

Montgomery, James, 1771–1854. Poet and editor. In 1796 he became editor of the *Sheffield Iris* and was twice imprisoned for political articles for which he was held responsible. He published several volumes of poems and some of his verses were printed in the *London Magazine* between 1821 and 1825. He also wrote some well known hymns.

Lamb did not think much of his poetry and said that the only good poem he had written was the 'Last Man'. No poem by Montgomery with this title is known and both Ainger and Lucas think Lamb referred to the poem 'The Common Lot.' Major Butterworth agreed. When in 1824 Montgomery was compiling an Album to be sold in aid of child chimney-sweepers, Lamb sent him a copy of Blake's poem 'The Chimney Sweeper.'

Moody, John, 1727–1812. Irish actor. First appeared on the stage in Jamaica, but later came to London and played at Drury Lane and the Haymarket. Made a success in Irish parts, partly on account of his broad Cork accent. He was praised by Charles Churchill in *The Rosciad.* He was famous as Teague in *The Committee.* Boaden states that 'his manner was peculiar, but he was a valuable actor and most respectable man.' He is mentioned by Lamb in his essay 'On Some of the Old Actors' and there is a second reference in that part of the essay in the *London Magazine* for October 1822 which was omitted from the Elia volume. Here Lamb writes of 'The immovable features of Moody, who afraid of o'stepping nature, sometimes stopped short of her.'

Moore, Thomas, 1779–1852. Irish poet. Educated at Trinity College, Dublin. Studied law at the Middle Temple. Was appointed Admiralty Registrar at Bermuda, but left the duties to a deputy who involved him in considerable trouble through dishonesty. Moore published many volumes of poems, his *Irish Melodies*, 1807, bringing him fame. He was able to sing his own songs and his ready wit made him a social success. He wrote a life of Byron in 1830. He was friendly with a large number of distinguished people and was well known in the Lamb circle.

Lamb's 'Sonnet. To ... Barry Cornwall' printed in the *London Magazine* in September 1820 contained a reference to Moore under his pseudonym of 'Little', but when the poem was reprinted in *Album Verses* the line was altered. When the famous dinner at Monkhouse's took place in April 1823 at which Coleridge, Wordsworth, Moore, Lamb and Rogers were present, Lamb sat next to Moore and the latter records in his *Diary* that Lamb was 'full of villainous and abortive puns', but he adds some excellent things came from him. They also talked about Defoe and Lamb said he was collecting the works of the Dunciad heroes. Lamb told Moore that he received £170 for two years' contributions of Elia essays to the *London Magazine*.

More, Hannah, 1745–1833. Dramatist, novelist and religious writer. A friend of Garrick who introduced her to Dr Johnson, Burke, Horace Walpole, Reynolds and Mrs Montagu. Her works included a novel, *Coelebs in Search of a Wife*, 1809, and a tract which led to the formation of the Religious Tract Society. Several of Lamb's letters refer to Hannah More and in one to Coleridge on 7 June 1809 he says he borrowed a copy of *Coelebs in Search of a Wife* and wrote the following verse in it

> If ever I marry a wife
> I'll marry a landlord's daughter
> For then I may sit in the bar
> And drink cold brandy-and-water.

Lucas suggests that Lamb's remark in his letter to J. Howard Payne in January 1823 about 'Plura' coming to see him may have referred to Hannah More.

More, Paul Elmer, 1864–1937. American author, editor and critic. Educated at Washington University and Harvard University. Taught Sanscrit at Harvard and was a lecturer at Princeton. Author of *Shelburne Essays*, 14 volumes, 1904–35. The Second and Fourth series both have essays on Charles Lamb. The Second also has an essay on 'The First Complete Edition of Hazlitt.' At one time he edited *The Nation*.

Morgan, John James, d.1820. Friend of Coleridge and Lamb. Was at school at Christ's Hospital. Coleridge stayed with the Morgans at Hammersmith after he left Basil Montagu's house in annoyance in 1810 and remained there for some time, later he stayed with them at Calne in Wiltshire. The Lambs were friends of the Morgans and Lamb described their circle as 'frank-hearted.' About 1819 Morgan lost a fortune of between £10,000 and £15,000 and shortly afterwards suffered a paralytic stroke. Southey wrote to Grosvenor Bedford in December 1819 saying he was raising funds for Morgan and had himself given an annuity of £10 p.a., while Lamb had given the same amount. The Lambs had stayed with the Morgans when they were at Calne and when they spent a holiday at Brighton in 1817 Mrs Morgan was with them. About 1828 Mrs Morgan seems to have kept a school.

Morgan, Peter Frederick, b.1930. Professor of English, University College of Toronto, Canada. Editor of *The Letters of Thomas Hood*,

1971. Contributed 'Taylor & Hessey: Aspects of their Conduct of the *London Magazine*' to *Keats-Shelley Journal*, 1958; 'Izaak Walton, Lamb and Thomas Hood' to *Charles Lamb Bulletin*, May 1961; and 'Charles Lamb and Thomas Hood: Records of a Friendship' to *Tennessee Studies in Literature*, 1964.

Morley, Edith Julia, 1875–1964. Emeritus Professor of the English Language, University of Reading. Among her books are *Blake, Coleridge, Wordsworth, Lamb &c. being selections from the Remains of Henry Crabb Robinson,* edited by E.J. Morley, 1922; *The Correspondence with the Wordsworth Circle,* 1927; *Henry Crabb Robinson in Germany,* 1929; *The Life and Times of Henry Crabb Robinson,* 1935; and *Henry Crabb Robinson on Books and their Writers,* 1938.

Morley, Frank Vigor. Mathematician and publisher. Educated at Oxford where he was a Rhodes Scholar. Author of *Lamb Before Elia,* 1932, reprinted 1935. He also wrote *Dora Wordsworth: Her Book,* 1924.

Morpurgo, Jack Eric, b.1918. Literary critic and historian. Educated at Christ's Hospital and in Canada and U.S.A. In 1970 was appointed Professor of American Literature at Leeds University. Has done much editorial work with Penguin publications and has been Director of the National Book League. Edited *Charles Lamb and Elia* for Penguin Books in 1948; Leigh Hunt's *Autobiography,* 1949; Shelley's *Letters,* Marlowe's *Edward II* and Trelawny's *Last Days of Shelley and Byron,* 1952. He was a member of the Committee of Old Blues which edited *The Christ's Hospital Book,* 1953.

Moxey or **Moxhay.** Lamb's letter to Hone on 21 May 1830 mentions Moxey, who, according to W.C. Hazlitt, was the owner of an eating house in Threadneedle Street, and was helpful to Hone and to William Hazlitt's son. Lamb also mentions him in a letter to Hone on 7 February 1831. He is said to have professed admiration for Lamb's writings. One 'Mockshay' is said to have attended Mary Lamb's funeral in 1847. Moxhay, a biscuit baker, had large contracts with the East India Company.

Moxon, Edward, 1801–58. Publisher and poet. First apprenticed to a bookseller in Wakefield, but came to London in 1817. Was employed by Longman & Co, 1821–27, then with Hurst, Chance & Co of St Paul's Churchyard. In 1830 started as a publisher on his own with the financial help of Samuel Rogers, the banker poet, who lent him £500. His office was first at 64 New Bond Street, but in 1833 he moved to 44 Dover Street.

His earliest publication was Lamb's *Album Verses,* 1830, and he also published *Satan in Search of a Wife,* 1831; *The Essays of Elia* (new edition) and *The Last Essays of Elia*, 1833; *Dramatic Specimens* (third edition, but first with the Garrick Plays), 1835; Lamb's *Prose Works* in three volumes, 1836; Lamb's *Poetical Works*, 1836; Talfourd's edition of the *Letters*, 1837; the first collected edition of the *Prose and Poetry*, 1840; and Talfourd's *Final Memorials*, 1848. The collected works were frequently reprinted by Moxon.

In 1826 Lamb first met Moxon, who became a frequent visitor to the Lambs at Enfield, sometimes bringing his brother and sisters. He became attracted to Emma Isola and in 1833 they were married. There are numerous references to the marriage in the letters.

Moxon became well known as a publisher, particularly of poetry, and among those whose work he issued were Tennyson, Allan Cunningham, Coleridge, B.W. Procter, Southey, Wordsworth, Talfourd, Rogers, Knowles, W.S. Landor, Thomas Hood, Thomas Campbell, Shelley, Henry Taylor, Robert Browning and Coventry Patmore, as well as Monckton Milnes and Isaac and Benjamin D'Israeli. He was particularly noted for the neatness and delicacy of the format of his publications, as well as for their notable literary content.

He also published *The Englishman's Magazine* in 1831 and *The Reflector* in 1832. Lamb contributed to both periodicals, but neither publication was successful and they were short lived.

Moxon's own poetry was not the equal of that of his authors, but he issued several volumes of verse. In 1826 *The Prospect and other Poems* was dedicated to Samuel Rogers and in 1829 *Christmas* was dedicated to Lamb; his *Sonnets* were privately printed 1830–35. Lamb reviewed the first part of the *Sonnets* in *The Athenaeum* on 13 April 1833. In 1835 Moxon wrote a *Memoir of Charles Lamb* that was printed privately and reprinted in *Leigh Hunt's London Journal* and in *Chambers Edinburgh Journal*. When Moxon issued *The Last Essays of Elia* in 1833 John Taylor, the publisher of the *London Magazine*, set up a claim to copyright that Moxon resisted successfully with Lamb's help.

Lamb left his books to Moxon, but they remained with Mary Lamb until her death. When Moxon eventually received them he is said to have selected sixty books that Lamb had annotated and to have destroyed the remainder! (*See* separate entry, Library, Lamb's).

Moxon was friendly with many famous people. John Forster was a constant friend and edited *The Reflector* of 1832. Moxon was a regular visitor to Rogers's breakfasts, and in 1837 he went to Paris with Wordsworth and Crabb Robinson. In 1846 he spent a week with Wordsworth at Rydal Mount. After his death his business was carried on as a trust, but in 1871 Ward Lock & Co took it over.

Moxon, William. Barrister. Brother of Edward Moxon, who dedicated a volume of his *Sonnets* to him in 1830. In a letter to

Edward Moxon on 11 February 1833 Lamb asks him to bring his brother to visit him. He was one of the witnesses at the wedding of Edward Moxon and Emma Isola in July 1833. On 14 February 1834 Lamb wrote a short note to C.W. Dilke to say that William Moxon was beginning business as a solicitor and asking Dilke if he could help him.

Mulready, William, 1786–1863. Irish painter. Student of the Royal Academy in 1800. Helped John Varley with his pupils and married Varley's sister. Elected R.A. in 1816. Among his best known pictures are 'Choosing the Wedding Gown', 'The Sonnet' and 'The Bathers'. In 1840 he designed the first penny postage envelope. He also did a set of illustrations to *The Vicar of Wakefield.*

Mulready did the drawings to illustrate Lamb's *The King and Queen of Hearts* and also twenty plates for the *Tales from Shakespeare.* Lamb complained much about the Shakespeare illustrations, but rather as to the subjects chosen by Mrs Godwin than about the artist's work.

Munden, Joseph Shepherd, 1758–1832. English comedian. First appeared at Covent Garden in 1790 where he remained for many years; he also played at the Haymarket and eventually moved to Drury Lane. Among his best parts were Old Dornton in Holcroft's *The Road to Ruin* and Old Dozey in Dibdin's farce *Past Ten O'Clock and a Rainy Night.*' He was regarded as one of the greatest actors of his day.

Munden was a favourite of Lamb's and was also a friend. They first met about 1819 or 1820 and Lamb wrote a number or pieces praising his acting. 'On the Acting of Munden' appeared in *The Examiner* in November 1819, then in the *London Magazine* for October 1822 and again in *The Essays of Elia* in 1823. His skit 'Autobiography of Mr Munden' was in the *London Magazine* for February 1825, and after Munden's death, he wrote 'Munden the Comedian' in *The Athenaeum* in February 1832 in the form of a letter to the editor. 'Munden's Farewell' in the *London Magazine* in July 1824 has been attributed to Lamb, but it is unlikely to be his.

In Raymond's *Life of Elliston* there is a story of Elliston, Munden and Lamb travelling on an excursion from Leamington to Warwick Castle, when Munden left the carriage on the return journey, as Elliston maintained, so as to avoid paying his share of the fare. When Munden retired in 1824 Mary Lamb observed 'Sic transit gloria Munden.'

Others who greatly admired Munden's acting were Vincent Novello and Talfourd, and he is praised by both Hazlitt and Procter. The latter supports Lamb's eulogy of Munden in O'Keeffe's *Modern Antiques.* Procter said that after Munden's retirement Lamb almost entirely forsook the theatre. Lamb presented Munden with a copy of *The Essays of Elia* which he had inscribed to him.

Murray, Charles Olivier. b.1842. Book illustrator. Member of the Royal Society of Painters, Etchers and Engravers. Exhibited at the Royal Academy, 1872. Silver medal in Paris, 1900. He did more than one hundred illustrations for *Some Essays of Elia* published by Sampson Low, Marston, Searle & Rivington (n.d., but c.1890). The same illustrations were used in *A Dissertation upon Roast Pig* by the same publishers, but printed in colour by Edmund Evans. R. Paterson was the engraver of both books.

Murray, Harriet, 1783–1844. Actress. She appeared at Covent Garden and Drury Lane in many famous parts and is described as an actress of real genius. She played Cordelia in the production at Covent Garden in which G.F. Cooke played Lear. She married Henry Siddons, Sarah Siddons's eldest son, and helped him when he was manager of a theatre in Edinburgh. After his death she continued to manage the Edinburgh theatre.

In the *Morning Post* for 9 January 1802 is a notice of Cooke's Lear which was probably written by Charles Lamb. In it he praises Miss Murray as Cordelia and writes that 'She played the part with great delicacy and feeling, sweetness and simplicity.' Leigh Hunt in his essay 'Recollections of Old Actors' writes of her 'with her sweet voice and eyes, the latter a little too rolling.'

Mylius, William Frederick, 1776–1863. Schoolmaster at Christ's Hospital. He published anthologies of verse for schools, three of which contain poems by Charles and Mary Lamb. They were the *Junior Class-Book*, 1809; *Poetical Class-Book*, 1810; and *The First Book of Poetry*, 1811. He also published *A School Dictionary*. All these books were issued by Mrs Godwin at the Juvenile Library. Some of them also printed pieces from the Lamb's *Tales from Shakespeare* and *Mrs Leicester's School*. Mylius's books were very popular: by 1828 *The First Book of Poetry* had reached a tenth edition, *The Junior Class-Book* a seventh edition and *The Poetical Class-Book* a sixth edition.

In a note to the essay 'The Old and the New Schoolmaster', Percy Fitzgerald refers to Lamb's 'friend Mylius, a well known teacher'. I can find no evidence of the friendship, although no doubt Mylius would have been in touch with Lamb before including his poems in his books and they might well have met at Godwin's.

Negus, Mr. Lucas mentions in the *Life*, the story told to Canon Ainger by Mary Louisa Field of an incident during the performance of Richard II at her father's house in 1824. When a Mr Negus was announced by the butler Lamb called out 'Hand him round.' In an article in *The Bookman* for May 1925 entitled 'Charles Lamb and Griffiths Wainewright' there is an illustration of the original wrapper for February 1825 of a copy of the *London Magazine*. On the top is written the name 'Edwd Negus.'

Neil Bell. *See* Stephen Southwold.

Nether Stowey. A village in Somersetshire to the west of Bridgwater, on the Minehead Road and at the foot of the Quantock Hills. In 1794 S.T. Coleridge first visited it and came to know Thomas Poole, a local tanner, who was to become one of his staunchest friends. In 1796 Poole found for Coleridge a tiny wayside cottage at a rent of £7 a year and on December 31 he moved in with his wife and child. The accommodation was poor, but in a letter to Thelwall on December 17 Coleridge told him 'My farm will be a garden of one acre and an half' and adds that he will grow vegetables and corn and keep pigs. When Lamb heard about the 'farm' he asked 'And what does your worship know about farming?' The cottage garden adjoined that of Poole. Charles Lloyd also lived here for a time with the Coleridges but had left by March 1797.

In July 1797 Wordsworth and his sister came from Racedown to visit Coleridge at Nether Stowey and remained at the cottage for a fortnight from the 2nd of July. During this time Charles Lamb managed to persuade his superior at East India House to give him a week's leave and he came to spend it with Coleridge for the week of July 9–16. Unfortunately just before, Sara Coleridge had accidentally spilt some boiling milk on her husband's leg and he was mostly confined to the house. Lamb and the two Wordsworths explored the Quantocks, while at the cottage Coleridge composed his poem 'This lime tree bower my prison' which caused Lamb to lodge a strong protest at being described in it as 'gentle-hearted Charles.'

The Wordsworths were so greatly attracted by Coleridge that they decided to look for a house nearby and found and rented the mansion of Alfoxden Manor, three miles from Nether Stowey (*See* separate entry), to which they moved in July. Later that month John Thelwall arrived at Coleridge's cottage, an unexpected visitor claiming hospitality, and a few days later he and Coleridge walked over to Alfoxden and stayed for three days with the Wordsworths. Thelwall was known as a radical and reformer and it was during his visit that the amusing episode of the Government spy occurred, who had been sent down to watch the poets.

Coleridge and Wordsworth saw each other daily and at this period produced some of their best poetry. While living at Nether Stowey Coleridge wrote 'The Ancient Mariner', 'Christabel' and 'Kubla Khan' and his tragedy *Osorio* later named *Remorse*. Wordsworth wrote 'Peter Bell' and together they planned *The Lyrical Ballads*.

In the Spring of 1798 William Hazlitt visited Coleridge at Nether Stowey, and later gave a famous account of the visit in his essay 'My First Acquaintance with Poets' in *The Liberal*. Joseph Cottle also visited Coleridge at Nether Stowey. When they left Alfoxden in June 1798 the Wordsworths stayed with the Coleridges again for a week before moving to Bristol.

In the autumn of 1798 Coleridge left the cottage for London. His wife and family remained there and did not leave Nether Stowey finally until Coleridge took them to Greta Hall, Keswick, in July 1800. Coleridge again visited the village in December 1801 and January 1802 staying with his friend Thomas Poole, where Thomas Wedgwood was his fellow guest. Again in the summer of 1807 Coleridge and his family were Poole's guests at Nether Stowey.

It does not appear that Lamb ever visited the village again, but his week's holiday in the society of Coleridge was made additionally notable as his first meeting with Wordsworth and his sister. Mary Lamb did not accompany her brother to Nether Stowey.

Nethery, Wallace. Librarian of the Hoose Library of Philosophy, University of Southern California. Owner of a private press that has printed a number of small books and booklets about Charles Lamb. A collector of American editions of Lamb's works and American Eliana. Among the publications, mostly written by Mr Nethery, and printed at his private press are: *Mr H—— in America, or, Anonymous Redivivus*, 1956; *Eliana Americana, a footnote to the bibliography of Charles Lamb*, 1957; *Witches and Other Night Fears* (Charles Lamb), 1958; *Midnight Darlings on Broadway*, 1959; *The Essays of Elia, a Review by Edgar Allan Poe*, 1959; *A Note on the San Francisco Pioneer, and a little known Poem attributed to Charles Lamb*, 1959; *J.C. Bloem on Charles Lamb*, 1960; *Eliana Americana 1838–1848*, 1960; *Charles Lamb in America to 1848*, 1963; *Charles Lamb Bibliophile*, 1965; and *Eliana Americana 1849–1866*, 1971 (Plantin Press). Articles contributed to magazines include:

The American Book Collector
1960   Eliana Americana (December).
1961   Eliana Americana, 1838–1848 (March).
1962   Charles Lamb in America, 1849–1866 (February).
The above are substantially the same as in the booklets, but there are some changes.
1963   Privately, Please, an account of the private press (January).
1965   Review of *Peppercorn Papers* by Claude A. Prance (December).
Notes & Queries
1962   Charles Lamb to Janus Weathercock (May).

An account of Mr Nethery's private press appeared in the student newspaper of the University of South California in February 1963.

Newton, Alfred Edward, 1863–1940. American book collector and author who lived at Oak Knoll, Daylesford, Pennsylvania. The possessor of one of the finest libraries in America which was rich in English literature, particularly concerning Dr Johnson; it also had a notable Lamb collection. When the sale of Newton's library occurred in April, May and October 1941 at the Parke-Bernet Galleries, New York, the Lamb collection was included in the section sold on May 14–16 and it included the manuscript of 'Dream Children' (described by Newton as 'the finest essay in the English language), Lamb's copy of Fuller's *Holy & Profane State*, 1652, a number of A.L.S. including one to Fanny Kelly and copies of his works inscribed to various friends.

The Catalogue of the sale was a substantial publication in three volumes, superbly illustrated. Among the facsimiles of Lamb items were the manuscript of 'Dream Children, three A.L.S.'s and some title pages. The Lamb material comprised items 583–631 and the highest price reached was $7,500 for the 'Dream Children' manuscript.

Newton was the author of a number of books dealing with book collecting. They are highly entertaining, and have been described as in the manner of the eighteenth century essayists; they include *The Amenities of Book-Collecting*, 1918; *This Book-Collecting Game*, 1926; *The Greatest Book in the World*, 1926; *A Magnificent Farce and Other Diversions of a Book-Collector*, 1921; *End Papers*, 1931; *Derby Day*, 1934; and *Bibliography and pseudo-Bibliography*, 1936. The earlier volumes contain many references to Charles Lamb. Newton also wrote A *Tourist in Spite of Himself*, 1930, and two plays, *Dr Johnson*, 1923, and *Mr Strahan's Dinner Party*, 1930. It was his custom to send small privately printed brochures to his friends, usually at Christmas. One of these issued in 1938 concerns George Dyer.

Norris, Philip, d.1806. In his letter to Coleridge on 3 October 1796, just after the tragedy, Lamb states that 'Mr Norris of Christ's Hospital has been a father to me, Mrs Norris as a mother; tho' we had few claims on them.' 'Mr Norris' has been identified by Canon Ainger as Randal Norris and by E.V. Lucas as Richard Norris, Junior. Miss Phyllis G. Mann in her series of articles in the *C.L.S. Bulletin*, 1953–5, has much to say on the Norris family, children of Richard Norris, builder, but apparently no relation of Randal Norris. One son, Richard, seems to have been a surveyor at Christ's Hospital, whose death in 1792 means he cannot have been Lamb's friend. Another brother, Philip, the only married son living in 1796, Miss Mann identifies as the member of the family mentioned by Lamb.

Norris, Randal, 1751–1827. Librarian and Sub-Treasurer of the Inner Temple. Was admitted a student of the Inner Temple in 1778 but was not called to the Bar. Appointed Librarian in 1784 and Sub-Treasurer in 1801. He ceased to be Librarian in 1818. Norris's second wife was Elizabeth Faint of Widford, Hertsfordshire, and a friend of Mrs Field. Mary Lamb was bridesmaid (and/or a witness) at her wedding. Mrs Norris's brother, Joseph Faint, was Chief Butler of the Hall Society of the Inner Temple.

Randal Norris had two daughters Elizabeth and Jane and a son, Richard, who was deaf. After the father's death Lamb was active in help to the widow and children. He wrote his famous letter to Crabb Robinson on 20 January 1827 about his dead friend and in an endeavour to get financial aid for the family from the Benchers; eventually a pension of £70 was obtained. The daughters already had a school at Widford (Goddard House School), and E.V. Lucas records some pleasant reminiscences of it which he obtained from Mrs Coe, an old pupil of the school, and of the half-holidays that were granted when Lamb visited them.

Of Randal Norris Lamb said 'he was my friend and my father's friend all the life I can remember' and he added he was the 'last to call me Charley'. He has also amusing stories of Randal Norris's struggles with a black letter Chaucer, which he maintained had 'a deal of indifferent spelling.' Several letters are printed by Lucas to various members of the Norris family.

Lamb mentions Randal Norris in his essay 'The Old Benchers of the Inner Temple' and in his 'Letter of Elia to Robert Southey, Esquire', both printed in the *London Magazine* in September 1821 and October 1823 respectively. His letter 'A Death Bed' which describes the Norris family was printed in Hone's *Table Book* in 1827 and although reprinted in *The Last Essays of Elia* in 1833 was omitted in later editions in dererence to the wishes of the family.

Randal Norris's daughters each married a farmer named Tween who were brothers and one daughter gave Canon Ainger some reminiscences and relics of Lamb. Miss Mann has discovered further information about Randal Norris's parents. (*See C.L.S. Bulletin*, No. 198).

North, Ernest Dressel. American bibliographer. At one time a member of Scribner's staff in New York. Wrote a 'Bibliography of Charles and Mary Lamb' which was printed at the end of B.E. Martin's *In the Footprints of Charles Lamb*, 1891 and edited *Wit and Wisdom of Charles Lamb*. North opened the Grolier Club Lamb Exhibition in 1923.

Novello, Vincent, 1781–1861. Organist, composer, conductor and music publisher. He was also a singer, choir trainer and skilled viola player. Born in London, the son of an Italian father and an English mother, he married Mary Sabilla Hehl in 1808 and they had eleven children, several of whom became famous. In 1812 when Catalani, the Italian prima donna, was in London with an opera company at the Pantheon, Novello acted as both pianist and conductor. He was an original member of the Philharmonic Society when it was founded in 1813. In the British Museum Library Catalogue there are twenty-five pages devoted to Novello's works.

The Lambs were great friends of the Novellos and they visited one another from time to time. Leigh Hunt may have introduced them about 1816. The Novello's children have left pleasing accounts of Charles Lamb at the Novello's parties, that he enjoyed in spite of his alleged antipathy to music—an antipathy that may not have been so great as he pretended. Several letters exist from the Lambs to the Novellos and no doubt there would have been more had they lived further apart. Lamb and Novello had much in common, for Novello had great admiration for some of Lamb's favourite actors and had a great knowledge of Shakespeare's works. It is said that under the name of 'Mr Howard' Novello once played Falstaff in Henry IV at some private theatricals.

Lamb's first published writing about his friend occurs in his Elia essay 'A Chapter on Ears' that appeared in the *London Magazine* in March 1821. In 1830 he wrote verses 'Free Thoughts on Several Eminent Composers', printed in his *Poetical Works*, 1836, but which he sent to William Ayrton in May of that year and inscribed in Novello's Album for which it was originally written. In 1950 this Album came up for sale at Sothebys and was bought by the music publishers Novello & Co. Lamb also wrote verses 'The Sisters' addressed to some of Novello's children, which W.C. Hazlitt thought was composed about 1833.

In 1834 he contributed to *The Athenaeum* verses 'To Clara N' addressed to one of Novello's daughters. In a joking letter of 6 November 1828 to Vincent Novello Lamb included a 'Serenata for two voices. On the Marriage of Charles Cowden Clarke Esqre, to Victoria . . .' which he pretended to have composed for Novello to set to music. The letter is amusing in its assumption of musical knowledge that Lamb did not possess. Edmund Blunden has pointed out that Lamb plagiarized this serenata from John Hughes's *Poems on Several Occasions*, 1735.

Novello's wife was well liked by her husband's friends. She appears to have been a woman of strong character and was christened by Leigh Hunt 'the Wilful Woman', but she was popular and her children had great affection for her.

Mary Victoria Novello, the eldest daughter, married Charles Cowden Clarke and both became well known writers; another daughter, Clara Anastasia Novello, achieved fame as a singer, being known as the greatest English soprano of her time. By marriage she became the Countess Gigliucci. A son, Joseph Alfred, also a musician, carried on the music publishing business and greatly enlarged it.

The Novellos had many friends and among those who visited their house were Keats, Shelley, Hazlitt, Leigh Hunt, Edward Holmes and John Nyren. In 1829 Vincent Novello and his wife made a pilgrimage to Germany to make a presentation to Mozart's sister who was in financial difficulties.

Nyren, John, 1764–1837. Famous cricketer. One does not associate Lamb with cricket, although he had a cousin who was notable at the game. It is not recorded that Lamb and Nyren met, but they might well have done so and have enjoyed each other's company. E.V. Lucas in his *The Hambledon Men*, 1907, tells us that Nyren was a 'Roman Catholic gentleman of cultivated tastes, a good musician, a natural philanthropist and the friend of very intelligent men, among them Charles Lamb's friends, Leigh Hunt, Cowden Clarke and Vincent Novello.' Nyren was a visitor to Novello's musical evenings, and his wife, who was of German parentage, was also well educated. Nyren was the author of the famous book *The Young Cricketer's Tutor* to which was added *Cricketers of My Time*. It was published in 1833 edited by his friend Charles Cowden Clarke. Leigh Hunt reviewed it in his *London Journal* in 1834 and John Mitford had reviewed it in the *Gentleman's Magazine* in the previous year.

Ogilvie, J. Clerk at East India House with Lamb. Brother of Captain Ogilvie introduced to Barron Field in Lamb's letter of 16 August 1820 as going to Australia. Lamb says 'intimately connected with the family of the Whites, I mean of Bishopsgate Street'—perhaps Edward White, also Lamb's fellow clerk. Ogilvie of the East India House gave some reminiscences of Lamb to the Rev. Joseph H. Twichell who printed them in *Scribner's Magazine* in March 1876; they included Lamb's epigram on Wawd. Lamb insisted on calling his fellow clerk Lord Ogleby, after the character in Colman and Garricks' play *The Clandestine Marriage*. Ogilvie recounts that Lamb was neither a neat nor an accurate accountant, a fact confirmed by Lamb himself, who said he thought he lost £100 a year by his want of neatness.

Ollier, Charles, 1788–1859. Was at one time employed by Coutts & Co, bankers, but in 1817 started a publishing business with his brother, James. They had a remarkable list of authors, publishing almost all of Shelley's works during his lifetime. They also issued Keats's *Poems*, 1817; Hazlitt's *Characters of Shakespeare's Plays*, 1817; Leigh Hunt's *Foliage*, 1818; his *Hero and Leander*, 1819;

Poetical Works, 1819; and *The Months* in 1821, as well as Lamb's *Works* in 1818. They also published for B.W. Procter, J.C. Hare, and Thomas Medwin. In 1819 Olliers issued the first number of Leigh Hunt's *Literary Pocket Book* and in 1820 Volume I of *Ollier's Literary Miscellany* that contained T.L. Peacock's 'The Four Ages of Poetry'. The firm ceased business in 1823.

Charles Ollier wrote poetry and novels and in 1817 composed a 'Sonnet to Keats.' Lamb seems to have had friendly relations with Charles Ollier, invited him to his house when Hunt and Novello were there, wrote to him for help for one of the Norris girls and for a situation for Emma Isola. Lamb's 'Popular Fallacies' were mostly sent to Ollier who by 1825 had a sub-editorial position on Colburn's *New Monthly Magazine*. A letter in the autumn of 1823 to Ollier contains Lamb's only known reference to T.L. Peacock of the Examiner's Department of the East India House. Ollier contributed to the *Shelley Memorials* which Lady Shelley edited with Richard Garnett's help. He was a lifelong friend of Leigh Hunt and the latter wrote his obituary notice in *The Spectator* in June 1859.

Ollier, Edmund, 1827–86. Son of Charles Ollier, the publisher of Lamb's *Works* in 1818. As a child he is said to have 'sat in Mary Lamb's lap.' In 1867 he contributed some reminiscences of Lamb to an edition of the *Essays of Elia* in Hotten's Worldwide Library. At one time he edited *The Atlas*, wrote an obituary notice of Leigh Hunt in *The Spectator* in 1859 and in 1862 reviewed the *Correspondence of Leigh Hunt* there. In 1869 he edited Leigh Hunt's *Tale for the Chimney Corner*.

Olszewska, E.S. Fellow of the University of Leeds. Edited *The Essays of Elia, First Series*, for the University Tutorial Press of London, n.d.

O'Neill, Eliza, 1791–1872. Actress. Daughter of the actor-manager of the Droghedra theatre. After considerable success in the provinces she came to London and appeared at Covent Garden in 1814 where she played Juliet with even greater success. Among her other parts were Belvidera, and Isabella, both highly praised by Hazlitt writing in *The Champion*, who hailed her as 'by far the most impressive tragic actress we have seen since Mrs Siddons.' She was also excellent in comedy and played Lady Teazle. She appeared for the last time on the stage in 1819 as Mrs Haller in *The Stranger*. Subsequently she married William Becher who was later created a baronet. George Dawe painted her portrait in 1816.

Crabb Robinson has a number of references to her in his *Diary* and although he did not think her a great actress, he seemed pleased with her acting and appearance. He records going with Charles Lamb to see her at Covent Garden on 23 December 1814 and taking Mary Lamb to see her at the same theatre in *The Stranger* on 4 March 1815. Lamb mentions her in his letter to Wordsworth in May 1815.

Owlett, F.C. Author of *The Spacious Days and Other Essays*, 1937. The first essay reprints the address delivered to the Elizabethan Society in January 1937 and the second is the famous 'Eulogy of Marlowe'. Both are of such excellence that lovers of Charles Lamb's work should not fail to read them, dealing as they do with a period beloved by Elia. Owlett also delivered an address to the Elian Society on 17 March 1938 on 'Shakespeare and Charles Lamb', later reprinted as a pamphlet. He contributed to *The Bibliophile* in October 1908 an essay 'The Cat in Literature' which refers to Lamb and reproduces two illustrations from *Prince Dorus*.

Packer, John Hayman, 1730–1806. Actor. Originally a saddler but turned to the stage. Was at Drury Lane under Garrick. He was the original Freeman in *High Life below Stairs*, 1759. Said to be a reliable actor, but took mainly small parts. Played the part of Snake in the original production of *The School for Scandal* at Drury Lane in 1777 and was also in the cast of *The Critic* in 1779. In 1782 he played with Mrs Siddons in *Isabella*. In later life he appeared mainly in old man parts and in sentimental comedy. Remained at Drury Lane for most of his life and retired in 1805.

Mentioned by Lamb in his essay 'On Some of the Old Actors'. Lamb is likely to have seen him also when he appeared with Dicky Suett in *The Virgin Unmask'd*, the after piece to Godwin's *Antonio* on 13 December 1800.

Pagan, Anna M. Author of *Elia and his Friends* in Blackie's *Rambles in Biography* series. A small book of eighty pages but well illustrated with portraits. Also wrote *Dr Johnson and his Circle*.

Page, Frederick, 1879–1962. Author and editor. Worked for the Oxford University Press. Editor of *Notes & Queries*. In 1929 the Oxford University Press published *The Last Essays of Elia*, edited with an introduction by Edmund Blunden and notes by Frederick Page.

Paice, Joseph, d.1810. City merchant. A friend of Lamb's 'Old Bencher', Thomas Coventry. Paice took Lamb into his office at 27 Bread Street Hill at the suggestion of Samuel Salt soon after he left Christ's Hospital. He was also responsible for getting him into the South Sea House, of which he was a director, and finally into the East India Company with the help of his friend, Sir Francis Baring, the chairman of the company. Lamb repaid his debt to Paice in the affectionate description of him in his essay 'Modern Gallantry'.

Thomas Edwards, author of *Canons of Criticism*, was Paice's uncle, and his sonnet 'To Mr J. Paice' mentioned by Lamb in his essay is printed in Ainger's edition of the *Essays of Elia*. Lamb mentions Paice in a letter to Barton on 25 February 1830. Paice was also a friend of Samuel Richardson.

Palmer, John, 1742–98. Lamb in his essay 'On Some of the Old Actors' refers to 'the elder Palmer, 'Jack Palmer' and 'John Palmer', presumably all the same person. He also mentions 'Bob Palmer'. In addition, as Lucas points out, Lamb's remarks tend to confuse John Palmer with an earlier actor of the same name known as 'Gentleman Palmer', but who died in 1768.

Lamb's John Palmer first appeared at the Haymarket and then with Garrick at Drury Lane. He was particularly good as the original Joseph Surface, as Captain Absolute and as Richard Amlet in Vanbrugh's *The Confederacy*. He was also excellent as Falstaff and Sir Toby Belch. He was a most versatile actor as well as being competent and popular. Sheridan nicknamed him 'Plausible Jack'. In 1787 he build the Royalty Theatre in Wellclose Square. John Palmer is described by Lamb in his essay 'My First Play' as a friend of Francis Fielde, his godfather. There is also a reference to 'the specious form of John Palmer, with the special effrontery of Bobby' in the part of 'The Old Actors' printed in the *London Magazine* in October 1822 but omitted from the *Elia* volume.

Palmer, Robert, 1757–1805. Actor. Brother of John Palmer. Was articled to Grimaldi as a youth. Later acted at both Drury Lane and the Haymarket. He succeeded his brother in the part of Joseph Surface. Lamb refers to 'Bob Palmer' as John Palmer's brother and mentions him as Bobby in Townley's play *High Life below Stairs* in his essay 'On Some of the Old Actors'.

There was another actor named Robert Palmer, to whose parts John Palmer was said to have succeeded, apparently no relation of the brothers.

Pantisocracy. In 1794 Coleridge was on a walking tour into Wales with a friend and visited Oxford on the way, where he met Southey. During this time the Utopian scheme of Pantisocracy was hatched and was elaborated on Coleridge's return when he visited Southey at Bristol. The plan was for 'twelve gentlemen of good education and liberal principles to embark with twelve ladies' for the banks of the Susquehanna in America, to establish an ideal form of communism. Following Adam Smith's argument that there is not above one productive man in twenty, they agreed that two hours' labour a day would be enough to support them and the rest of the time was to be

devoted to the intellect. There was to be a good library and each
emigrant was to provide £125.

Coleridge, Southey and George Burnett were active in the scheme
and succeeded in obtaining agreement from a number of friends to
join them. Among these were Robert Lovell, Robert Favell, Samuel
Le Grice, Robert Allen, Shadrack Weeks (an old servant of Southey's
mother), Heath (a Bristol apothecary) and Edmund Seward. With
them were to go all the Miss Frickers, one of whom was already
Lovell's wife. Southey's mother also agreed to go and the number rose
to about twenty-seven.

The scheme was talked about during 1794–5 but gradually the
enthusiasts' interest waned. Southey married Edith Fricker and went
to Portugal, Coleridge married Sara Fricker and his centre of interest
changed, and Seward and Lovell died. By 1796 the scheme had been
abandoned. However when Coleridge was in London in 1794 the idea
was often discussed with Lamb during the evenings at the 'Salutation
and Cat' in Newgate Street, but there seems no suggestion that Lamb
ever actually proposed to join the idealists.

The most complete account of Pantisocracy is given by Thomas
Poole in a letter of 22 September 1794 to a Mr Haskins, who had
inquired about the scheme, and is printed in Mrs Sandford's *Thomas
Poole and his Friends*, 1888.

Paper Buildings. This building which comprised chambers in the
Temple adjoined the Temple Gardens. Lamb refers to them twice in
his essay on the Old Benchers. He quotes a line 'Of building strong,
albeit of Paper hight,' which both Lucas and MacKinnon suggest was
his own invention, but Walter Jerrold in his *Thomas Hood and
Charles Lamb*, 1930, pointed out that it occurs in a poem 'The
Lawyer' printed in the *London Magazine* for August 1821, the month
before the appearance of the essay on the Old Benchers. The poem has
been variously attributed to Hood, Reynolds, Lamb and Richard
Woodhouse. Lamb's second reference bewails the removal of the
frescoes of the Virtues from the end of Paper Buildings which he
describes as 'my first hint of allegory'.

Dickens refers to Paper Buildings in *Barnaby Rudge* where he
describes them as 'a row of goodly tenements, shaded by ancient trees
and looking at the back upon the Temple Gardens'. The building as
Lamb knew it was destroyed by fire in 1838.

Paris, Mrs. Sister of William Ayrton, the music critic and friend of
Lamb. She was the daughter of Dr Edmund Ayrton the musician and
she lived in Trumpington Street, Cambridge. It was in her house that
the Lambs first met Emma Isola who was staying with her aunt, Miss
Humphreys, her mother's sister. Mrs Paris's son was John Ayrton
Paris, the physician. There are several references to Mrs Paris in

Lamb's letters and in 1828, when she was staying in London, Mary Lamb in a letter to the Hoods says she has talked Charles into a headache.

Park, Roy. Fellow and Praelector in English at University College, Oxford. Writer of the bibliography of Charles Lamb in *The New Cambridge Bibliography of English Literature*, Vol. 3, 1969. Author of *Hazlitt and The Spirit of the Age*, 1971. Edited with introductions Vol. 9 of *Sale Catalogues of Libraries of Eminent Persons*, 1974, which covers Wordsworth, Southey, Moore, Barton and Haydon. Contributed articles on Hazlitt, Coleridge and Wordsworth to periodicals. See *Keats-Shelley Journal Annual Bibliography*. *Charles Lamb Bulletin*, July 1976, prints his Crowsley Memorial Lecture 'Charles Lamb and the Critical Tradition'. Edited *Lamb as a Critic*, 1980.

Parr, Dr Samuel, 1747–1825. Scholar. Educated at Harrow and Emmanuel College, Cambridge. Became assistant master at Harrow and later headmaster of schools at Colchester and Norwich. Took orders and finally settled at Hatton, Warwickshire, where he had a library of 10,000 volumes. As an ardent Whig he engaged in political controversy and was well known as a talker, although criticized by De Quincey. Parr, who was known to Dr Johnson, was a friend of Richard Farmer, Master of Emmanuel College, Cambridge, and well known to George Dyer.

Talfourd tells the story of a meeting between Dr Parr and Charles Lamb in which the former expressed surprise at Lamb's rate of smoking, and of Lamb's reply 'I toiled after it, sir, as some men toil after virtue.'

Parsons, Mrs. Sister of Sarah James, Mary Lamb's nurse. She was the daughter of the Rector of Beguildy in Shropshire and was also a nurse. In 1841 she undertook the care of Mary Lamb. Mrs Parsons lived in Alpha Road, St John's Wood.

Parsons, William, 1736–95. Comedian. Educated at St Paul's School. First appeared at Drury Lane in 1762. It was said that 'nobody can forbear laughing either *with* him or *at* him, whenever he opens his mouth.' Parsons was particularly good in old men's parts. When Garrick produced *The Beggar's Opera* in 1762 he played Filch and his wife Mrs Peachum. He was the original Sir Fretful Plagiary when Sheridan's *The Critic* was produced at Drury Lane in 1779. He was also notable as Foresight in Congreve's *Love for Love*. He frequently played at the Haymarket and particularly at Drury Lane.

Lamb praises him in his piece 'The New Acting' in *The Examiner* on 18 July 1813, and in the essay 'On the Artificial Comedy of the Last Century' and in 'On Some of the Old Actors', 'The Death of

Munden' and 'Barbara S——'. Parsons was also an able painter and exhibited at the Society of Artists.

Pasta, Judith, 1798–1865. Italian soprano and actress. After singing much on the Continent, she and her husband, who was a tenor, were engaged by William Ayrton in 1816 for the King's Theatre, Haymarket, at a joint salary of £400 for the season. Later she returned to Italy, but reappeared in London in 1824 in Rossini's *Otello* and other operas.

Leigh Hunt was enthusiastic about her in his *Autobiography* and says she was a great tragic actress as well as a fine singer. In an earlier essay entitled 'Madame Pasta' he had also written eulogistically of her. Hazlitt gave her high praise in his essay 'Madame Pasta and Mademoiselle Mars' in *The Plain Speaker*. Lamb mentions her in his letter of 25 February 1828 to Charles Cowden Clarke and complains that Leigh Hunt's *Companion* has 'too much of Madam Pasta'. In a letter to Moxon in June 1832 he thanks him for a copy of Procter's *English Songs*, which did not impress him and on Procter's poem 'To the Singer Pasta' he notes 'damn "Madame Pasty"'.

Pater, Walter Horatio, 1839–94. Critic. Educated at King's School, Canterbury, and Queen's College, Oxford. Fellow of Brasenose. Wrote *Appreciations*, 1889, which included chapters on Charles Lamb, Coleridge, Wordsworth and Sir Thomas Browne. Perhaps his best known books are *Marius the Epicurean*, 1885, and *Studies in the History of the Renaissance*, 1873.

Patmore, Peter George, 1786–1855. Author and editor. Son of a jeweller and silversmith on Ludgate Hill. He contributed a number of articles to magazines including *Blackwoods*, *The London Magazine*, *Retrospective Review*, *Westminster Review* and *New Monthly Magazine*. He was editor of the last journal from 1841–53. He had also been a dramatic critic. He wrote *Letters on England*, 1823; *British Galleries of Art*, 1824; and *Mirror of the Months*, 1826. His *Rejected Articles*, 1826 was a series of parodies of celebrated authors including Lamb, and is not a very able performance. He also published *Chatsworth, or The Romance of a Week* in 1844 and in 1854 *My Friends and Acquaintances*. At one time he was a reader and adviser to Colburn, the publisher.

Patmore was Secretary of the Surrey Institution and met Hazlitt at the time of the latter's lectures there. He was with Hazlitt at the famous fight between Neate and Hickman that forms the subject of one of Hazlitt's essays. Some of the letters in Hazlitt's *Liber Amoris* were written to Patmore. He was acquainted with many of the celebrities of his day and numbered among his friends Lamb, Hazlitt,

Leigh Hunt, John Scott, the Montagus, Count D'Orsay and Lady Blessington.

When John Scott, the editor of the *London Magazine*, was involved in the duel with Jonathan Christie that resulted in Scott's death, Patmore was his second. As the consequences might have been serious for Patmore he fled to France after the duel, but when the trial was held he was acquitted and returned to England.

Lamb and Patmore first met in 1826 at Hazlitt's lodgings and became friends. There are several most interesting letters from Lamb to him extant; one in 1827 concerns Hood's dog, Dash, which seems to have been with Patmore at the time; another later in the same year refers to the funeral of Lamb's cousin the bookbinder. Patmore's three volumes *My Friends and Acquaintances* are important for students of Lamb's life because he included a number of detailed reminiscences. They are reprinted in R.H. Stoddard's *Personal Recollections of Lamb, Hazlitt, and Others*, 1875, and most of it is included in Lucas's *Life*. Among the amusing information are details of the dog, Dash, the Lamb's servant, Becky, and of Wordsworth with Lamb at the Westwoods consuming quantities of sugar. After Lamb's death Patmore wrote some reminiscences of him in the *Court Magazine* in 1835.

Patmore had four children, the eldest of whom was Coventry Patmore, the Victorian poet.

Paul, Herbert Woodfield, b.1853. Author and politician. Educated at Eton and Corpus Christi College, Oxford. Called to the Bar, 1878. Author of *Stray Leaves*, 1906, which contains a chapter on Charles Lamb, being a review of Lucas's *Life*. *The Independent Review* for 1905 also carried his essay on 'Charles Lamb'.

Payne, John Howard, 1791–1852. American actor and dramatist. Appeared on the New York stage in such parts as Young Norval, Romeo and Hamlet. Came to England in 1813 and appeared at Drury Lane. At one time he leased Sadler's Wells to produce his own melodramas, but was not successful, although his play *Therese, or the Orphan of Geneva* was popular in 1821. He fled to France to escape his debts and subsequently lived in both London and Paris, mostly translating and adapting French plays for the English stage. He was friendly with Washington Irving and it is said that both Payne and Irving were in love with Mary Shelley.

He wrote many plays himself, including *Brutus; or the Fall of Tarquin*, 1818 and *Charles II*, 1824; his *Clari, or the Maid of Milan*, 1823, contained the song 'Home, Sweet Home' which made him famous. It had first been sung by Marie Tree in 1821. Because of his travels and this song his friends called him the 'Homeless Poet of Home'. In 1842 he became American Consul at Tunis.

Lamb was friendly with him around 1822 and he was with the Lambs during their visit to France and was of help to Mary Lamb. Several letters from Lamb to Payne exist and Lamb seems to have submitted some of Payne's plays to Covent Garden through his friend, Henry Robertson, the Treasurer. No doubt Lamb wished to repay Payne's kindness to them in Paris when Mary Lamb had been ill.

Payne, John Thomas. Bookseller. Nephew of Thomas Payne, bookseller of Pall Mall. When his uncle retired about 1825 he continued the business with the existing partner Henry Foss. The shop was at Schomberg House, Pall Mall. In April 1821 he married his cousin, Sarah Burney, daughter of Admiral James Burney, Lamb's friend. The wedding took place at St Margaret's, Westminster, and the clergyman officiating was the Rev. Charles Parr Burney, Vicar of St Paul's, Deptford, a cousin of the bride.

Charles and Mary Lamb were present and in the *London Magazine* for June 1825 Lamb had his essay 'The Wedding' which describes the event. Letters from Lamb to William Ayrton in 1823 mention that the Paynes are coming to dinner.

John Payne and his bride spent their honeymoon on the Continent and when in Vienna called on Beethoven, who saw no one, but on it being explained that Mrs Payne was the granddaughter of Dr Burney, the historian of music, Beethoven welcomed them and when they left presented them with a sheet of music he had just composed.

Crabb Robinson records in his *Diary* that Lamb hearing of De Quincey's literary difficulties said he should have employed as his publishers Pain and Fuss, i.e. Payne & Foss. After the firm ceased to exist in 1850 Sally Payne and her husband lived chiefly in Rome.

Peacock, Thomas Love, 1785–1866. Novelist and poet. Entered the East India Company in 1819 in the Examiner's Department and rose to be Chief Examiner and a very important member of the Company. He was the intimate friend of Shelley of whom he wrote memoirs in *Fraser's Magazine* between 1858 and 1862. His novels were *Headlong Hall*, 1816; *Melincourt*, 1817; *Nightmare Abbey*, 1818; *Maid Marian*, 1822; *The Misfortunes of Elphin*, 1829; *Crotchet Castle*, 1831; and *Gryll Grange*, 1861. Peacock's daughter married George Meredith.

Although Lamb and Peacock were both employed at East India House they do not seem to have been friends, yet they had much in common: they read many of the same books and both had a keen sense of humour and a dislike of pretence and hypocrisy. It would seem difficult to work for six years in the same building without being acquainted. Peacock was however in a rather higher grade than Lamb although a younger man. The feeling of precedence is sometimes strong in offices. B.W. Procter in his *Autobiographical Fragment*, 1877, states that he first met Lamb and Peacock at Leigh Hunt's, but he does not say that he met them there together, although he may have done so.

In a letter to Charles Ollier in the Autumn of 1823 Lamb regrets he cannot obtain a situation at East India House for a protégé of Ollier's and suggests that Peacock may have more influence with the directors. Peacock's 'The Four Ages of Poetry' had first appeared in Ollier's *Literary Miscellany in Prose and Verse* in 1820.

It is possible that Peacock obtained the position with the East India Company that was originally offered to John Scott in 1819. That offer came through Sir James Mackintosh, the Professor of Law at the East India College at Haileybury, and Scott was informed that 'the Directors are in want of a man of Talents to write their Dispatches', and a figure of £2,000 a year was mentioned, but perhaps this high figure was to be the ultimate salary. Scott, who was abroad at the time failed to get the appointment because his letter of acceptance was delayed: to the great benefit of the *London Magazine* and incidentally of Charles Lamb. Peacock's salary at the time of his entry was £600, the same as Lamb's after many years of service. (Further details of possible meetings between Lamb and Peacock may be found in C.A. Prance's *The Laughing Philosopher*, 1976).

Peake, Richard. Treasurer of Drury Lane Theatre for forty years. When Drury Lane was burnt down in 1809 he and his assistants at great personal risk saved the iron box containing the theatre's Charter. He figures in Lamb's essay 'Barbara S——' under the name of Ravenscroft. Lamb wrote a letter to Peake in August 1827 asking if he would help to find employment for a Miss Ibbs.

His son, Richard Brinsley Peake, became a well known dramatist. In 1823 he dramatised Mary Shelley's *Frankenstein* which was produced at Covent Garden. Lamb mentioned him in his 'New Pieces at the Lyceum' in *The Examiner* in 1819. Peake also wrote most of the 'At Homes' given by Charles Mathews at the Adelphi from 1829 onwards.

Pierson, Peter, 1739–1808. Barrister. One of Lamb's 'Old Benchers'. When Lamb entered the East India House in 1792 he had to give a bond for £500 and find two friends who would give similar bonds. Peter Peirson and John Lamb, the younger, vouched for Charles Lamb. When Peirson died in 1808 his place was taken by James White. Peirson (Lamb spells his name Pierson) is mentioned in the essay 'The Old Benchers of the Inner Temple'. He had a sister Susannah who is said to have unsuccessfully pursued Samuel Salt for forty years. Salt left her a legacy, the works of Pope, Swift, Shakespeare, Addison and Steele and a choice of books from his library. In

1809 she petitioned the Benchers for permission to place a tablet in the Temple Church to the memory of her brother.

Pemberton, Sophia. Married Charles Lloyd in 1799. They had ten children. She had a large dowry and a private income, so the reluctance of her parents to the marriage when first proposed is unlikely to have been financial since Lloyd's parents were also wealthy. She is mentioned in some of Lamb's letters. Her family lived at Birmingham as did the Lloyds.

Pentonville, Chapel Street. The Lamb family moved to No. 45 Chapel Street, Pentonville, in December 1796 soon after the tragic death of Elizabeth Lamb, Charles's mother. At the time the area was surrounded by gardens and fields and the house was near the Angel Tavern, not far from the private asylum at Islington where Mary Lamb was then living. After his father's death in 1799 Charles Lamb moved to No. 36 Chapel Street, where Mary Lamb rejoined him on her recovery. In this street lived the Quakeress Hester Savory about whom Lamb wrote verses: although he never met her he used to see her pass his house frequently and named her the 'Witch of End-door' because she lived at the last house in the street. Lamb left here in 1800 for Southampton Buildings. The Agricultural Hotel later occupied the site of No. 45, and No. 36 was occupied by a shop.

It is interesting to note that James Mill, who later worked at East India House in a superior position to that of Lamb, moved to 12 Rodney Terrace, Pentonville, in 1805 on his marriage to the daughter of a widow who managed a lunatic asylum at Hoxton.

Periodicals. Lamb contributed much to periodicals and among those which printed his work were:

Magazines.
The Athenaeum, Blackwood's Magazine, British Lady's Magazine & Monthly Miscellany (Mary Lamb), *The Champion, The Englishman's Magazine, The Examiner, The Gentleman's Magazine, The Indicator, Leigh Hunt's London Journal, The Literary Examiner, The London Magazine, The Monthly Magazine, The New Monthly Magazine, The Philanthropist, The Quarterly Review, The Reflector* (Leigh Hunt's), *The Reflector* (John Forster's), and *The Spectator*.
Newspapers.
The Albion, The Morning Chronicle, The Morning Post, The New Times, The Times, Felix Farley's Bristol Journal, The Mirror of Literature.
Other periodicals.
The Annual Anthology, 1799; *The Bijou,* 1828; *The Every Day Book,* 1825–6; *The Gem,* 1829 and 1830; *Recreations in Agriculture, Natural History, the Arts and Miscellaneous Literature,* 1800;

The Table Book, 1827; *The Year Book*, 1831; *The Cabinet*, 1824, 1825 and 1831.

Perry, James, 1756–1821. Proprietor and editor of *The Morning Chronicle*, the leading Whig paper of his time. Began life as an actor, then became a journalist. Was an editor for nearly forty years. In 1782 he had been the first editor of the *European Magazine*. In 1798 he was imprisoned in Newgate for three months and fined £50 on a charge of libel against the House of Lords. In 1810 he was tried before Lord Ellenborough for reprinting a paragraph from *The Examiner* about George III, but he defended himself ably and was acquitted.

Among his friends were Porson, who married Perry's sister, Holcroft, and many other famous people. Coleridge, Lamb, Hazlitt, Moore, John Campbell and Byron wrote for his paper *The Morning Chronicle*. Lamb refers to Perry in his essay on 'Newspapers Thirty-Five Years Ago' and states he contributed to Perry's paper. He published sonnets there.

Perry's daughter, Kate, described how Lamb used to play blind man's buff with her and her sisters when he came to their house. He would tell them not to tell the old people with whom he later played whist. Perry is said to have died worth £130,000.

Perry, John, d.1785. Steward at Christ's Hospital from 1761 to 1785. Mentioned by Lamb with admiration in both his essays on Christ's Hospital. The Steward was a very important official at Christ's Hospital, the Masters being concerned with teaching only, and the Steward with almost all other matters. Edmund Blunden described him as the 'Commanding Officer'.

Phillips, Edward, 'Ned'. Clerk to John Rickman. Earlier he had been employed by Thomas Poole on his Poor Law work. He was frequently in debt and Rickman agreed to help him. When in 1814 Rickman was made Clerk to the House of Commons, Phillips succeeded him as Speaker's Secretary. As he had made an early but unfortunate marriage, Rickman made it a condition of his new employment that he should remain unmarried. Lamb wrote an amusing letter to Coleridge on 13 August 1814 about Phillips' promotion.

He was a frequent visitor to Lamb's evening parties and was friendly with the Burneys. In his letter to Coleridge Lamb states that he has written amatory verses for Phillips, but they do not seem to have survived. He accompanied the Lambs in 1809 or 1810 when they visited Hazlitt at Winterslow. Hazlitt said of him 'a better fellow in his way breathes not'.

Phillips, Erasmus. Said to have been a Colonel and a member of Lamb's circle of card players, but little seems to be known about him.

Phillips, Molesworth, 1755–1832. Son of John Phillips and grandson of the first Viscount Molesworth, Baron Phillips. He was a Lieutenant Colonel of Marines and sailed with Captain Cook; he shot the savage who killed Cook. His first wife was Susan Burney, the sister of Fanny Burney and Admiral James Burney. After she died in 1800 he married Ann Maturin. He was a friend of Lamb, James Burney and the card playing circle who frequented Lamb's evening parties. He was also friendly with J.T. Smith, the author of *A Book for a Rainy Day*. Phillips had three children by Susan Burney and four by Ann Maturin. He wrote *A Chronological Account of the Discoveries in the South Seas*.

W.C. Hazlitt in his *Mary and Charles Lamb: Poems, Letters & Remains*, 1874, has a note which states that 'Colonel Phillips, of the Marines, one of the Wednesday-men, and as it was half-suspected at the time, a government spy.'

Phillips, Sir Richard, 1767–1840. Journalist, editor, bookseller and publisher. Before he came to London he was imprisoned for selling Paine's *Rights of Man* and he edited the *Leicester Herald* from gaol. He had a shop in St Paul's Churchyard and was publisher and editor of the *Monthly Magazine*. As a successful publisher he employed a number of hack writers and both George Burnett and George Dyer worked for him. Phillips was elected Sheriff of London in 1807 and knighted in 1808. He wrote and compiled books himself and contributed to periodicals over the signature 'Common Sense'. He was satirized by George Borrow in *Lavengro* as the vegetarian publisher, and Christopher North referred to him as 'the dirty little Jacobin'.

Phillips published *The Book of Ranks and Dignities* in 1805 that has doubtfully been attributed to Lamb. When Phillips published his *Public Characters of All Nations* in 1823, he included a paragraph on Lamb. There are references to him in Lamb's letters and he is said to have played whist with Lamb.

Pictures. Charles and Mary Lamb's first acquaintance with pictures was probably at Blakesware, the Plumer's house in Hertfordshire, which they visited as children. Although Charles Lamb maintained in his Blakesmoor essay that tapestry was so much better than painting 'not adorning merely but peopling the wainscots', he learnt to love pictures from the old family portraits in the long gallery at Blakesware—some of them by Lely, Lawrence and Reynolds. There were, too, perhaps of more importance to Lamb, prints of Hogarth on the walls.

Like all who live in London the Lambs had many opportunities to see famous collections of pictures and they came to love the work of the great masters. Prints after Leonardo da Vinci decorated their rooms as did those of Charles's favourite Hogarth. He spent much time visiting great collections, enjoying the Titians and Claudes and his enthusiasm is echoed in his letters to his friends.

John Lamb, the well-to-do bachelor brother, was a collector of pictures, which included the portrait of Milton bequeathed to Charles, and a number of other pictures that were sold at Christie's after his death. Perhaps his interest in pictures was aroused by childhood visits to Blakesware.

Charles Lamb's most famous writing on art is undoubtedly his essay 'On the Genius and Character of Hogarth', but his Elian essay on the 'Barrenness of the Imaginative Faculty in the Productions of Modern Art' shows familiarity with a number of pictures. Other writings on art include references in the essay 'My Relations' and in his comments on the Reynolds Gallery. In his essay 'On the Old Actors' in the *London Magazine* he describes some of the theatrical portraits in Charles Mathews's gallery. Crabb Robinson recorded in his *Diary* on 3 July 1814 that Lamb had no relish for landscape painting, but that his relish for historic painting was exquisite. Lamb himself said in a letter to Robert Lloyd, 22 July 1800, that the only species of paintings he valued were portraits of great men, no doubt an exaggerated statement.

There must certainly have been much talk of painting in Lamb's circle, for he numbered artists among his friends: William Hazlitt, B.R. Haydon, T.G. Wainewright, Edward Burney, F.S. Cary, Thomas Hood, Matilda Betham and George Dawe. He was also acquainted with Stoddart, John Hazlitt and Washington Allston.

William Hazlitt in *The Spirit of the Age* wrote 'Mr Lamb is a good judge of prints and pictures. His admiration for Hogarth does credit to both, particularly when it is considered that Leonardo is his next greatest favourite'. He adds that Lamb's worst fault is 'over-eagerness of enthusiasm'. Walter Pater in his *Appreciations* also notes that Lamb was a fine critic of painting. In a letter to Barton on 15 May 1824 Lamb praised the work of William Blake.

Pitman, Robert Birks, c.1796–c.1861. Clerk with Lamb at the East India House. After the *Essays of Elia* was issued in 1823 Pitman made out a list of the initials and asterisks contained in the volume and Lamb added his interpretations, and Pitman inserted it in his copy of the book. This list has been used by editors of Lamb's works and is known as Lamb's Key.

Thomas Allsop in his *Letters, Conversations and Recollections of S.T. Coleridge* gives a conversation between Lamb and his sister in which she asked why he had invited Pitman to the house instead of some of his older friends. Lamb replied that 'Pitman has been very civil to me, always asking me to go and see him; and when the smoking club at Don Saltero's was broken up, he offered me all the ornaments and apparatus, which I declined, and *therefore* I asked him here tonight'. Don Saltero's was a coffee-house and museum opened in 1695 by Salter, a barber. The relics were sold in 1799 but Lamb's comment is described by Allsop as 1826. Edmund Blunden suggested that perhaps there was a subsequent collection.

Samuel McKechnie in the *C.L.S. Bulletin*, No. 87, stated that Pitman was not an Established Clerk, but an Extra Clerk, and thus of a lower grade than Lamb, which was the reason for Lamb's declining his gift. One does not imagine that Lamb was much concerned with precedence, but may not have wanted to be under an obligation to his junior.

R.B. Pitman is sometimes confused with the Rev. John Rogers Pitman, 1782–1861, an old Blue, who visited Leigh Hunt in prison.

Plays about Charles Lamb. The lives of Charles and Mary Lamb have attracted a number of dramatists.

Charles Lamb by Alice Brown, a well known American novelist, New York 1925. A.B. Walkley wrote, 'It will please neither the devotees of Charles Lamb nor the amateurs of plays. All one can say is, it might have been worse'.

The Night of Mr H——, a Charles Lamb pastiche by Harold Brighouse, 1927.

Charles! Charles! by Laurence Housman, 1929. A dramatized version of the Haydon dinner.

Charles and Mary by Joan Temple, 1930, first performed at the Everyman Theatre, London, 4 February 1930, transferred to the Globe Theatre, 28 February 1930. Produced by Malcolm Morley. Mary Lamb was played by Joan Temple and Charles Lamb by Peter Ridgeway. The play was revived as follows:
1. Players Theatre, Covent Garden, April 28–May 8, 1938, with Joan Temple and Peter Ridgeway in their original parts. Broadcast by B.B.C., 16 October 1938.
2. By 'The New Players' of the City Literary Institute, Institute Theatre, Covent Garden, 22 July 1944.
3. At the Theatre Royal, York, by York Repertory Company, 13 November 1944.
4. As a radio play by B.B.C., 7 June 1947.
5. By the Dramatic Class of the Guildhall School of Music, 29 October 1948.
6. On television by B.B.C. in May 1949.
7. By the Thespian Society of Wellington, New Zealand, April 1950.
8. By the Charles Lamb Society's Dramatic Group at the Portcullis Theatre, London, March 26–27, 1953.
A reviewer in *The Times* on 5 February 1930 wrote 'Miss

Temple has written seriously and with insight of a most difficult subject, and that, without weak sentimentalism, her work does honour to the memory of a lovable and genuinely heroic man'.

The Man Without a Foe by P.G. Mann and A. Macdonald, first produced by the B.B.C. in February 1945. Revived by the Dramatic Group of the Charles Lamb Society, 21 January 1946.

A Convivial Evening at Charles Lamb's by F.V. Hallam. Read to the Charles Lamb Society Dramatic Group, 6 June 1947.

What a Lass... by Basil Francis (about Fanny Kelly), first performed by the Dramatic Group of the Charles Lamb Society at the Interval Club Theatre, London, 17–18 March 1949. The part of Charles Lamb was played by Basil Francis and that of Fanny Kelly by Mayre Lawson.

Chinese Crackling by Basil Francis, first performed by the Dramatic Group of the Charles Lamb Society at the Interval Club Theatre, London, April 19–20, 1951.

Brilliant Water by Margaret Brown (concerns Thomas De Quincey). Read by Dramatic Group of the Charles Lamb Society 24 November 1950.

Harriot by Basil Francis (about Harriot Mellon), first performed by the Dramatic Group of the Charles Lamb Society at the Portcullis Theatre, Monck Street, Westminster on 3 April 1954.

The Counting-House Clerk by Michael Voysey, performed on television by the B.B.C., 7 September 1956.

Only a Clerk; An Entertainment devised by Ernest G. Crowsley, performed at the Portcullis Theatre, London, 25 March 1960.

The Albatross by Howard Koch, first performed at the Theatre Royal, Stratford, London, 4 November 1963. Charles Lamb played by Emrys James and Mary Lamb by Olive McFarland. Directed by Ilya Chamberlain. The play was adversely criticized and withdrawn after one week.

The Frolic and the Gentle by Richard Wordsworth. A one-man show given by Richard Wordsworth, the actor, based on Lamb's letters and essays, first performed at The Stables Theatre, Hastings, 28 September 1974. Repeated in the school theatre at Christ's Hospital 15 February 1975, the Wordsworth Summer School and elsewhere.

Plumer Family. Owners of Blakesware, near Ware, Hertfordshire, and employers of Mary Field, Lamb's maternal grandmother. William Plumer, who was the member of the family for whom Mary Field worked after his mother's death, also owned Gilston Park. He died in 1821 or 1822. Richard Plumer, another member of the family, was Deputy Secretary of the South Sea Company in 1800 after Henry Man. He is described in Lamb's essay on the South Sea House as 'fine, rattle-headed Plumer'. Lamb suggests that Richard Plumer was an illegitimate son of Walter Plumer, but this fact is contested by his descendants as noted by Lucas in his notes to the Elia essay. Both Lucas in the *Life* and Hine in his *Charles Lamb in his Hertfordshire* give much information on the Plumer family and on Blakesware.

Plumley, W.D. Clerk in East India House with Charles Lamb. He was the son of a silversmith in Cornhill. Lamb refers to him in his essay 'The Superannuated Man' and in his undated letter to John Chambers (No. 310 in Lucas).

Pocock, Guy Noel, b.1880. Author, editor and schoolmaster. Educated at St John's College, Cambridge. In 1934 was on the staff of the B.B.C. Wrote novels, essays and school books. Edited and arranged *Letters of Charles Lamb*, 1946, in the new Everyman's Library edition in two volumes. The arrangement was based on Lucas's 1935 edition. With Sir Arthur Quiller-Couch he edited the King's Treasuries of Literature series.

Poole, John, 1782–1872. Dramatist and humorous writer. Wrote farces, burlesques and satires. In 1813 he produced for the benefit of Mr and Mrs Liston at Drury Lane his *Hamlet Travestie* with Charles Mathews as Hamlet. Among his plays were *Twixt the Cup and Lip* and *Lodgings for Single Gentlemen*. The former with *Paul Pry*, produced at the Haymarket in 1825 with Liston in the chief part, were his greatest successes. Charles Kemble and William Farren both appeared in his plays.

He contributed a number of items to the *London Magazine*, including a series of 'Beauties of the Living Dramatists', 'A Cockney's Rural Sports' which was praised by Lamb in a letter to J. Howard Payne in January 1823, and some papers on Sterne. Poole met Lamb in Paris on the latter's visit there in 1822.

Lucas suggested that Poole's play *Paul Pry*' owed something to Lamb's essay 'Tom Pry'. Thomas Hill has been suggested by others as the original of the name part, but Poole denied this and said that although based on an old lady he knew, it was really drawn from a number of persons.

Poole, Thomas, 1765–1837. A wealthy tanner living at Nether Stowey. Originally a partner with his father in the business. The friend and benefactor of Coleridge, even contributing to the cost of Hartley Coleridge's education at Oxford. Poole was a strong character and very likeable man, described by De Quincey, who had stayed with him, as 'a polished and liberal Englishman'. He also praised his house and library.

Among Poole's friends were Southey, Wordsworth, John Kenyon, Rickman, Clarkson and Sir Humphrey Davy. Lamb met him when he visited Coleridge at Nether Stowey. Several short letters exist from Lamb to Poole. He contributed a paper on the Slave Trade to Coleridge's *Watchman*. In common with Rickman, Poole had a keen interest in the Poor Laws and when George Rose's act was passed in 1803 Rickman gave Poole the work of supervising the London administration of the act. He had an office in Abingdon Street, Westminster, for the task, and it was during this time that Coleridge stayed there with him.

Pope, Alexander, 1763–1835. Actor and painter. Son of the manager of the Cork Theatre and nephew of Jane Pope, the celebrated actress. He appeared at Covent Garden in 1785 playing Oroonoko, Jaffier and Othello. He also played much at Drury Lane where his family had played for many years. He appeared in the name part of 'Tamerlaine' when Kean played Bajazet and he also played opposite Mrs Siddons. He was so successful as Hastings in 'Jane Shore' that he was brought back by the applause of the audience and is said to be, with Quinn, one of the only two tragedians ever to get an encore. Pope was a friend of Kean.

His first wife was Elizabeth Younge, 1744–97, an actress; his second wife Maria Ann Chapman, 1775–1803, also an actress; and his third wife was Clara Maria Wheatley, a painter.

Lamb mentioned him in his essay 'The Religion of Actors' and also in 'The Old Actors' as it appeared in the *London Magazine* in October 1822 where he wrote of 'Pope, the abdicated monarch of tragedy and comedy, in Harry the Eighth and Lord Townley'. Leigh Hunt was critical of his acting, but Hazlitt praised him as Strickland in Hoadley's *The Suspicious Husband*. Many anecdotes exist that show Pope to have been a great gourmand and an authority on food. He was also a painter.

Pope, Elizabeth, 1744–97. Actress, first wife of the actor, Alexander Pope. She was an excellent actress and was a favourite of Garrick, with whom she played many times. She also played with Charles Macklin. She had a wide range of characters including Lady Macbeth and Jane Shore and played many other leading parts.

Lamb mentions her in his essay 'The Old Actors' as it appeared in the *London Magazine* in October 1822. He refers to 'the first Mrs Pope' and her enchanting voice and he praises her as the Lady Quakeress in O'Keeffe's *The Young Quakers*.

Pope, Jane, 1742–1818. English comic actress. Played as a child with Garrick. Excelled in the parts of hoydens, chambermaids and pert ladies. She was called 'lively Pope' by Charles Churchill in *The Rosciad*. She was the original Mrs Candour in Sheridan's *The School for Scandal* and Tilburnia in *The Critic*. She played many of the parts formerly acted by Kitty Clive.

Hazlitt described her as 'the very picture of a duenna, a maiden lady, or antiquated dowager'. Leigh Hunt said she was admirable as Mrs Malaprop. One of her best parts was as Audrey in *As You Like It*. J.T. Smith in *A Book for a Rainy Day* calls her 'that comic and most exemplary child of nature' and he praises her as Miss Allscrip in Burgoyne's *The Heroes*. She played at Drury Lane from 1756 to 1808 when she retired.

Lamb praises her in his essay 'On the Artificial Comedy of the Last Century' and in his piece 'The New Acting' in *The Examiner*. She is also mentioned in 'The Religion of Actors' and in the essay 'The Old Actors' in the *London Magazine* in October 1822 as 'a gentlewoman ever, to the verge of ungentility, with Churchill's compliment still burnishing upon her gay Honeycomb lips'.

The Pope family was still connected with the theatre in the twentieth century in the person of the late W.J. Maqueen Pope, the historian of the theatre.

Porson, Richard, 1759–1808. Classical scholar. Educated at Eton and Cambridge. Fellow of Trinity College, appointed Professor of Greek at Cambridge in 1792. One of the very greatest of Greek scholars. He was Principal Librarian of the London Institute from 1806.

He was a friend of Manning and Rickman. Lamb in a letter to Southey in 1830 (No. 864 in Lucas) states he met Porson at Rickman's lodgings. No doubt they would have had something in common for Porson was well acquainted with Shakespeare and the Elizabethan dramatists and poets.

Portraits of the Lambs. Lamb's own feelings on portraits are expressed in his letter of 22 July 1800 to Robert Lloyd: 'In the Bodleian are many Portraits of illustrious Dead, the only species of painting I value at a farthing. But an indubitable good Portrait of a great man is worth a pilgrimage to go and see'. Immediately following in this entry are lists of the known portraits of Charles and Mary Lamb, and of John Lamb, their father. After this entry are three separate entries, describing the portraits of the three Lambs.

There are, of course, a number of sketches and portraits done by later artists, but all are based on the portraits of the brother and sister that are listed here. In some the artists have drawn on written descriptions of the Lambs to elaborate their work. There are also various memorial plaques, statues and portrait busts based on the authentic portraits, as well as such trophies as the Lamb Medal. A particularly interesting painting was that that formerly existed in Dr Williams's Library in Gordon Square, London, by Edward Armitage; Charles and Mary Lamb were included among the frescoes of Crabb Robinson and his friends. It is reproduced in E.V. Lucas's *At the Shrine of Saint Charles*, 1934. It no longer exists.

Lucas in the *Life of Lamb*, 1905, II 251, quotes Moxon as repeating a story that Lamb had 'once sat to an artist of his acquaintance for a whole series of the British Admirals, but for what publication we never heard!' Lucas states he has not traced the book. Could it have been intended for Southey's *Lives of the British Admirals*, 1833–37, issued in Lardner's Cabinet Cyclopaedia series? *See also* Memorials to Charles Lamb.

Charles Lamb

Artist	Date	Age of Subject
Robert Hancock	1798	23
William Hazlitt	1804	29
Edward White	c.1804	c.29
William Hazlitt	1805	30
Sir Henry Raeburn	c.1810–15	c.40
F. Croll	c.1810–15	c.40
G.F. Joseph	1819	44
E.V. Rippingille	c.1824	49
T. Wageman	1824–5	c.50
J. Brook Pulham	1825	50
Thornton L. Hunt	c.1825	c.50
Henry Meyer	1826	51
Henry Weekes	c.1827	c.52
G.F. Joseph	c.1830	c.55
F.S. Cary	1834	59
F.S. Cary	after 1834	59
D. Maclise	c.1835	59
George Dance		

John Lamb, Senior.

J.S. Vinter

Mary Lamb

William Hazlitt		
Thomas Hood	1827	
F.S. Cary	1829	65
F.S. Cary	1834	70
S.J. Arnold (reputed)	c.1815	

Portraits of Charles Lamb

Hancock. Chalk drawing by Robert Hancock of Bristol done in 1798. Now in the National Portrait Gallery. Engraving done by R. Woodman for Cottle's *Reminiscences of Coleridge and Southey*. Reproduced in Lucas's *Life*, 1905; Macdonald's *Last Essays of Elia*, 1903; and in many other books on Charles Lamb. Presumably this is the 'pencil drawing' owned by Francis Cunningham, Allan Cunningham's youngest son, that is mentioned in *John Francis*, 1888 II 353.

Hazlitt. Oil portrait by William Hazlitt done in 1804. Now in the National Portrait Gallery. It shows Lamb in the dress of a Venetian senator. In a letter to W.P. Sherlock on 15 November 1834 Lamb said this portrait was done for Dr Stoddart. De Quincey said it was more like John Hamilton Reynolds than Lamb. Reproduced in Talfourd's *Letters*, 1837; Lucas's *Life*, 1905; Macdonald's *Letters*, 1903; and frequently elsewhere. Mary Lamb mentions this portrait in her letter of 13 October 1804 to Mrs Coleridge. Lucas in *Letters*, 1935 I 381, says another version of this picture exists with Lamb holding a copy of *Rosamund Gray* in his hand.

Hazlitt. In P.P. Howe's *Life of William Hazlitt*, 1947, he lists among Hazlitt's paintings *Portrait of a Gentleman* (?Lamb), Royal Academy 1805'. On page 78 he refers to a *Portrait of a Gentleman* who may, for anything that we know to the contrary, have been Lamb'.

White. Pencil sketch attributed by Mrs G.A. Anderson to Edward White, a colleague of Lamb's at East India House. She found the picture in W.T. Spenser's shop in New Oxford Street and states that it is the Hazlitt portrait reversed and in contemporary dress. White had the Hazlitt oil painting in his possession in 1827. Reproduced in *The Bookman*, April 1924, in Mrs Anderson's article on Edward White.

Raeburn. Painting by Sir Henry Raeburn reputed to be of Charles Lamb. In Greig's *Life and Works of Raeburn* is a reference to a picture 'Charles Lamb (?) aet 30, 28 in. by 24 in., Marquand sale, New York, Jan 23, 1903, Laurie'. A note in *The Bookman* in December 1914 states the picture belonged to Mr F.H. Clarke and the story of its discovery is related and an illustration of the picture is given. It was probably painted in 1810 or 1815.

Croll. *The Bookman*, December 1914, mentions a 'very scarce engraved portrait' of Lamb by F. Croll, which is said to resemble the Raeburn portrait.

Joseph. George Francis Joseph painted a water colour portrait of Charles Lamb in 1819. It was done for Lamb's colleague William Evans, of the East India House, for insertion in an extra-illustrated copy of Byron's *English Bards and Scotch Reviewers*. Now in the British Museum. Reproduced in Lucas *Life*, 1905; Macdonald *Letters*, 1903; and in several other books on Lamb. Joseph also did

a water colour of Charles Lamb about 1830 which is now in the Henry
E. Huntington Library, California. Reproduced in Lucas *Letters*,
1935 II.

Rippingville. Edward Villiers Rippingville exhibited his picture
Travellers' Breakfast at the Suffolk Street Galleries in 1824. It in-
cluded Charles Lamb, Coleridge, Wordsworth, Dorothy Words-
worth, Southey, members of the Elton family and the artist himself.
The picture is now at Clevedon Court, Somerset, the home of the
Elton family.

Wageman. Drawing by Thomas Wageman done in 1824 or 1825.
An engraving was made by Finden. Reproduced in Talfourd *Letters*,
1837; Lucas *Life*, 1905; and elsewhere.

Pulham. James Brook Pulham in 1825 made an etching 'scratched
on copper from life' and described as 'Lamb chatting with his brother
clerks'. Pulham was a colleague at the East India House. This was a
caricature of Lamb that so incensed Procter that he protested to a
bookseller who displayed a copy in his window. Lamb sent a copy of
this portrait to Coleridge in June 1826 and remarked that the likeness
was stolen in one of his unguarded moments and he adds 'my friends
are pleased to think that he has not much flattered me'. William
Ayrton thought it like Lamb; De Quincey said the nose was exaggerated. There are said to be two versions, one superior to the other.
A copy was in the possession of J.C. Hotton that had Lamb's
autograph and another copy is in the Huntington Library.
Reproduced in Lucas *Life*, 1905.

Hunt. Drawing by Thornton Leigh Hunt made from memory and
showing Leigh, Hunt, Lamb, Hazlitt and Thornton Hunt. At one time
in the possession of Mrs Shelley Leigh Hunt. Reproduced Lucas *Life*,
1905.

Meyer. Painting by Henry Meyer done in 1826. Leigh Hunt
thought it the 'least unsatisfactory' portrait of Lamb. Crabb Robinson thought it a strong likeness. The original is now in the India Office
and a copy is in the National Portrait Gallery, which Lucas says is
smaller than the original. Another copy was owned by Sir Charles
Dilke. The original had once belonged to Talfourd and was bought
from his daughter by the India Office. An engraving of this picture
was used by Leigh Hunt as frontispiece to his *Lord Byron and his
Contemporaries* in 1828. Reproduced with portraits of others on the
frontispiece of the Galignani edition of *The Poetical Works of
Rogers ... Lamb and Kirke White*, Paris, 1829; Lucas *Life*, 1905;
Macdonald *Essays*, 1903; and in many other books about Lamb
including Barry Cornwall's *Charles Lamb*, 1866.

Weekes. A medallion portrait after a model by Henry Weekes,
included in Tilt's *The Authors of England*, 1838. The text of this
book was written by Henry F. Chorley. In the National Library of
Scotland is a letter dated 22 January 1827 from Allan Cunningham

to Edward Moxon asking for facilities for Henry Weekes to do a head of Lamb (Ms. 1706.38). The portrait is reproduced in Lucas *Life*, 1905. Chorley's book was reprinted in 1861.

Cary. Francis Stephen Cary, son of Rev. H.F. Cary, painted a portrait showing both Charles and Mary Lamb in 1834, now in the National Portrait Gallery. This portrait was praised in a letter from Emma Moxon to the artist (printed in Lucas *Letters* 1935 III 407) in which she says it is 'perfectly characteristic of Charles Lamb and his sister'. Cary said that the portraits were painted at his father's request and sittings were given once a month; it was unfinished at the time of Lamb's death. Reproduced in Barry Cornwall's *Charles Lamb*, 1866; Lucas *Life*, 1905; Macdonald's *Tales from Shakespeare*, 1903; and in many other books about Lamb.

Cary, In his *Diary* for 16 March 1858 Crabb Robinson states that Sir George Scharf, Keeper of the National Portrait Gallery, asked him to look at a painting of Charles Lamb by Cary. Robinson thought it bad and unlike Lamb. In a letter from Cary quoted in an article in *Scribner's Magazine* in 1881 (reprinted in Lucas *Letters* III 407), the artist says this could not have been the picture mentioned above and may have been a copy he made after Lamb's death, but abandoned as unsuccessful.

Maclise. In 1835 Daniel Maclise's sketch of Lamb appeared in *Fraser's Magazine*. It is a caricature and exists in two states. The first is signed 'Elia' in Greek and the finished sketch 'Yours ratherish unwell Chs Lamb'. Since Lamb died in 1834 this must have been from memory and the inscription copied from some other document, or it may have been done earlier. Reproduced in *Fraser's Magazine*, 1835; *The Maclise Portrait Gallery*, 1898; and Fitzgerald's *Charles Lamb*, 1866 (in part); Lucas *Life*, 1905, reproduces both the first and finished states. He says the first is probably the more like Lamb. It is in the South Kensington Museum. Leigh Hunt described the sketches as 'the most miserable of all'.

Dance. Lucas *Life*, 1905, states that a putative portrait of Charles Lamb by George Dance was in America in the possession of Dr Weir Mitchell. He adds that he has seen a photograph of it but does not believe it to be Lamb.

Portrait of John Lamb, Senior

A lithograph of Charles Lamb's father by J.A. Vinter was printed in Barry Cornwall's *Charles Lamb*, 1866, from a portrait said to be in the possession of Mrs Moxon. Reproduced in Lucas *Life*, 1905, and Macdonald *Letters*, 1903.

Portraits of Mary Lamb

Hazlitt. An oil painting said to be by William Hazlitt is reproduced in *Maids of Honour* by A.J. Green-Armitage, 1896. It was then in the possession of Mr C. Elkin Mathews and, if authentic, shows Mary Lamb at a younger age than any other known portrait of her. The same portrait is reproduced as frontispiece to *Stories for Children* edited by William Macdonald, 1903.

Hood. Thomas Hood did a caricature of Mary Lamb getting over a stile which Charles Lamb sent to Hone's *Table Book* in 1827. It shows only a side view, the face being hidden by a large bonnet and was used to illustrate some verses entitled 'Mrs Gilpin riding to Edmonton'. It is reproduced in Lucas *Life*, 1905, and in Macdonald *Essays and Sketches*, 1903. Apropos of Hood's sketch, Lamb mentions in his Mackery End essay that one of the Gladmans remembered Mary Lamb climbing over a stile.

Cary. The portrait of the brother and sister done by F.S. Cary in 1834 shows Mary Lamb at the age of seventy.

Cary. In George Wherry's *Cambridge and Charles Lamb*, 1925, is reproduced a portrait of Mary Lamb, attributed to F.S. Cary and then in Dr Wherry's possession. It is very like the portrait of Mary Lamb in the joint portrait of 1834, but is reversed and differs in other respects. It is said to have been painted in 1829. In 1951 Wherry's daughter, Mrs Beatrice Oldfield, presented this portrait to the Charles Lamb Society and it is now in their library.

Arnold. In October 1946 *Sothebys' Catalogue* listed a portrait in oils by S.J. Arnold described as of Mary Lamb. It was said to be full face in a blue dress. It was withdrawn before the sale. A reference had been made in the *Daily Telegraph* of 18 November 1942 where it was described as a half length by Samuel James Arnold, c.1815. In 1971 J. & G. Stevens Cox, antiquarian booksellers of Guernsey, published a pamphlet reproducing a portrait in their possession said to be of Mary Lamb and described as by J. Arnold that may be the portrait mentioned above. The owners suggest it was painted c.1790.

Powell, Mary, ?1761–1831. Actress. Was known as Mrs Farmer before she married William Powell, the Prompter at Liverpool and later at Drury Lane. Afterwards she married a Mr Renaud, but retained the name of Mrs Powell on the stage (Lamb refers to her as 'Powel' and 'Renard'). She first appeared at the Haymarket about 1787 as Alicia in *Jane Shore*. In 1788 she was at Drury Lane and the next year played Lady Anne to Kemble's Richard III. Among her other parts were Edmunda in Ireland's *Vortigern*, Andromache in *The Distressed Mother*, Almeira in *The Mourning Bride*, and Lady Macbeth. In 1812 she played Portia in Kemble's revival of *Julius Caesar*. She was excellent in tragedy and played with most of the great tragedians of her time. She was especially good as Euphrasia in *The Grecian Daughter*. She retired from the London stage in 1816.

Lamb saw her in Olivia in 1790 and he mentions her in his review of Kenney's *Debtor and Creditor* in *The Examiner* in 1814 where he calls her the 'finest woman on the stage'. He also praised her in the part of Olivia in his essay 'On Some of the Old Actors'.

Powell, William. Actor and later Promoter at Drury Lane. Married Mary Farmer, a well known actress. He played in Godwin's play *Antonio* in 1800 and perhaps in Holcrofts *The Vindictive Man* in 1806, both of which plays failed. He had acted previously with Tate Wilkinson in York and had been Prompter in Liverpool. Lamb mentions him in his letter to Manning on 5 December 1806. (Marrs II 249n suggests Snelling Powell may have appeared in Holcroft's play).

Powys, John Cowper, 1872–1963. Poet, essayist and novelist. Educated at Sherborne and Cambridge. The best known of a remarkable group of brothers. In 1955 he published *Visions and Revisions: A Book of Literary Devotions* that contains an essay on Charles Lamb in which he writes 'Elia's style is the only thing in English prose that can be called absolutely perfect'. In his introduction he writes, 'As a book-lover, O more than a book-lover! as a book-worshipper, it is impossible to touch *The Essays of Elia* without feeling that in Lamb we have the essayist who comes nearer to understanding the multifarious secret of the innermost soul of Shakespeare than anyone else who has ever been influenced by him'. Among his many other books are *The Pleasures of Literature*, 1938, and his *Autobiography*, 1934.

Praise of London. Charles Lamb, ever a Cockney, never lost his first love of the place of his birth. He was born and passed the first seven years of his life in the Temple and, as he said, 'a man would give something to have been born in such places.' London was to him the sum of his delights: the lighted shops of the Strand and Fleet Street, the theatres, 'the print shops, the old bookstalls, parsons cheap'ning books, coffee houses, steams of soups from kitchens, the pantomimes. London itself a pantomime and a masquerade.'

The letter to Thomas Manning on 28 November 1800 contains the first notable eulogy of London and it was to be repeated with variations to other correspondents and in Lamb's published writings at intervals during his lifetime. As Walter Pater wrote, Lamb felt 'the genius of places' and that of London seems to have entered his soul at birth and never left it.

His happiest years were spent in and around the Temple. When he left there finally in 1817 he told Dorothy Wordsworth it was an ugly wrench, but the move was only to Great Russell Street, Covent Garden, and he endeavoured to console himself with the thought that Covent Garden was 'the individual spot I like best in all the great city', because of its theatres; and he says it is dearer to him than any gardens of Alcinous.

In 1823 he and his sister decided that the bustle of London with the social activities of their friends, and their too frequent 'droppings in' were injurious to their health. The move to Colebrooke Cottage, Islington, then in the country, seemed wise, but the withdrawal from friends and the delights of London was felt keenly and the country soon palled on Lamb. His heart was in London and his walks were always towards it. He told Wordsworth in a letter as late as January 1830, 'In dreams I am in Fleet-market, but I wake and cry to sleep again.'

Many others have felt the magic of London, notably Dr Johnson; Leigh Hunt, too, felt its influence, but no one more keenly than Charles Lamb. It is interesting to trace the consistency of Lamb's devotion to the city of his birth as shown in his writings. Some of the principal references are in his letters (to Manning, 28 November 1800, February 1801, 15 February 1802; to Wordsworth, 30 January 1801, 22 January 1830, May 1833; to Robert Lloyd, 7 February 1801; to Dorothy Wordsworth, 21 November 1817) and in his essays ('The Londoner', *Morning Post*, 1 February 1802; 'A Town Residence', *The Examiner*, 12 September 1813; 'New Year's Eve', *London Magazine*, January 1821).

Prance, Claude Annett, b.1906. Has contributed to periodicals the following pieces that refer to Charles Lamb and his friends:

The Times Literary Supplement
1951 A Forgotten Skit by Charles Lamb (February 9). A report of the re-discovery of the skit 'Cockney Latin' that appeared in the *London Magazine* in November 1823, reprinted *C.L.S. Bulletin*, October 1951.

The Private Library
1962 A Charles Lamb Library (January), reprinted *C.L.S. Bulletin*, July and September 1962.
1974 James Crossley, Man of Law and Book Collector (Summer).
1981 Southey's The Doctor (Summer).

The American Book Collector
1970 Thomas Hood: An Eighteenth Century Bookseller (February).
1973 The Retrospective Review (July–August).
1974 The Laughing Philosopher: Some Thoughts on Thomas Love Peacock (March–April).

C.L.S. Bulletin (Re-named *Charles Lamb Bulletin* from January 1973).
1951 A Forgotten Skit by Charles Lamb (October), reprinted from *T.L.S.*
1953 Contemporary Reviews of Romantic Poetry (November).
1954 The London Magazine 1820–29 (March).
1957 One of Charles Lamb's Debtors (January), traces Edward

Thomas's debt to Lamb.
—— Charles Lamb in the Harvard Library (May).
1958 The English Romantic Poets and Essayists (May).
1961 Thomas Fuller 1608–1661, a tercentenary tribute (September).
1962 Augustan Studies (May).
—— Homage to Edmund Blunden (May).
—— Hazlitt, the London Magazine and the Anonymous Reviewer (July).
—— A Charles Lamb Library (July and September), reprinted from *The Private Library*.
1963 William Hazlitt (March).
—— Thomas Hood (November).
1964 Charles Lamb: The Evolution of Elia (September).
1967 Some British Romantics (January).
1968 Charles Lamb's Illustrators 1796–1967 (July and October).
1970 The Perfect Edition of Elia (July).
1971 Egomet: A Lover of Elia (October).
1973 Charles Lamb and some events in 1823 (July).
1974 Edward Verrall Lucas (October).
1975 Charles Lamb and 'The Retrospective Review' (January).
—— Charles Lamb's 'Free Thoughts'. (October).
1978 Charles Lamb's 'Golden Year' (October 1978 and April 1979).
1979 The Elian (October 1979).
1980 Charles Lamb and John Linnell (October 1980).
1982 *The Englishman's Magazine* (January 1982).

Lectured to the Charles Lamb Society on 14 March 1951 on *The London Magazine* (Reported in *C.L.S. Bulletin*, May 1951.) Author of *Peppercorn Papers: A Miscellany on Books and Book Collecting*, 1964, and *The Laughing Philosopher: A Further Miscellany on Books, Booksellers and Book Collecting*, 1976. Both books include some of the essays mentioned above and the former has two chapters on *The London Magazine* in its early years of 1820–21. Joint author with Dr Frank P. Riga of *Index to the London Magazine*, 1978.

Priestley, Joseph, 1733–1804. Clergyman and chemist and a Unitarian minister. His *History of Electricity*, 1767, won him election as a Fellow of the Royal Society. Best known as the discoverer of oxygen. Because of his sympathy with the French Revolution his house in Birmingham was looted by a mob. In 1794 he emigrated to America.

Both Coleridge and Lamb admired him as a theologian and philosopher in their early days. Lamb in a letter to Coleridge in May 1796 says 'I *have* seen Priestley ... I love & Honour him almost profanely,' and further praise is given in other letters. Priestley preached at the Gravel Pit Chapel in Hackney and it is possible that Lamb saw him there. In 1797 he was re-reading some of Priestley's works.

Procter, Bryan Waller, 1787–1874. Poet. Wrote under the name of 'Barry Cornwall'. Educated at Harrow. Articled to a solicitor at Calne, Wiltshire, and then came to London about 1807. Practised as a solicitor and was called to the Bar in 1831. In 1832 was appointed Metropolitan Commissioner of Lunacy, a position he retained for the rest of his life.

In 1815 he began his literary career with contributions to the *Literary Gazette*. Was a frequent contributor to the *London Magazine* from the first number in January 1820 until 1825 and he also contributed to the *Edinburgh Review*. His *Dramatic Scenes* appeared in 1819; *A Sicilian Story*, 1820; *Marcian Colonna*, 1820; *Mirandola*, 1821 (produced at Covent Garden with Macready, Charles Kemble and Miss Foote); *The Flood of Thessaly*, 1823; and *English Songs*, 1832. His *Charles Lamb: A Memoir* appeared in 1866 and *An Autobiographical Fragment* in 1877.

In October 1824 Procter married Anne Benson Skepper, stepdaughter of Lamb's friend, Basil Montagu. She is the 'pretty A.S.' of Lamb's essay 'Oxford in the Vacation' and in a letter to Leigh Hunt in 1825 Lamb writes 'Barry Cornwall has at last carried [?married] the pretty A.S. They are just in the treacle-moon. Hope it won't clog his wings—*gaum* we used to say at school'. For a time they lived with the Montagus at 25 Bedford Square, but about 1831 moved to Harley Street. Mrs Procter was a noted wit and by her brilliant qualities made her home one of the chief centres of London literary society for nearly fifty years. Although of a kindly nature, her sharp tongue earned for her from Kinglake the title of 'Our lady of bitterness'. It is amusing to note that her husband wrote a poem 'Advice on Marriage' beginning 'Never, boy, wed a wit'.

Procter himself was the friend of most of those prominent in art and letters during his lifetime. He first met Lamb at Leigh Hunt's about 1817 and the liking was mutual. He remained a close friend of the Lambs and he was named as one of Lamb's executors in the first will, but was not included in the second will. Many letters exist from Lamb to him and Elia praised some of his verses.

Procter contributed to the *London Magazine* in July 1825 an address 'To Charles Lamb' that was reprinted in his *English Songs*. He also wrote verses for Emma Isola's Album entitled 'To the Spirit of Italy'. In 1823 Procter gave Lamb an engraved portrait of Pope by J.H. Robinson after Charles Jervas that was framed and hung in the Lambs' sitting room. In his letter of thanks on 13 April Lamb speculates on what Pope is thinking when the portrait was done. In a letter to Procter in 1829 Lamb included his poem 'The Gypsy's Malison' that had appeared in *Blackwood's Magazine* in January of that year.

Procter's *Charles Lamb: A Memoir* was published thirty-two years after Lamb's death, and is an important work by one who knew Lamb intimately. Although not a learned or scholarly book, it is of great interest; it also has much on the contributors to the *London Magazine*, for which Procter had acted as sub-editor at one time. In his *Autobiographical Fragment* there are also reminiscences of Lamb.

The Procters had six children, one of whom, Adelaide, became the well known Victorian poetess.

Pronunciation of Elia. Lamb in a letter to John Taylor on 30 June 1821 said the pronunciation should be 'Ellia', which we assume to be 'Ell-ia'. Taylor in a letter to Elton said he thought Lamb pronounced it 'Elia' (rhyming with 'a liar'), seemingly supported by William Hone, who in the *Every Day Book* made it rhyme with 'aspire'. Lucas said that modern usage rhymes 'Elia' with 'Celia', that is 'Eel-ia', but this does not seem to follow Lamb's letter to Taylor. 'Ell-ia' or 'El-ia' seems supported by Professor G.L. Barnett in his essay 'The Pronunciation of Elia' in *Studies in Romanticism*, V. Autumn 1965, 51–55, and by John Unsworth in 'What's in a Name?' in the *Charles Lamb Bulletin*, January 1978, 104–109. (*See* also entry for F. Augustus Elia.)

Mrs Cowden Clarke records that Lamb himself remarked that Elia formed an anagram of 'a lie'. In a letter to Charles Ollier probably in December 1825 Lamb coins a variation of the name, for he tells Ollier to use 'L' as signature for the 'Popular Fallacies', reserving Elia' for essays more 'Eliacal'.

Publishers of Lamb's Works (in chronological order).

Joseph Cottle, Bristol. While not actually the publisher of any of Lamb's books he issued in 1796 Coleridge's *Poems on Various Subjects* with a Second Edition in 1797, both of which included poems by Lamb.

John and Arthur Arch, 23 Gracechurch Street, London. *Blank Verse*, 1798.

Lee and Hurst, 32 Paternoster Row, London. *A Tale of Rosamund Gray and old blind Margaret*, 1798.(There is also an edition in Birmingham issued by Thomas Pearson).

G.G. and J. Robinson, Paternoster Row, London. *John Woodvil*, 1802. This publisher had issued James White's *Original Letters of Sir John Falstaff in* 1796 and the name also appears on the title page of *Poems on Various Subjects* 1796 and 1797.

William and Mary Jane Godwin (The Juvenile Library), First at

Hanway Street (opposite Soho Square), then at 41 Skinner Street, Snow Hill, London. *The King and Queen of Hearts*, 1805; *Tales from Shakespeare*, 1807; *The Adventures of Ulysses*, 1808; *Mrs Leicester's School*, 1809; *Poetry for Children*, 1809; *Prince Dorus*, 1811; and *Beauty and the Beast*, 1811.

Longman, Hurst, Rees and Orme, Paternoster Row, London. *Specimens of English Dramatic Poets*, 1808.

John Bumpus, 'near the Gate', St John's Square, London. In 1813 Bumpus bought the remainder sheets of the *Specimens of English Dramatic Poets* from Longman and issued them with a new title page marked Second Edition.

C. and J. Ollier, Vere Street, Bond Street, London. *The Works of Charles Lamb*, 1818.

Taylor & Hessey, 93 Fleet Street and 13 Waterloo Place, London. *The Essays of Elia*, 1823. These publishers also issued the *London Magazine* from 1821–1825. During the period from January 1820 until June 1821 the magazine was published by Baldwin, Cradock and Joy of 47 Paternoster Row.

Edward Moxon, 64 New Bond Street, later Dover Street, London. *Album Verses*, 1830; *Satan in Search of a Wife*, 1831; *The Last Essays of Elia*, 1833; *Specimens of English Dramatic Poets* (with the Garrick Plays), 1835; *The Poetical Works of Charles Lamb*, 1836; *The Prose Works of Charles Lamb*, 1835; *The Letters of Charles Lamb*, 1837; *The Works of Charles Lamb*, 1840; *Final Memorials*, 1848; *Eliana*, 1864; *The Complete Correspondence and Works of Charles Lamb*, 1870. Moxon also published *The Englishman's Magazine*, 1831, and *The Reflector*, 1832–3.

Pulham, James Brook. Clerk in the Treasurer's Office at East India House and a colleague of Lamb. He is perhaps best known for the etching he made of Charles Lamb talking with his colleagues 'scratched on copper from life in 1825'. It was this etching which so much aroused Procter's wrath that he protested to the bookseller displaying a copy. Lamb gave Pulham the interleaved copy of George Wither's works that had been printed by Lamb's friend J.M. Gutch. The book that was annotated by Lamb passed subsequently to Swinburne. It contained on the fly-leaf a note in Pulham's handwriting of Lamb's adventures in the stocks. Only one short letter from Lamb to Pulham seems to exist, that written on 20 November 1826.

Pulham made a collection of material for a history of the East India Company that is now in the British Museum. He possessed a painting of the old East India House as it was between 1648 and 1726 and he made an etching of it. It is known as the 'Dutch' view because of a Dutch legend at the top.

Purnell, Thomas, 1834–89. Journalist. Educated at Trinity

College, Dublin. Was assistant secretary of the Archaeological Institute of Great Britain and Ireland 1862–6. Among his friends were Swinburne, Whistler, Joseph Knight and Mazzini. In 1870 was published *The Complete Correspondence and Works of Charles Lamb* in four volumes. This has an introductory essay on Lamb by Thomas Purnell and the title page adds that it is aided by the recollections of Emma Isola. W.C. Hazlitt seems to have been concerned with this edition, but to have given place to Purnell in the final editing. Hazlitt had a dispute with the publishers, E. Moxon, Son and Co. (Edward Moxon had died in 1858), and in a note to his edition of the *Letters of Charles Lamb*, 1886, Hazlitt claims the Purnell edition was really his, issued without his name and he adds that he did not see the proofs and 'the text and notes abound with blunders'.

Purnell attended the Lamb celebration dinner organized by Swinburne in 1875 and he is described by Edmund Gosse, who was also present, as 'a rather trying journalist'.

Quakers. Lamb was greatly drawn to Quakerism and told Coleridge in a letter in February 1797 that he had thoughts of turning Quaker, but changed his mind after attending a meeting and seeing a man 'under all the agitations and workings of a fanatic'. Some of his earliest friends were the Quaker family, the Lloyds of Birmingham; at Pentonville he fell in love with Hestor Savory, a Quakeress, without knowing her and wrote one of his most beautiful poems, 'Hester', about her. In 1822 he came to know intimately the Quaker poet Bernard Barton, who became one of his most frequent correspondents.

There are many references to Quakers in his letters and in his essays 'A Quakers' Meeting' and 'Imperfect Sympathies'. Some of the books written by Quakers were among his favourite reading, especially John Woolman's *Journal*, William Penn's *No Cross, No Crown* and George Fox's *Journal*. He also read William Sewel's *History of the Quakers*. Lamb dressed with a plainness that Hood said caused many people to mistake him for a Quaker. Miss Mann in *C.L.S. Bulletin* No. 146 states that there were Quakers in the family of Lamb's mother.

Quick, John, 1748–1831. Actor. Played at the Haymarket and Drury Lane, but for most of his career was at Covent Garden. He was a well known comedian and the original Tony Lumpkin and Bob Acres. He also played Launcelot Gobbo, Sir Andrew Aguecheek, Touchstone, Pistol and Dr Caius. He created the part of Cockletop in O'Keeffe's *Modern Antiques* in 1791. In 1798 he retired to Islington (Hornsey Row afterwards Will's Row), but in 1801–2 was back at Drury Lane and in 1809 was playing in the north of England. One of his best parts was the First Gravedigger in *Hamlet*. He was a favourite actor of George III.

Lamb mentions him in his essay 'The Old Actors' in the *London Magazine* in October 1822 as 'little Quick (the retired Dioclesian of Islington) with his squeak like a Bart'lemew fiddle'.

Quiller-Couch, Sir Arthur, 'Q', 1863–1944. Professor of English Literature at Cambridge University. Educated at Clifton College, Bristol, and Trinity College, Oxford. President of the Charles Lamb Society from its formation in 1935 until his death in 1944. He proposed the toast of 'The Immortal Memory' at the first Charles Lamb Society dinner in February 1936. In May 1939 he unveiled the bronze plaque to Charles Lamb at Christ's Hospital, Horsham.

Author of many books and well known as a novelist and critic. Among his books are *Adventures in Criticism*, 1896; *From a Cornish Window*, 1906; *On the Art of Writing*, 1916; *Studies in Literature*, 1918–29; *On the Art of Reading*, 1920; *Charles Dickens and Other Victorians*, 1925. He edited the *Oxford Book of English Verse*, 1900; *Oxford Book of Ballads*, 1910; and the *Oxford Book of English Prose*, 1925. The latter volume contains extracts from Lamb's writings. In *Adventures in Criticism*, in the chapter on Scott and Burns, 'Q' has this: 'There are certain people whose biographies *ought* to be long. Who could learn too much concerning Lamb?' He also published *Historical Tales from Shakespeare*, 1899.

Quillinan, Edward, 1791–1851. Army officer and poet. Born at Oporto. Served in the Peninsula War, but retired from the Army in 1821. He lived near Wordsworth after his retirement. He had married a daughter of Sir Egerton Brydges, but in 1822 she died as a result of a fire. He moved to Lee Priory in Kent but was always friendly with Wordsworth. In 1841 he married Wordsworth's daughter, Dora.

Quillinan wrote volumes of poetry, many of which were printed at Egerton Brydges's Lee Priory Press. In 1841 he published a three volume novel, *The Conspiritors*, based on his experiences in Spain and Portugal. He also translated *The Lusiad of Camoens* that was published after his death. Lamb wrote verses for the album of Rotha Quillinan, his daughter by his first wife, who was Wordsworth's goddaughter. He also contributed an acrostic to her album.

Raeburn, Sir Henry, 1756–1823. Scottish painter. The most famous and successful portrait painter of his time. Elected R.A. in 1815 and knighted in 1822. He lived for most of his life in Edinburgh. He is said to have painted a portrait of Charles Lamb aged about 30. Lucas in his *Life of Lamb*, 1905, states that the picture is in America, but he had not seen it. A portrait is reproduced in *The Bookman* for December 1914 which it is claimed is this picture. Raeburn was in

London when Lamb was twenty and again when he was thirty-five and the owner of the picture, Mr F.H. Clarke, suggested that it was painted in 1810 or 1815.

Railton, Herbert, 1858–1910. Black and white draughtsman and illustrator. Trained as an architect but gave up the career for book illustration. Came to London in 1885 and some of his earliest work appeared in *The Portfolio.* He illustrated the Jubilee Edition of *Pickwick Papers* in 1887, and in 1888 joined with Hugh Thomson in illustrating Tristram's *Coaching Days and Coaching Ways.* Some of his best work appeared in the *English Illustrated Magazine.* He also illustrated volumes in Dent's Mediaeval Towns Series: *The Story of Bruges,* 1901, and *The Story of Chartres,* 1902. He was a delicate and careful draughtsman, particularly successful with old buildings.

Railton illustrated *The Essays of Elia* and *The Last Essays of Elia* for Dent's Temple Library edition in 1888. In 1890 six etchings from drawings for these volumes were issued printed on vellum. *In the Footprints of Charles Lamb* by B.E. Martin, 1891, was illustrated by Herbert Railton and John Fulleylove, and some of Railton's drawings were used in Macdonald's edition of Lamb's *Works* in 1903. In *The Portfolio* for 1892 are some fine drawings by Railton illustrating W.J. Loftie's article on Inns of Court. He also illustrated Landor's *Pericles and Aspasia,* 1890, and the *Essays and Poems* of Leigh Hunt in 1891 for Dent's Temple Library.

Ramsey. Mentioned by Lamb in his essay 'All Fool's Day', where he describes him as 'honest R——, my fine old Librarian of Ludgate'. In the document known as 'Lamb's Key' Lamb has added that 'Ramsay was librarian of the London Library, Ludgate Street, now extinct'. Lamb's description in the essay is so intriguing that we should like to know more of this quaint character. Lucas admits that he has tried in vain to find out more about him, but he discovered that the London Library was established at 5 Ludgate Street in 1785, and that later the books were lodged in Charles Taylor's house in Hatton Garden and finally moved to the London Institute in Finsbury Circus.

Lamb's essay has 'Good Grenville S——, thy last patron, is flown'. On Lamb's Key someone, not Lamb, has written Granville Sharp, who died in 1813. We do not know exactly when Lamb wrote the Key, except that it must have been after 1823.

Randel, Fred V. Assistant Professor of English Literature, University of California, San Diego. Contributed 'Eating and Drinking in Lamb's Elia Essays' to *Journal of English Literary History,* March 1970. Author of *The World of Elia: Charles Lamb's Essayistic Romanticism,* 1975.

Rannie, David Watson, b.1857. Educated at Oriel College, Oxford.

Author of *Wordsworth and his Circle*, 1907, containing many references to the Lambs. Also contributed to the *Academy, Fortnightly Review* and *Oxford and Cambridge Review*.

Raymond, George, b.1765. Actor. Prompter at Drury Lane. Played in Holcroft's *'The Vindictive Man'* in 1806. Mentioned by Lamb in his letter to Manning on 5 December 1806. He came into conflict with Edmund Kean during the rehearsals for the latter's debut at Drury Lane in 1814. Wrote *Memoirs of Robert William Elliston comedian*, 1844–5, which relates amusing anecdotes of Lamb and Elliston.

Reade, John, 1733–1804. Barrister of the Inner Temple. Called to the Bar in 1758. A Bencher in 1792. His chambers were at 16 Mitre Court Buildings. One of Lamb's Old Benchers, the essay describes him as 'good humoured and personable.' The obituary notice in the *Gentleman's Magazine* remarks on his benevolence and adds 'he was the kindest of masters and the best of friends'.

Rees, J. Rogers. Author. Contributed to *Notes & Queries*, 1904–13, several items about Charles Lamb and his friends. Author of *The Diversions of a Bookworm*, 1886, which is dedicated to Alexander Ireland and has numerous references to Lamb; *The Pleasures of a Bookworm*, 1886, also had Lamb references; *The Brotherhood of Letters*, 1889; *With Friend and Book and In the Study and the Fields*, 1892, dedicated to Richard Le Gallienne.

Information about Rees is difficult to find; Mrs Anderson, who had corresponded with him, was seeking it without success in 1924. From the dedication of *In the Study and the Fields*, 'To my friends of the Fortnightly in Memory of Attic Nights', it seems he may have written for that publication. He appears to have been a friend of Alexander Ireland, Hobart Clark and Thomas Bailey Aldrich. In 1889 Richard Le Gallienne and his sister stayed with Rees at his house in Salisbury. He also appears to have lived in Cardiff, in Pembrokeshire and probably in Chester.

In a copy of *Palenque or The Ancient World. A Poem*, by Charles Lamb Esq (Saunders and Ottley), 1849, in my possession that formerly belonged to Rogers Rees, he has written his name and 'Sarum May 1912.' In the preface there is a reference to the name 'Aretzin' and Rees has noted against it 'Lamb's *Champion* productions signed R et R (Ar-et-ar: this Ar-et-zin).'

Rees contributed to the *Bibliographer*, 1884, Vol. V 'An Odd Corner in a Book-Lover's Study' which refers to his collection of Eliana. Vol. VI contained his 'The Romance and Reality of Dedications'. Both are reprinted in *The Pleasures of a Bookworm*. To *The Bookworm*, Vol. II, 1889, he contributed 'Book-lovers' Songs'.

Reid, John C., d.1972. Professor of English at Auckland University,

New Zealand. Was Vice President of the Charles Lamb Society. Author of *Thomas Hood*, 1963, containing many references to Charles Lamb. Lectured to the Charles Lamb Society on 19 April 1969 on 'Some Aspects of Popular Literature in the Age of Lamb' and on 10 January 1970 on 'Thomas Hood: Populariser of the Commonplace'.

Reiman, Donald Henry, b.1934. Librarian at the Carl Pforzheimer Library, New York. Treasurer of the Keats-Shelley Association of America. Contributed 'Thematic Unity in Lamb's Familiar Essays' to *Journal of English and Germanic Philology*, July 1965, and 'Social and Political Satire in "A Dissertation upon Roast Pig"' to the *Charles Lamb Bulletin* in July 1976. Editor of *The Romantics Reviewed: Contemporary Reviews of British Romantic Writers*, 9 vols., 1972, which includes reviews of Charles Lamb's works. Editor of Volumes V & VI of *Shelley and his Circle 1773–1822*, 1973. Author of *Percy Bysshe Shelley*, 1976. Author of *English Romantic Poetry 1800–1835, a Guide to Information Sources*, 1979.

Relics of Charles and Mary Lamb. Few relics exist, if the manuscripts and books bearing his autograph or annotations are excluded, for there were no dependants to preserve and cherish mementoes of a famous man. After Mary Lamb's death in 1847 all property passed to Emma Isola (Mrs Edward Moxon) as residuary legatee, but there seem to be no relics of Lamb in the family, even most of the books were sold. A few items have come to light, some of which are listed below:

A Pair of Silver Candlesticks given by Mary Lamb to Mrs Westwood in 1833 in acknowledgement of the care she had taken of Charles during her enforced absences. An illustration of them is given in an article by Mrs G.A. Anderson in *The Bookman* in July 1921. Daniel Maclise inserted a pair of candlesticks in his drawing of Lamb, but they are not the same as those given to Mrs Westwood and are probably imaginary additions. When Mrs Anderson wrote the original candlesticks were still in the possession of the Westwood family.

John Lamb's Pictures. In the article mentioned above Mrs Anderson gives details of some of the pictures formerly belonging to Charles's brother, John, sold at Christie's on 14 March 1822. There were fifty-five lots. A few of the pictures failed to reach the reserve and were returned to the widow. Some may still exist and, if found, might qualify as relics of the Lamb family. The collection included pictures by Claude, Canaletto, Poussin, Titian and Teniers.

Portrait of Mrs Reynolds. A pastel portrait of Lamb's old schoolmistress is also mentioned in Mrs Anderson's article as being preserved in the Westwood family and is illustrated in the article.

Bust of Thomas Manning. Mrs Anderson reproduces this bust which was then in the possession of the Rev. C.U. Manning. She points out that Lamb mentions a bust in his letter to Barton in the autumn of 1827 as one of his possessions, but it is not stated if this was of Manning and may be one of the heads moulded by Lamb's father. Several copies of the Manning bust seem to have been done.

China Jar from Canton. Alfred Ainger possessed a jar given him by his friend John Loder, who had purchased it at the sale of the Rev. John Mitford's effects. Mitford had been anxious to obtain a number of these jars and his friend, Bernard Barton, asked Charles Lamb if he could help. Lamb wrote to his friend, Samuel Ball, at Canton, and the jars were sent to England. There are references to them in Lamb's letters to Barton, 1824–27. There were forty-two jars sent from China which with their stands and the cases cost £6 while the freight cost £22. In a letter to John Loder, Ainger says his jar is one of his most cherished possessions, and he adds that he has many Lamb autographs and relics to show him. (*Life of Ainger* by Edith Sichel). These relics were mostly obtained from Mrs Arthur Tween, one of Randal Norris's daughters.

Bust of Samuel Salt. Ainger also owned a little plaster cast of the head of Samuel Salt which had been given him by Mrs Tween. This was the work of John Lamb senior, Charles's father. It is probably the same bust in wax that is reproduced in Lucas's *Life of Lamb*, 1905 I.8, lent by Miss Roscow, for she was a relation of Ainger's.

Lock of Lamb's hair formed part of Leigh Hunt's collection of locks of hair that ranged from Swift to Napoleon and Robert Browning and included Keats, Shelley, Mary Shelley, Procter, Hazlitt, Coleridge, and Wordsworth, as well as Lucretia Borgia. The lock was said to have been cut from Lamb's head on 7 July 1826. The collection is now preserved in the Library of the University of Texas.

Portrait of Shakespeare painted on a pair of bellows. Shown to Lamb by François Joseph Talma, the famous French actor, when Lamb visited France in 1822. Lamb and Talma believed in its authenticity, but it was later proved to be a forgery by Zincke. Lamb describes it in his letter to Barron Field on 22 September 1822. Lucas reproduces the portrait in his edition of the *Letters*, 1905, II.574. The bellows were then in the possession of Mr B.B. MacGeorge.

Portrait of Milton originally belonged to John Lamb junior and on his death passed to his brother, who treasured it greatly. Charles gave it to Emma Isola as a marriage portion in 1833. The picture which is mentioned in several of Lamb's letters is now·in the New York Public Library. It is reproduced in Lucas's edition of the *Letters*, 1905, I.460.

Jackson Relics. In 1923 a number of items described as 'relics of Charles Lamb' were sold on the death of Richard Charles Jackson. Their authenticity is in some doubt. *See* separate entry R.C. Jackson.

Wooden Armchair was originally in the Lambs' cottage at

Colebrooke Row, and when they left it was sold, with other furniture, to John Webb, whose soda water factory backed onto the cottage. The business eventually became John G. Webb & Co. Ltd., and the directors presented the chair to the Charles Lamb Society.

Religion and Charles Lamb. At Christ's Hospital it was the custom for the Bible to be read daily and the knowledge thus obtained had a material influence on the boys. Charles Lamb's prose style shows evidence of this and his frequent quotations from the Bible, both in his published writings and in his letters, bear witness to the extent of his Biblical knowledge.

In his early letters to Coleridge around 1796–8 he shows a religious mind. Later his attitude changed from Unitarianism to a relatively open mind, dropping away from all sects. As Thomas Hood said he was 'Nothing at all, which means that he was everything but a Bigot'. At one period he had thought of turning Quaker but this passed. Coleridge described him as 'profoundly religious' and said that when alone his reading was often a Bible or an old Divine.

Writing to Walter Wilson on 14 August 1801 Lamb tells him 'I have known the importance and reality of a religious belief'. To Southey in 1825 he wrote 'Being, as you know, not quite a Churchman'. He was a frequenter of churches, visited that at Widford when in the village, wrote an eulogy of Hollington Church-in-the-Wood, and complained to Southey of unfairness when the latter wrote that Lamb's work wanted a more religious feeling.

Lamb's writings on religion include his essays 'Unitarian Protests', 'The Religion of Actors', such poems as 'Living without God in the World' and a great many references in all his writings. Professor Barnett has analysed his Biblical quotations and found that he drew from the Old Testament much more frequently than the New, and that Psalms and Proverbs were the most quoted (*Evolution of Elia*, 1964.222).

Among Lamb's books were many theological works from Stackhouse's *History of the Bible*, a volume of his childhood, to the *Book of Martyrs*. The Quaker writers, John Woolman and William Penn were favourites, as was Jeremy Taylor. We know, too, that he read Thomas Aquinas, Saint Augustine, Richard Baxter, Bishop Berkeley and Bishop Hall. Such devotion to religious writers could not but have an influence on his mind.

Lamb was, in fact, interested in all religions, his taste was catholic, and perhaps the position is summed up by Edmund Blunden when he said 'We may collect from his writings that he honoured all sincere forms of worship'.

Katharine Anthony in *The Lambs*, 1948, puts forward the theory that Lamb's Aunt Hetty (Sarah Lamb) had been brought up a Roman

Catholic and that this was the religion of his father's family. His mother's family are said to have had Quaker members.

Rendall, Vernon Horace, b.1869. Author and editor. Educated at Elstree School, Rugby and Trinity College, Cambridge. Editor of *The Athenaeum*, 1901–16; Editor of *Notes & Queries*, 1907–12; on the staff of the *Saturday Review*, 1916–21; Literary editor of *English Review*, 1926–31. Author of *Wild Flowers in Literature*, 1934. He has also been a lecturer and a publisher's reader. Rendall read the proofs and compiled the Index to E.V. Lucas's three volume edition of *The Letters of Charles and Mary Lamb*, 1935, and Lucas frequently acknowledges his help in his notes. Among his contributions to *Notes & Queries* were 'Wordsworth and Lamb', 1 June 1935, and 'An Uncollected Letter of Lamb', 28 January 1939.

Reynolds, Elizabeth, d.1832. Daughter of Charles Chambers, Librarian of the Inner Temple. She had been Lamb's schoolmistress when she was young. She was separated from her husband and in reduced circumstances. Lamb allowed her a pension of £32 a year and she had a pension of £10 a year from the Temple Society, which Lamb and Randal Norris had helped her to get. Her father had also been a clerk to Samuel Salt for nearly sixty years.

Mrs Reynolds was often at Lamb's Thursday evening parties and we get glimpses of her in both his and his sister's letters. Thomas Hood described her at Lamb's house as 'an elderly lady, formal, fair and flaxen-wigged'. In *The Bookman* for July 1921 there is a photograph of a pastel portrait of her which had been given by Lamb to Thomas Westwood. It shows her as an attractive young woman, in some contrast to the elderly lady of Hood's description who had endured a hard life.

Hazlitt's essay 'On the Conversation of Authors' has 'Mrs R——, who being of a quiet turn loved to hear a noisy debate'. In his further essay 'On Persons One Would Wish to Have Seen' Mrs Reynolds is quoted as saying she would wish to see Pope talking with Patty Blount or riding by in a coach with Lady Mary Wortley Montagu, and she startled the company by adding 'and I *have* seen Goldsmith'; in fact he had lent her his own copy of *The Deserted Village*.

Reynolds, E.E. Editor of *A Shorter Lamb: Chosen Essays and Letters*, 1938.

Reynolds, Frederick, 1764–1841. English dramatist. Educated at Westminster School. First studied law at Middle Temple, but abandoned it for playwriting. In 1786 his play *Werter* was produced at Covent Garden for Miss Brunton's benefit. He wrote nearly one hundred tragedies and comedies, among which were *The Dramatist*, 1789, and *The Caravan; or the Driver and his Dog*, 1803. The star of this latter play, performed at Drury Lane, was a real dog who dived into a tank of water on the stage to save a child from drowning. Byron satirized Reynolds in his *English Bards and Scotch Reviewers*. From 1814 to 1822 he was engaged at Covent Garden as 'thinker' for the management and later occupied the same position for Elliston at Drury Lane.

Reynolds was a friend of Lamb's and in a letter to J.B. Dibdin on 9 September 1826 Lamb says Reynolds is to dine with him, when Coleridge would also be there. Lamb mentions him in his essay 'The Old Actors' as at the performance of Godwin's *Antonio*.

His son was Frederic Mansel Reynolds, the dramatist, who edited *The Keepsake* from 1828 to 1835 and in 1839. The 1829 volume contained a poem 'What is love?' signed 'M.L.' and attributed to Mary Lamb.

Reynolds, John Hamilton, 1794–1852. Solicitor and author. Son of George Reynolds, who had been educated at Christ's Hospital and later became Writing Master there, rejoicing in the schoolboy conferred title of 'Spongy' Reynolds——an allusion to his nose. John Hamilton Reynolds was educated at Shrewsbury School and St Paul's School. At the latter school he had R.H. Barham as a schoolfellow.

Although first a clerk in the Amicable Insurance Office and then a lawyer, Reynolds attention was much given to literature. His early poems were praised by Byron and in *The Examiner* Leigh Hunt linked him with Shelley and Keats. Although he did not fulfil his early promise he produced some notable works. His *Safie, an Eastern Tale* appeared in 1814, *The Naiad* in 1816 and in 1819 *Peter Bell,* a parody of Wordsworth that appeared just before the latter's own poem with the same title. *The Fancy* followed in 1820 and *The Garden of Florence and other Poems* in 1821. He collaborated with Thomas Hood in *Odes and Addresses to Great People* in 1825 which was reviewed by Charles Lamb in *The New Times*. Coleridge thought the latter volume was certainly by Lamb, who corrected this impression in his letter to Coleridge of 2 July 1825.

Reynold's claim to fame is not a little due to his intimate friendship with Keats, but he was also friendly with others of the Keats circle and with Thomas Hood, who married his sister, Jane. As a contributor to the *London Magazine* he was well known to Lamb and to its famous group of writers, and he attended the magazine dinners given by its publishers, Taylor & Hessey, where his light heartedness accorded well with Lamb's humour.

He contributed to a number of periodicals that, in addition to the *London*, included *The Champion*, *The Retrospective Review*, *The Sporting Magazine*, *Edinburgh Review*, *Westminster Review* and *The Athenaeum*. Of the latter journal he was part owner in its early years. His contributions to the *London* were numerous and interesting, mostly written under the pseudonym of 'Edward Herbert'. In February 1823 he contributed 'The Literary Police Office, Bow Street', an amusing skit that referred to Lamb. It is sometimes difficult to distinguish his work in the magazine from that of Thomas Hood, who was its sub-editor. Reynolds also wrote some of the monologues for the 'At Homes' given by Charles Mathews. Like Charles Lamb and Thomas Hood he was an admirer of Fanny Kelly. He was a member of the Garrick Club.

Reynolds became a member of the legal firm of Rice & Reynolds, but after Rice's death it did not prosper and Reynolds gave it up. During the last years of his life he was Assistant Clerk to the County Court at Newport in the Isle of Wight, but is said to have ended as a broken-down, discontented man.

Reynolds's mother, Charlotte Reynolds, wrote a book for children *Mrs Leslie and Her Grandchildren* in 1827 under the name of Mrs Hamerton, which Lamb praised in a letter to Thomas Hood.

Rhys, Ernest Percival, 1859–1946. Author, editor and poet. Edited *The Essays of Elia* with an introduction for the Scott Library series in 1890. Edited the Camelot Classics series and Everyman's Library series. His autobiography *Everyman Remembers* appeared in 1931. He was a friend of W.B. Yeats, Ernest Dowson and Lionel Johnson.

Rice, Rev. Edward, d.1853. Educated at Christ's Hospital, 1802–13. Proceeded to Cambridge and later returned to his old school as classical master and was Upper Master from 1836 to 1853. He held the Christ's Hospital living at Horley from 1827. He is described by Thomas Hood as a friend of Keats, and Hood wrote two sonnets to his son, There is a Rice Prize at Christ's Hospital. Miss Mann has shown that he was the son of the Rev. Bernard Rice, vicar of Alderminster, and he was brother of Vincent Rice, who witnessed Lamb's will. He was the clergyman who officiated at Thomas Hood's wedding and at Tom Keats's funeral. He resigned from Christ's Hospital in January 1853 and within a week in a moment of aberration hanged himself.

Rice, Vincent. Educated at Christ's Hospital and subsequently a colleague of Lamb's at East India House where he was in the Transfer Department. He was the only witness to Lamb's second will which was made on 9 October 1830, where his address is given as 3 Ruffords Row, Islington. Mrs Anderson in *The Bookman* in April 1924 states that as there was only one witness, Willis Henry Lowe of the India House, had to appear before the probate officials to swear to Lamb's signature. Miss Mann has shown that he was the eldest son of the Rev. Bernard Rice, vicar of Alderminster and he was at Christ's Hospital,

1800–1805 and at East India House, 1806–1839. Both his brothers, Edward and John Rice, were also educated at Christ's Hospital.

Rich, Samuel Morris, 1877–1949. Jewish schoolmaster and Lamb scholar and collector. Educated at King's College, Strand, and in 1898 joined the staff of the Jews' Free School. In 1921 he was offered the post of Head of the Religion School of the London Liberal Jewish Synagogue and in 1922 became Director of Correspondence Classes. Retired in 1938.

He contributed to many periodicals, including *The Schoolmaster, The Schoolmistress, The Teachers' World, The New Age, Jewish Guardian* and *The London Teacher.* In 1931 he published *The Elian Miscellany: A Charles Lamb Anthology* that reprinted many scarce items about Lamb: he had been a collector of Eliana for fifty years. He also published a volume of verse entitled *From a Teacher's Desk: A Sonnet Sequence,* 1923, reprinted 1950.

Rich was a member and finally Secretary of the Elian Society. He was a founder member of the Charles Lamb Society on its formation in 1935 and editor of the *C.L.S. Bulletin,* 1935–47. He was also Vice-Chairman and later Vice-President of the Society.

His collection of Eliana numbered about 750 items, including a unique set of fifteen volumes of mounted newspaper cuttings and extracts from magazines: each volume had been indexed. His library was contained in what he called his Lamb Room with furniture and prints of the Lamb period. The collection passed to the Charles Lamb Society on his death. An interesting account of Rich's library is included in William Kent's *London for the Literary Pilgrim,* 1949, under the heading 'Charles Lamb'; a portrait of Rich is reproduced. Among his contributions to periodicals are: 'Charles Lamb and the Jews', *Jewish Guardian,* 5 May 1922, and 'In re Elia and Others (A Defence of Schoolmasters)', *The Schoolmaster,* 1 November 1913. Both are reprinted in *The Elian Miscellany,* 1931.

Richards, George, 1767–1837. Poet and divine. Educated at Christ's Hospital, 1776–85. Proceeded to Trinity College, Oxford, where he won the Chancellor's Prize for an English essay in 1789 and the Earl Harcourt Prize in 1791. Became a Fellow of Oriel and subsequently Vicar of St Martin's-in-the-Fields, Fellow of the Society of Antiquaries and a Governor of Christ's Hospital. He published his Oxford Prize poem *Aboriginal Britons* in 1791 and in *English Bards and Scotch Reviewers,* Byron called it 'an excellent poem'.

> Where Richards wakes a genuine poet's fires
> And modern Britons justly praise their sires.

Lamb said it was the 'most spirited' of Oxford Prize poems. Richards also wrote *An Essay on the Characteristic Differences between An-*

cient and Modern Poetry, 1789; *Songs of the Aboriginal Britons*, 1792; and *Odin, a Drama* in 1804. The same year he wrote *The Christian*, a verse essay inscribed to his old schoolmaster, James Boyer. He also contributed to the *Gentleman's Magazine*. At Christ's Hospital he founded the Richard's gold medal for the best copy of Latin hexameters. Lamb mentioned him in his essay 'Christ's Hospital Five and Thirty Years Ago'.

Richardson, William. Accountant General at East India House in Lamb's time. Lamb complained to Coleridge in two letters in 1796 and 1797 that Richardson had delayed or cancelled his holidays owing to illness in the office.

Rickman, John, 1771–1840. Parliamentary official and statistician. Educated at Guildford Grammar School, Magdalen Hall and Lincoln College, Oxford. Was Secretary to Charles Abbot, Speaker of the House of Commons. Went to Dublin with Abbot when he became Chief Secretary for Ireland. In 1814 Rickman was appointed Second Clerk Assistant at the table of the House of Commons and in 1820 became Chief Clerk, a position he held until his death.

Rickman was interested in farming and soon after leaving Oxford he obtained, through George Dyer, the editorship of the *Commercial, Agricultural and Manufacturers' Magazine,* He wrote a pamphlet advocating the census that was partly responsible for his undertaking the work of the census in England.

He was the son of a clergyman who lived at Christchurch, Hampshire, and first met Southey there in 1797. They became close friends and Southey usually stayed with Rickman when he came to London. In 1800 Rickman was living at Southampton Buildings and was introduced to Lamb by George Dyer. From the first Lamb was delighted with his new friend and his letters contain several eulogies of Rickman. The first is in a letter to Manning on 3 November 1800, when he wrote 'He is a most pleasant hand: a fine rattling fellow, has gone through life laughing at solemn apes; himself hugely literate ... can talk Greek with Porson, politics with Thelwall, conjecture with George Dyer, nonsense with me, and anything with anybody'. Lamb seems to have had no reason to change his mind and Rickman was a frequent visitor to the evening parties. He was also musical and often gave musical evenings at his house attended by the Burneys, Alsager and William Ayrton, although it is doubtful if Lamb came to the concerts.

There are many references to Rickman in Lamb's letters and also letters to him. In July 1829 Lamb stayed with him during one of Mary Lamb's illnesses and in 1830 he met Porson at Rickman's house. In 1833 Rickman dined with Lamb at the 'Bell' to meet Godwin.

Rickman, although of severe exterior, was generous and helpful to his friends, but could not stand incompetence. He acted as Southey's literary agent when the latter was in Portugal; procured him a sinecure when he returned, and he helped Coleridge to get a ship to Malta. He also assisted his friends' protégés, for he gave employment to George Burnett and to Martin Burney, but was intolerant of their shortcomings. He took as his clerk, Edward Phillips, another of Lamb's wayward friends, but he turned out rather better than the others and actually succeeded Rickman as Speaker's Secretary when the latter was promoted. In addition to Southey and members of Lamb's circle in London, Rickman was friendly with Henry Taylor, the poet, and in 1806 toured Holland with Southey and Taylor.

As well as his work as 'Census-taker' Rickman wrote an article on the Poor Laws, to which Southey added a small amount and sent to the *Quarterly Review*, where it was published in April 1818 under the title of 'The means of improving the People'. Rickman also supplied Southey with material for articles in the *Edinburgh Review* and the *Annual Register*, and contributed articles to the *Medical Gazette* on the probability of life. In 1832 he published *A Comparative Account of the Population of Great Britain in the Years 1801, 1811, 1812 and 1831* and the next year an *Abstract of Returns* in three volumes.

When Rickman died in 1840 the House of Commons passed a resolution that praised his work in no uncertain terms. His ability is unquestioned and when a portrait of him was published in 1843 it bore the caption 'An honest man'.

Rickman, Thomas, 'Clio' Rickman, 1761–1834. Bookseller, publisher, author and reformer. His shop was first at 39 Leadenhall Street and then at 7 Upper Marylebone Street. He was a friend of Thomas Paine, who wrote the second part of *The Rights of Man* in Rickman's house in London. He contributed verse to the *Sussex Weekly Advertiser* under the name of 'Clio' and published *Poetical Scraps*, two volumes of his collected verse in 1803. In 1796 he had edited *A Select Collection of Epigrams*. John Hazlitt painted his portrait.

Thomas Moore relates in his *Diary* that at the famous dinner party on 4 April 1823 when Coleridge, Rogers, Wordsworth and Lamb were present, he heard the latter quote Clio Rickman's epitaph on Thomas Tipper, the Newhaven brewer, who knew Hudibras by heart. This, misquoted by Lamb, was a favourite of his and he copied it into his Commonplace Book. 'Clio' Rickman was an ancestor of E.V. Lucas, as was another Thomas Rickman, the architect. W.C. Hazlitt stated in *Four Generations of a Literary Family* that 'Clio' Rickman was related to Lamb's friend, John Rickman.

Ridgway, Athelstan. Editor of *The Essays of Elia*, 1921, in Dent's series 'The King's Treasuries of Literature'. Included with his selection of Lamb's writing are Ridgway's own 'A Memoir to Charles Lamb' and 'Charles Lamb as a Writer'.

Riga, Frank Peter, b.1936. Professor of English, Canisius College, Buffalo, New York. Author of *The Uncollected and Apocryphal Poems of John Hamilton Reynolds*, doctoral dissertation, Buffalo, 1967. Has contributed a number of reviews of books on writers of the Romantic period to the *Library Journal*, including a review of Tim Chilcott's *A Publisher and his Circle: The life and work of John Taylor, Keats's Publisher*. Joint author with Claude A. Prance of *Index to the London Magazine* (1820–29), 1978. Received National Endowment for the Humanities grant, summer 1977.

Rippingille, Edward Villiers, ?1798–1859. English subject painter, writer and lecturer on art. Exhibited at the Royal Academy. Lived in Bristol in early years. Pictures taken from English rural life include *Travellers' Breakfast* (*see* Portraits of Lamb), *Enlisting, Scene in a Gaming House, A Country Post Office*, and *Progress of Drunkenness*. Contributed to the *Art Journal* and *Bentley's Magazine*.

Ritchie, Joseph, ?1788–1819. Explorer who was also a hospital surgeon. Left England in 1818 to try to penetrate via Fezzan to Timbuctoo, but died in Africa. An account of the expedition was published by Captain G.F. Lyon, a member of the party, in 1821. Poems by Ritchie were printed in the *London Magazine* in April 1821. His poem 'A Farewell to England' was printed in Alaric Watts's *Poetical Album* in 1829.

He met Keats through Haydon and was at the famous party at Haydon's studio in December 1817 when Lamb teased the Comptroller of Stamps. Lamb drank Ritchie's health as that of 'the gentleman we are going to lose'. He was a friend and schoolfellow of Rev. Richard Garnett and he knew Samuel Ireland, the Shakespeare forger.

Roberts, H.A. President of the Amicable Society of Blues in 1922. Author of *The Records of the Amicable Society of Blues and its Predecessors from 1629 to 1895*, Cambridge, 1924 (printed for private circulation), which contains the record of Lamb's attendance at the dinner at the London Tavern on 11 February 1817 and reproduces in facsimile two minutes concerning the function.

Roberts, Richard Ellis, b.1879. Author and editor. Educated at Merchant Taylors School and St John's College, Oxford. Fellow of the Royal Society of Literature. Contributed an essay on 'Charles Lamb' to *Essays by Divers Hands*, XIII, 1934. Among his books are *Samuel Rogers and his Circle*, 1910; *Reading for Pleasure*, 1928; and *Life as Material*. He contributed to *The Bookman, Daily News, English*

Review, New Statesman, Observer and *London Mercury*. He was also on the staff of the *Pall Mall Gazette*, Literary Editor of *The New Statesman* and editor of *Life and Letters*, 1934–5.

Roberts, William, b.1862. Author of *The Book-Hunter in London*, 1895, a fascinating book that contains a number of references to Charles Lamb. He was editor of *The Bookworm* to which he contributed many articles, as he did to *Booklore*, 1885, *Nineteenth Century* and *Fortnightly Review*. He wrote *Rare Books and their Prices*.

Robertson, Henry. Treasurer of Covent Garden Theatre. Friend of Lamb, Leigh Hunt, the Novellos and Cowden Clarke. Robertson was, with Edward Holmes and Cowden Clarke, 'A passionate Mozartian'. He had an excellent voice and Clarke describes him as 'one of the very best amateur singers'. He was frequently to be found at Novello's musical evenings and seems to have been very popular. Mary Cowden Clarke (Novello's daughter) writes of 'lively Henry Robertson' and her husband called him 'one of the most delightful of associates for good temper, good spirits, good taste in all things literary and artistic'. Lamb described him as a very good fellow in his letter to Payne in November 1822. Lamb's friend, John Howard Payne, had submitted his play *Grandpa* to Covent Garden through the Lambs, and Lucas prints a letter from Robertson to Mary Lamb on 9 February 1823 returning the play as unsuitable for Covent Garden and telling her that Kemble suggests it might suit the English Opera House. Lamb also negotiated with Covent Garden through Robertson about payment for Payne's play *Ali Pacha* and other plays in 1822. Robertson contributed to Leigh Hunt's *Examiner* articles on opera. Leigh Hunt wrote a 'Sonnet to Henry Robertson, John Gattie and Vincent Novello'.

Robinson, Anthony, 1762–1827. A Dissenting Minister who later went into business as a sugar refiner. Robert Hall was a fellow student with him at one time. He was a friend of Henry Crabb Robinson, but not a relative. He published several pamphlets and articles in reviews.

Crabb Robinson introduced him to Lamb and Hazlitt, and he entertained them at his house occasionally. He subscribed with Crabb Robinson and Lamb to send young Tom Holcroft to his brother in India. Anthony Robinson was instrumental in getting Hazlitt's first book *An Essay on the Principles of Human Action* published by Johnson in 1805. In 1812 Hazlitt borrowed £30 from him.

Crabb Robinson records in his *Diary* going to Covent Garden in March 1815 with Robinson's son, Anthony, and Mary Lamb. A later entry in the *Diary* concerns the disappearance of Anthony Robinson, Junior, who was a medical student and Crabb Robinson makes the horrific suggestion that he may have been a victim of Burke and Hare, the resurrection men.

When Anthony Robinson, Senior, died in 1827, Crabb Robinson wrote an obituary notice of him in *The Monthly Repository*. After his death his widow moved to Enfield where she lived opposite the Lambs.

Robinson, Henry Crabb, 1775–1867. Barrister and diarist. Born at Bury St Edmunds. Articled to an attorney in Colchester, he first came to London in 1796 and took lodgings in Drury Lane. He again worked in an attorney's office and soon became a keen playgoer, seeing both Mrs Siddons and Mrs Jordan. There are many references to the theatre in his *Diary*. He was at one time a war correspondent of *The Times* and later foreign editor. He subsequently visited Germany where he met Goethe, Schiller, Schelling, the Schlegels and Kotzebue. He also met Madame de Staël and he returned to England in 1805.

Crabb Robinson was called to the Bar in 1813 and joined the Eastern Circuit of which he later became the leader. He retired from the Bar in 1828. Because of his conversational powers he was a well known figure in society, meeting most of the important people of his time. For some years he lived with John Dyer Collier who introduced him to John Walter of *The Times*.

He started his famous *Diary* in 1811 and continued it until 1867. To it we are indebted for an enormous amount of interesting information on his life and times, and particularly on his friends. There are a great many references to Lamb and his circle in the Diary, for Robinson was one of his intimate friends and a frequent visitor to his house.

Robinson was introduced to both Lamb and Wordsworth by his friend, Catherine Buck, who became the wife of Thomas Clarkson, the abolitionist. He was present at the performance of Lamb's play *Mr H——*, and later attended Hazlitt's lectures. In 1812 he was responsible for bringing about the reconciliation between Coleridge and Wordsworth. In 1822 he was in Paris and of great help to Mary Lamb there.

In his *Diary* for 4 April 1823 Robinson gives an account of the famous dinner at Monkhouse's at which he was present with Wordsworth, Coleridge, Lamb, Moore, Rogers, Gillman, Mrs Wordsworth and Miss Hutchinson. (Lamb describes it in his letter to Barton on 5 April 1823). Robinson sent a fuller account than that in the *Diary* to *The Athenaeum* where it was printed on 25 June 1853, in which he differs from Moore as to those present as given in the latter's diary.

Crabb Robinson's *Diary, Reminiscences and Correspondence* was first published in 1869 edited by Thomas Sadler, and reprinted in 1872. In 1922 E.J. Morley published *Blake, Coleridge, Wordsworth, Lamb &c. being Selections from the Remains of Henry Crabb Robin-*

son and in 1938 she published her *Henry Crabb Robinson on Books and their Writers* in three volumes. There have been other selections from it, including one published in 1966 of Robinson's references to the theatre: *The London Theatre 1811–1866.* Edited by Eluned Brown for the Society for Theatre Research. The original *Diary* is in Dr Williams's Library in London.

Robinson, William. Lamb's letter of 11 October 1802 to Coleridge mentions Robinson as 'a good-natured young man, who was a little time at Xts, is now in the India House'. He appears to have travelled to Devonshire with Coleridge at one time. Samuel KcKechnie in the *C.L.S. Bulletin* No. 89 states that Robinson was a clerk in the Transfer Office. In 1805 he was sent out to the East India Company's office at Prince of Wales' Island, Penang, as Assistant Accountant and later became Accountant General there.

Rogers, Daniel, c.1760–1829. Eldest brother of Samuel Rogers, the banker poet. He married his cousin, Martha Bowles, and incurred his father's displeasure by doing so. He lived at Wassall Grove, near Stourbridge as a country squire. Lamb had met him at Samuel Rogers's house in St James's Place and on his death he wrote to his brother enclosing a sonnet he had written.

Rogers, Henry, d.1832. Banker, said to be the working head of the family business. Youngest brother of Samuel Rogers, the poet. Lamb had met him at his brother's house in St James Place. He said in a letter of August 1831 to Moxon that it was at Henry Rogers's house he had met the artists 'Daniels and Westall'. He had also met Thomas Stothard and John Wolcot there. Rogers retired from the banking firm in 1824 and his place was filled by his nephew Samuel Sharpe.

Rogers, John. Author of *With Elia and his Friends in Books and Dreams,* 1903. At one time he owned the copy of *The Essays of Elia* in which R.B. Pitman had inserted Lamb's Key.

Rogers, Samuel, 1763–1855. Poet and banker. Entered his father's bank and eventually became principal partner in the firm of Welch & Rogers. He was keenly interested in literature and the fine arts all his life. Became well known as a leader in society and a patron of the arts, and his breakfasts attended by celebrities became famous. Macaulay called him the 'Oracle of Holland House'. In 1803 he went to live in St James's Place where he assembled a notable collection of pictures, which at his death realized £50,000. At one time he lived in Paper Buildings in the Temple. He had considerable powers as a conversationalist and a sarcastic and bitter wit, but he was generous and Fanny Kemble said he had the kindest heart and unkindest tongue of anyone she knew. He helped a number of literary friends:

Robert Bloomfield, Thomas Moore and Sheridan; he procured a pension for H.F. Cary, obtained for Wordsworth his sinecure as Distributor of Stamps and saw the Prime Minister about Coleridge's pension. Rogers was offered the position of Poet Laureate on Wordsworth's death but declined it. He helped Edward Moxon to start in business in 1830 by lending him £500.

Rogers published his *Pleasures of Memory* in 1792; *Columbus*, 1810; *Jacqueline*, 1814; *Human Life*, 1819; and *Italy*, 1822. Moxon published editions of Rogers's *Poems* and *Italy* that were lavishly illustrated by J.M.W. Turner and Thomas Stothard at enormous cost.

Samuel Rogers was well known to Lamb. Both were at the famous party at Monkhouse's in April 1823 with 'half the poetry of England' as Lamb described it. Several letters exist from Lamb to Rogers. In one of 22 March 1829 Lamb wrote on the death of Rogers's eldest brother, Daniel, and enclosed a sonnet to Samuel Rogers that he had written. Rogers's reply Lamb described as 'the prettiest letter I ever read', and said it contained the sentence about his brother 'He was the only person in the world in whose eyes I always appeared young'. In 1830 Rogers sent Lamb a copy of the beautiful illustrated edition of his *Italy* and in 1833 came the illustrated *Poems*. The latter book brought from Lamb in his letter of thanks the statement that Rogers's *Pleasures of Memory* was the first school present Lamb had given to Emma Isola. He has too, his famous comments on illustrated books 'I am jealous of the combination of the sister arts. Let them sparkle apart'. Lamb had at this time written his sonnet 'To Samuel Rogers' which had appeared in *The Times* of 13 December 1833. He also wrote verses 'To T. Stothard. On his Illustrations to the Poems of Mr Rogers' which had appeared in *The Athenaeum* on 21 December of that year.

Rollins, Hyder Edward, 1889–1958. Professor of English Literature, Harvard University. Editor of *The Keats Circle. Letters and Papers 1816–1878*, 2 vols., 1948, Cambridge, Massachusetts, which contains many references to Charles Lamb, particularly in the letters of J.A. Hessey. Rollins was also editor of *The Letters of John Keats 1814–1821*, 2 vols., 1958, and *More Letters and Papers of the Keats Circle*, 1955.

Rooper, Rev. T.R., d.1865. In Sadler's edition of Crabb Robinson's *Diary and Correspondence* is a letter sent to Thomas Robinson on 5 November 1847 that mentions that Crabb Robinson had met Rooper at dinner and describes him as follows: 'a clergyman. A man of family and fortune. He was connected with old Plumer, the Herts M.P. whom he visited as a boy, when he played with Charles Lamb whose grandmother was the housekeeper'. This must have been at Blakesware.

Rooper was said to be a clergyman of the moderate Evangelical school, but very tolerant of the opinion of others.

In E.J. Morley's *Henry Crabb Robinson on Books and their Writers* Robinson is quoted as noting that he dined with Rooper on 9 January 1837. On 30 October 1847 is a note on which the letter to Thomas Robinson is probably based, which repeats that Rooper played with Charles Lamb as a child, but adds that he was a connection of Archbishop Whateley's family, who were great friends of 'old Plumer'.

Robinson seems to have forgotten he had met Rooper earlier than 1847, for he also notes in his *Diary* on 13 December 1831 that he dined with Rooper in his house in Brunswick Square to look at paintings by Sir Joshua Reynolds.

Rosenbach, Abraham Simon Wolf, 1876–1952. Famous American bookseller. A great many of the rarer Lamb items such as Emma Isola's Album, the manuscript of 'Dream Children' and the scarcer children's books passed through Dr Rosenbach's hands. There are references to some of them in *Rosenbach: A biography*, 1960, by Edwin Wolf 2nd and John Fleming. Rosenbach himself wrote several books about his adventures in the sale rooms, among which are *Books and Bidders*, 1927, and *A Book Hunter's Holiday* 1936. He also wrote *The Unpublishable Memoirs*, 1924, a series of short stories concerning book collecting.

Ross, Ernest Carson, 1897–1955. Professor of English, University of Oklahoma, 1939–55. Educated at the University of Virginia. Author of *The Ordeal of Bridget Elia*, 1940, and *Charles Lamb and Emma Isola*, 1950. The latter was a pamphlet of forty pages designed as a reply to Neil Bell's novel *So Perish the Roses* and Katharine Anthony's *The Lambs*. It was issued as Elian Booklet No. 1 by the Charles Lamb Society. Professor Ross lectured to the Charles Lamb Society in January 1938 on 'The Last Days of Bridget Elia' and contributed to the *C.L.S. Bulletin* two short pieces: 'Who was at the Monkhouse's Dinner Party?' July 1942, and 'Who was at Charles Lamb's Funeral?' September 1946.

Russell, John Fuller, 1814–84. Theological writer. Son of Thomas Cloutt, an independent minister, who adopted the name of Russell about 1820. Became perpetual curate of St James's, Enfield. He had been educated at Peterhouse, Cambridge. Wrote to Lamb in 1834 and sent the manuscript of a metrical novel *Emily de Wilton* for criticism. Lucas prints two short notes from Lamb containing the required comments and Russell visited Lamb at Edmonton several times. He published reminiscences of Lamb in *The Guardian* of 6 May 1874 and again in *Notes & Queries* in 1882, reprinted in *The*

Bookman January 1897 and in Blunden's *Charles Lamb his life recorded by his contemporaries*.

Russell, Samuel Thomas, c.1769–1845. Actor. First appeared on the stage as a child, and by 1795 had reached Drury Lane, where he played Charles Surface. In 1812 he was stage manager at the Surrey Theatre under Elliston, later at the Olympic and in 1819 at Drury Lane. In 1814 he played at the Haymarket and in 1837–8 was stage manager there. His most celebrated character was Jerry Sneak in Foote's *Mayor of Garratt*. Among his other well known parts were Copper Captain in *Rule a Wife and have a wife* and Paul Pry. He is described by Mrs Mathews as 'the prince of oral hoaxers' and because of the guileless expression with which he carried them out Charles Mathews nicknamed him 'His Innocence'. Lamb praises him in his piece 'The New Acting' in *The Examiner*. Russell was a close friend of William Dowton, the actor.

Russell Street, Covent Garden. The Lambs moved to No. 20 Great Russell Street, Covent Garden, in October 1817 in rooms over the shop of a Mr Owen, an ironmonger or brazier. It was on the north side, west of Bow Street, with Covent Garden Theatre seen from the back windows and Drury Lane within sight from the front. Lamb said in his letter to Dorothy Wordsworth on 21 November 1817, 'We are in the individual spot I like best in all this great city'.

B.W. Procter stated that Lamb lived in the corner house which would be No. 21 and was on the site of Will's Coffee House, but there seems some doubt as to whether it was Nos. 20 or 21, the same landlord owning both houses. Possibly the Lambs' rooms extended over both. In her letter to Dorothy Wordsworth on 21 November 1817 Mary Lamb writes that they are at No. 20, but it is probable that only one number would be given if the rooms covered both.

George Daniel, who first met Lamb in 1817, described the accommodation as 'light, airy, and convenient lodgings' but as reached 'after winding up a narrow pair of stairs'. The Lambs remained there until August 1823 when they moved to Islington. At No. 19 or 20 was the second hand bookseller, Barker, from whom Lamb bought his famous copy of Beaumont and Fletcher, described in his essay 'Old China', which was written while he was living in Great Russell Street. Barker had, however, left the shop when Lamb lived there.

In Lamb's day the street was divided into Great Russell Street running from Covent Garden and Little Russell Street at the other end. The house has been rebuilt since Lamb's time.

Rutt, John Towill, 1760–1841. Politician and man of letters. Educated at St Paul's School and subsequently followed a mercantile career. He was a Unitarian and a leading member of the Gravel-Pit congregation at Hackney. A friend of Crabb Robinson, George Dyer, Gilbert Wakefield and Joseph Priestley. He was one of those who provided bail for Wakefield at his trial. He edited Gilbert Wakefield's *Memoirs*, 1804; the *Works of Joseph Priestley*, 1817–32; and the *Diary of Thomas Burton 1656–9* in 1828. He was a student of Pepys and a regular contributor to the *Monthly Repository*. He also wrote in *The Christian Reformer*.

Lamb's friend, T.N. Talfourd, married Rutt's daughter, Rachel. In November 1826 Lamb wrote to his friend, Brook Pulham, asking for facilities to be given to Rutt to see some manuscripts in East India House concerning Cromwell. Crabb Robinson in his *Diary* on 21 May 1828 records being at Talfourd's with the latter's sister-in-law, Miss Anne Rutt, the Lambs and Wordsworth.

Rydal Mount. A house about one and one-half miles from Grasmere and the same distance from Ambleside, standing immediately above Rydal Water. Wordsworth and his sister came here in 1813 and remained there for the rest of their lives.

Ryle, Charles. Clerk at East India House. Co-executor and trustee of Lamb's will with T.N. Talfourd. Lucas prints a number of notes from Lamb to Ryle, in some of which Lamb asks if he can stay with Ryle. In March 1830 he congratulates Ryle on his promotion. Ryle attended the funerals of both Charles and Mary Lamb.

Sadler, Thomas, 1822–91. Divine. Educated at University College, London. Studied at Bonn and Erlangen. Minister at Rosslyn Hill Chapel, Hampstead, where he remained from 1846 until his death. Because of his knowledge of German universities he was entrusted with the editorship of Crabb Robinson's *Diary*. In 1869 Sadler published *The Diary, Reminiscences and Correspondence of Henry Crabb Robinson* (selections) in three volumes. A revised edition, the third, in two volumes appeared in 1872 with Augustus De Morgan's 'Recollections' of Robinson included. There are an enormous number of references to Charles Lamb in the *Diary*, and sometimes passages are included by Sadler that were not reprinted in the later edition of E.J. Morley. He also wrote a *Memoir of Edwin T. Field*, 1872. He was Senior Trustee of Dr Williams's Library where the *Diary* is kept and he was Visitor of Manchester New College.

Sage, Dean. American Lamb collector whose library was sold 13–14 November 1935 in New York at the American Art Association Anderson Galleries.

Sala, George Augustus, 1828–96. Journalist and novelist. Studied art and became a book illustrator and scene painter before turning to literature. Founder and editor of *Temple Bar*. Was on the staff of the

Daily Telegraph. In 1868 was published *The Correspondence and Works of Charles Lamb*, Vol. 1, with an introductory essay by G. A. Sala. No further volumes were published at this time, but subsequently this volume was re-issued with three others as *The Complete Correspondence and Works of Charles Lamb*, 1870, in which Sala's introduction was replaced by one by Thomas Purnell. W.C. Hazlitt in a footnote to his edition of the *Letters of Charles Lamb*, 1886, I.xiv, claims that he was responsible for this edition that was issued without his name.

Sala's mother, Henrietta Simon, 1789–1860 sang at Covent Garden in 1827 in Mozart's *Marriage of Figaro'*. She later acted with Braham. His brother, Charles Sala, 1823–57, was educated at Christ's Hospital and became an actor in Macready's Company.

Salary, Lamb's. When Charles Lamb was employed at the South Sea House in 1791–2 he received 10s. 6d. weekly. At the India House he received no salary for the first three years from his entry in 1792 until 1794, but was given an annual grant of £30. In 1795 his salary started at £40. By 1801 it was £100 p.a. and then rose by £10 annually until 1809 when on the transfer of William Marter to another office, Lamb received an additional £20. In 1815 it was £240, but because of the re-organization of the office work was increased to £480 in 1816. By 1819 it had reached £600 and by 1821 £700. It remained at this figure until 1825 when it was increased to £730. (Frederick Page in the notes to the O.U.P. edition of the *Last Essays of Elia*, 1929, gives the final figure as £675).

Lamb retired on 29 March 1825 and received a pension of £450 annually, less a deduction of £9 a year towards a pension for Mary Lamb. After her brother's death she received a pension from the East India Company of £120 a year. The Company had a rule that £10 of an employee's salary must be set aside each year for a holiday.

Salt, Samuel, d.1792. Barrister, Bencher and Sub-Treasurer of the Inner Temple. Called to the Bar in 1753. Elected a Bencher in 1782. He had chambers at No. 2 Crown Office Row where Charles Lamb was born. Salt was M.P. for Liskeard, Cornwall, from 1768 until 1784 and had Edward Gibbon as his fellow member for part of the time. He retired from Parliament in 1790. Salt's wife died in 1747 but he never remarried. Lamb says he was pursued unsuccessfully by Susannah Peirson, a sister of one of his fellow Benchers. He was a director of the South Sea Company and a Governor of Christ's Hospital, as well as a number of hospitals, including the Foundling Hospital. J.T. Smith in his *A Book for a Rainy Day* stated that Salt told him he was one of the four who buried Sterne, but MacKinnon seems doubtful of this.

Charles Lamb's father, John Lamb, senior, was servant and clerk to Samuel Salt for nearly forty years and in his will Salt left him £500 South Sea Stock and £200 to Mrs Lamb. He also left legacies to Susannah Peirson that included books she might choose from his library. This library was, no doubt, the 'spacious closet of good old English reading' in which Charles and Mary Lamb browsed in their childhood.

Salt was partly responsible for Lamb's entry into Christ's Hospital, the South Sea House and perhaps the East India Company as well. Miss Ann Manning in her *Family Portraits* states that Thomas Coventry placed Lamb at Christ's Hospital, so he may have joined with Samuel Salt. The actual guarantor was Timothy Yeats. Salt had also obtained for John Lamb, junior, Charles's elder brother, his position with the South Sea Company and may well have placed him in Christ's Hospital before that.

Lamb refers to Salt in his essay 'The Old Benchers of the Inner Temple'. Sir F.D. MacKinnon in *The Times Literary Supplement* of 5 June 1937 (reprinted in *Inner Temple Papers* 1948) joins issue with Lamb's picture of Salt and maintains that he was not the 'absent-minded nincompoop' of the Elia essay.

When William Plumer of Blakesware married the daughter of Viscount Falkland in 1760 Samuel Salt was one of the trustees, a fact discovered by Reginald Hine. He notes also that the Duchess of Portland referred to Salt as 'the Saline gentleman'. Lucas in the *Life* reproduces a bust of Salt modelled in wax by John Lamb. Ainger in a letter to Dykes Campbell in 1891 mentions that he had a plaster head of Salt.

Salutation and Cat. An inn at 17 Newgate Street, London, where Coleridge and Lamb used to meet about 1794–5. Coleridge stayed there for a time. The landlord was Thomas May. Lamb mentions the inn in several letters to Coleridge in 1797. It was burnt down in 1884.

Sargus, Mr. Lamb's tenant at Button Snap. When the cottage was sold in 1815 Lamb wrote to Sargus to inform him. Mrs Anderson suggested that he was an illiterate labourer since Lamb's letter had to be read to him.

Savage, Basil. Editor of *Charles Lamb Bulletin*, 1972–77, and joint editor with Mary R. Wedd, 1977–79. Contributed to the *Charles Lamb Bulletin* 'The Georgian Playhouse Exhibition', October 1975; 'Charles Lamb in Print', January 1976; 'Jane Austen Bicentenary Exhibition' April 1976; and 'Charles and Mary Lamb in Russell Street', July 1977.

Savory, Hester, 1777–1803. A young Quaker living at Pentonville about whom Lamb wrote a poem 'Hester' in 1803. She was the daughter of Joseph Savory, a Quaker goldsmith in the Strand. Lamb used to see her passing his house in Chapel Street, Pentonville, between 1800 and 1803. She married Charles Stoke Dudley in July 1802 and died in February 1803. Lamb said he had fallen in love with her although he had never spoken to her. He called her the 'Witch of Enddoor' because she lived at the last house in the street. She was buried in Bunhill Fields.

Lamb probably had her in mind when he referred to 'Beautiful Quakers of Pentonville' in his letter to Manning of 28 November 1800 in one of his eulogies of London. She had a brother, A.B. Savory, and two sisters, Anna and Martha Savory.

A Thomas Savory and a William Savory were both clerks in East India House and W.C. Hazlitt stated that William entered on the same day as Lamb. Thomas was probably the one mentioned in Lamb's letter to Coleridge of 29 June 1796; he was in the Treasurer's Office, but was transferred to the Accountant's Office. Both Thomas and William Savory resigned from the East India House. *The London Kalendar* for 1815 lists N.N. Savory as a clerk to the Private Warehouse Keeper at East India House. Lucas *Poems & Plays*, 1903, prints a portrait of Hester Savory.

Scargill, William Pitt, 1787–1836. Unitarian minister and novelist. Educated at Christ's Hospital, 1794–1802, where he was contemporary with Leigh Hunt. His novels, which were published anonymously, included *Elizabeth Evanshaw*, 1827; *Blue-Stocking Hall*, 1827; *Rank and Talent*, 1829; *Atherton*, 1831; and *The Autobiography of a Dissenting Minister*, 1832. In 1815 he had written *Essays on Various Subjects* and the following year *Moral Discourses principally intended for young People*.

The book which interests Elians most is his *Recollections of a Blue Coat Boy*, 1829, which he dedicated to Elia. In his letter of 24 October 1831 to Moxon, Lamb says, 'The Rev Mr S——. whose name you left illegible (is it *Sea-gull?*) never sent me any book on Christ's Hospital by which I could dream that I was indebted to him for a dedication'.

Cowden Clarke sent some books published by Hunt and Clarke to Lamb in May 1928, one of which Carl Woodring stated in the *Harvard Library Bulletin*, 1956, was *Penelope; or Love's Labour Lost* by Scargill; Lamb praised it, although he did not know who the anonymous author was. Mary Lamb read Scargill's *Rank and Talent* and Charles Lamb mentions it in his letter to Clarke on 2 February 1829 saying it is being read also by Mrs May (neé Mary Gisburne). Crabb Robinson mentions *Penelope* in his *Diary* on 29 May 1828.

Scargill also contributed to *The Athenaeum* essays which Edmund Blunden described as 'bold-thinking' and as helping to establish the journal.

Schneider, Duane, b.1937. Professor of English, Ohio University, Athens, Ohio. Professor Schneider is preparing a bibliography of Lamb studies, 1900–1973. Contributed 'The Lucas Edition of Lamb's Letters: Corrections and Notes' to *Notes & Queries*, May 1974.

Scott, Henry. At Christ's Hospital with Lamb, 1780–89. Referred to by Lamb in his essay 'Christ's Hospital Five and Thirty Years Ago' as 'poor S——' and noted in Lamb's Key that 'Scott, died in Bedlam'. *The Christ's Hospital Book*, 1953, prints verses by Scott 'Sic Vos Non Vobis' from James Boyer's *Liber Aureus*, 1785.

Scott, John, 1783–1821. Editor. Born at Aberdeen and educated there, where he had Byron for a schoolfellow. He came to London and became a journalist, first with *The Censor*, then as editor of *The Statesman*; and afterwards as editor of *Drakard's Paper*, the name of which was changed to *The Champion* during his editorship. He left *The Champion* in 1817 and travelled on the Continent. In 1819 Scott was offered a position with the East India Company, but he was in Italy at the time and through the delay of letters failed to get the position. Later the same year Scott accepted the editorship of Baldwin, Cradock & Joy's new monthly journal, *The London Magazine*, which began publication in January 1820 and was most successful; Scott seemed to have the ability to attract first class contributors and to draw from them some of their best work. He had in the magazine Lamb's Elia essays, Hazlitt's *Table Talk* and many other excellent contributions. He wrote much in the journal himself.

During the latter part of 1820 a quarrel developed between the *London* and *Blackwood's Magazine*. Unfortunately it became so serious that challenges to a duel were issued, at first between Scott as editor of the *London* and J.G. Lockhart as the supposed editor of *Blackwood's*. Although this duel did not materialize, a duel took place in February 1821 between Scott and Jonathan Christie, Lockhart's second, that resulted in Scott's being fatally wounded. Scott's second was P.G. Patmore, who subsequently fled to France but was acquitted at the inevitable trial.

Scott had married Caroline, a daughter of Paul Colnagi, the print dealer, and both Scott and his wife were friends of Keats and Haydon. He had probably met Lamb when the latter contributed to *The Champion*; it was during his editorship of the *London* that Lamb began to contribute his Elia essays, starting in August 1820. A few notes exist from Lamb to Scott. There is no doubt that John Scott was an editor of genius and that he published some of Charles Lamb's best work.

Scott wrote *A Visit to Paris in 1814*, 1815, and *Paris Revisited by Way of Brussels in 1815*, 1816, both of which Thackeray described in *The Newcomes* as 'famous good reading'. Scott's portrait by Seymour Kirkup is in the National Gallery of Scotland, Edinburgh.

Scott, Sir Walter, 1771–1832. Poet, novelist, critic and biographer. Educated at Edinburgh High School and Edinburgh University. Became an advocate. His son-in-law was John Gibson Lockhart.

Haydon records in his *Memoirs* that Lamb and Scott met at breakfast at his studio on 7 March 1821 when Procter and Wilkie were there. A few years earlier Scott had invited Lamb to Abbotsford, but there is no record that he went. Scott's name occurs from time to time in Lamb's letters and in October 1822 Lamb appealed to Scott for a subscription for Godwin. Scott sent £10 to Lamb who replied on 29 October 1822 thanking him for the donation and for a renewal of his invitation to visit him.

Scribner, Charles, 1854–1930. American publisher. Educated at the College of New Jersey (Princeton). Chairman of Scribners. A great lover of books, his Lamb collection was one of the three most important of his time, the other two being those of A. Edward Newton and J.A. Spoor. The Scribner Collection was presented to Princeton University by his son in memory of his father. See description of the collection by J.S. Finch in *Princeton University Chronicle*, 1945 and 1946.

Seward, Edmund, c. 1771–95. Friend of Robert Southey and with him at Balliol College, Oxford. Seward matriculated in 1789. In 1793 he accompanied Southey on a walking tour of the Cotswolds to Evesham and Worcester. He was one of those who agreed to join in the scheme of Pantisocracy, but he was of a prudent nature and subsequently expressing doubts withdrew in 1794. When he died in 1795 Southey wrote a poem entitled 'The Dead Friend'. In a letter to Grosvenor Bedford on 15 June 1795 Southey wrote 'he taught me all that I have of good'. Although there is no record that Seward and Lamb ever met, the latter must have heard about Seward when his friends were full of the Pantisocracy scheme.

Shelley, Mary Wollstonecraft, 1797–1851. Novelist. Daughter of William Godwin and his first wife, Mary Wollstonecraft, In 1814 she left England for the Continent with Percy Bysshe Shelley, but they returned in the following year and were married in 1816 on the death of Shelley's first wife. They went to Italy again in 1818 and were there until 1822 when Shelley was drowned. Mary Shelley returned to England in 1823.

As Godwin's daughter she would have known the Lambs from her childhood and, although Lamb did not much like Shelley, his feelings for Mary Shelley were kind. In 1823 he wrote to her to ask her to tea when the Novellos were coming. In July 1827 his letter to her mentions he is at work on his play *The Wife's Trial* and he adds that he is teaching Latin to Emma Isola 'Tis like feeding a child with chopped hay from a spoon. Sisyphus his labours were as nothing to it'. Lucas in *Letters*, 1935, III.111, prints a letter from Mary Shelley to Mary Lamb.

Mary Shelley's best known work is her novel *Frankenstein*, 1818, but she also wrote *Valperga*, 1823; *The Last Man*, 1826; *The Fortunes of Perkin Warbeck*, 1830; *Lodore*, 1835; and *Falkner*, 1837. She edited Shelley's poems in 1839. Her son, Percy, succeeded to the baronetcy when his grandfather died in 1844.

Shelley, Percy Bysshe, 1792–1822. Poet and dramatist. Educated at Eton and University College, Oxford. He was expelled from the University with his friend T. Jefferson Hogg, for issuing a pamphlet *The Necessity of Atheism*. He married Harriet Westbrook in 1811, but eloped to the Continent with Mary Godwin in 1814. They were married in 1816 and Shelley was drowned in Italy in 1822.

Although Shelley admired Lamb, the liking was not returned, and Lamb is said to have actively disliked Shelley and thought little of most of his poetry. He made disparaging remarks on Shelley in his letter to Barton of 9 October 1822.

Shelley's poem 'Letter to Mary Gisborne' has some lines following his description of Leigh Hunt that appear to refer to Lamb, although he is not actually named. They refer to 'his eternal puns'. Leigh Hunt writing to Shelley on 8 July 1819 about the latter's poem 'Rosalind and Helen' in *The Examiner* said 'I was rejoiced to find also that Charles Lamb was full of it'. Shelley praised Lamb's *Rosamund Gray*.

Shepard, Ernest Howard, b.1879. Artist. Illustrated *Everybody's Lamb*, 1933, the selection of Lamb's essays, letters and miscellaneous prose edited by A.C. Ward.

Shepard was educated at St Paul's School and studied at the Royal Academy Schools. He exhibited at the Royal Academy in 1901 and drew for *Punch* from 1907, being elected to the Punch Table in 1921. He has illustrated many books, including work by A.A. Milne and Kenneth Grahame. His best known illustrations are to *Winnie the Pooh*, 1926; *Everybody's Pepys*, 1926; *The Golden Age*, 1928; *Everybody's Boswell*, 1930; *Dream Days* 1930; and *The Wind in the Willows*, 1931. He is noted for the delicacy of his touch and the firmness of his line.

Shepherd, Richard Herne, 1842–95. Bibliographer and editor. In 1861 he published an essay on 'The School of Pantagruel' and later edited Blake's *Poems*, Shelley's *Poems*, Chapman's *Works* and a number of other works. In 1872 he edited *Poetry for Children* by

Charles and Mary Lamb, published in a beautiful little edition by Basil Montagu Pickering. In 1877 he issued a revised edition following the discovery of the complete book in Australia. In 1874 he issued *The Complete Works in Prose and Verse of Charles Lamb* in which he reproduced the original text as far as he could. He included a facsimile of a page of the essay 'A Dissertation upon Roast Pig'. In 1878 his *Waltoniana* appeared, described as 'an agreeable pasticcio of biographical and bibliographical gossip'. In 1879 he obtained £150 damages from *The Athenaeum* for an 'injurious review' of his revised edition of Lamb's *Poetry for Children*.

Shepherd, Thomas Hosmer, c. 1817–42. Topographical artist. He did a large number of drawings of London in the early nineteenth century. A first series was published in 1829 entitled *London and its Environs in the Nineteenth Century*, which reproduces the drawings of many places well known to Lamb and as he saw them. The text was by James Elmes. The book was reprinted in 1970. We owe to Shepherd's industry many drawings of important buildings long since swept away. Many hundreds of his drawings are in the British Museum.

Sheridan, Thomas, 1775–1817. Poet. Son of Richard Brinsley Sheridan. At one time he held a commission in the Army, but later became an assistant to his father, who he was very like, having all his extravagant ways. He was appointed Colonial Paymaster at the Cape of Good Hope in the hope that his health might improve, but he died there.

In a letter from Mary Lamb to Sarah Hazlitt on 10 December 1808 she says Charles Lamb has written some scenes in a 'speaking pantomime', the rest to be done by Tom Sheridan and his father. She says Charles's share is done and sent in.

Tom Sheridan married Caroline Callander, a noted beauty. Of her Frances Kemble said 'Mrs Sheridan, the mother of the Graces, more beautiful than anybody but her daughters'. She was the authoress of three novels.

Sherlock, William P., fl.1800–20. Artist, son of William Sherlock, the portrait painter. Exhibited at the Royal Academy 1801–10, particularly water colours. He illustrated Dickinson's *Antiquities of Nottinghamshire*, 1801–6, and did etchings of his own works and those of David Cox and Thomas Girtin. His series of water colours of London views are in the British Museum. He has been described as an artist of considerable merit.

On 15 November 1834 Lamb wrote to Sherlock in reply to a request, stating that the portrait done for Dr Stoddart was not in Lamb's possession. W.C. Hazlitt in *The Lambs*, 1897, notes against this letter 'Probably the Macmillan copy', and Lucas thinks this may refer to the Hazlitt portrait in the National Portrait Gallery or to the slightly different replica.

Shore, William Teignmouth, b.1865. Author and editor. Wrote under the pseudonym of 'E.G.O.' Was editor of *The Academy and Literature* from 1903 to 1905. Author of *Egomet by E.G.O.*, 1905, which contains references to Lamb by one who was well versed in Elia's works and who loved old books and old times. (See 'Egomet: A Lover of Charles Lamb' by Claude A. Prance in *C.L.S. Bulletin*, October 1971). Shore also wrote books on Dickens, Count D'Orsay and Shakespeare and contributed to the *Fortnightly Review*.

Siddons, Henry, 1774–1815. Actor and theatre manager. Eldest son of the famous Mrs Siddons. Educated at Charterhouse. Joined Covent Garden company where he first appeared in 1801 and remained with them until 1805, when he moved to Drury Lane. In 1809 he became manager of the Edinburgh Theatre where he received the encouragement of Sir Walter Scott. His ability as an actor has been questioned and is said to have suffered by comparison with his relatives, the Kembles. Perhaps his greatest success was the stranger in Thompson's play of that name in 1797 (or Sheridan's amended version). He married Harriet Murray, an excellent actress who played at Covent Garden and Drury Lane with success.

Lamb praised Henry Siddons as Edgar in his review of Cooke's *Lear* in the *Morning Post* on 9 January 1802. He played in Holcroft's *Vindictive Man* at Drury Lane on 20 November 1806 when it failed, as Lamb related in a letter to Manning at Canton. Siddons wrote several plays, for one of which *Time's A Tell Tale*, 1807, Charles Lamb wrote an epilogue, but the play was received badly and Lamb's epilogue was replaced by another on the second night. It was produced at Drury Lane and Harriot Mellon played the leading part of Lady Delmar. Siddons also published *Practical Illustrations of Rhetorical Gesture and Action, adapted to the English Drama* in 1807.

Siddons, Sarah, 1755–1831. Actress, daughter of Roger Kemble and sister of J.P. Kemble and Charles Kemble. She was said to have been the greatest tragic actress of the English stage. She married William Siddons, also an actor. Among her close friends were Mrs Piozzi and Sir Thomas Lawrence. Her first great success in London was as Isabella in *The Fatal Marriage*, but her most famous part was Lady Macbeth, and she dominated the stage for many years.

Lamb and Coleridge seem to have combined in writing a sonnet to her in 1794 which was printed in volumes of poems by both of them. In his essay 'My First Play' Lamb mentions seeing Mrs Siddons in

Isabella and refers to her in 'On the Custom of Hissing at the Theatre' and in the essay 'On the Tragedies of Shakespeare'. Lamb's mother is said to have borne a physical resemblance to Mrs Siddons.

Hazlitt in his *Characters of Shakespeare's Plays* writing of Mrs Siddons as Lady Macbeth said 'We can conceive of nothing grander. It was something above nature. It seemed almost as if a being of a superior order had dropped from a higher sphere to awe the world with the majesty of her appearance. Power was seated on her brow, passion emanated from her breast as from a shrine; she was tragedy personified ... To have seen her in that character was an event in every one's life, not to be forgotten'.

Simmons, Ann. Said to be the 'Alice W——' of Lamb's essays and the 'Anna' of his sonnets. Lucas said that Ann Simmons lived at Blenheims, near Blakesware. She married a silversmith and pawn-broker named John Thomas Bartram of Princes Street, Leicester Square. Southey mentions in a letter to his wife on 16 May 1799 that Lamb told him he had dined with his Anna after she was married. It is thought that Lamb's love for Ann Simmons was discouraged by Mrs Field, his grandmother, on the grounds of insanity in the Lamb family. References in Lamb's works that may be to Ann Simmons are in 'Dream Children' and in 'New Year's Eve', Alice W——n; in 'Love Sonnets', Fair-hair'd maid and Anna; in 'Dramatic Fragments: the Dying Lover', Anna; and in 'The Old Familiar Faces', Fairest among women.

Reginald Hine in his *Charles Lamb and his Hertfordshire* states that J.T. Bartram came probably from Hertfordshire. Ann Bartram had two daughters and one son; one daughter, Maria, married William Coulson, the surgeon and brother of Lamb's friend, Walter Coulson.

Skepper, Anne Benson, 1799–1888. Daughter of Mrs Skepper, the third wife of Basil Montagu. She married B.W. Procter in 1824. Mrs Procter was a lady of strong character, a witty and delightful talker said to have had few equals and no superior in her day. Although possessing a caustic wit she had great kindness of heart. For much of their early married life the Procters lived with the Montagus. She is said to have piqued herself on being as good a hater as she was a friend, and Lamb loved a good hater. Her youthfulness in old age is commemorated in James Russell Lowell's verses to her:

> I know a young girl of seventeen
> Who tells me she is seventy.

Mrs Procter knew most of the celebrated people of her day. Both she and her husband were friends of the Lambs and as Anne Skepper she was known to them before her marriage. In his essay 'Oxford in the

Vacation' Lamb writes of 'Mrs M ... with pretty A.S. at her side'. Charles Dickens said that no matter how brilliant the men were who surrounded her—and they were all that London had of the best— she always gave the last and wittiest rejoinder. *See also* B.W. Procter.

Smith, Harry Bache. Famous American librettist, playwright and book collector. Music critic, dramatic critic and author of the words and lyrics of more than two hundred comic operas and musical comedies. Author of *A Sentimental Library*, 1914, which describes his famous collection of association copies of books and other items. Among them were Lamb's copy of Drayton, with nineteen folio pages filled with Lamb's writing; A.L.S. to Fanny Kelly; a copy of *Works*, 1818, inscribed by Lamb to her; *Essays of Elia*, 1823, inscribed to her; and the manuscript of 'Dream Children'. Many other notable books were included, such as *Pickwick Papers* inscribed to Mary Hogarth, the manuscript of Keats's 'On First Looking into Chapman's Homer', and numerous MSS, ALSS and first editions of other authors. The whole collection was bought by Dr Rosenbach in 1914· for $79,000.

In 1936 a sale catalogue of Smith's collection of nineteenth century authors was issued by the Anderson Galleries, which included more Lamb items, among them some ALSS and many valuable items of Coleridge, De Quincey, Hazlitt and Leigh Hunt, as well as Claire Clairmont's Journal of 1818. Smith contributed to *Scribner's Magazine*, the *Century*, *Harpers* and the *Atlantic Monthly* and he was the author of *Will Shakespeare: Player*, 1893; *Lyrics and Sonnets*, 1894; *Stage Lyrics*; *Early Letters of Charles Dickens*; *First Nights and First Editions*; and *I Knew Them When*.

Smith, Herbert Grant, 1883–1974. Lamb scholar and collector. Editor of the *C.L.S. Bulletin*, 1948–72. Author of *Houses with Memories: A Series of Elian Cameos*, verses read to the Charles Lamb Society on 10 July 1948, but not published. Much of his writing appears in reports and accounts of meetings in the *Bulletin*. He contributed to *John O'London's Weekly* on 8 March 1946 an article 'Charles Lamb and His Bible'. This was an address delivered to the Charles Lamb Society in November 1945; it was reprinted privately in December 1968 as a pamphlet. He also contributed to the same journal on 4 February 1949 a letter entitled 'Lamb's Rent' and on 18 February 1949 one entitled 'Why Lamb Flitted'.

Smith, Horace, 1779–1849. Poet and novelist. Was first a City merchant and insurance broker, but later became a stock broker. With his brother, James Smith, a solicitor, he published in 1812 the enormously successful *Rejected Addresses*, which comprised humorous addresses supposed to have been submitted for the reopening of Drury Lane Theatre after its rebuilding.

Horace Smith was a friend of Shelley, Keats, Leigh Hunt, Charles Mathews, Barron Field and John Scott, the editor of the *London Magazine*. When Scott was involved in the fatal duel in 1821, he asked Smith to be his second, but the latter could not act and P.G. Patmore took his place.

Smith contributed poems and prose to the *London Magazine*, some of which was reprinted in his *Gaieties and Gravities* in 1825. He also wrote in 1813 *Horace in London* with his brother, *Brambletye House*, 1826, and *The Tin Trumpet*, 1836.

Charles Lamb in a letter to Wordsworth of 26 April 1819 referred to 'the sneering brothers—the vile Smiths'. There had been a parody of Wordsworth entitled 'The Baby's Debut' in the *Rejected Addresses*. Perhaps Lamb later overcame his dislike, for when writing to James Kenney in 1822 he says he has agreed to meet Moore at Horace Smith's house, but the meeting did not take place then. There is also a reference to Smith in a letter of J. Howard Payne in January 1823. In July 1824 he tells his friend Marter that the best of the items in the *New Monthly Magazine* are by Horace Smith.

Smith, John Thomas, 1766–1833. Son of Nathaniel Smith, principal assistant to Joseph Nollekens, the eccentric sculptor. As a youth John Smith was a pupil of Nollekens and later became his assistant. In 1798 he applied for the position of drawing master at Christ's Hospital, but did not obtain it, in spite of the support of his application by half the artists in London it would seem by the list printed in his *A Book for a Rainy Day*.

In 1816 he became Assistant Keeper of the Drawings and Prints at the British Museum, a position he retained for the rest of his life. Among the books he wrote were *Ancient Topography of London*, 1815; *Vagabondiana or Etchings of remarkable Beggars*, 1815–17; *The Streets of London*; and a number of other works on London. His *Nollekens and his times* appeared in 1828 and *A Book for a Rainy Day* in 1845. In the latter book Smith refers to his 'friend Charles Lamb'. Lucas was unable to trace any reference to Smith made by Lamb, but in the British Museum there is a framed autograph poem by Lamb dated 9 August 1830 and addressed 'To J.T. Smith, Keeper of Prints at the British Museum'. Probably Lamb's poem was contributed for Smith's album, which also contained verses on Shakespeare by Elizabeth Benger, the friend of George Dyer.

Smith stated in his *Rainy Day* book that Samuel Salt told him he was one of the four who buried Sterne. Smith claimed to be a friend of Colonel Phillips, Lamb's friend who had sailed with Captain Cook and who knew Dr Johnson.

Smith, Mrs. 'The biggest woman in Cambridge' is how Lamb described her in his letter of 8 January 1821 to Dorothy Wordsworth, and he elaborates on her size and activities. In his paper 'The Gentle Giantess' in the *London Magazine* in December 1822 he further describes her under the name of the Widow Blacket of Oxford. Crabb Robinson records in *Diary* for 18 July 1820 that when at Cambridge on circuit he played whist with Mrs Smith and the Lambs who were staying there.

Smith, Percy J. Typographer. In 1910 he issued a privately published booklet reprinting Charles Lamb's *The Child Angel: A Dream*. It was printed at the Chiswick Press and the pictures and other decorations were drawn and engraved on wood by Percy J. Smith. Five hundred copies only were printed on handmade paper. In 1935 Holbrook Jackson gave an opening speech at an exhibition of Percy Smith's typographical work at the First Edition Club.

Smith, William, ?1730–1819. English actor known as 'Gentleman Smith', because of his elegant appearance and manners. Educated at Eton and St John's College, Cambridge. He was sent down from Cambridge and took to the stage, first appearing at Covent Garden in 1753. He moved to Drury Lane in 1774 and in 1777 was the first Charles Surface, his best part. He also played as Macbeth with Mrs Siddons. He retired in 1788, but in 1789 reappeared as Charles Surface for the benefit of his friend, Tom King, the original Sir Peter Teazle. Smith married a sister of Lord Sandwich, which elicited Foote's quip, 'Art thou not Romeo, *and a* Montague?' (Montagu was the family name of Lord Sandwich).

Lamb refers to him in his piece 'Miss Kelly at Bath' in *Felix Farley's Bristol Journal* in 1819. In his essay 'On the Artificial Comedy of the last Century' Lamb says Smith had retired by the time he first saw *The School for Scandal* and the part was taken by John Kemble. Mary Lamb mentions him as 'our old neighbour' in her letter of 23 December 1806 to Mrs Clarkson and adds 'I well remember him the first season of the *School for Scandal*; he was ("I being a young thing then") a prodigious favourite with me'.

Sotheran. In 1934–35 Henry Sotheran Ltd., booksellers of 43 Piccadilly, London, issued No. 13 of their *Piccadilly Notes* devoted to Charles Lamb Centenary Number. It included pages from Emma Isola's Album and many rare items by and concerning Charles Lamb. Facsimiles are given of many of them. A Supplement was issued that included a silhouette portrait of Emma Isola. The collection was priced at £1,150.

South Sea House. The South Sea Company was incorporated in 1710 by an act that gave it the monopoly of trading in the Pacific

Ocean and along the East coast of South America. The famous Bubble was the financial scheme proposed by the company to the Government whereby the Directors offered to pay off part of the National Debt in return for the exclusive right of trading in the South Seas. The scheme came to grief in 1720, but the company continued to exist until well in the nineteenth century. The monopoly came to an end in 1806 and the company itself in 1853.

The Old South Sea House building was in Old Broad Street, but was vacated by the company in the middle of the eighteenth century and let as offices and dwelling apartments, when it moved to Threadneedle Street. The latter was the office known to Charles Lamb, who worked there as a clerk in the Examiner's Office from 1 September 1791 to 8 February 1792 at a salary of 10s.6d. a week. His brother, John Lamb, had entered the South Sea Company about 1778 and by 1792 was Deputy Accountant and subsequently became Accountant with a suite of rooms allotted to him.

The old building in Old Broad Street was destroyed by fire in 1826 and the City Club was built on the site; that in Threadneedle Street was re-built in 1902–3 as offices for the British Linen Bank.

Among the directors of the South Sea Company were some of Lamb's 'Old Benchers', including Thomas Coventry, Peter Peirson and Samuel Salt, Peirson being also Deputy Governor and Salt a Sub-Governor. Richard Johnson was Standing Counsel for the company. Another director was Joseph Paice who was largely responsible for Charles Lamb's entry there.

The old clerks mentioned by Lamb in his famous essay 'The South Sea House were William Evans, cashier; John Tipp, accountant before John Lamb; Henry Man, deputy secretary; Richard Plumer, deputy secretary after Man; Thomas Maynard, chief clerk in the Old Annuities and Three Per Cents; and Thomas Taine, deputy cashier. By the time Lamb's essay appeared the South Sea Company no longer traded, but only received interest on its capital with the Government. F. Augustus Elia was the Italian clerk at South Sea House from whom Lamb took his famous pseudonym.

Southampton Buildings, Chancery Lane. Lamb moved to 27 Southampton Buildings, Chancery Lane, Holborn, in the summer of 1800. His old schoolfellow, J.M. Gutch, who was a law stationer there offered the Lambs rooms. As Lamb said in his letter to Coleridge (probably in July), Gutch knew their story and Mary Lamb's liability to further attacks of insanity, and his kindness was much appreciated. Lamb was pleased with the accommodation which comprised three rooms (including servant) for less than £34 a year. Six weeks after the move Mary Lamb rejoined her brother after recovering from one of her attacks. On Ladyday 1801 the Lambs left this address to move to 16 Mitre Court, Inner Temple. Again in 1809 the

Lambs came to Southampton Buildings from March to the end of May, but this time to No. 34.

Several of the houses in these buildings have associations with Lamb's friends: Hazlitt lived at No. 9 in 1820 at the house of Mr Walker, a tailor, whose daughter, Sarah, was the cause of Hazlitt's infatuation as related in his *Liber Amoris*; the Southampton Coffee House was situated at No. 21, where Hazlitt spent much of his time and where he wrote his essay 'Coffee House Politicians'; John Rickman had rooms at No. 33 in 1800 and was there introduced to Lamb by George Dyer, as Lamb tells Manning in his letter of 3 November 1800.

In July 1830 the Lambs, who were then living at Enfield, again stayed at 34 Southampton Buildings until November of that year. The landladies were the Misses Buffam and the Lambs used these rooms as their headquarters on their occasional visits to London, as did Emma Isola. In a letter of 3 February 1831 to Moxon, Lamb asks him to collect some books he had left at Miss Buffam's, some to be returned to Novello and some to Talfourd. His last known letter, on 22 December 1834 to Mrs George Dyer, mentions a book of Cary's that he had collected from Miss Buffam's house.

Southampton Buildings have been rebuilt since Lamb's day, but both Lamb and Hazlitt were represented in a series of medallions of famous men formerly on the outside of the new building; the Lamb medallion was moved in 1965 to Button Snap, Hertfordshire, when further rebuilding took place.

Southern, Henry, 1799–1853. Journalist, editor and diplomat. Entered Trinity College, Cambridge, in 1814; later a member of one of the Inns of Court, but not called to the Bar. Founded and edited *The Retrospective Review*, 1820–28, the last two years with Nicholas Harris Nicolas, was co-editor of the *Westminster Review* with John Bowring from 1824, and editor of *The London Magazine* from 1825–28. He also contributed to *The Atlas*, *Spectator*, and *Examiner*. In 1833 he went as private secretary to the English Ambassador to Spain. He became Minister to the Argentine Confederation in 1848 and went to Brazil in 1851.

After Taylor & Hessey sold *The London Magazine* to Southern in 1825 Lamb continued to contribute for a time, but he had almost ceased by the end of the year: a few items appeared in 1826 which may be by Lamb. However, during 1825 Southern printed in the *London* such essays as 'Barbara S——', 'The Last Peach', 'The Superannuated Man', 'The Wedding' and 'The Convalescent'.

Southern was known to Crabb Robinson, Basil Montagu and J.H. Reynolds, as well as to Lamb. Robinson records a party at his rooms which included Southern, Barron Field and Carlyle and notes 'Southern left the party because he could not endure Carlyle.'

Southey, Robert, 1774–1843. Poet. Born at Bristol and educated at Westminster School from which he was expelled. He was later at Balliol College, Oxford. As a young man he was an ardent believer in the utopian scheme of Pantisocracy with his friend Coleridge, whom he had first met in 1794. Later in life he became a Tory. In 1795 he married Edith Fricker, whose sister Sara had just married Coleridge. He then went to Portugal to his uncle, but returned in 1796 and settled in Bristol. In 1803 he and his family moved to Greta Hall, Keswick, where Coleridge lived with them. When Coleridge left his family Southey was largely responsible for their support. He was appointed Poet Laureate in 1813.

He wrote many poems, of which the shorter ones are best known today. His outstanding work was his *Life of Nelson*, 1813. but he was a voluminous writer and his books included *A History of the Peninsula War*, 1823–32, and the fascinating volumes of *The Doctor* published anonymously, 1834–47. He was also a frequent writer in the *Quarterly Review*.

Lamb and Southey first met in 1795 and in time became firm friends. Southey was mentioned with Lamb in the attack made by *The Anti-Jacobin* in 1798. The two were in contact for most of their lives and Lamb gave Southey a copy of his *Works* in 1818. The only difference of opinion seems to have been in 1823 when Southey writing in the *Quarterly Review* remarked that Lamb's *Elia* volume lacked a sound religious feeling. This brought forth Lamb's famous 'Letter of Elia to Robert Southey Esquire' in the *London Magazine* for October 1823. Southey did not resent this and wrote a kind letter direct to Lamb in reply, so that all antagonism between them was forgotten.

There are numerous letters between the two authors that show their liking for one another and that they had a considerable number of friends in common. When William Jerdan criticized Lamb's *Album Verses* adversely in the *Literary Gazette* in 1830 Southey published verses in *The Times* defending Lamb. Among Southey's closest friends were John Rickman, Wordsworth and Grosvenor Bedford.

Southwold, Stephen, 1887–1964. Novelist who wrote mostly under the name of 'Neil Bell'. Author of *So Perish the Roses*, 1940, a novel on the life of Charles Lamb. It is stated in the Author's Note to this book that Lamb 'died, to leave behind him, contrived without set purpose by his friends for his memorial, the most spurious legend that has ever distorted the truth and betrayed a man of genius'. In this novel the suggestion is made that Charles Lamb was in love with Emma Isola. Other books include *Cover his Face*, 1943, a novel on the life of Chatterton and many other novels. His autobiography *My Writing Life* appeared in 1955.

Spoor, John A. American book collector of Chicago. The possessor of a notable library among which was his famous Lamb collection, said to be the greatest Lamb library in private hands when his books came up for sale in 1939. His collection had formed the basis of Luther S. Livingston's *A Bibliography of the First Editions in Book Form of the Writings of Charles and Mary Lamb*, 1903.

The sale of his library took place on April 26–8 and May 3–5, 1939, at the Parke Bernet Galleries in New York. The Lamb material comprised items 517–57 and realized a total of $33,685. Among these the outstanding item was Emma Isola's Album, which itself fetched $22,700. Other important items were John Lamb's *Poetical Pieces*; Charles Lamb's own copy of his will in his handwriting; *The King and Queen of Hearts*, 1806; *Tales from Shakespeare*, 1807; *Poetry for Children*, 1809; and the famous interleaved copy of Wither. There were also many other first editions in original boards. The sale catalogue of this collection, which is in two parts, is full of valuable bibliographical information and contains some facsimiles, including the first page of Emma Isola's Album, Lamb's will, a MS list of his works and Keats's sonnet 'To my Brother' from the Album.

Starkey, Benjamin. Usher at William Bird's Academy in Fetter Lane. William Hone in his *Every-Day Book* for 9 July 1825 gave extracts from a pamphlet issued by Starkey in 1818, *Memoirs of the Life of Benj. Starkey, late of London, but now an inmate of the Freeman's Hospital, in Newcastle*. This pamphlet gave Lamb the idea for his paper on 'Captain Starkey' which appeared in the *Every-Day Book* on 21 July 1825. Both Charles and Mary Lamb had attended Mr Bird's Academy.

Stephens, Catherine, 1794–1882. English singer and actress. Studied under Gesualdo Lanza and Thomas Welsh. Performed in the provinces and first appeared at Covent Garden in September 1813 as Mandane in Arne's *Artaxerxes* and in October as Polly in the *Begger's Opera* at Drury Lane. She played mainly at Covent Garden, 1813–22, and in Elliston's company at Drury Lane, 1823–7. Among her best parts were Ophelia, Desdemonia and Polly. In the latter part she was praised highly by both Hazlitt and Leigh Hunt. She was a great favourite with the former. Talfourd also remarked that she was as attractive in 1830 as when he first saw her in 1814 in *Love in a Village* at Covent Garden. She also had a successful career as a concert soprano.

Lamb mentions her in his review of Barron Field's *Poems* in *The Examiner* in 1820. She retired in 1835 and in 1838 married the fifth Earl of Essex. She was a close friend of Fanny Kelly, a lifetime friendship that lasted until they both died in 1882, aged 88 and 92 respectively.

Stephens, Rev. Lancelot Pepys, 1766–1833. (Spelt 'Stevens' by Lamb). Schoolmaster. Educated at Christ's Hospital from 1774–84, then proceeded to Pembroke College, Cambridge. He returned to Christ's Hospital as Under Grammar Master and as Feilde's successor. Lamb says he was the 'First Grecian' of his time, 'kindest of boys and men'. He and A.W. Trollope were said to be inseparable companions. He was a master at Christ's Hospital when Leigh Hunt was there and he describes him as 'short and fat, with a handsome cordial face'. Miss Mann has discovered that Stephens was the son of the keeper of Tom's Coffee House in Devereux Court and Thomas Coventry's protégé at the school (*C.L.S. Bulletin*, No. 198).

Stevens, John Edgar, b.1921. Professor of Medieval and Renaissance English, University of Cambridge. Educated at Christ's Hospital and Magdalene College, Cambridge. Gave Crowsley Memorial Lecture on 'The Romantic Humourist' to the Charles Lamb Society in 1977. President of Charles Lamb Society from 1980.

Stevenson, Miss. Actress. She later became Mrs Wiepperts. Mentioned by Lamb in his review in *The Examiner* in July 1819 of Richard Brome's 'Jovial Crew' as 'a fine open-countenanced lass, with glorious girlish manners'. In the same journal in August in reviewing 'New Pieces at the Lyceum' he wrote 'Miss Stevenson with her delicious mixture of the school-girl and the waiting maid.' She is also mentioned in his letter in February 1823 to John Howard Payne as suitable for Payne's play *Grandpa* had she been younger. She played Melesinda in the performance of *Mr H——* organized by Charles James Mathews in 1822.

Stoddard, Richard Henry, 1825–1903. American poet and critic. Literary editor of the *New York Mail & Express*. In 1875 he edited *Personal Recollections of Lamb, Hazlitt and Others*, New York, in the Bric-a-Brac series, which reprints P.G. Patmore's reminiscences of these authors, as well as some of those of W.C. Hazlitt concerning his grandfather. The 'Others' of the title are Thomas Campbell and the Countess of Blessington. Other volumes in the same series, edited by Stoddard, included Moore and Jerdan and Dickens and Thackeray. Stoddard published his *Recollections Personal and Literary* in 1903.

Stoddart, Sir John, 1773–1856. Barrister of Lincoln's Inn and journalist. Educated at Salisbury Grammar School and Christ's Church, Oxford. In 1803 went to Malta as Judge Advocate and remained there until 1807. Coleridge went to Malta during this time as private secretary to Sir Alexander Ball, the Governor, and at first stayed with Stoddart, but eventually they quarrelled and parted. Stoddart became leader writer of *The Times* in 1812, but his extreme opinions and diatribes against Napoleon that persisted after hostilities ceased brought about a quarrel with Walter, and Stoddart left the paper in 1817. He started a rival journal *The Day and New Times*, subsequently altered to *The New Times* and remained its editor for a number of years. In 1826 he again went to Malta and became Chief Justice and Justice of Vice Admiralty Court. He was knighted in 1826.

Stoddart translated some of Schiller's works in 1796 and 1798 and from the French an *Account of the Committee of Public Safety* in 1797. At one time he wrote for the *Glasgow Herald*. In 1801 he published *Remarks on the Local Scenery and Manners of Scotland*. Originally a Jacobin in politics he later changed his views. His hatred of Napoleon earned him the nickname of 'Dr Slop'. He has been described, however, as a thoroughly upright man.

John Stoddart became Lamb's bondsman at East India House in 1821 on the death of John Lamb. Both Charles and Mary Lamb were friendly with Stoddart and particularly with his sister, Sarah, who became William Hazlitt's first wife. He is mentioned in several of their letters and Lamb wrote an amusing letter to Stoddart on 9 August 1827 full of news of his friends.

Stoddart disliked his brother-in-law, William Hazlitt, although it was from his house that his sister was married. Stoddart married Isabella, daughter of Rev. Sir Henry Moncrieff, Bart. She wrote tales under the name of 'Mrs Blackford' between 1823 and 1850.

Stoddart, Sarah, c.1775–1842. Sister of Sir John Stoddart and first wife of William Hazlitt. She was the daughter of Lieutenant John Stoddart, R.N. (retired) of Salisbury. She was a close friend of Mary Lamb and there are a number of letters to her from the Lambs. She sometimes stayed with them in London. In 1804 she went to Malta to stay with her brother and was there during the time Coleridge was in Malta.

She made several attempts to get married before she met Hazlitt as Mary Lamb's letters show. She and William Hazlitt were married on 1 May 1808 at St Andrews Church, Holborn; Charles Lamb and her brother and his wife were present and Mary Lamb was bridesmaid. It was originally intended that she should be married from the Lambs' but her brother insisted it should be from his house. She had inherited some property from her father. She was divorced from Hazlitt in 1822. She was described by Sir Leslie Stephen as a woman of considerable reading and vigorous understanding.

Stoke Newington. It has been suggested that Balmes House on the Kingsland Road may be the 'madhouse at Hoxton' where Charles Lamb spent six weeks in 1796. (*Islington Gazette*, 21 June 1940). In 1816 and for a few years afterwards the Lambs had lodgings at 14

Kingsland Road, Dalston. In 1820 they took rooms in Stoke Newington without giving up their Russell Street house, for the sake of rest and quiet. A letter from Mary Lamb to Mrs Novello in the Spring of 1820 is dated from 'Newington' and one dated 28 March 1820 from Mary Lamb to Fanny Kelly has the address 'Mrs Bedford's, Church Street, Newington'. Charles Lamb in his Christ's Hospital essay in the *Gentleman's Magazine* states that as a schoolboy he made excursions to the New River near Newington.

Stothard, Thomas, 1755–1834. English painter and book illustrator. In 1778 became a student at the Royal Academy. Elected A.R.A., 1792, and R.A., 1794. In 1812 he became librarian of the Royal Academy. He illustrated many books including *Peter Wilkins*, *Robinson Crusoe*, *The Pilgrim's Progress*, *The Vicar of Wakefield*, Cowper's *Poems*, the works of Richardson, Fielding, Smollett and Sterne, and with J.M.W. Turner, Samuel Rogers's *Italy* and *Poems*.

Stothard was one of Lamb's favourite artists and he wrote verses 'To T. Stothard. Esq. On His Illustrations of the Poems of Mr Rogers' that were printed in *The Athenaeum* for 21 December 1833. However Lamb preferred Blake's 'Canterbury Pilgrims' to that of Stothard. Lamb had met Stothard at the rooms of Samuel Rogers's brother, Henry. There is a record of Lamb dining at Cary's house at the British Museum when Rogers and Stothard were there. The artist at this period was doing some of the illustrations for Rogers's *Poems*, 1833, and although he was nearly stone deaf seemed to enjoy all the jollity that was going on. Stothard painted a picture of the St Matthew's Day at Christ's Hospital in 1799 (Boyer's last speech day). It is reproduced in part in Lucas's *Life*, 1905, and the whole painting in *The Christ's Hospital Book*, 1953.

Stuart, Daniel, 1766–1846. Editor. Originally apprenticed to the King's Printer, he later became Deputy Secretary of the Society of the Friends of the People. He also became a journalist and wrote for the *Morning Post* and *Argus*. In 1796 he became owner and editor of the former paper but sold it in 1802 or 1803. From 1803 to 1811 he was part owner and editor of *The Courier*. He married in 1813 Mary, daughter of Major Andrew Schalch of the Royal Artillery. In 1814 he lived in Harley Street and in 1817 bought Wykham Park, an estate near Banbury of about 300 acres. In 1822 he sold *The Courier* and retired. He became Deputy Lieutenant and in 1823 served as High Sheriff.

During Stuart's editorship of the *Morning Post* and *The Courier* he has among his contributors Lamb, Mackintosh, Wordsworth, Praed, Southey and Coleridge. In 1838 Stuart wrote anecdotes of Coleridge, Wordsworth and Lamb in the *Gentleman's Magazine*. His sister, Catherine, married Sir James Mackintosh.

Lamb's paper on G.F. Cooke in *Richard the Third* and his essay 'The Londoner', with the piece on Lear were contributed to the *Morning Post* during Stuart's editorship. Under Daniel Stuart *The Morning Post* rose to a power and prestige hitherto unattained by any other English newspaper.

Suett, Richard, 'Dicky', 1755–1805. Comedian. As a boy he sang in the choir at Westminster Abbey. In 1769 he sang at Ranelagh and he also appeared at the Grotto and Marylebone Gardens. In 1771 he joined Tate Wilkinson and remained with him for nine years, receiving the largest salary Wilkinson ever paid to an actor. In 1780 he appeared at Drury Lane, Wilkinson having generously released him from his contract to accept a tempting offer from Sheridan. He played there as Ralph in *Maid of the Well*. He also appeared at the Haymarket during the summer seasons. He was at his best when playing Shakespeare's fools.

Lamb has a long description of him as one of his favourite actors in his essay 'The Old Actors' that appeared in the *London Magazine* in October 1822. He called him the 'Robin Goodfellow of the stage'. He is also mentioned in 'On the Acting of Munden'. Leigh Hunt said he had 'a laugh like a peal of giggles'. Off the stage he was said to be melancholy but given to practical jokes and outrageous puns. There is a painting of him by John Graham in the Victoria & Albert Museum.

Sugdens. A letter of Lamb to Moxon on 14 July 1831 states 'Our next 2 Sundays will be choked up with all the Sugdens.' Philip Sugden, who married Frances Westwood, the daughter of Lamb's landlord, was a schoolmaster at Enfield, and Lamb wrote to Mrs Morgan on 17 June 1828 seeking pupils for the school that had just opened. In Harvard Library is a copy of *John Woodvil*, 1802, with an inscription, 'Mr Sugden with C. Lamb's best regards'. It had formerly belonged to James Dykes Campbell and was item 202 in his sale catalogue. Mary Lamb wrote lines in Frances Westwood's album that referred to Philip Sugden.

Swinburne, Algernon Charles, 1837–1909. Poet. Educated at Eton and Balliol College, Oxford. Among his important works were *Atalanta in Calydon*, 1865; *Poems and Ballads*, 1866; *Songs before Sunrise*, 1871; *Erechtheus*, 1876; *Poems and Ballads* (Second Series), 1878; *Tristram of Lyonesse*, 1882; and *Poems and Ballads* (Third Series), 1889. He also wrote much critical prose including volumes on Congreve, Blake, Victor Hugo and numerous introductions, as well as articles for the *Encyclopaedia Britannica*.

He was a lifelong lover of the early dramatists and said that his interest in them was due to reading Lamb's *Specimens of Dramatic*

Poets while at Eton. His letters contain a number of references to
Lamb and praise of his work. A letter of May 1867 to Gerald Massey
praises Lamb's poetry. The following year he wrote verses on Barry
Cornwall after reading Lamb's tribute to Procter in the *London
Magazine*; the verses were printed in his *Poems and Ballads* (Second
Series) with the title 'Age and Song'. In October 1882 in a letter to
A.H. Bullen he referred to 'the hideous and vilely edited six volumes
of Moxon's Lamb'.

Swinburne had possessed the copy of George Wither's poems annotated by Lamb (*see* separate entry for J.M. Gutch). He wrote an
article about it in the *Nineteenth Century* in January 1885 that was
reprinted in his *Miscellanies* in 1886 with the title of 'Charles Lamb
and George Wither'. In it he has this sentence, 'The most beloved of
English writers may be Goldsmith or may be Scott: the best beloved
will always be Charles Lamb'.

Among Swinburne's prose works that refer to Lamb are the following:

Essays and Studies, 1875 (in essay on Ford).
George Chapman: A Critical Essay, (introduction to the *Works of
     Chapman*).
Nineteenth Century, January 1886 (essay on Thomas Middleton,
     reprinted in revised form as introduction to the Mermaid
     Edition of *Middleton's Plays* and in *The Age of Shakespeare*).
Nineteenth Century, January 1887 (essay on Dekker).
The Age of Shakespeare, 1908 (dedicated to the Memory of Charles
     Lamb and containing a Dedicatory Poem about Lamb's
     Dramatic Specimens, and with references to Lamb in the
     book).

He also wrote his well known sonnet 'On Lamb's Specimens of the
Dramatic Poets' that begins

> If all the flowers of all the fields on earth
> By wonder-working summer were made one.

Swinburne was responsible for organizing the centenary Charles
Lamb Dinner on 10 February 1875 (*see* separate entry Lamb
Dinners).

Swinnerton, Frank Arthur, b.1884. Novelist and critic. At one time
on the staff of the *Manchester Guardian*, later a publisher's reader.
Has written under the name of 'John O'London' in *John O'London's
Weekly*. President of the Royal Literary Fund. He has written more
than fifty books. He assisted William Macdonald in his edition of the
Works of Charles Lamb, 1903, and in 1944 gave a talk on Macdonald
to the Charles Lamb Society. There are references to Charles Lamb

in *Swinnerton: An Autobiography*, 1937, and in *The Bookman's London*, 1951, Swinnerton devotes several pages to Lamb.

Among his contributions to *John O'London's Weekly* are: 'Lamb was not "gentle"', 18 March 1938; 'Charles Lamb's Love Story', 1 September 1950; 'Elia Again', 30 May 1952; and 'Friend of Poets' (Moxon), 20 June 1952. Swinnerton edited Hazlitt's *Conversations of James Northcote Esq. R.A.* in 1949.

Talfourd, Sir Thomas Noon, 1795–1854. Judge and dramatist. The son of a brewer at Reading, he was educated at Mill Hill School where he was the first pupil and at Reading Grammar School under Dr Valpy. He read law with Joseph Chitty, the special pleader, and was called to the Bar in 1821, became a serjeant-at-law in 1833 and a judge of the common pleas in 1849. In 1822 he married Rachel Rutt, daughter of John Towill Rutt, and one son was named Charles Lamb Talfourd. He was M.P. for Reading and in 1837 introduced the Copyright Bill (Talfourd's Act) that was passed with modifications in 1842. Charles Dickens dedicated *Pickwick Papers* to him.

Talfourd wrote much for periodicals including *The Pamphleteer*, *London Magazine*, *Retrospective Review*, *New Monthly Magazine*, *The Examiner*, *Quarterly Review*, and contributed to both the *Morning Chronicle* and the *Manchester Guardian*. His play *Ion*, 1835, was produced successfully at Covent Garden in May 1836. Other plays include *The Athenian Captive*, 1838, and *Glencoe*, 1839. He also wrote poems, *Vacation Rambles and Thoughts*, 1845, and in 1841 his famous speech in the defence of Moxon, who had been prosecuted for publishing Shelley's works, was printed.

In 1820 Talfourd wrote 'Remarks on the Writings of Charles Lamb' in the *New Monthly Magazine* and in the same year he had in the *Retrospective Review* references to Lamb in his essays on Rhymer and Wallace. In 1837 his *The Letters of Charles Lamb, with a Sketch of his Life* appeared, to be followed in 1848 by *Final Memorials of Charles Lamb*.

Talfourd met Lamb early in 1815 through William Evans, the owner of *The Pamphleteer*, and they became firm friends. Lamb introduced Talfourd to Wordsworth as 'my only admirer', and he was named as executor and trustee in both the wills Lamb made. As Lamb's friend and first biographer much valuable information about Charles and Mary Lamb is found in his writings. Talfourd lived in the Inner Temple at the time he was introduced to Lamb in rooms on the next staircase to the Lambs. After Lamb's death he did much to help Mary Lamb.

Talma, François Joseph, 1763–1826. French actor. Was educated in England. First appeared at the Comédie Française in 1787. He was the first to play Roman parts in a toga instead of a modern dress. A supporter of the French Revolution he opened the Théâtre de la République. Napoleon had a great admiration for Talma, who became one of the foremost actors on the French stage.

Lamb was introduced to him by John Howard Payne on his visit to Paris in 1822 and they had supper together. Lamb in his letter of 22 September 1822 tells Barron Field about the bellows Talma had bought with a supposed portrait of Shakespeare on it, but it was eventually proved to be a forgery by an artist named Zincke.

Tame, Thomas. Deputy cashier at the South Sea House in 1793 under William Evans. Described by Lamb in his essay 'The South Sea House'. Lucas says that Tame was appointed deputy accountant four or five years after Lamb left the Company.

Tave, Stuart Malcolm, b.1923. American Professor of English and Lamb scholar. Educated at Columbia University and Harvard. D.Phil, Oxford, 1950. Author of *The Amicable Humorist*, 1960, and *New Essays of De Quincey*, 1966. Contributed to *The English Romantic Poets and Essayists* in 1957 the valuable chapter on 'Charles Lamb—Criticism' (revised edition, 1966; third revised edition edited by Frank Jordan, 1972).

Tayler, Charles Benjamin, 1797–1875. Curate of Hadleigh, Suffolk, later Rector of Otley. Friend of Bernard Barton. Lamb tells Barton in his letter of 23 January 1824 that Tayler had called on him. Lamb liked him but found his books 'too Parsonish'. In April 1828 he asks Barton to thank Tayler for a gift of books and says he can't afford to subscribe for books. In 1823 Tayler published *May You Like It*, which Lucas says is the book referred to by Lamb. He was a voluminous writer, publishing sermons, stories, religious books and biographies. *The British Museum General Catalogue of Printed Books* has more than three pages devoted to him.

Taylor, Sir Henry, 1800–86. Dramatist. Entered the Navy, but left it to become a clerk in the Civil Service where he eventually rose to hold important appointments in the Colonial Office. He was knighted in 1872. He wrote several plays including *Isaac Commenus*, 1827, and *Philip van Artevelde*, 1834, his best known play. He also wrote poetry and prose. He was the author of the well known lyric 'If I had the wings of a dove'. He contributed to the *London Magazine* and the *Quarterly Review*.

Lamb met Taylor at a party at Gillman's in Highgate on 10 June 1824 when the latter talked of the similarities between the Christian and Mahometan religions, which produced Lamb's query on finding Taylor hunting for his hat, 'Are you looking for your turban, sir?' Later someone sent Taylor's *Philip van Artevelde* to Lamb who was not impressed with it. Taylor was a friend of Southey and accompanied him on his continental tours in 1825 and 1826. His *Autobiography* appeared in 1877.

Taylor, John, 1781–1864. Publisher and bookseller, the son of a bookseller. Originally an assistant with Lackington, he moved to Vernor & Hood and then in 1806 started his own publishing business with J.A. Hessey, whom he had met at Lackington's. The firm built up a list of authors that included Keats, Clare, Hazlitt, Lamb, Cary, Coleridge, Landor, Darley, De Quincey, Hood and Carlyle. Taylor gave some of his authors considerable help and he is particularly remembered as Keats's first publisher and for the assistance he gave John Clare. The business was carried on at 93 Fleet Street and in 1822 a further office was opened at 13 Waterloo Place.

In 1821 following the death of John Scott, Taylor & Hessey bought *The London Magazine* from Baldwin, Cradock & Joy, and shortly afterwards acquired Gold & Northhouse's *London Magazine*. Taylor acted as editor of the combined periodical, but with his work as a book publisher he found his editorial duties rather more than he could manage. Eventually the journal declined and Taylor & Hessey sold it to Henry Southern in 1825.

Taylor wrote much himself, being greatly interested in financial, economic and, particularly, currency problems and in Biblical criticism. Among his books were volumes on the identity of Junius. He wrote for the *London Magazine* 'A Visit to John Clare' in November 1821 and there are other items by him in the magazine.

As the publishers of the *London Magazine* Taylor & Hessey gave periodical dinners to their contributors which became famous. The firm's achievement in publishing in their magazine such items as Lamb's *Essays of Elia*, De Quincey's *Confessions of an English Opium-Eater* and Hazlitt's *Table Talk* give them an important position in publishing history. John Taylor seems to have been the dominant partner and the relationship with Hessey was friendly, but in 1825 they decided to dissolve partnership. Taylor continued as a publisher, mainly of educational books, and he became bookseller and publisher to the newly established London University. He retired in 1853.

A few short notes exist from Lamb to Taylor, mostly about contributions to the *London Magazine*: in that for 30 June 1821 Lamb gives the correct pronunciation of Elia as 'Ellia'. When the *Last Essays of Elia* were published by Moxon in 1833 Taylor set up a claim for copyright, but Moxon eventually won.

Taylor, William, 1765–1836. Philosopher and critic. German scholar. Lived at Norwich. A friend of George Burnett and Robert Southey, he was also known to Crabb Robinson and there are numerous references in the latter's *Diary*. He first met Robinson in

1798 and encouraged him to read German literature. He was George Borrow's instructor in German and made translations from that language as well as writing much on German literature. Robinson noted that the Lambs were at a party on 24 February 1811 when Taylor was also present.

Temple, Joan, d.1965. Actress and dramatist. Born in London. Studied at R.A.D.A. and gained the Bancroft Gold Medal. Toured the provinces and played at theatres in London, including the Kingsway, Court, New and Ambassadors. Was with J.B. Fagan's company in Manchester and played Olivia in *Twelfth Night*. The author of a number of plays including *Charles and Mary*, 1930, and *No Room at the Inn*, 1945. She is also part author of a play about Keats, produced at the Century Theatre, Westbourne Grove, in February 1936. *Charles and Mary* is a play about the Lambs in which the author played the part of Mary Lamb at the first production in 1930. On 8 July 1947 she broadcast on the B.B.C. Far Eastern Services programme 'A Talk about Charles Lamb'. *See* separate entry, Plays about Charles Lamb.

Terry, Daniel, ?1780–1829. English actor and playwright. Friend of Sir Walter Scott and James Ballantyne. Originally trained as an architect, but turned to the stage. He played in Henry Siddons's company at Edinburgh in 1809 and first appeared in London at the Haymarket in 1812 as Lord Ogleby in *The Clandestine Marriage*. In 1825 in conjunction with Frederick Yates he bought the Adelphi Theatre, but he got into financial difficulty. He played in Shakespeare and in Sheridan, and is said to have been an excellent actor who had a considerable knowledge of the older English drama.

It is likely that Lamb had him in mind in his essay 'The Religion of Actors' when he wrote 'Mr T——y ... a member of the Kirk of Scotland'. In a letter to Hone in the summer of 1825 he asks him to send his farce *The Pawnbroker's Daughter* to Terry at the Adelphi.

Theatres in Lamb's Time. From the seventeenth to the nineteenth centuries the London theatres were dominated by the two great patent houses of Drury Lane and Covent Garden, which by their old established legal monopoly restricted the activities of rival theatres largely to musical entertainments and plays given when the two giants were closed in the summer. There were, however, many attempts to by-pass the monopoly, some of which did so fairly successfully.

Towards the end of the eighteenth century the emphasis was on individual actors, but around the turn of the century and for at least the first two decades afterwards, performances tended to degenerate into elaborate productions notable mainly for the visual effect. This change was due to the enormous size of the patent theatres. Drury Lane held 3,600 people, and as Lamb's friend, John Rickman said, when the audience could not hear it wanted at least to see. Even here the poor lighting arrangements, mainly candles and oil lamps until around 1815 when gas lighting was introduced, retarded much of the actor's work. In such large theatres the actors tended to indulge in rant and bombast, which was not conducive to good acting. Obviously there were many exceptions and some fine performances, and at least some playgoers were able to describe minutely the facial expressions of the actors.

Audiences were frequently noisy and unruly, but they usually got fairly good value for their money, at least in quantity. Performances often began between 6:00 P.M. and 7:00 P.M. and generally went on until midnight, with half price after 9:00 P.M.. The programme normally contained three items: a one act play, a full length drama and a farce. At the smaller theatres there was a good deal of music in the entertainments, for a musical play with no fewer than six songs did not infringe the monopoly of the patent houses.

Living for most of his life in central London, Lamb's favourite theatres were Drury Lane and Covent Garden, but he also visited others; there are records of his attendance at the Lyceum, Olympic, Haymarket and Sadler's Wells. When living at Islington from 1823 the latter theatre was almost on his doorstep; after his retirement his visits to the theatre were reduced greatly.

In his delightful essay 'My First Play' Lamb tells of a childhood visit, but he wrote so much about the theatre that perhaps the background to the playhouses in Lamb's time is best given by listing some important theatrical events during his lifetime, the London theatres, his writings on the subject and some of his friend's plays.

That there was much discussion of the theatre in his circle is certain since he numbered among his friends actors such as Liston, Munden, Fanny Kelly, Fanny Burrell, John Philip Kemble, Charles Kemble, Charles Mathews, Elliston and Macready. Other friends included the dramatists Thomas Holcroft, James Kenney, J.S. Knowles and John Howard Payne, while he was acquainted with the theatrical managers S.J. Arnold and Richard Wroughton, and he knew Henry Robertson, the treasurer of Covent Garden and friend of the Novellos.

Many of his friends were also dramatic critics and among the foremost writers on the theatre of their time; such were Hazlitt and Leigh Hunt, while others not quite so notable included Talfourd, Hood, Reynolds, Darley and in Lamb's later years, John Forster.

The London Theatres
Theatre Royal. Drury Lane, 1663. Managers included J.P. Kemble, 1788–1802, and S.J. Arnold, 1812.

Theatre Royal. Covent Garden, 1732. Managers included J.P. Kemble, 1803–17, and Charles Kemble, 1817–32.

King's Theatre. Haymarket, 1705. Manager, W. Taylor.

Theatre Royal, 'Little Theatre in the Hay'. Haymarket, 1720.

Lyceum. Wellington Street, Strand, 1809; English Opera House from 1816. Manager, S.J. Arnold.

Olympic. Wych Street, Drury Lane, 1806.

Sadler's Wells. Near New River Head, Islington, 1753.

Surrey Theatre. St George's Fields, 1809.

Other theatres of less importance during Lamb's lifetime were the Royal Coburg, later the Old Vic, 1818; Royalty, 1787; Regency, 1815; Sans Pareil, 1806; San Souci, 1791; and Astley's Amphitheatre and Pantheon.

Memorable Theatrical Events during Lamb's Lifetime

1775   Mrs Siddons failed as Portia at Drury Lane. *The Rivals* produced at Covent Garden.

1776   Garrick retired from the stage and Drury Lane passed to Sheridan.

1777   *The School for Scandal* first produced at Drury Lane.

1780   *The Belle's Stratagem* first produced at Covent Garden.

1782   Mrs Siddons returned to Drury Lane in triumph.

1785   John Philip Kemble first appeared at Drury Lane.

1785   Mrs Jordan first appeared at Drury Lane.

1788   J.P. Kemble, actor-manager at Drury Lane.

1789   Last appearance of Charles Macklin, as Shylock.

1790   Munden first appeared at Covent Garden.

1791–4 Drury Lane closed for re-building, the Company playing at the Haymarket.

1794   Sheridan re-opened Drury Lane. J.P. Kemble and Mrs Siddons played there.

1800   G.F. Cooke as Richard III at Covent Garden.

1803   J.P. Kemble and Mrs Siddons left Drury Lane for Covent Garden.

1808   Covent Garden destroyed by fire.

1809   O.P. Riots at Covent Garden on increase in price of seats on re-opening.
Drury Lane burnt down.

1810   'Romeo' Coates at Theatre Royal, Haymarket.

1812   Drury Lane re-opened with S.J. Arnold as manager.
Mrs Siddons farewell performance, but she re-appeared in 1815 and 1817.

1814   Edmund Kean at Drury Lane as Shylock and Richard III.

1816   Macready at Covent Garden.

1817   J.P. Kemble retired and was succeeded as manager of Covent Garden by Charles Kemble.

1819   R.W. Elliston lessee of Drury Lane.
1824   Charles Kemble's King John with Planché's costumes.
1825   John Poole's *Paul Pry* with Liston and Madam Vestris (114 performances).
1828   Grimaldi's farewell at Drury Lane.
1829   Fanny Kemble as Juliet at Covent Garden.
1833   Edmund Kean appeared at Covent Garden for the last time.

Lamb's Writings on the Theatre

Essays and criticism

G.F. Cooke's *Richard the Third, Morning Post*, 1802.
G.F. Cooke in *King Lear, Morning Post*, 1802.
Specimens of English Dramatic Poets, 1808.
'On the Custom of Hissing at the Theatre', *Reflector*, 1811.
'On the Tragedies of Shakespeare', *Reflector*, 1812.
'The New Acting', *Examiner*, 1813.
'Play-house Memoranda', *Examiner*, 1813.
'Mrs Gould (Miss Burrell) in *Don Giovanni in London*', *Examiner*, 1818.
'Characters of Dramatic Writers', *Works*, 1818, but reprinted from *Specimens*, 1808.
Richard Brome's *Jovial Crew, Examiner*, 1819.
Isaac Bickerstaff's *Hypocrite, Examiner*, 1819.
'New Pieces at the Lyceum', *Examiner*, 1819.
'Miss Kelly at Bath', *Felix Farley's Bristol Journal*, 1819.
'On the Acting of Munden', *Examiner*, 1819.
'My First Play', *London Magazine*, December 1821.
'The Old Actors', *London Magazine*, February, April and October 1822.
'Biographical Memoir of Mr Liston', *London Magazine*, January 1825.
'Autobiography of Mr Munden', *London Magazine*, February 1825.
'Barbara S——', *London Magazine*, April 1825.
'Stage Illusion', *London Magazine*, August 1825.
'The Religion of Actors', *New Monthly Magazine*, 1826.
'Shakespeare's Improvers', *Spectator*, 1828.
'To the Shade of Elliston', *Englishman's Magazine*, August 1831.
'Ellistoniana', *Englishman's Magazine*, August 1831.
'The Death of Munden', *The Athenaeum*, 1832.
Some of the above were reprinted with omissions in the two *Elia* volumes.

Plays

John Woodvil, 1802 (written c.1798).
Mr H——, 1806 (written 1805–6).

The Witch, 1818 (written 1798).
The Wife's Trial, 1828 (written 1827).
The Pawnbroker's Daughter, 1830 (written 1825).
Prologues
Godwin's *Faulkener*, 1807.
Coleridge's *Remorse*, 1813.
Knowles's *The Wife* , 1833.
Epilogues
Godwin's *Antonio*, 1800.
Siddons's *Time's a Tell-Tale*, 1807.
Kenney's *Debtor and Creditor*, 1814.
Richard II (amateur), 1824.
Knowles's *The Wife*, 1833.
Poems
Verses on Mrs Siddons, 1796 (in Coleridge's *Poems on Various Subjects*).
To Miss Kelly, *Morning Chronicle*, 1813.
To a celebrated performer ... *Morning Chronicle*, 1819.
Dramatic Fragment, *London Magazine*, January 1822 (excerpt from *John Woodvil*).

Some Plays by Lamb's Friends Acted on the Stage during his Lifetime
1792 T. Holcroft's *The Road to Ruin* at C.G. (February 18).
1800 W. Godwin's *Antonio* at D.L. (December 13).
1801 T. Holcroft's *Deaf and Dumb* at D.L. (February 24).
1803 James Kenney's *Raising the Wind* at C.G. (November 5).
1806 T. Holcroft's *The Vindictive Man* at D.L. (November 20).
1807 W. Godwin's *Faulkener* at D.L. (December 16).
    Henry Siddons's *Time's a Tell-Take* at D.L.
1813 S.T. Coleridge's *Remorse* at D.L. (January 23).
1814 James Kenney's *Debtor and Creditor* at C.G. (April 20).
1815 James Kenney's *The Fortunes of War* at C.G. (May 17).
1818 J.H. Payne's *Brutus* at D.L.
1820 J.S. Knowles's *Virginius* at C.G. (May 17).
1822 J.H. Payne's *Ali Pacha* at C.G. (October 19).
1823 J.H. Payne's *Clari or the Maid of Milan* at C.G. (May).
1823 James Kenney's *Sweethearts and Wives* at Haymarket (July 7).
—— J.S. Knowles's *Caius Gracchus* at D.L. (November 18).
1825 John Poole's *Paul Pry* at Haymarket (September 13).
—— J.S. Knowles's *William Tell* at D.L. (May 11).
1828 J.S. Knowles's *The Beggar's Daughter* at D.L. (November 22).
1832 J.S. Knowles's *The Hunchback* at C.G. (April 5).
1833 J.S. Knowles's *The Wife* at C.G. (April 24).

Thelwall, John, 'Citizen', 1764–1834. Studied divinity, then articled to an attorney of the Inner Temple, but gave up the law to become an enthusiastic Jacobin reformer. He was a good orator. He was imprisoned in the Tower on a charge of high treason in 1794 with Hardy, Horne Tooke and others, but they were acquitted. In 1797 he abandoned Republicanism for farming in Wales. Later he became a teacher of elocution, particularly for those who stammered. His school was in Lincoln's Inn Fields, but it subsequently moved to Brixton.

He published *Poems upon Various Subjects* in 1787, followed by other volumes of verses, and he wrote and lectured on reform. About 1818 he bought *The Champion* and in 1822 issued *The Poetical Recreations of The Champion*, which contained twelve poems by Lamb, some reprinted from *The Examiner*.

Lamb first met Thelwall about 1797 when the latter was a close friend of Coleridge. There are references to Thelwall in Lamb's letters and he numbered among his friends Southey, George Dyer, Hazlitt, Lamb, Talfourd and Crabb Robinson. In the latter's *Diary* there are many glimpses of him, including one of Thelwall's family and pupils (mostly stutterers) performing Milton's *Comus*! Lamb is said to have occasionally visited him at the school. Thelwall attended the meeting in 1809, at which Lamb was present, to try to help Holcroft's widow and family. During Thelwall's ownership of *The Champion*, 1818–20, Lamb contributed a number of poems. Although such an ardent reformer, Thelwall is described as an amiable man in private life.

Thomas, Philip Edward, 1878–1917. Poet and essayist. Educated at St Paul's and Lincoln College, Oxford. Thomas was influenced in his prose writings by Lamb's works. He first read them at Oxford, possibly with the guidance of W. Warde Fowler, sub-rector of Lincoln, who was a great lover of Elia. There are many references to Lamb in Thomas's books and he is either mentioned or quoted in all the following: *Horae Solitariae*, 1902; *Oxford*, 1903; *The Heart of England*, 1906; *The Book of the Open Air*, 1908; *Richard Jefferies*, 1909; *Rose Acre Papers* and *Feminine Influence on the Poets*, 1910; *Swinburne* and *George Borrow*. 1912; *Walter Pater*, 1913; *A Literary Pilgrim in England*, 1917; and *Cloud Castle*, 1922.

Thomas also refers to Elia in some of his letters, in one of which he states that Lamb is glorious, but he adds that he 'doesn't touch me deeply'. Perhaps this was because he had been obliged to write reviews of Lamb in *The Academy* three times in three months. They were on the *Works of Charles and Mary Lamb*, edited by E.V. Lucas, Vols. VI and VII (10 June 1905); Jules Derocquigny's *Charles Lamb sa vie et ses oeuvres* (26 August); and E.V. Lucas's *Life of Charles Lamb* (30 September). Thomas's poetry, which does not show

Lamb's influence, was first published under the name of 'Edward Eastaway'. *See* 'One of Charles Lamb's Debtors' in C.A. Prance's *Peppercorn Papers*, 1964.

Thomas, Sarah. Lucas in his note to a letter to Dr Cresswell in 1831 (*Letters*, 1935, III 312–3) states that Sarah Thomas was the only daughter of Rev. Anthony Keighley Thomas, Chaplain to the Forces at Woolwich. She appears to have been a friend of Dr Cresswell. Lamb wrote an acrostic to her that she did not like; he replaced it with another.

Thompson, Alexander Hamilton, 1873–1952. Author and editor. Educated at Clifton College and St John's College, Cambridge. Professor of History, University of Leeds, 1924. Edited *The Essays of Elia* (Pitt Press series), Cambridge, 1913, and *Lamb: Miscellaneous Essays*, 1921. Wrote the chapter on Charles Lamb in the *Cambridge History of English Literature*, Vol. XII, and contributed to other volumes. Editor of various English classics, including *Romantic Poets*, 1915–22, 6 vols. Wrote *History of English Literature*, 1901, and a number of books on medieval subjects.

Thompson, Marmaduke, c.1776–1851. Clergyman. At Christ's Hospital with Lamb. He became a Grecian and proceeded to Pembroke College, Cambridge. He went to the Far East as a missionary and became the Senior Chaplain of the East India Company at Madras. He returned to England and married a niece of Charles Sumner, Bishop of Winchester, who gave him the living of Brightwell, Berkshire, where he remained as Rector for twenty years.

In his early days he was friendly with Lamb and sometimes stayed with him. In a letter of October 1799 to Robert Lloyd, Lamb says that Thompson is with him, that he is in love, and 'like a man in a barrel of spikes'. Lamb adds that he is 'heartily sick of his domesticating with me'. Lamb dedicated *Rosamond Gray* to him in 1798 and also presented him with a copy of *Blank Verse by Charles Lamb and Charles Lloyd*, 1798. In the latter volume Thompson noted against the poem 'The Old Familiar Faces' sentences from Lamb's letters that throw some light on its composition. They were printed by Major Butterworth, who owned the book, in *The Bookman* in July 1921, and are reprinted by Lucas in *Letters*, 1935, I. 121, although he does not follow Butterworth accurately.

Lamb's letter to Robert Lloyd of 25 February 1809 refers to taking the two Lloyds to see the 'madness of young parson Thompson of Cambridge'. In his essay on 'Christ's Hospital Five and Thirty Years Ago' Lamb refers to 'Marmaduke T——, mildest of missionaries'.

Thomson, Joseph C. Typographer and bibliographer. Wrote *Bibliography of the Writings of Charles and Mary Lamb*, Hull, 1908.

He was also the author of bibliographies of Dickens, Tennyson and Swinburne. Contributed to *The Bookman's Journal and Print Collector*, 21 January 1921, an article on 'The "How" and "Why" of Cancel Pages'.

Thornton, Sir Edward, 1766–1852. Diplomatist, son of William Thornton, innkeeper. Educated at Christ's Hospital, 1773–85. Proceeded to Pembroke College, Cambridge, and elected a Fellow, 1798. He held a number of diplomatic posts including those of Chargé d'Affaires in Washington and Minister Plenipotentiary to Sweden and Portugal. Lamb mentions him in his essay 'Christ's Hospital Five and Thirty Years Ago' as a 'tall, dark, saturnine youth, sparing of speech, with raven locks.'

Thurlow, Edward Hovell, Baron Thurlow, 1781–1829. Poet. Educated at Charterhouse and Magdalen College, Oxford. Held various appointments, including that of one of the principal registrars of the diocese of Lincoln. His wife was Mary Catherine Bolton, an actress. Among his works were *Poems on Several Occasions*, 1813; *Selected Poems*, 1821; and *Angelica*, 1822. He was a frequent contributor to the *Gentleman's Magazine*. A great lover of Sir Philip Sidney's poems, he edited Sidney's *The Defence of Poesy* in 1810 and wrote verses to him. In his essay 'Defence of the Sonnets of Sir Philip Sidney' in the *London Magazine* in September 1823 Lamb added a footnote maintaining that some of Thurlow's verses were worthy of praise and he printed there his favourite of Thurlow's sonnets, 'To a Bird that haunted the waters of Lacken in the Winter', which he says 'for quiet sweetness, and unaffected morality, has scarcely its parallel in our language'. Lamb copies this sonnet into his Commonplace Book and read it aloud to De Quincey, who liked it.

Some of his contemporaries ridiculed Thurlow's verses; Moore attacked them in the *Edinburgh Review*, and he and Byron were very merry when reading them at Samuel Rogers's house, all three of whom are said to have collapsed into 'a state of unextinguishable laughter'. They were, as Lamb said, entitled to something better than neglect upon the score of exquisite diction alone.

Tibble, John William, 1901–72, and **Anne,** d.1980. Professor Tibble was Professor of Education at the University of Leicester, 1946–66; he was also Director of the University of Leicester School of Education until 1966. He and his wife were joint authors of *John Clare: A Life*, 1932, and revised edition 1972; *The Prose of John Clare*, 1951; and *The Letters of John Clare*, 1951; all three works refer to Charles Lamb. In 1956 they issued *Clare: his Life and Poetry*. Professor Tibble also edited *The Poems of John Clare*, 1935, and lectured to the Charles Lamb Society on 13 October 1952 on

'John Clare, Peasant, Poet, Prisoner'. Mrs Tibble gave the Centenary Address on 'John Clare 1793–1864, Tradition in his Character and in his poetry' on 11 April 1964. She contributed 'John Clare and his doctors' to *Charles Lamb Bulletin*, October 1973, and edited John Clare's *The Midsummer Cushion*, 1980 (with R.K.R. Thornton).

Ticknor, George, 1791–1871. American historian and biographer. Was Professor of Belles-Lettres and French and Spanish at Harvard, 1819–35. His principal work was his *The History of Spanish Literature*, 1849. He also wrote a *Life of Prescott*, 1864, and he was President of the Boston Public Library. In his *Life, Letters and Journal*, 1876, I. 294, occurs a passage derogatory to the Lamb circle which seems to arise from lack of knowledge of such people as Hazlitt, Lamb, Leigh Hunt and Godwin. Ticknor admits, however, that he met them only twice, once at dinner at Godwin's and once at a party at Hunt's. George Ticknor was a cousin of William Davis Ticknor, the publisher, founder of the firm of Ticknor & Fields.

Tidswell, Charlotte. Actress. Played in Lamb's *Mr H——* in 1806 when it was damned. In his letter to Manning on 13 December 1800 about Godwin's *Antonio*, Lamb wrote 'Miss Heard—except Miss Tidswell, the worst actress ever seen or *heard*'. Charlotte Tidswell, known as 'Aunt Tid', brought up Edmund Kean from the age of two. Through her influence she got him accepted at the Haymarket in 1806, and in 1813 she was partly responsible for his engagement at Drury Lane by Elliston.

Tillotson, Geoffrey, 1905–69. Professor of English Literature in the University of London, Birkbeck College. Former President of the Charles Lamb Society who frequently lectured to the members. He edited the new Everyman Edition of *The Essays of Elia and Last Essays of Elia* in 1962, to which he contributed an introduction. In 1966 he contributed to *Some British Romantics* (edited by J.V. Logan *et al*) 'The historical importance of certain "Essays of Elia"'. Among his other books are *On the Poetry of Pope*, 1938; *Essays in Criticism and Research*, 1942; *Criticism and the nineteenth century*, 1951; *Thackeray the novelist* 1954; and *Augustan Studies*, 1961.

Tillyard, Eustace Mandeville Wetenhall, 1889–1962. Master of Jesus College, Cambridge. In 1923 he edited with an introduction and short notes *Lamb's Criticism* (a selection). Tillyard wrote much on Milton and on Shakespeare.

Tipp, John. Accountant at the South Sea House until about 1805 or 1806, when John Lamb, Charles's brother, succeeded him. Lamb gives a delightful account of Tipp in his essay 'The South-Sea House'.

Adapting Fielding, Lamb says 'he thought an accountant the greatest character in the world, and himself the greatest accountant in it'.

Tobin, James Webbe. 1767–1814. Brother of John ·Tobin, the solicitor and dramatist. Friend of Coleridge, Lamb and Godwin. Coleridge stayed with him at Barnard's Inn, Holborn, in March 1804 just before going to Malta. Lamb's letter to Wordsworth on 26 June 1806 mentions that Tobin called and they talked about *Mr H——*, and plays by Tobin's brother, John, whose rejected play *The Honey Moon* was successfully produced a few weeks after its author's death in 1804. James Tobin is mentioned in Lamb's essay 'Christ's Hospital Five and Thirty Years Ago' as 'my friend Tobin', and also in 'Detached Thoughts on Books and Reading'. The Tobin family belonged to the West Indies where they were planters. Thomas Allsop relates how Coleridge told him that Tobin pestered him with stories of Godwin's dullness and on his departure Godwin would drop in to say that Tobin was more dull than ever.

Tomalin, J. Friend of Crabb Robinson and the Colliers. He helped John Payne Collier to make a shorthand report of Coleridge's lectures in 1811. Robinson records in his *Diary* that both Lamb and Tomalin were at a party at his rooms on 24 February 1811. He also notes that Tomalin dined with him on 20 October 1811 when Coleridge was also present.

Towers, Isabella Jane. Born Isabella Jane Clarke, sister of Charles Cowden Clarke. She and her husband lived in Little Warner Street, Clerkenwell, for a time and her brother lived with them. Later they lived at Standerwick in Somersetshire, where William Hazlitt walked over from Winterslow to see them. She was the author of children's books among which were *The Children's Fireside, The Young Wanderer's Cave* and *The Wanderings of Tom Starboard*. She also wrote verses and her 'Stanzas to a Fly that had survived the Winter of 1822', were printed by Leigh Hunt in his *Literary Examiner*; later he printed her verses 'To Gathered Roses' in his *London Journal*.

Lamb wrote verses for Mrs Towers's album in 1828, although he states that he knew her only as Charles Clarke's sister. Later she sent him one of her books for children. (See *Keats-Shelley Journal*, XXVIII, 1979).

Tregaskis, James. Bookseller. In 1927 James Tregaskis & Son of 66 Great Russell Street, London, issued No. 932 of their Caxton Head Catalogues entitled 'An Important Collection of Some of the Rarer Works of Charles Lamb together with some "Lambiana".' It comprised twenty-four items, mostly Lamb's children's books. The whole collection was offered for £5,000, but would, after 31 January 1927, be sold separately. The highest single price asked was £2,700 for *The King and Queen of Hearts*, 1805.

Trewin, John Courtenay, b.1908. Author and dramatic critic. Educated at Plymouth College. Has been a journalist on a number of papers; was dramatic critic of *Punch*, *John O'London's Weekly*, *Illustrated London News* and other publications. Author of many books, including *The Shakespeare Memorial Theatre*, 1932; *The English Theatre*, 1948; *Mr Macready*, 1955; and *Benson and the Bensonians*, 1960. *The Night has been unruly*, 1957, contains a chapter entitled 'A Lamb's Tale' on the failure of *Mr H——* at Drury Lane in 1806. Trewin edited the *Tales from Shakespeare* in 1965 and Macready's *Journals*, 1967.

Trollope, Rev. Arthur William, 1768–1827. Schoolmaster and classical scholar. At Christ's Hospital with Lamb (C.H. 1775–87). Proceeded to Pembroke College, Cambridge, where he gained many distinctions. Was Upper Grammar Master at Christ's in succession to James Boyer and remained there from 1799 to 1826. Trollope was secretary of the Amicable Society of Blues in 1810. In a letter to Coleridge on 26 August 1814, Lamb says, 'Old Jimmy Boyer is dead at last. Trollope has got his living, worth £1000 a year net'. The living was at Colne Engaine. Lamb mentions Trollope in his essay on Christ's Hospital. He resigned from the school in 1826. His son, William Trollope, 1798–1863, who was educated at Christ's Hospital and later became a classical master there, wrote *The History of Christ's Hospital*, 1834.

Truss. Lamb's letter of 1 September 1817 to Charles Chambers refers to 'Truss' and his playing at Leamington. Lucas says we know nothing of Truss and suggests it may be a misreading of Twiss for Horace Twiss, Mrs Siddons's nephew. There were, however, two 'Trusses' in the East India House in Lamb's early days: William H Truss, a clerk in the Auditor's Office, and John Truss in the Accountant's Office.

Tuer, Andrew White, 1838–1900. Author and publisher. Partner in the firm of Field & Tuer of The Leadenhall Press, London. Published *Beauty and the Beast* 1887 (with an introduction by Andrew Lang), and *Prince Dorus*, 1889 and 1890–1 (with an introduction by A.W. Tuer). Author of *1000 Quaint Cuts from Books of Other Days*, 1886; *A History of the Horn-Book*, 1896; *Pages and Pictures from Forgotten Children's Books*, 1898; and *Stories from Old-Fashioned Children's Books*, 1899. Edited *The Paper and Printing Trades Journal*, 1872–95.

Turnbull, John M., 1884–1950. Lamb scholar. Born in Scotland.

Educated in Jersey. Worked in London, then in 1908 was ostrich farming and mining in South Africa and Rhodesia until 1914. Served in the First World War in South West Africa, England and France. Studied forestry at Edinburgh University and became a Government Forestry officer, 1921 to 1946, when he retired to Pretoria.

At the time of his death he was working with H. Buxton Forman on a new edition of the *Essays of Elia* collated from the MSS. He had an alphabetical index of 2,600 references selected from the two series of Elia. His collection of Eliana (about 350 items) passed to the Charles Lamb Society in 1953.

He contributed frequently to periodicals, among which were the following.

The Bookman
1924   Lamb's 'Poor Relations' (February)
1925   Charles Lamb and Griffiths Wainewright (May).
1927   John Lamb and the Eton boys (January).
1928   William Jerdan and a sonnet by Charles Lamb (July).
1929   Lamb and Leigh Hunt: Two Characteristic Preferences (April).
1930   Charles Lamb: Some Side-lights from Barry Cornwall (August).

The Bookman's Journal and Print Collector
1921   An Elian Incongruity (April 8).

C.L.S. Bulletin
1948   Lamb (?) and 'London Fogs' (January).
──────   Some ask'd how pearls did grow (May).
1949   Pink Stockings (May).
──────   Appeal from M. Buxton Forman and John M. Turnbull for help in new edition of *Essays of Elia* (November).
1950   Poems by George Dyer 1802—verses by J.M.T. (May).
──────   An Elian Make-Weight (July). Refers to the Confessions of H.F.V.H. Delamore (reprinted from *Notes & Queries*).

Notes & Queries
1924   An Elian Annotation (September 27).
1928   Wordsworth's Part in the Production of Lamb's *Specimens* (February 18).
──────   A Matter-of-lie Man (May 26).
1946   An Elian Annotation (December 14)
1947   London Fogs (August 23).
1948   Lamb's Multiple Portrait (March 6).
1949   An Elian Make-Weight (January 22).
──────   The Originally Intended Destination of Lamb's Confessions of a Drunkard. (August 6).
──────   Lamb's Parallel between the Prince Regent and King Belshazzar (December 24).

1950 Earliest Disinterested Recognition of Charles Lamb as a Poet (February 18).

Review of English Studies
1927 A Retort to Elia (January).

The Times Literary Supplement
1924 Letter about Lamb's lines 'In the Album of Catherine Orkney' (December 25).
1928 Lamb's 'Mr Sea-Gull' (September 6).
1929 Wordsworth's 'Flying Tailor' (October 24).
1930 An Unrecorded Issue of Lamb's *Album Verses* (March 20).
1931 Reynolds, Hood and Mary Lamb (November 5).
1932 Cancels in *Last Essays of Elia* (June 23).
1949 Two Lamb Poems (February 5).

Tuthill, Sir George Leman, 1772–1835. Physician to several London hospitals. A friend of Lamb and Manning, he was the latter's fellow mathematician at Caius College, Cambridge, and Manning stayed with him from time to time at his house in Cavendish Square, London. He was caught in Paris at the outbreak of the war with France and was detained there with other Englishmen for several years. It is said that he was released only on his wife's personal application to Napoleon. He was back in Cambridge by 1807. In 1816 he took his M.D. and in 1820 he was knighted.

Manning and Tuthill went for a fortnight's holiday together to the Isle of Wight and Devonshire in 1802. It was probably through his friend's influence that Manning was able to study medicine at Westminster Hospital before going to China.

In 1810 Tuthill was prescribing 'water treatment' for Mary Lamb, and Crabb Robinson records that Charles had adopted the same treatment in sympathy. In 1811 Tuthill was defeated as candidate for the post of physician to St Luke's Hospital for the insane, but he was successful later. In 1825 as physician to Westminster Hospital he was co-signatory with James Gillman in the medical report on Charles Lamb which enabled him to retire from the East India Company. Lamb tells Gillman in an amusing letter on 8 March 1830 that he recently visited his friend, Tuthill, at St Luke's and was shown over the Hospital. Later he tells Basil Montagu that Tuthill could vouch for the character of Miss James's sister, Mrs Parsons, a nurse. Lamb in a letter to Manning on 5 December 1806 called Tuthill 'a noble fellow'.

Tween, Jane, d.1891. Daughter of Randal Norris; her mother was a native of Widford and knew Lamb's grandmother and Ann Simmons, Lamb's 'fair hair'd maid'. Jane Norris had kept a school at Widford with her sister, Elizabeth, and both sisters married farmers who were brothers named Tween: Jane Norris became Mrs Arthur Tween and Elizabeth Mrs Charles Tween. Jane gave Ainger some reminiscences of Lamb that he published in his essay 'How I traced Charles Lamb in Hertfordshire' in his *Lectures and Essays*, 1905. Elizabeth Tween died in 1894.

Twopenny, Richard, c.1727–1809. Stock broker to the Bank of England. Lamb includes him as one of his Old Benchers, but this is a mistake. Twopenny had chambers in Serjeant's Inn and was a neighbour and friend of Thomas Coventry, but he was never a Bencher. After his retirement he lived at West Malling. Lamb reports that Twopenny was very thin.

Upcott, William, 1779–1845. Antiquary, topographer and autograph collector. Said to be a natural son of the painter, Ozias Humphry. First a bookseller's assistant with R.H. Evans of Pall Mall, then with John Wright of Piccadilly. When Porson was appointed librarian of the London Institution, Upcott became his assistant and continued there when William Maltby succeeded Porson.

He was concerned with a *Biographical Dictionary of Living Authors of Great Britain and Ireland and a Chronological Register of their Publications*, 1816, of which John Watkins and Frederick Shoberl were the principal authors. This publication listed both Charles and Mary Lamb. Upcott compiled *A Bibliographical Account of the Principal Works relating to English Topography*, 1818, and in 1836 published a *Catalogue of Original Letters, MSS, and State Papers. Collected by William Upcott, of Islington*. He owned a large collection of books, MSS, prints and drawings. His collection of letters was said to number 32,000, of which many passed to the British Museum when sold after his death. When Henry Colburn brought out the first edition of Evelyn's *Diary* in 1818 it was said to be at Upcott's suggestion and that he revised the proofs for the press.

In 1827 Lamb wrote a short autobiography for Upcott which it seems was intended for a proposed second edition of the *Biographical Dictionary*; it was quoted by John Forster in the *New Monthly Magazine* in 1835. Upcott lived in a cottage in Islington not far from Lamb's Colebrooke Cottage. Upcott's library was sold in 1846 for £4,125.

Vaughan, Richard, 'Hell-Fire Dick'. Coach driver, who drove the 'Telegraph' from the 'Sun' in Trumpington Street, Cambridge, half way to London, where he met the London coach; the two drivers then exchanged coaches and 'Hell-Fire Dick' made the return journey to Cambridge. Mentioned by Mary Lamb in her letter of 20 August 1815 to Sara Hutchinson as driving her and her brother 'in great triumph' into Cambridge.

Vestris, Madame, 1797–1856. Italian actress, singer and dancer; a famous comédienne. Born Lucia Elizabeth Bartolozzi and grand-daughter of the famous engraver, Francesco Bartolozzi. She married Armand Vestris, but he left her after a few years and he died in 1825.

She had first appeared in Italian opera, but in 1820 played at Drury Lane with John Braham in James Cobb's *Siege of Belgrade* as Lilla, a part created for her. She also appeared in Cobb's *Haunted Tower* and in *Artaxerxes'*. She was particularly popular in 'breeches' parts, under Elliston as Macheath in *The Beggar's Opera* and in Moncrieff's burlesque of *Don Giovanni in London*, as well as in Bishop's version of *The Marriage of Figaro'*. In 1831 she took over the Olympic Theatre and made a great success of it. In 1838 she married Charles James Mathews and together they managed Covent Garden and then the Lyceum.

She was well known as a singer and in 1825 sang 'Cherry Ripe' at the Haymarket in the character of Phoebe in *Paul Pry*. The song became immensely popular; she also sang it at Vauxhall Gardens.

Lamb mentions her in his essay 'The Religion of Actors' and in 'Ellistoniana'. Crabb Robinson has many references to her in his *Diary* and was very favourably impressed with her.

Wadd, Henry. Son of Rev. Dr Wadd. Clerk at East India House with Lamb in the Accountant's Office. He seems to have been dis-tinguished for his stupidity. In 1811 Crabb Robinson notes in his *Diary* that Wadd had thrown a pen full of ink at Lamb and caused him considerable eye trouble. Lamb, writing to Walter Wilson in 1822, called him 'A sad shuffler' and he had composed an epigram on Wadd:

> 'What Wadd knows, God knows,
> But God knows *what* Wadd knows.'

Sometimes his name appears as 'Wawd'.

Waddy, John. Actor. Played the Earl of Kent to G.F. Cooke's Lear at Covent Garden in 1802. Lamb refers to him in his review of the play in the *Morning Post* on 9 January 1802, where he says he was a little coarse, but a good picture of blunt honesty in his humble dis-guise as Caius. He also played at the Haymarket in 1807.

Wageman, Thomas Charles, c.1787–1863. Portrait painter. Ex-hibited at the R.A., Suffolk Street, and the New Water Colour Society from 1816 to 1857. Painted many actors, including John Fawcett as 'Autolycus'; he also did a portrait of Thomas Stothard. Most of his theatrical portraits were engraved by Thomas Woolnoth. In 1824 or 1825 he did a drawing of Charles Lamb known as the 'Wageman portrait' showing a full face view of his subject, and many times reproduced.

Wainewright, Thomas Griffiths, 1794–1847. Painter and prose writer. Son of a solicitor of Gray's Inn and grandson of Dr Ralph Griffiths, founder of the *Monthly Review* and publisher of John Cleland's *Fanny Hill.* Wainewright was educated at Greenwich Academy of which Dr Charles Burney, the classical scholar and a distant relative, was headmaster. For a short time after leaving school he worked in the studio of Thomas Phillips, the portrait painter and while there he painted a portrait of Byron. He left after a few months and in 1814 was gazetted Ensign in the 16th Bedfordshire Regiment of Foot, but sold his commission the following year. He seems to have lived the life of a dilettante, although he did paint and contribute articles to periodicals. In 1821 he first exhibited at the Royal Academy and continued to do so for some years.

As an author his principal contributions were to the *London Magazine,* beginning in January 1820 and continuing until early in 1823. His articles were of a light hearted nature mainly dealing with the arts, and were highly praised by Lamb. He wrote under the pseudonyms of 'Janus Weathercock', 'Egomet Bonmot' and 'Cornelius Van Vinkbooms', and in some of his articles he has pleasant references to Elia and other contributors to the *London.* He claimed also to have written for the rival *London Magazine* of Gold and Northhouse, but some of the articles said to be by him are by W.F. Deacon. Apart from his work for periodicals it seems that his only published work was a booklet of forty-five pages in rhymed couplets entitled *Some Passages in the Life of Egomet Bonmot Esq., edited by Mr Mwaughmaim and now first published by Me,* 1825.

To his friends he was a dandy, art critic, painter and something of a man of leisure, but in the 1820s his extravagance landed him in debt. He was married in 1821 to Eliza Frances Ward, and they lived in lavish apartments at 49 Great Marlborough Street. Many of his friends were entertained there, including Lamb, Clare, Hood, Cunningham, Cary, Procter, Hazlitt, Dilke and Talfourd and others of the *London Magazine* circle. In 1827 he moved to Linden House at Turnham Green with his uncle, who died soon afterwards in mysterious circumstances. At this house both Lamb and Cary visited him in 1829 and Procter the following year. W.C. Hazlitt said that Lamb wrote verses in the album of Mrs Wainewright's sister, Madeleine Abercromby, but that they had disappeared.

Wainewright had been left certain funds in trust by his grandfather and to obtain the capital he forged the signatures of the trustees. The £5,000 thus received soon disappeared and afterwards some involved transactions in life assurance took place, followed by the death of the assured, Mrs Wainewright's half-sister. A great deal of litigation took place, for the insurance company refused to pay and won their case. Wainewright, who had lived in France for a time because of his debts, returned to England in 1837 when he was arrested on a charge of forgery. He finally pleaded guilty and was sentenced to be transported for life. He spent the rest of his days as a convict in Van Diemen's Land.

Curiously he was never tried for murder, although it seems highly likely that he was responsible for the death by poisoning of two, if not three, people and that his wife was at the very least an accessory.

Among the pictures painted by Wainewright, some of which were exhibited at the Royal Academy were *A Romance from Undine*, 1821; *Paris in the Chamber of Helen*, 1822; *The Milkmaid's Song*, 1824; *Scene from "Der Freischütz"* ' 1825; and *Sketch from La Gerusalemme Liberata*, 1825.

Waldens, The. Mr & Mrs Walden let lodgings at their house in Church Street, Edmonton, to mental patients, Mr Walden having been a keeper in a mental home. Mary Lamb had been there from time to time during her attacks, and in 1833 Charles Lamb felt that it would be best if she was there permanently. He decided to live there with her and in May the move was made. This was their last move together, but Mary Lamb remained there for some years after her brother's death in 1834. B.W. Procter wrote to Talfourd in 1841 to tell him that Mrs Walden was neglecting Mary and a move was then arranged to the house of Mrs Parsons, Miss James's sister in St John's Wood.

Wales, William, ?1734–98. Master at Christ's Hospital in charge of the Mathematical School in Lamb's day. Although Lamb was not in this part of the school he describes Wales and his scholars, known as the King's Boys, in his essay 'Recollections of Christ's Hospital' in the *Gentleman's Magazine* in 1813. Wales was said to be an excellent mathematician and to have been co-navigator with Captain Cook; thus he may well have known James Burney, for he had also been at Otaheite. Leigh Hunt mentions Wales in his *Autobiography*, although like Lamb he was in the Grammar School.

Warburton. Owner of a private asylum in Whitmore Road, Hoxton. Miss Sarah James, Mary Lamb's nurse, and her three sisters had all been nurses there. One sister, Mrs Trueman, was married to a keeper at the asylum. John Hollingshead, Sarah James's nephew, described it as an aristocratic madhouse in 1830. Lamb mentions it in his letter to Basil Montagu, probably in 1830, and in a letter of 1 February 1826 to a Mr Hudson he had stated that it was possible to hire a nurse for a mental patient at Warburton's, and the cost was twenty-eight shillings a week.

Ward, Alfred Charles. Author and editor. Editor of *Everybody's Lamb*, 1933 (illustrations by E.H. Shepard), and author of *The Frolic and the Gentle*, 1934, a centenary study of Charles Lamb. Other works include *Landmarks in Western Literature*, 1932, and *The Illustrated History of English Literature*, 1953, in three volumes, the last of which contains numerous references to Lamb. He also wrote *A Literary Journey through War Time Britain*, 1943, and revised G.H. Mair's *English Literature 1430–1939* in the Home University Library series. In 1945 he edited *Specimens of English Dramatic Criticism XVII–XX Centuries* which includes Charles Lamb, Leigh Hunt, William Hazlitt and Thomas Barnes.

Ward, Sarah. Actress, wife of Henry Ward, manager of the Manchester theatre. She played Lady Randolph to the Norval of West Digges in the first production of *Douglas* in Edinburgh in 1756. She later acted in Charles Coffey's *The Devil to Pay* and *The Merry Cobbler*, and Lamb described her in his essay 'The Old Actors' as matchless in Lady Loverule.

Warren, Samuel, 1807–77. Novelist. Studied medicine, afterwards became a barrister. Was Recorder of Hull and M.P. for Midhurst. Author of *Passages from the Diary of a late Physician* and *Ten Thousand a Year*. He also contributed to *Blackwood's Magazine* and wrote on legal subjects. Crabb Robinson records that he invited Warren to breakfast on 17 April 1834 when Lamb and Barron Field were also there. Lamb did not like Warren who was a great talker.

Watts, Alaric Alexander, 1797–1864. Poet and journalist. First an usher at a school in Fulham, then a journalist. Editor of several provincial papers, including the *Manchester Courier*, founded the *United Service Gazette* and contributed to the *Literary Gazette*. He published several volumes of poems and edited *The Literary Souvenir* from 1825–35 and its continuation *The Cabinet of British Art* from 1835–38. He also wrote a memoir for Turner's *Liber Fluviorum*, 1853.

Watts sent Lamb a volume of his poems in 1822 and what was no doubt an advance copy of his *Literary Souvenir* in December 1824. Watts was known as a cantankerous editor and tended to air his woes in the prefaces to his Annuals. Writing to William Blackwood in December 1821 he says 'Charles Lamb delivers himself with infinite pain and labour of a silly piece of trifling every month in this magazine [i.e. the *London*], under the signature of Elia'. He also told Blackwood he could give him the names of the contributors to the *London*, and sent a list of items and their supposed writers, most of which is incorrect (MS in National Library of Scotland). Lamb contributed his 'Saturday Night' to *The Gem*, 1830, edited by Watts.

In the *Literary Souvenir*, 1832, Watts printed verses entitled 'Charles Lamb'.

Waudby, Roberta F.C. Artist. Designed and illustrated The Aldine Chapbooks for J.M. Dent. The series, which was issued in wrappers about 1930, included *Dream Children and The Child Angel, The Praise of Chimney-Sweepers, Witches and Other Night Fears* and *Mrs Battle's Opinions on Whist*, as well as Leigh Hunt's *The Old Lady* and *The Maid-Servant*. Other authors in the series included Kenneth Grahame, W.H. Hudson, William Canton and Washington Irving.

Wawd, Henry (or **Wadd**), ?1784–1834. Clerk in the Accountant's Office, East India House with Lamb. He was noted for his stupidity and in a letter of December 1822 to Walter Wilson, Lamb called him 'a sad shuffler'. Crabb Robinson's *Diary* for 21 July 1811 relates that Lamb had met with an accident caused by Wawd throwing a pen full of ink into his eye. Lamb wrote an epigram on Wawd:

> What Wadd knows, God knows
> But God knows *what* Wadd knows.

Wedd, Mary L.R. Principal Lecturer in English, Goldsmiths' College, London. Joint editor with Basil Savage of *The Charles Lamb Bulletin* from 1977 to 1979. Editor from 1979. Gave lecture to the Charles Lamb Society in 1977 entitled 'All Fool's Day', reprinted in *Charles Lamb Bulletin*, October 1979. Contributed 'Dialects of Humour—Lamb and Wordsworth' to *Charles Lamb Bulletin*, July 1977.

Weekes, Henry, 1807–77. Sculptor. Born at Canterbury. A.R.A., 1851. R.A., 1865. Exhibited at the Royal Academy, British Institution and Suffolk Street Gallery. He was assistant to Sir Francis Legatt Chantry. In 1838 was published *The Authors of England* with text by H.F. Chorley and medallion portraits of literary characters engraved by A. Collas; a portrait of Lamb was included, engraved from a model by H. Weekes. In 1827 Allan Cunningham had asked Moxon for facilities for Henry Weekes to do a head of Lamb. Weekes also did the Shelley Memorial in Christchurch Abbey, Hampshire.

Wells, Charles Jeremiah, 1800–79. Poet and solicitor. Educated at John Clarke's school at Edmonton where he had Keats's brother, Tom, for a schoolfellow. Friendly with John Keats, but played a practical joke on Tom by fabricating a love correspondence with a fictitious lady, which caused Tom considerable pain and greatly annoyed his brother. John Keats's sonnet 'To a Friend who sent me some roses' was written to Wells in 1816. Friend of Hazlitt in the essayist's later years and erected a tombstone over Hazlitt's grave at St Anne's, Soho, and some say wrote an epitaph for it, although the epitaph has also been credited to R.H. Horne. Wells published *Stories from Nature*, 1822, and his best known work, *Joseph and his Brethren*, under the pseudonym of H.L. Howard in 1823; the latter was praised by both Rossetti and Swinburne. His last years were spent in France.

Lamb knew him and wrote a letter in 1822 thanking him for a copy of his *Stories from Nature* and inviting him to Dalston.

Wesley, Sarah, 1760–1828. Daughter of Charles Wesley and niece of John Wesley. A friend of Elizabeth Benger and said to be a woman of great culture. Lamb's letter in April 1800 to Coleridge says 'You encouraged that mopsey, Miss Wesley, to dance after you, in the hope of having her nonsense put in a nonsensical Anthology. We have pretty well shaken her off, by that simple expedient of referring her to you'.

Westwood, Frances. Daughter of Thomas Westwood, senior, who married in 1828 a Mr Sugden, a schoolmaster. Lamb wrote a letter to Mrs Morgan on 17 June 1828 to try to get pupils for the school which had just opened. Lamb speaks of him as 'my friend'. In 1827 and 1828 the Lambs wrote verses in Frances Westwood's album. The new school was at Peckham.

Westwood, Thomas (Senior). In September 1827 the Lambs moved to The Poplars, Chase Side, Enfield, next door to which lived the Westwood family. Thomas Westwood, senior, had been a haberdasher in Bow Lane, but after his retirement was an agent for the Phoenix Insurance Company, and lived at Enfield with his wife and two children, Thomas and Frances. In October 1829 the Lambs gave up their house and lodged with the Westwoods until May 1833. At first Lamb described them as an 'honest pair', but after a time his views changed and he came to dislike them. Lamb's long and famous letter to Wordsworth on 22 January 1830 describes Westwood as having '*one anecdote*, upon which and about forty pounds a year he seems to have retired in green old age'. By 1831 he had found them mean and extortionate and relates the amusing incident of being charged sixpence extra for tea supplied to Wordsworth when he visited Lamb because 'the elderly gentleman had taken such a quantity of sugar in his tea'. Lamb also describes Westwood in his letter to Gillman on 30 November 1829.

Westwood, Thomas (Junior), 1814–88. Poet. Son of Thomas Westwood, Lamb's landlord. Lamb found him an appointment in the counting house of his friend, Charles Aders. Later he went to Belgium and obtained a remunerative post as Brussels director and secretary of the Tournay and Jurbise Railway. His hobbies were literature and angling. The former was stimulated by Lamb who lent him books and introduced him to the Elizabethan dramatists, Defoe, Fielding and other of Lamb's favourites. Mary Lamb taught him Latin and he received much kindness from the brother and sister. Lamb seems to have encouraged his interest in angling as well, at least from the literary and bibliographical side. Westwood remembered Lamb's enthusiasm for Walton and in due course himself wrote *The Chronicle of 'The Compleat Angler'* in 1864. In the Preface he has pleasant sketches of Lamb at Enfield. His best known work was *A New Bibliotheca Piscatoria* 1861. He also published a number of volumes of poetry and in a pamphlet *Twelve Sonnets and an Epilogue,* 1884, he refers to Elia. The reminiscences of Lamb left by Thomas Westwood are among the most interesting about Elia's later years. In *Notes & Queries* in 1882 Westwood wrote, 'When my scanty honours are counted, let not this be overlooked. To have been Miss Kelly's frog-catcher and Bridget Elia's carpenter—that is surely something!' Westwood's reminiscences of Lamb are contained in the preface to *The Chronicle of the Compleat Angler,* 1864; in *Notes & Queries,* 'Recollections of Charles Lamb' (22 September 1866), Two Unpublished Poems (1870), 'Witches and Other Night Fears' (23 November 1872), and 'Charles Lamb: Supplementary Reminiscences' (20 May 1882); in *A Literary Friendship,* 1914; and in *The Angler's Notebook,* 1884.

Wewitzer, Ralph, 1748–1825. Jewish actor. A Londoner, he was first a jeweller, but turned to the stage. Appeared at Covent Garden in 1773 as Ralph in *The Maid of the Mill.* Subsequently played in Dublin, but returned to London and appeared at the Haymarket in 1780 and with the Drury Lane company at the King's Theatre in 1791. He was particularly good in French, German and Jewish parts and was said to be the best stage Jew of his time. He had been manager of the Royalty Theatre, Welclose Square, in 1789 but was not successful there.

Wewitzer invented pantomimes and was known as an inveterate punster. He was also a French scholar. He wrote *A Theatrical Pocket Book, or brief Dramatic Chronology* in 1814 and was also the author of *Dramatic Reminiscences.* He is said to have had a share in arranging the marriage of Harriot Mellon and for a short time was a member of her household. He played Landlord Pry in Lamb's *Mr H——* at Drury Lane in 1806. Wewitzer's sister was an actress and singer and appeared at Covent Garden.

Wharry, John, 1745–1812. Barrister of the Inner Temple. Called to the Bar in 1767 and a Bencher in 1801. His chambers were in Mitre Court Buildings. Lamb in his essay on the Old Benchers describes him as 'attenuated and fleeting' and with a peculiar gait of three steps and a jump.

Wherry, George Edward. Surgeon. Author of *Cambridge and Charles Lamb*, 1925, which also contains contributions from E.V. Lucas and Sir Edmund Gosse. It describes the Charles Lamb Dinners held at Cambridge from 1909 to 1914 and has a chapter on George Dyer. In 1951 Mrs Beatrix Oldfield, the daughter of George Wherry, presented to the Charles Lamb Society a collection of material concerning Lamb known as the 'George Wherry Collection of Eliana'. It included a portrait in oils of Mary Lamb by F.S. Cary, a series of water colours of haunts of Charles Lamb by Paul Braddon and material relating to the Lamb dinners at Cambridge.

White, Edward. Clerk at East India House in the Accountant's Office with Lamb. Friend of Lamb and Hazlitt. There are several glimpses of White in Lamb's letters. In a letter to John Howard Payne in late 1822 he introduces him as a friend who is visiting Paris and says White knows Paris thoroughly. To Leigh Hunt in December 1827 he says White has the Hazlitt portrait of Lamb and lives in Kentish Town, but is still working at East India House. C.W. Cope, the painter, in his *Reminiscences* says that White was an excellent judge of art and a diligent amateur painter, and that he attended Lamb's weekly parties frequently. At the time Cope was friendly with White, the latter lived in Chelsea. Crabb Robinson also records meeting him at Lamb's.

Mrs Anderson in her article in *The Bookman* in April 1924 tells of finding a sketch of Lamb in W.T. Spencer's bookshop in London that she thinks is the Hazlitt portrait reversed and in contemporary dress. She makes out a good case for Edward White as the artist. White was present when Hazlitt died. Lamb has a reference to the Whites of Bishopsgate Street, in his letter of 16 August 1820 to Barron Field, perhaps this reference was to Edward White's family.

White, James, 'Jem White', 1775–1820. Son of Samuel White of Bewdley, Worcestershire. Educated at Christ's Hospital, being admitted on the presentation of Thomas Coventry 19 September 1783. He left in 1790 and became a clerk in the Treasurer's Office at his old school where he remained for many years. *The London Kalendar* for 1815 lists James White as Assistant Clerk to Christ's Hospital. In 1800 he founded an advertising agency in Warwick Square, moving to Fleet Street in 1808. It still exists as R.F. White & Sons Ltd. James White's first client was Christ's Hospital and it is understood that the Company still has this account. White married Margaret Faulder, the daughter of a Bond Street bookseller, and one son, Richard Faulder White, carried on the advertising agency after his father's death.

White is described as an attractive character, full of fun and kindness. Lamb and White were friends from their schooldays and saw much of one another, particularly around the turn of the century. As early as 1796 *Original Letters &c. of Sir John Falstaff* appeared. Although written by White he undoubtedly had some help from Lamb who, some think, wrote the Preface and possibly made suggestions on the rest of the work. There are several references to the book in Lamb's letters, he encouraged his friends to publicise it and, as late as 1819, wrote a review of it in Leigh Hunt's *Examiner*. Lamb always had a great affection for the *Falstaff Letters* and never lost an opportunity to praise it. When in 1832 Landor visited him at Edmonton he gave his visitor a copy of the book. White was known as 'Sir John' among his friends.

During the period following the tragedy in Lamb's family, White and Lamb were inseparable. Another friend, Charles Lloyd, lived for a time with White. Later there are references in Crabb Robinson's *Diary* to White being at Lamb's parties.

The best known reference to White is in Lamb's essay 'The Praise of Chimney-Sweepers' where he describes the annual feast that White organized for the children employed as chimney sweepers, 'those tender novices' as Lamb calls them. White was 'host and waiter' at a 'solemn supper held in Smithfield'. Lamb says that he and John Fenwick also acted as waiters. The festivities were probably much more lively than Mrs Montagu's annual feast to the sweeps. Lamb also refers to White in a footnote to his essay 'On the Old Actors' in connection with an anecdote of James Dodd, the actor. Hazlitt mentions White in his essay 'On the Conversation of Authors'. It seems that it was James White who persuaded Lamb to write lottery puffs. When Godwin was in financial difficulties in 1811 White joined with Crabb Robinson in helping him. When Peter Peirson, one of Lamb's bondsmen at East India House, died, White took his place.

In 1805 White made a tour of South Wales with a 'Mr B', possibly a Mr Barker, and kept a manuscript journal which is now in the British Museum. Miniatures of White and his wife were painted by Sir William Newton, later the Court painter to William IV. A portrait of James White was reproduced in the *World's Press News* of 1 June 1951.

Lamb wrote in his famous essay on chimney sweepers that White 'carried away with him half the fun of the world when he died—of my world at least'.

When in 1961 a burglar broke into the offices of R.F. White & Son in Fleet Street, he stole a copy of *Falstaff's Letters*, two miniatures and two original letters.

Wilde, Sir Thomas, 1782–1855. Barrister who became Lord Chancellor. Educated at St Paul's School. Articled to his father, an attorney, and in 1811 entered at Inner Temple. Was called to the Bar in 1817. He was retained for the defence of Queen Caroline in 1820, became a serjeant-at-law in 1824 and eventually M.P. for Newark on Trent on 1831 after four attempts.

Martin Burney read briefs for him, and Wilde was a neighbour of Lamb's at Enfield. When he contested the Newark election in 1829 a number of election squibs were written for him and it has been suggested that Lamb was responsible for some of them (Lucas gives the evidence in his edition of Lamb's *Poems and Plays*, 1903, 341). Martin Burney was one of his helpers at the election.

In Lamb's *Album Verses*, 1830, are verses 'In the Autograph Book of Mrs Serjeant W——', which he wrote for Mrs Wilde, the first wife of Serjeant Wilde. Lucas prints a letter from Lamb to Mrs Wilde enclosing a copy of his *Album Verses*.

Wilde was known to Leigh Hunt. Crabb Robinson records on 28 May 1824 going to Westminster to hear Serjeant Wilde 'in defence of the British Press for a libel on Mr Chetwynd'. He praises his acuteness and adds 'He will soon be at the head of the Common Pleas'. Wilde was subsequently appointed solicitor-general, attorney-general, chief justice of the Common Pleas, Lord Chancellor and was created Baron Truro in 1850.

Will, Lamb's. Dated 9 October 1830. In a letter of 9 September 1823 to Thomas Allsop Lamb states that he is going to make his will and asks if Allsop will be one of the executors. He added that he was also going to ask Talfourd and Procter to be executors. Allsop replied at once agreeing to the request. Nothing further appears to have been heard of this will and, if it was ever completed, it must have been destroyed when a new one was made in 1830.

Lucas prints a letter to Talfourd (No. 860) in which Lamb writes that he encloses a rough draft of a proposed will and that he will have it drawn up properly if Talfourd agrees and, if so, he will submit it to Charles Ryle. In the J.A. Spoor Sale Catalogue is a letter to Talfourd dated 11 October 1830 stating that Ryle approves the draft and has the original will.

In this will Lamb bequeaths all his property to T.N. Talfourd and Charles Ryle in trust for his sister, Mary, the residue to go to Emma Isola. The will was drawn and executed wholly in Lamb's handwriting and was witnessed by Vincent Rice of 3 Ruffords Row, Islington.

Lamb died on 27 December 1834 and attached to the will at Somerset House are affidavits sworn by Talfourd and Ryle on 13 January 1835 and a statement that 'the whole of the Personal Estate and effects of the said deceased does not amount in Value to the sum of Fifteen hundred pounds.' The will was proved on 16 January 1835 and Willis Henry Lowe of the East India House certified that he knew and was well acquainted with Charles Lamb and that the will was in his handwriting. The certificate by Lowe was required because only one witness's name appeared on the will instead of the customary two.

A facsimile of Lamb's will was included as a supplement to No. 110 of the *C.L.S. Bulletin* in January 1953. It had also been printed in the Sale Catalogue of J.A. Spoor in 1939. The Will is printed in Edmund Blunden's *Charles Lamb: His Life Recorded by his Contemporaries*, 1934, and in E.V. Lucas's *Letters*, 1935, III.291–2.

Willey, Basil, 1897–1978. Professor of English Literature, University of Cambridge, 1946–64. Fellow of Pembroke College and President 1958–64. Educated at University College School and Peterhouse, Cambridge. Vice President of the Charles Lamb Society from 1950. Author of *The Seventeenth-century Background*, 1934; *The Eighteenth-century Background*, 1940; *Coleridge on Imagination and Fancy*, 1946; *Nineteenth-century Studies: Coleridge to Mathew Arnold*, 1949; *More Nineteenth-century Studies*, 1956. Edited *Essays and Studies*, 1958 (Vol. XI.N.S.) which contains 'Coleridge's Debt to Charles Lamb' by Basil Willey. Lectured to the Charles Lamb Society in March 1957 on 'Charles Lamb and Coleridge's *Annus Mirabilis*'. Several times the Guest of Honour at the Charles Lamb Society celebrations. Gave the Crowsley Memorial Lecture 'Charles Lamb and S.T. Coleridge' to the Charles Lamb Society in 1972.

Williams, Grace Joanna. Wife of the Rector of Fornham (or Thornham), Suffolk. In 1828 Emma Isola became a governess in the Rector's family. In 1830 Emma was ill at Fornham with an attack of brain fever, and when she recovered Charles Lamb went to fetch her. There are a number of letters extant from Lamb to Mrs Williams mostly concerned with Emma Isola. Lamb wrote acrostics to Mrs Williams and to her two daughters, Joanna and Louisa Clare. Mrs Williams replied with another acrostic on Charles Lamb's name which Lucas prints in Vol. III of his edition of the *Letters*, 1935.

Lamb met Mrs Williams's husband on his return journey from Fornham in 1830. The Rev. Williams had been tutor to W.B. Donne and Lamb's letter to Mrs Williams on 21 April 1830 is addressed 'Mrs Williams, W.B. Donne Esq, Mattishall, East Dereham, Norfolk'.

Williams, Orlo Cyprian, 1883–1967. Author. Educated at Eton and Balliol College, Oxford. Principal Clerk to the Committee and Private Bill Office, House of Commons. In 1911 he edited *The Essays of Elia* for the Oxford University Press and wrote an introduction and notes to it. He also wrote *Lamb's Friend the Census-Taker: Life & Letters of John Rickman*, 1911, and the volume on *Charles Lamb* in Duckworth's Great Lives series in 1934. For Martin Secker's 'The Art & Craft of Letters' series he wrote *The Essay* in 1914 which contains numerous references to Lamb, and in which Williams describes himself as 'a worshipper at the shrine of Charles Lamb'. He was a contributor to the *Times Literary Supplement*, *The Times*, *Edinburgh Review*, *Blackwoods*, *London Mercury*, *Athenaeum* and *National Review*.

Willis, Nathaniel Parker, 1806–67. American journalist and poet. Educated at Yale. His publications include *Fugitive Poetry*, 1829; *Pencillings by the Way*, 1835; *Melanie and Other Poems*, 1836 and *People I Have Met*. He was in England in 1834, 1835 and 1837 and sent to his paper the *New York Mirror* sketches of the people he had met. Crabb Robinson records in his *Diary* that on 19 June 1834 the Lambs had breakfast with him when N.P. Willis was also there. He had been introduced to Robinson by Landor and had specially asked to meet the Lambs. In his *Pencillings by the Way* he has left an interesting account of the meeting. Not all Willis's writings about the people he had met were approved by those concerned, for he had represented himself as an attaché to the American Legation instead of a journalist. Robinson says that Landor was annoyed with him and that Lady Blessington did not invite him to her house again. However, his account of the Lambs does not seem to have upset anyone.

Wilson, D.G. Chairman of Charles Lamb Society since 1974. Lectured to the Royal Society of Medicine on 'Imagination and Insight' in October 1970. (Summarized in *Charles Lamb Bulletin*, April 1972.) Contributed 'Charles Lamb and Bloomsbury' to *Charles Lamb Bulletin*, April 1979.

Wilson, John, 'Christopher North', 1785–1854. Barrister, journalist, poet and essayist. Born in Paisley and educated at Paisley Grammar School, Glasgow University and Magdalen College, Oxford. Won the Newdigate Prize for Poetry and became a noted athlete. Lived in the Lake District and was a friend of Wordsworth, Southey, Coleridge and De Quincey. Later he moved to Edinburgh. Was a frequent contributor to *Blackwood's Magazine* and possibly one of the editors. He was jointly responsible with J.G. Lockhart and James Hogg for the famous 'Chaldee Manuscript' in 'Maga'. Wilson became Professor of Moral Philosophy in Edinburgh University in 1820.

He published volumes of poetry, *The Isle of Palms*, 1812, and *The City of Plague*, 1816. His best known work is in the *Noctes Ambrosianae*, 1822–35. Wilson praised Lamb in the *Noctes* and in his 'Metricum Symposium', but was critical of Lamb's 'Letter to Robert Southey, Esq'. On 11 July 1832 Lamb and Wilson met for the first time, and as far as we know, the only time. Wilson called on Lamb at Enfield accompanied by Alexander Blair and Edward Moxon. Lamb took the opportunity to ask for a contribution for Emma Isola's

Album which was promised, but does not seem to have been given. In 1833 Lamb wrote a short note to Wilson enclosing a book, probably a copy of *The Last Essays of Elia*, and reminding him of his promise of album verses, and he adds 'Would you like now and then to hear from Elia?' In a letter to William Blackwood in the Spring of 1829 Lamb praised the *Noctes* and in another of 29 June 1830 he says that Wilson liked 'The Wife's Trial' which had appeared in *Blackwood's Magazine* in 1828.

Wilson, John Gideon, 1876–1963. Bookseller. Chairman and Managing Director of J. & E. Bumpus Ltd., of 477 Oxford Street, London (alas, no longer there). He came to London in 1910 from Glasgow, worked as a publisher with Messrs Constable for two years, then joined Jones & Evans, booksellers of Queen Street, Cheapside. After the First World War he went to Bumpus then at No. 350 on the north side of Oxford Street; later the business moved to the south side near Marble Arch. Wilson eventually became a director and head of the Company.

During his period with Bumpus he organized a number of book exhibitions in their Court Room, one of which in 1934 was devoted to Charles Lamb. For this the material was drawn from Wilson's extensive collection of Eliana. He was President and Chairman of the Elian Society. Wilson still continued his association with Jones & Evans Ltd., and was a director of that company until his death.

Wilson, John Iliffe. Educated at Christ's Hospital. Author of *A Brief History of Christ's Hospital*, 1820, which reprinted Lamb's essay on Christ's from the *Gentleman's Magazine* of 1813. The book was reprinted in an enlarged form in 1821 and had reached a seventh edition by 1842. There is no record that Lamb and Wilson ever met, but it is probable that the latter may have corresponded with Lamb to obtain permission to reprint Lamb's essay. Wilson was known to Leigh Hunt and described George Dyer as his friend.

Wilson, Walter, 1781–1847. Clerk at East India House. Later became a bookseller with Maxwell of Bell Yard, Temple Bar, and in 1806 took the bookshop at Mewsgate, Charing Cross, formerly occupied by the younger Thomas Payne and his famous father. After inheriting money from his relation, John Walter of *The Times*, he became one of the proprietors of the newspaper and entered himself at the Inner Temple. He does not seem to have practised at the Bar but devoted himself to literature.

He wrote *The History and Antiquities of Dissenting Churches and Meeting Houses in London* in four volumes, 1808–14. In 1822 he announced his life of Defoe, but the *Memoirs of the Life and Times of Daniel Defoe* in three volumes did not appear until 1830. In 1834 he moved to Bath and at the time of his death he was still one of the proprietors of *The Times*.

Wilson had a large collection of the publications of Daniel Defoe and a considerable library as well as many coins and prints. The books were sold in 1847 comprising 3,438 lots which realized £1,993. He bequeathed his manuscripts to Dr Williams's Library.

Wilson was a friend of Charles Lamb for many years. As early as 1801 Lamb wrote him a letter of apology for a prank on a trip to Richmond in which Lamb nearly succeeded in upsetting the boat. In December 1822 and February 1823 there are letters from Lamb to him about Defoe when Wilson was collecting information for his *Memoir*. Wilson dined with Lamb in May 1828 and Crabb Robinson says that they had not met for twenty years. In a letter in August 1832 Lamb tells Wilson he might do verses for Mrs Wilson's album, but there is no evidence that he did so.

In 1829 Lamb wrote his 'Estimate of De Foe's Secondary Novels' for Wilson's *Memoir of De Foe* and the latter printed it with Lamb's letter of 16 December 1822. In 1836 Wilson wrote some recollections of Lamb that were printed in *The London Mercury* in December 1934.

Macdonald states in *Critical Essays*, 1903, 335, that Wilson had been a schoolfellow of Lamb's, but no other evidence of this seems to be known and Blunden does not mention it. Lamb was at Christ's from 1782 to 1789 and, as Wilson was not born until 1781, he could only have been there during Lamb's last years at the school.

Winbolt, Samuel Edward, 1868–1944. Schoolmaster. Educated at Christ's Hospital where he became a Grecian and won the Charles Lamb Medal in 1886, passing to Corpus Christi, Oxford. He returned to the school as classics and history master and retired in 1929. He edited *The Poetry and Prose of Coleridge, Lamb and Leigh Hunt (The Christ's Hospital Anthology)*, 1920. He also wrote *James Boyer, A Memoir*, 1936, with notes and an appreciation by Rev. P.J. Boyer. He contributed to *The Times, Evening News* and *The Listener*. In 1940 he presented his Charles Lamb Medal to the Charles Lamb Society.

Winch, William, d.1806. At Christ's Hospital with Lamb and Coleridge. In his letter to Coleridge of 11 October 1802 Lamb says 'Billy Winch' is doing extremely well, having gone out to India on the Bengal Establishment as a Cadet. He was said to be courting his Colonel's daughter. He was promoted Captain in the 1st Regiment of Native Infantry in 1805 but died in 1806.

Winchester, Caleb T. American Professor. Author of *A Group of English Essayists of the Early Nineteenth Century*, New York, 1910.

Windham, William, 1750–1810. English politician. M.P. for Norwich. Chief Secretary for Ireland in 1783. In 1794 Pitt made him Secretary at War, with a seat in the Cabinet. He was a friend of Dr Johnson and a member of both The Literary Club and the Essex House Club.

John Lamb addressed his pamphlet on Lord Erskine's Bill for the prevention of cruelty to animals to Windham, who had opposed the Bill on the grounds that it was not a subject for legislation, although he agreed with the principle expressed.

Winged Horse, The. A Marble Relief by John Michael Rysbrack originally erected in 1739 on the staircase of the Inner Temple, but removed in 1816. Charles Lamb in his essay 'The Old Benchers of the Inner Temple', written in 1821, lamented the loss of the figure. In 1866 the Clock Tower containing the main staircase to the Inner Temple was rebuilt and the carving of the Winged Horse found and re-erected. The Clock Tower was damaged by bombs in 1941, but the Horse survived and when the Temple buildings were repaired and re-built it was re-placed in the Benchers' entrance hall over the doorway into Church Court.

A photograph of the Winged Horse appeared in *The Times* on 16 January 1936, and it is also reproduced in E.V. Lucas's *At the Shrine of Saint Charles,* 1934.

Winter, Sally. Mentioned by Lamb in his essay 'Distant Correspondents' as 'The blooming Miss W——r (you remember Sally W——r).' Lamb's Key gives the name as Sally Winter, but nothing of her seems to have been known until Miss Mann discovered that she was born at Wareside and baptized at Widford in 1782 (*C.L.S. Bulletin* No. 146).

Winterslow. A village in Wiltshire, six miles east of Salisbury. In May 1808 William Hazlitt married Sarah Stoddart who lived near and owned a cottage at Winterslow; after the marriage, which took place in London, they settled down in the country on her property, Middleton Cottage.

In October 1809 the Lambs stayed at Winterslow with the Hazlitts. The visit lasted a month and Mary Lamb wrote to Sarah Hazlitt afterwards about the 'dear, quiet, lazy, delicious month!' Lamb told Coleridge they had daily walks from eight to twenty miles and saw Wilton, Salisbury and Stonehenge. In July 1810 the Lambs again stayed with the Hazlitts at Winterslow, Ned Phillips and Martin Burney accompanying them. Mary Lamb's letter just before the visit makes elaborate plans for helping with the household expenses, without hurting Hazlitt's pride. On the return journey to London, Hazlitt went with his friends as far as Oxford.

When he first went to Winterslow Hazlitt was still a painter, but he gradually turned to writing as a means of livelihood. Some of his lectures and the famous series of essays collected under the name of Winterslow were written at the cottage. His son, William Hazlitt (Mr Registrar Hazlitt), was born there in September 1811 and Hazlitt lived there until about 1812. After the estrangement with his wife he lived at Winterslow Hut. The country around attracted him greatly and he spent some of the happiest days of his life there. From time to time he returned for rest and quiet and his essay 'A Farewell to Essay Writing' was dated from Winterslow in February 1828.

There are references to the Lambs' visits to Winterslow in their letters of 1809 and 1810 and Hazlitt mentions them in his essay 'On the Conversation of Authors' and also in 'A Farewell to Essay Writing'.

Winwar, Frances, b.1900. Author of *Farewell the Banner 'Three Persons and One Soul ...' Coleridge, Wordsworth and Dorothy*, which contains many references to Lamb (n.d., but about 1937). Also wrote *The Romantic Rebels*, 1935.

Wolcot, John, 'Peter Pindar', 1738–1819. Satirist and poet. Studied medicine at Aberdeen and was at one time a clergyman, but returned to medical practice. Came to London in 1780 and started to write satires. Among his works were a mock-heroic poem, *The Lousiad*, 1786, and attacks on George III and Boswell. Lamb was acquainted with his work. In a letter to Wordsworth on 28 April 1815 he says he had once heard 'old obscene beastly Peter Pindar' say he knew what good verse was. Lamb once met him at the house of Henry Rogers, brother of the poet, Samuel Rogers. Crabb Robinson records in his *Diary* that he met Wolcot at dinner at Thelwall's in 1811 but that he felt disgust and all but contempt for him.

Wood, Sir Matthew, 1768–1843. Municipal and political reformer. Alderman and twice Lord Mayor of London and M.P. for the City. A champion of Queen Caroline when she was rejected by her husband, George IV. Lamb wrote 'Sonnet to Matthew Wood, Esq. Alderman and M.P.' beginning 'Hold on thy course uncheck'd, heroic Wood!' which appeared in *The Champion* in May 1820. Wood was a Governor of Christ's Hospital. He was Trustee to the Duke of Kent and Queen Victoria created him a baronet.

Woodberry, George Edward, 1855–1930. American poet and critic. Professor of Comparative Literature at Columbia University, 1891–1904. Author of *Makers of Literature*, New York, 1900, which includes chapters on Charles Lamb, Coleridge, Shelley, Landor, Wordsworth and Sir George Beaumont. The chapter on Lamb originally appeared in 1892 in the edition of *The Essays of Elia* published by Little, Brown & Co. He also wrote *Studies in Letters and Life* and *The Appreciation of Literature*.

Woodcock, George. Author of *William Godwin*, 1946, which contains many references to Charles Lamb. In 1950 he edited for The Grey Walls Press a selection of *The Letters of Charles Lamb* with an introduction and notes. It was based on Lucas's edition of 1935.

Woodring, Carl R, b.1919. American Professor of Literature at Columbia University. Author of 'Charles Lamb in the Harvard Library' in the *Harvard Library Bulletin*, 1956, a most valuable account of the greatest interest to students of Lamb. He also contributed to the same periodical 'Lamb takes a holiday' in 1960. To the *Keats-Shelley Memorial Bulletin* in 1959 he contributed 'The Hunt Trials'. Among his books are *Victorian Samplers: William and Mary Howitt*, 1952; *Politics in the Poetry of Coleridge*, 1961; *Wordsworth*, 1965; and *Politics in English Romantic Poetry*, 1970. He also wrote an introduction to the Houtchens's *Leigh Hunt's Political and Occasional Essays*, 1962. *Charles Lamb Bulletin*, April–July 1975 printed his 'Lamb's Hoaxes and the Lamb Canon'.

Woodthorpe, Henry (Senior), d.1825. Educated at Christ's Hospital, but before Lamb's day. He was the secretary of The Amicable Society of Blues, 1788–9, and President in 1790 and 1803. From 1801 to 1825 he was Town Clerk of London and at the ceremony of the laying of the first stone of New London Bridge in 1825 he read aloud the Latin inscription on the copper plate to be placed beneath the stone. He was chairman of the dinner on 11 February 1817 when Lamb was the guest of the Amicable Society of Blues.

Woodthorpe, Henry (Junior). Educated at Christ's Hospital. Son of Henry Woodthorpe, Senior, also an old Blue. He succeeded his father as Town Clerk of London, 1825–43. He was Secretary of The Amicable Society of Blues in 1809 and President in 1816 and 1830. He attended the stone laying ceremony of New London Bridge in 1825. When it was decided to invite Lamb to dine with the Amicable Society on 11 February 1817 Woodthorpe as President made the arrangements.

   Although in receipt of an excellent salary as Town Clerk, Woodthorpe was excessively generous to friends and relations and in 1837 was in the Fleet prison for debt. He was a Vice-President and one of the trustees of the Benevolent Society of Blues and also a Governor of Christ's Hospital.

Wordsworth, Dora, 1804–47. Daughter of William Wordsworth. Married Edward Quillinan in 1841. She visited the Lambs in 1817 with her parents. Lamb wrote verses for Dora Wordsworth's album.

She wrote *A Journal of a Few Month's Residence in Portugal* and *Glimpses of the South of Spain*.

Wordsworth, Dorothy, 1771–1855. Sister of William Wordsworth. Described by Professor de Selincourt as 'probably the most remarkable and most distinguished of English writers who never wrote a line for the general public'. Her *Journals* were printed in their entirety for the first time in 1941. In 1829 she had a nervous breakdown and for the rest of her life was an invalid. Lamb had first met her at Nether Stowey in 1797 and she and her brother became close friends of the Lambs and visited them occasionally in London. There are numerous letters from both Charles and Mary Lamb to Dorothy Wordsworth, all of great interest. Sometimes Lamb sent his verses and those of his sister to her. Coleridge in a letter to Cottle in July 1797 described her as Wordsworth's 'exquisite sister'.

Wordsworth, John, 1772–1805. Brother of William Wordsworth. He was Captain of the East Indiaman *Earl of Abergavenny* which was wrecked off Portland Bill in February 1805 when he was drowned. Lamb refers to the accident in several letters to Wordsworth and on the poet's behalf saw various members of the crew who had survived to try to establish what had happened. An inquiry on the loss of the vessel was held by the Court of Directors of the East India Company. Wordsworth's poem 'Character of the Happy Warrior' is said to have been inspired by his brother's character; Wordsworth also wrote 'Elegiac Verses in memory of my brother, John Wordsworth'.

Wordsworth, William, 1770–1850. Poet Laureate. Educated at Hawkshead School and St John's College, Cambridge. His first published work appeared in 1793. With Coleridge he issued *The Lyrical Ballads* in 1798: the second edition with the famous preface came in 1800. He settled at Grasmere in the Lake District in 1799 and married his cousin Mary Hutchinson in 1802. In 1813 he moved to Rydal Mount and the same year was appointed a Distributor of Stamps for Westmorland. Published *The Excursion* in 1814 and *Peter Bell* and *The Waggoner* in 1819. He was appointed Poet Laureate in 1843 on the death of Robert Southey.

Wordsworth first met Charles Lamb at Nether Stowey in 1797. The poet and his sister had come to Racedown to visit Coleridge who was living near (*see* entry for Nether Stowey) and Lamb visited Coleridge in July of that year. Both William and Dorothy Wordsworth remained life long friends of the Lambs and many letters between them have been preserved. Wordsworth dedicated his volume *The Waggoner* to Charles Lamb. In 1835 he wrote a poem to be engraved on Lamb's tombstone, but it was too long to use. The same year he wrote 'Extempore Effusion upon the death of James Hogg' which contained the lines:

> And Lamb, the frolic and the gentle,
> Has vanished from his lonely hearth.

By this time Wordsworth, having reached old age, had survived most of his friends.

Owing to Wordsworth's importance as a poet, there are many volumes devoted to his life and his work; in most of them Charles Lamb appears.

Wrench, Benjamin, 1778–1843. Comedian. Joined Tate Wilkinson's company at York, played many parts at Bath and appeared at the Lyceum when it was used by the Drury Lane Company in 1809. Played at Drury Lane with Elliston, Dowton, Bannister, Fanny Kelly and Harriot Mellon. In 1815 he left Drury Lane to play at the Lyceum; later he played in the provinces. In 1826 he was at Covent Garden. Among his best parts were Charles Surface, Dr Pangloss and Captain Absolute. Wrench was still playing in 1840 when he took the part of Captain Dudley Smooth in Bulwer's *Money* at the Haymarket.

Lamb writes of him as 'easy natural Wrench' in his review of Brome's *Jovial Crew* in *The Examiner* in 1819. Lamb mentions him in his review of Isaac Bickerstaffe's *Hypocrite* and in 'New Pieces at the Lyceum'. Lamb also refers to him in his essays 'Ellistoniana' and 'Stage Illusion'.

Wright, Waller Rodwell, d.1826. Lawyer. Friend of Crabb Robinson who stated he was in training for the Bar in 1795. He became British Consul-General for the Republic of the Seven Islands (Ionian Islands), 1800–4. On his return to England he was appointed recorder for Bury St Edmunds and subsequently became President of the Court of Appeals at Malta. He wrote a volume of poems *Horae Ionicae*, 1809, which was praised by Byron, who also thought well of Wright's 'Ode on the installation of the Duke of Gloucester as Chancellor of Cambridge University'. Wright's tragedy *Orestes*, from the Italian of Alfieri, was included in the 1816 edition of *Horae Ionicae*.

Crabb Robinson records in his *Diary* for 21 June 1811 that he spent the evening with Lamb and his sister, Barron Field, Waller Wright and Mord Andrews. It was on this occasion that Lamb made his pun about punsters having no pockets, only 'a ridicule'.

Wroughton, Richard, 1748–1822. Actor and theatre manager. Born at Bath where he had a classical education and was apprenticed to a surgeon, but turned to the stage. He first appeared at Covent Garden in 1768 as Zaphna in *Mahomet* and remained at that theatre for seventeen years, playing principal parts in comedy. He joined

Samuel Arnold in the proprietorship of Sadler's Wells and acted as manager, but soon sold his share. In 1787 he appeared at Drury Lane and remained there for many years. He retired in 1798 but was persuaded by the Drury Lane management to return in 1800. Wroughton acted in Godwin's unsuccessful play *Antonio* on 13 December 1800. He was stage manager at Drury Lane. Among his best parts were Hamlet, Antonio, Sir Peter Teazle, Henry IV and Richard III. He was a great friend of Jack Bannister.

In February 1806 Mary Lamb took Charles's play *Mr H——* to Wroughton; in June they received a letter from him to say it had been accepted by the Proprietors; in October Charles took an amended copy to Wroughton. In her letter of 10 December 1808 Mary Lamb tells Sarah Hazlitt that 'through the medium of Wroughton, there came an invitation and proposal from T.S. [Tom Sheridan], that C.L. should write some scenes in a speaking Pantomime'. Lamb mentions him in 'The Old Actors' as printed in the *London Magazine* in October 1822. Macqueen Pope stated that his real name was 'Rotten', but he wisely changed it.

Wyatt. Comic singer and actor at Sadler's Wells. Lamb's letter of 9 September 1826 to J.B. Dibdin states that 'Liston and Wyat' are to dine with him the next day. In a letter to Moxon on 28 January 1834 Lamb writes that 'Wyatt' lived near the Bell, Edmonton, and knew Edmund Kean.

Yeats, Timothy, c.1713–92. Hop and brandy merchant of 2 St Mary's Hill, Billingsgate. He is the Governor who presented Lamb to Christ's Hospital in 1782, on behalf of his friend, Samuel Salt. Miss Mann has discovered much information about Yeats and his family, which is printed in the *C.L.S. Bulletin* Nos. 132 and 134, among which she states that Yeats presented Lamb because Salt's Presentations had already been used up for other children.

Young, Charles Mayne, 1777–1856. English actor. Educated at Eton and Merchant Taylors' School. First worked as a clerk in a West India house, but left it for the stage. Appeared at Liverpool in 1798, Manchester in 1804 and at the Haymarket in 1807, where he played Hamlet. He went to Covent Garden in 1808 and in 1811 played Macbeth to Mrs Siddons's Lady Macbeth. He appeared with a number of well known actors, including John Philip Kemble, Macready and Miss O'Neill. In 1822 at Drury Lane he played Othello and Iago on alternate nights with Edmund Kean. In 1823–4 he played with Kean at Covent Garden. He retired in 1832.

Among his friends were Charles Mathews and Sir Walter Scott. In private life he was said to be a delightful companion. His acting was praised by Leigh Hunt. Charles Lamb does not seem to have men-

tioned him in his writings, but Crabb Robinson records that on 4
March 1815 he went with Mary Lamb to Covent Garden to see Young
in *The Stranger*, and on 30 November 1824 to the same theatre to see
Young in Planché's *The Woman Never Vexed* and saw the Lambs
there. On 11 March 1812 Robinson notes that he met Young at dinner
and records with awe that 'He is accustomed to call Mrs Siddons
"Sally".'

Chronology of the lives of Charles and Mary Lamb

(After the birth of Charles Lamb, his age is given as the first item in the entry after the year.)

1760   George III came to the throne.

1761   John Lamb married Elizabeth Field.

1762   W.L. Bowles born.

1763   John Lamb (Junior), born June 5. Samuel Rogers born. Boswell met Johnson.

1764   Mary Anne Lamb born December 3. William Hogarth died. Goldsmith's *The Traveller* published.

1765   Percy's *Reliques* published.

1766   Goldsmith's *Vicar of Wakefield* published.

1768   Goldsmith's *The Good Natured Man* first performed at Covent Garden.

1769   Shakespeare Jubilee at Stratford upon Avon organized by Garrick with Mrs Abington as the Comic Muse and Mrs Barry as the Tragic Muse.

1770   John Lamb (Junior) entered Christ's Hospital. William Wordsworth and Basil Montagu born. Chatterton died. Goldsmith's *The Deserted Village* published.

1771   Dorothy Wordsworth and Walter Scott born. Gray and Smollett died. *Humphry Clinker* published.

1772   S.T. Coleridge, H.F. Cary and Thomas Manning born.

1773   Goldsmith's *She Stoops to Conquer* first performed at Covent Garden. Boston tea-ships incident.

1774   Robert Southey born. Goldsmith died. John Woolman's *Journal* published.

1775   Charles Lamb born February 10. Jane Austen, John Hunt, M.G. Lewis, W.S. Landor, Crabb Robinson, James Smith and J.M.W. Turner born. Sheridan's *The Rivals* first performed at Covent Garden. American War of Independence (1775–83).

1776 1. Gibbon's *Decline and Fall*, Volume I, and Adam Smith's *Wealth of Nations* published.

1777 2. Thomas Campbell born. Chatterton's *Rowley Poems* published. Sheridan's *The School for Scandal* first performed at Drury Lane.

1778 3. John Lamb leaves Christ's Hospital. William Hazlitt born. Rousseau died. Fanny Burney's *Evelina* published.

1779 4. Mary Lamb took Charles to visit his great aunt at Mackery End. Thomas Moore and Horace Smith born. David Garrick died.

1780 5. Thomas Arne's *Artaxerxes* performed at Drury Lane, probably when first seen by Charles Lamb. Charles received lessons from the schoolmistress Mrs Reynolds, (1780–1). Gordon Riots occurred in June.

1781 6. Charles Lamb probably attended William Bird's Academy. Admission forms for Christ's Hospital signed March 30. Charles visited grandmother at Blakesware. Charles saw *The Way of the World* and *Robinson Crusoe*, (1781–2). Vincent Novello born. Crabbe's *The Library* published.

1782 7. Charles admitted to Christ's Hospital in July, but not formally received until October 9. Coleridge entered at the same time, having come from the Junior School at Hertford. Fanny Burney's *Cecilia* and Cowper's *Poems* published. Mrs Siddons returned in triumph to Drury Lane in *Isabella*'.

1783 8. Washington Irving born. Crabbe's *The Village* published. John Philip Kemble made his London début at Drury Lane.

1784 9. Bernard Barton, Allan Cunningham, Leigh Hunt and Sheridan Knowles born. Dr Johnson died.

1785 10. De Quincey, T.L. Peacock and John Wilson ('Christopher North') born. Cowper's *The Task* published. Mrs Jordan first acted at Drury Lane. Prince of Wales married Mrs Fitzherbert.

1786 11. Barron Field, W.J. Fox and B.R. Haydon born. Burns's *Poems* (Kilmarnock edition) and Beckford's *Vathek* published.

1782 12. Wordsworth at Cambridge, studied Italian under Agostino Isola. Charles Cowden Clarke, Edmund Kean, Mary R. Mitford and B.W. Procter born.

1788 13. Byron, Hook, Barham and Charles Ollier born. Gibbon's *Decline and Fall* completed. Warren Hastings impeached.

1789 14. Charles Lamb left Christ's Hospital on November 23. Before leaving he wrote his verses 'Mille Viae Mortis' in James Boyer's *Liber Aureus*. Blake's *Songs of Innocence*, Bowles's *Sonnets* and Gilbert White's *Natural History of Selborne* published. Lady Blessington born. The Bastille was stormed during French Revolution.

1790 15. Charles Lamb worked in Joseph Paice's office on Bread Street Hill. Benjamin Franklin and Adam Smith died.

1791 16. Charles Lamb entered the South Sea House on 1 September. Coleridge left Christ's Hospital and proceeded to Jesus College, Cambridge. Leigh Hunt entered Christ's Hospital on November 23. Boswell's *Life of Johnson*, Cowper's *Homer*, Paine's *Rights of Man* and D'Israeli's *Curiosities of Literature*, Volume I published. Louis XVI fled.

1792 17. Lamb left South Sea House on February 8 and entered East India House on April 5. Samuel Salt died on July 27 and Mary Field, Lamb's grandmother, on July 31. Southey expelled from Westminster; George Dyer took rooms in Clifford's Inn and remained there the rest of his life. Holcroft's *Road to Ruin* produced at Covent Garden. George Cruikshank, T.J. Hogg, Edward Irving, P.B. Shelley and Trelawny born. Sir Joshua Reynolds died. Samuel Rogers' *Pleasures of Memory* published.

1793 18. The Lambs probably moved from the Temple to Little Queen Street. Southey attended Balliol. Coleridge fled from Cambridge and enlisted in the Dragoons on December 2. John Clare and W.C. Macready born. Gilbert White died. Godwin's *Political Justice* published. During the reign of terror in France, Louis XVI and Marie Antoinette were executed. War with France began (1793–1803).

1794 19. The Lambs were living at No. 7 Little Queen Street. Charles was in love with 'Alice W——' (Ann Simmons), 1794–5. Coleridge discharged from the Dragoons in April and returned to Cambridge, but left in December without a degree. Lamb and Coleridge met at the 'Salutation and Cat' in Newgate Street in December. Lamb's 'Sonnet to Mrs Siddons' published in the *Morning Chronicle* on December 29. Coleridge and Southey first met in June at Oxford. Pantisocracy scheme discussed. Holcroft, Thelwall and others tried on a charge of high treason, but acquitted. Drury Lane Theatre rebuilt. Danton and Robespierre guillotined. Edward Gibbon died and J.G. Lockhart born. Blake's *Songs of Experience*, Coleridge's and Southey's *Fall of Robespierre*, Godwin's *Caleb Williams*, Paine's *Age of Reason* and Mrs Radcliffe's *Mysteries of Udolpho* published.

1795 20. Lamb and Southey first met in January. Coleridge and Wordsworth first met in Bristol in September. Wordsworth was living at Racedown. Coleridge lectured in Bristol and on October 4 married Sarah Fricker. On November 14 Southey married Edith Fricker and went to Spain and Portugal. In November and December Lamb spent six weeks in a mad house at Hoxton and wrote verses 'To my Sister' while there.

Keats, Darley, Carlyle and Talfourd born. Boswell died. Landor's *Poems* & W.H. Ireland's Shakespeare forgeries published. Warren Hastings acquitted. Napoleon campaigning in Italy.

1796   21. First extant letters written from Lamb to Coleridge. Coleridge's *The Watchman* published in March and his *Poems on Various Subjects* in April. Charles Lloyd's *Poems on the Death of Priscilla Farmer* and James White's *Original Letters of Sir John Falstaff* published. In July Lamb contributed a sonnet to the *Monthly Magazine*. Mary Lamb, temporarily insane, stabbed her mother on September 22. John Lamb injured his leg. On December 31 Charles Lamb, his father and his aunt moved to No. 45 Little Chapel Street, Pentonville. Coleridge moved to Nether Stowey in December: he had begun to take laudanum in November. Hartley Coleridge and J.H. Reynolds born. Robert Lovell and Robert Burns died. Fanny Burney's *Camilla*, Southey's *Joan of Arc* and M.G. Lewis's *The Monk* published.

1797   22. Charles Lloyd visited Lamb in London in January. Sarah Lamb (Aunt Hetty) died in February and in April Mary Lamb left the private asylum to move into lodgings in Hackney. Charles Lamb visited Coleridge at Nether Stowey July 9–16 and met William and Dorothy Wordsworth. The latter moved from Racedown to Alfoxden on July 16. In August Lamb visited Southey at Burton, Hampshire, accompanied by Charles Lloyd. Lamb contributed to the *Monthly Magazine* and Coleridge and Wordsworth planned the *Lyrical Ballads*. In June the second edition of Coleridge's *Poems* was published with contributions from Charles Lamb and Charles Lloyd. William Godwin married Mary Wollstonecraft on March 29, but she died in September, a week after her daughter, Mary, was born. Mary Lamb was again ill in December. Horace Walpole, John Wilkes and Charles Macklin died. *The Anti-Jacobin* was started. A great financial crisis occurred and the Bank of England suspended payments.

1798   23. In January Lamb wrote 'The Old Familiar Faces'. Lamb and Coleridge became estranged and in May Lamb wrote his 'Theses Quaedam Theologicae'. In May/June Lamb visited Charles Lloyd at Birmingham for two weeks. Lamb's *A Tale of Rosamund Gray* was published as well as *Blank Verse* by Charles Lloyd and Charles Lamb. On July 9 *The Anti-Jacobin* referred to Lamb in 'The New Morality' and on 1 August *The Anti-Jacobin Review and Magazine* had Gillray's cartoon of Lamb and Lloyd. Lamb was writing 'Pride's Cure' (*John Woodvil*) and Hancock did a chalk drawing of him. In the spring Coleridge and Hazlitt first met and in the autumn

Coleridge and the Wordsworths went to Germany. *Lyrical Ballads* (September), Landor's *Gebir* and Charles Lloyd's *Edmund Oliver* were published. Battle of the Nile fought.

1799   24. Robert Lloyd was in London with Lamb in January. John Lamb (Senior) died in April, after which Charles moved to No. 36 Chapel Street, Pentonville, where Mary joined him. In May Charles dined with his 'Anna', now married to J.T. Bartram. In October Lamb visited Widford and Blakesware and Wordsworth settled at Dove Cottage. Leigh Hunt left Christ's Hospital on November 20. Lamb visited Charles Lloyd at Cambridge and met Thomas Manning in December. Thomas Hood born. George Washington died. Campbell's *Pleasures of Hope* and Godwin's *St Leon* published. Napoleon appointed First Consul.

1800   25. Manning stayed with Lamb for three days in January. Lamb first met Godwin. Coleridge stayed with Lamb in Pentonville in March. In May Mary Lamb was ill and Charles stayed with James White. In June Charles moved to No. 27 Southampton Buildings and a little later visited Gutch's family at Oxford. In August Coleridge moved to Greta Hall, Keswick and Manning stayed with Lamb for a few days. In August Lamb wrote his amusing letter to Manning about George Dyer and Manning's *Algebra*. In October Lamb met Rickman through George Dyer and Fenwick's farce *The Indian* was produced at Drury Lane. In December Godwin's *Antonio* with Lamb's epilogue was produced at Drury Lane but failed. Lamb wrote his amusing letter to Manning on December 16 describing the failure. On December 27 Lamb wrote his famous letter to Manning about the Preface to George Dyer's *Poems*. Lamb wrote his imitations of Burton and 'Thekla's Song' for Coleridge. Extracts from *John Woodvil* were printed in *Recreations in Agriculture* in November. *John Woodvil* was refused by Kemble. Bloomfield's *Farmer's Boy* and Moore's *Anacreon* published. Derwent Coleridge, Macaulay and Henry Taylor born. Cowper and Amos Cottle died. Napoleon defeated the Austrians at Marengo.

1801   26. Lamb visited Manning at Cambridge on January 5 and wrote letters to Wordsworth in January and Manning in February containing eulogies of London. In March the Lambs moved to No. 16 Mitre Court Buildings, Kings Bench Walk. On July 8 Randal Norris married Elizabeth Faint; Mary Lamb was bridesmaid. In August Lamb indulged in a prank in a boat at Richmond for which he had to write a letter of apology to Walter Wilson. The Lambs spent their holiday at Margate in September. In October George Dyer was nursed at the Lambs and in November Charles wrote his amusing letter to Rickman describing George's complaint, which was lack of food. In November both Coleridge and Manning stayed in London and in December Godwin married Mrs Clairmont. The Second Edition of *Lyrical Ballads* was published in January, a German edition of *Rosamund Gray* appeared, as did Leigh Hunt's *Juvenilia* and Southey's *Thalaba*. Lamb was writing for *The Albion* and then for the *Morning Chronicle*. Battles of the Baltic & Copenhagen fought.

1802   27. Lamb was writing for the *Morning Post* ('The Londoner', G.F. Cooke &c). *John Woodvil* published in February at Lamb's expense. Manning went to Paris to study Chinese. Hester Savory married Charles Stoke Dudley on 1 July. In August/September the Lambs visited Coleridge at Keswick for three weeks. Wordsworth visited Calais, but later in London was taken to Bartholomew Fair by Lamb. On September 24 Lamb wrote his fine letter to Manning describing his visit to the Lakes. Wordsworth married Mary Hutchinson on 4 October. Sara Coleridge born. Cobbett's *Political Register* and the *Edinburgh Review* started. Peace of Amiens declared.

1803   28. In February Lamb first met the Burneys. On 9 February Hester Savory died and Lamb wrote his poem 'Hester'. On February 19 Lamb wrote his famous letter to Manning about going to China. Mary Lamb became ill in March while Coleridge was staying with the Lambs. In July the Lambs visited the Isle of Wight with the Burneys and went to Sadler's Wells with Southey and Rickman. Lamb wrote for the *Morning Post* on the theme of pink stockings. Hayley's *Life of Cowper*, Godwin's *Life of Chaucer*. James Burney's *History of Discoveries in the South Seas*, Volume I, published. T.L. Beddoes, George Borrow, R.W. Emerson, R.H. Horne, Douglas Jerrold, Bulwer Lytton, John Wordsworth and R.S. Surtees born. Second War with France started.

1804   29. Lamb contributed to the *Morning Post*. Coleridge was in London in March and sailed for Malta on 9 April. Hazlitt and Lamb met in the spring and in October Hazlitt painted Lamb's portrait. The Lambs went to Richmond for a month's holiday in August/September. Laman Blanchard, Benjamin Disraeli and Dora Wordsworth born. William Blake tried for sedition and published his *Jerusalem*. Napoleon proclaimed Emperor.

1805   30. Captain John Wordsworth drowned on February 5. De Quincey met Lamb, probably early in the year. Lamb wrote his 'Farewell to Tobacco'. Mary Lamb was ill from June to August. Godwin started the Juvenile Library. Lamb's *King and Queen of Hearts* published. W.H. Ainsworth and Mazzini born. Hazlitt's *Principles of Human Action*,

Southey's *Madoc*, Scott's *Lay of the Last Minstrel* and Cary's *Inferno* published. Nelson killed in the Battle of Trafalgar on October 21. Battle of Austerlitz fought.

1806 31. Sarah Stoddart stayed with the Lambs for three weeks in January. In February Lamb was helping George Burnett with his *Specimens of English Prose Writers* and took a room to write undisturbed. Wrote *Mr H——*. Lamb met Crabb Robinson and R.W. Elliston and started his Wednesday evening parties. Manning sailed for China in May, *Mr H——* was accepted for Drury Lane in June and in July Lamb spent his holiday at home. During the spring the Lambs had been writing the *Tales from Shakespeare*. In August Coleridge returned to England and stayed with the Lambs. On November 20 Holcroft's *The Vindictive Man* failed at Drury Lane and on 10 December Lamb's *Mr H——* shared the same fate. Mrs Inchbald started to publish her *British Theatre*. E.B. Barrett and J.S. Mill born. C.J.Fox and William Pitt died.

1807 32. *Tales from Shakespeare* published in January. Coleridge and De Quincey met. In June Lamb visited the Clarksons at Bury St Edmunds. Mary Lamb became ill. Lamb worked at the British Museum on his *Dramatic Specimens*. In October Hazlitt became engaged to Sarah Stoddart. Godwin's *Faulkener* and Henry Siddons's *Time's-a-Tell Tale* both produced at Drury Lane. Byron's *Hours of Idleness*, Moore's *Irish Melodies*, Hunt's *Critical Essays on the performers of the London Theatres*, and Wordsworth's *Poems in Two Volumes* published. The Slave Trade was abolished.

1808 33. Coleridge lectured at the Royal Institution, January/ April. Wordsworth was in London and met Crabb Robinson at the Lambs on March 15. Hazlitt married Sarah Stoddart on 1 May, Mary Lamb was bridesmaid. Lamb's *Specimens of Dramatic Poets*, *Adventures of Ulysses* and *Mrs Leicester's School* published. Leigh Hunt started *The Examiner*. In December Lamb wrote scenes for a 'speaking pantomime'. Scott's *Marmion* and Southey's *Chronicles of the Cid* published. Covent Garden Theatre burnt down. Peninsula War began.

1809 34. The Lambs moved from Mitre Court Buildings to No. 34 Southampton Buildings in March and in May again to No. 4 Inner Temple Lane. Coleridge started *The Friend* in June. The Lambs' *Poetry for Children* published as well as second editions of *Mrs Leicester's School* and *Tales from Shakespeare*. Lamb wrote lottery puffs. The Lambs visited the Hazlitts at Winterslow in September/October. De Quincey settled at Dove Cottage in November. Wordsworth's *Convention of Cintra* and Byron's *English Bards and Scotch Reviewers* published and the *Quarterly Review* founded. Drury Lane Theatre burnt down in February. Edward FitzGerald, Alfred Tennyson, Charles Darwin, W.E. Gladstone, Abraham Lincoln and E.A. Poe born. Thomas Holcroft & Tom Paine died.

1810   35. John Lamb's pamphlet *A Letter to the Right Hon. William Windham* published in January or February. In July the Lambs visited the Hazlitts at Winterslow. During the summer Dorothy Wordsworth visited the Lambs. Coleridge and Wordsworth estranged, October–November. Coleridge living with the Morgans in London in November. Crabb Robinson first met Coleridge. Scott's *Lady of the Lake* and Southey's *Curse of Kehama* published. Thornton Leigh Hunt born.

1811   36. Crabb Robinson began his famous *Diary*. Mary Lamb was ill in the spring. Charles wrote for Leigh Hunt's *Reflector* ('Genius and Character of Hogarth' in October issue). In September/October Charles spent his month's holiday at home and shortly afterwards Mary went to Richmond for a week staying with Mrs Burney. *Prince Dorus* and *Beauty and the Beast* published. Leigh Hunt's *Examiner* was prosecuted for an article on army flogging, but acquitted. Shelley was expelled from Oxford and he married Harriet Westbrook. In October Robert Lloyd died and in November Lamb's 'Memoir' was printed in the *Gentleman's Magazine*. In November Coleridge lectured at the London Philosophical Society. Mylius's *First Book of Poetry*, Jane Austen's *Sense and Sensibility*, Scott's *Don Roderick* and Shelley's *The Necessity of Atheism* published. Charles Kean and Thackeray born. George Burnett died.

1812   37. Hazlitt lectured at the Russell Institution on the History of Philosophy in January. The Hazlitts moved to London to No. 19 York Street, Westminster, and the curious christening party for Hazlitt's son took place. Lamb continued to write for the *Reflector* (the essay on Shakespeare's plays appeared in March), and he contributed 'The Triumph of the Whale' to *The Examiner*. Later in the year the Hunts were prosecuted for a libel on the Prince Regent and sentenced to imprisonment. In August Lamb became the owner of Button Snap. William Gifford attacked Lamb in the *Quarterly Review*. Coleridge lectured at the Surrey Institution. Drury Lane Theatre re-opened. Byron's *Childe Harold*, Cantos I and II, and Horace and James Smith's *Rejected Addresses* published. Robert Browning, Dickens and John Forster born. Spencer Percival assassinated. Napoleon retreated from Moscow.

1813   38. Coleridge's *Remorse* produced at Drury Lane on January 23 with Prologue by Lamb who attended the performance. On February 3 Leigh Hunt imprisoned in Horsemonger Lane

Gaol where he was frequently visited by the Lambs. Lamb's 'Confessions of a Drunkard' printed in *The Philanthropist* and his 'Recollections of Christ's Hospital' in the *Gentleman's Magazine*. His 'Table Talk' appeared in *The Examiner*. In June Mary Lamb was ill at Windsor. Southey appointed Poet Laureate. Byron's *Giour* and *Bride of Abydos*, Jane Austen's *Pride and Prejudice*, Southey's *Life of Nelson* and Shelley's *Queen Mab* published.

1814   39. The Lambs changed their weekly parties to monthly functions to lessen the strain on their health. Lamb wrote an epilogue for Kenney's play *Debtor and Creditor*. In October Lamb's review of Wordsworth's *Excursion* was printed in the *Quarterly Review*. The Lambs discovered four untenanted rooms at their Inner Temple Lane lodgings and Mary Lamb's letter of 2 November to Barbara Betham gave interesting details of the use they made of them. In December Mary Lamb was writing her article 'On Needle-Work' and made herself ill by overwork. Shelley and Mary Godwin left England together on 28 July accompanied by Claire Clairmont. Edmund Kean first appeared in London. Cary's *Dante* (complete), Byron's *Corsair*, Jane Austen's *Mansfield Park*, Leigh Hunt's *Feast of the Poets*, J.H. Reynolds's *Safie* and Scott's *Waverley* published. James Boyer, Lamb's old schoolmaster, died. Napoleon exiled to Elba.

1815   40. Lamb's poem 'To T.L.H.' published in *The Examiner* on 1 January. Lamb and Talfourd first met. On 3 February Leigh Hunt left prison, and later with Hazlitt started the 'Round Table' essays in the *Examiner*. In May Wordsworth was in London and Leigh Hunt and Wordsworth met. Lamb and Barron Field visited Mackery End. In August the Lambs visited Cambridge. Mary Lamb was ill in September. Lamb sold Button Snap. On 25 December Lamb wrote an amusing letter to Manning full of nonsense. Wordsworth's *White Doe of Rylstone* and Scott's *Guy Mannering* published. Priscilla Wordsworth (née Lloyd) died in October. Napoleon left Elba in March and returned to France. Battle of Waterloo fought June 18. Napoleon exiled to St Helena in July.

1816   41. On February 17 Fanny Kelly was fired at by a lunatic at Drury Lane Theatre. On 16 April Coleridge went to live with James Gillman. The work at East India House was reorganized and Lamb's salary doubled. Leigh Hunt and Keats met. In July the Lambs spent a month's holiday at Calne, Wiltshire, with the Morgans; in the autumn they lived in lodgings at Dalston for ten weeks. It was probably this year that Lamb met the Novello family. Following the death of Harriet Shelley, Shelley married Mary Godwin in December.

Macready appeared at Covent Garden. Jane Austen's *Emma*, Byron's *Childe Harold*, Canto III, Coleridge's *Christabel* (with Kubla Khan), Hazlitt's *Memoirs of Thomas Holcroft*, Leigh Hunt's *The Story of Rimini*, Peacock's *Headlong Hall*, Shelley's *Alastor*, J.H. Reynolds's *The Naiad* and Scott's *The Antiquary* published. Byron left England for the last time. Charlotte Brontë born. Sheridan and Herbert Southey died. Elgin Marbles placed on view in London. Spa Fields Riots occurred.

1817   42. On 11 February Lamb attended the annual dinner of the Amicable Society of Blues as a guest at the London Tavern. Mary Lamb was ill in April. In the summer the Lambs visited Brighton with Mrs Morgan. William Hone was tried for blasphemy, but acquitted. During the autumn Manning returned to England, and in October the Lambs moved from Inner Temple Lane to No. 20 Great Russell Street, Covent Garden. *Blackwood's Magazine* in October attacked Leigh Hunt in an article 'The Cockney School of Poetry'. On December 28 the famous party in Haydon's studio occurred with Wordsworth, Keats and others, at which Lamb teased the Comptroller of Stamps. Lamb seems to have met Keats for the first time this year. Hazlitt dedicated his *Characters of Shakespeare's Plays* to Lamb and other books published were Keats's *Poems*, Coleridge's *Biographia Literaria* and *Sibylline Leaves*, Godwin's *Mandeville*, Moore's *Lalla Rookh*, Peacock's *Melincourt* amd Hazlitt's *Round Table*. Both *Blackwood's Magazine* and the *Literary Gazette* were founded. G.H. Lewes and H.D. Thoreau born. Jane Austen died.

1818   43. Coleridge lectured on Shakespeare and poetical literature January/March. Coleridge met Thomas Allsop. On 18 February Lamb wrote a fine letter to Mrs Wordsworth. Lamb contributed to the *Examiner*. In June Lamb's *Works* were published by the Olliers and he visited Birmingham. Keats was attacked in the April issue of the *Quarterly Review* (issued in September). In December Coleridge lectured on philosophy and on Shakespeare. Shelley finally left England. Jane Austen's *Northanger Abbey and Persuasion*, Leigh Hunt's *Foliage*, Hazlitt's *Lectures on the English Poets* and *A View of the English Stage*, Keats's *Endymion*, Peacock's *Nightmare Abbey*, Susan Ferrier's *Marriage*, Shelley's *Revolt of Islam*, Mary Shelley's *Frankenstein*, Scott's *Rob Roy* and *Heart of Midlothian* published. Leigh Hunt's *Literary Pocket Book* started. Emily Brontë born. Queen Charlotte died.

1819   44. Lamb sent a number of contributions to the *Examiner*. In May Charles Lloyd was in London and later introduced Macready to Lamb. Wordsworth published *The Waggoner* in

May dedicated to Charles Lamb. On 20 July Charles Lamb proposed marriage to Fanny Kelly, but she refused him. In November Lamb's sonnet on Miss Kelly was printed in the *Morning Chronicle*. In August Lamb visited Cambridge. In the autumn William Wordsworth (Junior) stayed with the Lambs. Byron's *Don Juan*, Cantos I & II, Barron Field's *First Fruits of Australian Poetry*, Hazlitt's *Lectures on the English Comic Writers*, Leigh Hunt's *Hero and Leander and Bacchus and Ariadne*, Wordsworth's *Peter Bell*, Scott's *Ivanhoe* and Charles Lloyd's *Nugae Canorae* published. Leigh Hunt's *Indicator* started in October. T.L. Peacock entered the East India House in the Examiner's Department. Queen Victoria born. Peterloo Massacre took place.

1820   45. On 1 January the *London Magazine* and *Retrospective Review* started, as well as a second *London Magazine* owned by Gold and Northhouse. In May Southey was in London and Wordsworth was there in June. In July the Lambs visited Cambridge and met Emma Isola. In August Lamb's first contribution appeared in the *London Magazine*, 'Recollections of the South Sea House', and he had items in it every month for the rest of the year. He also contributed to *The Champion*, *The Indicator*, *The Examiner*, *Morning Chronicle* and *The New Times*. He first met Thomas Allsop. Mary Lamb became ill in September. Emma Isola spent Christmas with the Lambs. Keats sailed for Italy in September. Clare's *Poems*, Barton's *Poems*, Keats's *Lamia and Isabella and Hyperion*, Hazlitt's *Lectures on the Dramatic Literature of the Age of Elizabeth*, Leigh Hunt's *Amyntas* (dedicated to Keats), Peacock's *Four Ages of Poetry*, J.H. Reynolds's *The Fancy*, Shelley's *The Cenci* (first London edition), and *Promethus Unbound*, published. Sheridan Knowles's *Virginius* produced at Covent Garden. George III and James White died. Queen Caroline tried.

1821   46. Lucas *Life*, II.60, calls 1821 'Lamb's golden year' when the best of the Elia essays were written. *The London Magazine* included 'Mrs Battle's Opinions on Whist', 'All Fools' Day', 'My Relations', 'Mackery End in Hertfordshire', 'Imperfect Sympathies', 'The Old Benchers of the Inner Temple', 'Witches and other Night Fears', and 'My First Play'. ('Dream Children', although written in 1821, was not printed until January 1822). In January B.W. Procter's play *Mirandola* was produced at Covent Garden. On February 27 John Scott, editor of Baldwin's *London Magazine*, died as the result of a duel. On 7 March Lamb met Sir Walter Scott. On 14 April Sarah Burney, the Admiral's daughter, married her cousin John Payne and the Lambs attended the wedding.

Lamb met Charles Mathews at Gillman's in May, the same month the *London Magazine* was sold by Baldwin, Cradock & Joy to Taylor & Hessey. In June the Lambs spent a holiday at Margate and in July Charles met Mrs Barbauld. Taylor & Hessey gave the first dinner to their contributors in July. Thomas Hood became sub-editor of the *London Magazine* and met Lamb. On 26 October John Lamb died and Mary Lamb became ill. Leigh Hunt embarked to join Byron and Shelley in Italy, but did not sail until the following year. Admiral Burney died on November 17. Clare's *Village Minstrel*, Hazlitt's *Table Talk*, Charles Lloyd's *Desultory Thoughts in London*, Leigh Hunt's *The Months*, Scott's *Kenilworth* and Shelley's *Adonais* published. Keats, Mrs Inchbald, Mrs Piozzi, Queen Caroline and Napoleon died.

1822   47. Lamb contributed to the *London Magazine* every month during the year. On 14 March John Lamb's pictures were sold at Christies. In May the Hunts eventually left England for Italy. In June the Lambs went to France to visit James Kenney at Versailles. Mary Lamb became ill and did not return to England until the end of August or the beginning of September. On 8 July Shelley was drowned. In August Lamb and Barton first met. In September the first number of Leigh Hunt's *The Liberal* appeared containing Byron's 'Vision of Judgment'. Hazlitt was divorced from his first wife. De Quincey's *Confessions of an English Opium-Eater* (reprinted from the *London Magazine* of 1821), Beddoes's *Bride's Tragedy*, Darley's *Errors of Ecstasie*, Washington Irving's *Bracebridge Hall*, Peacock's *Maid Marian*, Rogers's *Italy*, Part I, Scott's *Fortunes of Nigel* and *Peveril of the Peak*, Shelley's *Hellas* and *The Poetical Recreations of The Champion* published. The 'Noctes Ambrosianae' started in *Blackwood's Magazine*.

1823   48. *The Essays of Elia* published (actually issued in December 1822). Lamb contributed to the *London Magazine* every month except August. On 9 January Lamb wrote his famous letter to Barton about giving up the bank. On 4 April the notable dinner occurred at Monkhouse's with Wordsworth, Coleridge, Moore, Rogers, Crabb Robinson and Lamb. In May the Lambs were at Dalston and in June they went to Hastings for a holiday. At the end of July they moved to Colebrooke Cottage, Islington. Mary Lamb was ill in September, the month Lamb made his first will. In October Lamb's 'Letter of Elia to Robert Southey Esq' appeared in the *London Magazine*. In November Southey was in London when his differences with Lamb were finally made up. During November Charles Lamb dined at the Mansion House and George

Dyer walked into the New River at Islington. The Lambs adopted Emma Isola. Byron sailed for Greece. John Philip Kemble died. Hazlitt's *Liber Amoris*, Hunt's *Literary Examiner*, Moore's *Loves of the Angels* and Scott's *Quentin Durward* published.

1824   49. In April Manning and Wordsworth were both in London. In May George Dyer married Honor Mather, and Lamb's friend J.S. Munden retired from the stage. Lamb wrote to Barton on May 15 praising Blake's work. In June the Lambs spent their holiday at home. Barron Field returned from New South Wales in June and later Lamb attended an amateur performance of Richard II at Henry Field's house, for which he had written an epilogue. Edward Irving and Carlyle visited Lamb in July. In October B.W. Procter married Ann Skepper. Byron died in Greece. Barton's *Poetic Vigils*, Hazlitt's *Select British Poets*, Landor's *Imaginary Conversations*, and Mary Mitford's *Our Village* published.

1825   50. At the end of February Manning stayed with the Lambs. Earlier in the month Thomas Monkhouse had died. Lamb met Harrison Ainsworth. Brooke Pulham did his caricature of Lamb. On 29 March Lamb retired from East India House with a pension of £450 per annum. On 27 May Lamb attended the funeral of John Lamb's widow. Lamb's farce *The Pawnbroker's Daughter* was submitted to several theatres but rejected. Early in the year Taylor & Hessey sold the *London Magazine* to Henry Southern. During the spring and summer Lamb had a nervous breakdown. In July the Lambs joined the Allsops in Enfield. Mary Lamb was ill in September. Lamb contributed to the *London Magazine*, *Every Day Book*, *New Monthly Magazine* and *New Times*. The Hunts were back in England by December. Coleridge's *Aids to Reflection*, Hazlitt's *Spirit of the Age*, Hone's *Every Day Book*, Hood's and Reynold's *Odes and Addresses to Great People* and Horace Smith's *Gaieties and Gravities* published. John Poole's play *Paul Pry* was acted at the Haymarket. During the year there were great financial difficulties in the country and many banks failed.

1826   51. Lamb contributed his 'Popular Fallacies' to the *New Monthly Magazine* (January–June, September). Henry Meyer painted Lamb's portrait. On 30 June and 9 September Lamb wrote his interesting and amusing letters to John Bates Dibdin at Hastings. During the year Lamb read the Garrick Plays at the British Museum. William Hone was imprisoned for debt. Lamb contributed to the *Every Day Book*. Lamb met P.G. Patmore at Hazlitt's lodgings. Darley's *Labours of Idleness*, Hazlitt's *Plain Speaker*, Hood's *Whims and Oddities*,

P.G. Patmore's *Rejected Articles*, Scott's *Woodstock* and Mary Shelley's *The Last Man* published. William Gifford died. University College, London, founded.

1827   52. Randal Norris died on 20 January. In May Lamb wrote his poem 'On an Infant Dying as soon as born'. The Hoods stayed with the Lambs at Mrs Leishman's at Enfield during the summer and in July Hood made his caricature of Mary Lamb. Charles taught Latin to Emma Isola. In August Lamb sent his play *The Wife's Trial* to Charles Kemble. In September the Lambs moved from Islington to Chase Side, Enfield. Lamb contributed to the *Table Book* and *New Monthly Magazine*. Clare's *Shepherd's Calendar*, Darley's *Sylvia*, Barton's *The Widow*, Hood's *Plea of the Midsummer Fairies*, and Tennyson's *Poems by Two Brothers* published. William Blake died.

1828   53. In April Emma Isola became a governess with Mrs Williams at Fornham. Talfourd's son born and named Charles Lamb Talfourd. Both *The Athenaeum* and *The Spectator* started. Lamb contributed to *The Bijou* and *The Spectator*. Lamb's 'The Wife's Trial' printed in *Blackwood's Magazine*. *Elia. Second Series*, a pirated edition, published in America. Barton's *New Year's Eve*, Laman Blanchard's *Lyric Offerings*, Leigh Hunt's *Lord Byron and his Contemporaries* and J.T. Smith's *Nollekens and his Times* published.

1829   54. Martin Burney stayed with the Lambs in January. Lamb's poem 'The Gypsey's Malison' printed in *Blackwood's Magazine*. In April the Lamb's servant, Becky, left to get married and Mary Lamb was ill in May. In July the Lambs stayed in London for about ten days. Lamb contributed to *The Gem* which also printed Hood's 'Dream of Eugene Aram'. *The Poetical Works of Rogers, Campbell, J. Montgomery, Lamb and Kirke White* published by Galignani in Paris. Landor's *Imaginary Conversations, Second Series*, Walter Wilson's *Memoirs of the Life and Times of Daniel Defoe* (dated 1830) and Peacock's *Misfortunes of Elphin* published. Jerrold's *Black-eyed Susan* performed at the Surrey Theatre. In October the Lambs moved from their house at Enfield to the Westwood's next door. John Bates Dibdin died.

1830   55. In January Lamb's farce *The Pawnbroker's Daughter* printed in *Blackwood's Magazine*. On 22 January Lamb wrote a long interesting letter to Wordsworth eulogizing London and giving an account of the Westwoods. In February Emma Isola was seriously ill at Fornham and when she recovered Lamb went in April to fetch her. Moxon started as a publisher and in July issued Lamb's *Album Verses* as his first book; it was adversely reviewed in the *Literary Gazette*. In July the Lambs stayed at No. 34 Southampton Buildings. On 18 September William Hazlitt died. Lamb made his second will on 9 October. In November the Lambs returned to Enfield. During the year Charles contributed to *The Times*. *The Gem, Spectator* and *Examiner*. Leigh Hunt started *The Tatler* and *Fraser's Magazine* started and contained Maginn's 'Gallery of Illustrious Literary Characters' Cobbett's *Rural Rides*, Hazlitt's *Conversations with Northcote*, Moore's *Life of Byron*, and Southey's *Life of Bunyan* were published. Rogers's *Italy* was re-issued, illustrated by J.M.W. Turner and T. Stothard, & Hood's *Comic Annual* started. George IV died.

1831   56. *Satan in Search of a Wife* published by Moxon. On 2 November Carlyle visited Lamb and Wordsworth was a visitor in December. During the year Lamb wrote for *The Englishman's Magazine, The Athenaeum* and the *Year Book*. Peacock's *Crotchet Castle* and Trelawny's *Adventures of a Younger Son* published. R.W. Elliston and Mrs Siddons died.

1832   57. In February Lamb wrote an obituary notice of Munden who had died on 6 February. On 11 July Lamb met 'Christopher North' and on 28 September he was visited by Landor. Mary Lamb became ill. Mrs Reynolds died and Lamb's pension to her ceased. During the year Charles contributed to *The Athenaeum* and *The Reflector*. Lytton's *Eugene Aram*, Procter's *English Songs* and Genest's *Some Account of the English Stage* published. J.S. Knowles's *The Hunchback* and Jerrold's *Rent Day* were performed. Sir Walter Scott and Crabbe died. Reform Bill passed.

1833   58. *The Last Essays of Elia* published by Moxon. In April Emma Isola and Edward Moxon became engaged. Sheridan Knowles's play *The Wife* was produced at Covent Garden on 24 April with Prologue and Epilogue by Lamb. In May Mary Lamb was ill and the Lambs moved to the Walden's house at Edmonton. On 30 July Emma Isola and Moxon were married. During the year Lamb contributed to *The Athenaeum, The Times* and *The Mirror of Literature*. Hartley Coleridge's *Poems* and *Biographia Borealis*, Carlyle's *Sartor Resartus*, Nyren's *Young Cricketer's Tutor* and Southey's *Lives of the British Admirals* (1833–7) published. Edmund Kean died.

1834   59. Mary Lamb was ill in January. Leigh Hunt started his *London Journal* in April. Lamb contributed to *The Athenaeum*. In June Lamb had breakfast with the American, N.P. Willis, who later wrote reminiscences of Lamb. On 25 July Coleridge died. During the year F.S. Cary did his portrait of Charles and Mary Lamb. On 22 December Charles Lamb fell and injured his face: on 27 December he died at Edmonton. Lytton's *Last Days of Pompeii*, Henry Taylor's *Philip van Artevelde*, an elaborate illustrated edition of Rogers's *Poems*, Lowndes' *Bibliographer's Manual* and Southey's *The Doctor* Volumes I & II, published. Edward Irving died.

1835   Lamb buried at Edmonton on 3 January. Obituary notices appeared in many publications. The Maclise portrait of Lamb published in *Fraser's Magazine*. Moxon published the third edition of Lamb's *Dramatic Specimens* including the extracts from the Garrick Plays. Lamb's *Prose Works* published by Moxon. Clare's *Rural Muse*, Darley's *Nepenthe*, Coleridge's *Table Talk* and Wordsworth's *Yarrow Revisited* published. Sara Hutchinson, Charles Mathews and Cobbett died.

1836   Lamb's *Poetical Works* published and the *Prose Works* reissued, both by Moxon. Coleridge's *Literary Remains*, Hazlitt's *Literary Remains*, Allsop's *Letters, Conversation and Recollections* and Landor's *Pericles and Aspasia* published. Talfourd's *Ion* produced at Covent Garden with Macready. William Godwin died.

1837   Talfourd's *Letters of Charles Lamb*, Sara Coleridge's *Phantasmion*, *Pickwick Papers*, Cottle's *Early Recollections of S.T. Coleridge* published. Queen Victoria came to the throne.

1839   *Hood's Own* published.

1840   Moxon issued Lamb's *Works*. Thomas Manning died.

1841   Mary Lamb moved from the Waldens to Mrs Parsons' house in Alpha Road, St John's Wood. Moxon prosecuted for publishing Shelley's *Queen Mab*. George Dyer died.

1842   Allan Cunningham died.

1843   Southey died and Wordsworth became Poet Laureate. Macaulay's *Critical and Historical Essays* published.

1844   H.F. Cary died.

1845   Thomas Hood died.

1846   Barron Field, Darley and B.R. Haydon died.

1847   Mary Lamb died on 20 May, aged 82.

1848   Talfourd's *Final Memorials* published.

1849   Bernard Barton, Hartley Coleridge and Horace Smith died.

1850   Leigh Hunt's *Autobiography* published. Wordsworth died.

1851   Basil Montagu and Mary Shelley died. Macready retired from the stage.

1858   Edward Moxon died.

1859   Leigh Hunt, De Quincey and Washington Irving died.

1891   Emma Isola (Mrs Moxon) died at Brighton.

Abbreviated family tree of James Burney

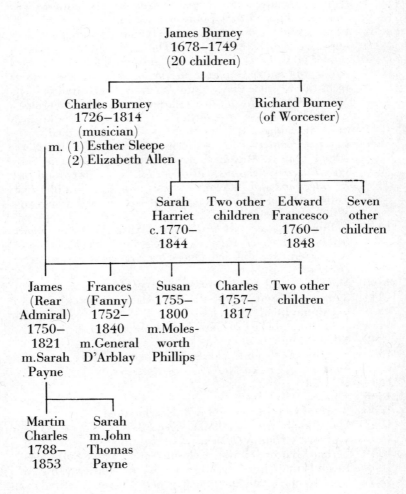

James Burney
1678–1749
(20 children)

Charles Burney
1726–1814
(musician)
m. (1) Esther Sleepe
(2) Elizabeth Allen

Richard Burney
(of Worcester)

Sarah
Harriet
c.1770–
1844

Two other
children

Edward
Francesco
1760–
1848

Seven
other
children

James
(Rear
Admiral)
1750–
1821
m.Sarah
Payne

Frances
(Fanny)
1752–
1840
m.General
D'Arblay

Susan
1755–
1800
m.Moles-
worth
Phillips

Charles
1757–
1817

Two other
children

Martin
Charles
1788–
1853

Sarah
m.John
Thomas
Payne

Abbreviated family tree of Samuel Taylor Coleridge

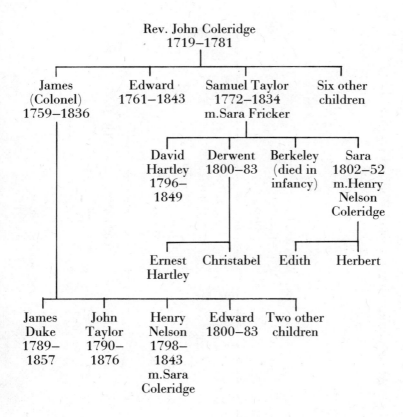

Abbreviated family tree of William Hazlitt

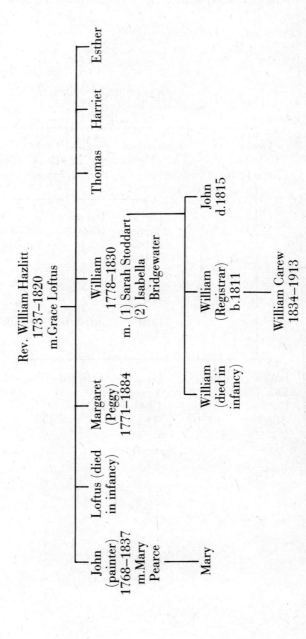

Abbreviated family tree of Charles and Robert Lloyd

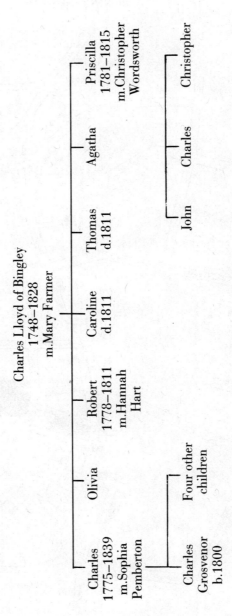

Charles Lloyd of Bingley
1748–1828
m.Mary Farmer

Charles
1775–1839
m.Sophia
Pemberton

Olivia

Robert
1778–1811
m.Hannah
Hart

Caroline
d.1811

Thomas
d.1811

Agatha

Priscilla
1781–1815
m.Christopher
Wordsworth

Charles
Grosvenor
b.1800

Four other
children

John

Charles

Christopher

Descendents of Agatha Lloyd included the poets Laurence Binyon and Stephen Phillips.

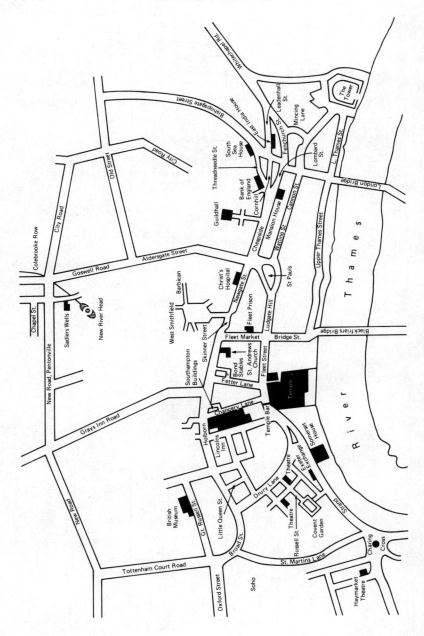

Sketch map of London in Lamb's time, c. 1800.

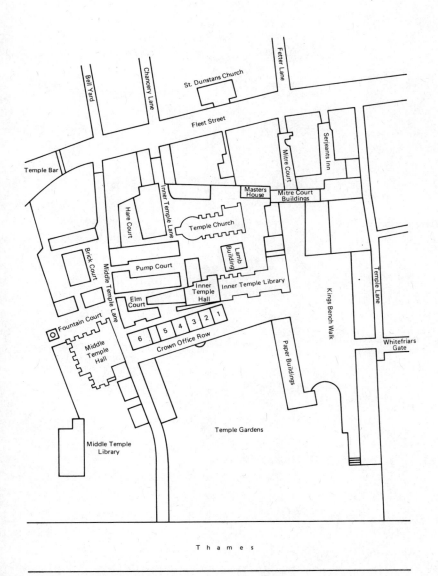

Sketch plan of the Temple in Lamb's time.

Index of actors, actresses, playwrights, dramatic critics, singers, music critics and plays

Index of artists and art collections

Index of contemporaries of Charles Lamb

Excluding those mentioned in other lists, except when they were particular friends of Lamb.

Index of late nineteenth- and twentieth-century writers on the period, including collectors of Lamb's books.

Index of non-biographical entries